W9-BJC-789

THE GIANT

$7 A MEAL COOKBOOK

701 INEXPENSIVE MEALS THE WHOLE FAMILY WILL LOVE

Chef Susan Irby, the Bikini Chef

Aadamsmedia
Avon, Massachusetts

Published by
Adams Media, a division of F+W Media, Inc.
57 Littlefield Street, Avon, MA 02322. U.S.A.
www.adamsmedia.com

ISBN 10: 1-4405-0635-3
ISBN 13: 978-1-4405-0635-2
eISBN 10: 1-4405-0904-2
eISBN 13: 978-1-4405-0904-9

Contains material adapted and abridged from *$5 a Meal College Cookbook*, by Rhonda Lauret Parkinson with B. E. Horton, MS, RD, copyright © 2010 by F+W Media, Inc., ISBN 10: 1-4405-0208-0, ISBN 13: 978-1-4405-0208-8; *The $7 a Meal Cookbook*, by Linda Larsen, copyright © 2009 by F+W Media, Inc., ISBN 10: 1-60550-109-3, ISBN 13: 978-1-60550-109-3; *The $7 a Meal Healthy Cookbook*, by Chef Susan Irby, copyright © 2009 by F+W Media, Inc., ISBN 10: 1-4405-0338-9, ISBN 13: 978-1-4405-0338-2; *The $7 a Meal Quick & Easy Cookbook*, by Chef Susan Irby, copyright © 2009 by F+W Media, Inc., ISBN 10: 1-4405-0223-4, ISBN 13: 978-1-4405-0223-1.

Printed in the United States of America.

10 9 8 7 6 5 4 3 2 1

Library of Congress Cataloging-in-Publication Data
is available from the publisher.

This publication is designed to provide accurate and authoritative information with regard to the subject matter covered. It is sold with the understanding that the publisher is not engaged in rendering legal, accounting, or other professional advice. If legal advice or other expert assistance is required, the services of a competent professional person should be sought.

—From a *Declaration of Principles* jointly adopted by a Committee of the American Bar Association and a Committee of Publishers and Associations

Many of the designations used by manufacturers and sellers to distinguish their product are claimed as trademarks. Where those designations appear in this book and Adams Media was aware of a trademark claim, the designations have been printed with initial capital letters.

This book is available at quantity discounts for bulk purchases.
For information, please call 1-800-289-0963.

CONTENTS

INTRODUCTION

The price of everything is skyrocketing these days. Remember when media pundits told us that "at least we're not paying $4 a gallon for gasoline like people in England"? That's now a reality. Gas prices, commodities futures, and the economy in general are forcing food prices up sharply. We have to take control of our budgets. In this book you'll learn how to shop in a grocery store, plan meals, write lists so you won't run out of food unexpectedly, and make a few meals out of practically nothing.

The price in this book has been calculated for the total recipe. Most magazines and books tell you the price per serving, which is accurate, but a recipe that claims to cost $3 per serving is almost $20 to feed six people. Recent issues of popular magazines offered budget meals with a cost per serving of $2.50 or less which is $10 for four, and a popular fast–food restaurant is bragging that you can feed your family for less than $4 a person. These meals are a deal! The number of servings in each recipe is only calculated after the calorie count is known, so you aren't being cheated by 100-calorie-a-serving treats masquerading as meals.

To cook successfully on a budget, you must follow a few rules. Making and abiding by a grocery list is one of the most important. Having a list in hand helps reduce temptation and will keep you focused on your goal. When you're busy comparing the prices of two kinds of chopped canned tomatoes, you'll be less likely to think about the freshly made chocolate chip cookies beckoning you from the bakery.

In this book, you'll find tips on how to avoid the traps that grocery store designers set for you. (Look high and low on the shelves because the most expensive products are placed at eye level.) And you'll learn how to get the best value for your money with a little secret called unit pricing.

The cost for each recipe was figured using NutriBase Clinical Version 7.0. To get the best representative cost for each ingredient, price lists at SimonDelivers.com, YourGrocery.com, and Peapod.com were used. Sale prices, discounts, and coupons were not included in the calculations, so you may find that prices in your area are higher or lower than those stated here. Every cook is different and so is every kitchen. These recipes were developed with cost savings in mind. Each recipe has the cost per serving, and many have a note to make the recipe more special and expensive if you want to splurge. Let's cook!

CHAPTER 1

COOKING ON A BUDGET

We used to joke that every time we turned around, prices went up. Now we know it's true! The price of oil, commodities speculation on the stock market, using food for fuel, the growing world population, and changing weather and climate all have an effect on food prices. Studies and surveys show that most of us are abandoning restaurants and fast food places and are trying to cook and eat at home. It's true: You can control your budget—and still eat very well, for very little—as long as you learn some new habits and follow a few simple rules.

IT'S ALL ABOUT THE PLAN

Everything should start with a plan, whether you're making a household budget, searching for a job, or trying to feed your family on less money. If you write lists, plan menus, and cut coupons you will save a significant amount of money, and you will be able to serve your family tastier and more nutritious food.

Cook at Home

Here's the most important rule: You will save money if you cook at home rather than spend your money in restaurants. The more work you do, and the simpler, more basic foods you buy, the more money you will save. This may sound daunting, but once you get into the habit of cooking it will take you less and less time and the skill will become second nature. Choose to make your own meals and you will control what's in the food you feed your family.

Eating "lower on the food chain" doesn't just mean avoiding beef, pork, and chicken. It also means eating foods that are as close to harvest condition as possible. A ripe peach will be less expensive than ice cream made with peaches or a bottled peach salsa. Manufactured foods will almost always cost more than the raw ingredients assembled by you.

Then begin by planning. Plan every meal. Plan for snacks and for the occasional evening out. Plan to use leftovers, and budget for special occasions. This may feel rigid, but you will realize that when you have meals planned for the week, you'll have more time for other things. The food you need will be in the house, you know what you'll prepare every day, and you won't have to spend time thinking about how you're going to get breakfast, lunch, and dinner on the table.

What's Cheaper?

A lot of your grocery savings will depend on what you buy. It's important to know that buying whole chicken breasts and deboning them yourself will not only cost less, but give you more for your money. The bones and skin can be saved to make chicken stock. In fact, for all of the recipes in this book I recommend buying bone-in, skin-on chicken breasts and removing the large breast muscle yourself. If you do this, a boneless, skinless chicken breast will cost you about a dollar. Buying them already boned and skinned will cost almost $2.00 apiece.

Surprisingly, butter costs about 10 cents a tablespoon, while the least expensive form of olive oil is 20 cents per tablespoon. When you're frying foods and want the best taste, butter and olive oil are the best choices. Use butter for the best flavor, and add a bit of the more expensive olive oil to raise the smoke point and keep the butter from burning.

Frozen and canned vegetables will usually be cheaper than fresh. And don't worry about the nutrition of these products. Processed produce has just as many vitamins as fresh; in many cases, even more because it's processed within a few hours of harvest. Fresh vegetables and fruits, especially when out of season, take days to get to the market and every day they lose vitamin content.

Buying a cheaper top round steak and marinating it overnight in the fridge will result in a tender and flavorful cut of beef that just takes a bit more work than plopping a tenderloin or ribeye on the grill. And buying that same steak and pounding it with flour makes Swiss steaks cheaper than you'll find in a frozen dinner. Make your own hamburgers rather than buying pre-formed patties. You get the idea!

Unit pricing is one of the best tools to budget shopping. Look at the price per ounce to see if that huge box of pasta is a better buy than the smaller one. Most grocery stores have unit pricing tags on the shelves right under the product. You can also bring a calculator to the store to figure it out for yourself. Just divide the price by the number of ounces in the product and compare.

Look at the price of a head of lettuce versus the bagged, "pre-washed" assembled salads. The price is more than double, for less product! The lesson? The more work you do in the kitchen, the more money you will save.

LOOK AT YOUR SPENDING HABITS

When you draw up a budget, it's important to look at how you have spent money in the past. We fall into habits and patterns and do what's easiest, especially when our lives are busy and stressful. By taking a close look at how you spend money on food, you can save a lot and eat better at the same time.

Look through your checkbook and credit card receipts and add up how much you've spent on food, eating out at restaurants, fast food stops, and trips to the convenience store in the last two months. Break down the different categories, add everything up, and then decide where you want to cut down.

Do you eat out because you love certain cuisines? Learn to make those foods at home, and not only will you be saving money, but you'll learn something about the world. The cooking methods, herbs and spices, and foods from world cuisines are usually quick to make, easy, and inexpensive.

If you're like most Americans, you spend a lot of money eating out; in fact, almost 50 percent of our food budget is spent on food not prepared at home. While it's fun to eat out, you can do the same thing at home for less than half the cost. Mexican, Chinese, Greek, and even French cuisine and recipes can easily be made in your own kitchen for a fraction of restaurant food. It's just as authentic, you don't have to worry about food safety or the nutrition of the food, and you can make cooking and baking a family event.

THE INDISPENSABLE LIST

All right, let's get serious. To start cooking on a budget, first you need to know what you have in the house, what your family likes to eat, and what you know you can cook. Then you have to make a list every time you go grocery shopping. And stick to it!

Record the Evidence

To get started, go through your pantry, fridge, and freezer and take stock. For two weeks make a list of the staples your family uses. For instance, every week you may buy milk, bread, cereal, ground beef, carrots, tomatoes, and rice. Use these foods to create a master list to save time. Then post that master list on the refrigerator, and when you run out of a food make a note on the list.

The rest of your list should come from ingredients you need for your planned meals. Note the amounts you'll need and any specifics on the list. When you go shopping, abide by the list. But at the same time, be open to change! You may find that there are in-store specials on certain foods, especially meats, which may change your meal plan. Be flexible and look for good buys.

Easy List Making

Websites can again be a valuable source of information. Many sites like webmomz.com and ehow.com offer printable grocery list forms already divided into categories that you just fill in. And you can personalize the list too, adding your staple items that you buy every week.

For some fun browsing on the web, as well as ideas for shopping lists, take a look at grocerylists.org, which is a collection of grocery lists found abandoned on supermarket floors and in parking lots. It's fun to see what other people buy, and you can learn something too!

In some cases, you may want to include quantity on your list, especially for more expensive items like spices or seafood. For instance, you can buy small amounts of spices and nuts in bulk bins at most food co-ops. Unless you know that you will use that food again, this is the cheapest way to shop.

Now follow the list. It should be your guide when you're in the store. Concentrating on it will help keep you focused on the foods you need and will help distract your attention from foods that look and smell tempting, but that aren't in your budget. You'll also discover that shopping this way will take less time and be less stressful.

USING COUPONS

You've seen those news stories where a woman buys a full cart of groceries for $2.18. While that is possible, saving that much money on groceries with coupons is practically a full-time job and requires double-couponing as well as buying many prepackaged and processed foods. By using these tips and shopping wisely, you can use coupons to save 10–20 percent from your grocery bill.

When you are looking for a coupon, think about these things:

- Will the coupon make that item the cheapest in unit pricing?
- Will you be able to use all of the food before the expiration date?
- Does your family like this food, and will they eat it?
- Is the food nutritious or junk food?
- Can you easily use the food in your regular in meal planning?
- Request coupons from manufacturers by calling the 800 numbers on their products.

Spend a little money and buy a loose-leaf notebook, along with a file folder to hold menus and coupons. You can arrange the folder in several ways: according to the types of food, according to the layout of your grocery store, or according to expiration date. Be sure you understand what food the coupon applies to, and buy that exact product. And go through the folder often, making a note of which coupons you want to use and which ones are close to their expiration date.

Sign up for coupon sites on the Internet that offer free, printable coupons, like coolsavings.com, smartsource.com, retailmenot.com/coupons/food, and thegrocerygame.com. Then each week you'll be reminded via e-mail to check those sites for new coupons. Be sure to only use coupons for foods you know your family likes. And look for "free" coupons, which will let you try a product before you spend money on it.

Make sure to read the fine print on the coupons carefully. Sometimes you can use more than one coupon on a product, and if that product happens to be on sale, the savings can really add up. More often, you need to purchase a specific size and brand of product that matches the coupon exactly.

If a store runs out of an item you have a coupon for, or that is on sale, ask for a raincheck, then keep that raincheck in the coupon folder. When the item is restocked, the grocery store will mail you a notice, and you can buy it at the sale price.

GROCERY SHOPPING

Grocery stores are planned to keep you in the store for a long period of time and to encourage you to spend the most money possible. After all, the grocer needs to make a profit! But when you know the tricks they use, you can learn to avoid them and save money while still feeding your family well.

Know the Store

Many stores offer "reward plans" that can help you save money. Some stores offer discounts on gasoline tied to the amount of food you buy. Others have punch cards that you can redeem for special products or money off when the card is full. Learn about these programs and use as many as you possibly can.

Learn the layout of the stores you patronize most often, so you can get in and out as quickly as possible and so you don't waste time looking for products. If you can't find a product fairly quickly, ask! Any store employee will be able to tell you where something is located.

Many stores offer a printed map, right next to the coupon fliers at the store entrance. This can be a great way to learn the layout quickly, and it can point you to bargains. If the store has a clearance aisle or section it should be marked on the map. Then use the map to organize your list for the next shopping trip.

You can also get help at the butcher counter. You can always ask if the butcher will cut a larger roast or steak into a smaller portion for you at the same price as the full cut. Ask if she'll divide up a package of chicken drumsticks or wings. She's also a great source of information if you have questions about how to prepare a certain cut of meat.

And when you're looking for something, avoid products placed at eye level. That's the "premium space" that brand name producers want, and where the highest priced products are located. Also avoid "end caps," those displays at the end of the aisle. Products that are placed there appear to be on sale, when more often they are not.

Check Your Receipt

Even with digital machines and scanners, there will be mistakes on your receipt. Check to make sure that the correct prices, especially sale prices, are on your receipt, that the coupons you turn in are properly redeemed for the correct price, and that there weren't any products that were scanned twice.

If you do find a mistake, don't go back to the cashier. Go directly to the service counter and speak to someone there. That way you'll get your money back, you won't hold up a line, and the correct price or discount will be programmed into all the checkout computers.

Shop Once a Week

Most budget books tell you to shop only once a week. If you are organized and know that you'll use the food you buy within that time, this is a smart idea, not only for your food budget, but your gasoline budget as well.

Why doesn't the CPI reflect the price increases we are seeing?

The CPI, or Consumer Price Index, used to be calculated using a fixed "basket" of products, priced at prevailing market costs. But in the 1990s, the Fed changed the system, substituting cheaper goods for more expensive ones. This new calculation, called "geometric weighting," gives more emphasis to goods that are decreasing in price.

But if you let food go to waste, if you throw a frozen pizza into the oven instead of slicing the vegetables and making that quiche you had planned, it's better to shop more often and buy less at one time. This works best if a grocery store with good prices is on your route home from work or school. Combine errands to save on gas, but make sure to shop for groceries last. Perishable and frozen foods should go directly from the grocery store to your fridge and freezer, as quickly as possible.

The number of times you shop in a week also depends on how far you are from a grocery store. If there is one with reasonable prices and good stock within walking distance, you can shop more often, look for buys, and take advantage of coupons and sales.

WASTE: THE BUDGET BUSTER

The biggest budget buster isn't that $8 steak or $4 gallon of milk. It's waste! Americans throw away as much as 45 percent of the food they buy. If you spend $800 a month on food, you may be throwing away more than $300 a month. Whether it's a head of lettuce that languishes in the fridge until it wilts, or a bag of chicken breasts imperfectly wrapped so it develops freezer burn, food is easy to waste.

How Long Do Foods Last?

How long should perishable products be kept on the counter or in the fridge until they're no longer safe or wholesome? There are some fairly rigid rules about how soon food should be used before it must be frozen or thrown away. On manufactured and dairy products, and on some meat products, be sure to scrupulously follow the expiration dates stamped on the package. For others, here are some general rules.

TABLE 1-1: SHELF LIFE

FOOD	ON COUNTER	REFRIGERATOR	FREEZER
Apples	3 days	3 weeks	Cook first, 6 months
Strawberries	1 day	3 days	Flash freeze, 4 months
Berries	1 day	2 days	4 months

TABLE 1-1: SHELF LIFE (continued)

FOOD	ON COUNTER	REFRIGERATOR	FREEZER
Onions	3 weeks	Not recommended	Cooked, 6 months
Potatoes	1 month	Not recommended	Cooked, 6 months
Mushrooms	1 day	3 days	8 months
Celery	1 day	1 week	Not recommended
Ground meat	Not recommended	3 days	6 months
Eggs	Not recommended	3 weeks	Separated, 3 months
Cheese	Not recommended	3 weeks	6 months

Leftovers have to be planned into your budget to make another meal. Spend a little money to get reusable good quality food containers that will hold the food until you're ready to use it. Always refrigerate food promptly, know what's in your fridge and freezer, and plan your weekly meals with leftovers in mind.

Food Savers

There are some products you can buy that can help reduce waste. Green Bags made by Evert-Fresh do work, although some sources say the food doesn't stay fresh as long as claimed. The bag should keep your strawberries and asparagus fresh and wholesome for 5–7 days, which is 3–4 days longer than produce.

You can also look into vacuum sealers, which remove the air from food containers to help prevent freezer burn. Of course, you can get close to the same result this way: Use a heavy-duty freezer bag, seal it almost to the end, then insert a straw and suck out as much air as possible. Seal the bag, label, and freeze immediately.

BUY IN BULK

Bulk buying has long been the secret of organizations, schools, and restaurants. Food is almost always cheaper bought in large quantities. But you don't have to lug home gallon size cans of peaches or 12 loaves of bread to take advantage of bulk buying.

If you have storage space, and scrupulously follow expiration dates and rotate food, you can save lots of money buying in bulk, especially from bulk bins at co-ops. Bring your own containers, and be sure to mark everything on masking tape placed on the container: date of purchase, the name of the item, quantity, and expiration dates, if any.

Be sure to follow cleanliness instructions when buying in bulk. Put on gloves when you remove food from a bulk bin, and use the tongs or scoops supplied. Ask about expiration dates and times for food. And be sure to place food in tightly sealed, clean containers and store food in a cool, dark place.

You could also share costs with another family if you want to buy in bulk. Pair up with another family or two and buy mayonnaise, canned fruit, milk, cereal, and meat in large quantities, then divide them equally.

LEARN TO COOK

Cooking isn't difficult; it just takes some time to become familiar with new terms and some practice sessions to learn some skills. Watch cooking shows on television; that's one of the best ways to learn how to cook and bake.

You can find lots of places that offer cooking e-courses and information online for free. Go to the library and take out a basic cookbook and read through it. You can always ask questions on online forums. Your local extension service, through the university in your state, is also a good resource for cooking information, as well as recipes and food safety tips.

Here are some basic rules for cooking and baking:

- First read through the recipe
- If you don't understand words or terms, look them up
- Make sure you have the ingredients and utensils on hand
- Follow the directions carefully

- Be sure you understand how to measure ingredients
- Measure flour by lightly spooning it into the measuring cup, then level off top
- Start checking the food at the shortest cooking time
- Understand doneness tests
- Make sure meat is cooked to a safe internal temperature

Some supermarkets and specialty stores also occasionally offer cooking classes. Take the time to ask neighbors, family, and friends about teaching you to cook. Once you've learned the basic rules about cooking and baking, you'll be able to save money so many ways.

It may feel a little awkward and strange during your first forays into the kitchen, but as with any skill, the more you practice, the easier it will become. And when you see your budget balancing and the amount of money you save, you'll be encouraged to stick with it. There are more advantages to cooking for yourself too; you'll spend more time with family, enjoy the family table, and teach your kids how to cook and feed themselves, which will set them up for life.

Now let's get started in the kitchen with these delicious and easy recipes that cost less than $7 to prepare, and feed at least four people.

CHAPTER 2

APPETIZERS AND SAUCES

Spinach Pesto

 Serves 10; serving size ¼ cup

- ~ **TOTAL COST:** $4.89
- ~ **CALORIES:** 105.85
- ~ **FAT:** 9.94 g
- ~ **PROTEIN:** 3.42 g
- ~ **CHOLESTEROL:** 1.83 mg
- ~ **SODIUM:** 335.75 mg

1 (10-ounce) package frozen spinach, thawed
⅓ cup fresh basil leaves
2 teaspoons dried basil leaves
3 tablespoons lemon juice
½ cup chopped walnuts
1 teaspoon salt
⅛ teaspoon white pepper
⅓ cup grated Parmesan cheese
¼ cup olive oil
¼–⅓ cup water

Frozen chopped spinach not only reduces the cost of pesto, but it adds nutrients and fiber. A four-serving package of ready-made pesto costs $4.50.

1. Drain thawed spinach in a colander, pressing with your fingers to remove excess water. Combine in blender or food processor with basil, dried basil, lemon juice, walnuts, salt, pepper, and cheese. Process until finely chopped.
2. While processor is running, slowly add olive oil until a thick paste forms. Add water as needed until a smooth thick sauce forms. Serve immediately or cover and refrigerate up to 3 days. Freeze up to 3 months.

Spiced Cream Cheese–Stuffed Mushrooms

Serves 12

- ~ **PREP TIME:** 8 minutes
- ~ **COOK TIME:** 12 minutes
- ~ **TOTAL COST:** $4.58
- ~ **CALORIES:** 25
- ~ **FAT:** 2 g
- ~ **CARBOHYDRATES:** 1 g
- ~ **PROTEIN:** .5 g
- ~ **CHOLESTEROL:** 7 mg
- ~ **SODIUM:** 20 mg

1 tablespoon prepared horseradish
4 ounces cream cheese, softened
2 teaspoons lemon juice
Pinch five spice powder
24 large button or cremini mushrooms, wiped clean, stems removed

Cream cheese is a great foundation for many appetizer recipes as it blends well with other flavors and is easy to spread. Substitute lighter Neufchatel cheese if you desire.

Preheat oven to 350°F. In small bowl, mix prepared horseradish with half of the cream cheese. In a separate bowl, combine lemon juice, five-spice powder, and remaining cream cheese. Spoon approximately 1 level teaspoon cream cheese/horseradish mixture into half the mushroom caps. Spoon the cream cheese/lemon mixture into the other half of the mushroom caps. Place all mushrooms on a parchment-lined baking sheet. Bake for 10 to 12 minutes until cream cheese is heated through.

Five-Spice Powder
Five-spice powder is native to China and features 5 main spices with additional secondary spices.

Big Batch Guacamole

 Serves 9

~ **TOTAL COST:** $4.24

~ **CALORIES:** 195.54

~ **FAT:** 7.57 g

~ **PROTEIN:** 7.93 g

~ **CHOLESTEROL:** 3.39 mg

~ **SODIUM:** 147.73 mg

1½ cups dried lima beans
1 cup chopped onion
3 tablespoons lemon juice
½ teaspoon salt
1 tablespoon butter, melted
¼ teaspoon cayenne pepper
2 ripe avocados

Yes, you can buy premade guacamole, but it's full of fillers and artificial ingredients, and it still costs more per serving, because each serving of this guacamole is a full ⅓ cup.

1. The day before you want to serve the dip, sort the lima beans, discarding any foreign objects. Rinse thoroughly and drain well. Combine in heavy saucepan with cold water to cover and chopped onion. Cover, bring to a boil, reduce heat, and simmer for 1 hour until very tender. Refrigerate cooked beans overnight in the cooking liquid.
2. When you want to serve the dip, combine lemon juice, salt, butter, and cayenne pepper in a food processor. If necessary, drain the bean mixture; add the cooled bean and onion mixture to the lemon juice mixture and process until smooth. Then peel and slice the avocados; add to processor and process again until smooth. Serve immediately, or cover and refrigerate up to 8 hours before serving.

Herbed Sour Cream Dip

Serves 8

~ **PREP TIME:** 8 minutes

~ **CHILL:** 1 hour

~ **TOTAL COST:** $3.75

~ **CALORIES:** 128

~ **FAT:** 12 g

~ **PROTEIN:** 2 g

~ **CHOLESTEROL:** 22 mg

~ **SODIUM:** 51 mg

2 cups sour cream, low-fat okay
¼ cup mayonnaise
2 tablespoons fresh dill, chopped, or 1 tablespoon dried dill
2 tablespoons green onion, chopped
2 tablespoons chives, chopped
1 tablespoon fresh Italian parsley, chopped
Sea salt and black pepper to taste

Although in the onion family, chives are not the same as green onions. Chives are smaller and therefore more pungent in flavor. Used here with the green onion, this dip takes on a crisp, refreshing flavor. If you have a lemon on hand, add a squeeze of lemon juice or pinch of lemon zest for extra flavor punch without adding fat or calories.

Mix all ingredients together, cover and chill. Serve with vegetables such as celery, carrots, or broccoli florets.

Quick and Easy Tip

Recipes don't get much easier than this. When out-of-town guests arrive for a weekend, have some of this on hand for an easy, inexpensive snack.

Smoked Salmon on Sliced Cucumber

 Serves 8

- ~ **PREP TIME:** 15 minutes
- ~ **TOTAL COST:** $6.99
- ~ **CALORIES:** 99
- ~ **FAT:** 3 g
- ~ **CARBOHYDRATES:** 1 g
- ~ **PROTEIN:** 15 g
- ~ **CHOLESTEROL:** 19 mg
- ~ **SODIUM:** 1,695 mg

6 ounces smoked salmon, flaked and diced
2 tablespoons red onion, finely diced
1 tablespoon capers, chopped
1 teaspoon fresh chives or dill, chopped
1 tablespoon olive oil
Sea salt and black pepper to taste
1 cucumber, sliced

Because I am the Bikini Chef, foods that are figure flattering are my specialty. I try to use cucumbers whenever I can as a low-cal, refreshing, and delicious alternative to crackers or bread.

In medium mixing bowl, combine all ingredients except for cucumber slices. Mix gently with a fork until the olive oil is evenly distributed. Arrange cucumber slices on a serving platter. Use a small teaspoon to mound ¾ teaspoon of salmon mixture onto center of each cucumber slice.

> **Presentation Tip**
> When slicing cucumber, make green stripes by leaving alternating strips of green peel when peeling the cucumber. Then slice the cucumber.

Parmesan Crisps with Apricots and Thyme

 Serves 8

- ~ **PREP TIME:** 5 minutes
- ~ **COOK TIME:** 30 minutes
- ~ **TOTAL COST:** $6.92
- ~ **CALORIES:** 101
- ~ **FAT:** 3 g
- ~ **CARBOHYDRATES:** 14 g
- ~ **PROTEIN:** 2 g
- ~ **CHOLESTEROL:** 6 mg
- ~ **SODIUM:** 95 mg

½ cup apricot preserves
¼ cup dried apricots, finely chopped
2 tablespoons water
1 tablespoon honey
½ teaspoon fresh thyme, leaves chopped
1½ cups Parmigiano-Reggiano cheese, grated

Parmigiano-Reggiano cheese is an authentic Italian cheese that is very dense and actually lower in fat content that other cheeses.

1. Preheat oven to 350°F. Line baking sheet with parchment paper. In heavy saucepan, combine preserves, apricots, water, honey, and thyme leaves. Bring to a simmer. Simmer for 5 to 8 minutes, stirring frequently, until dried apricots are softened and mixture is thickened. Remove from heat and let cool slightly.
2. Meanwhile, using a tablespoon, place mounds of cheese 4 inches apart on prepared baking sheet. Gently pat to form 2-inch rounds. Bake for 4 to 6 minutes or until cheese is melted and turns light golden brown. Let crisps cool for 5 minutes on baking sheet, then transfer to paper towels. Serve with apricot mixture.

Garlic Toast

Serves 10

- ~ **TOTAL COST:** $3.20
- ~ **CALORIES:** 254.01
- ~ **FAT:** 10.68 g
- ~ **PROTEIN:** 5.55 g
- ~ **CHOLESTEROL:** 17.27 mg
- ~ **SODIUM:** 390.26 mg

16 slices Whole Wheat French Bread (Chapter 3)
4 tablespoons butter, softened
3 tablespoons olive oil
5 cloves garlic, minced
½ teaspoon salt
¼ teaspoon lemon pepper

Garlic toast, or bruschetta, is a basic appetizer. It can be topped with everything from salsa to cheese to caramelized onions for a hearty snack.

1. Preheat broiler. Place bread slices on cookie sheet. Broil one side of bread slices until golden. Remove from oven and turn over.
2. In small bowl, combine butter, olive oil, garlic, salt, and lemon pepper and mix well. Spread onto Bread slices. Return to broiler. Broil slices, watching carefully, until butter mixture bubbles and turns golden brown. Serve immediately.

Roasted Garlic

Serves 6

- ~ **TOTAL COST:** $2.42
- ~ **CALORIES:** 50.05
- ~ **FAT:** 2.32 g
- ~ **PROTEIN:** 1.28 g
- ~ **CHOLESTEROL:** 0.0 mg
- ~ **SODIUM:** 198.00 mg

2 heads garlic
1 tablespoon olive oil
Pinch salt
1 teaspoon lemon juice

Believe it or not, roasted garlic is a fabulous treat eaten all by itself. You can spread it on bread, mash it into some cream cheese for a sandwich spread, or add to sauces.

1. Preheat oven to 400°F. Peel off some of the outer skins from the garlic head, leaving the head whole. Cut off the top ½-inch of the garlic head; discard top.
2. Place on a square of heavy-duty aluminum foil, cut side up. Drizzle with the olive oil, making sure the oil runs into the cloves. Sprinkle with salt and lemon juice.
3. Wrap garlic in the foil, covering completely. Place on a baking sheet and roast for 40–50 minutes or until garlic is very soft and golden brown. Let cool for 15 minutes, then serve or use in recipes.

Freezing Roasted Garlic
Make a lot of Roasted Garlic. When the garlic is cool, squeeze the cloves out of the papery covering; discard the covering. Place the garlic in a small bowl and work into a paste. Freeze in ice cube trays until solid, then place in heavy-duty freezer bags, label, and freeze up to 3 months.

Bean Nachos

Serves 6–8

~ **TOTAL COST:** $6.16
~ **CALORIES:** 269.10
~ **FAT:** 12.59 g
~ **PROTEIN:** 12.16 g
~ **CHOLESTEROL:** 24.58 mg
~ **SODIUM:** 628.85 mg

4 cups tortilla chips
1 (15-ounce) can refried beans
1 cup canned pinto beans
1 tablespoon chili powder
1 cup chunky salsa
1 jalapeño chile, seeded and chopped
1 cup shredded Cheddar cheese
1 cup shredded part skim Mozzarella cheese
¼ cup chopped parsley

The combination of smooth refried beans along with chunky whole beans is really nice in these nachos. This appetizer is hearty enough to be a main dish to serve four.

1. Preheat oven to 400°F. Place tortilla chips on a large rimmed baking sheet and set aside. In medium saucepan, combine refried beans, pinto beans, chili powder, and salsa. Heat over medium heat until mixture just begins to bubble, stirring frequently.
2. Pour bean mixture evenly over chips. Sprinkle with chile and cheeses. Bake at 400°F for 15–20 minutes until cheeses melt and begin to bubble.
3. Sprinkle with parsley and serve with sour cream and Big Batch Guacamole (this chapter), if desired.

Reuben Dip with Swiss Cheese

Serves 10

~ **PREP TIME:** 8 minutes
~ **COOK TIME:** 30 to 35 minutes
~ **TOTAL COST:** $6.99
~ **CALORIES:** 111
~ **FAT:** 17 g
~ **CARBOHYDRATES:** 5 g
~ **PROTEIN:** 7 g
~ **CHOLESTEROL:** 40 mg
~ **SODIUM:** 413 mg

1 (8-ounce) package cream cheese, softened
½ cup Thousand Island dressing
1 cup Swiss cheese, shredded
¼ pound sliced corned beef, chopped
1 cup sauerkraut, drained

This recipe is made in honor of the classic Reuben sandwich, which contains all the ingredients listed here except for cream cheese.

1. Preheat oven to 375°F. In medium bowl, beat cream cheese until fluffy. Stir in ¼ cup Thousand Island dressing and ½ cup Swiss cheese. Mix well to combine. Spread in bottom of 9" oven-safe pie plate. Top cream cheese mixture with corned beef and sauerkraut, spreading evenly to cover. Drizzle with remaining ¼ cup Thousand Island dressing and top with remaining cheese. Cover with foil.
2. Bake in oven for 30 minutes until cheese melts and mixture is hot.

Serving Tip
This dip is great served hot with pretzels, celery, or whole-grain crackers.

Hot and Spicy Popcorn

 Serves 8; serving size 2 cups

~ **TOTAL COST:** $4.84
~ **CALORIES:** 319.96
~ **FAT:** 25.82 g
~ **PROTEIN:** 7.27 g
~ **CHOLESTEROL:** 41.53 mg
~ **SODIUM:** 997.29 mg

4 quarts popped popcorn
½ cup butter, melted
3 tablespoons olive oil
3 tablespoons chili powder
1 teaspoon dried oregano leaves
2 teaspoons salt
1 teaspoon red pepper flakes
1 cup shelf–stable Parmesan cheese

The cheapest popcorn is the kind you buy in the large glass containers. Pop it in an air popper, or on the stovetop over medium high heat.

1. Preheat oven to 300°F. For 4 quarts of popcorn, start with ½ cup unpopped kernels. Place in air popper, or in large stockpot over medium high heat. When kernels start to pop, shake pan constantly over heat. Remove from heat when popping slows down. Remove any unpopped kernels.
2. In medium saucepan, combine butter and olive oil and melt over medium heat. Remove from heat and add chili powder, oregano, salt, and red pepper flakes. Place popcorn in two large baking pans. Drizzle butter mixture over popcorn. Sprinkle each pan with Parmesan cheese; toss to coat.
3. Bake for 15–20 minutes, stirring twice during baking time, until popcorn is crisp and cheese is melted. Serve warm or cool and store in air tight container up to 3 days.

Roasted Red Pepper Bruschetta

Serves 6

~ **PREP TIME:** 15 minutes
~ **COOK TIME:** 12 minutes
~ **TOTAL COST:** $6.81
~ **CALORIES:** 157
~ **FAT:** 5 g
~ **PROTEIN:** 5 g
~ **CHOLESTEROL:** 2 mg
~ **SODIUM:** 904 mg

1 sourdough baguette, cut into ½-inch slices
1 jar roasted red bell peppers, drained and chopped
¼ cup fresh basil leaves, chopped
2 tablespoons grated Parmesan cheese
1 garlic clove, chopped
2 tablespoons extra virgin olive oil
1 tablespoon balsamic vinegar
Sea salt and black pepper to taste

Roasted red bell peppers add depth to the most basic of ingredients like the recipe here. If you have time, roast your own—but be aware, they do make a little mess. If not, these marinated ones work just fine!

1. Line a baking sheet with parchment paper. Preheat oven to 250°F. Place baguette slices on baking sheet and place in oven. Let baguette slices rest in oven while you prepare the bruschetta. The low temperature of the oven will not burn the baguette, and for this appetizer, the crunchier the baguette the better!
2. In a medium mixing bowl, place peppers, basil, cheese, garlic, olive oil, and balsamic. Toss well. Season with salt and pepper as desired.
3. Remove baguette slices from oven. Place on serving tray and top with bruschetta. Serve immediately.

Celery Crisps with Cheese

 Serves 12

~ **PREP TIME:** 10 minutes
~ **CHILL:** 1 hour
~ **TOTAL COST:** $4.58
~ **CALORIES:** 76
~ **FAT:** 6 g
~ **PROTEIN:** 3 g
~ **CHOLESTEROL:** 8 mg
~ **SODIUM:** 82 mg

12 long celery stalks with leaves attached, if possible
6 ounces cream cheese, room temperature
½ cup nonfat cottage cheese
¼ cup yellow onion, chopped
2 tablespoons nonfat milk
12 large pimento-stuffed green olives, cut into ¼-inch-thick slices
Paprika for garnish

Stuffed celery is also a great snack for in-between meals. When watching your calorie intake, substitute low-fat cream cheese.

1. Cut celery sticks in half, crosswise, to create 24 sticks. In food processor, combine cream cheese, cottage cheese, and onion. Process at high speed for 4 minutes until smooth. If the texture is very thick, add the milk a little at time to reach desired spreading consistency.
2. Using a knife, spread the mixture into the hollows of the celery stalk, dividing it evenly among the stalks. Push the olive slices into the spread along the entire length of stalk. Wrap in plastic wrap and chill well. Just before serving, unwrap and sprinkle with paprika.

Suave Fruit Salsa

 Serves 8; Serving size ½ cup

~ **TOTAL COST:** $4.85
~ **CALORIES:** 65.81
~ **FAT:** 0.11 g
~ **PROTEIN:** 0.61 g
~ **CHOLESTEROL:** 0.0 mg
~ **SODIUM:** 151.57 mg

1 (8-ounce) can crushed pineapple
1 (8-ounce) can sliced peaches
1 cucumber
¼ cup peach preserves
1 jalapeño pepper, minced
½ cup finely chopped red onion
½ teaspoon salt
⅛ teaspoon cayenne pepper
2 tablespoons lemon juice

This delicious salsa can be served with corn or tortilla chips, or used as a sauce on grilled fish or chicken. Purchased fruit salsa costs $6.99 for the same amount.

1. Drain pineapple, reserving ¼ cup juice. Drain peaches, reserving 2 tablespoons juice. Chop peaches and combine with pineapple in medium bowl.
2. Peel cucumber, cut in half, remove seeds, and chop. Add to bowl with pineapple. In a small bowl, combine reserved juices, preserves, jalapeño, red onion, salt, pepper, and lemon juice and mix well. Pour over pineapple mixture and toss gently. Serve immediately or cover and refrigerate up to 2 days.

Quick and Easy Tip
Make 1 or 2 days ahead of time to save time on day of party. However, do not freeze. Cheeses do not freeze well because of the moisture they contain.

Roasted Cayenne Peanuts

Serves 12

~ **PREP TIME:** 5 minutes
~ **COOK TIME:** 20 minutes
~ **TOTAL COST:** $5.48
~ **CALORIES:** 211
~ **FAT:** 17 g
~ **CARBOHYDRATES:** 6 g
~ **PROTEIN:** 9 g
~ **CHOLESTEROL:** 0 mg
~ **SODIUM:** 7 mg

1 egg white
2 tablespoons curry powder
¼ teaspoon cayenne pepper
Pinch of sea salt
1 teaspoon sugar
3 cups unsalted peanuts, shelled

Walnuts or almonds are also delicious with this recipe. If you like, use 1 cup of each!

1. Preheat oven to 300°F. Line 2 baking sheets with parchment paper. In medium mixing bowl, whip egg white until frothy. Add curry powder, cayenne, salt, and sugar. Whisk until well blended. Add peanuts and stir until evenly coated.
2. Spread nuts in single layer on the baking sheets. Roast, uncovered, for about 20 minutes, until the nuts are dry and toasted. Stir and turn the nuts at least 2 times during the roasting process. Remove nuts from oven and transfer to separate parchment sheet to cool.

Baking Tip
When roasting any kind of nut in oven or on stovetop, watch them carefully as they may seem slow to roast, but once they begin, they can burn quickly and easily.

Parmesan-Spinach Croquettes

Serves 10

~ **PREP TIME:** 15 minutes
~ **COOK TIME:** 20 minutes
~ **TOTAL COST:** $6.99
~ **CALORIES:** 201
~ **FAT:** 11 g
~ **PROTEIN:** 7 g
~ **CHOLESTEROL:** 107 mg
~ **SODIUM:** 432 mg

2 packages frozen spinach, thawed and well drained
½ cups dry herb-seasoned bread stuffing mix
5 eggs
1 cup yellow onion, finely chopped
¾ cup butter, melted
½ cup Parmesan cheese, grated
¾ cup fresh Italian parsley, chopped
1½ teaspoons garlic powder
½ teaspoon dried thyme
½ teaspoon black pepper
½ teaspoon sea salt

This dish is traditional to Italy; however, the Italians usually use ricotta cheese instead of the Parmesan chosen here.

Preheat oven to 375°F. In a large bowl, combine all ingredients and mix well. Form into 1- to 1¼-inch balls (croquettes) and place on a baking sheet lined with parchment paper. Bake for 15 to 20 minutes. Serve warm.

Quick and Easy Tip
Croquettes may be frozen and stored until needed. When cooking straight from freezer, do not thaw. Place directly on a baking sheet and bake for 20 to 25 minutes.

Citrus-Glazed Shrimp

 Serves 4

- ~ **PREP TIME:** 8 minutes
- ~ **COOK TIME:** 3 minutes
- ~ **TOTAL COST:** $6.85
- ~ **CALORIES:** 150
- ~ **FAT:** 5 g
- ~ **PROTEIN:** 23 g
- ~ **CHOLESTEROL:** 172 mg
- ~ **SODIUM:** 168 mg

1 orange, zested and juiced
1 shallot, diced
½ teaspoon capers, drained
black pepper to taste
1 tablespoon olive oil
¾ pound large shrimp, peeled, tails on

Try this recipe in place of the traditional cocktail shrimp.

1. In a bowl, combine orange zest and juice, shallots, capers, and oil.
2. In a skillet over medium heat, heat orange mixture. When heated, add shrimp and black pepper, and cook until just done, about 2 to 3 minutes. Remove from heat and serve with toothpicks.

Quick and Easy Tip
Reserve any leftover citrus sauce as a side dipping sauce for the shrimp. Frozen, cooked shrimp also work well for this recipe. Just make sure they are thawed before cooking and only cook for 30 to 45 seconds to heat and coat with citrus mixture.

Cheesy Tomato Bruschetta

Serves 8

- ~ **TOTAL COST:** $4.36
- ~ **CALORIES:** 307.55
- ~ **FAT:** 9.43 g
- ~ **PROTEIN:** 10.84 g
- ~ **CHOLESTEROL:** 12.93 mg
- ~ **SODIUM:** 670.00 mg

¼ cup tomato paste
2 tablespoons olive oil
1 (14-ounce) can diced Italian tomatoes, drained
3 cloves garlic, minced
1 teaspoon dried basil leaves
¾ cup grated Parmesan cheese
16 slices Whole Wheat French Bread (Chapter 3)

This quick and easy appetizer can be served as a lunch, along with some fresh fruit and a simple green salad.

1. Preheat broiler in oven; set oven rack 6 inches from heat source.
2. In medium bowl, combine tomato paste and olive oil; blend well until smooth. Add remaining ingredients except for bread and mix gently.
3. Slice bread into 16½-inch slices and place on broiler pan; set aside. Broil bread slices until golden on one side, about 1–3 minutes. Turn and broil until light golden brown on second side. Remove from oven and top with tomato mixture. Return to oven and broil for 3–5 minutes or until tomato topping is bubbly and begins to brown. Serve immediately.

About Tomato Paste
Tomato paste is made by concentrating fresh tomatoes until almost all the water is evaporated. It is very flavorful, and can be found in flavored varieties.

Antipasto Platter

Serves 8

- ~ **PREP TIME:** 15 minutes
- ~ **TOTAL COST:** $6.80
- ~ **CALORIES:** 356
- ~ **FAT:** 11 g
- ~ **CARBOHYDRATES:** 6 g
- ~ **PROTEIN:** 5 g
- ~ **CHOLESTEROL:** 52 mg
- ~ **SODIUM:** 764 mg

2 (4-ounce) jars mushrooms, undrained
1 (8-ounce) package frozen artichoke hearts, thawed
   and drained
¾ cup Italian salad dressing
1 bunch asparagus spears, stalks trimmed
1 jar roasted red bell peppers, drained
8 ounces Cheddar cheese, cubed or sliced
8 ounces Swiss or provolone cheese, cubed or sliced
½ pound thinly sliced salami

Antipasto platters are the perfect appetizer for a last minute party or for surprise guests as it requires no cooking and tastes delicious! There is no hard-and-fast rule about how to serve your antipasto platter, so serve with or without bread and crackers and feel free to use your favorite combinations of cheeses and vegetables. Marinated olives are also a nice touch.

In a bowl, combine mushrooms, artichoke hearts, and salad dressing. Toss well. On a serving platter, arrange asparagus, red peppers, cheeses, and salami. Place artichoke hearts and mushrooms in a decorative bowl for serving and place on the platter. Serve chilled or room temperature using toothpicks.

Crostini with Roasted Garlic and Herbs

Serves 6

- ~ **PREP TIME:** 3 minutes
- ~ **COOK TIME:** 30 minutes
- ~ **TOTAL COST:** $4.99
- ~ **CALORIES:** 110
- ~ **FAT:** 1 g
- ~ **CARBOHYDRATES:** 21 g
- ~ **PROTEIN:** 4 g
- ~ **CHOLESTEROL:** 3 mg
- ~ **SODIUM:** 220 mg

2 heads garlic
¼ cup extra-virgin olive oil
1 sourdough baguette, sliced into ½-inch slices and
   toasted
1 bunch fresh Italian parsley, chopped

Roasted garlic makes for an easy appetizer for any party. Spread on baguette slices, as here, or serve with roasted peppers and goat cheese.

1. Preheat oven to 400°F. Slice tops off each garlic head (or bulb) revealing the sliced cloves inside. Place both bulbs on aluminum foil and pour olive oil over each. Wrap foil around garlic and place in center of rack of oven and bake for 30 minutes.
2. Remove garlic from oven, place in center of serving platter, and arrange baguette slices around garlic; top garlic with fresh parsley and serve.

Cucumber Cups of Baked Chicken with Spicy Salsa and Cilantro

 Serves 6

~ **PREP TIME:** 8 minutes
~ **TOTAL COST:** $3.75
~ **CALORIES:** 92
~ **FAT:** 3 g
~ **CARBOHYDRATES:** 5 g
~ **PROTEIN:** 7 g
~ **CHOLESTEROL:** 4 mg
~ **SODIUM:** 314 mg

2 cucumbers, peeled and cut into 1- to 1¼-inch sections
½ cup hot salsa
½ cup romaine lettuce, finely chopped
⅓ cup red onion, finely diced
¼ teaspoon garlic salt
⅔ cup baked chicken, diced
⅓ cup pepper jack or other Mexican-style cheese, shredded
2 tablespoons fresh cilantro, leaves chopped
Pinch black pepper to taste

Cucumbers are relatively neutral in flavor so filling them with foods that are highly flavorful creates a perfect balance of flavors. Plus, they are extremely low in calories and great for snacking any time of day.

1. Prepare cucumber cups by scooping ¾ of the center of the cucumber using a melon baller. Place cups upside down in a single layer on paper towels for about 10 minutes before using to drain.
2. In medium mixing bowl, combine all ingredients except cucumber. Toss with fork to combine. Arrange cucumber cups on serving platter. Using a teaspoon, fill each cup with chicken mixture. Top with any additional cilantro.

Cucumber Cups of Goat Cheese, Black Olives, and Herbs

 Serves 4

~ **PREP TIME:** 8 minutes
~ **TOTAL COST:** $6.25
~ **CALORIES:** 106
~ **FAT:** 8 g
~ **CARBOHYDRATES:** 1 g
~ **PROTEIN:** 5 g
~ **CHOLESTEROL:** 20 mg
~ **SODIUM:** 155 g

2 cucumbers, peeled and cut into 1- to 1¼-inch-thick sections
4 ounces goat cheese, plain or herbed, crumbled
4 ounces canned, pitted black olives, chopped
2 tablespoons fresh Italian flat leaf parsley, leaves chopped
2 tablespoons fresh basil, julienned
Black pepper to taste

If you don't have a melon baller, use a small teaspoon or even a measuring teaspoon to scoop out the cucumber. The key is to leave a ¼- to a ½-inch layer of cucumber to support the filling.

1. Prepare cucumber cups by scooping ¾ of the center of the cucumber using a melon baller. Place cups upside down in a single layer on paper towels for about 10 minutes before using to drain.
2. In mixing bowl, combine goat cheese, olives, parsley, basil, and pepper. Toss with fork to combine. Arrange cucumber cups on serving platter. Using a teaspoon, fill each cup with goat cheese mixture until nicely mounded on top. Garnish with chopped parsley before serving.

Feta-Stuffed Grape Leaves

 Serves 6

~ **PREP TIME:** 15 minutes
~ **COOK TIME:** 20 minutes
~ **TOTAL COST:** $6.87
~ **CALORIES:** 54
~ **FAT:** 1 g
~ **CARBOHYDRATES:** 9 g
~ **PROTEIN:** 1 g
~ **CHOLESTEROL:** 4 mg
~ **SODIUM:** 574 mg

1 teaspoon olive oil
1 leek, rinsed, finely chopped
1 cup white rice
2 cups vegetable broth
2 ounces feta cheese, crumbled
Pinch black pepper
1 small jar grape leaves, drained, rinsed, and separated
¼ bunch fresh oregano, leaves chopped

Stuffed grape leaves are commonly associated with Mediterranean dishes. Add golden currants and chopped hazelnuts for a variation on this delicious recipe.

1. Heat oil over medium heat in medium-size sauce-pan. Add leeks and oregano. Toss them in oil; add rice and toss again. Pour stock in with rice mixture and stir. Cover and cook approximately 15 to 20 minutes, until rice is thoroughly cooked. Cool rice in a medium-size mixing bowl, then add feta and pepper.
2. Lay out grape leaf. Place spoonful of rice mixture on center of leaf, then fold each end over the other and seal tightly. Repeat until all grape leaves and rice mixture are used.

Creamy Crab Wontons

Serves 10

~ **PREP TIME:** 20 minutes
~ **COOK TIME:** 7 minutes
~ **TOTAL COST:** $7.00
~ **CALORIES:** 126
~ **FAT:** 9 g
~ **PROTEIN:** 4 g
~ **CHOLESTEROL:** 22 mg
~ **SODIUM:** 182 mg

3 fresh basil leaves, chopped or ½ teaspoon dried basil
¾ pound canned lump crabmeat
¾ cup sour cream, low-fat okay
Black pepper to taste
1 package square or round wontons
2 cups canola oil

These appetizers are best served warm or hot. Prepare them ahead of time and fry just before guests arrive, but be sure to wear an apron so you don't get dirty!

1. Combine basil, crab, sour cream, and pepper. Mix well.
2. Remove wontons from wrapper and place ½ to 1 tablespoon crab mixture in center of wonton. Using your fingertip, spread a little water around the edges. Pinch edges of wonton together to seal.
3. In a medium skillet, heat oil. When oil is hot, add crab wontons and fry until golden brown. Remove from skillet and drain on paper towels.

Quick and Easy Tip
Wonton wrappers come in handy for lots of dishes, including ravioli. The key is not to overfill them so they stay sealed when cooking. Fry, as they are here, or bake them for a crispy cracker.

Citrus-Broiled Pears with Gorgonzola

 Serves 10

- ~ **PREP TIME:** 10 minutes
- ~ **COOK TIME:** 5 minutes
- ~ **TOTAL COST:** $5.75
- ~ **CALORIES:** 71
- ~ **FAT:** 2 g
- ~ **PROTEIN:** 1 g
- ~ **CHOLESTEROL:** 2 mg
- ~ **SODIUM:** 40 mg

2½ teaspoons olive oil
5 Anjou or Bartlett pears, quartered but not peeled
½ cup gorgonzola cheese, crumbled
1 teaspoon honey
2 oranges, zested and juiced
Pinch black pepper

Pears were a staple at Beccofino Ristorante & Wine Bar, Florence, Italy, where I worked for then Executive Chef Francesco Berardinelli. There I learned cheeses go well with pears as with this recipe. In Italy, we also served mascarpone (Italian cream cheese) with our pears.

1. Preheat broiler. Lightly grease baking sheet with 1 teaspoon of oil. Toss pears with remaining oil and place skin side down on the baking sheet. Sprinkle cheese over the pears and drizzle with honey. Sprinkle with zest and a little pepper.
2. Place under broiler and cook until browned. Serve warm.

> **Quick and Easy Tip**
> Serve any leftovers for breakfast the next day with waffles or use cooked pears as an addition to the Basic Muffins (Chapter 3).

Apple Chutney

 Yields 2 cups; serving size ¼ cup

- ~ **TOTAL COST:** $2.95
- ~ **CALORIES:** 55.03
- ~ **FAT:** 0.07 g
- ~ **PROTEIN:** 0.26 g
- ~ **CHOLESTEROL:** 0.0 mg
- ~ **SODIUM:** 149.03 mg

2 apples
1 onion, chopped
2 cloves garlic, minced
¼ cup brown sugar
¼ cup apple cider vinegar
1 tablespoon grated ginger root
½ teaspoon salt
⅛ teaspoon pepper
1 teaspoon cinnamon
½ teaspoon nutmeg

In the store, a bottle of mango chutney costs at least $5.00 for an 8-ounce bottle. This recipe doesn't use mango, but it has the same spices and characteristics.

1. Peel and core apples and chop. Combine in large saucepan with onion, garlic, sugar, and remaining ingredients.
2. Bring to a simmer and simmer, stirring frequently, for 20–30 minutes or until chutney is thick and fairly smooth. Store, covered, in refrigerator for up to 1 week. Can be frozen for longer storage.

Spicy Jalapeño Black Bean Dip

 Serves 8

- ~ **PREP TIME:** 15 minutes
- ~ **COOK TIME:** none
- ~ **TOTAL COST:** $2.28
- ~ **CALORIES:** 112
- ~ **FAT:** 1 g
- ~ **PROTEIN:** 6 g
- ~ **CHOLESTEROL:** 0 mg
- ~ **SODIUM:** 413 mg

2 (15-ounce) cans black beans, drained
2 jalapeño peppers, seeded and chopped
2 cloves garlic, chopped
1 tomato, seeded and chopped
2 tablespoons fresh cilantro, minced
Pinch sea salt and black pepper

For a spicier dip, leave in the jalapeño seeds. Just beware—those seeds can be pretty hot. Also, if you overspice your mouth, drink milk to calm the heat. Water will only flare it!

Combine the beans, jalapeños, and garlic in a food processor. Purée until smooth. Transfer to a bowl. Add the tomato, cilantro, salt, and pepper. Mix well and serve with raw vegetables or pita slices.

Quick and Easy Tip
Food processors are great. If you don't have one, save up and invest in one as they are easier to use and easier to clean than blenders!

Cream Cheese Dip with Fresh Dill

 Serves 8

- ~ **PREP TIME:** 10 minutes
- ~ **CHILL TIME:** 20 minutes to 2 hours
- ~ **TOTAL COST:** $4.14
- ~ **CALORIES:** 85
- ~ **FAT:** 12 g
- ~ **CARBOHYDRATES:** 4 g
- ~ **PROTEIN:** 4 g
- ~ **CHOLESTEROL:** 28 mg
- ~ **SODIUM:** 184 mg

1 (8-ounce) package cream cheese, softened
½ cup low-fat mayonnaise
½ cup plain nonfat yogurt
1 tablespoon fresh dill, chopped
2 fresh garlic cloves, chopped
Pinch sea salt

This tasty and simple dip is perfect served with cucumber slices, carrot sticks, and celery for a truly low-fat treat.

In medium bowl, beat cream cheese until soft and fluffy. Add mayonnaise and yogurt and mix well. Stir in dill, garlic, and salt until combined. Serve immediately, or cover and refrigerate for 20 minutes to 2 hours before serving.

Avocado and Cantaloupe with Raspberry Vinaigrette

 Serves 8

~ **PREP TIME:** 10 minutes

~ **COOK TIME:** none

~ **TOTAL COST:** $6.99

~ **CALORIES:** 63

~ **FAT:** 7 g

~ **CARBOHYDRATES:** 5 g

~ **PROTEIN:** 1 g

~ **CHOLESTEROL:** 0 mg

~ **SODIUM:** 11 mg

¼ cup olive oil
3 tablespoons raspberry vinegar
1 tablespoon honey
¼ teaspoon ground ginger or ½ teaspoon fresh ginger
Pinch sea salt
2 avocados, peeled
½ cantaloupe, seeds removed

Avocados are fairly high in calories and fat, but they contain the good fat that your body needs for energy. They also have no cholesterol and are naturally low in sodium!

1. In medium bowl, combine olive oil, 2 tablespoons vinegar, honey, ginger, and salt. Mix well using wire whisk. Cut avocados into chunks, or make balls using a melon baller. Sprinkle remaining tablespoon vinegar over prepared avocado.

2. Use a melon baller to scoop cantaloupe into small balls. Place cantaloupe and avocado in serving bowl and drizzle raspberry vinaigrette over all. Serve in martini glasses or sherbet glasses for an elegant predinner appetizer presentation.

Creamy Spinach Pesto Spread

 Serves 8

~ **TOTAL COST:** $4.11

~ **CALORIES:** 159.27

~ **FAT:** 14.32 g

~ **PROTEIN:** 3.57 g

~ **CHOLESTEROL:** 32.01 mg

~ **SODIUM:** 213.35 mg

1 tablespoon olive oil
½ cup finely chopped onion
2 cloves garlic, minced
¾ cup Spinach Pesto (this chapter)
⅛ teaspoon pepper
1 tablespoon lemon juice

This spread is delicious on an antipasto platter. Set it out, with small knives, next to some good crusty bread, celery sticks, and bell pepper strips.

1. In a heavy saucepan, cook onion and garlic in olive oil over medium heat until tender, about 5 minutes. Remove to small bowl and let cool. Stir in Spinach Pesto.

2. In medium bowl, beat cream cheese with whipping cream until smooth and fluffy. Add pepper and lemon juice and beat again.

3. Add the Pesto mixture to the cream cheese mixture and stir just until Pesto is swirled into the cream cheese. Spoon into serving bowl or press into a plastic wrap-lined bowl. Cover and chill for 3–4 hours. Serve with small knives, or unmold and serve immediately.

Egg Rolls

Makes 12

- ~ **TOTAL COST:** $6.56
- ~ **CALORIES:** 242.50
- ~ **FAT:** 4.57 g
- ~ **PROTEIN:** 6.85 g
- ~ **CHOLESTEROL:** 16.49 mg
- ~ **SODIUM:** 315.54 mg

½ pound ground pork
1 carrot, shredded
2 cloves garlic, minced
¼ cup finely chopped green onions
1 cup shredded cabbage
2 tablespoons low-sodium soy sauce
1 tablespoon mustard
2 tablespoons cornstarch
1 tablespoon water
1 (12-count) package egg or spring roll wrappers

To make a dipping sauce, mix 3 tablespoons soy sauce with 1 teaspoon sugar, 1 tablespoon mustard, and 1 tablespoon vinegar.

1. In a large skillet, brown ground pork until almost done. Add carrot and garlic; cook and stir for 4–6 minutes or until pork is cooked. Remove from heat, drain well, and add green onions, cabbage, soy sauce, and mustard.
2. Combine cornstarch and water in small bowl and blend well.
3. To form egg rolls, place one wrapper, point-side down, on work surface. Place 3 tablespoons filling 1 inch from corner. Brush all edges of the egg roll wrapper with cornstarch mixture. Fold point over filling, then fold in sides and roll up egg roll, using cornstarch mixture to seal as necessary.
4. Fry the rolls in peanut oil heated to 375°F for 2–3 minutes, turning once, or until deep golden brown. Egg rolls may be frozen after frying; flash freeze, then package and freeze up to 3 months. To reheat fried egg rolls: Place frozen egg rolls on baking sheet. Bake at 375°F for 10–12 minutes or until crisp and hot.

Egg Roll Variations
Egg rolls are a delicious way to repackage leftovers so they don't seem like leftovers—at all! Cooked chopped chicken, steak, roasts, hamburger, or sausage all make excellent egg roll fillings. You can freeze leftover egg roll wrappers and use them anytime; just let thaw on the counter for 20–30 minutes.

Gingerbread Fruit Dip

 Serves 8; serving size 3 tablespoons

- ~ **TOTAL COST:** $3.14
- ~ **CALORIES:** 197.39
- ~ **FAT:** 12.94 g
- ~ **PROTEIN:** 2.65 g
- ~ **CHOLESTEROL:** 37.51 mg
- ~ **SODIUM:** 99.40 mg

1 (8-ounce) package cream cheese, softened
½ cup sour cream
⅓ cup brown sugar
¼ cup light molasses or maple syrup
2 tablespoons chopped candied ginger
½ teaspoon ground ginger
½ teaspoon cinnamon
¼ teaspoon nutmeg

This dip is wonderful served with fresh fruits like apple and pear slices, banana slices, and strawberries.

In medium bowl, beat cream cheese until light and fluffy. Gradually add sour cream, beating until smooth. Add sugar and beat well. Gradually add molasses and beat until smooth. Stir in remaining ingredients. Cover and chill for at least 3 hours before serving with fresh fruit.

Candied Ginger

Candied ginger is also known as crystallized ginger, made of pieces of ginger root simmered in a sugar syrup, then rolled in sugar. You can make your own by combining ¾ cup sugar with ¾ cup water and bring to a simmer. Add ½ cup peeled and chopped fresh ginger root; simmer for 25 minutes. Drain, dry, then roll in sugar to coat. Store in airtight container up to 3 weeks.

Cream and Cranberry Spread

Serves 12

- ~ **TOTAL COST:** $6.52
- ~ **CALORIES:** 193.57
- ~ **FAT:** 12.62 g
- ~ **PROTEIN:** 2.96 g
- ~ **CHOLESTEROL:** 29.22 mg
- ~ **SODIUM:** 77.36 mg

1 (15-ounce) can whole berry cranberry sauce
1 teaspoon orange zest
2 tablespoons frozen orange juice concentrate
1 (8-ounce) package cream cheese
1 cup sour cream
2 tablespoons brown sugar
½ cup sliced almonds, toasted

Serve this tart and creamy dip with crackers (trans fat-free!), slices of toasted French bread, and breadsticks for dipping.

1. In medium bowl, combine cranberry sauce with orange zest; mix well and set aside. In large bowl, combine orange juice concentrate, cream cheese, sour cream, and brown sugar and beat until combined.
2. On large serving plate, spread cream cheese mixture into an even layer. Spoon cranberry mixture evenly over the cream cheese layer. Sprinkle with toasted almonds and serve immediately, or cover and chill for 4–6 hours before serving.

Spinach Puffs with Parmesan Cheese

 Serves 10

- ~ **PREP TIME:** 15 minutes
- ~ **COOK TIME:** 20 minutes
- ~ **TOTAL COST:** $6.93
- ~ **CALORIES:** 215
- ~ **FAT:** 11 g
- ~ **CARBOHYDRATES:** 15 g
- ~ **PROTEIN:** 4 g
- ~ **CHOLESTEROL:** 123 mg
- ~ **SODIUM:** 182 mg

2 packages frozen spinach, thawed and well drained
2 cups dry herb-seasoned bread stuffing mix
6 eggs
1 cup yellow onion, finely chopped
½ cup butter, melted
¾ cup Parmesan cheese, grated
¾ cup fresh Italian parsley, chopped
1½ teaspoons garlic powder
½ teaspoon dried thyme
½ teaspoon black pepper
½ teaspoon sea salt

This dish is traditional to Tuscany, Italy; however, they use ricotta cheese instead of the Parmesan cheese used here.

Preheat oven to 375°F. In a large bowl, combine all ingredients and mix well. Form into 1- to 1¼-inch balls (puffs) and place on a parchment-lined baking sheet. Bake for 15 to 20 minutes. Serve warm.

> **Make-Ahead Tip**
> Puffs may be frozen and stored until needed. When cooking straight from freezer, do not thaw. Place directly on baking sheet and bake for 20 to 25 minutes.

Rolled Eggplant with Ricotta

 Serves 6

- ~ **PREP TIME:** 15 minutes
- ~ **COOK TIME:** 12 minutes
- ~ **TOTAL COST:** $5.75
- ~ **CALORIES:** 110
- ~ **FAT:** 5 g
- ~ **CARBOHYDRATES:** 12 g
- ~ **PROTEIN:** 5 g
- ~ **CHOLESTEROL:** 8 mg
- ~ **SODIUM:** 114 mg

1 medium eggplant (about 1 pound), sliced very thinly, ⅛-inch thick
½ cup rice flour
Sea salt and black pepper
½ cup olive oil
1 cup ricotta cheese
¼ cup black olives, chopped
¼ cup Parmesan cheese, grated

Add a little lemon zest to the ricotta cheese for extra flavor but not extra calories!

1. Preheat oven to 350°F. Salt eggplant slices and stack them on a plate. Let sit under a weight (another plate weighted down) for about ½ hour to let brown juices out. Pat eggplant slices with paper towels to dry. In mixing bowl, place flour and season with salt and pepper. Heat oil to hot but not smoking. Dip slices in flour and fry until almost crisp, about 2 minutes per side.
2. Drain fried slices on paper towels. Place spoonful of ricotta cheese and a little chopped olive on the end of each slice. Roll and secure with a toothpick. Sprinkle rolls with Parmesan cheese and bake for 8 minutes. Serve warm.

Cheesy Filo Rolls

Yields 24 rolls

~ **TOTAL COST:** $4.17
~ **CALORIES:** 93.09
~ **FAT:** 6.21 g
~ **PROTEIN:** 2.37 g
~ **CHOLESTEROL:** 13.87 mg
~ **SODIUM:** 151.77 mg

6 tablespoons Spinach Pesto (this chapter)
1 (3-ounce) package cream cheese, softened
¾ cup grated Parmesan cheese, divided
1 teaspoon dried Italian seasoning
16 (15" × 9") sheets filo dough, thawed
⅓ cup butter, melted

This savory little appetizer is perfect for special occasions. It's easy to make and is very impressive.

1. Preheat oven to 375°F. In small bowl, combine Pesto, cream cheese, and ¼ cup Parmesan cheese; mix well and refrigerate. In small bowl, combine ½ cup cheese and Italian seasoning and mix well.
2. Work with one filo sheet at a time, keeping the rest covered. Place one sheet on work surface and brush with melted butter. Sprinkle with ¼ of the Parmesan cheese mixture. Lay second filo sheet on top of first.
3. Starting with 9-inch side, cut stack into three 3" × 15" strips. Place 2 teaspoons cream cheese filling at 3-inch edge of each strip. Carefully roll up strip.
4. Place each roll seam side down on Silpat-lined cookie sheets. Brush each with butter. Repeat with remaining sheets of filo, butter, Parmesan cheese mixture, and cream cheese filling. Bake for 15–20 minutes or until pastries are golden brown. Cool for 15 minutes, then serve. Store leftovers in the refrigerator.

Filo Dough
Filo, or phyllo, or fillo dough is very thin dough that you find in the freezer section of the supermarket. Thaw it overnight in the refrigerator. Place on counter, cover with waxed paper, then a damp towel. You should work quickly because the dough can dry out fast. Don't worry about tears or rips; just layer on another sheet.

Ricotta–Gorgonzola Torta with Lemon

 Serves 6

- ~ **PREP TIME:** 10 minutes
- ~ **COOK TIME:** 30 minutes
- ~ **TOTAL COST:** $6.97
- ~ **CALORIES:** 202
- ~ **FAT:** 14 g
- ~ **CARBOHYDRATES:** 6 g
- ~ **PROTEIN:** 12 g
- ~ **CHOLESTEROL:** 21 mg
- ~ **SODIUM:** 137 mg

12-ounces fresh whole-milk ricotta cheese
4 ounces or ½ cup Gorgonzola cheese, crumbled
1 teaspoon fresh oregano, leaves chopped
1 teaspoon fresh lemon zest
1 teaspoon fresh lemon juice
Sea salt and black pepper to taste
3 egg whites, beaten stiff with hand mixer or standing
  mixer
½ cup hazelnuts, chopped and toasted

Springform pans have a latch on the side allowing the pan to expand and contract, making it easy to remove after baking. If you don't have one, use a cake ring instead.

Preheat oven to 350°F. In food processor, mix together cheeses, oregano, lemon zest, lemon juice, salt, and pepper until smooth. Place in a bowl and fold in beaten egg whites until combined. Transfer cheese mixture into a 9" springform pan lined with parchment paper or sprayed with nonstick spray. Bake for 30 minutes or until slightly golden. Remove from oven, sprinkle with hazelnuts, cool slightly, and serve.

Marinated Boneless Chicken Wings

Serves 8

- ~ **PREP TIME:** 10 minutes
- ~ **COOK TIME:** 20 minutes
- ~ **TOTAL COST:** $6.89
- ~ **CALORIES:** 95
- ~ **FAT:** 1 g
- ~ **PROTEIN:** 10 g
- ~ **CHOLESTEROL:** 29 mg
- ~ **SODIUM:** 223 mg

2 pounds chicken tenders
⅓ cup soy sauce
¼ cup apple cider vinegar
2 tablespoons Dijon mustard
¼ cup honey
¼ cup brown sugar
1 teaspoon salt
1 teaspoon hot sauce
4 cloves garlic, chopped
½ cup yellow onion, minced

Buffalo chicken wings are a must for any party, especially Super Bowl! Using chicken tenders here saves on calories and cleanup!

1. Cut chicken tenders in half crosswise. In a mixing bowl, combine all ingredients except chicken and mix well. Add chicken tenders, seal bag, and marinate in refrigerator for 2 hours or overnight.
2. In a large saucepan, drizzle in some of the marinade and heat over medium heat. Add chicken and remaining marinade. Cover sauce pan with lid and cook for 10 minutes or until chicken is cooked through. Remove from pan and serve!

Baked Cheese Loaf

Serves 8

~ **PREP TIME:** 8 minutes
~ **COOK TIME:** 12 minutes
~ **TOTAL COST:** $6.96
~ **CALORIES:** 313
~ **FAT:** 22 g
~ **PROTEIN:** 6 g
~ **CHOLESTEROL:** 20 mg
~ **SODIUM:** 391 mg

1½ cups sour cream
¼ cup gorgonzola cheese
¼ cup shredded fontina cheese
1 package Pepperidge Farm puff pastry sheets
2 tablespoons olive oil

Appetizers usually indicate someone's having a party or get-together, and there is nothing better than cheese to make guests happy.

1. Preheat oven 350°F. Line a baking sheet with parchment paper. In a mixing bowl, combine sour cream and cheeses. Blend well.
2. Roll out pastry sheet and coat with olive oil. Spread cheese mixture on top. Roll up dough like a jelly roll into a log. Slice the log into 1-inch slices.
3. Place on baking sheet and bake for 12 minutes or until pastry is puffed and golden. Serve warm.

> **Quick and Easy Tip**
> Prepare log ahead of time and keep in the refrigerator. Do not freeze as sour cream and cheese tend not to freeze well.

Taco Dip

Serves 8

~ **PREP TIME:** 8 minutes
~ **COOK TIME:** none
~ **TOTAL COST:** $6.98
~ **CALORIES:** 375
~ **FAT:** 17 g
~ **PROTEIN:** 8 g
~ **CHOLESTEROL:** 24 mg
~ **SODIUM:** 312 mg

1 (8-ounce) container sour cream
½ teaspoon chili powder
2 cups shredded iceberg lettuce
1 tablespoon fresh cilantro, leaves chopped
1 tablespoon fresh Italian parsley, chopped
1 tablespoon fresh chives, chopped
8 ounces sharp Cheddar cheese, shredded
2 medium ripe tomatoes, seeded and chopped
1 bag tortilla chips

Serve this with extra hot sauce on the side for those who really like the spice!

Blend sour cream and chili powder together and spread mixture into a 13" x 9" inch baking dish or other deep serving platter. Sprinkle lettuce, herbs, cheese, and tomatoes on top. Serve with nacho chips.

> **Quick and Easy Tip**
> Add a can of refried beans to the bottom of the baking dish before putting sour cream for a more traditional taco dip. They are inexpensive and taste good!

Grilled Vegetable Kebabs

Serves 8

- **PREP TIME:** 18 minutes
- **COOK TIME:** 10 minutes
- **TOTAL COST:** $5.25
- **CALORIES:** 49
- **FAT:** 0 g
- **PROTEIN:** 1 g
- **CHOLESTEROL:** 0 mg
- **SODIUM:** 1 mg

1 large yellow onion, cut into eighths
1 red bell pepper, cut into 2-inch squares
1 green bell pepper, cut into 2-inch squares
1 yellow bell pepper, cut into 2-inch squares
8 cremini or button mushrooms, stems removed and halved
2 tablespoons olive oil
Sea salt and black pepper to taste
8 wooden skewers about 5 to 6 inches long

Presoak wooden skewers for about 45 minutes. If 5- to 6-inch skewers are not available, purchase the long ones and cut them with kitchen scissors to the desired length.

1. Preheat grill or broiler. Place all vegetables in a bowl. Pour in olive oil, add sea salt and pepper to taste. Toss vegetables to coat.
2. Skewer vegetables in random order such as red bell pepper slice, onion slice, mushroom slice, green bell pepper slice, onion slice, mushroom slice, and yellow bell pepper slice.
3. Place the skewers on the grill or under the broiler, paying close attention as they cook as they can easily burn. Try to turn the vegetables only once or twice as the vegetables become tender while cooking and can fall off the skewer. Cook until the vegetables are fork tender, about 6 minutes.

Chicken Herb Meatballs

Serves 6

- **PREP TIME:** 20 minutes
- **COOK TIME:** 20 minutes
- **TOTAL COST:** $5.83
- **CALORIES:** 190
- **FAT:** 18 g
- **PROTEIN:** 23 g
- **CHOLESTEROL:** 85 mg
- **SODIUM:** 221 mg

2 slices bread, toasted
1 pound ground chicken
¼ cup dried cranberries
½ cup pecans, chopped, or pecan pieces, chopped
1 egg
¼ teaspoon cinnamon
¼ teaspoon curry powder
½ teaspoon fresh thyme leaves or dried thyme
Sea salt and black pepper
1 jar mango chutney or other favorite jam or chutney

Meatballs are always great for appetizer parties as they are filling for guests who arrive super hungry. You could also serve these as a meal with rice and vegetables for your family.

1. Preheat oven to 350°F. Line a baking sheet with parchment paper. In a small bowl, soak the bread in water for 1 minute or until wet. Squeeze out liquid and set aside.
2. In a larger mixing bowl, combine bread with remaining ingredients. Shape the mixture into balls. Place balls on a baking sheet and cover with foil. Bake about 20 minutes. Serve with jam or chutney.

Meatballs with Chili Pepper Glaze

 Serves 8

~ **PREP TIME:** 8 minutes
~ **COOK TIME:** 20 minutes
~ **TOTAL COST:** $6.38
~ **CALORIES:** 230
~ **FAT:** 13 g
~ **CARBOHYDRATES:** 5 g
~ **PROTEIN:** 2 g
~ **CHOLESTEROL:** 27 mg
~ **SODIUM:** 500 mg

1 16-ounce package frozen mini-meatballs
1 tablespoon olive oil
1 yellow onion, chopped
Sea salt and black pepper to taste
¾ cup chili sauce
½ cup peach jam
¼ cup water

You can make your own meatballs if you prefer, but there are so many delicious, affordable premade meatballs available that it makes sense to save yourself the time of rolling them.

Bake meatballs as directed on package. Meanwhile, heat olive oil in heavy saucepan and add onion, salt, and pepper. Cook and stir until onion is starting to turn brown and caramelize. Add chili sauce, peach jam, and water; stir, and bring to a boil. Add the cooked meatballs and stir to coat. Serve hot.

Spicy and Sweet Flavors
Chili peppers and peaches may not sound like they go together; however, any time you have a spicy ingredient, the sweetness of fruit helps balance out the spice to make for a perfect blend of flavors.

Curried Empanadas

Yields 32 empanadas

~ **TOTAL COST:** $4.55
~ **CALORIES:** 54.26
~ **FAT:** 2.62 g
~ **PROTEIN:** 1.08 g
~ **CHOLESTEROL:** 6.25 mg
~ **SODIUM:** 123.52 mg

1 tablespoon olive oil
½ cup finely chopped onion
1 tablespoon curry powder
2 cups garlic and onion mashed potatoes
½ teaspoon salt
⅛ teaspoon cayenne pepper
32 (3- to 4-inch) wonton wrappers
4 tablespoons butter, melted

Read labels carefully! These products should be trans fat–free; be sure that no ingredient with the word 'hydrogenated' is in the ingredient list.

1. Preheat oven to 375°F. In heavy saucepan, heat olive oil over medium heat. Add onion and curry powder; cook and stir for 4–5 minutes until onions are tender. Remove from heat and add crumbles, potatoes, salt, and pepper and stir together.
2. Place 6 wonton wrappers on work surface. Place 1 tablespoon filling in center of wrapper. Brush edges of wrapper with water. Fold wrapper over filling, forming a triangle. Press edges to seal. Place on ungreased cookie sheet and brush with butter. Bake for 8–12 minutes or until empanadas are light golden brown. Cool for 15 minutes, then serve.

Eggplant Caviar

Serves 6

~ **TOTAL COST:** $5.46
~ **CALORIES:** 172.41
~ **FAT:** 15.33 g
~ **PROTEIN:** 3.56 mg
~ **CHOLESTEROL:** 0.0 mg
~ **SODIUM:** 198.02 mg

1 large eggplant
¼ cup olive oil
½ cup finely chopped onion
4 cloves garlic, minced
3 tablespoons lemon juice
½ teaspoon salt
⅛ teaspoon pepper
½ cup chopped toasted walnuts

Eggplant takes on a smoky taste when roasted; combined with onion and lemon juice it does taste a bit like caviar—only better for you!

1. Preheat oven to 375°F. Peel eggplant and slice into ½-inch rounds. Drizzle half of the olive oil on the bottom of a roasting pan and arrange eggplant in the oil. Drizzle remaining olive oil over eggplant. Roast for 20 minutes.
2. Remove pan from oven and sprinkle onion and garlic over eggplant. Return to oven and roast for 10–20 minutes longer or until eggplant is soft and onion and garlic are tender.
3. Place in medium mixing bowl and sprinkle with lemon juice, salt, and pepper. Using a fork, mash eggplant mixture until partially smooth. Fold in nuts and serve immediately or omit nuts and cover and refrigerate up to 24 hours before serving. Fold in walnuts just before serving.

Toasting Nuts

Toasting nuts brings out their flavor and makes a little go a long way. To toast nuts, preheat an oven (or the toaster oven) to 350°F. Spread nuts in a single layer on a baking sheet. Toast for 8–12 minutes, shaking pan once during cooking time, until the nuts are fragrant and a bit darker in color. Let cool completely before chopping.

Poppy Popcorn

 Yields 18 cups; 18 servings

- **TOTAL COST:** $6.75
- **CALORIES:** 290.06
- **FAT:** 16.89 g
- **PROTEIN:** 3.47 g
- **CHOLESTEROL:** 16.96 mg
- **SODIUM:**217.99 mg

4 quarts air-popped popcorn
1 cup walnut pieces
1 cup pecan pieces
10 tablespoons butter
¾ cup sugar
1 cup brown sugar
⅓ cup corn syrup
1 teaspoon salt
½ teaspoon baking soda
2 teaspoons vanilla
1 cup milk chocolate chips

This crunchy and crisp mixture makes a lot of sweetened popcorn and nuts. It's perfect for the holidays.

1. Preheat oven to 350°F. Carefully remove unpopped kernels from popcorn. Place remaining popcorn in two large baking pans. Spread pecans and walnuts on a cookie sheet. Toast for 8 minutes, stirring once during baking time. Add sliced almonds and toast 3–5 minutes longer until nuts are fragrant. Cool completely and mix with popcorn.
2. In large saucepan, combine butter, sugar, brown sugar, corn syrup, honey, and salt. Bring to a boil over high heat; reduce heat to medium and boil for 5 minutes. Remove from heat and stir in baking soda; mixture will foam up. Stir in vanilla, then spoon mixture evenly over popcorn mixture. Toss to coat and spread evenly in pans.
3. Reduce oven heat to 250°F. Bake popcorn mixture for 1 hour, stirring every 20 minutes during baking time. While mixture is baking, grind chocolate chips in blender or food processor. When popcorn mixture is golden, remove from oven and sprinkle ground chocolate evenly over both pans. Let stand for 10 minutes, then stir. Let cool completely, break into pieces, and stir in airtight container.

Shrimp Quiches

 Makes 36; serves 12

- ~ **TOTAL COST:** $6.98
- ~ **CALORIES:** 266.80
- ~ **FAT:** 15.38 g
- ~ **PROTEIN:** 8.26 g
- ~ **CHOLESTEROL:** 80.47 mg
- ~ **SODIUM:** 371.23 mg

2 9-inch Angel Pie Crusts (Chapter 15)
½ cup finely chopped onion
1 tablespoon butter
2 eggs
⅓ cup heavy cream
1 (4-ounce) can tiny shrimp, drained
½ teaspoon dried marjoram leaves
¼ teaspoon salt
⅛ teaspoon pepper
¾ cup shredded Swiss cheese

Wow—shrimp quiches seem so expensive, yet when served as an appetizer they are quite affordable. And impressive!

1. Using a 2-inch cookie cutter, cut 36 rounds from pie crusts. Place each in a 1 ¾-inch mini muffin cup, pressing to bottom and sides. Set aside.
2. Sauté onion in butter until tender. Beat eggs with cream in medium bowl. Add drained shrimp, onion, marjoram, salt, and pepper, and mix well.
3. Sprinkle 1 teaspoon cheese into each muffin cup and fill cups with shrimp mixture. Bake at 375°F for 15–18 minutes or until pastry is golden and filling is set. Serve immediately.

Cheesy Potato Chips

Yields 12 cups; serving size 1 cup

- ~ **TOTAL COST:** $2.57
- ~ **CALORIES:** 59.01
- ~ **FAT:** 3.26 g
- ~ **PROTEIN:** 1.96 g
- ~ **CHOLESTEROL:** 2.93 mg
- ~ **SODIUM:** 305.65 mg

1 russet potato (about 1 pound)
1 lemon, juiced
2 cups canola oil
½ cup finely grated Parmesan cheese
1 teaspoon salt, or to taste

Making your own potato chips is fun. For best results, use the powdered Parmesan cheese in the green can.

1. Fill a large bowl with cold water and add ice cubes and lemon juice, along with the lemon rind. Peel potato and cut into very thin chips (about ⅓-inch) using a food processor, a mandoline, or a vegetable peeler. Place into water as soon as chips are formed.
2. In large heavy pan, heat canola oil to 375°F. Working with a handful of potato chips at a time, remove from water and drain on kitchen towels, then pat dry with paper towels.
3. Drop chips into the oil; fry for 3–6 minutes, turning with slotted spoon, until chips are light golden brown. Remove and place onto paper towels; sprinkle hot chips with a mixture of cheese and salt. Repeat with remaining chips and salt mixture. Cool completely, then store in airtight container up to 3 days.

Traditional Hummus

Serves 6

- ~ **PREP TIME:** 7 minutes
- ~ **COOK TIME:** none
- ~ **TOTAL COST:** $2.44
- ~ **CALORIES:** 61
- ~ **FAT:** 2 g
- ~ **PROTEIN:** 12 g
- ~ **CHOLESTEROL:** 0 mg
- ~ **SODIUM:** 718 mg

1 cup garbanzo beans, drained
2 garlic cloves
1 lemon, zested and juiced
2 teaspoons extra virgin olive oil
Sea salt and black pepper to taste
¼ cup fresh Italian parsley, chopped, or 2 teaspoons
   dried parsley

Hummus is always a crowd pleaser. Add tomato wedges to the serving platter for added color.

In a food processor or blender, purée the garbanzo beans, garlic, and lemon zest and juice. While purée-ing, drizzle in the olive oil until well combined. Remove the mixture and season to taste with salt and pepper. Sprinkle with parsley when serving. Serve with crackers or Melba toast.

Quick and Easy Tip
Serve with celery stalks for a low-fat, low-cost appetizer that your friends and guests will love.

Dip of Eggplant and Herbs

Serves 6

- ~ **PREP TIME:** 15 minutes
- ~ **COOK TIME:** 10 minutes
- ~ **TOTAL COST:** $4.40
- ~ **CALORIES:** 88
- ~ **FAT:** 6 g
- ~ **PROTEIN:** 4 g
- ~ **CHOLESTEROL:** 4 mg
- ~ **SODIUM:** 16 mg

1 large eggplant
1 tablespoon olive oil
3 cloves garlic, minced
½ cup yogurt, low-fat or nonfat is okay
½ cup sour cream, low-fat or nonfat is okay
1 tablespoon fresh rosemary, chopped
1 tablespoon fresh basil, chopped
1 tablespoon fresh Italian parsley, chopped
Sea salt and black pepper to taste

A lot of people don't get that excited when they hear the word eggplant, but it makes for a tasty appetizer and is almost always a hit at parties.

1. Preheat oven to 375°F and line a baking sheet with parchment paper.
2. Slice eggplant lengthwise and drizzle with olive oil and garlic. Cover with foil and place on baking sheet. Bake in oven for 10 minutes. Remove from oven and place in plastic bag to sweat.
3. Spoon the eggplant pulp into a food processor or blender, and pulse. Add the yogurt and sour cream ¼ cup at a time, and blend until it reaches the consistency of thick sauce. Add the herbs and blend well. Season with salt and pepper to taste. Refrigerate until ready to use.

Roasted Roma Tomatoes with Herbs

 Serves 4

~ **PREP TIME:** 8 minutes
~ **COOK TIME:** 11 minutes
~ **TOTAL COST:** $2.52
~ **CALORIES:** 32
~ **FAT:** 2 g
~ **PROTEIN:** 1 g
~ **CHOLESTEROL:** 0 mg
~ **SODIUM:** 3mg

4 Roma or plum tomatoes
3 cloves garlic
¼ cup fresh thyme, leaves removed from stems
Sea salt and black pepper to taste
Extra virgin olive oil for drizzling after baked

This appetizer was a favorite at the restaurant I worked for in Florence, Italy. We would bake hundreds of tomatoes each day and serve as an appetizer on our regular menu.

1. Preheat oven to 385°F.
2. Cut the tomatoes into quarters and remove seeds. Lay out each quarter in a single layer on a baking sheet lined with parchment paper. Mince the garlic, and chop the thyme slightly to open up the flavors. Sprinkle the tomatoes with the garlic, thyme, sea salt, and black pepper.
3. Bake in the oven for approximately 10 to 12 minutes. Then remove and serve on top of crackers, Melba rounds, and drizzle with olive oil. Or, skip the carbs and calories and enjoy the Italian way with olive oil!

Creamy and Crunchy Hummus

 Yields 3 cups; serving size ¼ cup

~ **TOTAL COST:** $3.54
~ **CALORIES:** 110.29
~ **FAT:** 5.98 g
~ **PROTEIN:** 3.48 g
~ **CHOLESTEROL:** 2.81 mg
~ **SODIUM:** 213.00 mg

1 tablespoon olive oil
5 cloves garlic, sliced
1 (15-ounce) can garbanzo beans
½ cup mashed sweet potato
3 tablespoons lemon juice
½ teaspoon salt
⅛ teaspoon pepper
⅓ cup sour cream
½ cup chopped walnuts

Sweet potato adds great color and nutrition to classic hummus. To make it easy, use canned sweet potatoes, drained and mashed.

1. In small saucepan, heat olive oil over medium heat. Add sliced garlic; cook and stir until garlic turns light brown; do not let it burn. Remove from heat and cool until warm.
2. Combine with remaining ingredients except walnuts in blender or food processor; blend or process until smooth. Stir in walnuts and serve, or cover and chill before serving.

Buffalo Mozzarella with Tomatoes and Basil

 Serves 8

~ **PREP TIME:** 10 minutes
~ **TOTAL COST:** $7.00
~ **CALORIES:** 98
~ **FAT:** 9 g
~ **CARBOHYDRATES:** 0 g
~ **PROTEIN:** 4 g
~ **CHOLESTEROL:** 20 mg
~ **SODIUM:** 85 mg

8 ounces buffalo mozzarella
1 bunch fresh basil leaves, stems removed
6 Roma tomatoes, sliced
Extra-virgin olive oil
Sea salt and black pepper

Extra-virgin olive oil is the best oil to use when drizzling foods for flavor. When cooking, however, use olive oil, as it has a higher burning temperature.

Slice mozzarella into 2-inch slices. Arrange on platter by placing tomato slice first, then basil leaf, then cheese. When finished, drizzle with olive oil and sprinkle with just a pinch of salt and pepper. Enjoy!

Insalata Caprese
Insalata caprese is the Italian name to this simple yet delicious salad that was made famous by the Italian island of Capri for which this salad is named.

Roasted Red Pepper Aioli

 Serves 6

~ **PREP TIME:** 8 minutes
~ **COOK TIME:** none
~ **TOTAL COST:** $3.99
~ **CALORIES:** 83
~ **FAT:** 5 g
~ **PROTEIN:** 3 g
~ **CHOLESTEROL:** 7 mg
~ **SODIUM:** 796 mg

1 (7-ounce) jar roasted red peppers, drained
1 tablespoon balsamic vinegar
½ tablespoon fresh mint leaves, chopped
⅓ cup low-fat cottage cheese
⅓ cup mayonnaise
2 cloves garlic
Sea salt and black pepper to taste

Aioli is a traditional Mediterranean dip that can also be used as a sauce for fish or chicken.

Combine the roasted red peppers and vinegar in a food processor. Purée until smooth. Add the mint, cottage cheese, mayonnaise, garlic, salt, and pepper. Process until smooth. Serve with raw vegetables, crostini, or pita wedges.

Quick and Easy Tip
Usually aioli is made by combining eggs and oil in a food processor; however, using mayonnaise saves time and reduces the health risk that comes with consuming raw eggs.

Beefy Mini Pies

Makes 24

~ **TOTAL COST:** $5.64

~ **CALORIES:** 122.57

~ **FAT:** 7.27 g

~ **PROTEIN:** 4.69 g

~ **CHOLESTEROL:** 31.40 mg

~ **SODIUM:** 263.34 mg

1 (10-ounce) package refrigerated flaky dinner rolls
½ pound ground beef
1 small onion, chopped
2 cloves garlic, minced
1 cup shredded Colby cheese
2 eggs
⅓ cup light cream
½ teaspoon dried dill weed

Include these pies in an appetizer buffet, or serve them to guests before dinner with a glass of red wine.

1. Preheat oven to 350°F. Remove rolls from package and divide each roll into 3 rounds. Place each round into a 3-inch muffin cup; press firmly onto bottom and up sides.
2. In a heavy skillet, cook ground beef with onion and garlic until beef is done. Drain well. Place 1 tablespoon beef mixture into each dough-lined muffin cup. Sprinkle cheese over beef mixture. In small bowl, beat together eggs, half-and-half, and dill weed. Spoon this mixture over beef in muffin cups, making sure not to overfill cups.
3. Bake at 350°F for 10–13 minutes or until filling is puffed and set. Flash freeze in single layer on baking sheet. When frozen solid, wrap, label, and freeze.
4. To thaw and reheat: Thaw pies in single layer in refrigerator over-night. Bake at 350°F for 7–9 minutes or until hot.

Grilled Beef Skewers

 Serves 4

- ~ **PREP TIME:** 16 minutes
- ~ **COOK TIME:** 15 minutes
- ~ **TOTAL COST:** $6.99
- ~ **CALORIES:** 235
- ~ **FAT:** 27 g
- ~ **PROTEIN:** 27 g
- ~ **CHOLESTEROL:** 56 mg
- ~ **SODIUM:** 53 mg

¾ pound sirloin beef
¼ cup walnuts, chopped
2 garlic cloves
1 tablespoon olive oil
½ cup dry red wine such as Merlot
Sea salt and black pepper

Sirloin is a quality cut of beef and is much less expensive than filet. Marinades also tenderize beef, allowing you to use less choice cuts for certain recipes such as this one.

1. Thinly slice and skewer the beef; skewers do not need to be pre-soaked. Place beef skewers in a large rectangular baking dish.
2. In food processor or blender, finely grind the walnuts and add garlic, oil, wine, and pinch of salt and pepper. Blend well. Pour mixture over beef skewers, coating well. Cover and refrigerate for 15 minutes or up to 2 hours.
3. Preheat oven to 400°F. Bake skewers, covered, for 15 minutes. Serve hot.

> **Quick and Easy Tip**
> Sharp knives are essential to slicing beef; however, before slicing, place beef in freezer for about 15 minutes and beef will become more firm making it easier to slice.

CHAPTER 3

BREAD

Freezer Wheat Rolls

 Yields 24 rolls

~ **TOTAL COST:** $1.91
~ **CALORIES:** 102.01
~ **FAT:** 2.21 g
~ **PROTEIN:** 2.95 g
~ **CHOLESTEROL:** 8.81 mg
~ **SODIUM:** 101.76 mg

2 (0.25-ounce) packages active dry yeast
½ cup warm water
¼ cup brown sugar
1½ cups whole wheat flour

1 teaspoon salt
1 egg
3 tablespoons oil
2–3 cups all-purpose flour

Frozen brown–and–serve rolls make entertaining so easy. These rolls are hearty yet light, perfect served warm with some softened butter.

1. In large mixing bowl, combine yeast and warm water; stir until dissolved. Let stand for 10 minutes, or until yeast starts to bubble. Add sugar, whole wheat flour, salt, egg, and oil and beat with an electric mixer for 2 minutes.
2. By hand, gradually stir in bread flour until the mixture forms a medium soft dough. Turn dough out onto lightly floured surface and knead until smooth and elastic, about 8 minutes. Clean bowl and grease with butter. Place dough in bowl, turning to grease top. Cover and let rise in warm place for 1 hour until double.
3. Grease two cookie sheets with unsalted butter. Punch down dough and divide into 24 pieces. Roll each ball between your hands to form a smooth ball. Place on prepared cookie sheets, cover with a kitchen towel, and let rise for 30–40 minutes until double.
4. Preheat oven to 300°F. Bake the rolls for 15–20 minutes, reversing cookie sheets halfway during cooking, until the rolls are puffed and firm to the touch, but not browned. Let rolls cool on cookie sheets for 5 minutes, then remove and place on a wire rack to cool. Place in hard–sided freezer containers and freeze up to 3 months.
5. To serve, let frozen rolls stand at room temperature for 1 hour. Then bake in preheated 400°F oven for 10–15 minutes or until rolls are golden brown and hot. Brush with more butter and serve.

Forming Dinner Rolls

You can shape these rolls other ways, if you'd like. Flatten the balls, spread with butter, and then fold over to form Parker House Rolls. Divide each ball into 3 pieces and place in a muffin cup for Cloverleaf Rolls. And for knots, roll each ball into a roll, then tie loosely into a knot and fold ends under. Let rise and bake as directed.

Cinnamon Biscotti

 Yields 32 biscotti

- ~ **TOTAL COST:** $2.87
- ~ **CALORIES:** 171.94
- ~ **FAT:** 3.68 g
- ~ **PROTEIN:** 4.02 g
- ~ **CHOLESTEROL:** 27.46 mg
- ~ **SODIUM:** 100.56 mg

2 (0.25-ounce) packages dry yeast
½ cup warm water
½ cup butter
1 cup sugar, divided
1 teaspoon salt
2 teaspoons cinnamon, divided
2 cups boiling water
3 eggs
7–8 cups all purpose flour

Your own homemade biscotti are so delicious. It's difficult to find biscotti at a bakery or coffee shop for less than a dollar each. Make your own and save!

1. In small bowl, combine yeast with ½ cup water and set aside. In large bowl, combine butter, ¾ cup sugar, salt, and 1 teaspoon cinnamon. Pour boiling water over and stir until butter melts. Let stand until just warm. Beat in eggs and yeast mixture. Add 5 cups flour, a cup at a time, beating well after each addition.
2. Then stir in enough flour to make a firm dough. Knead on floured surface until smooth, about 5 minutes. Place in greased bowl, turning to grease top. Cover and let rise until doubled, about 1 hour.
3. Punch down and divide into four balls. Grease 2 cookie sheets with unsalted butter. On prepared cookie sheets, roll out balls into 5" × 8" rectangles. Cover and let rise until doubled, about 30 minutes.
4. Preheat oven to 350°F. Bake loaves until light golden brown and set, about 25–35 minutes. Let cool on wire racks for 30 minutes. Increase oven temperature to 400°F.
5. Then slice each loaf into eight 1-inch pieces. In small bowl, combine ¼ cup sugar with 1 teaspoon cinnamon. Dip both cut sides of slices into cinnamon sugar and return to cookie sheets. Bake again, turning once, until brown and crisp, about 5 minutes on each side. Cool completely on wire racks.

Double Cornbread

 Yields one 9" × 9" baking pan (or 9 pieces)

~ **TOTAL COST:** $2.38

~ **CALORIES:** 241.56

~ **FAT:** 10.37 g

~ **PROTEIN:** 5.09 g

~ **CHOLESTEROL:** 57.62 mg

~ **SODIUM:** 179.89 mg

1 cup frozen corn, thawed

1 cup all-purpose flour

1 cup yellow cornmeal

¼ cup sugar

¼ cup vegetable oil

½ cup sour cream

2 eggs, beaten

½ teaspoon baking powder

½ teaspoon baking soda

½ teaspoon salt

What do you do with all the bags of frozen corn that have about ¼ of a cup rattling around at the bottom? Save them up and use in this fabulous quick bread recipe, of course.

1. Preheat oven to 325°F. Grease a 9" × 9" pan with solid shortening and set aside. Place half of the corn in a blender or food processor and process until as smooth as possible. Mix with whole kernel corn in large mixing bowl. Add remaining ingredients and stir just until combined.
2. Pour batter in greased pans. Bake for 40–50 minutes or until cornbread is golden brown around the edges and a toothpick inserted in the center comes out clean. Serve warm.

> **Northern Versus Southern Corn Bread**
> There is a great debate brewing over what ingredients should be included in cornbread. In the Southern United States, white cornmeal and no sugar are the rule, and the cornbread must be baked in a cast iron skillet. In the North, yellow cornmeal and sugar are usually used, and the bread is cakier and smoother. Which is better? Depends on which one you ate first!

Whole Wheat French Bread

 Yields 1 loaf (or 16 slices)

~ **TOTAL COST:** $1.80

~ **CALORIES:** 109.53

~ **FAT:** 1.88 g

~ **PROTEIN:** 3.38 g

~ **CHOLESTEROL:** 3.16 mg

~ **SODIUM:** 150.58 mg

1 (0.25-ounce) package active dry yeast

1¼ cups warm water

¼ cup orange juice

½ cup sour cream

1 teaspoon salt

1 tablespoon brown sugar

1–½ cups whole wheat flour

1–½ to 2 cups all-purpose flour

Bakery breads have skyrocketed in price, much more than the price of flour. Making your own is fun and easy, and saves a lot of money.

1. In large bowl, combine yeast with warm water and let stand for 10 minutes. Add orange juice, sour cream, salt, and brown sugar along with the whole wheat flour and ½ cup all-purpose flour and beat well.
2. Cover this sponge with a towel and let rise in warm place for 2 hours. Then add enough remaining all–purpose flour to make a firm dough. Turn onto floured surface and knead until smooth and elastic, about 5 minutes. Place in greased bowl, turning to grease top. Cover and let rise for 45 minutes.
3. Punch down dough and roll or pat into a 12" × 8" rectangle. Roll up tightly, starting with the 12-inch side. Roll on floured surface to a 14-inch long cylinder. Place on lightly floured cookie sheet, cover, and let rise for 30 minutes.
4. Preheat oven to 375°F. Carefully cut a few slashes on the top of the loaf. Bake for 25–35 minutes or until bread sounds hollow when tapped with fingers. Cool completely on a wire rack.

Brown Bread

 Yields 1 loaf (or 16 slices)

- **TOTAL COST:** $1.99
- **CALORIES:** 158.75
- **FAT:** 3.86 g
- **PROTEIN:** 3.56 g
- **CHOLESTEROL:** 22.08 mg
- **SODIUM:** 74.08 mg

⅓ cup rolled oatmeal
1–½ cups all-purpose flour
1 cup whole wheat flour
1 teaspoon baking powder
1 teaspoon baking soda
¼ cup brown sugar
¼ cup sugar
¼ cup butter
⅓ cup light molasses
1 egg, beaten
1 cup buttermilk
⅓ cup water

This classic recipe makes a delicious and inexpensive old-fashioned meal when paired with Rich Baked Beans (Chapter 11).

1. Preheat oven to 350°F. Grease a 9" × 5" loaf pan with solid shortening and set aside. Place oatmeal in small saucepan. Toast over medium heat until fragrant, about 3–5 minutes. Cool completely, then grind in food processor or blender.
2. In large bowl, combine oatmeal, all purpose flour, whole wheat flour, baking powder, baking soda, brown sugar, and sugar and mix well. Cut in butter until particles are fine.
3. In small bowl, combine molasses, egg, buttermilk, and water and mix well. Add to flour mixture all at once, and stir just until combined. Pour batter into prepared pan. Bake for 50–60 minutes until dark brown and firm. Cool completely.

Whole Wheat Flour

Store whole wheat flour in the freezer to make it last longer. It is more expensive than all-purpose flour, so take care of it! Decant it into a hard sided freezer container, label with the date you purchased the product, and freeze for up to 6 months. You can use it straight from the freezer, or let it stand at room temperature for 30 minutes first.

Flatbread with Onion

 Serves 10

- **PREP TIME:** 10 minutes
- **CHILL:** 1 hour
- **COOK TIME:** 8 minutes
- **TOTAL COST:** $2.70
- **CALORIES:** 100
- **FAT:** 1 g
- **PROTEIN:** 3 g
- **CHOLESTEROL:** 19 mg
- **SODIUM:** 329 mg

3½ cups plain flour
½ teaspoon sea salt
1 cup cold water, adding up to ¼ cup extra if needed
1 large yellow onion, chopped
1 teaspoon olive oil

The great thing about basic flatbread is that you can add almost any flavorful ingredient you like. This recipes uses chopped fresh onion. You can also sauté the onion for about 5 minutes and then add to the mixture for a slightly different flavor.

1. Sift together flour and salt. Mix flour and water in mixer using a large dough hook for 3 minutes or until all ingredients are incorporated and the dough is formed. Add onion and incorporate into dough. Let dough rest for 1 hour in the refrigerator. Form dough into approximately 20 small balls. On a floured surface, use a floured rolling pin to roll out dough into circles about ½-inch thick.
2. Lightly grease skillet with oil and heat to medium heat. Add flatbread and cook about 4 minutes per side, using tongs to flip, or until lightly browned on each side.

Quick and Easy Tip
Developing a feel for how much to knead your dough comes with time and experience. If you overwork it, you overdevelop the gluten in the dough, making it tough. This causes the bread to have a chewy, unpleasant texture. A few quick motions should be all the kneading your dough needs.

Whole Wheat Flatbread with Herbs

 Serves 10

~ **PREP TIME:** 8 minutes
~ **CHILL:** 1 hour
~ **COOK TIME:** 8 minutes
~ **TOTAL COST:** $3.12
~ **CALORIES:** 112
~ **FAT:** 1 g
~ **PROTEIN:** 4 g
~ **CHOLESTEROL:** 18 mg
~ **SODIUM:** 330 mg

3 cups whole wheat flour
1 cup plain flour
½ teaspoon sea salt
1 cup cold water, plus up to an extra ¼ cup if needed
2 tablespoons fresh thyme, stems removed, leaves chopped
2 tablespoons fresh rosemary, stems removed, leaves chopped
1 teaspoon olive oil

When adding water to dough, add a little at a time to incorporate into mixture. If dough still feels too dry, add a little more water.

1. Sift together flour and salt. Mix flour and water in mixer using a large dough hook for 3 minutes or until all ingredients are incorporated and the dough is formed. Add herbs and incorporate into dough. Let dough rest for 1 hour in the refrigerator. Form dough into approximately 20 small balls. On a floured surface, use a floured rolling pin to roll out dough into circles about ½-inch thick.
2. Lightly grease skillet with oil and heat to medium heat. Add flatbread and cook about 4 minutes per side, using tongs to flip, or until lightly browned on each side.

Basic Flatbread

 Serves 10

~ **PREP TIME:** 10 minutes
~ **CHILL:** 1 hour
~ **COOK TIME:** 8 minutes
~ **TOTAL COST:** $2.20
~ **CALORIES:** 100
~ **FAT:** 0.8 g
~ **PROTEIN:** 3 g
~ **CHOLESTEROL:** 18 mg
~ **SODIUM:** 326 mg

4 cups plain flour
½ teaspoon sea salt
1⅓ cups cold water
1 teaspoon olive oil

For a little sweetness, add 1 tablespoon of honey to the dough.

1. Sift together flour and salt. Mix flour with water in a mixer using a large dough hook for 3 minutes or until ingredients are incorporated and the dough is formed. Let dough rest for 1 hour in the refrigerator.
2. Once chilled, form dough into small balls, approximately 20 balls. On floured surface, use a floured rolling pin to roll out each ball into a circles about ½-inch thick. Lightly grease skillet with oil and heat to medium heat. Add flatbread and cook about 4 minutes per side, using tongs to flip, or until lightly browned on each side.

Quick and Easy Tip
Once the flatbread is cooked, drizzle with olive oil and sprinkle with sea salt and freshly chopped rosemary leaves.

Mexican Cornbread

 Serves 9

- ~ **PREP TIME:** 5 minutes
- ~ **COOK TIME:** 23 minutes
- ~ **TOTAL COST:** $2.79
- ~ **CALORIES:** 223
- ~ **FAT:** 7 g
- ~ **PROTEIN:** 5 g
- ~ **CHOLESTEROL:** 6 mg
- ~ **SODIUM:** 749 mg

1 cup buttermilk
¼ cup frozen corn kernels, thawed
¼ cup vegetable or canola oil
1 egg
1¼ cups pancake mix
¾ cup yellow cornmeal
½ teaspoon paprika

Adding the corn kernels makes for a Mexican-style cornbread. You can also add roasted red bell peppers and cheese.

1. Preheat oven to 400°F. Grease a 9-inch square baking pan and set aside. In a medium bowl, combine buttermilk, corn kernels, oil, and egg, and beat with a wire whisk. Stir into dry ingredients just until combined. Pour into prepared pan.
2. Bake for 17 to 23 minutes or until edges are golden brown and top springs back when touched with finger. Serve warm with butter.

Quick and Easy Tip
Leftover cornbread can be crumbled and used as bread crumbs for other dishes such as baked chicken.

Grilled Garlic Bread

Serves 6

- ~ **PREP TIME:** 5 minutes
- ~ **COOK TIME:** 10 minutes
- ~ **TOTAL COST:** $6.00
- ~ **CALORIES:** 172
- ~ **FAT:** 6 g
- ~ **PROTEIN:** 3 g
- ~ **CHOLESTEROL:** 22 mg
- ~ **SODIUM:** 400 mg

½ cup extra virgin olive oil
4 cloves garlic, crushed and minced
Pinch onion salt
3 tablespoons butter, melted
1 teaspoon fresh Italian parsley, chopped
1 loaf French bread

Garlic bread is the best and customary accompaniment to most Italian dishes. Just be sure to serve fresh parsley with it for those who have intense garlic breath.

Preheat grill or grill pan. Combine all ingredients, except bread, in a mixing bowl, stirring well. Using a pastry brush, brush butter mixture on both sides of bread slices. Wrap entire loaf in aluminum foil and put on the grill or grill pan. Turn after 5 minutes and heat for another 5 minutes.

Quick and Easy Tip
The secret to great garlic bread is mixing all the ingredients together with melted or super softened butter. That way, all the flavors meld together and coat the bread evenly.

Tex-Mex Gougère

Serves 6

- **TOTAL COST:** $4.51
- **CALORIES:** 338.97
- **FAT:** 17.70 g
- **PROTEIN:** 15.33 g
- **CHOLESTEROL:** 189.32 mg
- **SODIUM:** 572.39 mg

¼ cup butter
¼ cup minced onion
1 clove garlic, minced
2 tablespoons chopped drained pimentos
2 tablespoons diced green chiles, drained
1 cup milk
½ teaspoon salt
⅛ teaspoon pepper
1¼ cups flour
2 teaspoons chili powder
4 eggs
1 cup diced Muenster cheese
1 tablespoon evaporated milk
2 tablespoons finely grated Cotija cheese

Gougère is a classic French quick bread made from pate a choux pastry. Tex-Mex seasonings add a nice twist to this cheesy and crisp bread. Served with a green salad, it's an excellent lunch dish.

1. Preheat oven to 375°F. Melt butter in large saucepan over medium heat and cook onion and garlic until tender, 4–5 minutes. Add pimentos and chiles; cook and stir for 1–2 minutes.
2. Add milk, salt, and pepper and bring to a rolling boil. All at once, add the flour and chili powder and cook and stir over medium heat until the mixture forms a ball and cleans the sides of the pan.
3. Remove from heat and add eggs, one at a time, beating well after each addition. Fold in Muenster cheese. Line a cookie or baking sheet with Silpat silicon liner or foil. Grease foil with solid shortening.
4. Scoop out dough in spoonfuls the size of an egg and arrange into an 8-inch ring on the liner, edges just touching, leaving the center open. Spoon a smaller ring of dough spoonfuls on top. Brush bread with milk and sprinkle with Cotija cheese.
5. Bake the bread at 375°F for about 35–45 minutes, or until the bread is puffy, deep golden brown, and firm. Serve immediately.

Breadsticks with Parmesan Cheese

 Serves 8

~ **PREP TIME:** 8 minutes
~ **COOK TIME:** 16 minutes
~ **TOTAL COST:** $5.04
~ **CALORIES:** 172
~ **FAT:** 8 g
~ **PROTEIN:** 2 g
~ **CHOLESTEROL:** 22 mg
~ **SODIUM:** 390 mg

3 tablespoons butter
2 cloves garlic, minced
½ cup Parmesan cheese, grated
¼ cup Romano cheese, grated
½ teaspoon dried Italian seasoning
1 11-ounce can refrigerated breadstick dough

Breadsticks are great with soup, salad, or just by themselves. Keep them stored in an airtight container for freshness.

1. Preheat oven to 375°F. Line baking sheets with parchment paper and set aside. In a microwave-safe dish, place butter and garlic. Cook on full power for 1 minute, until garlic is fragrant. Pour butter mixture onto a shallow plate and let stand for 5 minutes.
2. Meanwhile, on another shallow plate, combine cheeses and Italian seasoning mix. Open dough and separate into 8 breadsticks; cut each in half crosswise to make 16 breadsticks. Dip each breadstick into butter mixture, then roll in cheese mixture to coat. Place on baking sheets, about 2 inches apart. Bake breadsticks for 12 to 16 minutes or until they are puffed and light golden brown.

Two-Cheese Garlic Bread

 Serves 6

~ **PREP TIME:** 5 minutes
~ **COOK TIME:** 21 minutes
~ **TOTAL COST:** $6.56
~ **CALORIES:** 165
~ **FAT:** 4 g
~ **PROTEIN:** 5 g
~ **CHOLESTEROL:** 14 mg
~ **SODIUM:** 292 mg

1 loaf French bread
4 cloves garlic, minced
½ tablespoon cayenne pepper
2 tablespoons fresh Italian flat-leaf parsley, leaves chopped
½ cup butter
1 teaspoon lemon pepper
¼ cup Parmesan cheese
¼ cup cheddar cheese

This crispy bread is perfect with spaghetti and meatballs or a salad. Use leftovers to make bread crumbs or croutons.

1. Slice bread into ¼-inch thick slices. In a heavy skillet, heat olive oil over medium heat and sauté garlic until soft and fragrant, about 2 to 3 minutes. Pour oil and garlic into medium bowl and let stand for 10 minutes. Add butter, lemon pepper, cayenne, parsley, and cheeses and mix well.
2. Preheat broiler. Spread butter mixture onto both sides of bread. Place on a baking sheet and broil about 6 inches from heat source for 3 to 5 minutes, until light brown. Turn and broil for 3 minutes on second side, until light brown and crisp. Pay attention because broiling bread can result in burned bread if not watched carefully.

Yeast Pizza Crust

Makes 3 crusts; serves 18

- **TOTAL COST:** $3.08
- **CALORIES:** 189.40
- **FAT:** 4.36 g
- **PROTEIN:** 4.72 g
- **CHOLESTEROL:** 0.0 mg
- **SODIUM:** 195.42 mg

3 cups all-purpose flour
1½ cups cornmeal
1 tablespoon dry yeast
1 tablespoon sugar
1½ teaspoons salt
5 tablespoons olive oil
2 cups warm water
1½ cups whole wheat flour

Make a bunch of these crusts and keep them in your freezer; then when you want pizza, pull out a crust, bake it as directed, top it with fun toppings, bake again, and eat!

1. In large bowl combine 1 cup white flour, cornmeal, dry yeast, sugar, salt, pepper, and olive oil; mix well. Add warm water and beat until a batter forms. Cover and let stand for 30 minutes. Add whole wheat flour and enough remaining white flour to form a firm dough.
2. Knead dough for 8 minutes on floured board. Place dough in greased mixing bowl, turning to grease top. Cover and let rise in warm place for 1 hour. Punch down dough and divide into 6 balls. Sprinkle work surface with flour and roll out each ball into 12-inch circle. Place dough on cookie sheets and flash freeze.
3. When dough is frozen solid, wrap well, label, and seal. To use, bake frozen rounds at 400°F for 10–15 minutes, until just beginning to brown. Top with pizza ingredients and bake according to pizza recipe.

Pizza Crusts

If you have some frozen pizza crusts on hand, you are literally minutes away from a hot, fresh, inexpensive pizza. Spice up plain tomato sauce with some mustard and chopped onion, stew cooked meat and shredded cheese over the top, and bake until the crisp is golden and the cheese melted and bubbly.

Whole Grain Oatmeal Bread

Yields 2 loaves; 24 servings

- ~ **TOTAL COST:** $4.15
- ~ **CALORIES:** 158.74
- ~ **FAT:** 3.46 g
- ~ **PROTEIN:** 4.85 g
- ~ **CHOLESTEROL:** 24.47 mg
- ~ **SODIUM:** 124.69 mg

1 cup warm water
2 (¼-ounce) packages active dry yeast
¼ cup honey
1 cup milk
1 cup regular oatmeal
1 teaspoon salt
3 tablespoons butter
2 eggs
1½ cups whole wheat flour
3½ to 4½ cups all-purpose flour
2 tablespoons butter

This hearty bread is delicious toasted and spread with whipped honey or jam. Bread with this character usually costs about $3.00 a loaf.

1. In small bowl, combine water and yeast; let stand until bubbly, about 5 minutes. Meanwhile, in medium saucepan combine honey, milk, oatmeal, salt, and 3 tablespoons butter. Heat just until very warm (about 120°F). Remove from heat and beat in egg. Combine in large bowl with whole wheat flour and 1 cup ball-purpose flour. Add yeast mixture and beat for 1 minute. Cover and let rise for 30 minutes.
2. Gradually stir in enough remaining all-purpose flour to make a firm dough. Turn onto floured surface and knead until dough is elastic, about 10 minutes. Place in greased bowl, turning to grease top. Cover and let rise for 1 hour. Punch down dough, divide in half, and form into loaves. Place in greased 9" × 5" loaf pans, cover, and let rise for 30 minutes.
3. Bake in preheated 350°F oven for 25–30 minutes or until golden brown. Brush each loaf with 1 tablespoon butter, then remove to wire racks to cool.

Rolls or Bread?

Any yeast bread mixture can be made into rolls. Just divide the dough into 2-inch balls and roll between your hands to smooth. Place on greased cookie sheets about 4 inches apart. Cover and let rise for 30–40 minutes. Then bake at 375°F for 15–25 minutes until deep golden brown.

Cinnamon Platters

 Yields 18 sweet rolls

- ~ **TOTAL COST:** $3.96
- ~ **CALORIES:** 169.56
- ~ **FAT:** 3.30 g
- ~ **PROTEIN:** 3.62 g
- ~ **CHOLESTEROL:** 13.44 mg
- ~ **SODIUM:** 42.47 mg

1 (¼-ounce) package instant-blend dry yeast
2¼ to 2¾ cups all-purpose flour
¼ teaspoon salt
1 teaspoon cinnamon
1 tablespoon honey
2 tablespoons brown sugar
¼ cup orange juice
1 tablespoon butter
½ cup water
1 egg
½ cup dried currants
1 cup sugar
½ cup finely chopped walnuts
2 teaspoons cinnamon

These crisp and flat rolls are a perfect treat for a special occasion, like Christmas morning or Mother's Day. Bakery sweet rolls are usually at least 50¢ each.

1. In large bowl, combine yeast, 1 cup all-purpose flour, salt, 1 teaspoon cinnamon, and cardamom and mix well. In small saucepan, combine honey, brown sugar, orange juice, and water; heat until very warm. Add to flour mixture and beat for 2 minutes.
2. Add egg and beat for 1 minute. Stir in enough remaining all-purpose flour to form a stiff batter. Stir in currants. Cover and let rise for 1 hour.
3. Stir down dough. Line cookie sheets with parchment paper or foil. On plate, combine sugar, walnuts, and 2 teaspoons cinnamon and mix well. Drop dough by spoonfuls into the sugar mixture and toss to coat. Place on prepared cookie sheets and flatten to 1/8-inch thick circles.
4. Preheat oven to 400°F. Bake pastries for 13–16 minutes or until light golden-brown and caramelized. Let cool on cookie sheets for 2 minutes, then remove to wire rack to cool.

Oat-Bran Dinner Rolls

 Yields 30 rolls

- ~ **TOTAL COST:** $4.19
- ~ **CALORIES:** 100.84
- ~ **FAT:** 1.58 g
- ~ **PROTEIN:** 3.30 g
- ~ **CHOLESTEROL:** 9.36 mg
- ~ **SODIUM:** 55.45 mg

1½ cups water
¾ cup quick-cooking oats
½ cup oat bran
¼ cup brown sugar
2 tablespoons butter
1 cup buttermilk
1 egg yolk
2 (¼-ounce) packages active dry yeast

2 to 3 cups all-purpose flour, divided
1½ cups whole wheat flour
½ teaspoon salt
2 tablespoons honey
1 egg white, beaten
2 tablespoons oat bran

These excellent rolls are light yet hearty, with a wonderful flavor and a bit of crunch.

1. In medium saucepan, bring water to a boil over high heat. Add oats, oat bran, brown sugar, and butter and stir until butter melts. Remove from heat and let cool to lukewarm.
2. Meanwhile, in microwave-safe glass cup, place buttermilk. Microwave on medium for 1 minute or until lukewarm (about 110°F). Sprinkle yeast over milk; stir and let stand for 10 minutes.
3. In large mixing bowl, combine 1 cup all-purpose flour, whole wheat flour, and salt. Add honey, cooled oatmeal mixture, softened yeast mixture, and egg yolk and beat until smooth. Gradually add enough remaining all-purpose flour to form soft dough.
4. Turn onto lightly floured board and knead until smooth and elastic, about 5–7 minutes. Place in greased bowl, turning to grease top. Cover and let rise for 1 hour or until dough doubles.
5. Punch down dough and divide into thirds. Divide each third into 10 pieces. Roll balls between your hands to smooth. Place balls into two 9-inch round cake pans. Brush with egg white and sprinkle with 2 tablespoons oat bran. Cover and let rise until doubled, about 45 minutes.
6. Preheat oven to 375°F. Bake rolls for 15–25 minutes or until firm to the touch and golden brown. Remove from pans and cool on wire racks.

Hearty White Bread

 Yields 4 loaves (or 48 slices)

- **TOTAL COST:** $4.18
- **CALORIES:** 151.05
- **FAT:** 1.41 g
- **PROTEIN:** 3.30 g
- **CHOLESTEROL:** 0.26 mg
- **SODIUM:** 159.23 mg

½ cup warm water
2 (0.25–ounce) packages active dry yeast
1 tablespoon sugar
4 cups warm water
½ cup sugar
6 cups all-purpose flour
1 cup dry milk powder
3 teaspoons salt
¼ cup oil
5–6 cups all-purpose flour

Dry milk powder is not only less expensive than regular milk, but it makes the bread fluffier. Technically, the powder is a 'finely divided solid,' which improves mouth feel.

1. In large mixing bowl, combine ½ cup water with the yeast and 1 tablespoon sugar. Mix well and let stand for 10 minutes, until foamy. Add remaining warm water, ½ cup sugar, 6 cups flour, dry milk powder, salt, and oil and beat until smooth. Cover and let rise for 30 minutes.
2. Stir down batter. Gradually add remaining flour until soft dough forms. Turn out onto lightly floured board and knead until smooth and elastic, about 8 minutes. Place in greased bowl, turning to grease top. Let rise until doubled, about 1½ hours. Punch down again.
3. Divide dough into four parts. On lightly floured surface, pat or roll each part into a 12" × 7" rectangle. Tightly roll up, starting with 7-inch side; seal edge. Place in prepared pans; cover and let rise until doubled, about 35–45 minutes. Preheat oven to 350°F. Bake bread for 30–40 minutes or until golden brown. Turn out onto wire racks to cool.

Freezing Bread
Making big batches of bread and then freezing the results harkens back to Grandma's day—or maybe great-grandma's! Bread freezes beautifully as long as you follow a few rules. First, let the bread cool completely. Then slice it and package the slices in freezer bags. Label the bags and freeze up to 3 months. To thaw, just toast!

Peanut Butter Bread

 Yields 1 loaf (or 12 slices)

- **TOTAL COST:** $2.73
- **CALORIES:** 309.97
- **FAT:** 11.11 g
- **PROTEIN:** 7.94 g
- **CHOLESTEROL:** 24.35 mg
- **SODIUM:** 274.38 mg

½ cup peanut butter
2 tablespoons butter or margarine
1 cup brown sugar
1 egg
2 cups all-purpose flour
1 teaspoon baking soda
¼ teaspoon salt
1 cup buttermilk
¼ cup peanut butter
⅓ cup brown sugar
⅓ cup all-purpose flour

Peanut butter is a high quality and inexpensive form of protein when combined with grains. This hearty loaf is great for breakfast on the run; one slice will fill you up.

1. Preheat oven to 350°F. Grease an 8" × 4" loaf pan with solid shortening and set aside. In large bowl, combine ⅓ cup peanut butter, butter, and 1 cup brown sugar and beat until blended. Add egg and beat well. In small bowl, combine 1¾ cups flour, baking soda, and salt. Add dry ingredients alternately with buttermilk to peanut butter mixture.
2. For streusel topping, in small bowl, combine ¼ cup peanut butter and ⅓ cup brown sugar and blend well. Add ⅓ cup flour and blend until crumbs form. Pour batter into prepared pan and sprinkle streusel over loaf. Bake for 45–55 minutes or until toothpick comes out clean when inserted into loaf. Cool on wire rack.

Artisan Whole Wheat Bread

 Yields 3 loaves (or 48 slices)

- ~ **TOTAL COST:** $5.36
- ~ **CALORIES:** 105.65
- ~ **FAT:** 2.22 g
- ~ **PROTEIN:** 2.75 g
- ~ **CHOLESTEROL:** 1.27 mg
- ~ **SODIUM:** 77.15 mg

¾ cup warm water
2 (0.25-ounce) packages active dry yeast
1 tablespoon honey
⅓ cup vegetable oil
2 cups warm water
1½ teaspoons salt
½ cup honey
4 cups all-purpose flour
4–5 cups whole wheat flour
2 tablespoons butter, softened

It's difficult to make whole wheat bread without using some white flour. This proportion is just about perfect. And the several risings help develop the flavor of the wheat.

1. In a small bowl, combine ¾ cup water with yeast and 1 tablespoon honey; set aside for 10 minutes. In a large bowl, combine oil, 2 cups water, ½ cup honey, and salt. Add yeast mixture, then stir in flour. Beat for 5 minutes. Cover and let rise for 30 minutes.
2. Stir down dough and gradually add enough whole wheat flour to form a soft dough. Turn out onto floured surface and knead in enough remaining flour until the dough is smooth and elastic, about 5–7 minutes. Place in greased bowl, turning to grease top. Cover and let rise until doubled, about 1 hour.
3. Grease three 9" × 5" loaf pans with solid shortening and set aside. Punch down dough and divide into three parts and roll or pat into 7" × 12" rectangles. Spread each with one third of the butter and tightly roll up, starting with 7-inch side. Place each in prepared loaf pan. Cover and let rise for about 30–40 minutes until bread has almost doubled. Preheat oven to 350°F. Bake bread for 40–50 minutes or until deep golden brown. Turn out onto wire racks to cool.

Almost Sourdough Rolls

Yields 24 rolls

~ **TOTAL COST:** $3.51
~ **CALORIES:** 117.53
~ **FAT:** 1.88 g
~ **PROTEIN:** 3.98 g
~ **CHOLESTEROL:** 11.74 mg
~ **SODIUM:** 112.17 mg

3½ to 4 cups all purpose flour
1 cup whole wheat flour
1 teaspoon salt
2 (0.25-ounce) packages instant blend dry yeast
1 tablespoon honey
1 cup buttermilk
½ cup sour cream
½ cup water
1 tablespoon apple cider vinegar
1 egg, separated
2 tablespoons oat bran

The sour cream and vinegar give these rolls a slightly sour flavor. To make them even crisper, spray with some cold water halfway through the baking time.

1. In large bowl, combine 1 cup all-purpose flour, whole wheat flour, 3 tablespoons wheat germ, salt, and yeast; stir until blended. In small saucepan, combine honey, buttermilk, sour cream, and water and heat over low heat until warm to the touch. Add to flour mixture along with vinegar and egg yolk and beat for 2 minutes.

2. Stir in enough remaining all purpose flour with a spoon until a soft dough forms. On floured surface, knead in enough remaining flour until the dough is elastic, about 5–8 minutes. Place dough in greased bowl, turning to grease top. Cover and let rise until doubled, about 1 hour.

3. Punch dough down and divide into 24 balls. Place balls on two greased cookie sheets. In small bowl, beat egg white until frothy and gently brush over rolls. Sprinkle with oat bran, cover with a kitchen towel, and let rise for 30–40 minutes.

4. Place a 9-inch square pan with 1 inch of water on the bottom rack of oven. Preheat oven to 350°F. Bake for 15–25 minutes or until rolls are golden brown and sound hollow when tapped. Remove from cookie sheets and cool on wire rack.

Producing Crusty Rolls

To make rolls and breads with a crisp crust, there are two things you can do. One is to brush the dough with a slightly beaten egg white. Another is to create a moist environment in the oven. Place a pan with some water in the bottom rack of the oven, or spray the rolls with a bit of water before they bake and once during baking time.

Raisin Spice Swirl Bread

 Yields 2 loaves; 24 slices

- **TOTAL COST:** $5.01
- **CALORIES:** 194.52
- **FAT:** 4.92 g
- **PROTEIN:** 4.10 g
- **CHOLESTEROL:** 28.84 mg
- **SODIUM:** 95.42 mg

2 (0.25-ounce) packages active dry yeast
½ cup warm water
¾ cup buttermilk
⅓ cup butter
¾ cup brown sugar, divided
½ teaspoon salt
2 teaspoons cinnamon, divided

¼ teaspoon nutmeg
⅛ teaspoon ground cloves
1½ cups raisins
2 eggs
½ cup whole wheat flour
4 to 5 cups all purpose flour
3 tablespoons butter, softened

Putting raisins into the dough rather than just in the cinnamon swirl makes this bread easier to slice. It is fabulous toasted, or use it in any French toast recipe. Good quality raisin bread costs at least $3.50 for one loaf.

1. In large bowl, combine yeast and warm water; set aside. In large saucepan, combine milk, butter, ¼ cup brown sugar, salt, 1 teaspoon cinnamon, nutmeg, cloves, and raisins. Heat over medium heat until butter melts. Set aside to cool to lukewarm.
2. Add milk mixture to yeast mixture along with eggs; beat well. Beat in whole wheat flour. Gradually add enough all purpose flour to form a soft dough, beating well after each addition. Turn dough onto floured surface and knead in enough remaining flour until dough is smooth and elastic. Place dough in greased bowl, turning to grease top. Cover and let rise until doubled, about 1 hour.
3. In small bowl, combine softened butter with ½ cup brown sugar and 1 teaspoon cinnamon. Punch down dough and divide into two parts. On lightly floured surface, roll out each part to a 7" × 12" rectangle. Spread each with the butter mixture. Roll up tightly, starting with 7-inch end. Pinch edges to seal. Place into prepared pans, cover, and let rise until doubled, about 45 minutes.
4. Preheat oven to 350°F. Bake bread for 30–45 minutes, or until bread is golden brown. Turn out onto wire racks to cool.

Cornmeal Focaccia

 Yields 2 loaves; 12 servings

~ **TOTAL COST:** $3.13

~ **CALORIES:** 175.02

~ **FAT:** 5.55 g

~ **PROTEIN:** 4.28 g

~ **SODIUM:** 154.62 mg

~ **CHOLESTEROL:** 1.83 mg

1½ to 2½ cups all-purpose flour

1 (¼-ounce) package instant-blend dry yeast

1 cup water

1 tablespoon honey

4 tablespoons olive oil, divided

½ teaspoon salt

2 teaspoons dried oregano leaves

1 cup cornmeal

2 tablespoons cornmeal

¼ cup grated Romano or Cotija cheese

Focaccia is a perfect bread to serve as a side to chili or a hearty stew.

1. In large bowl, combine 1 cup flour and yeast and mix well. In microwave-safe glass measuring cup, combine water, honey, 2 tablespoons olive oil, and salt. Microwave on 50 percent power for 1 minute or until mixture is very warm.

2. Add to flour mixture; beat for 2 minutes. Stir in rosemary, oregano, ½ cup cornmeal, and masa harina and beat for 1 minute.

3. Add enough remaining all-purpose flour to make a soft dough. Cover and let rise for 30 minutes.

4. Divide dough in half. Grease two 12-inch round pizza pans with unsalted butter and sprinkle with 2 tablespoons cornmeal. Divide dough into two parts and press each part into prepared pans. Push your fingertips into the dough to make dimples. Drizzle remaining olive oil over the dough; sprinkle with cheese. Let stand for 20 minutes.

5. Preheat oven to 425°F. Bake bread for 13–18 minutes or until deep golden brown. Cool on wire racks.

Garlic Herb Focaccia

 Serves 10

- ~ **PREP TIME:** 5 minutes
- ~ **RESTING TIME:** 2 hours
- ~ **COOK TIME:** 1 hour
- ~ **TOTAL COST:** $5.90
- ~ **CALORIES:** 236
- ~ **FAT:** 3 g
- ~ **PROTEIN:** 7 g
- ~ **CHOLESTEROL:** 11 mg
- ~ **SODIUM:** 197 mg

2 teaspoons olive oil
1¼-ounce package dry active yeast
½ cup warm water, not hot and not cold
6 cups plain flour
¼ teaspoon sea salt
2 cups water
½ bunch fresh basil, leaves finely chopped
3 cloves garlic, minced

If you are making bread dough from scratch (not using a bread mix), go easy on yourself the first time. Getting the feel for the right amount of moisture can be a little tricky at first, but don't worry, even professional chefs make mistakes.

1. Lightly grease a 13" x 9" baking pan with 1 teaspoon olive oil. In a small bowl, stir together the yeast and warm water. Let stand for 5 minutes, until foamy. Sift together the flour and salt. Add yeast mixture into flour mixture by hand or using mixer. If doing by hand, gently incorporate yeast mixture into flour mixture. If using mixer, use dough hook, and combine mixture on slow speed for about 3 minutes or until dough forms together. Remove from bowl, cover with a clean but damp kitchen towel. Let rest on a floured surface for about 1 hour.
2. Combine basil and garlic in a small bowl. Place dough in prepared pan, forming as desired. Using your fingers, gently press garlic-basil mixture into dough. Cover with kitchen towel and let rest again in warm place for about 1 hour.
3. Preheat oven to 425°F. Bake bread for 1 hour, until lightly golden brown.

> **Quick and Easy Tip**
> This is definitely a make-ahead recipe. Make the day before and keep wrapped in aluminum foil or airtight container. To make it crispier, drizzle a little olive oil on the crust before baking. To make the bread softer, brush the crust with oil immediately after it comes out of the oven.

Cinnamon Glazed Bagels

 Yields 12 bagels

- ~ **TOTAL COST:** $5.22
- ~ **CALORIES:** 432.31
- ~ **FAT:** 9.09 g
- ~ **PROTEIN:** 10.90 g
- ~ **CHOLESTEROL:** 6.31 mg
- ~ **SODIUM:** 233.19 mg

1 (0.25-ounce) package active dry
  yeast
½ cup warm water
1½ cups milk
2 tablespoons butter, melted
¾ cup sugar, divided
3 teaspoons cinnamon, divided

2 teaspoons salt, divided
5½ to 6½ cups all-purpose flour
1 cup raisins
1 cup chopped walnuts
1 egg white, lightly beaten
⅓ cup sugar

Your own homemade bagels are so delicious! These special treats are
hearty and chewy, with a wonderful cinnamon flavor. Bakery bagels
can cost $1.00 apiece.

1. In a large mixing bowl, combine yeast with ½ cup warm water. Stir
   and let stand for 10 minutes. Add milk, orange juice, melted butter,
   ¼ cup sugar, 2 teaspoons cinnamon, salt, and whole wheat flour;
   beat for 1 minute. Gradually add 3 cups bread flour. Add raisins
   and walnuts. Turn dough onto floured surface and knead in enough
   remaining bread flour until the dough is stiff, smooth, and elastic,
   about 10 minutes.
2. Place dough in greased bowl, turning to grease top. Cover and let
   rise until doubled, about 1 hour. Punch down and divide into four
   parts. Divide each part into three balls. Flatten balls until they are
   about 4 inches in diameter. Punch a hole in the center and gently
   stretch the rings until the hole is about 1½ inches wide. Place on
   greased baking sheets and let rise until doubled, about 30 minutes.
3. Bring a large pot of water to a boil; add ½ cup sugar and 1 teaspoon
   salt. Drop three bagels at a time into the boiling water and let rise to
   the top. Boil for 1 minute, remove, drain, and place on greased baking sheets.
4. Preheat oven to 425°F. Bake bagels until browned, about 15 minutes. In small bowl, combine ⅓ cup sugar and 1 teaspoon cinnamon
   and mix well. Remove bagels from oven. Brush with egg white and
   sprinkle with cinnamon sugar. Return to oven and bake for 5–12 minutes longer until deep golden brown. Let cool on wire racks.

Quick Pizza Crust

 Serves 6

~ **TOTAL COST:** 53¢
~ **CALORIES:** 263.71
~ **FAT:** 11.95 g
~ **PROTEIN:** 4.88 g
~ **CHOLESTEROL:** 0.68 mg
~ **SODIUM:** 281.90 mg

1 tablespoon cornmeal
2 cups all-purpose flour
1 teaspoon baking powder
½ teaspoon salt
⅓ cup solid shortening
⅓ cup water
⅓ cup milk

You don't need yeast to make this pizza crust. This one is flaky and light and is made in a flash. It's easy to triple this recipe and bake three crusts; freeze two and top one for dinner.

1. Preheat oven to 425°F. Grease a 12-inch pizza pan with solid shortening and sprinkle with cornmeal. In large bowl combine flour, baking powder, and salt and mix well. Cut in shortening until particles are fine. Add water and milk and stir until a dough forms. Press into prepared pizza pan and bake for 10 minutes.
2. Remove crust from oven and top as desired. Bake at 425°F for 15–25 minutes or until crust is crisp and cheese is melted and beginning to brown. Let cool for 5 minutes and slice to serve.

Orange-Blueberry Muffins

 Serves 10

~ **PREP TIME:** 3 minutes
~ **COOK TIME:** 10 minutes
~ **TOTAL COST:** $6.60
~ **CALORIES:** 84
~ **FAT:** 7 g
~ **PROTEIN:** 4 g
~ **CHOLESTEROL:** 2 mg
~ **SODIUM:** 179 mg

1 (9-ounce) blueberry quick bread mix
5 tablespoons orange juice
¾ cup milk
¼ cup oil
1 egg
½ cup powdered sugar

Mini muffins are perfect quick breakfast or snack for kids.

1. Preheat oven to 375°F. Line 44 mini muffin cups with paper liners and set aside. In a large bowl, combine quick bread mix, 4 tablespoons orange juice, milk, oil, and egg and stir just until dry ingredients disappear. Fill prepared muffin cups two-thirds full of batter. Bake for 10 to 15 minutes or until muffins spring back when gently touched with finger. Cool for 3 minutes, then remove to wire rack.
2. In a small bowl combine powdered sugar and 1 tablespoon orange juice; drizzle this mixture over the warm muffins and serve.

Quick and Easy Tip
Make muffins ahead of time and store in airtight containers, then reheat for best taste and texture. To reheat, place muffins on microwave-safe dish, cover with paper towels, and heat for 10 seconds per muffin, until warm.

Apple Quick Bread

 Makes 2 loaves; serves 16

- ~ **TOTAL COST:** $6.03
- ~ **CALORIES:** 326.77
- ~ **FAT:** 11.86 g
- ~ **PROTEIN:** 5.15 g
- ~ **CHOLESTEROL:** 69.26 mg
- ~ **SODIUM:** 244.04 mg

3 medium apples
½ cup butter, softened
⅓ cup vegetable oil
1 cup sugar
1 cup brown sugar
2 teaspoons cinnamon
4 eggs
3 ½ cups flour
1 teaspoon baking soda
½ teaspoon baking powder
½ teaspoon salt
1 cup buttermilk
1 teaspoon vanilla

This is great bread for breakfast on the run. You can add a glaze if you like: Combine 1 cup confectioners' sugar, ½ teaspoon vanilla, and 2 to 3 tablespoons milk and mix well, then drizzle over loaves.

1. Preheat oven to 325°F. Generously grease and flour two 9" × 5" loaf pans and set aside. Peel and core apples and chop finely, by hand or in a food processor.
2. In large bowl, combine chopped apples, butter, sugar, cinnamon, and eggs. Stir for 2–3 minutes, until blended. Add remaining ingredients and mix well to blend. Pour batter into prepared baking pans.
3. Bake at 325°F for 60–75 minutes, until dark golden brown. Cool bread in pans for 5 minutes, then turn out of pans and cool on wire rack.

Tex-Mex Beer Bread

Serves 8

- ~ **TOTAL COST:** $1.89
- ~ **CALORIES:** 222.89
- ~ **FAT:** 4.91 g
- ~ **PROTEIN:** 4.85 g
- ~ **CHOLESTEROL:** 11.45 mg
- ~ **SODIUM:** 324.92 mg

2½ cups flour
½ teaspoon salt
1 teaspoon baking powder
½ teaspoon baking soda
⅓ cup yellow cornmeal
2 teaspoons chili powder
1 (12-ounce) can beer
3 tablespoons butter, melted

Serve this super-easy bread hot out of the oven with butter seasoned with chili powder, oregano, and cumin to taste. It's excellent served with any soup or chili, and perfect when you want hot bread at the last minute.

1. Preheat oven to 375°F. In large bowl, combine dry ingredients and stir with a wire whisk. Add beer and melted butter and mix just until blended.
2. Spray 9" × 5" loaf pan with nonstick cooking spray and dust with a little flour. Pour batter into prepared pan. Bake at 375°F for 50–55 minutes or until bread is firm and light golden brown and pulls away from edge of pan. Serve warm.

Self-Rising Flour

Self-rising flour is sold primarily in the Southern United States. It combines flour with salt and baking powder, in proportions of ½ teaspoon salt and 1½ teaspoons baking powder per cup of flour. You can make your own and use less salt to help control your family's sodium intake.

Cinnamon Oat Scones

Serves 6

~ **PREP TIME:** 6 minutes
~ **COOK TIME:** 15 minutes
~ **TOTAL COST:** $4.56
~ **CALORIES:** 300
~ **FAT:** 12 g
~ **PROTEIN:** 4 g
~ **CHOLESTEROL:** 38 mg
~ **SODIUM:** 265 mg

2 cups plain flour
⅔ cup oatmeal
⅓ cup brown sugar
1½ teaspoons baking powder
½ teaspoon cinnamon
6 tablespoons butter
2 eggs
6 tablespoons heavy cream
1 tablespoon sugar

Try adding chopped nuts, raisins, or dried cranberries. Serve the scones hot with butter, honey, or jam.

1. Preheat oven to 400°F. Line a baking sheet with parchment paper and set aside. In a large bowl combine flour, oatmeal, brown sugar, baking powder, and half the cinnamon. Cut in butter until particles are fine.
2. In a small bowl, combine eggs and 5 tablespoons cream and beat until smooth. Add to oatmeal mixture and mix until a dough forms. Shape into a ball and press into a 9-inch circle on a baking sheet. Cut dough into 8 wedges and separate slightly. Brush with remaining 1 tablespoon cream and sprinkle with 1 tablespoon sugar mixed with remaining cinnamon. Bake for 12 to 15 minutes until edges are golden brown. Serve hot with butter.

Basic Muffins

Serves 6

~ **PREP TIME:** 12 minutes
~ **COOK TIME:** 20 minutes
~ **TOTAL COST:** $1.43
~ **CALORIES:** 307
~ **FAT:** 7 g
~ **PROTEIN:** 6 g
~ **CHOLESTEROL:** 28 mg
~ **SODIUM:** 31 mg

2 cups plain flour
¼ cup granulated sugar
1 tablespoon baking powder
½ teaspoon sea salt
1 large egg
1 cup low-fat milk
⅓ cup canola oil

Add blueberries, nuts, or smashed ripe bananas to this basic mix for fresh, tasty muffins in a pinch.

1. Preheat the oven to 400°F. Grease well a 12-cup muffin tin, or line with paper cups. Sift together the flour, sugar, baking powder, and salt. Place the sifted dry ingredients into a bowl and make a well in the center. In a second bowl, beat the egg lightly. Add the milk and oil and combine. Pour the egg mixture into the well in the dry ingredients and combine quickly, until dry ingredients are just moistened. Some lumps will remain in the batter.
2. Fill the muffin cups about ⅔ full. Bake about 20 minutes, or until the center tests done when toothpick inserted comes out clean.

Quick and Easy Tip
Muffins are a great snack for kids after school. When making, make two batches and keep some in the freezer for quick access.

Pumpkin Bread

Serves 10

- ~ **PREP TIME:** 5 minutes
- ~ **COOK TIME:** 1 hour
- ~ **TOTAL COST:** $4.50
- ~ **CALORIES:** 170
- ~ **FAT:** 6 g
- ~ **PROTEIN:** 3 g
- ~ **CHOLESTEROL:** 36 mg
- ~ **SODIUM:** 338 mg

1 cup plain flour
¼ cup whole wheat flour
¾ cup sugar
½ teaspoon ground cinnamon
1 (3-ounce) package instant butterscotch pudding mix
½ teaspoon baking soda
½ teaspoon baking powder
½ cup butter, melted
2 eggs
1 cup canned pumpkin pie filling

Quick breads use baking soda and powder for leavening. For best results, measure all ingredients carefully and mix wet and dry ingredients until just combined. Overmixing makes the bread tough.

1. Preheat oven to 400°F. Spray a 9" x 5" loaf pan with nonstick cooking spray. In a large bowl, combine flour, whole wheat flour, sugar, cinnamon, pudding mix, baking soda, and baking powder, and stir to blend. Add melted butter, eggs, and pumpkin pie filling and stir just until blended. Pour into prepared pan.
2. Place bread in oven and bake for 1 hour, or until when toothpick inserted comes out clean. Remove from oven and let cook on rack for about 10 minutes. Using a table knife, loosen bread by going around sides of pan. Turn loaf pan upside down, transferring bread to plate. Slice and serve.

Banana Muffins

Yields 12–15 muffins*

- ~ **COST:** $0.20
- ~ **CALORIES:** 150
- ~ **FAT:** 5 g
- ~ **CARBOHYDRATES:** 22 g
- ~ **PROTEIN:** 3 g
- ~ **CHOLESTEROL:** 20 mg
- ~ **SODIUM:** 150 mg

1 egg
1 cup milk
¼ cup vegetable oil
¾ teaspoon baking soda
¾ teaspoon baking powder
⅛ teaspoon salt
1½ cups all-purpose flour
3 tablespoons liquid honey
1 cup mashed banana (about 2 bananas)
¼ teaspoon ground cinnamon

1. Preheat oven to 375°F. Grease a muffin pan.
2. In a small bowl, add the egg to the milk and beat lightly. Add the vegetable oil and stir to combine.
3. In a large bowl, stir the baking soda, baking powder, and salt into the flour until well blended.
4. Add the egg mixture to the flour mixture and stir to form a batter. Stir in the honey, banana, and ground cinnamon. Stir until combined but do not beat.
5. Spoon the batter into the muffin tins so that they are about ⅔ full. Bake for 20 to 25 minutes or until a toothpick inserted into the middle of a muffin comes out clean. Let cool for 5 minutes before serving. Store the muffins in a sealed tin.

*Nutrition information and price per serving based on the recipe serving 12.

Raspberry Oatmeal Muffins

Yields 12 muffins

- ~ **TOTAL COST:** $3.17
- ~ **CALORIES:** 224.56
- ~ **FAT:** 8.03 g
- ~ **PROTEIN:** 3.83 g
- ~ **CHOLESTEROL:** 27.08 mg
- ~ **SODIUM:** 255.59 mg

1 cup all-purpose flour
½ cup whole wheat flour
½ cup brown sugar
¼ cup ground oatmeal
1 teaspoon cinnamon
2 teaspoons baking powder
½ teaspoon salt
1 cup leftover Nutty Oatmeal (Chapter 4)
1 egg
¼ cup butter, melted
3 tablespoons vegetable oil
1 cup frozen raspberries

Ground oatmeal is the secret ingredient in these muffins; it adds texture and a slightly nutty flavor.

1. Preheat oven to 400°F. Line 12 muffin cups with paper liners; set aside. In large bowl, combine all purpose flour, whole wheat flour, brown sugar, ground oatmeal, cinnamon, baking powder, and salt and mix well.
2. In small bowl, combine Oatmeal, egg, butter, and vegetable oil and mix well. Add to dry ingredients and stir just until combined. Fold in raspberries. Spoon batter into prepared muffin cups.
3. Bake muffins for 18–23 minutes or until they are set and golden brown. Let stand for 5 minutes, then remove from muffin cups and cool on wire rack. Serve warm.

> **Quick and Easy Tip**
> It's important to use pumpkin pie filling and not canned pumpkin purée because the pie filling has spices that add flavor to the bread.

CHAPTER 4

BREAKFAST ON A BUDGET

Basic Pancakes

Serves 5

~ **PREP TIME:** 10 minutes
~ **COOK TIME:** 6 minutes
~ **TOTAL COST:** $2.42
~ **CALORIES:** 180
~ **FAT:** 7 g
~ **PROTEIN:** 5 g
~ **CHOLESTEROL:** 33 mg
~ **SODIUM:** 36 mg

1 cup plain flour
1 tablespoon granulated sugar
2½ teaspoons baking powder
¼ teaspoon sea salt
1 egg
1 cup low-fat milk
2 tablespoons canola oil

Pancakes are very inexpensive and also filling. For maximum health benefit, buy low-cal syrup if possible and be sure to check your local paper for the weekly special. Next time syrup is on special, buy two and set one aside in your pantry!

1. Combine the flour, sugar, baking powder, and salt in a bowl by stirring. Then, make a well in the middle of the mixture. In a separate bowl, beat the egg using a fork and thoroughly combine with the milk and oil. Add the liquid to the flour mixture and stir quickly until moistened; the batter will have some lumps.
2. Preheat a greased or buttered griddle or skillet over medium-high heat. Cook pancakes on the hot griddle, using about ¼ cup batter per cake. Cook about 2 or 3 minutes on each side; pancakes are ready to turn when the tops have broken bubbles on the surface and the edges appear dry.

Quick and Easy Tip
For added flavor and nutrition, add a tablespoon of fresh or canned fruit, such as blueberries, to each pancake when you first pour the batter onto the griddle. If using canned fruit, make sure to drain the liquid.

Buttermilk Pancakes

 Makes 16 pancakes

- ~ **TOTAL COST:** $2.12
- ~ **CALORIES:** 137.81
- ~ **FAT:** 6.45 g
- ~ **PROTEIN:** 3.74 g
- ~ **CHOLESTEROL:** 35.41 mg
- ~ **SODIUM:** 113.24 mg

2 cups flour
2 teaspoons baking powder
½ teaspoon baking soda
2 tablespoons sugar
¼ teaspoon salt
2 eggs
2 cups buttermilk
3 tablespoons vegetable oil
1 teaspoon vanilla
Solid vegetable shortening

Classic buttermilk pancakes are so easy to make and are unbelievably inexpensive.

1. In large bowl, combine all dry ingredients and mix well with wire whisk to blend.
2. In small bowl, beat together eggs, buttermilk, oil, and vanilla until smooth. Pour into dry ingredients and stir just until dry ingredients are blended; do not overmix.
3. In a nonstick skillet, rub a small amount of solid vegetable shortening and heat over medium heat. Pour ¼ cup batter for each pancake. Cook until bubbles form on surface and edges begin to brown, about 3–4 minutes. Carefully flip pancakes and cook 2 to 3 minutes longer, until pancakes are fluffy and golden brown; serve immediately. Repeat with remaining batter.

Peanut Butter Pancakes

 Makes 8 pancakes; serves 4

- ~ **TOTAL COST:** $1.38
- ~ **CALORIES:** 397.32
- ~ **FAT:** 19.45 g
- ~ **PROTEIN:** 13.74 g
- ~ **CHOLESTEROL:** 55.41 mg
- ~ **SODIUM:** 443.24 mg

1 cup flour
1 teaspoon baking powder
½ teaspoon baking soda
¼ teaspoon salt
1 egg
2 tablespoons brown sugar
1 cup buttermilk
6 tablespoons peanut butter
2 tablespoon vegetable oil
1 teaspoon vanilla
Solid vegetable shortening

These rich pancakes have a wonderful taste. Serve them with butter and grape jelly. To help prevent sticking, spray the spatula with a nonstick cooking spray.

1. In large bowl, combine flour, baking powder, baking soda, and salt, and mix well with wire whisk to blend.
2. In small bowl, beat together eggs, brown sugar, buttermilk, peanut butter, oil, and vanilla until smooth. Pour into dry ingredients and stir just until dry ingredients are blended; do not overmix.
3. In a nonstick skillet, rub a small amount of solid vegetable shortening and heat over medium heat. Pour ¼ cup batter for each pancake. Cook until bubbles form on surface and edges begin to brown, about 3–4 minutes. Carefully flip pancakes and cook 2–3 minutes longer, until pancakes are fluffy and golden brown; serve immediately. Repeat with remaining batter.

Chicken Sausage Patties

 Serves 6

- **TOTAL COST:** $4.53
- **CALORIES:** 235.53
- **FAT:** 12.63 g
- **PROTEIN:** 23.43 g
- **CHOLESTEROL:** 71.06 mg
- **SODIUM:** 523.70 mg

1 medium Granny Smith apple, peeled
½ cup finely chopped onion
2 cloves garlic, minced
3 tablespoons margarine, divided
1 teaspoon salt
½ teaspoon dried thyme leaves
⅛ teaspoon cayenne pepper
1 pound chicken pieces

When you make your own sausage patties you can control what goes into them. You can reduce or omit the salt if you'd like.

1. Finely chop the apple, and combine with the onion, garlic, and 2 tablespoons margarine in a small saucepan. Cook over medium heat, stirring frequently, until onion is tender. Remove from heat, pour into large bowl, and let cool, about 20 minutes.
2. Add salt, thyme, and cayenne pepper to onion mixture and blend well. Remove skin and bones from chicken (reserve for Chicken Stock, Chapter 6). In food processor, grind chicken with the pulse feature until mixture is even. Add to onion mixture and mix well with hands just until blended.
3. Form mixture into six patties. In large nonstick skillet, melt 1 tablespoon margarine. Cook chicken patties, turning once, for 8–12 minutes or until patties are deep golden brown and chicken is thoroughly cooked, 165°F. Serve immediately, or freeze for longer storage.

Ground Chicken
Once chicken or other poultry is ground it should be used within 24 hours. Mix dark and light meat together for best taste and lower cost. Save the skin and bones when you work with chicken until you have enough to make Chicken Stock (Chapter 6). Place them in the freezer in a large bag or hard-sided container marked for the stock recipe.

Breakfast Pizza

 Serves 4

~ **TOTAL COST:** $4.29
~ **CALORIES:** 452.55
~ **FAT:** 30.90 g
~ **PROTEIN:** 27.61 g
~ **CHOLESTEROL:** 300.99 mg
~ **SODIUM:** 823.55 mg

4 whole wheat pita breads
1 (3-ounce) package cream cheese, softened
2 tablespoons margarine
4 eggs, beaten
2 tablespoons milk
¼ teaspoon salt
2 Chicken Sausage Patties (Chapter 4), chopped
1 cup shredded Cheddar cheese

If you like, you could add any cooked vegetables such as mushrooms, asparagus, or red bell peppers to these cute pizzas.

1. Preheat oven to 400°F. Place pita breads on a cookie sheet and spread each with ¼ of the cream cheese; set aside.
2. Heat butter in small skillet over medium heat. In small bowl, combine eggs with milk and salt and beat well. Pour into skillet. Cook and stir until eggs are set but still moist, about 5 minutes. Divide among Pita Breads.
3. Top with chopped Chicken Patties and cheese. Bake for 10–15 minutes or until pizzas are hot and cheese melts and begins to bubble. Let cool for 5 minutes and serve.

Blueberry Yogurt Smoothie

 Serves 4

~ **TOTAL COST:** $4.67
~ **CALORIES:** 130.86
~ **FAT:** 2.05 g
~ **PROTEIN:** 4.03 g
~ **CHOLESTEROL:** 6.74 mg
~ **SODIUM:** 46.18 mg

1¼ cups frozen blueberries
1 cup orange juice
¼ cup dry milk powder
¾ cup plain yogurt
1 (8-ounce) can crushed pineapple, undrained
½ teaspoon vanilla

Frozen concentrated orange juice is a better buy than the jugs. The jugs are usually made from concentrate anyway, so you're paying for water and a bit of work.

In blender or food processor, combine all ingredients. Blend or process until smooth and thick. Serve immediately.

Frozen Fruit
Frozen fruit is usually much less expensive than fresh fruit, especially when it's out of season. Buy loose or dry pack fruit, in which the fruit is individually frozen. It's easier to use and looks more like the real thing than fruits packed in juices or syrup. With loose pack, you can remove just the amount you need and return the rest to the freezer.

Fresh Fruit with Yogurt and Mint

 Serves 6

~ **PREP TIME:** 10 minutes
~ **TOTAL COST:** $4.05
~ **CALORIES:** 184
~ **FAT:** 2 g
~ **CARBOHYDRATES:** 19 g
~ **PROTEIN:** 21 g
~ **CHOLESTEROL:** 10 mg
~ **SODIUM:** 189 mg

6 cups plain nonfat yogurt
¼ fresh cantaloupe, peeled and thinly sliced
¼ fresh honeydew melon, peeled and thinly sliced
2 fresh kiwi, peeled and sliced
1 fresh peach, thinly sliced
1 fresh plum, thinly sliced
½ pint fresh raspberries
6 mint sprigs, leaves chopped

Add crunchy granola, if you like, for extra protein, energy, and flavor.

Spoon yogurt into serving bowls and arrange the fruit around the rim, sprinkling raspberries on top. Garnish with freshly chopped mint.

Prosciutto-Wrapped Figs with Honey

 Serves 4

~ **PREP TIME:** 15 minutes
~ **COOK TIME:** 5 minutes
~ **TOTAL COST:** $6.89
~ **CALORIES:** 159
~ **FAT:** 9 g
~ **CARBOHYDRATES:** 7 g
~ **PROTEIN:** 8 g
~ **CHOLESTEROL:** 28 mg
~ **SODIUM:** 640 mg

4 ounces prosciutto, thinly sliced
4 fresh figs, quartered
1 teaspoon honey
2 tablespoons fresh-squeezed lemon juice
2 tablespoons extra-virgin olive oil
Sea salt and black pepper as needed
Toothpicks for serving

Fresh figs are ideal for this recipe but you can also enjoy figs dried when fresh figs are out of season. Prepare the dried figs in the same way as this recipe and if your budget allows, add goat or blue cheese for extra delicious flavor!

Trim excess fat from prosciutto strips and cut prosciutto in half, lengthwise. Wrap each of the fig pieces with a strip of prosciutto. Combine remaining ingredients in a small bowl and whisk well. Spoon over figs and serve with toothpicks.

Buying Prosciutto
Purchase prosciutto freshly sliced from the meat department at most grocery stores or purchase presliced and packaged near the specialty deli meat counter.

Multigrain Pancakes

Makes 12 pancakes

~ **TOTAL COST:** $1.38
~ **CALORIES:** 132.27
~ **FAT:** 3.60 g
~ **PROTEIN:** 4.07 g
~ **CHOLESTEROL:** 19.67 mg
~ **SODIUM:** 137.78 mg

1½ cups flour
¼ cup whole wheat flour
¼ cup finely ground oatmeal
1½ teaspoons baking powder
½ teaspoon baking soda
3 tablespoons sugar
¼ teaspoon salt
1 egg
1¼ cups buttermilk
2 tablespoons vegetable oil
1 teaspoon vanilla
Solid vegetable shortening

This batter can be used to make waffles, too. Top them with honey, syrup, or just some berries and a sprinkling of powdered sugar.

1. In large bowl, combine all dry ingredients and mix well with wire whisk to blend.
2. In small bowl, beat together egg, buttermilk, oil, and vanilla until smooth. Pour into dry ingredients and stir just until dry ingredients are blended; do not overmix.
3. In a nonstick skillet, melt a small amount of butter over medium heat and pour ¼ cup batter for each pancake. Cook until bubbles form on surface and edges begin to brown, about 3–4 minutes. Carefully flip pancakes and cook 2–3 minutes longer, until pancakes are fluffy and golden brown; serve immediately. Repeat with remaining batter.

High-Protein Pancakes
Serves 4

~ **PREP TIME:** 8 minutes
~ **COOK TIME:** 10 minutes
~ **TOTAL COST:** $2.96
~ **CALORIES:** 185
~ **FAT:** 4 g
~ **PROTEIN:** 14 g
~ **CHOLESTEROL:** 124 mg
~ **SODIUM:** 382 mg

3 eggs, separated
¾ cup small-curd cottage cheese, low-fat
½ teaspoon sea salt
½ cup plain flour
1 tablespoon granulated sugar

These protein-packed pancakes are a calorie-efficient way to start your day. Skip the syrup completely or go with ½ tablespoon of butter. Tastes terrific, keeps calories down, and saves on costs!

Combine the eggs, cottage cheese, and salt in a blender (or food processor) and blend until smooth. Add the flour and sugar and blend again. Pour onto a hot, well-greased griddle, keeping pancakes no larger than 4 inches in diameter. Cook until golden brown, turning once. These pancakes will take longer to cook through than Basic Pancakes.

Quick and Easy Tip
Extra calories can add up at the end of the day leading to extra, unwanted pounds. Use nonfat or low-fat cottage cheese here to help balance out heavier meals at the end of the day.

Sausage Bake

- ~ **PREP TIME:** 15 minutes
- ~ **COOK TIME:** 20 minutes
- ~ **TOTAL COST:** $6.93
- ~ **CALORIES:** 447
- ~ **FAT:** 30 g
- ~ **PROTEIN:** 18 g
- ~ **CHOLESTEROL:** 59 mg
- ~ **SODIUM:** 918 mg

¾ pound ground sausage, mild or medium
1 puff pastry sheet, Pepperidge Farm preferred
2 tablespoons grated Cheddar cheese
2 tablespoons grated Parmesan cheese
Pinch sea salt

Puff pastry is available at most grocery stores and is located near the frozen pie shells. Pepperidge Farm is usually the only brand available and is a good quality product. The package contains 2 puff pastry sheets, so use one for this recipe and save the other one for another quick meal!

1. Preheat oven to 400°F. Line a baking sheet with parchment paper and set aside. In a heavy skillet, cook sausage over medium heat until golden brown and cooked, about 5 to 7 minutes. Drain off grease.
2. Unfold puff pastry sheet and place on parchment or wax paper. In a small bowl, combine cheeses and mix well. Sprinkle cheese mixture over the puff pastry and gently press cheese mixture into pastry; roll to a 12" x 18" rectangle. Spread cooked sausage over pastry and roll up like a log. Press edges of pastry to seal.
3. Place pastry on lined baking sheet and bake for 12 to 18 minutes until puffed and golden brown. Slice "loaf" and serve hot.

Quick and Easy Tip
Cook sausage and prepare "loaf" the day before and keep in the refrigerator, or prepare one week ahead and keep in the freezer, securely wrapped. Remove from refrigerator or freezer when ready to bake. If baking direct from freezer, allow an extra 5 minutes cooking time.

Scrambled Egg Crepes

Serves 6

~ **TOTAL COST:** $5.93
~ **CALORIES:** 452.96
~ **FAT:** 24.45 g
~ **PROTEIN:** 24.33 g
~ **CHOLESTEROL:** 415.45 mg
~ **SODIUM:** 548.54 mg

1 cup all-purpose flour
1¼ cups milk
10 eggs, divided
3 tablespoons butter, melted
½ teaspoon salt, divided
¼ cup sour cream
2 tablespoons butter
1 cup shredded Swiss cheese
1 cup shredded Cheddar cheese

This recipe is great for brunch when you have company or as a late-night dinner. It elevates scrambled eggs to a gourmet dish; for about a dollar a serving!

1. In a blender or food processor, combine flour, milk, three eggs, 3 tablespoons melted butter, and ¼ teaspoon salt and blend or process until smooth. Let stand for 15 minutes.
2. Then heat an 8-inch nonstick skillet over medium heat and brush with ½ tablespoons butter. Pour ¼ cup batter into skillet and turn and twist skillet to spread batter evenly. Cook until the crepe can be moved, about 2 minutes, then carefully flip and cook 30 seconds on other side. Flip out onto kitchen towel. Repeat, making 8 crepes in all; do not stack hot crepes.
3. Preheat oven to 350°F. In medium bowl, beat remaining 6 eggs with sour cream and ¼ teaspoon salt. Melt remaining 1½ tablespoons butter in the nonstick skillet and pour in eggs. Cook, stirring frequently, until eggs are set but still moist.
4. Place crepes, light side up, on work surface. Divide eggs among the crepes and sprinkle with half of each of the cheeses. Roll up crepes and place, seam side down, in 9-inch glass baking dish. Sprinkle with remaining cheeses. Bake for 10–15 minutes or until cheeses melt. Serve immediately.

Crepes

Crepes are quite easy to make, and they help you turn leftovers into a fancy dish. For the best crepes, make sure the batter is very smooth. Let it stand for a few minutes before cooking. Also, quickly turn and twist the skillet as soon as the batter hits the hot surface so the crepes are thin and even.

Simple Corn Crepes

 Serves 6

- ~ **PREP TIME:** 6 minutes
- ~ **COOK TIME:** 12 minutes
- ~ **TOTAL COST:** $1.02
- ~ **CALORIES:** 80
- ~ **FAT:** 3 g
- ~ **CARBOHYDRATES:** 8 g
- ~ **PROTEIN:** 3 g
- ~ **CHOLESTEROL:** 53 mg
- ~ **SODIUM:** 237 mg

2 eggs
1 cup milk or buttermilk
Pinch sea salt
1 cup corn flour
2 teaspoons sugar (optional)
2 tablespoons butter, melted
Canola oil for frying

Traditionally associated with French cuisine, crepes are a light pancake that are perfect for brunches or even dessert.

1. Place eggs, milk, and salt in a food processor and blend until smooth. With the motor on low, slowly add flour and sugar. Scrape down sides of bowl, turn back to low speed, and add butter.
2. Heat nonstick skillet over medium heat and add 2 teaspoons of oil. Pour in batter to make crepes. Tilt pan to spread batter evenly. Place crepes on parchment paper dusted with a little corn flour to prevent sticking. To store, place in Ziploc bag in refrigerator or freezer. Serve them with fresh fruit or cheese.

Breakfast Bread Pudding

Serves 8

- ~ **PREP TIME:** 5 minutes
- ~ **COOK TIME:** 50 minutes
- ~ **TOTAL COST:** $6.76
- ~ **CALORIES:** 373
- ~ **FAT:** 11 g
- ~ **CARBOHYDRATES:** 24 g
- ~ **PROTEIN:** 15 g
- ~ **CHOLESTEROL:** 46 mg
- ~ **SODIUM:** 398 mg

½ teaspoon extra-virgin olive oil
5 eggs
¼ cup low-fat milk
¼ cup plain yogurt
2 ounces blue cheese
3 slices seedless rye bread, torn into large pieces
3 slices pumpernickel bread, torn into large pieces
Ground black pepper

Substitute sourdough or wheat bread if you prefer.

Preheat oven to 375°F. Grease 2-quart casserole dish with oil. In mixing bowl, beat the eggs. Add the milk, yogurt, and cheese. Place bread pieces in prepared casserole dish, then pour egg mixture over. Bake for 40 to 50 minutes, until mixture is set and the top is golden brown. To serve, cut into squares and season with pepper.

Breakfast Sandwiches

Serves 6

~ **TOTAL COST:** $5.18
~ **CALORIES:** 336.89
~ **FAT:** 18.32 g
~ **PROTEIN:** 14.83 g
~ **CHOLESTEROL:** 236.65 mg
~ **SODIUM:** 424.54 mg

2 tablespoons butter
1 green bell pepper, chopped
2 cups frozen hash brown potatoes
6 eggs
¼ cup milk
½ teaspoon salt
⅛ teaspoon pepper
1 cup shredded Swiss cheese
3 pita breads, halved

These sandwiches taste like those at your local drive–through, but better. Plus, they're about half the price. If you don't like to eat bell peppers in the morning, leave them out.

1. In large skillet, melt butter over medium heat. Add bell pepper; cook and stir until crisp tender, about 3 minutes. Add potatoes; cook, stirring occasionally, until potatoes are tender and beginning to brown.
2. In medium bowl, combine eggs, milk, salt, and pepper and beat well. Pour into skillet with vegetables. Cook, stirring occasionally, until eggs are scrambled and set. Sprinkle cheese over, remove from heat, cover, and let stand for 3 minutes. Divide egg mixture among pita breads and serve immediately.

Nutty Oatmeal

Serves 5

~ **TOTAL COST:** $2.62
~ **CALORIES:** 413.43
~ **FAT:** 19.64 g
~ **PROTEIN:** 12.08 g
~ **CHOLESTEROL:** 13.43 mg
~ **SODIUM:** 518.98 mg

2 cups regular oatmeal
2 tablespoons butter
1 cup chopped walnuts
3 cups water
½ cup milk
½ cup brown sugar
1 teaspoon salt
½ teaspoon cinnamon
⅛ teaspoon nutmeg

Toasting the oatmeal and the nuts brings out the best flavor in this simple recipe. Serve it with some cold milk or cream poured over the top.

1. Place oatmeal in large skillet over medium high heat. Toast, stirring constantly, for 5–6 minutes or until oatmeal is fragrant and begins to brown around the edges. Remove to large saucepan.
2. In same skillet, melt butter and add chopped walnuts. Toast over medium heat, stirring constantly, until nuts are toasted; set aside. Add water, milk, salt, cinnamon, and nutmeg to oatmeal in saucepan.
3. Bring to a boil over high heat, then reduce heat to low and simmer 5–6 minutes until oatmeal is tender. Add brown sugar and nuts, stir, then cover oatmeal and let stand for 3 minutes. Stir and serve.

No-Oat Oatmeal

 Serves 4

- ~ **PREP TIME:** 2 minutes
- ~ **COOK TIME:** 45 to 60 minutes
- ~ **TOTAL COST:** $2.28
- ~ **CALORIES:** 85
- ~ **FAT:** 1 g
- ~ **CARBOHYDRATES:** 15 g
- ~ **PROTEIN:** 4 g
- ~ **CHOLESTEROL:** 0 mg
- ~ **SODIUM:** 30 mg

1½ cups soy milk
1½ cups water
1 cup brown rice
1 tablespoon honey
¼ teaspoon nutmeg
8 tablespoons fresh fruit (optional)

This recipe is perfect for the person who is looking for a healthy, tasty alternative to oatmeal.

Place all ingredients except fresh fruit in a medium-size saucepan. Bring the mixture to a slow simmer and cover with a tight-fitting lid. Simmer for 45 to 60 minutes, until the rice is tender and done. Serve in bowls, topped with your favorite fresh fruit.

Chilled Swiss Oatmeal (Muesli)

Serves 6

- ~ **PREP TIME:** 15 minutes
- ~ **REFRIGERATE TIME:** 25 minutes or overnight
- ~ **TOTAL COST:** $5.60
- ~ **CALORIES:** 183
- ~ **FAT:** 10 g
- ~ **PROTEIN:** 6 g
- ~ **CHOLESTEROL:** 2 mg
- ~ **SODIUM:** 61 mg

2 cups quick-cooking rolled oats
½ cup orange juice
¾ cup chopped prunes, raisins, or currants
⅓ cup chopped nuts or wheat germ
¼ teaspoon salt
¼ cup honey
1¼ cups low-fat milk

Most muesli has to be cooked, and that's why this one is so great to have on hand for breakfast or snacks.

Place the oats in a bowl and pour the juice over them; toss till it is evenly absorbed. Stir in the fruit, nuts, and salt. Pour the honey over the mixture and toss until evenly combined. Stir in the milk. Cover and refrigerate at least 8 hours. Do not cook; serve cold with brown sugar and additional milk or cream if desired.

Quick and Easy Meals
Try making two batches of this recipe, as you can make it ahead and hold it in the refrigerator for up to one week. Or, because it's freezer friendly, seal it in a Ziploc and enjoy in a month!

Stretch Your Scrambled Eggs

Serves 6

~ **TOTAL COST:** $2.93
~ **CALORIES:** 220.98
~ **FAT:** 14.59 g
~ **PROTEIN:** 13.48 g
~ **CHOLESTEROL:** 439.39 mg
~ **SODIUM:** 373.79 mg

2 tablespoons butter
12 eggs
⅓ cup 1% milk
⅓ cup sour cream
½ teaspoon salt
⅛ teaspoon pepper

Even though the price of eggs has doubled in the last year, they are still one of the cheapest sources of complete protein.

1. Place a large saucepan with 1½ inches of water over medium heat and bring to a simmer. Place slightly smaller saucepan in the water, add butter; let melt. In large bowl, combine eggs, milk, sour cream, salt, and pepper and beat well.
2. Pour egg mixture into melted butter in top saucepan. Cook, stirring occasionally, for about 30–40 minutes or until eggs are set and creamy. Serve immediately. You can also cook the eggs in a skillet directly over medium heat, stirring frequently, for about 5–7 minutes.

How to Cook Eggs

Eggs are best cooked quickly over medium-low heat. Heat the pan with the fat you're using before you add the eggs to reduce sticking.

Vegetable Egg Scramble

Serves 6

~ **PREP TIME:** 12 minutes
~ **COOK TIME:** 10 minutes
~ **TOTAL COST:** $5.42
~ **CALORIES:** 67
~ **FAT:** 5 g
~ **PROTEIN:** 6 g
~ **CHOLESTEROL:** 157 mg
~ **SODIUM:** 53 mg

1 teaspoon olive oil
3 scallions (green onions), minced
2 cloves garlic, minced
½ pound mushrooms, sliced
1 green bell pepper, chopped
1 (8-ounce) can kernel corn, drained
6 eggs
Sea salt and black pepper to taste

Vegetables are a great way to include extra flavor and nutrients to a dish without adding fat!

1. In a large skillet, heat the oil over medium heat. Add the scallions, garlic, mushrooms, bell pepper, and corn. Sauté, stirring occasionally, until the vegetables are tender, about 5 minutes.
2. Meanwhile, beat the eggs lightly in a bowl. Add the eggs to the vegetables, season with salt and pepper, and scramble until thoroughly cooked. Serve at once.

Quick and Easy Tip

Precook your vegetables the day before or use canned vegetables; just make sure they are drained really well or they will make your eggs soggy.

Scrambled Eggs with Lox

 Serves 4

~ **PREP TIME:** 15 minutes
~ **COOK TIME:** 10 minutes
~ **TOTAL COST:** $3.98
~ **CALORIES:** 184
~ **FAT:** 8 g
~ **CARBOHYDRATES:** 5 g
~ **PROTEIN:** 14 g
~ **CHOLESTEROL:** 264 mg
~ **SODIUM:** 703 mg

6 eggs
½ cup low-fat milk
1 (3-ounce) package cream cheese, softened
1 teaspoon fresh dill, chopped
Salt and pepper to taste
3 ounces lox or smoked salmon
1 tablespoon butter, unsalted

Salmon has a high content of omega-3 fatty acids, which are great for your heart and skin.

Using a wire whisk, beat eggs and milk together. Add cream cheese and combine thoroughly. Stir in dill, salt, pepper, and lox. Melt butter in 10-inch skillet over medium heat. Pour in egg mixture and scramble egg mixture until thickened but still moist.

Extra Nutrients
Fresh spinach is a natural and healthy addition to this recipe. If you have some on hand, add about ½ cup fresh spinach leaves to the skillet with the dill and other ingredients for a recipe that is packed full of flavor and nutrients without adding unwanted fat and calories.

Roasted Red Pepper Omelet

Serves 1

~ **PREP TIME:** 8 minutes
~ **COOK TIME:** 10 minutes
~ **TOTAL COST:** $1.94
~ **CALORIES:** 222
~ **FAT:** 11 g
~ **PROTEIN:** 32 g
~ **CHOLESTEROL:** 336 mg
~ **SODIUM:** 73 mg

2 eggs
Sea salt and black pepper to taste
¼ cup cooked spinach, drained (frozen is okay)
2 tablespoons grated Parmesan cheese
2 tablespoons red roasted peppers, chopped

Omelets are perfect for customizing—make yours and add your favorite touches, then have the rest of your family choose their own additions.

1. In a small mixing bowl, beat eggs until well combined using wire whisk or fork. Coat a nonstick skillet with nonstick spray (see Easy Omelet, this chapter, for uncoated skillet directions) and heat slightly over medium heat.
2. Add eggs to skillet and salt and pepper to taste. Cook on medium until eggs are just setting. Add spinach, cheese, and red peppers to center of eggs. Fold omelet over and cook for 2 minutes.
3. Flip omelet and cook for an additional 2 minutes.

Quick and Easy Tip
Be sure to use a spatula to lift edges of omelet and tilt skillet to drain off excess egg in the center of the omelet. This helps prevent burning your omelet while waiting for the center to finish cooking.

Easy Omelet

Serves 1

- ~ **PREP TIME:** 4 minutes
- ~ **COOK TIME:** 8 minutes
- ~ **TOTAL COST:** $1.47
- ~ **CALORIES:** 194
- ~ **FAT:** 15 g
- ~ **CARBOHYDRATES:** 6 g
- ~ **PROTEIN:** 12 g
- ~ **CHOLESTEROL:** 306 mg
- ~ **SODIUM:** 89 mg

2 eggs per omelet
1 tablespoon low-fat milk
Cooking spray if using nonstick skillet or omelet pan
2 teaspoons butter if using uncoated skillet or omelet pan

The idea of making an omelet often intimidates people but don't let it scare you. The key to an omelet is in the folding. If you don't fold it perfectly every time, don't worry—you can always have scrambled eggs or a frittata, an open-faced omelet.

1. Beat the eggs and milk in a bowl until combined; do not allow them to become frothy. Spray the nonstick skillet and heat slightly over medium heat, or if using an uncoated skillet, melt the butter over medium heat, tilting the skillet to coat the bottom.
2. Pour in the eggs; stir gently with a fork while they thicken to distribute the eggs from top to bottom. Stop stirring when the eggs begin to set. As the eggs thicken, lift the edges of the omelet and allow the uncooked eggs to flow underneath. Allow to cook until the bottom is golden and the top is set but shiny. With a long, flat spatula, gently loosen the edge of the omelet and fold the omelet in half toward you. With the help of the spatula, slide the omelet out of the pan and onto a plate. If making multiple omelets, cover them with foil to keep warm.

Customize Your Omelet

To add additional ingredients like cheese, meat, or vegetables, distribute them down the center of the omelet when the top is set but still shiny and before folding the omelet. Use approximately 1/3 cup if adding only one ingredient; if using multiple ingredients, distribute accordingly to equal approximately 1/3 cup.

French Toast

 Serves 4

- ~ **TOTAL COST:** $2.60
- ~ **CALORIES:** 325.82
- ~ **FAT:** 12.04 g
- ~ **PROTEIN:** 14.32 g
- ~ **CHOLESTEROL:** 79.60 mg
- ~ **SODIUM:** 484.15 mg

1 (12-ounce) can evaporated milk
1 egg, beaten
1 teaspoon vanilla
2 tablespoons powdered sugar
3 tablespoons butter
8 slices whole wheat bread

French Toast is an ideal way to use up stale bread. In fact, if the bread is stale it will make better French Toast! Serve with jam and powdered sugar.

1. Preheat griddle over medium heat. In shallow bowl, combine milk, egg, vanilla, and powdered sugar and beat until smooth.
2. Melt butter on skillet. Add bread to egg mixture, four slices at a time, and let stand for 1–2 minutes, turning once, to absorb egg mixture.
3. Immediately place coated bread in sizzling butter on griddle. Cook over medium heat for 5–6 minutes, turning once, until golden brown. Serve immediately.

Vegetarian Omelet

Serves 1

- ~ **PREP TIME:** 10 minutes
- ~ **COOK TIME:** 10 minutes
- ~ **TOTAL COST:** $1.68
- ~ **CALORIES:** 298
- ~ **FAT:** 24 g
- ~ **CARBOHYDRATES:** 5 g
- ~ **PROTEIN:** 20 g
- ~ **CHOLESTEROL:** 424 g
- ~ **SODIUM:** 332 mg

2 eggs
Sea salt and black pepper to taste
1 Roma tomato, chopped
2 tablespoons cremini mushrooms, chopped
1 tablespoon green onion, chopped

Since this recipe serves one person, have each person in your family add their favorite vegetables and perhaps even some cheese to customize their omelet.

1. In small mixing bowl, beat eggs until well combined using wire whisk or fork. Coat a nonstick skillet with nonstick spray (see Easy Omelet, this chapter, for uncoated skillet instructions) and heat slightly over medium heat.
2. Add eggs to skillet and salt and pepper to taste. Cook on medium until eggs are just setting. Add tomatoes, mushrooms, and onions to center of eggs. Fold omelet over and cook for 2 minutes.
3. Flip omelet and cook for an additional 2 minutes or until done.

Cheesy Fruit Omelet

 Serves 4

- ~ **TOTAL COST:** $4.38
- ~ **CALORIES:** 332.97
- ~ **FAT:** 22.83 g
- ~ **PROTEIN:** 19.62 g
- ~ **CHOLESTEROL:** 465.10 mg
- ~ **SODIUM:** 641.81 mg

1 apple, peeled and chopped
½ cup finely chopped onion
2 tablespoons butter or margarine, divided
8 eggs
2 tablespoons water
½ teaspoon salt
1 cup shredded Colby cheese

Omelets are easy, as long as you pay attention and keep moving the egg mixture. You could use any fruits or veggies you'd like in the filling.

1. In large nonstick skillet, melt 1 tablespoon butter over medium heat. Add apples and onion; cook and stir until tender, about 5 minutes. Remove from skillet and set aside.
2. In medium bowl, combine eggs with water and salt; beat until fluffy. Return skillet to heat, add remaining tablespoon butter to skillet and pour in egg mixture. Cook without stirring over medium heat for 2 minutes. Then, using a rubber spatula, gently run it under the edges of the omelet, lifting to let the uncooked egg flow underneath. Shake pan occasionally to prevent sticking.
3. When eggs are almost cooked but still moist on top, add apple filling to half of the omelet and sprinkle with cheese. Cover and cook for 2–3 minutes longer, then fold over and slide onto serving plate. Serve immediately.

Omelet Tricks
To make the best omelet, be sure to beat the egg mixture well, and cook the omelet quickly. To speed up the cooking, gently lift the edges of the egg as they start to set, letting the uncooked egg flow underneath. Make sure that the diners are ready for the omelet because they should be eaten immediately. And don't overcook them; cook just until the egg is set.

Golden Apple Omelet with Cheese

 Serves 2

- ~ **PREP TIME:** 15 minutes
- ~ **COOK TIME:** 15 minutes
- ~ **TOTAL COST:** $3.28
- ~ **CALORIES:** 175
- ~ **FAT:** 22 g
- ~ **PROTEIN:** 15 g
- ~ **CHOLESTEROL:** 322 mg
- ~ **SODIUM:** 250 mg

4 eggs
1 Golden Delicious apple, peeled, cored, and sliced
2 tablespoons butter, divided
1 tablespoon water
Sea salt and black pepper to taste
2 tablespoons crumbled blue cheese
2 tablespoons grated Parmesan cheese

Pears also taste great with this recipe. For a lighter omelet, leave out the blue cheese and save on calories and your pocketbook!

1. In a small mixing bowl, beat eggs using wire whisk or fork until combine.
2. Sauté the apple in 1 tablespoon butter until barely tender; remove from the pan.
3. Combine eggs, water, salt, and pepper until blended. Heat remaining butter in an omelet pan or skillet; add egg mixture. Cook slowly, lifting the edges to allow the uncooked portion to flow under. Arrange the apple slices on half of the omelet. Sprinkle with the cheeses; fold in half. Cook an additional 2 minutes or until done. Transfer to plate for serving.

Italian-Style Frittata

 Serves 4

- ~ **PREP TIME:** 15 minutes
- ~ **COOK TIME:** 10 minutes
- ~ **TOTAL COST:** $6.36
- ~ **CALORIES:** 163
- ~ **FAT:** 11 g
- ~ **PROTEIN:** 14 g
- ~ **CHOLESTEROL:** 328 mg
- ~ **SODIUM:** 267 mg

8 eggs
1 tablespoon white or yellow onion, chopped
1 tablespoon green or red bell peppers, chopped
1 ounce ham or turkey, chopped
⅓ cup grated Cheddar cheese

A frittata is an open-faced omelet that originated in Italy. Frittatas taste delicious and are easier to cook than an omelet because you don't have to fold them.

1. In a medium mixing bowl, beat eggs using wire whisk or fork until combined.
2. Coat an ovenproof, nonstick skillet with nonstick spray (see Basic Omelet instructions for uncoated skillets). On medium-high heat, add onions, peppers, and ham to skillet. Sauté for 2 minutes.
2. Add eggs to skillet and cook for 2 to 3 minutes. Place cheese on top of frittata, then place skillet in oven under the broiler and broil for 2 to 3 minutes or until cheese melts and eggs are set. Remove from pan and serve.

Quick and Easy Tip

Frittatas are like omelets but more sturdy. They are usually baked in the oven or cooked on the stovetop and finished under the broiler. As with omelets, be sure to lift edges of frittata with a spatula to help prevent sticking.

Parmesan Frittata

Serves 4

- ~ **PREP TIME:** 10 minutes
- ~ **COOK TIME:** 10 minutes
- ~ **TOTAL COST:** $4.44
- ~ **CALORIES:** 258
- ~ **FAT:** 15 g
- ~ **PROTEIN:** 11 g
- ~ **CHOLESTEROL:** 315 mg
- ~ **SODIUM:** 680 mg

8 eggs
5 slices day-old toast
2 tablespoons butter
1 small white or yellow onion, chopped
Sea salt and black pepper to taste
1 tablespoon grated Parmesan cheese

If you prefer, substitute your favorite cheese or, better yet, whatever you have in your refrigerator.

1. In a small mixing bowl, beat eggs using wire whisk or fork. Set aside.
2. Place toast in plastic bag and roll over it with a rolling pin to crush. In ovenproof skillet, melt butter over medium heat and add onions and crushed bread crumbs. Sauté 3 minutes. Add eggs, salt and pepper, and cheese. Cook until eggs are setting. Turn on broiler and place skillet under broiler. Broil for 1 minute or until eggs are cooked.

Quick and Easy Tip

Anytime you have leftover toast, save in a plastic bag and keep in freezer if not using within a day or two. Toast can be used not only for this recipe but as croutons for salad or in meatloaf or hamburgers. Add veggies into this recipe and serve for dinner as a meal!

Oven-Baked Eggs with Ham and Fresh Herbs

Serves 4

- ~ **PREP TIME:** 5 minutes
- ~ **COOK TIME:** 20 to 25 minutes
- ~ **TOTAL COST:** $3.24
- ~ **CALORIES:** 88
- ~ **FAT:** 14 g
- ~ **CARBOHYDRATES:** 2 g
- ~ **PROTEIN:** 17 g
- ~ **CHOLESTEROL:** 80 mg
- ~ **SODIUM:** 582 mg

2 tablespoons butter, unsalted
3 ounces ham, thinly sliced
3 large eggs
1 teaspoon Dijon mustard
¼ cup nonfat plain yogurt
¾ cup Cheddar cheese, shredded
2 teaspoons fresh chives, chopped
2 teaspoons fresh Italian flat-leaf parsley, chopped

Italian flat-leaf parsley has milder, more crisp flavor that curly parsley. It's more attractive than curly parsley and more popular with chefs.

Preheat oven to 375°F. Lightly grease 4 (6-ounce) ramekins with the butter. Line the ramekins with the ham. Combine eggs, Dijon, and yogurt, and mix well. Stir ¼ cup cheese into egg mixture. Add half the chives and parsley to mixture, and stir well. Spoon mixture into the prepared ramekins. Sprinkle with the remaining cheese and herbs. Bake for 20 to 25 minutes, until golden and set. Garnish with remaining herbs.

Healthy Tip

Fresh herbs are a great way to add flavor and color without adding fat and calories. As the Bikini Chef, I use fresh herbs in almost every recipe I make.

Oven-Baked Frittata

Serves 8

~ **PREP TIME:** 10 minutes
~ **COOK TIME:** 1 hour
~ **TOTAL COST:** $6.72
~ **CALORIES:** 208
~ **FAT:** 8 g
~ **CARBOHYDRATES:** 12 g
~ **PROTEIN:** 9 g
~ **CHOLESTEROL:** 11 mg
~ **SODIUM:** 134 mg

2 baking potatoes, peeled and sliced into ¼-inch slices
1 each yellow and red bell peppers, seeded and chopped
1 large red onion, roughly chopped
2 teaspoons olive oil
Sea salt and black pepper to taste
5 whole eggs
1 cup plain nonfat yogurt
1 cup skim milk
3 ounces fontina cheese, grated

Frittatas are open-faced omelets that are usually cooked on the stovetop and then finished in the oven. Here, everything is cooked in the oven making it much simpler!

1. Preheat oven to 375°F. Toss potatoes, peppers, and onion in oil. Season with salt and pepper. Place vegetables on parchment-lined baking sheet and roast in oven for about 20 minutes. While vegetables are baking, whisk together eggs, yogurt, milk, and cheese in a mixing bowl and set aside.
2. Remove vegetables from oven and transfer to baking dish. Layer vegetables in dish and pour yogurt mixture over vegetables. Place baking dish in oven and bake until egg mixture is completely set, about 30 to 40 minutes.

Lowering Fat in Recipes
Cooking with nonfat yogurt and low-fat or nonfat milk helps to cut down on your fat intake, and therefore calories, but most often does not sacrifice flavor.

Baked Bread Crumb Frittata

 Serves 4

~ **TOTAL COST:** $4.38
~ **CALORIES:** 329.13
~ **FAT:** 20.62 g
~ **PROTEIN:** 22.17 g
~ **CHOLESTEROL:** 348.48 mg
~ **SODIUM:** 756.13 mg

2 tablespoons butter or margarine, divided
1 tablespoon olive oil
1 cup frozen spinach, thawed and drained
3 slices leftover Garlic Toast (Chapter 2), crumbled
6 eggs
½ cup cottage cheese
½ teaspoon salt
1 cup shredded Swiss cheese

Frittatas are like heavy omelets. They can be eaten hot, warm, or cold, so they are perfect for breakfast on the run; just wrap a slice in a napkin and go!

1. Preheat oven to 375°F. Grease a 9-inch pie plate with 1 tablespoon butter and set aside. In medium skillet, melt 1 tablespoon butter with the olive oil over medium heat. When the butter foams, add spinach; cook and stir until liquid evaporates. Remove spinach from skillet and set aside.
2. Add Toast crumbs to the skillet; cook and stir over medium heat until coated with butter mixture. Remove from heat.
3. In medium bowl, beat eggs with cottage cheese and salt. Add spinach and Swiss cheese and mix well, then pour into prepared pie plate.
4. Bake for 20 minutes or until almost set. Remove from oven and sprinkle with Toast crumbs and cheese. Bake for 10–20 minutes longer until frittata is set and top is browned. Cool for 5 minutes, then slice to serve.

Hot Pepper and Salsa Frittata

 Serves 4

~ **TOTAL COST:** $4.36
~ **CALORIES:** 301.08
~ **FAT:** 20.47 g
~ **PROTEIN:** 19.55 g
~ **CHOLESTEROL:** 435.33 mg
~ **SODIUM:** 439.79 mg

2 tablespoons vegetable oil
½ cup finely chopped onion
2 cloves garlic, minced
½ green bell pepper, chopped
1 jalapeño pepper, minced
8 eggs
¼ cup milk
4 tablespoons grated Parmesan cheese
½ cup shredded mozzarella cheese
½ cup salsa
2 tablespoons chopped cilantro

Once you know how to make a frittata, the sky's the limit. Flavor them with cooked apples, mushrooms, pesto, meats, and cooked vegetables. They're a great way to use leftovers.

1. In large nonstick ovenproof skillet, heat oil over medium heat. Add onion, garlic, green bell pepper, and jalapeño pepper; cook and stir until crisp-tender, about 4 minutes.
2. In medium bowl beat eggs, milk, and Parmesan cheese until combined. Pour into skillet. Cook frittata, running spatula around edge as it cooks, until eggs are soft set and light brown on the bottom.
3. Preheat broiler. Sprinkle frittata with mozzarella cheese. Place frittata 6 inches from heat and broil for 4–7 minutes, watching carefully, until the top is browned and set. Top with salsa and cilantro and serve immediately.

Yes, Eggs Benedict
 Serves 6

- **TOTAL COST:** $6.39
- **CALORIES:** 410.81
- **FAT:** 25.34 g
- **PROTEIN:** 21.62 g
- **CHOLESTEROL:** 417.78 mg
- **SODIUM:** 536.00 mg

3 English muffins
2 tablespoons butter, softened
¼ cup sour cream
¼ cup mayonnaise
2 tablespoons heavy cream
2 tablespoons lemon juice
1 tablespoon butter, melted
10 eggs
⅓ cup milk
2 tablespoons butter
½ teaspoon salt
⅛ teaspoon white pepper
⅔ cup chopped ham
1 cup shredded Swiss cheese

The expensive parts of Eggs Benedict are the Hollandaise sauce and the Canadian bacon. This recipe solves that by making a "fake" Hollandaise and folding some chopped ham into the scrambled eggs.

1. Preheat broiler. Split English muffins and spread each with some of the 2 tablespoons butter. Place on broiler pan and broil until golden brown; set aside. In blender or food processor, combine mayonnaise, sour cream with cream, lemon juice, and 1 tablespoon melted butter. Blend or process until smooth. Set aside.
2. In large bowl, combine eggs, milk, salt, and pepper and beat until frothy. In large saucepan melt 2 tablespoons butter; add egg mixture and cook over medium heat, stirring frequently, until eggs are creamy but not quite set. Stir in ham and continue cooking until eggs are set.
3. Top each toasted English muffin with some of the cheese, a spoonful of the egg and ham mixture and a spoonful of the sauce. Broil for 2–3 minutes or until heated through; serve immediately.

Bruschetta of Eggs, Tomatoes, and Peppers

 Serves 4

- ~ **PREP TIME:** 6 minutes
- ~ **COOK TIME:** 5 minutes
- ~ **TOTAL COST:** $3.56
- ~ **CALORIES:** 375
- ~ **FAT:** 11 g
- ~ **CARBOHYDRATES:** 34 g
- ~ **PROTEIN:** 9 g
- ~ **CHOLESTEROL:** 44 mg
- ~ **SODIUM:** 381 mg

½ loaf Italian or French bread
½ cup extra-virgin olive oil
¼ cup pesto (in the refrigerated pasta section)
2 eggs
1 red bell pepper, seeded and chopped
¼ cup mozzarella cheese, shredded
1 medium tomato, seeded and diced

Traditionally, bruschetta is an Italian appetizer of toasted bread rubbed with fresh garlic and topped with extra-virgin olive oil. This version is a combination of Italian- and American-style bruschetta.

1. Slice the bread into 4¾-inch lengthwise slices. Brush 1 side of each with a bit of the oil; toast on grill or grill pan. When that side is toasted, brush oil on the other side, flip, and toast that side.
2. Place the toasted bread on a baking sheet, and spread with pesto. Mix eggs with bell pepper. Heat the remaining oil in sauté pan to medium temperature; add the egg mixture and cook omelet style. Cut the omelet and place on the bread; top with cheese and tomatoes.

Mini Pastry Puffs

Serves 12

- ~ **PREP TIME:** 15 minutes
- ~ **COOK TIME:** 20 minutes
- ~ **TOTAL COST:** $1.22
- ~ **CALORIES:** 52
- ~ **FAT:** 2 g
- ~ **PROTEIN:** 2 g
- ~ **CHOLESTEROL:** 26 mg
- ~ **SODIUM:** 16 mg

2 eggs
⅔ cup low-fat milk
⅔ cup plain flour
1 tablespoon canola oil

This recipe is a favorite with adults and kids alike!

1. Preheat oven to 425°F. Spray mini muffin pans with baking spray and set aside.
2. Combine all ingredients in a medium bowl and beat well with wire whisk until batter is blended and smooth. Pour 1 tablespoon of batter into each prepared muffin cup. Bake for 15 to 22 minutes or until puffs are deep golden brown and are puffed. Serve immediately.

Quick and Easy Tip
Puffs "puff up" without any leavening in the batter because it contains lots of gluten and liquid. When the popovers are placed in the hot oven, the batter almost explodes with steam, and the gluten keeps the shell together.

Pita Scramblers Sandwiches

 Serves 4

- ~ **TOTAL COST:** $4.91
- ~ **CALORIES:** 418.48
- ~ **FAT:** 28.35 g
- ~ **PROTEIN:** 24.07 g
- ~ **CHOLESTEROL:** 380.80 mg
- ~ **SODIUM:** 882.35 mg

2 pita breads
⅓ pound pork sausage
6 eggs
⅓ cup sour cream
½ teaspoon salt
⅛ teaspoon pepper
1 cup shredded Cheddar cheese
1 tomato, chopped
2 green onions, chopped

Other vegetables, like chopped red bell pepper, chopped mushrooms, or summer squash, could be substituted for the tomatoes. These sandwiches are great for lunch or breakfast.

1. Cut pita breads in half and set aside. In large skillet, cook sausage until brown; drain off fat. In medium bowl, combine eggs, sour cream, salt, and pepper and beat well. Add to skillet with sausage; cook and stir until eggs are set but still moist.
2. Sprinkle with cheese, remove from heat, and cover. Let stand for 4 minutes. In small bowl, combine tomato and green onion.
3. Spoon egg mixture into Pita Breads and top with tomato mixture. Serve immediately.

> **Egg Safety**
> Did you know that it's not safe to eat poached or fried eggs done "softly set" or "over easy"? Eggs must be fully cooked to be safe. In other words, the yolk must be set and firm. You can use pasteurized eggs and still eat them softly set, but they are very expensive. This recipe solves that problem by making an egg sandwich with scrambled eggs.

Peach and Raspberry Soufflé

Serves 4

- **TOTAL COST:** $3.70
- **CALORIES:** 353.90
- **FAT:** 13.13 g
- **PROTEIN:** 10.51 g
- **CHOLESTEROL:** 330.70 mg
- **SODIUM:** 228.17 mg

1 cup chopped frozen peaches, thawed
2 tablespoons butter or margarine
2 tablespoons flour
⅛ teaspoon salt
¼ cup sugar, divided
½ cup reserved peach juice
3 tablespoons raspberry jelly
½ teaspoon dried thyme leaves
6 egg yolks
6 egg whites
¼ teaspoon cream of tartar

Your guests should always be waiting for the soufflé, not vice versa. This delicate soufflé is an elegant treat for a fancy brunch, for pennies.

1. Preheat oven to 400°F. Drain peaches, reserving juice. Add enough water to peach juice to equal ½ cup, if necessary.
2. In medium pan, melt butter over medium heat. Add flour and salt; cook and stir for 3 minutes until bubbly. Add 1 tablespoon sugar, reserved peach juice, and jelly; stir until mixture bubbles and thickens. Remove from heat and whisk in thyme, egg yolks and drained peaches. Set aside.
3. In large bowl, combine salt with egg whites and cream of tartar; beat until foamy. Gradually beat in remaining 3 tablespoons sugar until stiff peaks form.
4. Stir a dollop of the egg white mixture into peach mixture, then fold in remaining egg whites. Spray the bottom of a 2-quart casserole dish with nonstick cooking spray and pour soufflé batter into the dish. Bake for 35–45 minutes or until soufflé is puffed and deep golden brown. Serve immediately.

Raspberry–Cream Cheese Biscuits

Serves 7

- ~ **PREP TIME:** 15 minutes
- ~ **COOK TIME:** 10 minutes
- ~ **TOTAL COST:** $2.48
- ~ **CALORIES:** 279
- ~ **FAT:** 7 g
- ~ **PROTEIN:** 7 g
- ~ **CHOLESTEROL:** 6 mg
- ~ **SODIUM:** 33 mg

3 cups plain flour
2 tablespoons baking powder
¾ teaspoon sea salt
3 tablespoons shortening
¾ cup orange juice or low-fat milk
1 3-ounce package cream cheese
2 tablespoons raspberry all-fruit spread or jam
2 tablespoons sugar for sprinkling tops

Raspberries are pretty, delicious, and can be enjoyed in muffins, as they are here, or in salads, desserts, and even entrées. When cooking with them, be sure to stir them gently as they are delicate little berries!

1. Preheat the oven to 450°F. Sift together the flour, baking powder, and salt. Cut in the shortening until the mixture resembles coarse crumbs. Add the orange juice and beat to form a soft dough. Turn the dough onto a surface well dusted with flour and knead 10 times. Roll or pat the dough till it's ½-inch thick. Cut rounds with a biscuit cutter or a 2½-inch round cutter (a drinking glass can be used). Place the rounds on an ungreased cookie sheet.
2. Soften the cream cheese. Add the jam and mix until marbled but not thoroughly combined. Spoon about 1 teaspoon onto the center of each round. Sprinkle with sugar. Bake 8 to 10 minutes, or until golden brown.

Quick and Easy Tip
To save time and possibly money, replace flour, baking powder, salt, and shortening by using 3 cups of biscuit mix such as Bisquick. This will only save money if your pantry is lacking in all of the ingredients.

Quiche Lorraine

Serves 5

- ~ **PREP TIME:** 15 minutes
- ~ **COOK TIME:** 25 minutes
- ~ **TOTAL COST:** $4.35
- ~ **CALORIES:** 207
- ~ **FAT:** 16 g
- ~ **PROTEIN:** 15 g
- ~ **CHOLESTEROL:** 209 mg
- ~ **SODIUM:** 447 mg

2 slices bacon
1 medium onion, chopped
1½ tablespoons canola oil
6 eggs
1½ cups shredded Swiss cheese
1 small pinch nutmeg
Sea salt and black pepper to taste

Quiche is delicious and not something you think of every day. You can also make mini-quiche and serve as an appetizer!

1. Preheat the broiler. Cook the bacon in a skillet until hard. Drain well, crumble, and reserve. Slice the onion very thinly. In a 10-inch ovenproof skillet, heat the oil and sauté the onion for about 2 minutes.
2. Beat the eggs well. Stir in the cheese, nutmeg, salt and pepper, and bacon. When the onions have finished cooking, stir to distribute evenly (do not drain), and pour the egg mixture over them. Reduce the heat to medium low and cook until set but still moist on top, about 8 minutes. Immediately put the skillet in the broiler, about 5 inches from the flame or element, and cook until the top is done but not browned.

Anything Quiche

Serves 6

- ~ **TOTAL COST:** $4.00
- ~ **CALORIES:** 398.63
- ~ **FAT:** 22.79 g
- ~ **PROTEIN:** 19.62 g
- ~ **CHOLESTEROL:** 185.63 mg
- ~ **SODIUM:** 764.05 mg

1 Angel Pie Crust (Chapter 15), unbaked
½ to 1 cup cooked leftover meat
½ to 1 cup cooked leftover vegetables
1 cup shredded Colby or Muenster cheese
4 eggs
½ cup milk
½ cup sour cream
2 tablespoons all-purpose flour
½ teaspoon salt
⅛ teaspoon pepper
¼ cup grated Parmesan cheese

Any leftover or bits and pieces of cooked food can be used in a quiche. Add you need is eggs, milk, and cheese.

1. Preheat oven to 375°F. In Pie Crust, arrange meat, eggs, and cheese; set aside.
2. In medium bowl, combine eggs, milk, sour cream, flour, salt, and pepper and beat well with wire whisk or eggbeater until smooth. Pour into Pie Crust and sprinkle with Parmesan cheese.
3. Bake for 25–35 minutes or until quiche is puffed and set, and top is beginning to brown. Let stand for 5 minutes, then slice to serve.

Double Egg Quiche

Serves 6

- ~ **TOTAL COST:** $4.81
- ~ **CALORIES:** 450.32
- ~ **FAT:** 28.09 g
- ~ **PROTEIN:** 20.34 g
- ~ **CHOLESTEROL:** 323.30 mg
- ~ **SODIUM:**656.39 mg

4 hard-cooked eggs
1 cup shredded Swiss cheese
1 Angel Pie Crust (Chapter 15), unbaked
4 eggs
½ cup light cream
¼ cup milk
1 tablespoon mustard
2 tablespoons all-purpose flour
½ teaspoon salt
⅛ teaspoon pepper
1 cup frozen peas, thawed
¼ cup grated Parmesan cheese

Using sliced hard-cooked eggs along with an egg custard in this quiche makes it extra–rich.

1. Preheat oven to 350°F. Peel and slice hard-cooked eggs. Layer with Swiss cheese in the bottom of Pie Crust; set aside.
2. In medium bowl, combine eggs, cream, milk, mustard, flour, salt, and pepper and mix well with wire whisk until blended.
3. Sprinkle peas over ingredients in Pie Crust and pour egg mixture over. Sprinkle with Parmesan cheese. Bake for 45–55 minutes or until quiche is puffed and golden brown. Serve immediately.

Hard Cooked Eggs

To hard cook eggs, cover eggs by 1 inch with water. Bring to a boil over high heat. When water comes to a full boil, cover the pan and remove from heat. Let stand for 15 minutes for large eggs. Then place pot in the sink, uncover, and let cold water run into the pan until the eggs are cold. Crack, peel, and use.

French Toast with Citrus Compote

Serves 4

~ **TOTAL COST:** $4.28
~ **CALORIES:** 379.94
~ **FAT:** 10.46 g
~ **PROTEIN:** 8.67 g
~ **CHOLESTEROL:** 120.49 mg
~ **SODIUM:** 346.13 mg

1 orange
1 large red grapefruit
½ cup sugar, divided
1 cup orange juice, divided
1 teaspoon vanilla
2 eggs
8 slices cracked wheat bread
2 tablespoons butter or margarine

This citrus compote can be served with any pancakes, waffles, French Toast, or even hot cooked oatmeal. One-fourth of the compote provides 100 percent of your DV requirement for Vitamin C.

1. Peel and chop orange and grapefruit and place in small bowl. In small saucepan, combine sugar with ½ cup orange juice and bring to a simmer. Simmer for 5–6 minutes or until slightly thickened; pour over orange mixture and set aside.
2. In shallow bowl, combine remaining ¼ cup sugar with ½ cup orange juice, vanilla, and eggs, and beat well. Heat a nonstick pan over medium heat and add butter.
3. Dip bread into egg mixture, turning to coat. Cook in hot butter over medium heat for 6–8 minutes, turning once, until bread is crisp and deep golden brown. Serve with citrus compote.

Basic Waffles

Serves 3

~ **PREP TIME:** 10 minutes
~ **COOK TIME:** 5 minutes
~ **TOTAL COST:** $1.84
~ **CALORIES:** 401
~ **FAT:** 41 g
~ **PROTEIN:** 17 g
~ **CHOLESTEROL:** 110 mg
~ **SODIUM:** 110 mg

2 cups plain flour
4 teaspoons baking powder
¼ teaspoon sea salt
2 eggs
1¾ cups low-fat milk
½ cup canola oil

If your family loves waffles, consider investing in a waffle iron. They are not too expensive and will bring joy to your family for years to come.

Preheat waffle iron following manufacturer's instructions. Stir together the flour, baking powder, and salt, and make a well in the middle of the mixture. Beat the eggs lightly, then beat in the milk and oil until well combined. Add all at once to the dry ingredients and combine until just moistened. Batter will have a few lumps.

Quick and Easy Tip

Use the manufacturer's directions to determine how much batter to use per waffle; use about 1 cup for a standard 7-inch circular waffle. Do not open the iron while the waffle is cooking! Remove with a fork to avoid burning your fingers.

French Toast with Fresh Fruit

 Serves 2

~ **PREP TIME:** 15 minutes
~ **COOK TIME:** 15 minutes
~ **TOTAL COST:** $4.54
~ **CALORIES:** 325
~ **FAT:** 10 g
~ **CARBOHYDRATES:** 24 g
~ **PROTEIN:** 13 g
~ **CHOLESTEROL:** 74 mg
~ **SODIUM:** 380 mg

½ teaspoon olive oil
3 small loaves challah bread, sliced into 2½- to 3-inch-thick slices
1 cup seasonal fresh fruit, such as strawberries, diced
4 eggs
¼ cup skim milk
1 cup orange juice
¼ cup nonfat plain yogurt
1 tablespoon confectioners (powdered) sugar

Look for challah bread in your grocery store bakery.

1. Preheat oven to 375°F. Line baking sheet with parchment paper. Prepare bread slices by cutting a slit into the bottom of the crust, forming a pocket. Fill pockets with diced fruit.
2. In large mixing bowl, beat eggs and milk. Dip bread into egg mixture, letting it fully absorb the mixture then removing quickly. Place bread on baking sheet. Bake for 10 minutes on 1 side, flip and bake 10 minutes more.
3. While bread is baking, pour the orange juice in small saucepan. Boil until reduced by half and mixture becomes syrupy. Remove bread from oven, cut in half diagonally. Serve each with a dollop of yogurt, drizzle of juice, and sprinkle of sugar.

Sausage Quiche

 Serves 6

~ **TOTAL COST:** $6.17
~ **CALORIES:** 481.65
~ **FAT:** 28.12 g
~ **PROTEIN:** 20.05 g
~ **CHOLESTEROL:** 169.70 mg
~ **SODIUM:** 823.17 mg

½ pound pork sausage
1 onion, chopped
1 green bell pepper, chopped
2 tablespoons all-purpose flour
½ teaspoon salt
⅛ teaspoon pepper
1 (12–ounce) can evaporated milk
3 eggs
1 cup shredded Cheddar cheese
½ cup shredded Swiss cheese
1 Angel Pie Crust (Chapter 15), unbaked

A quiche is always an elegant lunch or dinner, and it's easy to make too.

1. Preheat oven to 400°F. In large saucepan, cook sausage and onion over medium heat, stirring to break up sausage, until pork is browned, about 5–7 minutes. Drain fat. Add bell pepper to saucepan; cook and stir for 1 minute longer.
2. Sprinkle with flour, salt, and pepper; cook and stir for 3 minutes. Add milk; cook and stir until thickened.
3. In large bowl, beat eggs until foamy. Stir sausage mixture into eggs. Sprinkle cheeses into Pie Crust and pour sausage mixture over. Bake for 25–35 minutes or until quiche is puffed, set, and top is beginning to brown.

Crisp French Toast

 Serves 4

- ~ **TOTAL COST:** $2.91
- ~ **CALORIES:** 496.83
- ~ **FAT:** 14.71 g
- ~ **PROTEIN:** 14.69 g
- ~ **CHOLESTEROL:** 130.04 mg
- ~ **SODIUM:** 734.83 mg

8 slices whole wheat bread
2 eggs, beaten
⅓ cup milk
2 tablespoons sugar
½ teaspoon cinnamon
2 cups finely crushed leftover cereal flakes
2 tablespoons butter

French toast is easy to make and it's an inexpensive way to stretch bread. You could use cracked wheat, white, or multigrain bread in this simple recipe.

1. In shallow bowl, combine eggs, milk, sugar, and cinnamon and beat until smooth. Dip each slice of bread into the egg mixture, letting stand for 1 minute, turn over, and then dip into crushed cereal to coat.
2. In large skillet over medium high heat, melt butter. When it's melted and foamy, add the coated bread pieces, two to three at a time. Cook on first side for 3–5 minutes until golden brown. Carefully turn and cook on second side for 2–4 minutes until golden brown and crisp. Serve immediately.

Whole Grain Waffles

Serves 6

- ~ **TOTAL COST:** $2.43
- ~ **CALORIES:** 360.62
- ~ **FAT:** 8.82 g
- ~ **PROTEIN:** 12.69 g
- ~ **CHOLESTEROL:** 122.41 mg
- ~ **SODIUM:** 450.21 mg

1 cup all-purpose flour
¾ cup whole wheat flour
1 cup cornmeal
2 teaspoons baking powder
½ teaspoon baking soda
⅛ teaspoon salt
3 egg yolks
2 tablespoons butter or margarine, melted
2 cups buttermilk
3 egg whites
¼ cup sugar

Homemade waffles taste so much better than frozen. You can use them for breakfast with fresh fruit, or omit the sugar and serve them for dinner with some Homemade Chili (Chapter 6).

1. In medium bowl, combine flour, whole wheat flour, cornmeal, baking powder, baking soda, and salt, and mix well.
2. In small bowl, combine egg, melted butter, and buttermilk and mix well. Add to flour mixture and stir just until combined.
3. In large bowl, beat egg whites until foamy. Gradually add sugar, beating until stiff peaks form. Fold into flour mixture.
4. Spray waffle iron with nonstick cooking spray and heat according to directions. Pour about ¼ cup batter into the waffle iron, close, and cook until the steaming stops, or according to the appliance directions. Serve immediately.

Waffles with Fresh Fruit Syrup

Makes 6 waffles

- **PREP TIME:** 10 minutes
- **COOK TIME:** 15 minutes
- **TOTAL COST:** $4.46
- **CALORIES:** 379
- **FAT:** 22 g
- **CARBOHYDRATES:** 42 g
- **PROTEIN:** 8 g
- **CHOLESTEROL:** 68 mg
- **SODIUM:** 48 mg

½ cup orange juice
½ cup apple juice
½ cup sugar
2 tablespoons honey
Juice of 1 lemon
1½ cups fresh berries such as raspberries, blueberries, or strawberries
2 cups plain flour
4 teaspoons baking powder
¼ teaspoon sea salt
2 eggs
1¾ cups low-fat or nonfat milk
½ cup canola oil

Citrus syrups are delicious served over bowls of fresh fruit or used as a glaze for chicken.

1. Make syrup by heating orange juice, apple juice, sugar, honey, and lemon juice over medium heat in small-quart boiler. Bring to a boil and reduce liquid by half. Add berries and simmer for 1 minute. Remove from heat and set aside to cool.
2. Preheat waffle iron following manufacturer's instructions. Stir together the flour, baking powder, and salt, and make a well in the middle of the mixture. Beat the eggs lightly, then beat in the milk and oil until well combined. Add all at once to the dry ingredients and combine until just moistened. Batter will have a few lumps.
3. Use the manufacturer's directions to determine how much batter to use per waffle; use about 1 cup for a standard 7-inch circular waffle. Do not open the iron while the waffle is cooking! Remove with a fork to avoid burning your fingers. Serve waffles with syrup.

Waffles

Waffles are essentially batter based cakes which is why they work perfectly with all different textures and flavors of toppings. Feel free to experiment with your favorite flavors and create your own waffles.

Huevos Rancheros

Serves 4

~ **TOTAL COST:** $6.20

~ **CALORIES:** 446.55

~ **FAT:** 28.09 g

~ **PROTEIN:** 23.04 g

~ **CHOLESTEROL:** 404.65 mg

~ **SODIUM:** 1050.21 mg

1 cup enchilada sauce

3 tablespoons vegetable oil

4 (6-inch) corn tortillas

7 eggs

¼ cup heavy cream

½ teaspoon salt

⅛ teaspoon pepper

3 green onions, chopped

1 cup refried beans

1 cup shredded Cheddar cheese

1 avocado, peeled and sliced

This hearty dish makes a perfect breakfast when you have a busy day ahead; it will keep you going for hours! Serve it with cold orange juice and some fresh fruit.

1. Heat enchilada sauce in medium saucepan. Meanwhile, heat vegetable oil over medium heat in large skillet. Fry tortillas, turning once, until crisp, about 1 minute on each side. Remove to paper towels to drain. Drain off all but 1 tablespoon vegetable oil.
2. Beat eggs with cream, salt, and pepper until smooth; add green onion and pour into hot oil. Scramble eggs over medium heat, stirring occasionally, until eggs are cooked through but still moist. Meanwhile, place beans in another small saucepan and warm over medium heat.
3. When ready to eat, spread refried beans over the crisp tortillas. Top with a spoonful of enchilada sauce and a generous portion of eggs. Top with more sauce, sprinkle with cheese, and top with avocado; serve immediately.

CHAPTER 5

SALADS

Caesar Salad

Serves 6

- ~ **PREP TIME:** 15 minutes
- ~ **TOTAL COST:** $2.94
- ~ **CALORIES:** 96
- ~ **FAT:** 7 g
- ~ **CARBOHYDRATES:** 1 g
- ~ **PROTEIN:** 1 g
- ~ **CHOLESTEROL:** 5 mg
- ~ **SODIUM:** 108 mg

2 tablespoons low-fat mayonnaise
Juice of ½ lemon
1 teaspoon Worcestershire sauce
1 teaspoon Dijon mustard (Grey Poupon recommended)
Black pepper to taste
3 tablespoons extra-virgin olive oil
¼ cup Parmesan cheese, grated
1 head romaine lettuce, washed, dried, and cut into bite-sized pieces
1 cup croutons (optional)

Croutons add fat and calories that aren't needed. If you can resist, skip the croutons and add a healthy protein such as diced, baked chicken or grilled salmon.

In medium mixing bowl, combine mayonnaise, lemon juice, Worcestershire sauce, mustard, and pepper. Whisk well until blended. Whisk in olive oil. Add cheese and lettuce and toss to coat. Top with croutons, if desired.

Chopping Lettuce
Tearing lettuce can bruise the lettuce, making the tender leaves turn brown. An easy way to slice romaine is to cut off the end, slice the head lengthwise into planks, then turn the sliced planks sideways and slice into 1-inch slices.

Caesar Salad with Grilled Steak

Serves 4

- ~ **PREP TIME:** 10 minutes
- ~ **COOK TIME:** 10 minutes
- ~ **TOTAL COST:** $6.93
- ~ **CALORIES:** 282
- ~ **FAT:** 17 g
- ~ **PROTEIN:** 21 g
- ~ **CHOLESTEROL:** 52 mg
- ~ **SODIUM:** 708 mg

6 cups romaine lettuce
2 tablespoons Parmesan cheese, grated
¼ cup Caesar dressing, your favorite
8 ounces grilled, lean steak

A classic Caesar is always good. Add grilled steak for a new twist and extra protein for a complete meal.

In a large mixing bowl, combine lettuce, cheese, and dressing and toss well to coat. Add steak on top of salad when serving.

Quick and Easy Tip
Sirloin cut into strips or flank steak works well for this salad and is less expensive than filet.

Grilled Chicken Caesar Salad with Pepper Jack Cheese

Serves 4

~ **PREP TIME:** 8 minutes
~ **COOK TIME:** 10 minutes
~ **TOTAL COST:** $5.48
~ **CALORIES:** 283
~ **FAT:** 13 g
~ **PROTEIN:** 22 g
~ **CHOLESTEROL:** 68 mg
~ **SODIUM:** 213 mg

1 pound boneless chicken breasts, skin removed
Sea salt and pepper to taste
3 tablespoons olive oil
¼ cup Caesar dressing
1 teaspoon green pepper sauce
6 cups romaine lettuce
¼ cup pepper jack cheese, grated

Caesar salads are easily customizable depending on your family's tastes. Try grilled chicken, as here, or barbecue chicken, or blackened salmon. It's a great way to make this salad a meal and not just a side dish.

1. Cut chicken into cubes, toss in a mixing bowl and add salt, pepper, and oil and toss to coat. Heat a medium skillet over medium heat. Add chicken and cover with lid. Cook until done, about 8 to 10 minutes. Turn off heat and set aside.
2. Separately, in a mixing bowl, add remaining ingredients and toss well. When serving, serve in bowls and add chicken on top.

Tuna Salad

Serves 4

~ **PREP TIME:** 15 minutes
~ **COOK TIME:** none
~ **TOTAL COST:** $4.56
~ **CALORIES:** 200
~ **FAT:** 11 g
~ **PROTEIN:** 21 g
~ **SODIUM:** 374 mg

2 cans tuna fish in water, drained
1 stalk celery, chopped
1 tablespoon yellow onion, diced
Sea salt and pepper to taste
½ cup mayonnaise, low-fat if desired
1 teaspoon prepared mustard
⅓ cup red seedless grapes, halved, optional
1 hard-boiled egg, chopped
6 cups spring mix lettuce
1 tomato, sliced

Tuna salad is perfect as a snack, on sandwiches or, as here, on a bed of lettuce with tomatoes. My favorite way to eat it is right out of the mixing bowl with saltine crackers!

In a mixing bowl, combine all ingredients except lettuce and tomato and mix well. Place lettuce on a plate. Top with scoops of tuna and sliced tomatoes.

Quick and Easy Tip

A surefire way to save money is to make this easy tuna salad recipe yourself. Don't waste money on premade, packaged tuna salad, which is more expensive and doesn't taste near as good! Substitute chicken if you prefer.

Black Bean Salad with Romaine

 Serves 8

- **PREP TIME:** 15 minutes
- **CHILL TIME:** 15 to 20 minutes
- **TOTAL COST:** $6.93
- **CALORIES:** 92
- **FAT:** 2 g
- **CARBOHYDRATES:** 14 g
- **PROTEIN:** 3 g
- **CHOLESTEROL:** 1 mg
- **SODIUM:** 530 mg

1 (15-ounce) can black beans, rinsed and drained
1 (12-ounce) can yellow corn kernels, drained
½ cup red onion, chopped
½ cup green bell pepper, chopped
2 cloves garlic, chopped
¾ cup low-fat Italian dressing
½ teaspoon Tabasco sauce
½ teaspoon chili powder
Sea salt and black pepper to taste
1 head romaine lettuce, washed, dried, and chopped
    into 2-inch pieces

Beans are a natural source of protein; however, if you need extra protein, this is a great recipe to add chicken or turkey.

In large mixing bowl, combine all ingredients except lettuce. Toss well. Chill for 15 to 20 minutes. Remove from refrigerator, add lettuce, and toss well. Serve immediately.

Taco Salad

 Serves 4

- **PREP TIME:** 8 minutes
- **COOK TIME:** none
- **TOTAL COST:** $5.36
- **CALORIES:** 233
- **FAT:** 2 g
- **PROTEIN:** 4 g
- **CHOLESTEROL:** 5 mg
- **SODIUM:** 251 mg

6 cups iceberg lettuce, washed, dried, and largely
    chopped
2 tomatoes, diced
½ cup black beans, drained
1 medium yellow onion, chopped
½ cup kernel corn, drained
½ cup Cheddar cheese, grated
1 jalapeño pepper, sliced
½ packet taco seasoning or ¼ cup salsa
Tortilla chips (optional)

You can make this dish spicy by adding hot sauce, or cool it down by adding a dollop of sour cream. Either way, this recipe is family pleaser!

Place all ingredients in a large mixing bowl except tortilla chips. Toss well and serve with chips, if desired.

Quick and Easy Tip
With a well stocked pantry, this salad can be made using canned foods such as diced tomatoes, green chilis, even sliced jalapeños come canned. Just be sure to drain them well. Also, if you have some leftover cooked chicken, dice it up and throw it in for extra flavor and protein!

Tex-Mex Pasta Salad

 Serves 6

~ **TOTAL COST:** $6.79
~ **CALORIES:** 435.95
~ **FAT:** 6.67 g
~ **PROTEIN:** 18.70 g
~ **CHOLESTEROL:** 28.30 mg
~ **SODIUM:** 590.23 mg

½ cup mayonnaise
1 cup plain yogurt
¼ cup milk
1 cup chunky salsa
1 green bell pepper, chopped
1 jalapeño pepper, minced
1 Slow Cooker Simmered Chicken Breast (Chapter 7),
  diced
¼ cup grated Parmesan cheese
2 cups frozen corn
1 (16-ounce) package gemelli pasta

Pasta salads are a great choice during the summer months. Make the salad in the morning or evening, then let it marinate until serving time.

1. Bring a large pot of water to a boil. Meanwhile, in large bowl, combine mayonnaise, yogurt, milk, and salsa, and mix well. Stir in bell pepper, jalapeño pepper, chicken, and cheese and mix well. Place corn on top of salad mixture.
2. Cook pasta according to package directions, drain, and stir into salad mixture while hot. Stir gently to coat all ingredients with dressing, cover, and refrigerate for 1–2 hours to blend flavors.

Mixed Greens with Radicchio and Oranges in Honeyed Vinaigrette

Serves 6

~ **PREP TIME:** 15 minutes
~ **TOTAL COST:** $6.08
~ **CALORIES:** 130
~ **FAT:** 10 g
~ **CARBOHYDRATES:** 8 g
~ **PROTEIN:** 1 g
~ **CHOLESTEROL:** 0 mg
~ **SODIUM:** 0 mg

¼ cup apple cider vinegar
1 tablespoon honey
Sea salt and black pepper to taste
¼ cup extra-virgin olive oil
6 cups mixed greens, washed and dried
3 oranges, peeled, membranes removed
2 heads radicchio, chopped

Radicchio is a leafy vegetable that has a slightly bitter taste. This honey vinaigrette helps to balance the bitterness of the leaves. Radicchio is also delicious grilled, which mellows the bitter flavor.

1. In a large mixing bowl, combine vinegar, honey, salt, and pepper. Whisk well to combine. Add olive oil while whisking. Mix thoroughly.
2. Separately, combine mixed greens, oranges, and radicchio and toss to combine. Add into vinaigrette and toss to coat.

Pasta Cabbage Salad

Serves 6

- ~ **TOTAL COST:** $6.44
- ~ **CALORIES:** 396.32
- ~ **FAT:** 10.33 g
- ~ **PROTEIN:** 13.07 g
- ~ **CHOLESTEROL:** 11.25 mg
- ~ **SODIUM:** 525.91 mg

½ cup mayonnaise
½ cup plain yogurt
½ cup zesty Italian salad dressing
1 head cabbage
1 green bell pepper, chopped
2 cups frozen peas
1 (12–ounce) package penne pasta

Add a can of tuna or chicken and this becomes a hearty main dish salad.

1. Bring a large pot of salted water to a boil. Meanwhile, in large bowl combine mayonnaise, yogurt, and salad dressing and mix well.
2. Wash cabbage and cut in half. Remove corn and cut crosswise into ¼-inch thick pieces. Add to mayonnaise mixture in bowl. Add bell pepper and mushrooms.
3. Place frozen peas in a colander. Cook pasta in boiling water until al dente according to package directions. Drain over peas in colander and add to salad mixture. Toss gently to coat and serve immediately or cover and chill for 3–4 hours before serving.

Pasta Salad with Breast of Chicken

 Serves 6

- ~ **PREP TIME:** 10 minutes
- ~ **COOK TIME:** 5 minutes
- ~ **CHILL TIME:** 1 hour
- ~ **TOTAL COST:** $6.74
- ~ **CALORIES:** 227
- ~ **FAT:** 4 g
- ~ **CARBOHYDRATES:** 13 g
- ~ **PROTEIN:** 24 g
- ~ **CHOLESTEROL:** 61 mg
- ~ **SODIUM:** 462 mg

Pinch sea salt (for pasta water)
1 head fresh broccoli, chopped
3 cups cooked chicken breast, chopped
½ pound pasta shells, cooked and drained
2 large tomatoes, chopped
½ red onion, chopped
Black pepper to taste
1 cup Italian dressing

Pasta salad recipes are very fun to make because you are not limited to just these ingredients. Feel free to use your favorite type of pasta, perhaps bow-tie or corkscrew, and add shredded carrots, black olives, or red bell peppers for a variation on this already simply delicious dish.

1. In large pot filled ¾ with water, bring water to a boil. Add pinch of salt, then add broccoli and allow to boil for 20 seconds. Remove broccoli from boiling water and transfer to colander to drain.
2. In large mixing bowl, combine broccoli, chicken, pasta, tomatoes, onion, and pepper. Pour dressing over and toss well to coat. Cover and chill before serving.

Napa Cabbage with Mustard Ginger Dressing

 Serves 6

- ~ **PREP TIME:** 20 minutes
- ~ **CHILL TIME:** 1 hour
- ~ **TOTAL COST:** $5.86
- ~ **CALORIES:** 79
- ~ **FAT:** 1 g
- ~ **CARBOHYDRATES:** 18 g
- ~ **PROTEIN:** 1 g
- ~ **CHOLESTEROL:** 3 mg
- ~ **SODIUM:** 26 mg

4 cups napa (Chinese) cabbage, shredded
1 (8¼-ounce) can crushed pineapple, drained
1 (8-ounce) can sliced water chestnuts, drained
¼ cup scallions, chopped
¼ cup low-fat mayonnaise
1 tablespoon mustard
1 teaspoon peeled and grated fresh gingerroot

Chinese cabbage is a light, crispy cabbage more like a lettuce than traditional green or red cabbage. As with any salad green, toss with dressing just before serving to avoid soggy cabbage.

In medium mixing bowl, combine cabbage, pineapple, water chestnuts, and scallions. Toss to combine. Cover and chill. In small mixing bowl, whisk together mayonnaise, mustard, and ginger. Cover and chill. When ready to serve, pour mayonnaise mixture over cabbage mixture and toss well to coat.

Mixed Greens with Dijon Vinaigrette

Serves 4

- ~ **PREP TIME:** 10 minutes
- ~ **TOTAL COST:** $3.81
- ~ **CALORIES:** 116
- ~ **FAT:** 14 g
- ~ **CARBOHYDRATES:** 0 g
- ~ **PROTEIN:** 2 g
- ~ **CHOLESTEROL:** 5 mg
- ~ **SODIUM:** 95 mg

¼ cup apple cider vinegar
2 tablespoons lemon juice
2 cloves garlic, minced
1 tablespoon Dijon mustard
Sea salt and black pepper to taste
¼ cup extra-virgin olive oil
10 to 12 ounces mixed greens, washed and dried
¼ cup Parmesan cheese, grated

Try using mustard vinaigrettes for cooking chicken, fish, and vegetables. The mustard gives foods a flavor lift without adding fat and calories, plus it's inexpensive!

In large mixing bowl, combine vinegar, lemon juice, garlic, and mustard. Whisk well to combine. Add salt and pepper as desired (about 1 pinch each). Drizzle in olive oil and whisk again to combine. Add mixed greens and cheese. Toss well to coat. Serve immediately.

Making Your Own Dressing
When making an olive oil–based dressing, use extra-virgin olive oil and whisk in the olive oil last to get an even, thick consistency as well as bring out the delicious olive oil flavor.

Wild Rice Salad with Fresh Tomatoes and Basil

 Serves 4

- ~ **PREP TIME:** 15 minutes
- ~ **RESTING TIME:** 20 minutes
- ~ **TOTAL COST:** $6.67
- ~ **CALORIES:** 197
- ~ **FAT:** 7 g
- ~ **CARBOHYDRATES:** 26 g
- ~ **PROTEIN:** 2 g
- ~ **CHOLESTEROL:** 0 mg
- ~ **SODIUM:** 0 mg

2 cups cooked wild rice
3 large vine-ripe tomatoes, seeded and chopped
3 green onions, chopped
3 tablespoons fresh basil, chopped
1 clove garlic, chopped
Sea salt and black pepper as desired
2 tablespoons extra-virgin olive oil

Wild rice is a positive alternative to white rice. It is flavorful, has more nutrients, and has different layers of textures for a true palate pleaser.

In large mixing bowl, place rice, tomatoes, onion, basil, and garlic. Season with salt and pepper as desired. Drizzle oil over rice mixture and toss to combine. Let stand at room temperature about 20 minutes before serving to allow flavors to combine.

Chicken Salad with Cucumber and Melon

 Serves 4

- ~ **PREP TIME:** 15 minutes
- ~ **TOTAL COST:** $6.47
- ~ **CALORIES:** 356
- ~ **FAT:** 13 g
- ~ **CARBOHYDRATES:** 7 g
- ~ **PROTEIN:** 29 g
- ~ **CHOLESTEROL:** 89 mg
- ~ **SODIUM:** 301 mg

2 ½ cups cooked chicken breast, chopped
1½ cups honeydew melon or cantaloupe, peeled, seeded, and cut into 2-inch cubes
1½ cups cucumber, peeled and diced
1½ cups seedless green grapes
½ cup low-fat mayonnaise
2 tablespoons plain nonfat yogurt
1½ teaspoons cider vinegar
Pinch sea salt and black pepper
⅓ cup fresh cilantro, leaves chopped
2 tablespoons fresh lime juice (about 1 large lime)

This is a great recipe to serve for brunch or a ladies luncheon. Serve them in papaya boats for a beautiful, unique presentation that is also delicious!

In a large mixing bowl, combine chicken, melon, cucumber, and grapes. Separately, in small mixing bowl, whisk together remaining ingredients. Pour over chicken mixture and toss to combine. Cover and chill for at least 1 hour before serving.

Money-Saving Tip
This is a great recipe for leftover chicken breasts. You can also substitute turkey breasts or canned tuna, if you prefer.

Romaine Lettuce with Pears and Goat Cheese

 Serves 4

- ~ **PREP TIME:** 10 minutes
- ~ **TOTAL COST:** $5.12
- ~ **CALORIES:** 201
- ~ **FAT:** 18 g
- ~ **CARBOHYDRATES:** 7 g
- ~ **PROTEIN:** 3 g
- ~ **CHOLESTEROL:** 10 mg
- ~ **SODIUM:** 23 mg

¼ cup extra-virgin olive oil
¼ cup champagne or apple cider vinegar
6 cups romaine lettuce
1 bartlett pear, seeded and diced
2 tomatoes, diced
2 tablespoons toasted walnuts
¼ cup goat cheese, crumbled

Goat cheese and pears are two of my favorite combinations, but you can substitute apples and gorgonzola for another tasty variation.

In large mixing bowl, whisk together oil and vinegar until well combined. Add all other ingredients and toss well.

Mediterranean Salad with Feta and Kalamata Olives

 Serves 4

- ~ **PREP TIME:** 15 minutes
- ~ **TOTAL COST:** $5.97
- ~ **CALORIES:** 181
- ~ **FAT:** 18 g
- ~ **CARBOHYDRATES:** 5 g
- ~ **PROTEIN:** 1 g
- ~ **CHOLESTEROL:** 5 mg
- ~ **SODIUM:** 704 mg

¼ cup extra-virgin olive oil
¼ cup balsamic vinegar
6 cups romaine lettuce
2 tomatoes, diced
1 cucumber, diced
½ cup kalamata olives, pitted, chopped
2 pepperoncini, diced
¼ cup red onions, diced
½ cup feta cheese, crumbled

The Mediterranean diet mainly consists of fresh fruits, fresh vegetables, and olive oil, which is said to lower cholesterol, blood pressure, and monounsaturated fat.

In large mixing bowl, whisk together oil and vinegar. Whisk until well combined. Add remaining ingredients and toss well to coat.

Health-Conscious Vinaigrettes
Making your own vinaigrettes is easy and is usually healthier than bottled dressings, which tend to be higher in sodium and preservatives and contain more chemically processed ingredients.

Curried Chicken Salad with Mango Chutney

 Serves 6

~ **PREP TIME:** 15 minutes
~ **CHILL TIME:** 1 hour
~ **TOTAL COST:** $6.76
~ **CALORIES:** 138
~ **FAT:** 8 g
~ **CARBOHYDRATES:** 8 g
~ **PROTEIN:** 15 g
~ **CHOLESTEROL:** 46 mg
~ **SODIUM:** 272 mg

½ cup low-fat mayonnaise
2 tablespoons mango or other chutney
Fine zest of 1 lemon
1 tablespoon lemon juice
1 teaspoon sea salt
1 teaspoon curry powder
2 cups cooked chicken breasts, diced
1 cup celery, chopped
¼ cup red onion, chopped
½ pint fresh strawberries, sliced in half
6 lettuce leaves

Chutneys are great for cooking, as they are very versatile and are available in many flavor combinations. Use them for topping pork, turkey, or even fish, or mix with cream cheese for a delicious and easy spread.

In large mixing bowl, stir together mayonnaise, chutney, lemon juice, lemon zest, salt, and curry powder. Mix well. Add the chicken, celery, and onion. Toss well and cover. Chill for up to 1 hour. Just before serving, add strawberries and toss gently. Place lettuce leaves on serving platter. Place chicken mixture on lettuce leaf.

Chinese Chicken Salad

Serves 6

~ **PREP TIME:** 15 minutes
~ **COOK TIME:** 10 minutes
~ **TOTAL COST:** $6.89
~ **CALORIES:** 535
~ **FAT:** 40 g
~ **CARBOHYDRATES:** 23 g
~ **PROTEIN:** 21 g
~ **CHOLESTEROL:** 26 mg
~ **SODIUM:** 69 mg

¼ cup sugar
Pinch sea salt and black pepper
½ cup plus 2 tablespoons peanut oil
6 tablespoons rice vinegar
¼ cup sliced almonds
¼ cup sesame seeds
8 green onions, chopped
1 head cabbage, grated or minced
2 cups cooked chicken breast, chopped
2 packages ramen noodles, broken

Chinese chicken salad is always a hit. Add mandarin oranges for extra flavor, color, and, of course, vitamin C.

1. In a small mixing bowl, combine sugar, salt, pepper, ½ cup peanut oil, and vinegar. Set aside.
2. Heat remaining 2 tablespoons oil on large skillet over medium heat. Add almonds and sesame seeds. Sauté until lightly browned, about 2 minutes. Add the onions and cabbage. Sauté for 5 minutes, or until tender. Add the chicken, sauté for 1 minute. Add the noodles and stir to combine. Add vinegar mixture, tossing well to coat. Serve.

Pecan-Crusted Chicken Salad

 Serves 4

~ **PREP TIME:** 15 minutes
~ **COOK TIME:** 20 minutes
~ **TOTAL COST:** $6.48
~ **CALORIES:** 349
~ **FAT:** 22 g
~ **PROTEIN:** 23 g
~ **CHOLESTEROL:** 59 mg
~ **SODIUM:** 54 mg

1 pound boneless chicken breasts, skin removed
¼ cup plus 1 tablespoon extra virgin olive oil
Sea salt and pepper to taste
½ cup pecans, finely chopped
¼ cup balsamic vinegar
6 cups romaine lettuce
2 tablespoons raisins
4 Roma tomatoes, diced
¼ cup carrots, chopped

Pecans add both flavor and a crunchy texture to chicken, turkey, even fish. And nuts contain healthy oils and proteins that are good for your skin.

1. Preheat oven to 380°F. Line a baking sheet with parchment paper. Coat chicken with 1 tablespoon of olive oil. Season with salt and pepper. Press pecans gently onto chicken. Place chicken on baking sheet, cover with foil, and bake for 20 minutes or until done.
2. Separately, in a large mixing bowl, whisk together remaining oil and vinegar. Toss in all other ingredients and coat well. When chicken is cooked, allow to cool slightly. Serve salad in bowls and top with chicken.

Mixed Greens with Balsamic Vinaigrette and Dried Cranberries

Serves 4

~ **PREP TIME:** 10 minutes
~ **COOK TIME:** none
~ **TOTAL COST:** $4.84
~ **CALORIES:** 143
~ **FAT:** 10 g
~ **CARBOHYDRATES:** 12 g
~ **PROTEIN:** 1 g
~ **CHOLESTEROL:** 0 mg
~ **SODIUM:** 2 mg

¼ cup balsamic vinegar
¼ cup extra-virgin olive oil
Sea salt and pepper to taste
6 cups mixed greens
1 red bell pepper, seeded and diced
1 medium red onion, diced
1 large tomato, diced
1 cucumber, diced
2 tablespoons dried cranberries

Balsamic vinaigrette is simply balsamic vinegar whisked together with extra virgin olive oil. Create your own variation by adding a pinch of sugar, a squeeze of lemon and orange juice, and some fresh herbs (such as thyme).

In large mixing bowl, whisk together vinegar, oil, salt, and pepper. Add remaining ingredients and toss well to coat.

Mixed Greens
Mixed greens can usually be purchased two ways at the grocery store: in bulk or in prepackaged bags. Buy them in bulk, when possible, as the greens taste more fresh and you control the quantity you need.

Red Leaf Lettuce with Feta Cheese

 Serves 4

~ **PREP TIME:** 15 minutes
~ **COOK TIME:** none
~ **TOTAL COST:** $6.04
~ **CALORIES:** 175
~ **FAT:** 19 g
~ **CARBOHYDRATES:** 1 g
~ **PROTEIN:** 2 g
~ **CHOLESTEROL:** 5 mg
~ **SODIUM:** 103 mg

6 cups red leaf lettuce
1 large tomato, sliced into wedges
1 large red onion, thinly sliced
4 ounces feta cheese, crumbled
2 tablespoons balsamic vinegar
2 cloves garlic, minced
5 tablespoons extra-virgin olive oil
Sea salt and black pepper to taste

If you don't have feta cheese, try goat cheese, brie, or even white cheddar for a tasty twist.

In mixing bowl, place lettuce, tomato, onion, and feta cheese. Toss well. Separately, in small mixing bowl, whisk together vinegar, garlic, oil, salt, and pepper. Mix well. Pour vinaigrette over greens mixture and toss to coat.

Red and Green Leaf Salad with Spiced Nuts

 Serves 4

~ **PREP TIME:** 8 minutes
~ **COOK TIME:** none
~ **TOTAL COST:** $6.98
~ **CALORIES:** 341
~ **FAT:** 27 g
~ **PROTEIN:** 5 g
~ **CHOLESTEROL:** 10 mg
~ **SODIUM:** 22 mg

¼ cup extra virgin olive oil
¼ cup balsamic vinegar
3 cups red leaf lettuce
3 cups green leaf lettuce
½ cup mandarin oranges, canned okay, just drain well
¼ to ½ cup spiced nuts
¼ cup feta cheese, crumbled

Leftover nuts add a delicious and nutritious twist on salad. Try spiced nuts.

In a mixing bowl, whisk together oil and vinegar. Add remaining ingredients and toss to coat.

> **Quick and Easy Tip**
> Red and green leaf lettuce is more nutritious than iceberg, so use whenever possible.

Grilled Vegetable Salad

 Serves 4

~ **PREP TIME:** 10 minutes
~ **COOK TIME:** 10 minutes
~ **TOTAL COST:** $6.52
~ **CALORIES:** 175
~ **FAT:** 18 g
~ **CARBOHYDRATES:** 7 g
~ **PROTEIN:** 1 g
~ **CHOLESTEROL:** 0 mg
~ **SODIUM:** 3 mg

¼ cup plus 2 tablespoons olive oil
1 red bell pepper, seeded and chopped
1 shallot, peeled and diced
1 cup broccoli florets
4 asparagus spears, chopped
1 fresh ear of corn, kernels cut off cob
Salt and pepper to taste
¼ cup balsamic vinegar
6 cups romaine lettuce, chopped

This is a great salad for a barbecue! For outdoor grilling, grill corn whole and cut the kernels off the cob after grilling.

1. Heat 2 tablespoons oil over medium to medium-high heat on a grill pan or in sauté skillet. Add red bell pepper, shallot, broccoli, asparagus, and corn and sprinkle with pinch of salt and pepper. Cook until vegetables are tender, about 5 minutes.
2. In mixing bowl, whisk together remaining oil and vinegar. Add lettuce and other vegetables. Toss well and serve.

Three-Bean Salad

 Serves 8

~ **PREP TIME:** 10 minutes
~ **CHILL TIME:** 4 hours or overnight
~ **TOTAL COST:** $4.56
~ **CALORIES:** 118
~ **FAT:** 7 g
~ **CARBOHYDRATES:** 6 g
~ **PROTEIN:** 2 g
~ **SODIUM:** 95 mg

½ cup sugar
⅓ cup canola oil
⅔ cup apple cider vinegar
Sea salt and pepper to taste
1 16-ounce can French-cut green beans, drained
1 16-ounce can yellow beans, drained
1 16-ounce can red kidney beans, drained
1 yellow onion, chopped

An easy salad that takes no time to throw together, three-bean salad is healthy, delicious and fits with any budget! Go easy on the sugar to avoid unwanted calories.

In large mixing bowl, whisk together sugar, vinegar, oil, salt, and pepper. Whisk well. Add in beans and onions. Mix well. Chill at least 4 hours or overnight, stirring occasionally, if desired.

Romaine Lettuce with BBQ Chicken

 Serves 4

- ~ **PREP TIME:** 10 minutes
- ~ **COOK TIME:** 20 minutes
- ~ **TOTAL COST:** $6.36
- ~ **CALORIES:** 256
- ~ **FAT:** 13 g
- ~ **CARBOHYDRATES:** 10 g
- ~ **PROTEIN:** 22 g
- ~ **CHOLESTEROL:** 62 mg
- ~ **SODIUM:** 1,176 mg

1 pound boneless chicken breast, skin removed
2 tablespoons olive oil
1 cup barbecue sauce
¼ cup Italian or ranch dressing
1 large head romaine lettuce, chopped
1 large tomato, diced
1 cucumber, diced
½ medium red onion, diced

This is a great salad to serve as a meal. Kids even like it because of the sweet barbecue sauce, but they usually want you to leave out the onions.

1. Chop chicken into 1- to 2-inch cubes. In mixing bowl, coat chicken with olive oil. Preheat skillet to medium heat. Add chicken and ⅓ cup water. This helps prevent burning. Cover with lid and let chicken cook, about 8 to 10 minutes, adding water if needed. When cooked, remove from heat and toss with barbecue sauce. Set aside.
2. In separate mixing bowl, pour in dressing. Add remaining ingredients and toss to coat. Add chicken and serve.

Smoked Turkey Salad with Grapes

 Serves 4

- ~ **PREP TIME:** 12 minutes
- ~ **COOK TIME:** none
- ~ **TOTAL COST:** $6.92
- ~ **CALORIES:** 301
- ~ **FAT:** 11 g
- ~ **CARBOHYDRATES:** 25 g
- ~ **PROTEIN:** 26 g
- ~ **CHOLESTEROL:** 84 mg
- ~ **SODIUM:** 275 mg

3 cups smoked turkey breast, chopped
1 cup celery, chopped
½ cup green seedless grapes, halved
½ cup red seedless grapes, halved
½ cup low-fat mayonnaise
¼ cup plain yogurt, nonfat okay
1 tablespoon honey
Juice of 1 lemon
Sea salt and black pepper to taste

Serve this delicious salad on wheat bread or a toasted bagel as a sandwich—or for a fun presentation, serve in a martini glass on a small bed of mixed greens.

1. In a large mixing bowl, combine turkey, celery, and grapes. Set aside.
2. In separate mixing bowl, combine remaining ingredients. Add the yogurt mixture to the turkey and lightly toss to coat.

Smoked Foods
Smoking foods is an excellent way to add tons of flavor without adding fat and calories. If you really like smoked foods, invest in a stovetop smoker. You can smoke practically anything right in your kitchen.

Salad of Orzo, Red Bell Pepper, and Fresh Herbs

 Serves 4

~ **PREP TIME:** 15 minutes
~ **COOK TIME:** none
~ **TOTAL COST:** $6.48
~ **CALORIES:** 188
~ **FAT:** 10 g
~ **CARBOHYDRATES:** 20 g
~ **PROTEIN:** 3 g
~ **CHOLESTEROL:** 0 mg
~ **SODIUM:** 0 mg

¼ cup extra-virgin olive oil
2 cups fresh basil leaves, finely chopped
4 cloves garlic, finely chopped
½ cup fresh Italian flat-leaf parsley, finely chopped
Sea salt to taste
1 pound orzo pasta, cooked al dente and drained
 thoroughly
1 red bell pepper, seeded and diced
½ red onion, finely chopped

Sometimes called *Italian rice*, orzo is made from wheat semolina flour. In the United States, orzo is considered to be a rice-shaped pasta slightly smaller than a pine nut.

In mixing bowl, whisk together oil, basil, parsley, garlic, and salt. Add the orzo, red pepper, and red onion. Toss well to combine.

Spinach Salad with Grilled Salmon

 Serves 2

~ **PREP TIME:** 15 minutes
~ **COOK TIME:** 5 minutes
~ **TOTAL COST:** $6.43
~ **CALORIES:** 405
~ **FAT:** 24 g
~ **CARBOHYDRATES:** 12 g
~ **PROTEIN:** 19 g
~ **CHOLESTEROL:** 47 mg
~ **SODIUM:** 121 mg

¼ cup extra-virgin olive oil
¼ cup balsamic vinegar
Sea salt and black pepper to taste
5 ounces salmon fillet, grilled, skin off, broken into
 pieces
2 cups fresh spinach leaves, washed and dried
½ cup red grapes, sliced in half
1 tablespoon dried cranberries

Both salmon and spinach are very healthy foods. Salmon is high in omega-3 fatty acids, which are great for your skin, and spinach is high in beta carotene, which helps fight against cancer.

In a large mixing bowl, whisk together olive oil, balsamic vinegar, salt, and pepper. Whisk together well. Add salmon, spinach, grapes, and cranberries. Toss to combine and serve.

Cooking Tip
The easiest way to grill salmon is to coat it with a little olive oil, sea salt, and pepper, place it on a piece of aluminum foil, and broil it in the oven. It only takes about 5 minutes and it's easy on cleanup!

Fresh Spinach Salad with Roasted Turkey

 Serves 2

- ~ **PREP TIME:** 15 minutes
- ~ **COOK TIME:** none
- ~ **TOTAL COST:** $5.88
- ~ **CALORIES:** 306
- ~ **FAT:** 22 g
- ~ **CARBOHYDRATES:** 5 g
- ~ **PROTEIN:** 19 g
- ~ **CHOLESTEROL:** 48 mg
- ~ **SODIUM:** 32 mg

¼ cup balsamic vinegar
1 squeeze fresh lemon
Sea salt and black pepper to taste
¼ cup extra-virgin olive oil
2 cups fresh spinach leaves, washed and drained
4 ounces honey-roasted turkey breast, chopped
1 tomato, chopped
1 Gala or Fuji apple, chopped

Turkey is often less thought of for everyday recipes but it is lower in fat than chicken and is a tasty, healthy substitution for chicken, beef, and pork recipes.

In large mixing bowl, combine vinegar, lemon, salt, and pepper and whisk together. Drizzle in olive oil while whisking. Add spinach, turkey, tomato, and apple. Toss well to coat.

Tip for Tossing Salads
The easiest way to make sure all your greens are coated with the vinaigrette is to place your vinaigrette or dressing in the bottom of the salad bowl first, before you add the greens and any other ingredients. Then, toss from the bottom up until all greens are coated.

Cucumber Salad with Sesame Vinaigrette

Serves 2

- ~ **PREP TIME:** 10 minutes
- ~ **COOK TIME:** none
- ~ **TOTAL COST:** $4.48
- ~ **CALORIES:** 63
- ~ **FAT:** 16 g
- ~ **CARBOHYDRATES:** 1 g
- ~ **PROTEIN:** 0 g
- ~ **CHOLESTEROL:** 0 mg
- ~ **SODIUM:** 2 mg

1 teaspoon sugar
3 tablespoons rice wine vinegar
Sea salt and black pepper, as needed
3 tablespoons sesame oil
2 large cucumbers, partially peeled and diced
1 teaspoon jalapeño pepper, chopped

Sesame oil is the natural oil extracted from sesame seeds. It provides a distinctive flavor different than that of olive or canola oil and is widely used in Asian cooking.

In mixing bowl, combine sugar, vinegar, salt, and pepper. While whisking, drizzle in the sesame oil. Add cucumber and jalapeño and toss to combine.

Sesame Oil Substitution
If you don't cook a lot, you may not have sesame oil in your pantry. If you don't, don't stress; substitute olive oil or canola oil.

Wild Rice Salad with Chicken and Walnuts

Serves 4

- ~ **PREP TIME:** 10 minutes
- ~ **COOK TIME:** 15 minutes
- ~ **CHILL TIME:** up to 1 hour
- ~ **TOTAL COST:** $5.84
- ~ **CALORIES:** 332
- ~ **FAT:** 13 g
- ~ **CARBOHYDRATES:** 19 g
- ~ **PROTEIN:** 34 g
- ~ **CHOLESTEROL:** 93 mg
- ~ **SODIUM:** 365 mg

1 4.3 ounce package wild rice

¼ cup olive oil

3 tablespoons balsamic vinegar

3 cups cooked chicken, cut into bite-sized pieces

4 scallions, chopped

3 tablespoons Parmesan cheese, grated

Juice of 1 lemon

½ cup toasted walnuts, whole or chopped

1 cup cherry tomatoes, sliced

Wild rice is a species of plants that grow in small lakes and streams. Wild rice is naturally high in protein and fiber and low in fat.

1. Prepare rice according to package directions. In small bowl, whisk together oil, vinegar, and lemon. When rice is ready, stir in the chicken and scallions; add the vinegar mixture and cheese. Toss well to coat. Pour into a serving dish and chill for up to 1 hour.
2. Garnish salad with walnuts and cherry tomatoes.

> **Cooking Wild Rice**
> Certain grains of wild rice take up to 45 minutes to cook. Read the package directions when purchasing to make sure you buy quick-cooking wild rice.

Winter Greens Salad with Green Beans and Blue Cheese Vinaigrette

 Serves 4

- ~ **PREP TIME:** 15 minutes
- ~ **COOK TIME:** 5 minutes
- ~ **TOTAL COST:** $7.00
- ~ **CALORIES:** 102
- ~ **FAT:** 4 g
- ~ **CARBOHYDRATES:** 14 g
- ~ **PROTEIN:** 4 g
- ~ **CHOLESTEROL:** 6 mg
- ~ **SODIUM:** 129 mg

1 bunch watercress
2 heads Belgium endive
1 small red onion
½ pound green beans

Vinaigrette
⅓ cup balsamic vinegar
⅓ cup vegetable oil
⅓ cup extra-virgin olive oil
1 tablespoon chopped chives
¼ pound blue cheese
Sea salt and ground black pepper

Fresh asparagus tips also taste great with this salad. Prepare them the same way as the green beans.

1. Rinse watercress and break into bite-size pieces. Cut endives diagonally into 3 or 4 sections each, discarding cores. Slice red onion into thin rings.
2. In 3 quarts of rapidly boiling salted water, cook green beans in 2 separate batches until just tender, about 5 minutes, then plunge them into salted ice water to stop the cooking process. Drain them and then combine with greens and onions.
3. Whisk together vinegar, vegetable oil, olive oil, and chives. Roughly break the blue cheese into vinaigrette; stir with a spoon, leaving some large chunks. Season with salt and pepper. Pour ⅓ cup of vinaigrette onto greens. Reserve remaining vinaigrette in refrigerator for up to 2 weeks. Arrange salad onto 4 plates, with onions and green beans on top.

Tatsoi Greens with Orange-Sesame Vinaigrette

 Serves 4

~ **PREP TIME:** 10 minutes
~ **COOK TIME:** none
~ **TOTAL COST:** $4.21
~ **CALORIES:** 89
~ **FAT:** 2 g
~ **CARBOHYDRATES:** 4 g
~ **PROTEIN:** 2 g
~ **CHOLESTEROL:** 0 mg
~ **SODIUM:** 64 mg

6 cups tatsoi
¼ cup Orange-Sesame Vinaigrette (Chapter 5)
½ cup red onion, sliced paper-thin

Wash and dry the tatsoi leaves, then toss gently with one half of the vinaigrette. Distribute onto 4 salad plates. Arrange sliced onions atop each salad, and finish with a final spoonful of vinaigrette.

Tatsoi Greens

Tatsoi greens, also called spinach mustard greens, are customary to Asian cuisine. They have a soft, creamy texture and subtle flavor.

Orange-Sesame Vinaigrette

 Yields about 1¼ cups

~ **PREP TIME:** 10 minutes
~ **COOK TIME:** none
~ **TOTAL COST:** $2.55
~ **CALORIES:** 64
~ **FAT:** 2 g
~ **CARBOHYDRATES:** 4 g
~ **PROTEIN:** 2 g
~ **CHOLESTEROL:** 0 mg
~ **SODIUM:** 64 mg

Zest of ½ orange
Zest of ½ lime
1 pickled jalapeño pepper, with juice, chopped
¼ cup Japanese rice wine vinegar
¼ cup orange juice concentrate
1½ teaspoons Dijon mustard
Few drops sesame oil
¼ cup peanut oil
¼ cup olive oil
Salt and freshly ground black pepper

Use this vinaigrette on any salad or even for cooking chicken!

Combine zests, pickled jalapeño and brine, rice vinegar, orange concentrate, Dijon mustard, and sesame oil in a blender. Blend on medium speed, slowly drizzling in the peanut and olive oils. Season to taste with salt and pepper.

Tomato Crostini Salad

Serves 4

- ~ **PREP TIME:** 8 minutes
- ~ **COOK TIME:** none
- ~ **TOTAL COST:** $2.85
- ~ **CALORIES:** 124
- ~ **FAT:** 5 g
- ~ **PROTEIN:** 2 g
- ~ **CHOLESTEROL:** 0mg
- ~ **SODIUM:** 175 mg

2 cups diced red tomatoes, any variety
¼ cup red onion, finely chopped
Sea salt and black pepper to taste
1½ tablespoons extra virgin olive oil
Juice of one lemon
2 cups day-old country bread, cut into ½-inch cubes and air dried overnight
¼ cup fresh Italian parsley, chopped

Italians keep pretty much everything simple. I think that's why the world is so attracted to everything Italian. The simplicity is the beauty of this recipe.

In a medium mixing bowl, toss tomatoes with onion, salt, pepper, olive oil, and lemon juice. Throw in bread cubes and parsley and toss again. Serve immediately.

Quick and Easy Tip

This is a great recipe for those bread pieces you have no idea what to do with. Save the end pieces or other bits of leftover bread and let them air dry overnight or toast them off in a 225°F oven for 25 minutes and store them in an airtight container for later use.

Pear-Feta Salad

Serves 4

- ~ **PREP TIME:** 10 minutes
- ~ **COOK TIME:** none
- ~ **TOTAL COST:** $5.01
- ~ **CALORIES:** 201
- ~ **FAT:** 18 g
- ~ **PROTEIN:** 3 g
- ~ **CHOLESTEROL:** 10 mg
- ~ **SODIUM:** 23 mg

¼ cup extra virgin olive oil
¼ cup champagne or apple cider vinegar
6 cups romaine lettuce
1 Bartlett pear, seeded and diced
2 tomatoes, diced
2 tablespoons toasted pine nuts
¼ cup feta cheese, crumbled

The sweetness of the fruit, nuttiness of the pine nuts, and the creamy sharpness of the cheese blend together for mouth-watering goodness in this recipe.

In a large mixing bowl, whisk together oil and vinegar until well combined. Add all other ingredients and toss well.

Quick and Easy Tip

Buy feta cheese in blocks and crumble yourself. If you can refrain from eating it while cooking, you may just have enough left for your salad!

Arugula Greens with Balsamic Vinaigrette and Goat Cheese

 Serves 6

- ~ **PREP TIME:** 12 minutes
- ~ **COOK TIME:** none
- ~ **TOTAL COST:** $6.18
- ~ **CALORIES:** 126
- ~ **FAT:** 12 g
- ~ **CARBOHYDRATES:** 1 g
- ~ **PROTEIN:** 4 g
- ~ **CHOLESTEROL:** 16 mg
- ~ **SODIUM:** 39 mg

¼ cup extra-virgin olive oil
¼ cup balsamic vinegar
2 tablespoons lemon juice
1 tablespoon shallot, minced
Sea salt and black pepper to taste
5 cups loosely packed arugula greens
1 tablespoon fresh basil leaves, finely chopped
5 ounces goat cheese, crumbled

Shallots are part of the onion family. Their flavors are more condensed so you don't need as many shallots as onion when cooking.

Combine the oil, vinegar, lemon juice, shallot, salt, and pepper in a large mixing bowl and whisk together. Add remaining ingredients and toss to coat.

Salad Serving Tip
Tossing salad too early will cause greens to become limp and soggy. To ensure crisp greens, toss salad with vinaigrette just before serving, or, for buffet style service, serve vinaigrette on the side.

Fruit and Vegetable Salad with Apple Cider Vinaigrette

 Serves 4

- ~ **PREP TIME:** 10 minutes
- ~ **COOK TIME:** none
- ~ **TOTAL COST:** $5.68
- ~ **CALORIES:** 149
- ~ **FAT:** 11 g
- ~ **PROTEIN:** 1 g
- ~ **SODIUM:** 1 mg

⅓ cup olive oil
⅓ cup apple cider vinegar
Pinch of granulated sugar
6 cups shredded romaine lettuce
8 cherry tomatoes, halved
1 apple, such as Gala, seeded and cubed
½ cup golden raisins
1 cup mandarin oranges

Fruit salad doesn't always have to mean only fruit. The key, however, is to use fresh fruit, not canned cocktail fruit, which is overly mushy because it has been sitting in syrup for a long time.

In a mixing bowl, whisk together oil, vinegar, and sugar. Add remaining ingredients and toss to coat.

Quick and Easy Tip
Substitute your favorite fruits in this recipe. For added flavor, texture, and protein, add in toasted nuts if you have them on hand.

Broccoli Medley

Serves 5

~ **PREP TIME:** 8 minutes
~ **COOK TIME:** 5 minutes
~ **TOTAL COST:** $5.38
~ **CALORIES:** 128
~ **FAT:** 8 g
~ **PROTEIN:** 2 g
~ **CHOLESTEROL:** 8 mg
~ **SODIUM:** 161 mg

4 cups fresh broccoli florets
½ cup mayonnaise
2 tablespoons balsamic vinegar
2 tablespoons granulated sugar
⅓ cup raisins
¼ cup sunflower seeds
¼ cup red onion, chopped
1 cup frozen peas, thawed

This recipe gives broccoli a new twist.

1. Fill a large-quart boiler ¾ with water, bring to a boil, and add 1 teaspoon salt. Add broccoli florets and let boil for 10 seconds. Quickly remove and transfer to a bowl filled with ice or ice water. Drain well.
2. In a separate bowl, combine mayonnaise, vinegar, and sugar. Whisk together well. Add remaining ingredients and toss to coat.

Quick and Easy Tip
Ever wonder why the vegetables at nice restaurants look so beautiful? It's not because they are special vegetables that cost more. They bring out the colors by blanching, as this recipe does with the broccoli. The ice bath stops the cooking process so vegetables don't get overcooked and limp.

Salad of Jicama and Mango with Black Beans

Serves 4

~ **PREP TIME:** 15 minutes
~ **COOK TIME:** none
~ **TOTAL COST:** $6.89
~ **CALORIES:** 102
~ **FAT:** 1 g
~ **PROTEIN:** 1 g
~ **CHOLESTEROL:** 0 mg
~ **SODIUM:** 3 mg

1 cup peeled and diced jicama
⅓ cup mango, diced
½ cup canned black beans, drained and rinsed
½ cup diced red onion
⅓ cup mandarin oranges, drained
2 tablespoons fresh lime juice
2 tablespoons fresh orange juice
2 tablespoons fresh cilantro, chopped
Pinch sea salt and black pepper

Jicama is a Mexican vine, and the edible part is the root. It is high in fiber and up to 90 percent water.

1. Combine the jicama, mango, black beans, red onion, and mandarin oranges in a medium bowl and toss to mix.
2. Separately, mix together the lime juice, orange juice, cilantro, salt, and pepper in a bowl. Pour over jicama mixture and toss well. Let stand at room temperature for 10 minutes to allow flavors to blend.

Quick and Easy Tip
This is the perfect salad for a brunch. Make the day before and keep in the refrigerator until ready to serve.

Spring Roll Salad

 Serves 2–4 *

- ~ **COST:** $1.76
- ~ **CALORIES:** 160
- ~ **FAT:** 3.5 g
- ~ **CARBOHYDRATES:** 32 g
- ~ **PROTEIN:** 5 g
- ~ **CHOLESTEROL:** 0 mg
- ~ **SODIUM:** 280 mg

1 cup mung bean sprouts
1 carrot
1 red bell pepper
1 (14-ounce) can baby corn
2 teaspoons olive oil
3 teaspoons soy sauce
1 tablespoon red wine vinegar
1 teaspoon granulated sugar

1. Wash the vegetables. Drain the mung bean sprouts thoroughly. Peel the carrot and cut into thin strips about 2 inches long. Cut the red pepper in half, remove the seeds, and cut into thin strips about 2 inches long. Rinse the baby corn in warm water and drain thoroughly.
2. Combine the olive oil, soy sauce, red wine vinegar, and sugar in a jar and shake well. Toss the salad with the dressing. Wait about 30 minutes to serve to allow the flavors to blend.

Festive Fruit Salad

Serves 1–2*

- ~ **COST:** $2.62
- ~ **CALORIES:** 310
- ~ **FAT:** 1.5 g
- ~ **CARBOHYDRATES:** 78 g
- ~ **PROTEIN:** 2 g
- ~ **CHOLESTEROL:** 0 mg
- ~ **SODIUM:** 15 mg

2 apples
2 bananas
1 orange
1¾ cups canned pineapple chunks, with juice
2 tablespoons sweetened coconut flakes, optional

1. Wash the apples and cut into slices. Peel the bananas and cut diagonally into 1-inch pieces. Peel the orange and separate into segments.
2. Place the fruit in a large bowl with the pineapple chunks and juice. Cover and refrigerate until ready to serve. Sprinkle with the sweetened coconut flakes, if desired.

*Nutrition information and price per serving based on the recipe serving 4.

*Nutrition information and price per serving based on the recipe serving 2.

Rainbow Salad with Fennel

 Serves 2

- ~ **COST:** $2.23
- ~ **CALORIES:** 190
- ~ **FAT:** 7 g
- ~ **CARBOHYDRATES:** 32 g
- ~ **PROTEIN:** 4 g
- ~ **CHOLESTEROL:** 5 mg
- ~ **SODIUM:** 260 mg

1 carrot
1 red bell pepper
2 cups shredded red cabbage
2 tablespoons, plus 2 teaspoons low-fat mayonnaise
3 teaspoons liquid honey
1 fennel bulb

1. Wash the carrot and red pepper. Grate the carrot (there should be ½ to ⅔ cup of grated carrot). Cut the red pepper into thin strips.
2. Mix together the carrot, red pepper, and cabbage in a bowl. Mix the mayonnaise with the honey. Toss the vegetables with the mayonnaise mixture.
3. Rinse the fennel under running water and pat dry. Trim off the top and bottom of the fennel bulb. Cut the fennel into quarters, remove the core in the middle, and cut into thin slices. Garnish the coleslaw with the fennel.

Cobb Salad

 Serves 4

- ~ **PREP TIME:** 7 minutes
- ~ **COOK TIME:** 20 minutes
- ~ **TOTAL COST:** $6.92
- ~ **CALORIES:** 224
- ~ **FAT:** 18 g
- ~ **PROTEIN:** 19 g
- ~ **CHOLESTEROL:** 51 mg
- ~ **SODIUM:** 563 mg

¼ cup water
⅔ cup honey Dijon dressing
8 ounces boneless chicken breast, skin removed
6 cups romaine lettuce
4 ounces sliced deli ham
4 Roma tomatoes, sliced
½ cup cremini mushrooms, sliced
2 tablespoons Swiss or provolone cheese, chopped

This recipe is packed with protein and flavor. Enjoy as a side salad or as a meal.

1. In a medium saucepan over medium heat, add water and ⅓ cup honey Dijon dressing. Mix with a wooden spoon. Add chicken and cover. Cook until chicken is cooked through, adding water if needed to prevent burning, about 20 minutes depending upon thickness of chicken.
2. In a large mixing bowl, combine all other ingredients except remaining dressing. Pour remaining dressing over ingredients and toss well to coat. When chicken is cooked, place salad in serving bowls and top with equal portions of chicken. Drizzle any remaining sauce over salad, if desired.

Quick and Easy Tip
Premade salad dressings can be used as marinades or to make sauces.

CHAPTER 6

SOUPS

Chicken Stock

 Yields 12 Cups

- ~ **TOTAL COST:** $3.31
- ~ **CALORIES:** 98.86
- ~ **FAT:** 5.94 g
- ~ **PROTEIN:** 4.78 g
- ~ **CHOLESTEROL:** 21.78 mg
- ~ **SODIUM:** 242.64 mg

1½ pounds chicken wings or bones
1 onion, chopped
2 carrots, chopped
1 tablespoon olive oil
11 cups water
3 cloves garlic, minced
2 celery stalks, chopped
¼ cup chopped celery leaves
2 teaspoons salt
½ teaspoon pepper

Use your slow cooker to make chicken stock for a big batch with almost no work at all. Freeze in 1 cup portions or in ice cube trays.

1. Preheat oven to 400°F. Place chicken, onions, and carrots on baking sheet and drizzle with olive oil. Roast for 30–40 minutes or until chicken begins to brown.
2. Combine roasted chicken, onions, and carrots with all ingredients in a 5–6 quart slow cooker. Cover and cook on low for 8–10 hours. When stock tastes rich and chickeny, strain and refrigerate overnight. The next day, remove the fat from the surface of the stock and discard. Freeze stock up to 3 months.

Mexican Beef Stew

 Serves 6

- ~ **PREP TIME:** 10 minutes
- ~ **COOK TIME:** 25 minutes
- ~ **TOTAL COST:** $6.12
- ~ **CALORIES:** 162
- ~ **FAT:** 8 g
- ~ **CARBOHYDRATES:** 6 g
- ~ **PROTEIN:** 17 g
- ~ **CHOLESTEROL:** 49 mg
- ~ **SODIUM:** 365 mg

2 tablespoons olive oil
1 yellow onion, chopped
1 pound ground beef
1 package taco seasoning
2 (15-ounce) cans chili beans, undrained
1 (16-ounce) package frozen corn
1 (14-ounce) can tomatoes with green chiles, undrained
2 cups water
1 tablespoon chili powder
½ teaspoon cumin
½ teaspoon cayenne pepper

Cumin is traditional to Indian, Mexican, and Cuban cuisines. A great source of iron, cumin brings out the sweetness of other ingredients in the recipe and helps balance out spicy foods.

In large saucepan over medium heat, heat olive oil. Add onions and sauté until tender, about 5 minutes. Add ground beef and cook until browned, about 5 minutes. Add remaining ingredients, stir, cover, and simmer for about 20 minutes, until flavors are combined.

Cowboy Soup

 Serves 4

- ~ **TOTAL COST:** $6.79
- ~ **CALORIES:** 435.67
- ~ **FAT:** 17.57 g
- ~ **PROTEIN:** 21.40 g
- ~ **CHOLESTEROL:** 53.38 mg
- ~ **SODIUM:** 925.64 mg

½ pound lean ground beef
1 onion, chopped
2 jalapeño chiles, minced
4 cloves garlic, minced
2 tablespoons flour
1 (10-ounce) can condensed tomato soup
1 tablespoon chili powder
1 teaspoon cumin
2 cups beef stock
3 cups water
1½ cups frozen corn
½ cup long-grain white rice
1 cup cubed processed American cheese

This thick soup, more like a stew, is an excellent choice for lunch on a cold winter day. Serve with warmed flour tortillas, sour cream, and Big Batch Guacamole (Chapter 2).

1. In heavy stockpot, cook beef, onion, chiles, and garlic over medium heat, stirring to break up beef, until browned, about 7–8 minutes. Add flour; cook and stir for 3–4 minutes until bubbly. Add soup, chili powder, cumin, and beef stock; bring to a boil, then cover and simmer for 5 minutes.
2. Stir in frozen corn and bring back to a simmer. Stir in the rice, cover, and simmer for 15–20 minutes until rice is tender. Stir in cheese until melted, and serve.

Tomato Soup

Serves 6

- ~ **PREP TIME:** 5 minutes
- ~ **COOK TIME:** 25 minutes
- ~ **TOTAL COST:** $4.90
- ~ **CALORIES:** 120
- ~ **FAT:** 2 g
- ~ **PROTEIN:** 4 g
- ~ **CHOLESTEROL:** 1 mg
- ~ **SODIUM:** 110 mg

2 tablespoons olive oil
1 medium chopped onion
2 cloves garlic, finely chopped
4 (32-ounce) cans whole, peeled tomatoes with juice
Sea salt and black pepper to taste

Tomato soup and grilled cheese sandwiches are as American as baseball and apple pie. This tomato soup recipe is so simple there is simply no excuse not to make it.

In a large-quart boiler over medium heat, heat olive oil until fragrant, about 1 minute. Add onion and garlic and cook for 8 minutes. Stir in tomatoes, with juice, and simmer about 20 minutes. Purée in a food processor, in batches, until smooth. Add salt and pepper to taste. Serve hot or cold.

> **Quick and Easy Tip**
> Using canned tomatoes saves on time and money in this recipe.

Vichyssoise

Serves 6

~ **TOTAL COST:** $4.30

~ **CALORIES:** 326.13

~ **FAT:** 8.66 g

~ **PROTEIN:** 9.04 g

~ **CHOLESTEROL:** 27.14 mg

~ **SODIUM:** 822.22 mg

2 tablespoons butter

2 onions, finely sliced

3 potatoes, peeled and diced

2 cups Chicken Stock (Chapter 6)

2 cups water

2 cups milk

½ teaspoon salt

⅛ teaspoon white pepper

½ cup heavy cream

2 tablespoons minced fresh parsley

This classic soup, which sounds so expensive, is just potato and leek soup, blended until smooth and chilled. Because leeks are expensive, onions are a good substitute.

1. In large pot, melt butter over medium heat. Add onions; cook and stir until translucent. Add potatoes, Stock, and water and bring to a simmer. Cover and cook until potatoes are tender, about 10–15 minutes.
2. Purée the soup either by using an immersion blender, a standard blender, or forcing the soup through a sieve. Return to pot. Add milk, salt, pepper, and cream and heat through. Soup can be served hot with a sprinkling of parsley, or chilled and served cold with some diced fresh chives.

> **Blending Hot Liquids**
> Hot liquids expand in the blender, so whether you're blending a soup or a sauce, don't fill the blender all the way to the top. Filling it half way and blending in batches is the safest way. Remember to cover the lid with a folded kitchen towel; hold onto the towel to keep the lid down.

Italian Minestrone

 Serves 8

- ~ **PREP TIME:** 10 minutes
- ~ **COOK TIME:** 35 minutes
- ~ **TOTAL COST:** $6.71
- ~ **CALORIES:** 156
- ~ **FAT:** 2 g
- ~ **CARBOHYDRATES:** 24 g
- ~ **PROTEIN:** 3 g
- ~ **CHOLESTEROL:** 3 mg
- ~ **SODIUM:** 343 mg

1 tablespoon olive oil
2 yellow onions, chopped
2 carrots, peeled and chopped
2 stalks celery, chopped
2 cloves garlic, chopped
1 (16-ounce) can chopped tomatoes, undrained
½ cup fresh green beans, trimmed and chopped
½ tablespoon fresh oregano, leaves chopped
8 cups water or chicken broth
2 cups cooked pasta, such as shells or rotini
⅓ cup Parmesan cheese, grated

Minestrone is a traditional Italian soup that can be made from whatever vegetables you have on hand. It is a very filling soup that is not expensive to make.

Heat oil in large stockpot (boiler) over medium heat. Add onion, carrots, celery, and garlic and sauté for 5 minutes. Stir in tomatoes, beans, oregano, and water and simmer for 25 minutes, uncovered. Add pasta and simmer for 5 minutes, until heated through. Sprinkle with cheese and serve.

Recipe Suggestion
If your budget allows, add a package of frozen meatballs to this already delicious pasta soup. Add them with the tomatoes and simmer for 25 minutes.

Spicy Gazpacho

Serves 6

- ~ **PREP TIME:** 15 minutes
- ~ **CHILL TIME:** 1 hour
- ~ **TOTAL COST:** $5.36
- ~ **CALORIES:** 112
- ~ **FAT:** 4 g
- ~ **CARBOHYDRATES:** 5 g
- ~ **PROTEIN:** 2 g
- ~ **CHOLESTEROL:** 0 mg
- ~ **SODIUM:** 350 mg

8 tomatoes, seeded and finely diced
2 cucumbers, peeled and finely diced
2 green bell peppers, seeded and finely diced
1 clove garlic, finely diced
2 tablespoons extra-virgin olive oil
1½ teaspoons red wine vinegar
2 teaspoons Worcestershire sauce
1 teaspoon sea salt
2 cups tomato juice
Dash hot sauce or more as desired

For dinner parties, serve this as an appetizer in little espresso cups. It tastes great, it's flavorful, and serving in cups makes it easy to enjoy! Make ahead of time as this recipe gets better with age.

Combine all ingredients and mix well, adding additional hot sauce as your tastes allow. Cover and refrigerate for 1 hour.

Tomato–Basil Soup

Serves 6

- **PREP TIME:** 10 minutes
- **COOK TIME:** 1 hour 10 minutes
- **TOTAL COST:** $6.99
- **CALORIES:** 126
- **FAT:** 2 g
- **CARBOHYDRATES:** 13 g
- **PROTEIN:** 4 g
- **CHOLESTEROL:** 1 mg
- **SODIUM:** 110 mg

2 tablespoons olive oil
1 yellow onion, chopped
6 cloves garlic, chopped
8 Roma tomatoes, chopped, or 1 large can diced tomatoes with juice
8 cups water or vegetable broth
¼ bunch fresh basil, leaves chopped
¼ bunch fresh Italian flat-leaf parsley, leaves chopped
¼ cup Parmesan cheese, grated
2 tablespoons capers, drained
Black pepper to taste

As the Bikini Chef, I always try to include fresh herbs in my recipes—even desserts—as a way to bring out the flavors of the foods without adding unwanted fat and calories.

Heat the oil in a large stockpot on medium for about 3 minutes. Add the onions and sauté for about 2 minutes. Add the garlic and sauté for about 2 minutes. Add the tomatoes. Reduce heat to low and add the vegetable broth. Simmer for 45 minutes, uncovered. Add the herbs and simmer for 20 minutes, uncovered. Sprinkle each serving with the Parmesan, capers, and pepper.

Preparation Tip

Puréed soups make for a nice presentation and are sort of in fashion. Puréeing is easily done in a blender. Just be sure to purée in batches so as not to overfill the blender. Overfilling can result in a soup explosion, burning your arm! Reserve the cheese, capers, and pepper for garnish when serving.

Fresh Vegetable Soup with Chicken

 Serves 4

- **PREP TIME:** 10 minutes
- **COOK TIME:** 42 minutes
- **TOTAL COST:** $6.56
- **CALORIES:** 135
- **FAT:** 2 g
- **CARBOHYDRATES:** 5 g
- **PROTEIN:** 23 g
- **CHOLESTEROL:** 59 mg
- **SODIUM:** 591 mg

3 tablespoons olive oil
1 yellow onion, chopped
½ head broccoli, chopped
2 carrots, peeled and chopped
1 red bell pepper, seeded and chopped
Salt and black pepper to taste
4 cups chicken broth
2 cups cooked chicken, diced
2 tablespoons Italian parsley, chopped

For an even more filling soup, add diced potatoes when you add the broccoli and carrots!

Heat oil in a large quart boiler over medium heat. Add the onions and cook until soft. Add broccoli, carrots, and peppers. Cook about 4 minutes. Add salt, pepper, and broth and bring to a simmer. Cook until vegetables are tender, about 25 minutes. Add the chicken and parsley, return to a simmer, and simmer for 8 minutes.

Cooking with Chicken

Chicken is a great item to have on hand either frozen in individual servings or cooked leftover chicken from another meal. Throw into soups such as this one for a quick, easy, and affordable meal.

French Onion Soup

 Serves 6

- **PREP TIME:** 15 minutes
- **COOK TIME:** 25 minutes
- **TOTAL COST:** $6.72
- **CALORIES:** 498
- **FAT:** 10 g
- **CARBOHYDRATES:** 74 g
- **PROTEIN:** 28 g
- **CHOLESTEROL:** 20 mg
- **SODIUM:** 132 mg

2 tablespoons olive oil
2 tablespoons butter plus ¼ cup butter softened
2 large yellow onions, chopped
2 tablespoons plain flour
1 quart beef broth
6 slices French bread
1 tablespoon fresh Italian flat-leaf parsley
2 garlic cloves, minced
2 cups Gruyère cheese, shredded

French onion soup is traditionally made with gruyere cheese, but if you prefer, you can substitute mozzarella or provolone for a milder flavor.

1. In large saucepan, combine olive oil and 2 tablespoons butter over medium heat until butter is foamy. Add onions; cook over medium heat for 10 minutes, stirring frequently, until onions brown around edges. Sprinkle flour over onions; cook and stir for 2 to 3 minutes.
2. Stir in broth, bring to a simmer, and cook for 10 minutes. Meanwhile, spread French bread slices with ¼ cup butter, parsley, and garlic. Toast bread until browned and crisp. Sprinkle with 1 cup cheese and toast until cheese melts. When serving soup, divide soup among bowls and top with remaining cheese. Float toasted cheese bread on top.

Chicken Divan Soup

Serves 4

~ **TOTAL COST:** $6.60
~ **CALORIES:** 372.67
~ **FAT:** 18.23 g
~ **PROTEIN:** 28.29 g
~ **CHOLESTEROL:** 75.14 mg
~ **SODIUM:** 898.15 mg

2 boneless, skinless chicken breasts
1 onion, chopped
2 cloves garlic, chopped
1 tablespoon olive oil
1 tablespoon butter
3 cups Chicken Stock (Chapter 6)
⅛ teaspoon pepper
1 (10-ounce) can condensed broccoli cheese soup
1 (10-ounce) package frozen chopped broccoli
1 cup grated Swiss cheese

This simple soup uses the flavors of Chicken Divan, or chicken topped with broccoli and cheese, in a new way. It's rich and luscious.

1. Cut chicken breasts into 1-inch pieces. In large saucepan, cook chicken, onion, and garlic in olive oil and butter over medium heat until vegetables are crisp-tender. Add Stock, pepper, and condensed soup; stir well. Simmer for 10–15 minutes, until chicken is thoroughly cooked.
2. Add cheese and stir over low heat until cheese melts and soup is blended. Serve immediately.

Chicken Noodle Soup

Serves 4

~ **TOTAL COST:** $2.42
~ **CALORIES:** 320.23
~ **FAT:** 8.38 g
~ **PROTEIN:** 19.93 g
~ **CHOLESTEROL:** 56.21 mg
~ **SODIUM:** 739.22 mg

Bones and trimmings from Slow Cooker Simmered Chicken Breasts (Chapter 7)
7 cups water
1 teaspoon salt
3 slices fresh ginger root
1 onion, sliced
1 bay leaf
1 tablespoon butter
1 onion, finely chopped
3 carrots, chopped
2 cups egg noodles
1 tablespoon lemon juice

You can make the broth ahead of time, then when you're ready to eat, cook the onion and carrots, add the broth, and simmer the egg noodles until tender.

1. Place bones and trimmings from chicken into a large pot and cover with water. Add salt, ginger root, onion, and bay leaf; bring to a boil. Reduce heat, cover, and simmer for 2 hours. Strain broth, discarding solids.
2. In large saucepan, combine butter, onion, and carrots; cook until tender, about 6–8 minutes. Add broth; bring to a simmer. Then add egg noodles; bring back to a simmer and cook until noodles are tender, about 8–10 minutes. Stir in lemon juice and serve immediately.

Grains and Beans Soup

 Serves 6

- ~ **TOTAL COST:** $4.67
- ~ **CALORIES:** 418.26
- ~ **FAT:** 5.88 g
- ~ **PROTEIN:** 20.82 g
- ~ **CHOLESTEROL:** 10.58 mg
- ~ **SODIUM:** 701.80 mg

1 tablespoon olive oil
1 onion, chopped
4 cloves garlic, minced
¾ cup dried split peas
¾ cup dried green lentils
¾ cup pearl barley
3 carrots, chopped
2 cups Chicken Stock (Chapter 6)
8 cups water
1 teaspoon salt
1 teaspoon dried thyme leaves
1 (14–ounce) can diced tomatoes, undrained
¾ cup bulgur

This fabulous soup is so rich, thick, and hearty. Because legumes and grains are so inexpensive, you can feed some hungry teenagers for a five dollar bill.

1. In large pot, heat olive oil over medium heat. Add onion and garlic; cook and stir until tender, about 5 minutes. Meanwhile, sort through peas and lentils, removing any debris; rinse and drain. Add beans to pot along with barley, carrots, Stock, and water. Bring to a boil, cover, reduce heat, and simmer for 30 minutes.
2. Add salt, thyme, and tomatoes. Bring to a simmer again and cook for 15–25 minutes longer until barley, peas, and lentils are tender. Stir in bulgur and remove from heat. Cover and let stand for 10–15 minutes, until bulgur is tender. Stir and serve immediately.

> **Cooking Times for Legumes**
> All legumes have different cooking times. You can still use them in the same recipe if you follow a couple of rules. Learn the cooking times, and add the ingredients at staggered times, working backward from the finish time. Use canned beans, which are more expensive, if you want to add all at once. And beans that are soaked overnight cook more quickly than those that have not soaked.

Cabbage-Tomato-Bean Chowder

 Serves 4

- ~ **TOTAL COST:** $5.00
- ~ **CALORIES:** 288.05
- ~ **FAT:** 8.15 g
- ~ **PROTEIN:** 12.98 g
- ~ **CHOLESTEROL:** 13.20 mg
- ~ **SODIUM:** 754.33 mg

1 tablespoon olive oil
1 onion, chopped
4 cloves garlic, minced
3 cups shredded green cabbage
1 (14-ounce) can diced tomatoes, undrained
1 (6-ounce) can tomato paste
2 cups Chicken Stock (Chapter 6)
3 cups water
1 teaspoon sugar
⅛ teaspoon white pepper
1 (15-ounce) can Great Northern beans, drained
⅓ cup half-and-half cream

Cabbage becomes sweet when cooked, and is a great complement to tender beans and tangy tomatoes. A tiny bit of sugar helps counteract the acid in the tomatoes.

1. In large saucepan, heat olive oil over medium heat. Add onion and garlic; cook and stir until crisp-tender, about 4 minutes. Add cabbage; cook and stir for 3 minutes longer.
2. Add tomatoes, tomato paste, chicken broth, sugar, and pepper. Cook and stir until tomato paste dissolves in soup. Then stir in beans and bring to a simmer. Simmer for 10 minutes, then add half-and-half. Heat until the soup steams, and serve.

> **Low-Sodium Tomato Products**
> Most supermarkets now carry many low-sodium or no-salt products; they're on the shelves right next to the regular products. You just need to be on the alert when purchasing these products: they are more expensive than regular products. You can also find some of these products, especially organic foods, on the Internet and at co-ops and health-food stores.

Cheese and Onion Soup

 Serves 4

- ~ **PREP TIME:** 8 minutes
- ~ **COOK TIME:** 15 minutes
- ~ **TOTAL COST:** $5.76
- ~ **CALORIES:** 315
- ~ **FAT:** 27 g
- ~ **PROTEIN:** 16 g
- ~ **CHOLESTEROL:** 77 mg
- ~ **SODIUM:** 497 mg

2 tablespoons butter
¼ cup yellow onion, chopped
½ cup celery, chopped
2 tablespoons plain flour
½ teaspoon ground cayenne pepper
¼ teaspoon dry mustard
½ tablespoon Worcestershire sauce
1 cup whole milk
1½ cups chicken broth, canned
2 cups cheddar cheese, grated
Sea salt and black pepper to taste
Paprika for garnish

If you love cheese, you will love this recipe. Be sure to keep an eye on it while cooking as cheese and milk tend to burn if not stirred constantly and supervised.

1. Melt butter in a medium saucepan over medium heat. add the onion and celery and cook until tender, about 4 minutes. Add the flour, cayenne, mustard, and Worcestershire, and mix to combine.
2. Add the milk and chicken broth and bring to a boil. Cook for 1 minute, stirring constantly. Reduce heat to low, add cheese, and stir frequently just until the cheese is melted. Add salt and pepper. When serving, sprinkle with paprika.

Cannelloni Chicken Soup

Serves 6

- ~ **TOTAL COST:** $6.50
- ~ **CALORIES:** 365.09
- ~ **FAT:** 14.42 g
- ~ **PROTEIN:** 31.78 g
- ~ **CHOLESTEROL:** 92.82 mg
- ~ **SODIUM:** 543.95 mg

1 pound boneless, skinless chicken thighs
1 onion, chopped
3 cloves garlic, minced
2 tablespoons butter
3 carrots, sliced
3 cups Chicken Stock (Chapter 6)
3 cups water
½ teaspoon salt
⅛ teaspoon white pepper
½ teaspoon dried marjoram leaves
1 (16-ounce) can cannelloni beans, drained
¼ cup grated Parmesan cheese

This hearty soup can be served without freezing by simmering for 40–45 minutes, then adding drained and rinsed cannelloni beans. Simmer soup for another 10–15 minutes, until slightly thickened.

1. Cut chicken into 1-inch pieces. Sauté chicken, onion, and garlic in olive oil and butter in large stockpot until chicken is browned and vegetables are crisp-tender. Add carrots; cook and stir 4–5 minutes.
2. Add Stock, water, salt, pepper, and marjoram and bring to a boil. Reduce heat, cover, and simmer for 30–35 minutes, until chicken is thoroughly cooked. Add beans and bring to a simmer. Sprinkle with cheese and serve.

47-Cent Split Pea Potage

Serves 8

~ **TOTAL COST:** $3.76
~ **CALORIES:** 412.12
~ **FAT:** 1.42 g
~ **PROTEIN:** 27.38 g
~ **CHOLESTEROL:** 0.0 mg
~ **SODIUM:** 350.58 mg

1 (1-pound) package split peas
9 cups water
3 carrots, sliced
2 potatoes, peeled and diced
1 onion, chopped
3 cloves garlic, chopped
1 teaspoon salt
⅛ teaspoon pepper
½ teaspoon dried thyme leaves
2 cups split peas
1 tablespoon mustard
1 tablespoon lemon juice

When you or a relative has ham for the holidays, ask for the ham bone and add it to this soup! It's full of flavor and adds a real richness to this simple and inexpensive recipe.

1. Rinse the 1 pound bag of split peas and sort to remove any debris. Combine all ingredients except split peas and mustard in large soup pot. Bring to a simmer, then reduce heat to low, cover, and simmer for 1½ hours or until peas fall apart.
2. Add 2 cups of rinsed split peas and bring back to a simmer. Simmer for 45–50 minutes until the just added peas are soft. Stir in mustard and lemon juice and let stand for 10 minutes, then serve.

Complete Proteins

Foods like split peas and other legumes are 'incomplete proteins;' your body can't use them unless missing amino acids are added. For a complete protein in a really inexpensive meal, add some grains. Freezer Wheat Rolls (Chapter 3) or Double Cornbread (Chapter 3) would be good and inexpensive choices.

Cream of Asparagus Soup

 Serves 6

- ~ **PREP TIME:** 10 minutes
- ~ **COOK TIME:** 30 minutes
- ~ **TOTAL COST:** $6.48
- ~ **CALORIES:** 269
- ~ **FAT:** 14 g
- ~ **PROTEIN:** 4 g
- ~ **CHOLESTEROL:** 27 mg
- ~ **SODIUM:** 432 mg

2 tablespoons olive oil
1 medium onion, chopped
4 cloves garlic, chopped
1 bunch fresh asparagus, including stalks, chopped
Sea salt and black pepper to taste
¼ cup white wine or Sherry
3 cups vegetable broth
1 (10-ounce) package frozen peas
2 cups sour cream
1 teaspoon dried basil

The alcohol in the wine cooks off, but before it cooks off, the alcohol extracts flavors from the other ingredients surrounding it to make a very tasty dish.

1. In a large-quart boiler, heat olive oil over medium heat until fragrant, about 1 minute. Add onion, garlic, asparagus, and salt. Cook 8 minutes, until onions are translucent but not browned. Add wine or Sherry and cook 1 minute. Add the broth. Simmer for 20 minutes, until asparagus is very tender. Remove from heat and stir in frozen peas.
2. Purée in food processor, in batches, until smooth. Transfer back to pot and heat to a simmer. Add sour cream, season with salt, pepper, and basil. Serve hot or cold.

> **Quick and Easy Tip**
> Not many soups afford you the choice between serving hot or cold. Prepare this one ahead of time and keep in the refrigerator. When ready to serve, your soup is well chilled.

Tuscan Bean Soup

Serves 8

~ **PREP TIME:** 5 minutes
~ **COOK TIME:** 25 minutes
~ **TOTAL COST:** $5.76
~ **CALORIES:** 276
~ **FAT:** 5 g
~ **CARBOHYDRATES:** 45 g
~ **PROTEIN:** 14 g
~ **CHOLESTEROL:** 16 mg
~ **SODIUM:** 717 mg

4 tablespoons extra-virgin olive oil
1 bunch green onion, chopped
3 cloves garlic, finely chopped
1 tablespoon fresh rosemary, stems removed, finely
   chopped
4 cups chicken broth
2 (32-ounce) cans great Northern beans with juice
½ cup ham or 1 ham bone
Sea salt and black pepper to taste

For my clients who love Italian gourmet food, this
is one of my pocket faves. Drizzle a little extra-virgin
olive oil on top when serving—you can't go wrong!

In large-quart boiler over medium heat, heat 1 tablespoon olive oil until fragrant, about 1 minute. Add onion and garlic and cook for 8 minutes. Add rosemary,
broth, beans, and ham (or ham bone). Bring to a boil.
Stir, cover, and reduce heat to simmer. Simmer 25 minutes. Season with salt and pepper as desired. Serve
and drizzle remaining olive oil over individual servings
for extra flavor.

Mushroom Soup with Parmesan

Serves 2

~ **PREP TIME:** 10 minutes
~ **COOK TIME:** 15 minutes
~ **TOTAL COST:** $4.50
~ **CALORIES:** 256
~ **FAT:** 17 g
~ **PROTEIN:** 4 g
~ **CHOLESTEROL:** 26 mg
~ **SODIUM:** 1223 mg

3 tablespoons butter
6 ounces assorted mushrooms
1 yellow onion, chopped
4 cups beef broth, canned
¼ cup dry Sherry wine or Merlot
Sea salt and pepper to taste
4 tablespoons Parmesan cheese, grated
½ tablespoon fresh thyme, leaves only

Cooking with fresh herbs is a great way to enhance
the flavor of foods without adding fat and calories.

1. Melt the butter in a medium skillet over medium
    heat. Add the mushrooms and onions. Cook, stir-
    ring frequently, until soft, about 8 minutes.
2. Add the beef broth, sherry, salt, and pepper.
    Simmer for 5 to 7 minutes. Taste and adjust the
    seasoning (add salt or pepper to taste). If too
    "winey," cook 5 minutes longer. To serve, ladle
    soup into bowls and garnish with fresh thyme
    leaves and parmesan.

Quick and Easy Tip
Thyme is a very versatile herb. Thyme blends well
with other herbs such as rosemary and pairs nicely
with beef, chicken, and fish.

Homemade Chili

 Serves 4

- ~ **TOTAL COST:** $5.65
- ~ **CALORIES:** 333.55
- ~ **FAT:** 10.59 g
- ~ **PROTEIN:** 22.88 g
- ~ **CHOLESTEROL:** 47.01 mg
- ~ **SODIUM:** 978.56 mg

½ pound ground beef
1 onion, chopped
3 cloves garlic, minced
1 (14-ounce) can diced tomatoes, undrained
1 (6-ounce) can tomato paste
4 cups water
⅛ teaspoon pepper
1 tablespoon apple cider vinegar
1 (15-ounce) can kidney beans, drained
1 tablespoon chili powder
2 tablespoons cornstarch
¼ cup water

This chili is so easy to make, and it's rich, thick, and satisfying, with 30 percent of the DV of vitamin A and 45 percent of the DV of vitamin C per serving.

1. In large stockpot, cook ground beef, onion, and garlic until beef is browned. Drain off fat.
2. Add remaining ingredients except cornstarch and ¼ cup water, bring to a boil, reduce heat, and simmer for 30–40 minutes until thickened, stirring frequently.
3. To thicken chili, combine cornstarch and ¼ cup water in small bowl and stir into saucepan. Simmer for 5–8 minutes until thick.

> **Canned vs. Homemade Chili**
> You can buy canned chili for about 90¢ a cup. But it's full of preservatives, artificial ingredients, and fillers, and is not as nutritious as homemade chili. Each serving of this chili is about 2 cups, for $1.41. If you have any left over, save it to use in "Neat" Sloppy Joes (Chapter 14) and Chili Quesadillas (Chapter 14).

Tomato Bisque

 Serves 4

~ **PREP TIME:** 15 minutes

~ **COOK TIME:** 12 minutes

~ **TOTAL COST:** $6.74

~ **CALORIES:** 261

~ **FAT:** 18 g

~ **PROTEIN:** 8 g

~ **CHOLESTEROL:** 44 mg

~ **SODIUM:** 397 mg

1 tablespoon olive oil

1 yellow onion, finely chopped

1 10-ounce container refrigerated Alfredo sauce

1½ cups chicken broth

1½ cups whole milk

2 (14-ounce) cans diced tomatoes, undrained

½ teaspoon dried basil leaves

¼ teaspoon dried marjoram leaves

Sea salt and black pepper to taste

Bisque is any kind of thick, creamy soup usually made with cream. Use this recipe as a base for seafood bisque and just add your favorite cooked seafood.

1. In a heavy saucepan, heat olive oil over medium heat and add onion. Cook and stir until onion is tender, about 4 minutes. Add Alfredo sauce and chicken broth; cook and stir with wire whisk until mixture is smooth. Add milk and stir; cook over medium heat for 2 to 3 minutes.

2. Meanwhile, purée undrained tomatoes in food processor or blender until smooth. Add to saucepan along with remaining ingredients and stir well. Heat soup over medium heat, stirring frequently, until mixture just comes to a simmer. Serve immediately.

> **Quick and Easy Tip**
> When a recipe calls for yellow or white onion, I always opt for the yellow onion as the flavors are somewhat similar and yellow onions can be substantially cheaper. Also, Alfredo sauce is a white creamy sauce that is found in the refrigerated dairy and cheese section of your grocery store.

Simple Gumbo

Serves 4

- ~ **PREP TIME:** 15 minutes
- ~ **COOK TIME:** 20 minutes
- ~ **TOTAL COST:** $6.88
- ~ **CALORIES:** 378
- ~ **FAT:** 7 g
- ~ **PROTEIN:** 34 g
- ~ **CHOLESTEROL:** 56 mg
- ~ **SODIUM:** 955 mg

1 (14½-ounce) can beef broth
1 (14½-ounce) can Italian stewed tomatoes
2 cups water
2 cups frozen hash brown potatoes
1 (10-ounce) package frozen mixed vegetables
8 ounces smoked sausage, sliced
⅛ teaspoon black pepper
2 tablespoons Parmesan cheese, grated
Sea salt and black pepper to taste

Gumbo is a popular dish made famous by New Orleans chefs. Traditional gumbo includes okra but okra can be hard to find. If you happen to find it at your local grocery store, add a cup along with the stewed tomatoes for extra flavor and a more thick consistency.

Combine beef broth, undrained stewed tomatoes, and water in a large-quart boiler. Bring to a boil. Stir in hash brown potatoes, mixed vegetables, sausage, and pepper. Return to boiling. Reduce heat and simmer, covered, for 5 to 10 minutes. Serve soup in bowls and sprinkle with Parmesan cheese and salt and pepper to taste.

Tortellini Soup
Serves 6

- ~ **PREP TIME:** 10 minutes
- ~ **COOK TIME:** 18 minutes
- ~ **TOTAL COST:** $6.72
- ~ **CALORIES:** 302
- ~ **FAT:** 28 g
- ~ **PROTEIN:** 29 g
- ~ **CHOLESTEROL:** 91 mg
- ~ **SODIUM:** 1062 mg

1 pound sweet Italian bulk sausage
1 (8-ounce) jar sliced mushrooms
4 cloves garlic, minced
3 (14-ounce) cans beef broth
1½ cups water
1 teaspoon dried Italian seasoning
½ teaspoon black pepper
1 (24-ounce) package frozen cheese tortellini

Tortellini are available both fresh or frozen. Frozen tend to be less expensive than fresh but are not lacking in flavor!

1. In a large saucepan over medium heat, brown sausage with mushrooms and garlic, stirring to break up sausage. When sausage is cooked, drain thoroughly. Add broth, water, Italian seasoning, and pepper to saucepan and bring to a boil over high heat. Reduce heat to low and simmer for 8 to 10 minutes.
2. Stir in frozen tortellini and cook, stirring frequently, over medium-high heat for 7 minutes or until tortellini are hot and tender. Serve immediately.

Quick and Easy Tip
Get tired of having plain pasta; this recipe is an easy and affordable way to enjoy pasta.

Spiced Corn and Cheese Soup

 Serves 6

~ **PREP TIME:** 10 minutes
~ **COOK TIME:** 15 minutes
~ **TOTAL COST:** $5.40
~ **CALORIES:** 370
~ **FAT:** 9 g
~ **PROTEIN:** 6 g
~ **CHOLESTEROL:** 31 mg
~ **SODIUM:** 871 mg

2 tablespoons olive oil
1 yellow onion, chopped
1 package taco seasoning mix
2 cups canned creamed corn
2 (10-ounce) cans chicken broth
1½ cups water
2 cups shredded pepper jack cheese
2 tablespoons plain flour

Serve this soup with salsa, sour cream, chopped avocado, and tortilla chips.

1. In a large-quart boiler, heat olive oil over medium heat. Add onion and sauté until crisp-tender, about 4 minutes. Sprinkle taco seasoning mix over the onions and stir. Then add corn, chicken broth, and water. Bring to a simmer and cook for 10 minutes, stirring occasionally.
2. Meanwhile, in a medium bowl, toss cheese with flour. Add to soup and lower heat; cook and stir for 2 to 3 minutes, until cheese is melted and soup is thickened. Serve hot.

Quick and Easy Tip
Make sure you stir the cheese almost constantly. If you allow the cheese to sit and melt, it tends to burn.

No-Peel Potato Soup

 Serves 6

~ **PREP TIME:** 10 minutes
~ **COOK TIME:** 20 minutes
~ **TOTAL COST:** $5.64
~ **CALORIES:** 325
~ **FAT:** 12 g
~ **PROTEIN:** 11 g
~ **CHOLESTEROL:** 35 mg
~ **SODIUM:** 683 mg

4 slices bacon
1 yellow onion, chopped
1 cup package cheesy scalloped potato mix
3 cups water
1 (15-ounce) can evaporated milk
2 cups frozen hash brown potatoes
½ teaspoon dried dill
½ teaspoon white pepper

Evaporated milk, not to be confused with sweetened condensed milk, is milk from which 60 percent of the water has been removed. The result is a more concentrated flavor. Because the milk comes in a can, it has a shelf life of months or sometimes years.

In heavy saucepan, cook bacon until crisp. Remove bacon, drain on paper towels, crumble, and set aside. Cook onion in bacon drippings until tender, about 5 minutes. Add potato mix and seasoning packet from potato mix along with remaining ingredients. Bring to a boil and simmer for 17 to 20 minutes, until potatoes are tender. Sprinkle with bacon and serve.

Quick and Easy Tip
Dehydrated potatoes, used here, are not expensive and you don't have to peel them. Plus, they save on cooking time.

Creamy Pea Soup

 Serves 4

~ **PREP TIME:** 15 minutes
~ **COOK TIME:** 12 minutes
~ **TOTAL COST:** $3.48
~ **CALORIES:** 149
~ **FAT:** 2 g
~ **PROTEIN:** 19 g
~ **CHOLESTEROL:** 2 mg
~ **SODIUM:** 47mg

2 (10-ounce) packages frozen green peas
2 cups water
3½ cups chicken broth
Juice of 1 lemon
1 clove garlic, minced
1 small yellow onion, chopped
Sea salt and black pepper to taste
¼ cup mint leaves, chopped
¼ cup plain yogurt

Add a little crispy bacon bits on top for a smoky flavor that complements the peas.

Cook the peas in 2 cups of boiling water for just a few minutes. Drain, reserving water for use later in the recipe. Purée peas in a food processor. Mix 2 cups of the cooking water, broth, and lemon juice in a saucepan. Add the puréed peas and bring to a simmer. Add garlic, onion, salt, and pepper. Turn off heat. Add the mint and stir to combine. Serve with a dollop of yogurt

Quick and Easy Tip
Keep a large bag of frozen peas in your freezer at all times. They are great as a snack right out of the freezer, or add some to rice for Italian *risi e bisi*!

Pumpkin Wild Rice Chowder

Serves 4

~ **TOTAL COST:** $4.68
~ **CALORIES:** 325.08
~ **FAT:** 7.73 g
~ **PROTEIN:** 9.89 g
~ **CHOLESTEROL:** 27.17 mg
~ **SODIUM:** 728.34 mg

3 carrots, sliced
3 potatoes, peeled and cubed
½ cup wild rice, rinsed
1 onion, chopped
4 cloves garlic, minced
1 (15-ounce) can solid pack pumpkin
1½ cups beef broth
2 cups water
2 teaspoons curry powder
½ teaspoon salt
¼ teaspoon white pepper
⅓ cup heavy cream

You can substitute half and half for the heavy cream if you'd like. This hearty chowder is thick and full of flavor.

1. Place carrots, potatoes, and wild rice in bottom of 4–5 quart slow cooker. In large skillet, heat olive oil over medium high heat. Add onion and garlic; cook and stir for 2 minutes.
2. Add pumpkin and beef broth to skillet. Cook and stir until mixture blends and comes to a simmer. Pour into crockpot; add water, curry powder, salt, and pepper and stir. Cover and cook on low for 8–9 hours, until wild rice is tender. Stir in heavy cream and cook for 20 minutes longer; serve.

Pasta e Fagioli

 Serves 8

~ **TOTAL COST:** $6.98
~ **CALORIES:** 427.15
~ **FAT:** 9.26 g
~ **PROTEIN:** 21.69 g
~ **CHOLESTEROL:** 12.18 mg
~ **SODIUM:** 524.44 mg

¾ pound dried navy beans
2 tablespoons vegetable oil
2 onions, chopped
5 cloves garlic, minced
3 stalks celery, chopped
8 cups water
⅛ teaspoon pepper
1 cup chopped ham
1 teaspoon dried Italian seasoning
1 (14-ounce) can diced tomatoes, undrained
1 (12-ounce) package ditalini or small shell pasta
¼ teaspoon red pepper flakes
½ cup Spinach Pesto (Chapter 2)
½ cup shredded Parmesan cheese

This dish is usually served as a soup, but this version is a very thick stew studded with beans, onions, and garlic.

1. Sort beans and rinse; drain, then cover with cold water. Let soak overnight. In the morning, drain beans and set aside.
2. In large soup pot, cook onion, garlic, and celery in olive oil until crisp-tender, about 4 minutes. Add the beans, water, and pepper, and bring to a boil. Reduce heat, then cover and simmer for 3 hours, stirring occasionally.
3. Using a potato masher, mash some of the beans. Add ham, Italian seasoning, tomatoes, pasta, and red pepper flakes to pot. Bring to a boil and cook until pasta is tender, about 6–8 minutes or according to package directions. Serve with Pesto and Parmesan cheese.

Pasta in Soup

When pasta is cooked directly in soup or stews, it takes a few minutes longer to reach al dente. But it will be more flavorful, because it absorbs herbs and spices from the broth or liquid while it is cooking. Just be sure to stir occasionally and taste the pasta until it reaches the perfect texture.

Cheese Vegetable Soup

Serves 6

~ **TOTAL COST:** $6.98
~ **CALORIES:** 330.08
~ **FAT:** 17.65 g
~ **PROTEIN:** 17.57 g
~ **CHOLESTEROL:** 50.96 mg
~ **SODIUM:** 603.79 mg

2 tablespoons butter
1 tablespoon olive oil
1 onion, chopped
2 stalks celery, sliced
3 carrots, sliced
3 tablespoons flour
1 teaspoon paprika
½ teaspoon salt
⅛ teaspoon pepper
3 cups vegetable broth
1 (14.5-ounce) can diced tomatoes, drained
2 cups milk
1½ cups cubed Havarti cheese

A hot vegetable soup is poured over cheese placed in soup bowls so the cheese slowly melts are you eat it. Yum!

1. In large pot, combine butter and olive oil over medium heat. When butter melts, add onion; cook and stir for 3 minutes. Add carrots; cook and stir 3 minutes longer. Stir in celery and cook for 1 minute. Add flour, paprika, salt, and pepper. Cook and stir for 2 minutes.
2. Add vegetable broth and tomatoes, bring to a simmer, and cook for 5–10 minutes until vegetables are tender. Slowly stir in milk and heat until the soup steams; do not boil. Place ¼-cup cheese in the bottom of each serving bowl and pour soup over. Serve immediately.

Corn Chowder with Pepper Jack Cheese

Serves 6

~ **PREP TIME:** 10 minutes
~ **COOK TIME:** 15 minutes
~ **TOTAL COST:** $4.90
~ **CALORIES:** 370
~ **FAT:** 10 g
~ **CARBOHYDRATES:** 40 g
~ **PROTEIN:** 6 g
~ **CHOLESTEROL:** 35 mg
~ **SODIUM:** 671 mg

2 tablespoons olive oil
1 yellow onion, chopped
1 package taco seasoning mix
2 cups canned creamed corn
2 (10-ounce) cans chicken broth
1½ cups water
2 cups shredded pepper jack cheese
2 tablespoons plain flour

Serve this soup with salsa, sour cream, or chopped avocado.

1. In large-quart boiler, heat olive oil over medium heat. Add onion and sauté until crisp-tender, about 4 minutes. Sprinkle taco seasoning mix over the onions and stir. Then add corn, chicken broth, and water. Bring to a simmer and cook for 10 minutes, stirring occasionally.
2. In medium bowl, toss cheese with flour. Add to soup and lower heat; cook and stir for 2 to 3 minutes, until cheese is melted and soup is thickened.

Cooking Tip
Stir cheese frequently as it tends to burn if it rests too long over heat.

Beef Barley Stew

Serves 4

~ **TOTAL COST:** $6.99
~ **CALORIES:** 476.50
~ **FAT:** 15.50 g
~ **PROTEIN:** 42.05 g
~ **CHOLESTEROL:** 70.27 mg
~ **SODIUM:** 903.24 mg

¾ pound beef stew meat
3 tablespoons flour
1 teaspoon paprika
1 teaspoon salt
⅛ teaspoon pepper
1 tablespoon olive oil
1 onion, chopped
3 cloves garlic, minced
1 teaspoon dried thyme leaves
4 carrots, sliced
3 cups beef broth
3 cups water
½ cup pearl barley
½ (29-ounce) can tomato puree
3 tablespoons tomato paste

This rich stew is perfect for a cold winter's day. Serve it with Oat Bran Dinner Rolls (Chapter 3) for a warming and easy meal.

1. Cut beef stew meat into 1-inch pieces. Sprinkle with flour, paprika, salt, and pepper and toss to coat. In large stockpot, heat olive oil over medium heat. Add cubes of beef; brown on all sides, stirring occasionally, about 10 minutes total. Remove beef from pot. Add onion and garlic; cook and stir until crisp tender, about 4 minutes.

2. Add thyme, carrots, and beef broth to pot; stir to loosen drippings from bottom of pan. Return beef to pot along with water. Bring to a boil, then reduce heat, cover pot, and simmer for 1 hour. Add barley, cover, and simmer for 25 minutes longer. Then stir in tomato purée and tomato paste; simmer for 20–30 minutes until beef, vegetables, and barley are tender, then serve.

Tomato Paste

Tomato paste is most often sold in 6-ounce cans. If a recipe doesn't call for a whole can, freeze the rest! Portion it into 2 tablespoon mounds and freeze. Then place the mounds in a food storage bag and freeze up to 3 months. You can also find tomato paste in a tube; just store it in the fridge and measure out the amount you need.

Bean and Sausage Chowder

 Serves 6

- ~ **TOTAL COST:** $6.80
- ~ **CALORIES:** 464.23
- ~ **FAT:** 6.02 g
- ~ **PROTEIN:** 29.44 g
- ~ **CHOLESTEROL:** 17.01 mg
- ~ **SODIUM:** 1074.34 mg

1 pound Great Northern beans
½ pound sweet Italian sausage
8 cups water
1 onion, chopped
4 cloves garlic, minced
3 potatoes, peeled and chopped
1 zucchini, chopped
1 (14-ounce) can diced tomatoes, undrained
1 (8-ounce) can tomato sauce
1 teaspoon salt
⅛ teaspoon pepper

This hearty soup is perfect for cold winter evenings. It stretches half a pound of Italian sausage to serve six people! To splurge, add some cooked link sausage.

1. Sort beans and rinse thoroughly. Drain and place in large pot; cover with water. Bring to a boil and boil for 2 minutes. Then cover pot, remove from heat, and let stand for 1 hour. Meanwhile, cook sausage in large skillet until browned; drain off all but 1 tablespoon drippings. Cook onion and garlic in drippings over medium heat until crisp tender, about 4 minutes.
2. Drain beans and rinse well. Cut sausage into 1-inch pieces. Combine in 4–5 quart slow cooker with 8 cups water, onion, garlic, and potatoes. Cover and cook on low for 8 hours. Then stir in zucchini, tomatoes, tomato sauce, salt, and pepper; cover and cook on low for 1–2 hours longer, until beans and potatoes are tender. If you'd like, you can mash some of the beans and potatoes, leaving others whole, for a thicker chowder.

Triple Corn Chowder

Serves 4–6

- ~ **TOTAL COST:** $4.70
- ~ **CALORIES:** 328.68
- ~ **FAT:** 15.23 g
- ~ **PROTEIN:** 11.04 g
- ~ **CHOLESTEROL:** 43.02 mg
- ~ **SODIUM:** 737.23 mg

1 onion, chopped
2 tablespoons butter
2 cups frozen corn
1 (15-ounce) can creamed corn
4 cups Chicken Stock (Chapter 6)
2 tablespoons masa harina (corn flour)
½ cup heavy cream
1 (4-ounce) can diced chiles
½ teaspoon cumin

Chowders are thicker than stews and usually have cheese or another dairy product in the recipe. Serve this hearty chowder with some breadsticks and a fruit salad.

1. In heavy saucepan, cook onion in butter until crisp-tender, about 4 minutes. Stir in frozen corn, creamed corn, and half of chicken broth; bring to a boil. Meanwhile, in small saucepan combine remaining chicken broth with masa harina; bring to a boil, stirring constantly.
2. Stir chicken broth and masa harina mixture into onion mixture along with cream, bell pepper, chiles, and cumin; simmer for 5–8 minutes, stirring frequently, until blended.

Using Dairy Products in Soups

When a soup recipe calls for milk or cream, be sure that you don't let the mixture boil after the dairy products are added. The casein protein in the milk can denature and cause curdling, which is undesirable. Just let the soup simmer briefly to heat through and be sure to stir the soup constantly.

Fish Chowder with Potatoes and Corn

 Serves 4

- ~ **PREP TIME:** 10 minutes
- ~ **COOK TIME:** 35 minutes
- ~ **TOTAL COST:** $6.99
- ~ **CALORIES:** 323
- ~ **FAT:** 12 g
- ~ **CARBOHYDRATES:** 25 g
- ~ **PROTEIN:** 28 g
- ~ **CHOLESTEROL:** 77 g
- ~ **SODIUM:** 1080 mg

1 tablespoon olive oil
½ yellow onion, diced
2 large baking potatoes, peeled and cut into 1- to
   2-inch cubes
2 ears corn, kernels cut off cob
1 leek, trimmed and sliced
½ pound cod, skin removed
16 ounces chicken broth
16 ounces low-fat milk
Sea salt and lemon pepper to taste

When making a chowder, it is best to use a less expensive fish such as cod because you are combining it with so many other layers of flavors. If you don't care for cod, substitute shrimp, clams, or mussels.

In large-quart boiler, heat oil on medium heat. Add onion and sauté until just tender, about 3 minutes. Add the potatoes, then stir in corn, leeks, and fish; sauté until leeks begin to wilt, about 6 minutes. Add broth and milk, and season with salt and pepper. Let simmer for 30 minutes, adding broth and milk as needed.

Split Pea Soup

 Serves 6

- ~ **TOTAL COST:** $6.21
- ~ **CALORIES:** 448.48
- ~ **FAT:** 9.39 g
- ~ **PROTEIN:** 26.89 g
- ~ **CHOLESTEROL:** 23.42 mg
- ~ **SODIUM:** 633.91 mg

1 pound dried split peas
3 cups water
3 cups Chicken Stock (Chapter 6)
1 onion, chopped
3 cloves garlic, chopped
3 carrots, chopped
1 tablespoon olive oil
2 tablespoons butter
1 cup cubed ham
1 teaspoon dried thyme leaves
1 (15-ounce) can creamed corn

Sautéing the ham in butter adds a subtle flavor. You can omit the ham or add cooked chicken breasts or leftover meatballs for a different taste.

1. Carefully pick over peas and discard any wrinkled peas or stones. Place in large stockpot, cover with water and broth, and bring to a boil. Reduce heat and simmer for about 1 hour, until peas are tender.
2. While peas are cooking, in heavy skillet sauté onion, garlic, and carrots in olive oil. Add vegetables to stockpot. In the same skillet, heat butter and add ham. Sauté for 3–4 minutes, until ham is slightly browned. Add to stockpot along with thyme and creamed corn. Simmer for 15–25 minutes more or until peas begin to dissolve and vegetables are tender. Stir and serve immediately.

Vegetable Soup with Brown Rice

Serves 8

- ~ **PREP TIME:** 15 minutes
- ~ **COOK TIME:** 30mintues
- ~ **TOTAL COST:** $6.85
- ~ **CALORIES:** 141
- ~ **FAT:** 0.5 g
- ~ **CARBOHYDRATES:** 28 g
- ~ **PROTEIN:** 5 g
- ~ **CHOLESTEROL:** 2 mg
- ~ **SODIUM:** 139 mg

1 tablespoon olive oil
½ cup yellow onions, diced
1 clove fresh garlic, minced
1 (16-ounce) package frozen California-blend vegetables
2 large baking potatoes, peeled and cubed
2 (14- to 16-ounce) cans vegetable broth
1 celery stalk, chopped
1 teaspoon dried Italian seasoning
1 teaspoon fresh oregano, leaves chopped
¼ cup fresh Italian flat-leaf parsley, leaves chopped
2 cups instant brown rice
2 cups water
Sea salt and black pepper to taste

Brown rice is similar to white rice in calories and carbohydrates, however, brown rice contains higher amounts of other nutrients such as vitamin B and magnesium.

In large boiler over medium heat, heat oil. Add onions and garlic and sauté until fragrant, about 3 minutes. Add vegetables, potatoes, broth, celery, herbs, rice, and water. Bring to a boil, reduce heat and simmer for 25 minutes, or until potatoes are tender. Add more water or broth, if needed. Season with salt and pepper as desired.

Purée of Broccoli Soup

Serves 5

- ~ **PREP TIME:** 15 minutes
- ~ **COOK TIME:** 20 minutes
- ~ **TOTAL COST:** $5.94
- ~ **CALORIES:** 126
- ~ **FAT:** 3 g
- ~ **CARBOHYDRATES:** 24 g
- ~ **PROTEIN:** 4 g
- ~ **CHOLESTEROL:** 6 mg
- ~ **SODIUM:** 315 mg

1 head broccoli, stems and florets chopped
1 medium onion, chopped
2 large baking potatoes, peeled and diced
2 cloves garlic, chopped
1½ cups vegetable broth
2 teaspoons fresh thyme, leaves chopped
Black pepper to taste
Pinch nutmeg
1½ cups low-fat milk
Sea salt to taste

The potatoes help make this puréed soup thick and creamy, but you can leave them out if you are concerned about your carb intake. Add a dollop of low-fat or nonfat sour cream when serving too add extra flavor with minimal fat and calories.

1. In a large-quart boiler, combine broccoli stems and florets, onion, potatoes, garlic, broth, thyme, pepper, and nutmeg. Bring to a boil. Reduce the heat, cover, and simmer for 15 minutes or until potatoes are tender.
2. In a blender or food processor, purée the soup, in batches if necessary, until smooth. Return to the saucepan. Add the milk. Heat through on medium heat without boiling, about 5 minutes. Season with salt to taste.

Pasta and Bean Soup

Serves 8

- ~ **PREP TIME:** 8 minutes
- ~ **COOK TIME:** 25 minutes
- ~ **TOTAL COST:** $5.28
- ~ **CALORIES:** 169
- ~ **FAT:** 3 g
- ~ **CARBOHYDRATES:** 28 g
- ~ **PROTEIN:** 9 g
- ~ **CHOLESTEROL:** 4 mg
- ~ **SODIUM:** 392 mg

3 tablespoons olive oil
1 medium onion, chopped
3 cloves garlic, chopped
1 teaspoon fresh oregano, leaves chopped
1 large can (16 ounce) tomato sauce
Sea salt and black pepper to taste
1 tablespoon Worcestershire sauce
2 large cans red beans, undrained
1 small bunch Italian parsley, chopped
6 cups vegetable broth or chicken broth
2 cups cooked pasta such as fusilli

In Italy, pasta fagiole is a very popular dish during the winter months. Substitute any canned beans you like.

1. In a large pot, heat olive oil over medium heat; add onions and garlic and sauté for 5 minutes or until onions are tender. Add oregano, tomato sauce, salt, pepper, and Worcestershire sauce. Bring to a simmer then add beans, parsley, and broth.
2. Bring to a boil. Add cooked pasta and bring back to boil for 1 minute.

Miso Soup

Serves 4

- ~ **PREP TIME:** 15 minutes
- ~ **COOK TIME:** 10 minutes
- ~ **TOTAL COST:** $4.56
- ~ **CALORIES:** 61
- ~ **FAT:** 2 g
- ~ **CARBOHYDRATES:** 8 g
- ~ **PROTEIN:** 3 g
- ~ **CHOLESTEROL:** 0 mg
- ~ **SODIUM:** 750 mg

¼ cup miso paste
3½ cups chicken broth
8 ounces medium to firm tofu, cubed
4 sprigs Italian parsley, chopped
4 cremini or button mushrooms, brushed and sliced
2 shitake mushrooms, sliced
Sea salt and black pepper to taste

The mystery of miso is that it is hard to make but this simple recipe will solve that for you!

In large-quart boiler, whisk the miso into 2 tablespoons of slightly warmed broth and blend well. Gradually add the miso liquid into the remaining broth. Bring the soup to a simmer. Add the tofu cubes, parsley, and mushrooms. Maintain a simmer until the mushrooms and tofu are heated. Do not boil or the soup will become bitter and cloudy. Serve soup in bowls and serve immediately. Season with salt and pepper as desired.

> **Miso**
> Miso is a fermented soybean paste that can be found in most well-stocked supermarkets. It lasts for a year or more if stored properly, and can be used to make aioli or as a substitute for peanut butter in some recipes.

Mexican Posole

 Serves 6

- **PREP TIME:** 15 minutes
- **COOK TIME:** 24 minutes
- **TOTAL COST:** $6.97
- **CALORIES:** 378
- **FAT:** 4 g
- **CARBOHYDRATES:** 43 g
- **PROTEIN:** 30 g
- **CHOLESTEROL:** 52 mg
- **SODIUM:** 663 mg

1 (16-ounce) package pork roast, chopped
1 (4-ounce) can chopped green chilies, undrained
2 (14-ounce) cans chicken broth
1 tablespoon chili powder
1 teaspoon ground cumin
1 teaspoon fresh oregano, leaves chopped
1 (15-ounce) can hominy, drained
2 cups (16 ounces) frozen corn
3 tablespoons plain flour
¼ cup water
Sea salt and black pepper to taste

Posole is a Mexican stew made with hominy, green chilies, and cubes of tender pork.

1. In large saucepan over medium heat, combine pork (with any juices), chilies, broth, chili powder, cumin, oregano, hominy, and corn. Bring to a boil over high heat, then reduce heat to low, cover, and simmer for 12 to 15 minutes until pork is hot and tender.
2. In small bowl, combine flour and water. Mix well until smooth. Stir into stew and raise to medium heat. Cook and stir until stew thickens, about 5 to 8 minutes. Season with salt and pepper as desired.

> **Hominy**
> Hominy is made by removing the bran and germ from the kernels of corn. It can be made by soaking the corn kernels in a weak solution of lye and water, or by physically crushing the corn. Yellow hominy is generally sweeter than the white. You can substitute barley for it in any recipe, if you prefer.

Meatball Soup with Vegetables

 Serves 6

- ~ **PREP TIME:** 10 minutes
- ~ **COOK TIME:** 20 minutes
- ~ **TOTAL COST:** $6.96
- ~ **CALORIES:** 237
- ~ **FAT:** 4 g
- ~ **CARBOHYDRATES:** 23 g
- ~ **PROTEIN:** 27 g
- ~ **CHOLESTEROL:** 92 mg
- ~ **SODIUM:** 468 mg

1 pound frozen meatballs
2 cups V8 juice or other tomato juice blend
2 cups frozen mixed vegetables
1½ cups beef broth
3 cups water
½ teaspoon dried Italian seasoning
½ teaspoon black pepper
1 cup vermicelli pasta noodles

This hearty soup is perfect for kids, as it contains many of their favorite ingredients, such as meatballs and pasta. Serve this as a quick snack after school instead of less healthy potato chips or fast food.

In large-quart boiler, combine all ingredients except pasta and mix gently. Bring to a boil over high heat, reduce heat, and let simmer for 10 minutes. Add pasta and simmer an additional 10 minutes, until pasta is tender.

Classic Chili with Beans

 Serves 4

- ~ **TOTAL COST:** $6.36
- ~ **CALORIES:** $326.90
- ~ **FAT:** 12.62 g
- ~ **PROTEIN:** 19.51 g
- ~ **CHOLESTEROL:** 39.76 mg
- ~ **SODIUM:** 1043.34 mg

½ pound ground beef
1 onion, chopped
3 cloves garlic, minced
½ (29-ounce) can tomato puree
1 (8-ounce) can tomato sauce
1 (6-ounce) can tomato paste
1 tablespoon chili powder
1 (15-ounce) can kidney beans
1 (4-ounce) can diced green chiles
1 cup water
⅛ teaspoon pepper

"Classic" chili doesn't have beans, but this recipe does. Beans help stretch the meat, add lots of fiber, and taste wonderful. So use them without shame.

1. In large saucepan, brown ground beef with onion and garlic until beef is cooked, stirring frequently. Drain if necessary.
2. Add remaining ingredients along and stir gently. Bring to a simmer, then cover pan and simmer soup for 20–30 minutes until flavors are blended.

Bean Soup with Bacon and Cheese

Serves 4

~ **PREP TIME:** 10 minutes
~ **COOK TIME:** 15 minutes
~ **TOTAL COST:** $6.84
~ **CALORIES:** 326
~ **FAT:** 16 g
~ **PROTEIN:** 22 g
~ **CHOLESTEROL:** 49 mg
~ **SODIUM:** 704 mg

2 slices bacon
1 yellow onion, chopped
1 (14-ounce) can diced tomatoes, undrained
2 (15-ounce) cans pinto beans, drained
2 cups chicken broth
1½ cups Cheddar cheese, shredded

Most kids love anything with cheese—that's why this soup is perfect for kids' lunches.

In a large saucepan, cook bacon until crisp. Drain bacon on paper towels, crumble, and set aside. Drain off all but 2 tablespoons bacon drippings. Cook onion in drippings over medium heat for 3 to 4 minutes. Add tomatoes, beans, and broth and bring to a simmer. Simmer for 10 to 12 minutes, then use a potato masher to mash some of the beans. Add reserved bacon, stir, and simmer for 5 minutes longer. Serve immediately and top with cheese. Or pour into warmed insulated thermoses for kids lunches or picnics.

Quick and Easy Tip
When buying bacon, the leanest cuts have the least amount of white marble. Some is okay, but just make sure there is more meat than fat!

Sausage Gumbo

Serves 4

~ **PREP TIME:** 15 minutes
~ **COOK TIME:** 30 minutes
~ **TOTAL COST:** $6.91
~ **CALORIES:** 388
~ **FAT:** 6 g
~ **CARBOHYDRATES:** 37 g
~ **PROTEIN:** 34 g
~ **CHOLESTEROL:** 52 mg
~ **SODIUM:** 1225 mg

8 ounces hot or mild Italian sausage, removed from casing
1 (14½-ounce) can beef broth
1 (14½-ounce) can Italian stewed tomatoes, undrained
2 cups water
2 baking potatoes, peeled and cut into 1- to 2-inch cubes
1 (10-ounce) package frozen mixed vegetables
1 teaspoon dried Italian seasoning
Sea salt and black pepper to taste

Other alternatives for this recipe include substituting chopped chicken or leaving out the potatoes and serving over white rice.

In large-quart boiler, sauté sausage until browned, breaking up pieces. Add beef broth, tomatoes, and water. Bring to a boil. Stir in potatoes, mixed vegetables, Italian seasoning, and salt and pepper. Return to boiling. Reduce heat and simmer, covered, 20 to 25 minutes, or until potatoes are tender.

Gumbo
True gumbo usually has fresh okra in it; however, fresh okra can be extremely hard to find. Use fresh green beans instead or just use frozen mixed vegetables as suggested here.

Black Bean Soup

 Serves 6

- ~ **TOTAL COST:** $5.80
- ~ **CALORIES:** 345.54
- ~ **FAT:** 3.50 g
- ~ **PROTEIN:** 23.62 g
- ~ **CHOLESTEROL:** 13.24 mg
- ~ **SODIUM:** 395.50 mg

1 pound dried black beans
1 onion, chopped
3 cloves garlic, minced
2 stalks celery, minced
2 jalapeño peppers, minced
1 tablespoon chili powder
1 teaspoon cumin
¼ teaspoon cayenne pepper
1 ham bone, if desired
4 cups water
3 cups Chicken Stock (Chapter 6)
2 tablespoons masa harina
⅓ cup water

Black beans, also called turtle beans, make the most wonderful soup. Their meaty flavor and creamy texture enhance the vegetables in this easy recipe.

1. Sort and rinse black beans and cover with cold water. Let stand overnight. In the morning, drain beans, discard soaking water, and combine in a 4- to 5-quart crockpot with remaining ingredients except masa harina and ⅓ cup water. Cover and cook on low for 8–10 hours until beans are soft.
2. Remove ham bone and take meat off the bone; chop and return to soup. Turn crockpot to high. In small bowl, mix masa harina with water and blend well. Stir into soup, mixing well. Cook on high for 30 minutes, stirring once during cooking, until soup is thickened.

Ham Bones

You can usually buy ham bones right in your supermarket's meat aisle. You may have to ask the butcher for the bones. A ham bone adds a rich flavor to soups, especially when long simmered as in crockpot recipes. If you can't find one, substitute 1 cup of chopped cooked ham.

Simple Oven Stew

  Serves 6

- **TOTAL COST:** $6.97
- **CALORIES:** 394.04
- **FAT:** 20.19 g
- **PROTEIN:** 18.51 g
- **CHOLESTEROL:** 61.04 mg
- **SODIUM:** 745.93 mg

1 pound ground beef
1 tablespoon olive oil
2 onions, chopped
4 carrots, sliced
3 cloves garlic, minced
1 (10.75-ounce) can cream of mushroom soup
2 cups water
3 russet potatoes, sliced
2 cups frozen peas
½ teaspoon dried tarragon leaves
½ teaspoon salt
⅛ teaspoon pepper

This easy and wholesome stew bakes in the oven so you can go about your day without worrying about it. Serve it with a gelatin salad and some breadsticks for a retro meal that evokes memories of the 1960s.

1. Brown ground beef in large skillet. Remove meat from skillet with slotted spoon and place in 3 quart baking dish. Drain all but 1 tablespoon of drippings from skillet. Add olive oil, then cook onion and carrots in drippings for 3–4 minutes until glazed. Add to beef in baking dish.
2. Add garlic, soup, and water to skillet and bring to a simmer, scraping any brown bits from the bottom of the skillet. Then pour into baking dish along with remaining ingredients and stir well. Cover tightly with foil and bake at 325°F for 1½ to 2 hours or until vegetables are tender and soup is bubbling.

Soup Science
Soup is one of the most forgiving recipes in all of food science. You can add almost anything to it, and leave everything out but the liquid. It's a great way to use leftover vegetables and meats. Just remember, if the ingredients are already cooked, add them at the very end; you just want to reheat them, not overcook them.

CHAPTER 7

CHICKEN AND TURKEY

Chicken Curry with Basmati Rice

 Serves 5

- ~ **PREP TIME:** 10 minutes
- ~ **COOK TIME:** 25 minutes
- ~ **TOTAL COST:** $6.85
- ~ **CALORIES:** 250
- ~ **FAT:** 2 g
- ~ **CARBOHYDRATES:** 21 g
- ~ **PROTEIN:** 35 g
- ~ **CHOLESTEROL:** 4 mg
- ~ **SODIUM:** 240 mg

2 cups basmati rice
4 cups water
Sea salt and red pepper flakes to taste
2 cloves garlic, chopped
1 yellow onion, chopped
Juice of 1 lemon
1 teaspoon cumin
½ cup fresh Italian parsley, chopped
1 cup low-fat yogurt
1 tablespoon curry powder
Tabasco to taste
1 pound boneless chicken breasts, skin removed, cut into 1- to 2-inch cubes

Curry is a blend of other spices, including turmeric and coriander, and is native to India.

1. Place rice and water in quart boiler. Bring to a boil, stir, reduce heat, cover, and simmer about 15 minutes. Add the salt and pepper flakes, garlic, onion, lemon juice, cumin, and parsley. Stir to combine, cover, and simmer an additional 2–3 minutes, if needed.
2. Turn broiler to high. In mixing bowl, combine yogurt, curry, and Tabasco. Toss chicken to coat. Place on aluminum foil and place under broiler for 5 minutes. Turn chicken and broil an additional 5 minutes or as needed until cooked through.
3. Mix cooked chicken into the rice and serve.

Chicken Veracruz

Serves 4

~ **TOTAL COST:** $6.80
~ **CALORIES:** 493.03
~ **FAT:** 25.04 g
~ **PROTEIN:** 45.93 g
~ **CHOLESTEROL:** 130.96 mg
~ **SODIUM:** 926.55 mg

4 bone-in, skin-on chicken breasts
¼ cup flour
½ teaspoon salt
⅛ teaspoon pepper
1 teaspoon paprika
1 tablespoon olive oil
1 tablespoon butter
1 onion, chopped
1 (14-ounce) can diced tomatoes, undrained
¼ cup water
⅓ cup sliced green olives

Chicken spiced with paprika and olives is a true feast. This easy recipe has lots of flavor and is delicious served over hot cooked rice or couscous.

1. Preheat oven to 375°F. On shallow plate, combine flour, salt, pepper, and paprika. Coat chicken in this mixture. In large saucepan, heat 2 tablespoons olive oil over medium heat. Add chicken, skin side down, and cook until browned. Remove chicken to a 2-quart casserole dish.
2. Add olive oil to saucepan and cook onion and garlic until tender, about 4 minutes, stirring to loosen pan drippings. Add tomatoes, water, and green olives and bring to a boil.
3. Pour sauce over chicken in casserole. Cover and bake for 40–50 minutes or until chicken is 170°F on a meat thermometer. Serve immediately.

Bone-In, Skin-On Breasts
Remember, for the most cost savings, purchase bone-in, skin-on breasts for all recipes that call for boneless, skinless chicken breasts. Remove the skin, then cut the large piece of meat away from the bone. Freeze the bones with the meat still on them, and the skin to make Chicken Stock (Chapter 6).

King Ranch Chicken Casserole

Serves 5

- ~ **TOTAL COST:** $6.83
- ~ **CALORIES:** 376.51
- ~ **FAT:** 14.01 g
- ~ **PROTEIN:** 20.63 g
- ~ **CHOLESTEROL:** 39.04 mg
- ~ **SODIUM:** 1177.90 mg

1 onion, chopped
3 cloves garlic, minced
1 tablespoon butter
1 tablespoon olive oil
1 cup frozen corn
½ (14.5-ounce) can diced tomatoes, undrained
2 Slow Cooker Simmered Chicken Breasts (this chapter), cubed
1 (15-ounce) can black beans, rinsed
1 (14-ounce) can cream of chicken soup
½ (4-ounce) can diced green chiles, drained
¼ cup evaporated milk
4 corn tortillas
2 teaspoons chili powder
½ teaspoon salt
⅛ teaspoon cayenne pepper
¾ cup shredded Cheddar cheese

This famous recipe is pure Tex-Mex comfort food. You can make it ahead of time and refrigerate until it's time to eat. Then add 15–20 minutes to the baking time; make sure the casserole is bubbling and thoroughly heated.

1. Preheat oven to 350°F. In skillet, cook onions and garlic in butter and olive oil until crisp-tender. Add frozen corn; cook and stir for 3 minutes until corn is thawed. Remove from heat and top with drained tomatoes. Set aside.

2. In medium bowl, combine chicken, black beans, soup, green chiles, and milk; stir. Cut tortillas into 1-inch strips. In small bowl, combine chili powder, salt, and cayenne pepper and mix. Sprinkle over tortillas and toss to coat.

3. Coat 9" × 13" baking dish with nonstick cooking spray. In the prepared dish, layer half of the chicken mixture, half of the tortillas, half of the onion mixture, and half of the cheese. Repeat layers, ending with cheese.

4. Bake casserole at 350°F for 40–50 minutes or until sauce is bubbling and cheese is melted and beginning to brown. Serve with salsa, sour cream, and guacamole.

Cheesy Chicken Quiche

 Serves 8

~ **TOTAL COST:** $6.08
~ **CALORIES:** 341.48
~ **FAT:** 20.57 g
~ **PROTEIN:** 17.64 g
~ **CHOLESTEROL:** 149.46 mg
~ **SODIUM:** 467.02 mg

2 tablespoons butter
1 onion, chopped
2 tablespoons all-purpose flour
½ teaspoon salt
⅛ teaspoon pepper
½ cup milk
⅓ cup sour cream
1 tablespoon mustard
4 eggs
2 Slow-Cooker Simmered Chicken Breasts (this chapter)
1 Angel Pie Crust (Chapter 15), unbaked
1 cup shredded Swiss cheese
3 tablespoons grated Parmesan cheese

Quiches are easy, and so inexpensive. You can fill this basic quiche recipe with everything from chopped ham to cheese.

1. Preheat oven to 350°F. In medium saucepan, melt butter over medium heat. Add onion; cook and stir until tender, about 5 minutes. Add flour, salt, and pepper; cook and stir until bubbly, about 3 minutes longer.
2. Stir in milk and cook until thick, about 3 minutes. Remove from heat and add sour cream and mustard. Beat in eggs one at a time, beating well after each addition.
3. Remove meat from Chicken and dice meat; save bones for Stock. Sprinkle in bottom of Pie Crust along with Swiss cheese. Pour egg mixture over all. Sprinkle with Parmesan cheese and bake for 40–50 minutes or until quiche is puffed and set.

> **Freezing Quiche**
> All quiches freeze beautifully. This is great if you have a small family; just make one quiche and you have another dinner ready. To freeze, cut quiches into individual serving sizes and place in a hard-sided freezer container. Freeze until firm, then store up to 3 months. To thaw, heat each slice in the microwave on high for 1–2 minutes.

Tomato Chicken in Buttermilk

Serves 4

- ~ **TOTAL COST:** $6.98
- ~ **CALORIES:** 309.38
- ~ **FAT:** 12.90 g
- ~ **PROTEIN:** 23.18 g
- ~ **CHOLESTEROL:** 68.46 mg
- ~ **SODIUM:** 382.01 mg

⅓ cup flour
1 teaspoon sugar
½ teaspoon salt
⅛ teaspoon pepper
½ teaspoon paprika
4 boneless, skinless chicken breasts
1 tablespoon olive oil
2 tablespoons butter
1 onion, chopped
1 (14-ounce) can diced tomatoes, drained
½ cup buttermilk
1 teaspoon dried dill weed
⅛ teaspoon pepper
½ cup sour cream
2 teaspoons cornstarch
⅓ cup grated Parmesan cheese

Buttermilk is an excellent low cost marinade ingredient that adds flavor to sauces. Save the juice from the drained tomatoes to add to spaghetti sauce or a beef broth.

1. On plate, combine flour, sugar, salt, pepper, and paprika; mix well. Roll chicken in flour mixture to coat. Heat olive oil and butter in large skillet over medium heat. Add chicken and brown on both sides, turning once, about 10 minutes. Add half of the green onions to skillet; cook for 2 minutes longer.
2. In a food processor, combine tomatoes, buttermilk, dill, and pepper; process until smooth. Pour over chicken and bring to a boil. Cover, reduce heat to low, and simmer until chicken is tender, about 20–25 minutes.
3. Add sour cream, cornstarch, and cheese and stir well. Simmer for 5–6 minutes longer to blend flavors; serve immediately over hot cooked rice.

Slow Cooker Simmered Chicken Breasts

 Serves 4

~ **TOTAL COST:** $4.40
~ **CALORIES:** 141.90
~ **FAT:** 3.07 g
~ **PROTEIN:** 26.68 g
~ **CHOLESTEROL:** 73.10 mg
~ **SODIUM:** 645.01 mg

4 bone-in, skin-on chicken breasts
1 teaspoon salt
⅛ teaspoon white pepper
½ cup water

This chicken is perfect for Raspberry Chicken Sandwiches (Chapter 14). Use it to make your own chicken salad too.

1. Sprinkle chicken with salt and pepper and arrange in 4–6 quart slow cooker. Pour water into slow cooker, cover, and cook on low, rearranging once during cooking, for 7–9 hours or until chicken is fully cooked.
2. Remove chicken to a baking dish and pour any juices remaining in slow cooker over. Cover and chill for 2–3 hours or until chicken is cold. Remove meat from chicken in large pieces and refrigerate up to 2 days, or freeze up to 3 months. Freeze skin and bones for making Chicken Stock (Chapter 6).
3. You can cook chicken thighs or drumsticks using this method too; just increase the cooking time to 8–10 hours.

Potato Chip Crusted Chicken

 Serves 4

~ **PREP TIME:** 10 minutes
~ **COOK TIME:** 25 minutes
~ **TOTAL COST:** $6.60
~ **CALORIES:** 470
~ **FAT:** 18 g
~ **PROTEIN:** 33 g
~ **CHOLESTEROL:** 63 mg
~ **SODIUM:** 378 mg

12 ounces potato chips
1 teaspoon freshly ground black pepper
2 tablespoons fresh chives, chopped
1 teaspoon dried thyme
4 boneless chicken breasts, skin removed
⅔ cup sour cream

The potato chips give a crunchy coating to this chicken, but don't add salt—there is enough on the potato chips.

1. In a food processor, chop potato chips until you have 1 cup crumbs. Mix crumbs together with pepper, chives, and thyme.
2. Preheat oven to 350°F. Coat baking dish with butter or spray with nonstick cooking spray. Lay chicken is dish and coat with sour cream, then sprinkle with potato chip mixture. Bake in oven for 25 minutes or until browned and crispy.

Quick and Easy Tip
Substitute chicken tenders for a quick and easy appetizer. Serve with barbecue sauce.

Chicken with Tomato Salsa and Green Peppers

Serves 4

- ~ **PREP TIME:** 10 minutes
- ~ **COOK TIME:** 15 minutes
- ~ **TOTAL COST:** $5.68
- ~ **CALORIES:** 420
- ~ **FAT:** 11 g
- ~ **PROTEIN:** 34 g
- ~ **CHOLESTEROL:** 6 mg
- ~ **SODIUM:** 790 mg

3 boneless chicken breast halves, skim removed
1 tablespoon olive oil
1 (15-ounce) jar mild or medium salsa
¾ cup chicken broth
½ cup green bell pepper, seeded and chopped
1 cup quick-cooking rice
½ cup Cheddar cheese, shredded

Try to keep a jar of salsa in your pantry for recipes like this!

Cut the chicken into 1-inch cubes. Heat oil in a large skillet and sauté chicken until cooked, about 8 minutes. Stir in salsa, chicken broth, and green pepper. Bring to a boil. Stir in the uncooked rice. Sprinkle with cheese, cover, and remove from heat. Let stand 5 minutes until rice is cooked.

Quick and Easy Tip
Salsa is a quick and easy way to spice up lots of dishes. Its combination of tomatoes, onions, and other ingredients is a perfect complement to rice, eggs, fish, pork, and more.

Easy-Baked Chicken Casserole

Serves 6

- ~ **PREP TIME:** 10 minutes
- ~ **COOK TIME:** 15 minutes
- ~ **TOTAL COST:** $6.97
- ~ **CALORIES:** 270
- ~ **FAT:** 15 g
- ~ **PROTEIN:** 23 g
- ~ **CHOLESTEROL:** 9 mg
- ~ **SODIUM:** 780 mg

2 cups cooked chicken, cubed
2 cups celery, sliced
½ cup almonds
½ teaspoon sea salt
½ yellow onion, finely chopped
Juice of 1 lemon
1 cup mayonnaise
½ cup Cheddar cheese, shredded
1½ cups crushed potato chips

Casseroles usually take tons of time to bake. With precooked chicken, you save about an hour of cooking time.

Preheat oven to 425°F. In lightly greased shallow quart baking dish, combine the chicken, celery, almonds, salt, onions, lemon juice, and mayonnaise. Sprinkle with cheese and potato chips. Bake for 15 minutes or until heated through.

Quick and Easy Tip
If the chicken is chopped small enough, this recipe is also great as an appetizer! Serve with additional potato chips as an appetizer.

Baked Chicken with Herb Stuffing

Serves 4

~ **PREP TIME:** 10 minutes
~ **COOK TIME:** 15 minutes
~ **TOTAL COST:** $6.99
~ **CALORIES:** 429
~ **FAT:** 17 g
~ **PROTEIN:** 54 g
~ **CHOLESTEROL:** 29 mg
~ **SODIUM:** 1596 mg

4 boneless chicken breasts, skin removed
1 (10-ounce) can cream of chicken soup
½ can water
1½ teaspoons curry powder
Juice of 1 lemon
½ cup Cheddar cheese, shredded
½ cup mayonnaise
1 (8-ounce) package herb stuffing mix

This recipe takes an hour to bake, but use that time to hang out with the family—watch a football game together or, if sunny, get outside and play some ball.

Preheat oven to 350°F. Lay chicken breasts in a 9" x 12" casserole. Combine the soup and water in a small bowl. Pour the soup mixture over chicken. Mix the remaining ingredients into the stuffing mix. Spread the stuffing mix over the chicken. Bake 1 hour. If the stuffing gets too brown, cover loosely with aluminum foil.

Quick and Easy Tip
Even though this recipe takes an hour to bake, use that baking time to do other things, like relax!

Skillet Chicken with Rice

Serves 4

~ **PREP TIME:** 10 minutes
~ **COOK TIME:** 15 minutes
~ **TOTAL COST:** $5.68
~ **CALORIES:** 420
~ **FAT:** 11 g
~ **CARBOHYDRATES:** 43 g
~ **PROTEIN:** 34 g
~ **CHOLESTEROL:** 6 mg
~ **SODIUM:** 570 mg

3 boneless chicken breast halves, skim removed
1 tablespoon olive oil
1 (15-ounce) jar mild or medium salsa
¾ cup chicken broth
½ cup green bell pepper, seeded and chopped
1 cup quick-cooking rice
Sea salt and lemon pepper to taste

Lemon pepper really does taste lemony and is a nice change to black pepper. It's great with chicken, fish, beef, and even on popcorn!

Cut the chicken into 1-inch cubes. Heat oil in large skillet and sauté chicken until cooked, about 8 minutes. Stir in salsa, chicken broth, and green pepper. Bring to a boil. Stir in the uncooked rice. Let stand, covered, 5 minutes until rice is cooked. Season with salt and lemon pepper.

Salsa!
Salsa is packed full of flavor and low in calories and fat. Use salsa to spice up eggs, grilled fish, and other poultry dishes.

Chicken Casserole with Red Bell Peppers

 Serves 6

- ~ **PREP TIME:** 10 minutes
- ~ **COOK TIME:** 15 minutes
- ~ **TOTAL COST:** $6.97
- ~ **CALORIES:** 270
- ~ **FAT:** 15 g
- ~ **CARBOHYDRATES:** 13 g
- ~ **PROTEIN:** 23 g
- ~ **CHOLESTEROL:** 39 mg
- ~ **SODIUM:** 680 mg

2 cups cooked chicken, cubed
2 cups celery, sliced
¼ cup almonds, chopped
½ teaspoon sea salt
½ yellow onion, finely chopped
Juice of 1 lemon
1 cup low-fat mayonnaise
1 red bell pepper, seeded and diced
½ cup Cheddar cheese, shredded
1½ cups crushed potato chips

Casseroles usually take tons of time to bake. With precooked chicken, you save about an hour of cooking time.

Preheat oven to 425°F. In lightly greased shallow quart baking dish, combine the chicken, celery, almonds, salt, onions, lemon juice, mayonnaise, and red bell peppers. Sprinkle with cheese and potato chips. Bake for 15 minutes or until heated through.

Lemon-Herbed Chicken

 Serves 5

- ~ **PREP TIME:** 10 minutes
- ~ **COOK TIME:** 15 minutes
- ~ **TOTAL COST:** $5.65
- ~ **CALORIES:** 398
- ~ **FAT:** 6 g
- ~ **CARBOHYDRATES:** 44 g
- ~ **PROTEIN:** 18 g
- ~ **CHOLESTEROL:** 21 mg
- ~ **SODIUM:** 671 mg

4 boneless chicken breasts, skin removed
1 (10-ounce) can cream of chicken soup
½ can water
1 teaspoon curry powder
Juice of 1 lemon
1 cup low-fat mayonnaise
1 (8-ounce) package herb stuffing mix

Baked chicken casseroles were a staple in my household growing up. They are easy to prepare and can be made ahead of time. Try cubing the chicken when making for kids.

Preheat oven to 350°F. Lay chicken breasts in a 9" x 12" casserole. Combine the soup and water in a small bowl. Pour the soup mixture over chicken. Mix the remaining ingredients into the stuffing mix. Spread the stuffing mix over the chicken. Bake 1 hour. If the stuffing gets too brown, cover loosely with aluminum foil.

Spicy Cornbread Chicken Tenders

 Serves 4

~ **PREP TIME:** 10 minutes

~ **COOK TIME:** 6 minutes

~ **TOTAL COST:** $3.85

~ **CALORIES:** 380

~ **FAT:** 9 g

~ **PROTEIN:** 28 g

~ **CHOLESTEROL:** 71 mg

~ **SODIUM:** 73 mg

1 cup plain flour
1 teaspoon sea salt
Red pepper flakes to taste
1 teaspoon baking powder
1 cup cornbread crumbs
1 egg, beaten
2 tablespoons milk
1 pound chicken tenders, cut into bite-sized pieces
Canola oil as needed, about 2 to 3 cups

Sea salt is a natural salt from the sea. It is more flavorful than iodized salt and is better for you because it is natural.

1. In a mixing bowl, combine flour, salt, pepper, and baking powder, then spread it on to parchment paper or wax paper.
2. On a separate sheet of parchment or wax paper, spread out cornbread crumbs. In a mixing bowl, beat egg and milk together using fork or wire whisk. Dredge the tenders in the flour mixture, then dip them in the egg mixture, and, lastly, coat them with breadcrumbs.
3. In a heavy-bottomed frying pan, heat ½ inch of oil to 365°F or until hot. Fry chicken tenders until golden, about 3 to 4 minutes. Drain on paper towels.

> **Quick and Easy Tip**
> To see if oil is hot enough for frying, insert spoon end of wooden spoon into oil. If the oil bubbles around the spoon, oil is ready.

Curried Chicken with Lentils

 Serves 4

- ~ **PREP TIME:** 10 minutes
- ~ **COOK TIME:** 25 minutes
- ~ **TOTAL COST:** $6.48
- ~ **CALORIES:** 250
- ~ **FAT:** 2 g
- ~ **PROTEIN:** 35 g
- ~ **CHOLESTEROL:** 4 mg
- ~ **SODIUM:** 240 mg

1 cup lentils

3 cups water

Sea salt and red pepper flakes to taste

2 cloves garlic, chopped

1 yellow onion, chopped

Juice of 1 lemon

1 teaspoon cumin

½ cup fresh Italian parsley, chopped

1 cup yogurt

1 tablespoon curry powder

Tabasco to taste

1 pound boneless chicken breasts, skin removed, cut into 1- to 2-inch cubes

Curry is a blend of other spices including turmeric and coriander and is native to India.

1. Place lentils and water in quart boiler. Bring to a boil, reduce heat, and simmer. Just before the lentils are cooked, about 25 minutes, add the salt and pepper flakes, garlic, onion, lemon juice, cumin, and parsley.
2. Turn broiler to high. In a mixing bowl, combine yogurt, curry, and Tabasco. Toss chicken to coat. Place on aluminum foil and place under broiler for 5 minutes. Turn chicken and broil an additional 5 minutes or as needed until cooked through.
3. Mix cooked chicken into the lentils and serve with rice, if desired.

Quick and Easy Tip

Use canned lentils and you'll save about 15 minutes of cooking time. The flavor is good and you have more time for family.

Grilled Turkey Cutlets with Lime

Serves 6

- ~ **PREP TIME:** 12 minutes
- ~ **COOK TIME:** 7 minutes
- ~ **TOTAL COST:** $6.48
- ~ **CALORIES:** 229
- ~ **FAT:** 4 g
- ~ **CARBOHYDRATES:** 8 g
- ~ **PROTEIN:** 28 g
- ~ **CHOLESTEROL:** 75 mg
- ~ **SODIUM:** 130 mg

2 large limes: 1 lime zested and juiced, 1 lime cut in wedges
⅓ cup plain yogurt
1 tablespoon canola oil
2 teaspoons fresh gingerroot, peeled, chopped
1 teaspoon ground cumin
1 teaspoon ground coriander
1 teaspoon sea salt
1 clove garlic, crushed
1½ pounds turkey cutlets
Fresh cilantro sprigs for garnish

The flavors of lime and cilantro compliment one another and bring life to this simple recipe. You can also add a hint of other citrus flavors, such as lemon and orange juice or zest, for another layer of flavor.

1. Heat grill. Place zest and juice in a large bowl. Add yogurt, oil, ginger, cumin, coriander, salt, and garlic to bowl with zest and juice. Mix until blended.
2. Add the turkey cutlets to the bowl with the yogurt mixture, stirring to coat the cutlets, but do not marinate as their texture will become mealy.
3. Place the turkey cutlets on grill. Cook cutlets 5 to 7 minutes until they just lose their pink color throughout. Serve with lime wedges. Garnish with cilantro sprigs.

Turkey Cutlets

Turkey cutlets are a choice cut that are perfect for the grill as they are not typically as thick as chicken and, therefore, take less time to cook.

Grilled Turkey with Toasted Almonds

 Serves 6

- ~ **PREP TIME:** 10 minutes
- ~ **COOK TIME:** 10 minutes
- ~ **TOTAL COST:** $5.32
- ~ **CALORIES:** 278
- ~ **FAT:** 9 g
- ~ **CARBOHYDRATES:** 14 g
- ~ **PROTEIN:** 16 g
- ~ **CHOLESTEROL:** 8 mg
- ~ **SODIUM:** 528 mg

2 tablespoons olive oil
1 cup sliced carrots
2 cups grilled turkey breast
1 (14-ounce) jar turkey gravy
½ cup low-fat milk
½ cup nonfat sour cream
Sea salt and black pepper to taste
½ cup whole almonds, toasted

Gravy can be tricky to make, so using premade gravy is an easy way to get the flavor and consistency you desire without going through a great hassle. Premade gravy is also a good trick to use for your Thanksgiving turkey. Use it as a base, adding drippings from your cooked turkey before serving.

In heavy saucepan over medium heat, heat oil. Add carrots and cook until crisp-tender, about 5 minutes. Add chopped turkey and stir. Add gravy, milk, sour cream, salt, and pepper, and stir to combine. Bring to a simmer and cook for 5 minutes until turkey is heated through. Top with almonds and serve.

Money-Saving, Time-Saving Tip
This is a perfect recipe for leftover Thanksgiving turkey. Not only do you get at least two meals in one, using leftovers saves on cooking time!

Skillet Picadillo with Turkey

Serves 6

- **PREP TIME:** 10 minutes
- **COOK TIME:** 15 minutes
- **TOTAL COST:** $6.78
- **CALORIES:** 222
- **FAT:** 11 g
- **CARBOHYDRATES:** 14 g
- **PROTEIN:** 25 g
- **CHOLESTEROL:** 35 mg
- **SODIUM:** 232 mg

2 tablespoons olive oil
1½ pounds ground turkey
1 clove fresh garlic, minced
½ teaspoon all-purpose seasoning
1 cup yellow onions, chopped
1 large tomato, diced
1 tablespoon tomato paste
2 teaspoons cumin
¼ cup fresh cilantro, leaves chopped
¼ cup golden raisins
1 cup baking potatoes, cut into 1-inch cubes
1 cup water

Picadillo is a Cuban dish usually made with ground beef. This lean turkey version is lower in fat and calories but maintains the delicious flavor.

1. In large skillet over medium heat, heat 1 tablespoon olive oil. Add turkey, olive oil, garlic, and all-purpose seasoning to skillet. Cook on medium high for 5 to 8 minutes, using a spatula to stir and chop turkey meat.
2. Add onions, tomatoes, tomato paste, cumin, and cilantro to skillet. Cook for 5 minutes on medium heat.
3. Add raisins, potatoes, and water. Simmer for another 8 to 10 minutes or until potatoes are tender.

Chicken Fried Rice

Serves 4

- **TOTAL COST:** $3.56
- **CALORIES:** 460.58
- **FAT:** 11.02 g
- **PROTEIN:** 18.45 g
- **CHOLESTEROL:** 124.25 mg
- **SODIUM:** 699.95 mg

1 ½ cups long-grain white rice
2 ½ cups water
2 tablespoons vegetable oil
1 onion, chopped
1 cup shredded carrot
2 eggs
1 Slow Cooker Simmered Chicken Breast (Chapter 7), diced
1 cup frozen peas
3 tablespoons soy sauce
2 tablespoons chicken broth
⅛ teaspoon pepper

Freezing freshly cooked rice helps dry it out so the finished product has nice separate grains. You could use brown rice for more nutrition; it cooks in about 30 minutes and the dish will cost $3.76.

1. Combine rice and water in heavy saucepan. Bring to boil over high heat. Reduce heat to low, cover pan, and cook rice until almost tender but still firm in the center, about 15 minutes. Spread rice on a baking sheet and freeze for 10 minutes.
2. When rice is done, heat vegetable oil in wok or large skillet. Add onion and carrot; stir-fry until tender, about 5 minutes. Add eggs and cook until set but still moist. Add Chicken, peas, and rice and stir-fry until hot.
3. Sprinkle with soy sauce, chicken broth, and pepper and stir-fry for 1–2 minutes, then serve immediately.

Sautéed Chicken with Roasted Garlic Sauce

- **TOTAL COST:** $6.96
- **CALORIES:** 247.01
- **FAT:** 7.78 g
- **PROTEIN:** 27.51 g
- **CHOLESTEROL:** 71.85 mg
- **SODIUM:** 358.61 mg

1 head Roasted Garlic (Chapter 2)
⅓ cup chicken broth
½ teaspoon dried oregano leaves
4 (4-ounce) boneless, skinless chicken breasts
¼ cup flour
¼ teaspoon salt
⅛ teaspoon pepper
1½ tablespoons olive oil

When roasted, garlic turns sweet and nutty. Combined with tender sautéed chicken, this makes a memorable meal.

1. Squeeze garlic cloves from the skins and combine in small saucepan with chicken broth and oregano leaves.
2. On shallow plate, combine flour, salt, and pepper. Dip chicken into this mixture to coat.
3. In large skillet, heat the olive oil. At the same time, place the saucepan with the garlic mixture over medium heat and bring to a simmer. Add the chicken to the hot olive oil; cook for 5 minutes without moving. Then carefully turn chicken and cook for 4–7 minutes longer until chicken is thoroughly cooked.
4. Stir garlic sauce with wire whisk until blended. Serve with the chicken.

Very Lemon Chicken

- **TOTAL COST:** $6.51
- **CALORIES:** 276.41
- **FAT:** 5.87 g
- **PROTEIN:** 27.86 g
- **CHOLESTEROL:** 92.14 mg
- **SODIUM:** 433.26 mg

4 boneless, skinless chicken breasts
2 tablespoons butter, melted
⅓ cup lemon juice
2 tablespoons honey
2 tablespoons apple jelly
1 tablespoon grated lemon zest
1 teaspoon dried thyme leaves
1 onion, chopped
2 cloves garlic, minced
½ teaspoon salt
⅛ teaspoon white pepper
½ teaspoon paprika

Lemon juice and lemon zest combine to make extremely tender chicken that is very well flavored.

1. Place chicken in 9" × 13" glass baking dish. In a small bowl, combine butter, lemon juice, honey, jelly, lemon zest, thyme, onion, and garlic; mix well. Pour over the chicken, cover, and refrigerate for 4 to 8 hours, turning chicken occasionally.
2. Preheat oven to 325°F. Sprinkle chicken with salt, pepper, and paprika. Cover dish with foil and bake for 30 minutes. Uncover and bake for 20–30 minutes longer or until chicken is thoroughly cooked. Serve immediately.

Chicken Cabbage Stir-Fry

Serves 4

~ **TOTAL COST:** $6.72

~ **CALORIES:** 307.21

~ **FAT:** 8.90 g

~ **PROTEIN:** 17.96 g

~ **CHOLESTEROL:** 35.57 mg

~ **SODIUM:** 413.61 mg

2 (4-ounce) boneless, skinless chicken breasts
2 tablespoons cornstarch
2 tablespoons lemon juice
2 tablespoons low-sodium soy sauce
½ teaspoon ground ginger
1 cup chicken broth
2 tablespoons peanut oil
4 cups shredded cabbage
1 onion, chopped
1 green bell pepper, sliced
1½ cups frozen peas, thawed

The combination of cabbage, chicken, and onion is delicious and very healthy.

1. Cut chicken into 1-inch pieces. In small bowl, combine cornstarch, lemon juice, soy sauce, and chicken broth. Add chicken and let stand for 15 minutes.
2. Heat oil in large skillet or wok. Drain chicken, reserving marinade. Add chicken to skillet; stir-fry until almost cooked, about 4 minutes. Remove chicken to a plate.
3. Add onion to skillet; stir-fry until onion is crisp-tender, about 4 minutes. Add bell pepper and cabbage; cook until cabbage wilts, about 4 minutes.
4. Stir marinade and add to skillet along with chicken and peas. Stir-fry until sauce bubbles and thickens and chicken is thoroughly cooked. Serve over hot cooked rice.

Stir-Frying

Stir-frying is one of the healthiest and quickest ways to cook. Once all the ingredients are prepared, the method takes 10 minutes or less. But all of the food must be prepared before the actual cooking begins. There is no time to chop or slice vegetables once the wok is hot and you start to stir-fry.

Kung Pao Chicken

Serves 4

~ **PREP TIME:** 10 minutes
~ **COOK TIME:** 15 minutes
~ **TOTAL COST:** $6.92
~ **CALORIES:** 260
~ **FAT:** 16 g
~ **PROTEIN:** 17 g
~ **CHOLESTEROL:** 70 mg
~ **SODIUM:** 338 mg

3 boneless chicken breasts, skin removed
1½ tablespoons peanut oil
1 dried red chili
⅓ cup peanuts
2 tablespoons water
2 tablespoons dry sherry
1 tablespoon soy sauce
1 teaspoon sugar
1 tablespoon chili sauce
1 teaspoon fresh ginger, peeled and chopped
2 cloves garlic, minced
2 scallions, chopped
2 teaspoons rice or apple cider vinegar
1 teaspoon sesame oil
4 cups cooked white rice

This recipe calls for peanut and sesame oils, both of which are good oils to have on hand for specialty dishes like this one.

Dice the chicken into 1-inch cubes. Heat the oil in a wok or skillet and add the chili. Add the chicken and peanuts and stir-fry until the chicken is cooked. Add the remaining ingredients, except the sesame oil and rice, and bring to a boil. Cook for a few minutes. Add the sesame oil and serve over rice.

Quick and Easy Tip
Plan your weekly meals ahead of time, perhaps on Sunday afternoon. Then if you are serving several dishes during the week that need rice, make the rice ahead of time and keep in the refrigerator.

Chicken Cutlets Parmesan

 Serves 4

- ~ **TOTAL COST:** $6.86
- ~ **CALORIES:** 305.49
- ~ **FAT:** 13.98 g
- ~ **PROTEIN:** 34.77 g
- ~ **CHOLESTEROL:** 130.13 mg
- ~ **SODIUM:** 559.86 mg

4 (4-ounce) boneless, skinless chicken breasts
1 egg
3 tablespoons dry breadcrumbs
⅛ teaspoon pepper
4 tablespoons grated Parmesan cheese
2 tablespoons vegetable oil
1 (8-ounce) can tomato sauce
1 teaspoon dried Italian seasoning
½ cup finely shredded part-skim mozzarella cheese

This classic dish is usually smothered in cheese, with deep-fried breaded chicken. This lighter version is just as delicious.

1. Preheat oven to 350°F. Spray a 2-quart baking dish with nonstick cooking spray and set aside. Place chicken on waxed paper, smooth side down, and cover with more waxed paper. Gently pound until chicken is about ⅓-inch thick.
2. In shallow bowl, beat egg until foamy. On plate, combine breadcrumbs, pepper, and Parmesan. Dip the chicken cutlets into the egg, then into the breadcrumb mixture, turning to coat.
3. In large saucepan, heat oil over medium heat. Add chicken cutlets; brown on both sides, about 2–3 minutes per side. Remove from pan and place in prepared baking dish. Add tomato sauce and Italian seasoning to saucepan; bring to a boil.
4. Pour sauce over cutlets in baking pan and top with mozzarella cheese. Bake for 20–30 minutes or until sauce bubbles and cheese melts and begins to brown. Serve with pasta, if desired.

Teriyaki Chicken

Serves 4

- ~ **PREP TIME:** 10 minutes
- ~ **MARINATE:** overnight
- ~ **COOK TIME:** 20 minutes
- ~ **TOTAL COST:** $6.58
- ~ **CALORIES:** 292
- ~ **FAT:** 12 g
- ~ **PROTEIN:** 32 g
- ~ **CHOLESTEROL:** 24 mg
- ~ **SODIUM:** 1083 mg

½ cup Italian dressing
½ cup teriyaki sauce
5 boneless chicken breast halves, skin removed

Italian dressing is useful for all sorts of things: pasta salad, poaching chicken breasts, and even for marinating steaks. It's a great trick to add lots of flavor without all the preparation!

Combine the Italian dressing and teriyaki sauce. Marinate the chicken in this mixture overnight. Grill over hot coals for about 20 minutes, turning chicken after 10 minutes. Cook until the meat is no longer pink and the juices run clear.

> **Quick and Easy Tip**
> Marinating foods is easy and infuses flavor into your protein product. This recipe calls for marinating overnight, making for super easy cooking the next day.

Hot-and-Spicy Peanut Thighs

Serves 4

- ~ **TOTAL COST:** $4.86
- ~ **CALORIES:** 332.41
- ~ **FAT:** 19.55 g
- ~ **PROTEIN:** 28.12 g
- ~ **CHOLESTEROL:** 94.26 mg
- ~ **SODIUM:** 429.88 mg

2 tablespoons peanut oil
4 (4-ounce) chicken thighs
½ cup barbecue sauce
1 tablespoon chili powder
⅛ teaspoon pepper
½ cup chopped peanuts

Serve this easy and spicy recipe with whole grain cornbread.

1. Preheat oven to 350°F. Drizzle a roasting pan with peanut oil and set aside. Pound chicken slightly, to ⅓-inch thickness.
2. In shallow bowl, combine barbecue sauce and chili powder and mix well. Dip chicken into sauce, then dip one side into peanuts. Place, peanut side-up, in prepared pan.
3. Bake for 30–40 minutes, or until chicken is thoroughly cooked. Serve immediately.

> **Coating for Poultry**
> When you're baking poultry that has a nut or bread-crumb coating, it's usually best to coat only the top side of the meat. The coating underneath can become mushy and fall off because of the moisture in the chicken. If you want to coat both sides, it's best to pan-fry or sauté the chicken.

Asian Chicken Stir-Fry

Serves 4

- ~ **TOTAL COST:** $6.89
- ~ **CALORIES:** 288.42
- ~ **FAT:** 13.42 g
- ~ **PROTEIN:** 21.07 g
- ~ **CHOLESTEROL:** 33.11 mg
- ~ **SODIUM:** 460.04 mg

2 (4-ounce) boneless, skinless chicken breasts
½ cup chicken broth
2 tablespoons low-sodium soy sauce
2 tablespoons cornstarch
2 tablespoons peanut oil
1 onion, sliced
3 cloves garlic, minced
1 tablespoon grated ginger root
1 yellow summer squash, sliced
1 cup sliced mushrooms
1 cup frozen peas
⅓ cup chopped unsalted peanuts

Yellow summer squash is a thin-skinned squash like zucchini. It has a mild, sweet flavor and can be found in any supermarket.

1. Cut chicken into strips and set aside. In small bowl, combine chicken broth, soy sauce, cornstarch, and sherry and set aside.
2. In large skillet or wok, heat peanut oil over medium-high heat. Add chicken; stir-fry until almost cooked, about 3–4 minutes. Remove to plate. Add onion, garlic, and ginger root to skillet; stir-fry for 4 minutes longer. Then add squash and mushrooms; stir-fry for 2 minutes longer.
3. Stir chicken broth mixture and add to skillet along with chicken and peas. Stir-fry for 3–4 minutes longer or until chicken is thoroughly cooked and sauce is thickened and bubbly. Sprinkle with peanuts and serve immediately.

Marinated Ginger Chicken

Serves 4

- ~ **PREP TIME:** 12 minutes
- ~ **MARINATE:** 4 hours
- ~ **COOK TIME:** 20 minutes
- ~ **TOTAL COST:** $4.32
- ~ **CALORIES:** 370
- ~ **FAT:** 9 g
- ~ **PROTEIN:** 20 g
- ~ **CHOLESTEROL:** 14 mg
- ~ **SODIUM:** 660 mg

1 (2- to 3-pound) whole frying chicken, cut into pieces, or 1 package whole, cut-up chicken pieces
½ cup lemon juice
½ cup canola oil
¼ cup soy sauce
1 teaspoon grated gingerroot or 1 tablespoon ground ginger
1 teaspoon onion salt
¼ teaspoon garlic powder

Fresh gingerroot is best for this recipe and is relatively inexpensive. Buy some fresh root and keep what you don't use in your freezer!

1. Place chicken in a shallow baking dish. In a small bowl, combine the lemon juice, oil, soy sauce, ginger, onion, and garlic powder. Pour over the chicken. Cover and refrigerate at least 4 hours or overnight, turning occasionally.
2. Grill or broil for about 20 minutes, turning after 10 minutes. Cook until the meat is no longer pink, basting frequently with marinade.

Quick and Easy Tip
Marinating is an easy way to infuse flavor into foods without a long cooking time. Here, soy sauce and ginger combine for spectacular flavor.

Chicken Picatta

Serves 4

- **PREP TIME:** 12 minutes
- **COOK TIME:** 20 minutes
- **TOTAL COST:** $5.98
- **CALORIES:** 202
- **FAT:** 9 g
- **PROTEIN:** 19 g
- **CHOLESTEROL:** 50 mg
- **SODIUM:** 721 mg

4 boneless, chicken breast halves, skin removed
Sea salt and black pepper to taste
2 tablespoons butter
1 teaspoon olive oil
½ cup chicken broth
¼ cup vermouth
Juice of 1 lemon
1 tablespoon capers, drained and rinsed
Lemon slices for garnish, if desired

Picatta is a cooking style using lemon, capers, and wine and is traditional to Italian cuisine. You can also substitute veal or pork.

1. Pat chicken dry. Season with salt and pepper. Melt butter with oil in a large heavy skillet over medium-high heat. Add the chicken and cook until springy to the touch, about 4 minutes per side. Remove from the skillet; keep warm.
2. Increase heat to high. Stir broth and vermouth into the skillet. Boil until reduced by half, scraping up any browned bits. Remove from heat. Mix in lemon juice and capers. Place chicken on plates and pour sauce over the chicken. Garnish with lemon slices.

Quick and Easy Tip
Vermouth is substituted for white wine here. Add a side of pasta for a heartier meal.

Lemon Chicken with Broccoli

Serves 4

- **PREP TIME:** 10 minutes
- **COOK TIME:** 20 minutes
- **TOTAL COST:** $6.89
- **CALORIES:** 382
- **FAT:** 11 g
- **PROTEIN:** 28 g
- **CHOLESTEROL:** 6 mg
- **SODIUM:** 760 mg

1 tablespoon olive oil
4 boneless chicken breast halves, skin removed
1 (10-ounce) can cream of broccoli soup
¼ cup low-fat milk or whole milk
Juice of 1 lemon
Pinch black pepper
4 thin lemon slices

Using the cream of broccoli soup as a base saves time but keeps the flavor of the dish.

Heat the oil in a skillet. Sauté the chicken breasts about 10 minutes, until browned on both sides. Pour off the fat. Combine the soup, milk, lemon juice, and pepper. Pour over the chicken. Top each chicken piece with a slice of lemon. Reduce heat to low and cover. Simmer 5 to 10 minutes until chicken is tender, stirring occasionally.

Quick and Easy Tip
Add in some fresh steamed broccoli florets, if you wish, for an even more nutritious meal without tons of extra time and money.

Curried Chicken Pot Pie

 Serves 6

- ~ **TOTAL COST:** $6.91
- ~ **CALORIES:** 493.95
- ~ **FAT:** 27.17 g
- ~ **PROTEIN:** 20.37 g
- ~ **CHOLESTEROL:** 65.49 mg
- ~ **SODIUM:** 857.15 mg

3 tablespoons butter
1 onion, chopped
¼ cup all-purpose flour
½ teaspoon salt
⅛ teaspoon pepper
1 tablespoon curry powder
1 cup Chicken Stock (Chapter 6)
⅓ cup light cream
2 Slow Cooker Simmered Chicken Breasts (this chapter), cubed
1 carrot, sliced
1 cup frozen peas, thawed
1 cup frozen hash brown potatoes, thawed
1 cup cubed Swiss cheese
1 Angel Pie Crust (Chapter 15), unbaked

Adding curry powder to chicken pot pie elevates it to a new realm. This comforting food is delicious for a cold winter's night.

1. Preheat oven to 400°F. In large saucepan, melt butter and add onion; cook and stir until crisp—tender, about 4 minutes. Sprinkle with flour, salt, and pepper, and curry powder; cook and stir until bubbly, about 3 minutes.
2. Add Chicken Stock and light cream to saucepan; cook and stir until sauce is thickened. Remove from heat and add cubed Chicken, carrots, peas, and potatoes. Fold in cheese.
3. Pour mixture into a 10-inch deep dish pie plate. Top with the Pie Crust and cut slits in the top to let steam escape. Bake for 25–35 minutes or until chicken mixture is bubbling and Crust is golden brown. Serve immediately.

Chicken Potato Pie

Serves 6

- **TOTAL COST:** $6.70
- **CALORIES:** 371.80
- **FAT:** 19.63 g
- **PROTEIN:** 22.15 g
- **CHOLESTEROL:** 187.41 mg
- **SODIUM:** 715.22 mg

For crust:

½ cup finely chopped onion
1 tablespoon olive oil
2 cups frozen hash brown potatoes, thawed
1 egg

For filling:

2 Slow Cooker Simmered Chicken Breasts (this chapter), cubed
1 cup frozen peas, thawed
1 cup shredded Swiss cheese
3 eggs
½ cup evaporated milk
½ teaspoon dried marjoram
½ teaspoon salt
⅛ teaspoon white pepper

Hash brown potatoes form a crust in this delicious main-dish pie. To serve immediately, bake as directed. Let the pie stand 10 minutes before slicing.

1. Preheat oven to 375°F. In heavy skillet, sauté onion in olive oil until tender. Remove from heat. Drain potatoes very well and add to skillet along with first egg. Mix well and press into well-greased 9-inch pie pan. Bake at 375°F for 15–20 minutes, until crust begins to brown.
2. Place chicken and peas in potato crust and sprinkle with cheese. In medium bowl beat eggs, milk, marjoram, salt, and pepper until blended. Pour egg mixture over cheese.
3. Bake at 375°F for 25–35 minutes, until filling is puffed and set. Run knife around edge of pie pan to loosen crust, then slice to serve.

Turkey Pot Pie

Serves 4

- **PREP TIME:** 15 minutes
- **COOK TIME:** 14 minutes
- **TOTAL COST:** $6.94
- **CALORIES:** 253
- **FAT:** 6 g
- **PROTEIN:** 26 g
- **CHOLESTEROL:** 57 mg
- **SODIUM:** 943 mg

1 tablespoon butter
½ yellow onion, diced
½ cup celery, chopped
1 can turkey or chicken gravy
¼ cup water
1 (10-ounce) package frozen mixed vegetables
1 cup turkey breasts, cut into cubes
¼ teaspoon black pepper
¼ teaspoon marjoram
1 can refrigerated biscuits

Pot pie is a wonderful dish for chilly days.

1. Preheat the oven to 400°F. In a medium oven-proof skillet, heat the butter over medium heat; sauté the onion and celery in the butter about 3 minutes. Stir in the gravy, water, vegetables, turkey, pepper, and marjoram. Bring to a boil, then remove from the heat.
2. Arrange the biscuits on top of the mixture. Bake 12 to 14 minutes, or until the biscuits are golden brown.

Quick and Easy Tip
Refrigerated biscuits make this dish the simplest ever.

Indian-Spiced Turkey

Serves 6

- **PREP TIME:** 12 minutes
- **COOK TIME:** 7 minutes
- **TOTAL COST:** $6.54
- **CALORIES:** 229
- **FAT:** 4 g
- **PROTEIN:** 28 g
- **CHOLESTEROL:** 75 mg
- **SODIUM:** 130 mg

2 large limes
⅓ cup plain yogurt
1 tablespoon canola oil
2 teaspoons fresh gingerroot, peeled and chopped
1 teaspoon ground cumin
1 teaspoon ground coriander
1 teaspoon sea salt
1 clove garlic, crushed
1½ pounds turkey cutlets
Fresh cilantro sprigs for garnish

Turkey cutlets are a choice cut that are perfect for the grill as they are not typically as thick as chicken and therefore take less time to cook.

1. Prepare a fire in a charcoal grill. Grate the peel and extract the juice from 1 lime. Place 1 teaspoon of grated peel and 1 tablespoon juice in a large bowl. Cut the other lime into wedges and set aside. Add yogurt, oil, ginger, cumin, coriander, salt, and garlic to the lime peel and juice, and mix until blended.
2. Just before grilling, add the turkey cutlets to the bowl with the yogurt mixture, stirring to coat the cutlets. Do not let the cutlets marinate in the yogurt mixture, as their texture will become mealy.
3. Place the turkey cutlets on the grill over medium-hot coals. Cook the cutlets 5 to 7 minutes, until they just lose their pink color throughout. Serve with lime wedges. Garnish with cilantro sprigs.

Cuban Skillet Turkey

 Serves 6

- ~ **PREP TIME:** 10 minutes
- ~ **COOK TIME:** 15 minutes
- ~ **TOTAL COST:** $6.78
- ~ **CALORIES:** 222
- ~ **FAT:** 11 g
- ~ **PROTEIN:** 25 g
- ~ **CHOLESTEROL:** 35 mg
- ~ **SODIUM:** 232 mg

2 tablespoons olive oil
1½ pounds ground turkey
1 clove fresh garlic, minced
½ teaspoon all-purpose seasoning
1 cup yellow onions, chopped
1 large tomato, diced
1 tablespoon tomato paste
2 teaspoons cumin
¼ cup cilantro, chopped
¼ cup raisins
1 cup baking potatoes, cubed
1 cup water

This Cuban dish, sometimes called picadillo, is typically made with ground beef. It's often used for stuffed potatoes and tacos and is commonly served with mixed vegetables.

1. In a large skillet over medium heat, heat 1 tablespoon olive oil. Add turkey, olive oil, garlic, and all-purpose seasoning to skillet. Cook on medium high for 5 to 8 minutes, using a spatula to stir and chop turkey meat.
2. Add onions, tomatoes, tomato paste, cumin, and cilantro to skillet. Cook for 5 minutes on medium heat.
3. Add raisins, potatoes, and water. Simmer for another 8 to 10 minutes.

> **Quick and Easy Tip**
> Serve this dish with Grilled Bananas with Honey (Chapter 15).

Baked Turkey Sausage with Zucchini

 Serves 6

~ **PREP TIME:** 10 minutes
~ **COOK TIME:** 40 minutes
~ **TOTAL COST:** $6.92
~ **CALORIES:** 231
~ **FAT:** 7 g
~ **PROTEIN:** 17 g
~ **CHOLESTEROL:** 51 mg
~ **SODIUM:** 680 mg

2 cups baking potatoes, cubed
2 cups turkey sausage, sliced
1 zucchini, sliced
1 yellow onion, chopped
½ cup chicken broth
½ teaspoon sea salt
¼ teaspoon black pepper
2 teaspoons plain flour
1 clove fresh garlic, minced
1 cup shredded mozzarella cheese

Sausages are spiced meats typically used for their powerful flavor. Substituting turkey sausage for your regular sausage is a healthy alternative that doesn't compromise flavor.

1. Coat a 9" x 13" baking dish with cooking spray or butter.
2. In a bowl, mix all ingredients except for mozzarella. Mix well and pour into sprayed dish. Top with mozzarella and cover with foil.
3. Bake at 365°F for 30 to 35 minutes.

Mom's Turkey Meatloaf

Serves 4

~ **TOTAL COST:** $5.26
~ **CALORIES:** 306.23
~ **FAT:** 15.95 g
~ **PROTEIN:** 23.85 g
~ **CHOLESTEROL:** 162.29 mg
~ **SODIUM:** 522.85 mg

⅓ cup chopped onion
⅓ cup chopped mushrooms
3 cloves garlic, minced
2 tablespoons butter
¼ cup dry bread crumbs
¼ cup evaporated milk
1 egg
½ teaspoon salt
⅛ teaspoon white pepper
½ teaspoon dried marjoram leaves
1 pound ground turkey, light and dark meat

This tender loaf is full of flavor. To serve without freezing, let fully cooked meatloaf stand, covered, 10 minutes before slicing.

1. Preheat oven to 350°F. In heavy skillet, cook onions, mushrooms, and garlic in olive oil until vegetables are tender. Remove from heat and set aside.
2. In large bowl, combine bread crumbs, milk, egg, salt, pepper, and marjoram and mix well. Add sautéed vegetable mixture and stir to blend. Add ground turkey and mix gently with hands.
3. Form mixture into oblong loaf and place on baking pan. Bake at 350°F for 50–60 minutes, until instant-read thermometer measures 170°F. Remove from oven, cover with foil, and let stand for 10 minutes, then slice to serve.

Oven-Baked Turkey with Fresh Herbs

Serves 6

~ **PREP TIME:** 10 minutes
~ **COOK TIME:** 25 minutes
~ **TOTAL COST:** $6.72
~ **CALORIES:** 263
~ **FAT:** 11 g
~ **CARBOHYDRATES:** 22 g
~ **PROTEIN:** 17 g
~ **CHOLESTEROL:** 51 mg
~ **SODIUM:** 500 mg

1 clove fresh garlic, minced
½ teaspoon all-purpose seasoning
1 cup yellow onions, chopped
4 cups bread stuffing
½ cup carrots, chopped
½ cup celery, chopped
1 cup cremini or button mushrooms, sliced
2 cups turkey sausage, sliced
1 cup chicken broth
1 tablespoon fresh Italian parsley, chopped
1 teaspoon fresh sage, leaves chopped
1 teaspoon fresh thyme, leaves chopped
2 large eggs

You can also remove the sausage from the casing, mix with the other ingredients and use it as a stuffing for a whole chicken. Or after baking, use this mix to stuff tomatoes or red bell peppers.

1. Preheat oven to 375°F. Mix all ingredients together well in a large bowl.
2. Coat a 9" x 13" baking dish with nonstick spray. Pour mixture into the dish and cover with foil. Bake for 25 minutes.
3. Remove foil and bake for another 5 minutes or until top is golden brown.

Nutty Chicken Fingers

Serves 4

~ **TOTAL COST:** $5.98
~ **CALORIES:** 354.56
~ **FAT:** 19.07 g
~ **PROTEIN:** 35.70 g
~ **CHOLESTEROL:** 69.51 mg
~ **SODIUM:** 298.97 mg

½ cup crushed cornflake crumbs
½ cup finely chopped walnuts
2 tablespoons chopped flat-leaf parsley
½ teaspoon garlic salt
¼ teaspoon pepper
4 boneless, skinless chicken breasts
3 tablespoons buttermilk

These little sticks of chicken are great for kids. Serve them with a dipping sauce by combining mayonnaise and mustard, or ketchup with a bit of salsa.

1. Preheat oven to 400°F. In shallow dish, combine crumbs, pecans, parsley, garlic salt, and pepper and mix well.
2. Cut chicken into strips about 3 inches long and ½-inch wide. Dip the chicken in the buttermilk, then roll in the crumb mixture to coat. Place in a 15" × 10" jelly roll pan.
3. Bake until chicken is tender and juices run clear when pierced with a fork, turning once halfway through cooking, about 12–15 minutes. Serve at once with a dipping sauce.

How to Chop Nuts

There are several ways to chop nuts. You can use a food processor, adding a bit of flour so the nuts don't stick. Or crush them with a chef's knife. And then there are nut choppers, which you can find at grocery stores.

Turkey Scallopini with Mascarpone

 Serves 5

~ **PREP TIME:** 10 minutes

~ **COOK TIME:** 35 minutes

~ **TOTAL COST:** $6.98

~ **CALORIES:** 340

~ **FAT:** 11 g

~ **CARBOHYDRATES:** 27 g

~ **PROTEIN:** 32 g

~ **CHOLESTEROL:** 49 mg

~ **SODIUM:** 364 mg

1 tablespoon olive oil

2 pounds boneless, skinless turkey breasts

Sea salt and black pepper to taste

2 yellow onions, chopped

1 stick unsalted butter

½ cup plain flour

4 cups low-fat milk

2 cups nonfat sour cream

1 cup mascarpone cheese

Mascarpone is Italian-style cream cheese and is most commonly used in making Italian desserts such as tiramisù.

1. Preheat oven to 400°F. Grease a large roasting pan with oil. Slice the turkey into thin scalloppini-like portions, and season with pepper. Place onions and turkey in roasting pan. Cover and roast for 20 minutes. Uncover and continue roasting for another 10 to 15 minutes.
2. While turkey is roasting, make the cheese sauce by melting butter in large saucepan over medium heat. Sprinkle in flour and stir with a wooden spoon. Whisk in the milk and sour cream, stirring constantly. Simmer until the sauce thickens, about 10 minutes. Remove from heat and stir in mascarpone cheese.
3. To serve, place roasted turkey on platter and drizzle with cheese sauce. Serve remaining sauce on the side.

Breaded Chicken with Mozzarella

 Serves 4

- ~ **TOTAL COST:** $6.63
- ~ **CALORIES:** 350.24
- ~ **FAT:** 17.28 g
- ~ **PROTEIN:** 38.07 g
- ~ **CHOLESTEROL:** 104.33 mg
- ~ **SODIUM:** 453.17 mg

4 boneless, skinless chicken breast halves
3 tablespoons low-fat buttermilk
3 tablespoons dry bread crumbs
¼ cup grated Parmesan cheese
1 teaspoon dried basil leaves
1 tablespoon olive oil
2 tablespoons butter
1 cup shredded part-skim mozzarella cheese
4 (½-inch) tomato slices

This super quick recipe is easy and delicious, especially when paired with a simple green salad and some buttered pasta. It also works for a laid-back lunch with guests.

1. Place chicken, smooth side down, between waxed paper. Working from the center to the edges, pound gently with a meat mallet or rolling pin until meat is ⅛ inch thick. Brush chicken with buttermilk and let stand for 10 minutes.
2. On plate, combine bread crumbs, Parmesan cheese, and basil leaves. Dip chicken into bread crumb mixture to coat both sides, pressing to adhere.
3. In a medium skillet, heat olive oil and butter over medium heat. Add chicken and sauté, turning once, until golden brown and cooked through, about 7–9 minutes total.
4. Reduce heat to low. Top chicken with mozzarella cheese and tomato. Cover pan and cook for 1 minute, then serve immediately.

> **Doubling Recipes**
>
> You can double most cooking recipes—that is, soups, broiled and grilled meats, and casseroles. Don't try to double baking recipes because they usually won't work. If you do double or even triple a recipe, be careful with seasonings. Use less than double and then add more if you think the recipe needs it.

Yogurt Chicken Paprika

 Serves 4

~ **TOTAL COST:** $6.23
~ **CALORIES:** 311.74
~ **FAT:** 13.09 g
~ **PROTEIN:** 31.20 g
~ **CHOLESTEROL:** 92.95 mg
~ **SODIUM:** 475.05 mg

4 boneless, skinless chicken breasts
⅛ teaspoon pepper
½ teaspoon salt
¼ cup flour
1 tablespoon olive oil
2 tablespoons butter
1 onion, diced
½ cup fat-free chicken broth
1 tablespoon lemon juice
2 tablespoons cornstarch
1 cup plain yogurt
1 teaspoon paprika

Yogurt and paprika are a classic combination when cooked with chicken. Serve this over brown rice.

1. Season chicken with salt and pepper. Roll in the flour to coat. In a large skillet, heat oil and butter over medium heat. Add chicken and brown on both sides, about 10 minutes total. Add onion, chicken broth, and lemon juice; bring to a simmer. Cover and simmer until tender and thoroughly cooked, about 10–12 minutes.
2. Meanwhile, combine cornstarch, yogurt, and paprika in a medium bowl. When chicken is cooked, remove from pan and drain off and discard half of the liquid in pan. Add yogurt mixture to pan drippings and bring to a simmer.
3. Simmer over low heat for 5 minutes, then return chicken to the pan. Simmer for another 3–4 minutes until sauce is slightly thickened. Serve immediately.

Chow Mein Chicken Salad

Serves 4

~ **TOTAL COST:** $6.28
~ **CALORIES:** 440.48
~ **FAT:** 18.03 g
~ **PROTEIN:** 27.16 g
~ **CHOLESTEROL:** 59.32 mg
~ **SODIUM:** 830.95 mg

4 large cabbage leaves
4 cups chopped cabbage
½ (8-ounce) package chow mein noodles
1 cup shredded carrots
3 Slow Cooker Simmered Chicken Breasts (this chapter)
1½ cups frozen peas, crisp thawed and drained
1 cucumber, peeled and chopped
½ cup Thousand Island salad dressing

This fresh salad is a good idea for using up leftovers after grilling chicken, and can be made with leftover turkey after Thanksgiving.

1. Line salad plates with the cabbage leaves, and top with chopped cabbage. Divide the chow mein noodles over the cabbage.
2. Top with carrots, chicken, peas, and cucumber. Drizzle with half of the dressing. Serve immediately, passing the rest of the dressing.

Chicken Avocado and Wild Rice Salad

 Serves 4

~ **PREP TIME:** 10 minutes
~ **COOK TIME:** 15 minutes
~ **CHILL:** up to 1 hour
~ **TOTAL COST:** $5.94
~ **CALORIES:** 332
~ **FAT:** 13 g
~ **PROTEIN:** 34 g
~ **CHOLESTEROL:** 93 mg
~ **SODIUM:** 365 mg

1 (4.3-ounce) package mixed white and wild rice
3 cups cooked chicken, cut into bite sized pieces
4 scallions, chopped
1 cup Italian dressing
2 ripe avocados, sliced
Juice of 1 lemon
½ cup toasted pine nuts or sliced almonds
1 cup cherry tomatoes

Wild rice adds color, flavor, and texture to this dish and is a refreshing alternative to plain white rice.

1. Prepare rice according to package directions. When rice is ready, stir in the chicken and scallions; add the dressing and toss well. Pour into a serving dish and chill for up to 1 hour.
2. Toss avocados with the lemon juice. Garnish salad with avocados, nuts, and cherry tomatoes.

Quick and Easy Tip
Certain wild rice packages take up to 45 minutes to cook. Make sure you buy quick-cooking wild rice when shopping.

Turkey Sausage Stuffing with Mushrooms

 Serves 6

~ **PREP TIME:** 10 minutes
~ **COOK TIME:** 25 minutes
~ **TOTAL COST:** $6.72
~ **CALORIES:** 263
~ **FAT:** 11 g
~ **PROTEIN:** 17 g
~ **CHOLESTEROL:** 51 mg
~ **SODIUM:** 500 mg

1 clove fresh garlic, minced
½ teaspoon all-purpose seasoning
1 yellow onion, chopped
4 cups bread stuffing
½ cup carrots, chopped
½ cup celery, chopped
1 cup cremini or button mushrooms, sliced
2 cups turkey sausage, sliced
1 cup chicken broth
1 tablespoon fresh Italian flat-leaf parsley, chopped
1 teaspoon dried or fresh sage
1 teaspoon dried thyme
2 eggs

Sometimes it can be frustrating buying fresh herbs for such a small amount needed in a recipe. If you don't have the good fortune to have a little herb garden and you only need a very small amount, such as here, then use dried herbs.

1. Mix all ingredients together well in a large bowl.
2. Coat a 9" x 13" baking dish with nonstick spray. Pour mixture into the dish and cover with foil.
4. Bake at 350°F for 25 minutes.
5. Remove foil and bake for another 5 minutes or until top is golden brown.

Southern Fried Chicken

 Serves 4

- ~ **PREP TIME:** 10 minutes
- ~ **COOK TIME:** 20 minutes
- ~ **TOTAL COST:** $6.92
- ~ **CALORIES:** 395
- ~ **FAT:** 14 g
- ~ **PROTEIN:** 35 g
- ~ **CHOLESTEROL:** 131 mg
- ~ **SODIUM:** 82 mg

1 whole chicken, cut into 8 pieces, or buy whole chicken pieces
1 cup buttermilk
1½ cups corn flour
1 teaspoon sea salt or to taste
1 teaspoon black pepper or to taste
1 teaspoon baking powder
1 egg, beaten
½ cup beer
1½ cups cornmeal
Canola oil for frying

If you don't have beer, don't worry, leave it out.

1. Place chicken in Ziploc bag with buttermilk and let rest in refrigerator while you prepare other ingredients.
2. In a large paper bag, mix together corn flour, salt, pepper, and baking powder. Add the chicken pieces to the corn flour mixture one at a time. Close the bag and shake until the chicken is well coated.
3. Separately, whisk together the egg and beer (if using, otherwise, just the egg). Spread the cornmeal on a large piece of parchment or waxed paper.
4. Bring 1 inch of oil to 365°F in a skillet or fryer. Fry the chicken for 20 to 25 minutes, turn every 4 or 5 minutes. Watch the chicken carefully to make sure it doesn't burn.

> **Quick and Easy Tip**
> Another tip for frying chicken is to preheat oven to 400°F. Fry chicken in a skillet until outer coating is crisp and browned, about 5 to 10 minutes. Then place chicken in a baking dish in oven to finish cooking, about 10 to 15 minutes.

Chicken Cacciatore

Serves 4

- ~ **PREP TIME:** 10 minutes
- ~ **COOK TIME:** 50 minutes
- ~ **TOTAL COST:** $6.94
- ~ **CALORIES:** 346
- ~ **FAT:** 6 g
- ~ **PROTEIN:** 32 g
- ~ **CHOLESTEROL:** 95 mg
- ~ **SODIUM:** 451 mg

1 cup plain flour
Sea salt and black pepper
1 teaspoon oregano, crumbled
¼ cup olive oil
1 teaspoon butter
1 yellow onion, diced
2 to 3 cloves garlic, minced
2 tablespoons fresh rosemary, chopped
2 cups mushrooms, brushed and chopped
2-pound chicken, cut into pieces
1 (16-ounce) jar marinara sauce
½ cup red wine
¼ cup Parmesan cheese
1 bunch fresh Italian parsley, chopped, for garnish

Add pasta to this recipe for a truly hearty meal.

1. In a mixing bowl, combine flour, salt, pepper, and oregano. Heat the oil and butter in a large skillet over medium heat until butter melts. Add onion, garlic, rosemary, and mushrooms and sauté for 5 minutes. Add chicken and sauté an additional 5 minutes.
2. Add the marinara sauce and red wine. Cover and simmer over low heat for 45 minutes. Remove cover and place chicken on platter, simmer sauce an additional 10 minutes. Serve and spoon sauce over chicken. Sprinkle with cheese and fresh parsley.

> **Quick and Easy Tip**
> To save time, precook chicken and add during final stages of cooking. This recipe gets better with age; prepare a day ahead and reheat on stovetop.

Marinated Chicken Skewers

Serves 4

- ~ **PREP TIME:** 15 minutes
- ~ **MARINATE:** 20 minutes
- ~ **COOK TIME:** 8 minutes
- ~ **TOTAL COST:** $6.32
- ~ **CALORIES:** 181
- ~ **FAT:** 7 g
- ~ **PROTEIN:** 26 g
- ~ **CHOLESTEROL:** 72 mg
- ~ **SODIUM:** 64 mg

1 tablespoon lemon juice
1 tablespoon water
1 tablespoon olive oil
½ teaspoon dried tarragon, crumbled
¼ teaspoon Tabasco sauce
¼ teaspoon sea salt
1 clove garlic, chopped
4 boneless chicken breasts, skim removed, cut into 1-inch cubes
1 red bell pepper, seeded and cut into 1-inch squares
2 zucchini, cut into 1-inch thick slices

People love anything on the grill. This marinade is not sugar based so the chicken will not burn as easily when on the grill.

1. In a small bowl, combine the lemon juice, water, oil, tarragon, Tabasco sauce, salt, and garlic. Place the chicken in a lock-top plastic bag and set in a deep bowl. Pour the lemon juice mixture into the bag, secure the top closed, and let the chicken stand for 20 minutes at room temperature, turning the bag frequently.
2. Preheat the broiler. Drain the chicken, reserving the marinade. Thread the chicken, bell pepper, and zucchini alternately onto 4 10- to 12-inch long skewers. Arrange the skewers on a broiler pan. Slip under the broiler 4 to 5 inches from the heat source. Broil, turning once and brushing occasionally with the reserved marinade until the chicken is tender and cooked through, about 8 minutes. Serve immediately.

Quick and Easy Tip

A great way to save time and stress is to marinate the chicken the day before and go ahead and prepare the skewers. Then, just heat the grill and cook!

Stir-Fry Chicken with Vegetables

 Serves 4

- ~ **PREP TIME:** 15 minutes
- ~ **COOK TIME:** 10 minutes
- ~ **TOTAL COST:** $6.44
- ~ **CALORIES:** 387
- ~ **FAT:** 11 g
- ~ **PROTEIN:** 29 g
- ~ **CHOLESTEROL:** 82 mg
- ~ **SODIUM:** 627 mg

2 tablespoons red wine
1 tablespoon soy sauce
½ teaspoon cornstarch
1 teaspoon sugar
1 tablespoon sea salt
1 tablespoon peanut oil
2 cups blanched broccoli florets
1 cup blanched, sliced carrots
½ cup yellow onion wedges
6 ounces boneless chicken breasts, skin removed, cut into thin strips
2 cups cooked rice

Stir-fry is a healthy way to cook. If you don't have a wok, don't worry; a skillet works fine.

1. In a small bowl, make the sauce by combining the red wine, soy sauce, cornstarch, sugar, and salt. Stir to dissolve the cornstarch. Set aside. In a wok heat the oil; add the broccoli, carrots, and onion. Cook, stirring quickly and frequently, until vegetables are tender and crisp and onions are browned. Stir in the chicken and stir-fry 2 more minutes.
2. Add the sauce to the chicken mixture and cook, stirring constantly, until the sauce is thickened, 2 to 3 minutes. Serve each portion over ½ cup cooked rice.

Quick and Easy Tip
Blanching the vegetables is a process that brings out the color of the vegetable while at the same time making them tender. Be sure not to overcook them as the vegetables will become mushy and not good for stir-fry.

Orange-Glazed Turkey Cutlets

Serves 4

- **TOTAL COST:** $5.97
- **CALORIES:** 278.64
- **FAT:** 11.51 g
- **PROTEIN:** 21.40 g
- **CHOLESTEROL:** 74.80 mg
- **SODIUM:** 387.51 mg

12 ounces turkey cutlets
3 tablespoons flour
½ teaspoon salt
⅛ teaspoon white pepper
1 tablespoon olive oil
2 tablespoons butter
1 cup orange juice
1 teaspoon Worcestershire sauce
2 tablespoons honey
½ teaspoon dried basil leaves

Turkey cutlets are also known as turkey tenders. If you can't find them, cut a turkey tenderloin into ½-inch thick slices and pound to ¼-inch.

1. Prepare cutlets. On plate, combine flour, salt, and pepper. Dredge cutlets in this mixture, shaking off excess. Heat olive oil and butter in large skillet over medium heat until foamy. Add cutlets and cook in batches, turning once, for 3–4 minutes per side, until turkey is thoroughly cooked. Remove cutlets to clean plate as they cook.
2. To make sauce, add remaining ingredients to the pan. Cook and stir over high heat until mixture reduces and thickens, about 4–5 minutes. Return turkey to saucepan and cook over medium heat, stirring occasionally, about 1–2 minutes or until cutlets are hot. Serve immediately.

Cutlets

Cutlets, or thinly sliced pieces of chicken or turkey, are used to prepare many dishes, including Turkey Piccata and Chicken Marsala. It can be difficult to find these, but it's easy to prepare them yourself. Cutlets cook very quickly, just a few minutes per side over medium heat. Be careful not to overcook them or they can become dry.

Spicy Turkey Enchiladas

 Serves 4

- ~ **TOTAL COST:** $6.99
- ~ **CALORIES:** 388.93
- ~ **FAT:** 17.49 g
- ~ **PROTEIN:** 22.47 g
- ~ **CHOLESTEROL:** 75.93 mg
- ~ **SODIUM:** 1039.45 mg

8 ounces ground turkey
1 tablespoon olive oil
1 tablespoon butter
1 onion, chopped
4 cloves garlic, minced
2 tablespoons flour
½ teaspoon salt
⅛ teaspoon cayenne pepper
½ cup chicken broth
1 (4-ounce) can diced green chilies, undrained
1 (8-ounce) can tomato sauce
2 tablespoons tomato paste
1 tablespoon chili powder
8 corn tortillas
1 cup shredded pepper Jack cheese
½ cup shredded Parmesan cheese

Look for ground turkey, dark and light meat. That type has more flavor and is much less expensive than ground turkey breast.

1. In large skillet, cook turkey until browned; remove from skillet with slotted spoon, place in medium bowl, and refrigerate. Drain skillet but do not wash or wipe.
2. In same skillet, heat olive oil and butter over medium heat. Add onion, garlic, and bell pepper; cook and stir until tender, about 5 minutes. Sprinkle with flour, salt, and pepper; cook and stir until bubbly.
3. Add chicken broth; cook, stirring frequently, until mixture thickens. Add chilies, tomatoes, tomato paste, and chili powder; simmer for 10 minutes. Add ½ cup of this sauce to the cooked ground turkey; stir in pepper Jack cheese and half of the Parmesan cheese.
4. Preheat oven to 350°F. Dip tortillas into the hot sauce, then place a few spoonfuls of the turkey mixture on each tortilla and roll up. Place, seam side down, in 13" × 9" glass baking dish, and cover with remaining tomato sauce. Sprinkle with remaining Cotija cheese. Bake for 20–25 minutes or until sauce begins to bubble. Serve immediately.

Crispy Chicken Patties

Serves 4

- ~ **TOTAL COST:** $5.89
- ~ **CALORIES:** 301.23
- ~ **FAT:** 13.95 g
- ~ **PROTEIN:** 26.75 g
- ~ **CHOLESTEROL:** 141.85 mg
- ~ **SODIUM:** 523.61 mg

1 tablespoon olive oil
¼ cup finely chopped onion
¼ cup finely chopped red bell pepper
2 tablespoons finely chopped mushrooms
1 slice Hearty White Bread (Chapter 3)
1 egg, beaten
½ teaspoon salt
⅛ teaspoon pepper
¼ teaspoon poultry seasoning
1 pound ground chicken breast
½ cup dried bread crumbs
2 tablespoons butter

Serve these patties on a bun with mustard and relish, or serve them on top of mashed potatoes, with creamed peas for a retro meal.

1. In large skillet, heat 1 tablespoon olive oil over medium heat. Add onion, bell pepper, and mushrooms; cook and stir until tender, about 4 minutes. Continue cooking, stirring frequently, until liquid evaporates. Remove from heat.
2. Make soft bread crumbs from the slice of bread. In medium bowl, combine bread crumbs, egg, salt, cayenne pepper, poultry season, and onion mixture; stir to combine. Add ground chicken and mix gently but thoroughly. Form into four patties. Dip patties in dried bread crumbs to coat.
3. Wipe out skillet. Add the butter; melt over medium heat. Add chicken patties; cook for 5 minutes on first side. Carefully turn; cook for 3–6 minutes on second side until juices run clear and chicken is thoroughly cooked.

Ground Chicken

You can usually purchase ground chicken at the supermarket; you may have to ask the butcher to grind some for you. You can also grind it yourself. Just take boneless, skinless chicken pieces and cut into 1-inch chunks. Place in food processor and pulse until the chicken is ground, but still has texture. Use the same day the chicken is ground.

Chicken Tetrazzini

 Serves 5

- ~ **TOTAL COST:** $6.89
- ~ **CALORIES:** 594.55
- ~ **FAT:** 22.95 g
- ~ **PROTEIN:** 29.56 g
- ~ **CHOLESTEROL:** 89.55 mg
- ~ **SODIUM:** 833.61 mg

1 tablespoon olive oil
2 tablespoons butter
1 onion, chopped
2 cloves garlic, minced
2 Slow Cooker Simmered Chicken Breasts (this chapter)
3 tablespoons all-purpose flour
½ teaspoon salt
⅛ teaspoon pepper
½ teaspoon thyme leaves
1 (12-ounce) package spaghetti pasta
1 cup Chicken Stock (Chapter 6)
½ cup light cream or whole milk
1 tablespoon mustard
½ cup sour cream
1 cup shredded Muenster cheese
¼ cup grated Parmesan cheese

This classic recipe looks complicated, but it goes together quickly. In addition, it makes a fabulous casserole to serve a crowd with only three chicken breasts!

1. Preheat oven to 350°F. Grease a 2-quart casserole dish and set aside. Bring a large pot of salted water to a boil. In large saucepan, combine olive oil and butter over medium heat. When butter melts, add onion and garlic; cook and stir until crisp-tender, about 4 minutes.
2. Remove meat from chicken; chop and set aside. Drain mushrooms, reserving juice. Add mushrooms to saucepan and cook for 1 minute. Sprinkle with flour, salt, pepper, and thyme leaves; cook and stir until bubbly, about 3 minutes.
3. Cook pasta until almost al dente according to package directions. Add Stock, light cream, and reserved mushroom liquid to flour mixture in saucepan and bring to a simmer. Cook until thickened, about 5 minutes.
4. Drain pasta and add to sauce along with chicken. Stir in mustard, sour cream, and Muenster cheese and pour into prepared casserole. Sprinkle with Parmesan cheese and bake for 30–40 minutes or until casserole bubbles and begins to brown on top. Serve immediately.

Turkey, Tomatoes, and Olives with Linguine

Serves 4

- ~ **PREP TIME:** 20 minutes
- ~ **COOK TIME:** 30 minutes
- ~ **TOTAL COST:** $7.00
- ~ **CALORIES:** 294
- ~ **FAT:** 14 g
- ~ **PROTEIN:** 32 g
- ~ **CHOLESTEROL:** 72 mg
- ~ **SODIUM:** 808 mg

2 teaspoons olive oil

1 yellow onion, chopped

3 cloves garlic, chopped

¾ pound turkey breast, skin removed, cut into bite-sized pieces

1 tablespoon fresh basil, chopped

½ teaspoon dried thyme

½ teaspoon dried rosemary

12 to 16 kalamata or other olives, pitted and chopped

1½ tablespoons capers, drained

2 tomatoes, chopped

2 cups chicken broth

1 tablespoon sea salt

1 pound linguine

1 cup grated Pecorino Romano cheese or Parmesan cheese

Pecorino Romano cheese is a wonderful Italian blended cheese, but it can get a little expensive. If your budget is tight, go with a more traditional Parmesan instead without sacrificing flavor.

1. In a large, deep skillet, heat the oil over medium heat. Add the onion and garlic and cook until the onion is translucent. Add the turkey, basil, thyme, and rosemary and sauté until the turkey is lightly browned. Stir in the olives, capers, and tomatoes and cook briefly, until the tomatoes begin to give off liquid. Remove the turkey from the skillet. Add the chicken stock, bring to a boil, and simmer over medium heat until the broth is reduced by half. Return the turkey to the sauce and stir well.

2. Meanwhile, in a large pot, bring at least 4 quarts of water to a rolling boil. Add 1 tablespoon salt. Add the linguine, stir to separate, and cook until al dente. Drain.

3. Transfer the linguine to the skillet and toss with the sauce until the sauce is evenly distributed. Transfer to a warm serving dish, top with the cheese, and serve.

Quick and Easy Tip

As with chicken, buy turkey when on special in bulk. Separate into individual family size servings and freeze for later use. Be sure to plan ahead, however, allowing turkey to thaw overnight in the refrigerator.

CHAPTER 8

PORK

Pork Fried Rice

 Serves 4

- ~ **TOTAL COST:** $5.09
- ~ **CALORIES:** 454.58
- ~ **FAT:** 13.02 g
- ~ **PROTEIN:** 16.45 g
- ~ **CHOLESTEROL:** 134.26 mg
- ~ **SODIUM:** 689.45 mg

1 ½ cups long-grain white rice
2 ½ cups water
2 tablespoons vegetable oil
1 onion, chopped
1 (7-ounce) butterflied boneless loin pork chop, diced
1 cup shredded cabbage
2 eggs
3 tablespoons soy sauce
2 tablespoons chicken broth
⅛ teaspoon pepper

Boneless loin pork chops give you the most meat per pound. They freeze very well; buy them when on sale, package in single chop portions, and freeze up to 3 months.

1. Combine rice and water in heavy saucepan. Bring to boil over high heat. Reduce heat to low, cover pan, and cook rice until almost tender but still firm in the center, about 15 minutes. Spread rice on a baking sheet and freeze for 10 minutes.
2. When rice is done, heat vegetable oil in wok or large skillet. Add onion, pork, and cabbage; stir-fry until vegetables are crisp-tender and pork is cooked, about 4–5 minutes.
3. Push onion and pork to side of wok. Add eggs and cook until set but still moist, about 1–2 minutes. Add rice and stir-fry until hot.
4. Sprinkle with soy sauce, chicken broth, and pepper and stir-fry for 1–2 minutes, then serve immediately.

Mexican Rice

Serves 6

- ~ **TOTAL COST:** $6.82
- ~ **CALORIES:** 342.64
- ~ **FAT:** 18.65 g
- ~ **PROTEIN:** 12.80 g
- ~ **CHOLESTEROL:** 52.72 mg
- ~ **SODIUM:** 1305.80 mg

¾ pound ground pork sausage
1 onion, chopped
1 tablespoon olive oil
1 tablespoon butter
1–½ cups long grain rice
2 cups water
1 (14–ounce) can diced tomatoes, undrained
1 (4–ounce) can green chiles, undrained
½ cup chili sauce
½ teaspoon salt
⅛ teaspoon pepper

You could add some olives or corn to this hearty recipe, or serve warmed corn tortillas and shredded cheese so your guests can make burritos.

1. In large saucepan, cook sausage and onion over medium heat, stirring frequently, until sausage is almost cooked. Drain. Add olive oil and butter to saucepan and stir in rice. Cook and stir for 2–4 minutes until rice turns opaque.
2. Add water, tomatoes, and remaining ingredients and bring to a boil. Cover, reduce heat, and simmer for 20–25 minutes or until rice is tender and liquid is absorbed. Let stand for 5 minutes, then stir and serve immediately.

Easy Lasagna

Serves 6

- **TOTAL COST:** $6.87
- **CALORIES:** 448.08
- **FAT:** 20.30 g
- **PROTEIN:** 25.15 g
- **CHOLESTEROL:** 122.15 mg
- **SODIUM:** 980.73 mg

8 ounces little uncased pork sausages, chopped
1 onion, chopped
3 cloves garlic, minced
1 (15-ounce) can tomato sauce
1 cup water
1 teaspoon dried Italian seasoning
1 cup part skim ricotta cheese
1 egg
½ teaspoon salt
¼ teaspoon pepper
1 cup shredded part skim mozzarella cheese
6 uncooked lasagna noodles
⅓ cup grated Parmesan cheese

Lasagna is a hearty casserole and a great way to stretch little pork sausages to serve six people. Part skim mozzarella and ricotta are cheaper than full fat versions.

1. In large skillet, brown sausages until partially cooked; drain. Add onion and garlic; cook and stir until sausage is cooked and vegetables are tender; drain. Add tomato sauce, water, and seasoning; mix well and bring to a simmer.
2. Meanwhile, in medium bowl combine ricotta, egg, salt, and pepper and mix well. Stir in mozzarella cheese.
3. In 9" × 9" baking dish, place ⅔ cup sausage mixture. Lay 3 uncooked lasagna noodles on top. Spread one third of ricotta filling over noodles and top with one third of the remaining ground beef mixture. Repeat layers twice, ending with ground beef mixture.
4. Cover tightly with foil and bake at 350°F for 1 hour. Uncover, sprinkle with cheese, and bake another 10–15 minutes, until casserole is bubbling and cheese browns.

Sausage and Greens with Pasta

 Serves 6

- ~ **TOTAL COST:** $6.05
- ~ **CALORIES:** 492.65
- ~ **FAT:** 12.61 g
- ~ **PROTEIN:** 20.60 g
- ~ **CHOLESTEROL:** 32.42 mg
- ~ **SODIUM:** 394.23 mg

½ pound pork sausage
1 onion, chopped
4 cloves garlic, chopped
1 pound chopped kale
½ teaspoon salt
1 cup Chicken Stock (Chapter 6)
1 tablespoon sugar
1 (16–ounce) package linguine pasta
½ teaspoon hot sauce
⅓ cup grated Parmesan cheese

Kale is an inexpensive and very hearty green that is full of vitamins, minerals, and fiber. It's delicious combined with sausage and served with pasta.

1. Bring a large pot of salted water to a boil. In large saucepan, cook sausage with onion and garlic, stirring to break up pork, until browned. Drain off all but 1 tablespoon drippings.
2. Add kale to skillet and sprinkle with salt. Let kale cook down for about 4–5 minutes, then add Chicken Stock and sugar. Cover pan and simmer for 10–15 minutes, until kale is tender.
3. Add pasta to boiling water; cook according to package directions until al dente. Drain and add hot sauce to pan with kale mixture; cook and stir for 2 minutes. Sprinkle with cheese and serve.

Cooking Dark Greens

Dark leafy greens include kale, collard greens, spinach, and mustard greens. They cook down dramatically in volume; 4 cups cooks down to about 1–2 cups. The longer the cooking time, the less bitter the greens will be. Clean them thoroughly by submerging in water in order to remove all the grit or sand.

Tex-Mex Turnovers

Serves 6

~ **TOTAL COST:** $6.78

~ **CALORIES:** 474.19

~ **FAT:** 22.71 g

~ **PROTEIN:** 14.40 g

~ **CHOLESTEROL:** 54.95 mg

~ **SODIUM:** 981.52 mg

½ pound ground pork sausage
1 onion, chopped
1 tablespoon chili powder
½ (15–ounce) can refried beans
24 (14" × 9") filo pastry sheets, thawed
¼ cup butter, melted
¾ cup salsa
1½ cups shredded Cheddar cheese

These turnovers are perfect for a party. You can make them about half this size by cutting the filo into two 14" × 4½" rectangles and serve as appetizers.

1. In large saucepan, combine sausage and onion over medium heat. Cook and stir until sausage is browned. Drain well, then add chili powder, cumin, refried beans, and water and mix well. Simmer for 5 minutes. Let cool for 20 minutes.
2. Unwrap filo sheets and cover with damp towel. Place one rectangle on work surface, brush sparingly with melted butter, and top with another rectangle. Repeat, using four sheets in all. Place about ¼ cup sausage mixture at short end of rectangle, leaving about a ½" border. Top with a spoonful of salsa and 2 tablespoons cheese.
3. Starting at short end, roll the filo over the filling. Fold sides in, then continue rolling to the end. Seal edge with melted butter. Brush with butter and place on cookie sheet.
4. Repeat with remaining filo, filling, salsa, and cheese, making six turnovers in all. Preheat oven to 375°F. Bake turnovers for 20–30 minutes or until pastries are golden brown. Serve with salsa and sour cream, if desired.

Sausage Stir-Fry

 Serves 4

¾ pound sweet Italian sausages

¼ cup water

¼ cup apple cider vinegar

3 tablespoons sugar

3 tablespoons ketchup

1 tablespoon soy sauce

1 tablespoon cornstarch

2 tablespoons water

1 tablespoon vegetable oil

1 onion, chopped

1 yellow summer squash, sliced

1 cup frozen broccoli florets, thawed

Serve this fresh-tasting stir-fry over hot cooked rice, and accompany with some canned peaches or apricots.

1. In large skillet, cook sausage and water over medium heat for 6–8 minutes, turning frequently during cooking time, until water evaporates and sausages begin to brown. Remove sausages to plate and cut into 1-inch pieces.
2. Drain fat from skillet but do not rinse. In small bowl, combine vinegar, sugar, ketchup, soy sauce, cornstarch, and water, and mix well; set aside.
3. Return skillet to medium-high heat and add oil. Heat until oil shimmers, then add onion. Stir-fry until onion is crisp-tender, about 3–4 minutes. Add squash and broccoli; stir-fry 4–5 minutes longer, or until broccoli is hot and squash is tender.
4. Stir ketchup mixture and add to skillet along with sausages. Stir-fry for 5–7 minutes until sausage pieces are thoroughly cooked and sauce bubbles. Serve immediately over hot cooked rice.

Cooking Rice

Rice expands to three times its bulk when cooked. Each serving is about ½ cup, so if you want to serve six people, cook 1 cup of rice to make 3 cups. Combine 1 cup long-grain rice with 2 cups water and a pinch of salt in a saucepan. Cover, bring to a boil, reduce heat to low, and simmer for 15–20 minutes until tender.

Risotto with Ham and Pineapple

 Serves 4

- **TOTAL COST:** $6.89
- **CALORIES:** 399.77
- **FAT:** 15.92 g
- **PROTEIN:** 14.37 g
- **CHOLESTEROL:** 32.81 mg
- **SODIUM:** 750.26 mg

2 cups water
2 cups chicken broth
1 tablespoon vegetable oil
1 tablespoon butter
1 onion, chopped
3 cloves garlic, minced
½ teaspoon dried thyme leaves
1 green bell pepper, chopped
1½ cups long-grain white rice
1 cup chopped ham
1 (8-ounce) can pineapple tidbits, drained
⅛ teaspoon pepper
¼ cup grated Parmesan cheese

Reminiscent of Hawaii, this risotto is delicious! Serve it with a green salad and some sherbet for dessert.

1. In medium saucepan, combine water and chicken broth and bring to a simmer over low heat. Keep warm. In large saucepan, heat olive oil and butter over medium heat. Add onion and garlic; cook and stir for 3 minutes. Add thyme, bell pepper, and rice; cook and stir for 4 minutes.
2. Start adding the broth, 1 cup at a time, stirring frequently. When 1 cup broth remains to be added, add ham, pineapple, and pepper to risotto. Add last cup of broth; cook and stir until rice is tender and creamy and liquid is absorbed. Stir in Parmesan, cover, let stand for 5 minutes, then serve.

Herb-Crusted Bone-In Pork Chops

 Serves 4

- **PREP TIME:** 10 minutes
- **COOK TIME:** 18 minutes
- **TOTAL COST:** $6.40
- **CALORIES:** 220
- **FAT:** 7 g
- **CARBOHYDRATES:** 16 g
- **PROTEIN:** 27 g
- **CHOLESTEROL:** 67 mg
- **SODIUM:** 210 mg

2 tablespoons fresh rosemary, leaves chopped
2 tablespoons fresh thyme, leaves chopped
2 tablespoons olive oil
4 pound bone-in pork chops
Sea salt and black pepper to taste
1 yellow onion, chopped
½ cup apple juice

Substitute boneless pork chops if you prefer, but you'll miss the added flavor that comes from the marrow of the bone.

1. In small mixing bowl, combine herbs and mix together. Lightly coat chops using 1 tablespoon olive oil. Season chops with salt and pepper, then coat with herb mixture.
2. In large saucepan, heat 1 tablespoon olive oil over medium-high heat. Add chops and brown on both sides, turning once. Transfer the chops to a plate and set aside. Add the onions and cook over medium heat until soft, about 3 minutes. Return chops to skillet and add apple juice. Reduce heat to low and cover with lid. Cook until tender, about 15 minutes.

Ham Sweet Potato Stir-Fry

Serves 4

~ **TOTAL COST:** $5.02

~ **CALORIES:** 269.34

~ **FAT:** 9.03 g

~ **PROTEIN:** 12.27 g

~ **CHOLESTEROL:** 23.49 mg

~ **SODIUM:** 998.34 mg

1 sweet potato

3 tablespoons low-sodium soy sauce

3 tablespoons ketchup

2 tablespoons brown sugar

2 tablespoons apple cider vinegar

1 cup Chicken Stock (Chapter 6)

2 tablespoons cornstarch

1 tablespoon vegetable oil

1 onion, chopped

1 cup sliced carrot

¼ cup water

1 cup frozen chopped broccoli, thawed and drained

1 cup cubed ham

The dense sweetness of sweet potatoes is a nice contrast to the chewy, salty ham in this easy dish.

1. Peel sweet potato and cut in quarters lengthwise, then cut into ¼" thick slices; set aside. In small bowl, combine soy sauce, ketchup, sugar, vinegar, Chicken Stock, and cornstarch.
2. In large skillet or wok, heat olive oil over medium high heat. Add onion and sweet potato; stir-fry for 4 minutes. Add carrot, then add water, cover, and simmer for 5–9 minutes or until sweet potato and carrots are tender.
3. Uncover skillet and add ham; stir-fry for 2 minutes. Then stir cornstarch mixture and add to skillet. Bring to a simmer and stir-fry until sauce thickens. Serve immediately over hot cooked rice.

> **Freezing Ham**
> Ham freezes well, but its texture will change and will become softer. You can freeze it up to 2 months. Use the thawed ham in recipes such as stir-fries and soups, not sandwiches. Ham will keep more of its quality if you freeze it in a liquid; pineapple juice is a good choice.

Thin Pork Chops with Mushrooms and Herbs

- **TOTAL COST:** $6.53
- **CALORIES:** 303.02
- **FAT:** 17.03 g
- **PROTEIN:** 17.94 g
- **CHOLESTEROL:** 78.74 mg
- **SODIUM:** 594.99 mg

3 tablespoons flour
½ teaspoon salt
⅛ teaspoon pepper
1 teaspoon dried thyme leaves
4 (3-ounce) boneless pork chops
2 tablespoons butter
1 onion, minced
1 cup sliced mushrooms
½ cup light cream

Serve this quick and easy dish with a rice pilaf and a green salad tossed with shredded carrots and radishes.

1. On shallow plate, combine flour, salt, pepper, and thyme leaves and mix well. Place pork between two sheets of waxed paper and pound until ½" thick. Dredge pork chops in this mixture, shaking off excess.
2. Heat olive oil in large skillet over medium heat. Add pork chops; brown on first side without moving, about 4 minutes.
3. Turn pork and add onion and mushrooms to the pan. Cook for 3 minutes, then remove pork from pan. Stir vegetables, scraping pan to remove drippings.
4. Add cream to pan and bring to a boil. Return pork to skillet, lower heat, and simmer pork for 2–4 minutes longer until pork is very light pink. Serve immediately.

Pounding Meat

Many meat dishes start by pounding the meat before it's seasoned and cooked. This reduces the cooking time and tenderizes the meat by breaking the fibers. It also makes the portion size look bigger, which is helpful for reducing saturated fat and cholesterol intake. Don't pound too hard, and use a meat mallet or rolling pin.

Panko-Crusted Pork Chops

Serves 4

- ~ **PREP TIME:** 8 minutes
- ~ **COOK TIME:** 18 minutes
- ~ **TOTAL COST:** $6.28
- ~ **CALORIES:** 381
- ~ **FAT:** 14 g
- ~ **CARBOHYDRATES:** 12 g
- ~ **PROTEIN:** 28 g
- ~ **CHOLESTEROL:** 62 mg
- ~ **SODIUM:** 367 mg

1 egg, beaten
½ cup milk
1 cup panko bread crumbs
1 teaspoon Italian seasoning
Sea salt and black pepper to taste
½ cup Parmesan cheese, grated
4 boneless pork chops, 1-inch thick
¼ cup canola oil

If you don't have Italian seasoning, substitute cayenne pepper, herbs de provence, or spice it up with chili powder.

1. Preheat oven to 375°F. In small mixing bowl, whisk together egg and milk to combine. In separate bowl, combine panko, Italian seasoning, salt, pepper, and cheese. Blend well.
2. Place pork chops between two pieces of plastic wrap and pound out to about ⅓-inch thick with mallet or rolling pin. Dredge pounded chops in egg mixture, then into panko mixture. Place on wire rack, if you have one. If not, just set aside.
2. On grill pan over medium heat, heat oil. Add chops and grill about 4 minutes on each side, or until crisp and golden on each side. Transfer chops to parchment-lined baking sheet and bake for about 10 minutes, or until chops are cooked through.

> **Panko Bread Crumbs**
> Panko bread crumbs are Japanese-style bread crumbs. They are very light, dry, and coarse. Usually they are located in your grocer's Asian food aisle. Use them anywhere your recipe calls for bread crumbs.

Wine-Poached Pork Chops with Sage

 Serves 4

~ **PREP TIME:** 10 minutes
~ **COOK TIME:** 35 minutes
~ **TOTAL COST:** $6.96
~ **CALORIES:** 217
~ **FAT:** 5 g
~ **CARBOHYDRATES:** 16 g
~ **PROTEIN:** 24 g
~ **CHOLESTEROL:** 65 mg
~ **SODIUM:** 175 mg

2 tablespoons fresh sage, finely chopped
2 cloves garlic, chopped
Sea salt and black pepper to taste
4 bone-in pork chops
2 tablespoons butter
¾ cup dry white wine
¼ cup apple juice

Apple juice is a great substitute for white wine when you are cooking just about anything. The sweetness of the apple juice compares to the sweetness of the wine, the only difference is the alcohol in wine actually helps to extract flavors.

1. Combine sage, garlic, salt, and pepper. Press mixture firmly into both sides of the pork chops. In large saucepan, melt butter over medium heat. Add chops and brown on both sides. Remove chops and set aside.
2. Add about ⅔ of the wine and 1 tablespoon of the apple juice, and bring to a boil. Return chops to pan, cover, and reduce heat. Simmer until chops are tender, about 25 to 30 minutes. When done, remove chops. Add remaining wine and juice to saucepan and boil down to a syrupy glaze, about 4 minutes. Pour over chops.

Italian-Seasoned Pork Cutlets with Lemon

Serves 4

~ **PREP TIME:** 10 minutes
~ **COOK TIME:** 5 minutes
~ **TOTAL COST:** $6.08
~ **CALORIES:** 345
~ **FAT:** 17 g
~ **CARBOHYDRATES:** 15 g
~ **PROTEIN:** 35 g
~ **CHOLESTEROL:** 50 mg
~ **SODIUM:** 336 mg

4 boneless pork cutlets
Sea salt and black pepper to taste
½ cup plain flour
2 eggs, beaten
1¼ cups Italian-seasoned bread crumbs
2 cups canola oil, as needed
1 lemon, halved

Famed chef Wolfgang Puck made a similar dish famous as it is native to his homeland of Austria.

1. Using meat pounder, cover cutlets with parchment or wax paper, and pound cutlets as thin as possible. Sprinkle with salt and pepper. Set up an assembly line with flour on one plate, eggs on another, and crumbs on a third. Coat each cutlet with flour, then egg, then bread crumbs.
2. Heat ¼ inch of oil in a large skillet over medium heat. Add as many cutlets as will fit without crowding. Cook until golden brown on each side, about 1½ minutes per side. Drain cutlets on paper towels. When serving, squeeze with a little lemon juice, removing any seeds.

Cayenne Pork Chops with Banana

 Serves 4

~ **PREP TIME:** 7 minutes
~ **COOK TIME:** 23 minutes
~ **TOTAL COST:** $6.79
~ **CALORIES:** 463
~ **FAT:** 23 g
~ **CARBOHYDRATES:** 33 g
~ **PROTEIN:** 49 g
~ **CHOLESTEROL:** 105 mg
~ **SODIUM:** 105 mg

4 thick pork chops, boneless
Sea salt to taste
1 teaspoon cayenne pepper
1 tablespoon olive oil
1½ cups dry white wine
¼ cup honey
1 cup red bell pepper, chopped
1 yellow onion, chopped
1 clove garlic, chopped
¼ cup apple juice
1 banana, peeled and sliced
2 cups hot cooked rice

As you can tell from the pork recipes I have shared, pork pairs nicely with all types of fruits. Feel free to experiment with other fruits such as pineapple, strawberries, and even mango!

Sprinkle chops with salt and cayenne pepper. In a large saucepan, heat 1 tablespoon oil over medium heat. Add pork chops and brown them on each side, about 2 minutes per side. Add wine, honey, bell pepper, onion, and garlic. Cover and simmer for 10 minutes. Stir in ¼ cup apple juice. Simmer, about 5 minutes. Add bananas and cook until pork is cooked through, about 4 minutes. Serve pork chops and bananas over cooked rice.

Baked Pork Chops with Sweet Raisin Crust

 Serves 6

~ **PREP TIME:** 10 minutes
~ **COOK TIME:** 35 minutes
~ **TOTAL COST:** $6.87
~ **CALORIES:** 215
~ **FAT:** 5 g
~ **CARBOHYDRATES:** 5 g
~ **PROTEIN:** 20 g
~ **CHOLESTEROL:** 82 mg
~ **SODIUM:** 191 mg

3 slices raisin bread, toasted and well crushed
¼ cup plain flour
Sea salt and black pepper to taste
1 cup milk
1 egg, beaten
6 pork chops

Bread crumbs don't have to be plain and boring. Using varieties of bread to add flavor to foods is a great way to maximize flavor without extra ingredients, which translates to less work for you and a more cost-effective recipe.

Preheat oven to 375°F. Line baking sheet with parchment paper. In medium mixing bowl, combine breadcrumbs, flour, salt, and pepper. In a separate bowl, whisk together milk and egg. Dredge chops in milk mixture, then in breadcrumb mixture. Place on baking sheet and bake for 15 minutes, turn, and continue baking for an additional 10 minutes or until chops reach an internal temperature of 160°F.

Herb-Crusted Pork Chops with White Wine Sauce

 Serves 4

- ~ **PREP TIME:** 10 minutes
- ~ **COOK TIME:** 40 minutes
- ~ **TOTAL COST:** $6.96
- ~ **CALORIES:** 217
- ~ **FAT:** 5 g
- ~ **PROTEIN:** 24 g
- ~ **CHOLESTEROL:** 65 mg
- ~ **SODIUM:** 175 mg

1 tablespoon fresh sage, chopped
1 teaspoon fresh rosemary, leaves chopped
2 cloves garlic, chopped
Sea salt and black pepper to taste
4 pork chops, about 1 inch thick
2 tablespoons butter
1 tablespoon olive oil
¾ cup dry white wine

Don't fear cooking with wine. The alcohol cooks out of the wine but extracts flavors from the other ingredients in the meantime.

1. Rub chops with the olive oil. Combine sage, rosemary, garlic, salt, and pepper. Press mixture firmly into both sides of the pork chops. In a large saucepan, melt butter over medium heat. Place in chops and brown on both sides. Remove chops and set aside.
2. Add about ⅔ of the wine and bring to a boil. Return chops to pan, cover, and reduce heat. Simmer until chops are tender, about 25 to 30 minutes. When done, remove chops. Add remaining wine to saucepan and boil down to a syrupy glaze, about 4 minutes. Pour over chops.

Pork Tenderloin Stuffed with Apricots and Raisins

 Serves 6

- ~ **PREP TIME:** 10 minutes
- ~ **COOK TIME:** 30 minutes
- ~ **TOTAL COST:** $6.88
- ~ **CALORIES:** 257
- ~ **FAT:** 5 g
- ~ **PROTEIN:** 32 g
- ~ **CHOLESTEROL:** 38 mg
- ~ **SODIUM:** 96 mg

3 dried apricots, chopped
¼ cup dried cranberries
2 tablespoons golden raisins
1 cup warm water
Juice of ½ lemon
2 pork tenderloins, about ¾ pound each
Worcestershire sauce
1 cup cornmeal
Sea salt and black pepper to taste
¼ cup olive oil

The tenderloin is so named because it is the most tender cut of pork.

1. Place dried fruit in a mixing bowl with the warm water and lemon juice. Let stand until most of the water is absorbed.
2. Preheat oven to 350°F. Make a tunnel through each tenderloin by using the handle of a wooden spoon, knife handle, or knitting needle. Stuff the fruit into the tunnels. Sprinkle both tenderloins (or roasts) with Worcestershire. Make a paste with cornmeal, salt, pepper, and olive oil. Spread it on the pork and roast for 30 minutes. The crust should be golden brown and the pork a healthy, cooked pink.

Apple-Stuffed Pork Chops with Pears

 Serves 4

- ~ **PREP TIME:** 10 minutes
- ~ **COOK TIME:** 45 minutes
- ~ **TOTAL COST:** $6.92
- ~ **CALORIES:** 312
- ~ **FAT:** 8 g
- ~ **PROTEIN:** 41 g
- ~ **CHOLESTEROL:** 105 mg
- ~ **SODIUM:** 86 mg

½ cup olive oil
2 apples, such as Granny Smith, cored, seeded, and chopped
1 yellow onion, chopped
1 tablespoon dried rosemary, chopped
¼ cup Italian parsley, chopped
½ cup cornbread crumbs
Sea salt and black pepper to taste
4 thick-cut pork rib chops
4 garlic cloves, chopped
Zest and juice of 1 lemon
½ cup chicken broth
½ cup dry white wine
1 teaspoon cornstarch mixed in 1 tablespoon water

Even at your local grocery store, the butcher can be helpful. Ask him to cut chops thick enough, about 1½ inches to 2 inches, and to cut a slit in each so as to be easily stuffed.

1. In a large saucepan, heat ¼ cup olive oil. Add apples, onion, and herbs and sauté until softened, about 5 minutes. Add the cornbread crumbs, salt, and pepper. Remove from heat and let cool. When cooled, stuff this mixture into the chops and secure with a toothpick.
2. Add ¼ cup olive oil to the saucepan and heat over medium heat. Add the stuffed chops and brown on each side. Add the remaining ingredients, except for the cornstarch-water mixture, and cover. Simmer for 40 minutes over low heat.
3. Place the chops on a warm platter and add the cornstarch-water mixture to the pork gravy in the saucepan to thicken. Add salt and pepper to taste. Serve chops and top with sauce.

Quick and Easy Tip
Prepare the apple mixture the day ahead and prestuff the pork chops.

Honey Mustard Pork Chops

Serves 4

- ~ **PREP TIME:** 10 minutes
- ~ **COOK TIME:** 12 minutes
- ~ **TOTAL COST:** $6.24
- ~ **CALORIES:** 198
- ~ **FAT:** 3 g
- ~ **PROTEIN:** 21 g
- ~ **CHOLESTEROL:** 61 mg
- ~ **SODIUM:** 247 mg

2 tablespoons honey
¼ cup Dijon mustard
1 tablespoon fresh rosemary, leaves chopped
1 tablespoon fresh thyme, leaves chopped
Sea salt and black pepper to taste
4 boneless pork chops, about 1 inch thick

Honey can be used as a sweetener for all kinds of dishes. Substitute for sugar in dressing recipes for a healthier dressing that has great flavor and consistency.

Preheat broiler. In a bowl, combine honey, mustard, herbs, and salt and pepper and whisk to combine well. Brush over the chops and place on aluminum foil. Then place under broiler and cook for about 5 minutes, turn once, baste with mustard mixture, and cook an additional 5 to 6 minutes or until pork reaches 160°F and is cooked through but still pinkish in color.

Quick and Easy Tip

Pork chops are a great item to buy in bulk and then freeze in family-size servings. Thaw in refrigerator overnight.

Cajun-Style Pork Chops with Pineapple

Serves 4

- ~ **PREP TIME:** 7 minutes
- ~ **COOK TIME:** 35 minutes
- ~ **TOTAL COST:** $6.99
- ~ **CALORIES:** 463
- ~ **FAT:** 22 g
- ~ **PROTEIN:** 39 g
- ~ **CHOLESTEROL:** 105 mg
- ~ **SODIUM:** 110 mg

4 thick pork chops, boneless
Sea salt to taste
1 teaspoon cayenne pepper
1 tablespoon olive oil
1½ cups dry white wine
1 cup red bell pepper, chopped
1 yellow onion, chopped
1 clove garlic, chopped
2 tablespoons soy sauce
1 (15-ounce) can pineapple chunks, liquid reserved
Hot cooked rice

This dish keeps the pork chops nice and moist.

Sprinkle chops with salt and cayenne pepper. In a large saucepan, heat 1 tablespoon oil over medium to medium-high heat. Add pork chops and brown them slowly on each side. Add wine, bell pepper, onion, and garlic. Cover and simmer for 25 to 30 minutes. Remove pork chops, add soy sauce, pineapple liquid and simmer, stirring, until thickened. Add the pineapple chunks and bring to a boil. Serve over pork chops with cooked rice.

Quick and Easy Tip

Keep cooked rice on hand in the refrigerator for simple, fast meals in a pinch.

Breaded Pork Cutlets

 Serves 4

~ **PREP TIME:** 10 minutes
~ **COOK TIME:** 3 minutes
~ **TOTAL COST:** $6.08
~ **CALORIES:** 345
~ **FAT:** 17 g
~ **PROTEIN:** 35 g
~ **CHOLESTEROL:** 50 mg
~ **SODIUM:** 336 mg

1 pound pork cutlets
Sea salt and black pepper to taste
½ cup plain flour
2 eggs, beaten
1¼ cups bread crumbs
2 cups canola oil

Another name for this dish is schnitzel, which translates to cutlets without bones. Schnitzel is traditional to Austria and has been made famous by Chef Wolfgang Puck, who is from Austria.

1. Cover cutlets with parchment or wax paper and use meat pounder to make them as thin as possible. Sprinkle with salt and pepper. Set up an assembly line with plates for flour, eggs, and crumbs. Coat each with flour, then egg, then crumbs.
2. Heat ¼ inch of oil in a large skillet over medium heat. Add as many cutlets as will fit without crowding. Cook until golden brown on each side, about 1½ minutes per side. Drain cutlets on paper towels and serve.

Quick and Easy Tip

Having your ingredients organized before cooking is the secret to making this recipe truly quick and easy. Heat your oil to hot, but not burning, before adding in cutlets to avoid overly oily cutlets.

Sautéed Pork Tenderloin with Fresh Spinach and Water Chestnuts

Serves 4

~ **PREP TIME:** 10 minutes
~ **COOK TIME:** 15 minutes
~ **TOTAL COST:** $6.94
~ **CALORIES:** 394
~ **FAT:** 19 g
~ **PROTEIN:** 42 g
~ **CHOLESTEROL:** 119 mg
~ **SODIUM:** 275 mg

¼ cup plain flour
1 pinch nutmeg
¼ teaspoon ground cloves
Sea salt and black pepper to taste
2¾-pound pork tenderloins, cleaned and trimmed
¼ cup olive oil
Juice from 1 lemon
1 teaspoon Worcestershire sauce
1 large bunch fresh spinach, washed, dried, stems trimmed
½ cup sliced water chestnuts

This is a delicious, quick weeknight meal.

In a large mixing bowl, combine flour, nutmeg, cloves, salt, and pepper and coat pork. Heat olive oil in a large saucepan over medium heat. Add pork and sauté about 6 minutes per side. Add lemon juice, Worcestershire sauce, spinach, and water chestnuts. Stir to wilt leaves. If pan is dry, drizzle with a bit more olive oil or add a tablespoon or 2 of water.

Quick and Easy Tip

When sautéing meats, add a tablespoon or 2 of water, white wine, apple juice, or Italian dressing if the pan needs a little moisture to prevent from burning.

Grilled Pork Tenderloin Stuffed with Shallots and Herbs

 Serves 4

~ **PREP TIME:** 5 minutes
~ **COOK TIME:** 18 minutes
~ **TOTAL COST:** $6.84
~ **CALORIES:** 232
~ **FAT:** 6 g
~ **PROTEIN:** 39 g
~ **CHOLESTEROL:** 112 mg
~ **SODIUM:** 79 mg

2 tablespoons unsalted butter
2 shallots, minced
2 tablespoons fresh rosemary, leaves chopped
1 tablespoon fresh basil, chopped
½ teaspoon ground coriander
4 pork chops, 1½ to 2 inches thick, a pocket cut from the outside edge
¼ cup olive oil
Sea salt and black pepper to taste

This is a perfect meal for a lazy afternoon feast.

1. In a large saucepan, heat the butter over medium heat. Add shallots and sauté until softened, about 4 minutes. Add herbs and sauté.
2. Stuff the chops with the shallot/herb mixture and rub with olive oil, salt, and pepper.
3. Heat an outdoor grill or use low broil of broiler and sear chops on each side, about 4 to 5 minutes per side for medium chops, depending upon thickness.

Quick and Easy Tip
Sauté the shallots and herbs and stuff the chops ahead of time. Go from refrigerator to grill and be ready to serve within minutes.

Roasted Pork Meatballs with Apples

 Serves 4

~ **PREP TIME:** 12 minutes
~ **COOK TIME:** 30 minutes
~ **TOTAL COST:** $6.98
~ **CALORIES:** 267
~ **FAT:** 5 g
~ **PROTEIN:** 37 g
~ **CHOLESTEROL:** 138 mg
~ **SODIUM:** 563 mg

5 thick slices day-old or toasted Italian bread loaf
2 tart apples, such as Granny Smith, peeled and finely chopped
1 yellow onion, chopped
2 sprigs fresh oregano, leaves chopped
1 tablespoon olive oil
1 pound ground pork
1 egg, lightly beaten
2 tablespoons chopped walnuts
Sea salt and black pepper to taste

These meatballs make great appetizers for various parties. They are a popular dish and are a tasty alternative to beef!

1. Preheat oven to 375°F. Line a baking sheet with parchment paper.
2. In a bowl, soak bread in water for 1 minute. Squeeze out liquid and set aside. In bowl, combine all ingredients and form the mixture into 2-inch balls. Place meatballs on a baking sheet. Bake for 30 minutes or until thoroughly cooked and golden brown. Drain on paper towels and serve.

Pork Ribs with Merlot Sauce

 Serves 5

- ~ **PREP TIME:** 10 minutes
- ~ **COOK TIME:** 15 minutes
- ~ **TOTAL COST:** $7.00
- ~ **CALORIES:** 230
- ~ **FAT:** 8 g
- ~ **PROTEIN:** 25 g
- ~ **CHOLESTEROL:** 65 mg
- ~ **SODIUM:** 482 mg

1 tablespoon olive oil
1 yellow onion, chopped
2 pounds thick pork ribs
6 plum tomatoes, diced
1 orange, zested and juiced
2 cups beef broth
4 sprigs fresh oregano, leaves chopped
1 cup Merlot wine
½ cup honey
Sea salt and black pepper to taste

This recipe is a quick way to enjoy ribs.

1. Preheat oven to 400°F. Heat oil in a large oven-proof saucepan over medium-high heat. Add the onions and ribs. Brown together, about 5 minutes per side for the ribs. Add the tomatoes and cook for 3 minutes. Add remaining ingredients.
2. Cover the pan and place in oven for 45 minutes. Uncover and cook an additional 15 minutes. Serve.

Quick and Easy Tip
Zesting an orange means to use a grater (or zester) and scrape the peel from the orange. Only zest the top layer of the fruit. Use zest in everything from dressings to desserts!

Sautéed Pork Sausage with Red Bell Peppers

 Serves 4

- ~ **PREP TIME:** 8 minutes
- ~ **COOK TIME:** 15 minutes
- ~ **TOTAL COST:** $6.75
- ~ **CALORIES:** 391
- ~ **FAT:** 29 g
- ~ **PROTEIN:** 215 g
- ~ **CHOLESTEROL:** 65 mg
- ~ **SODIUM:** 1052 mg

1 tablespoon olive oil
1 pound pork sausage, mild or medium
1 red bell pepper, seeded and chopped
1 shallots, chopped
2 garlic cloves, chopped
2 stalks celery, chopped
1 teaspoon fresh ginger, peeled and minced
1 oranges, zested and juiced
3 sprigs fresh thyme, leaves chopped
1 bay leaf
Sea salt and black pepper

Red bell peppers complement this recipe. They're great accents to grilled foods such as chicken or beef.

1. In a large saucepan, heat oil over medium-high heat. Brown the pork and sausage. Add the bell peppers, shallots, garlic, celery, and ginger. Reduce heat to medium and sauté for 5 minutes.
2. Add the orange juice and zest, thyme, and bay leaf. Season with salt and pepper and simmer, uncovered, for about 20 minutes.

Roasted Pork with Potatoes

 Serves 6

- ~ **PREP TIME:** 5 minutes
- ~ **COOK TIME:** 1 hours
- ~ **TOTAL COST:** $6.98
- ~ **CALORIES:** 389
- ~ **FAT:** 5 g
- ~ **PROTEIN:** 38 g
- ~ **CHOLESTEROL:** 37 mg
- ~ **SODIUM:** 227 mg

1 (2½-pound) pork roast, bone-in
2 cloves garlic, chopped
Sea salt and black pepper to taste
1 tablespoon olive oil
2 yellow onions, peeled and quartered
2 large baking potatoes, washed and cut into 2-inch chunks
2 sprigs fresh oregano, leaves chopped

This recipe takes awhile to cook, but it's easy to prepare.

Preheat oven to 375°F. Pierce the pork with a sharp knife in several places and insert garlic cloves with oregano leaves. Season with salt and pepper. Prepare roasting pan by pouring in oil. Place the pork roast in a roasting pan with a lid. Cover and roast for 40 minutes, add onions, potatoes, and oregano and stir. Roast uncovered for about 20 minutes, until the potatoes are fork-tender and the pork is cooked to an internal temperature of 160°F.

> **Quick and Easy Tip**
> For an even more nutritious, delicious meal, add carrots and celery!

Apple-Coated Baked Pork Chops

 Serves 6

- ~ **PREP TIME:** 10 minutes
- ~ **COOK TIME:** 15 minutes
- ~ **TOTAL COST:** $6.97
- ~ **CALORIES:** 215
- ~ **FAT:** 4 g
- ~ **PROTEIN:** 20 g
- ~ **CHOLESTEROL:** 82 mg
- ~ **SODIUM:** 241 mg

3 slices raisin bread
½ cup applesauce
6 cloves garlic
1 teaspoon olive oil
6 pork chops
Sea salt and black pepper to taste

Most kids love anything with cheese. That's why this soup is perfect for kids' lunches.

Preheat oven to 375°F. Line a baking sheet with parchment paper. Separately, toast the bread and grate into crumbs. In food processor or blender, purée applesauce, garlic, and oil and blend until smooth. Rub the chops with the applesauce mixture, coat with bread crumbs and place the coated chops on the baking sheet, and sprinkle with salt and pepper. Bake for 30 minutes, turn and bake for an additional 30 minutes or until done.

> **Quick and Easy Tip**
> Applesauce is the secret ingredient here. I use it as a base for many recipes including soups and other sauces.

Chili Pepper Pork with Potatoes

 Serves 6

~ **PREP TIME:** 8 minutes
~ **COOK TIME:** 1½ hours
~ **TOTAL COST:** $6.98
~ **CALORIES:** 293
~ **FAT:** 7 g
~ **PROTEIN:** 41 g
~ **CHOLESTEROL:** 112 mg
~ **SODIUM:** 84 mg

1 (2-pound) shoulder of pork (fat trimmed)
1 yellow onion, quartered
2 whole cloves
1 cinnamon stick
1 tablespoon whole peppercorns
2 garlic cloves, chopped
1 teaspoon cumin seeds
5 whole, fresh chili peppers, your choice of pepper
3 medium new potatoes, quartered
2 tablespoons apple cider vinegar

Here, the peppers are left whole so you gain maximum flavor without having to worry about the super spicy pepper seeds.

In a large-quart boiler, place pork, onions, cloves, cinnamon, peppercorns, garlic, cumin, and chili peppers. Add enough water to cover all. Cover and cook on low for 3 hours. Stir and add the potatoes. Cook about 1½ hours longer. Remove cloves, cinnamon stick, peppercorns, and chili peppers. Add the vinegar and stir to combine. Serve hot.

Stewed Pork with Horseradish

 Serves 6

~ **PREP TIME:** 10 minutes
~ **COOK TIME:** 1½ to 2 hours
~ **TOTAL COST:** $7.00
~ **CALORIES:** 213
~ **FAT:** 6 g
~ **PROTEIN:** 34 g
~ **CHOLESTEROL:** 89 mg
~ **SODIUM:** 322 mg

Sea salt and black pepper to taste
2 tablespoons canola oil
1½ pounds boneless pork, cut into bite-size pieces
1 yellow onion, chopped
1 carrot, peeled and sliced
1 rib celery, sliced
2 cans beef broth
½ cup cider vinegar
¼ cup prepared horseradish

Horseradish is a root that comes from the same plant family as mustard, wasabi, and cabbage. Prepared horseradish is grated horseradish root that has been mixed with vinegar, thereby preserving the flavor and color of fresh horseradish. Prepared horseradish will keep in your refrigerator for months before it darkens, which indicates it is losing its flavor.

In a large-quart boiler, heat butter and oil over medium heat. Add pork and cook until browned, about 3 minutes. Remove pork and set aside. Add onion, carrot, and celery and cook until onions are softened, about 8 minutes. Return the pork to the boiler and add beef broth and vinegar, and bring to a boil. Reduce the heat, cover, and simmer for 1½ hours or until pork is tender. Remove from heat, stir in horseradish and serve.

Paprika Pork Chops

 Serves 4

- ~ **PREP TIME:** 8 minutes
- ~ **COOK TIME:** 55 minutes
- ~ **TOTAL COST:** $6.90
- ~ **CALORIES:** 202
- ~ **FAT:** 8 g
- ~ **PROTEIN:** 33 g
- ~ **CHOLESTEROL:** 89 mg
- ~ **SODIUM:** 265 mg

1 cup sour cream
½ cup plain flour
1 tablespoon dried dill or 1½ tablespoons fresh dill
Sea salt and black pepper to taste
4 shoulder pork chops, 1-inch thick
4 tablespoons butter
1 yellow onion, chopped
2 cloves garlic, chopped
2 tablespoons paprika, or more, to taste
1 cup Chicken Broth (Chapter 6)

Paprika, or red pepper, is native to Hungary and can be either spicy or mild. Most Hungarian paprika purchased in stores is of the mild variety.

1. In a small mixing bowl, combine sour cream, 2 tablespoons flour, and dill. Set aside. In a separate mixing bowl, combine salt, pepper, and remaining flour. Dredge pork chops in flour-salt mixture. In a large saucepan, heat the butter over medium heat until browning. Add the chops and brown for about 5 minutes on each side. Remove chops and set aside. Add onion and garlic and cook until tender, about 3 to 4 minutes. Add paprika and chicken broth, increase heat, and bring to a boil to combine all the flavors in the pan.
2. Return chops to pan, reduce heat, cover, and simmer chops for 45 minutes or until tender. Remove chops again and stir in sour cream mixture and cook over medium heat until heated, stirring constantly until thick and smooth. Pour over the chops when serving.

Quick and Easy Tip
Sour cream is an easy way to make cream sauces without worrying too much about burning.

Fennel-Roasted Pork Shoulder with Apples

Serves 4

- ~ **PREP TIME:** 10 minutes
- ~ **COOK TIME:** 3 to 4 hours
- ~ **TOTAL COST:** $6.92
- ~ **CALORIES:** 340
- ~ **FAT:** 7 g
- ~ **PROTEIN:** 32 g
- ~ **CHOLESTEROL:** 128mg
- ~ **SODIUM:** 281 mg

1 (2-pound) boneless pork shoulder roasts
1 bulb fennel, cleaned and chopped
1 yellow onion, chopped
2 Granny Smith apples, cored and chopped (substitute pears if you prefer)
2 tablespoons olive oil
½ cup vegetable broth
Sea salt and black pepper to taste

Fennel is a vegetable that is often confused with the herb star anise because each has a mild licorice flavor. Dice or chop the fennel bulb as you would an onion and use the more bitter stalks for soups and stews.

Preheat oven to 375°F. Cut open the roast in half, sideways, creating a top and bottom and place inside up. Layer bottom half with fennel, onion, and apples. Place top half on and tie securely with butcher's twine. Coat with olive oil, salt, and pepper. Place in a roasting pan. Add broth and cover with foil. Roast (bake) for 1 hour. Uncover and roast an additional ½ hour longer until the pork is thoroughly cooked. Untie, slice, and serve.

> **Quick and Easy Tip**
> Pork shoulder is a fairly lean cut of pork that can be purchased bone in or bone out. Cooking a bone-in pork shoulder takes a little more time that boneless, however, the bone does add a little extra flavor to the meat.

Stroganoff with Pork

 Serves 6

- ~ **PREP TIME:** 9 minutes
- ~ **COOK TIME:** 45
- ~ **TOTAL COST:** $6.96
- ~ **CALORIES:** 326
- ~ **FAT:** 9 g
- ~ **PROTEIN:** 31 g
- ~ **CHOLESTEROL:** 96 mg
- ~ **SODIUM:** 513 mg

Sea salt and black pepper to taste
½ cup plain flour
1½ pounds boneless pork, cut into 2-inch chunks
2 tablespoons butter
2 garlic cloves, chopped
1 yellow onion, chopped
1½ cups chicken broth
2 teaspoons Worcestershire sauce
1 cup sour cream
¼ cup Italian parsley, chopped

Stroganoff, or stroganov, is a Russian dish that includes beef and sour cream. Delicious on its own, this dish is now traditionally served over rice or noodles. Here I have substituted pork for beef.

In a large mixing bowl, combine salt, pepper, and flour. Coat pork in flour mixture. In a large saucepan, heat butter over medium heat until browning. Add garlic and onion, and cook until tender. Add pork, broth, and Worcestershire sauce. Bring to a boil, reduce heat, cover, and simmer for 30 minutes, stirring occasionally. Gradually stir in sour cream and cook an additional 5 minutes. Garnish with the parsley.

Quick and Easy Tip
To serve with noodles, use 1 pound of egg noodles cooked in water and drained.

Skillet-Braised Pork with Horseradish

Serves 6

- ~ **PREP TIME:** 10 minutes
- ~ **COOK TIME:** 1½ to 2 hours
- ~ **TOTAL COST:** $7.00
- ~ **CALORIES:** 210
- ~ **FAT:** 6 g
- ~ **CARBOHYDRATES:** 4 g
- ~ **PROTEIN:** 34 g
- ~ **CHOLESTEROL:** 89 mg
- ~ **SODIUM:** 322 mg

2 tablespoons olive oil
1½ pounds boneless pork roast, cut into 1- to 2-inch cubes
1 yellow onion, chopped
1 carrot, peeled and chopped
1 rib celery, chopped
2 cans beef broth
Sea salt and lemon pepper to taste
¼ cup cider vinegar
¼ cup prepared horseradish

Fresh horseradish is a root related to mustard. Prepared horseradish is fresh horseradish that has been grated and mixed with vinegar to preserve flavor and color.

In large saucepan, heat oil over medium heat. Add pork and cook until browned, about 3 minutes. Add vegetables and cook until onions are softened, about 3 minutes. Add beef broth, salt, lemon pepper, vinegar, and horseradish and bring to a boil. Reduce the heat, cover, and simmer for 1½ hours or until pork is tender.

Citrus-Glazed Ham over Rice

 Serves 4

- ~ **PREP TIME:** 8 minutes
- ~ **COOK TIME:** 28 minutes
- ~ **TOTAL COST:** $6.38
- ~ **CALORIES:** 342
- ~ **FAT:** 11 g
- ~ **CARBOHYDRATES:** 24 g
- ~ **PROTEIN:** 25 g
- ~ **CHOLESTEROL:** 72 mg
- ~ **SODIUM:** 1695 mg

1 cup uncooked rice
2 cups water
½ cup orange marmalade
Sea salt and black pepper to taste
¼ cup orange juice
2 tablespoons balsamic vinegar
½ teaspoon fresh marjoram, leaves chopped
1 pound cooked ham, cut into cubes

This citrus sweet ham is also delicious served chilled with mixed greens and balsamic vinaigrette.

1. In medium-quart boiler, combine rice and 2 cups of water. Bring to a boil over high heat. Cover and reduce heat to low and simmer for about 18 minutes. Remove from heat and set aside.
2. Meanwhile, in large saucepan, combine all remaining ingredients except ham and bring to a boil. Reduce heat to low and simmer for about 4 minutes. Add ham and stir to combine. Cook until ham is heated through and sauce has thickened to a glaze, about 4 minutes. Serve over rice and drizzle with any remaining glaze.

Penne Pasta with Ham, Broccoli, and Cauliflower

Serves 6

- ~ **PREP TIME:** 8 minutes
- ~ **COOK TIME:** 20 minutes
- ~ **TOTAL COST:** $6.90
- ~ **CALORIES:** 302
- ~ **FAT:** 11 g
- ~ **CARBOHYDRATES:** 24 g
- ~ **PROTEIN:** 23 g
- ~ **CHOLESTEROL:** 46 mg
- ~ **SODIUM:** 365 mg

2 cups penne pasta
2 tablespoons olive oil
1½ cups frozen broccoli and cauliflower blend
2 tablespoons water
Sea salt to taste
2 cups cubed ham
1 (10-ounce) container four-cheese or Alfredo sauce
Black pepper to taste

Other vegetable combinations are also delicious in this recipe. Use sugar snap peas and shaved carrots, for example.

1. Bring a large pot of water to boil; cook penne according to package directions. Meanwhile, heat olive oil in large saucepan over medium heat. Add frozen vegetables; sprinkle with 2 tablespoons water and season lightly with salt. Cover and cook over medium heat for 4 to 5 minutes until vegetables are almost hot, stirring once during cooking time. Add ham and Alfredo sauce; bring to a simmer.
2. Drain pasta when cooked and add to saucepan with ham mixture. Stir gently, then simmer for an additional 4 minutes until vegetables and ham are hot. Season with pepper and serve.

Grilled Polish Sausages with Slaw

Serves 4

~ **PREP TIME:** 8 minutes
~ **COOK TIME:** 18 minutes
~ **TOTAL COST:** $6.98
~ **CALORIES:** 425
~ **FAT:** 19 g
~ **CARBOHYDRATES:** 45 g
~ **PROTEIN:** 28 g
~ **CHOLESTEROL:** 49 mg
~ **SODIUM:** 681 mg

5 polish sausages
1 cup beer
3 cups coleslaw mix
¾ cup Italian dressing
5 4-inch sourdough rolls, if desired

Polish sausage is also known as kielbasa and can be purchased smoked or fresh. In North America, the term polish sausage refers to any Eastern European sausage.

1. Prepare and preheat grill. Prick sausages with fork and place in saucepan with beer. Bring to a boil over high heat, then reduce heat to low and simmer for 5 minutes, turning frequently. Drain sausages and place on grill over medium coals; grill until hot and crisp, turning occasionally, about 5 to 7 minutes.
2. Meanwhile, combine coleslaw mix and dressing in medium bowl and toss. Toast rolls, cut side down, on grill. Make sandwiches using sausages, coleslaw mix, and buns.

Pork Quesadillas

Serves 4

~ **TOTAL COST:** 6.86
~ **CALORIES:** 463.36
~ **FAT:** 20.34 g
~ **PROTEIN:** 21.63 g
~ **CHOLESTEROL:** 63.36 mg
~ **SODIUM:** 221.17 mg

½ pound ground pork
1 onion, chopped
⅓ cup sour cream
1 cup shredded part-skim mozzarella cheese
1 avocado, chopped
1 jalapeño pepper, minced
8 (6-inch) corn tortillas
1 tablespoon vegetable oil

You can serve these toasty sandwiches with some salsa for dipping. This is a quick and easy idea for lunch for friends; serve with some fresh fruit.

1. In medium skillet, cook pork with onion, stirring to break up meat, until pork is browned and cooked through. Drain well and transfer to medium bowl; let stand for 10 minutes.
2. Stir in sour cream, cheese, avocado, and jalapeño pepper and mix gently. Divide mixture among half the tortillas, placing the remaining half of tortillas on top to make sandwiches.
3. Heat griddle and brush with vegetable oil. Place quesadillas on the griddle; cover and grill for 2–3 minutes on each side until tortillas are crisp and cheese is melted. Cut into quarters and serve.

Pork Chops with Cabbage

Serves 4

- ~ **TOTAL COST:** $6.98
- ~ **CALORIES:** 308.53
- ~ **FAT:** 10.03 g
- ~ **PROTEIN:** 22.59 g
- ~ **CHOLESTEROL:** 53.68 mg
- ~ **SODIUM:** 494.80 mg

4 (4-ounce) boneless pork chops
⅛ teaspoon white pepper
1 tablespoon vegetable oil
1 onion, chopped
4 cups chopped red cabbage
⅓ cup brown sugar
⅓ cup apple cider vinegar
1 tablespoon mustard

Cabbage is the ideal accompaniment to pork; a classic French addition. This recipe is tangy and sweet and the pork becomes very tender cooked this way.

1. Trim pork chops of any excess fat and sprinkle with pepper. Heat oil in large saucepan over medium heat. Brown chops on both sides, about 4 minutes total. Remove from saucepan and set aside.
2. Add onion, garlic, and cabbage to saucepan; cook and stir for 5–6 minutes or until cabbage starts to wilt. Return pork chops to pan.
3. In small bowl, combine brown sugar, vinegar, and mustard and mix well. Pour into saucepan and bring to a simmer. Cover and cook on low heat for 15–20 minutes or until cabbage is tender and pork is thoroughly cooked. Serve immediately.

Cabbage and Nutrition
Cabbage is a member of the cruciferous vegetable family, which also includes cauliflower and broccoli. These vegetables have phytochemicals called indoles which may help protect heart health. Cabbage is high in vitamin C, fiber, and folate. Red cabbage has more vitamin C and fiber than green cabbage.

Hot German Potato Salad

Serves 6

- **TOTAL COST:** 6.88
- **CALORIES:** 468.36
- **FAT:** 26.34 g
- **PROTEIN:** 11.63 g
- **CHOLESTEROL:** 53.36 mg
- **SODIUM:** 821.17 mg

5 russet potatoes
1 onion, chopped
3 cloves garlic, minced
3 tablespoons vegetable oil
¾ pound fully cooked Polish sausages, sliced
1 tablespoon butter
3 tablespoons all-purpose flour
1 teaspoon celery salt
⅛ teaspoon pepper
1 cup water
⅓ cup apple cider vinegar
¼ cup honey
½ cup sour cream

By leaving the skins on these potatoes, you're getting the most fiber, nutrition, and yield. Plus, because they've been roasted, they're crisp and delicious!

1. Preheat oven to 400°F. Cut potatoes into 1-inch pieces, including some skin with each piece. Place in large roasting pan with onion and garlic. Drizzle oil over all and toss. Roast for 30 minutes, turn vegetables with a spatula, return to oven, and roast for 40–45 minutes longer until potatoes are tender and skins are crisp.
2. When potatoes are done, brown Polish sausage in a large saucepan until crisp and hot; remove and add to pan with potatoes.
3. Add butter to drippings in saucepan and melt over medium heat. Add flour, celery salt, and pepper; cook and stir until bubbly, about 3 minutes. Add water, vinegar, and honey and bring to a boil. Stir in sour cream.
4. Add potato mixture to sauce in saucepan and mix gently until combined. Serve immediately.

Hot Salads

Hot salads may sound unusual to you, but they can be very delicious and very inexpensive, especially when made with potatoes. They are also hearty and filling, perfect for feeding teenage boys. Be sure to refrigerate the Hot German Potato Salad leftovers promptly; the next day, leftovers heat up perfectly in the microwave oven.

Asian Pork Stir-Fry

 Serves 4

- ~ **TOTAL COST:** $6.76
- ~ **CALORIES:** 294.75
- ~ **FAT:** 9.01 g
- ~ **PROTEIN:** 15.72 g
- ~ **CHOLESTEROL:** 37.90 mg
- ~ **SODIUM:** 396.46 mg

2 tablespoons low-sodium soy sauce
2 tablespoons honey
¼ cup chicken broth
1 teaspoon five spice powder
⅛ teaspoon pepper
1 tablespoon cornstarch
2 tablespoons vegetable oil
3 cloves garlic, minced
1 tablespoon minced ginger root
½ pound pork tenderloin, thinly sliced
1 cup sliced mushrooms
1 zucchini, sliced
1 cup frozen peas

Serve this delicious and spicy stir-fry over hot cooked brown rice, with chopsticks.

1. In small bowl, combine soy sauce, honey, chicken broth, five spice powder, and cornstarch and mix thoroughly with wire whisk. Set aside. Prepare the meat and all of the vegetables.
2. In large wok or large skillet, heat oil over medium-high heat. Add garlic and ginger; stir-fry for 2 minutes. Then add pork tenderloin slices; stir-fry for 3–4 minutes. Remove pork from wok.
3. Add mushrooms, zucchini, and peas to wok and stir-fry until crisp-tender, about 4 minutes. Return meat to wok. Stir soy sauce mixture and pour into wok. Stir-fry for 2–4 minutes or until sauce boils and thickens. Serve immediately over hot cooked rice.

Country Style Pork Kiev

Serves 4

- ~ **TOTAL COST:** $6.89
- ~ **CALORIES:** 296.14
- ~ **FAT:** 14.26 g
- ~ **PROTEIN:** 26.44 g
- ~ **CHOLESTEROL:** 100.79 mg
- ~ **SODIUM:** 530.43 mg

2 slices oatmeal bread
2 tablespoons grated Parmesan cheese
½ teaspoon dried basil leaves
½ teaspoon dried oregano leaves
½ teaspoon salt
3 tablespoons butter
1 (12 ounce) pork tenderloin
¼ cup Chicken Broth (Chapter 6)
2 tablespoons chopped parsley

Coating pork tenderloins with seasoned bread crumbs, then baking it in a butter sauce makes a wonderful elegant dish perfect to serve to company.

1. Preheat oven to 425°F. Make bread crumbs from oatmeal bread; mix in small bowl with Parmesan cheese, basil, oregano, and salt. Melt butter in small saucepan. Mix melted butter with the bread crumbs.
2. Place pork on a shallow roasting pan. Press crumb mixture onto the top and bottom sides of the pork tenderloin. Bake for 35–45 minutes or until pork registers 165°F on a meat thermometer and coating is brown and crisp.
3. Combine Chicken Broth and parsley. Bring to a boil over high heat and pour over tenderloin. Slice to serve.

Kung Pao Pork

Serves 4

- ~ **TOTAL COST:** $6.84
- ~ **CALORIES:** 304.32
- ~ **FAT:** 14.01 g
- ~ **PROTEIN:** 18.54 g
- ~ **CHOLESTEROL:** 51.60 mg
- ~ **SODIUM:** 739.23 mg

¾ pound boneless pork chops
3 tablespoons low-sodium soy sauce
3 tablespoons vegetable oil, divided
2 tablespoons apple cider vinegar
2 tablespoons cornstarch
1 tablespoon sugar
⅛ teaspoon pepper
1 jalapeño pepper, minced
1 cup Chicken Broth (Chapter 6)
1 green bell pepper, sliced

You can control the spiciness of this recipe by preparing the jalapeños. Discard the seeds and it will be milder; use the seeds for a hotter dish.

1. Cut pork into 2" × ⅛" slices. In medium bowl, combine soy sauce, 1 tablespoon canola oil, vinegar, cornstarch, sugar, pepper, and jalapeños, and mix well. Add pork and stir to coat. Cover and refrigerate for 1 hour.
2. Drain pork, reserving marinade. Heat a wok or large skillet over medium high heat. Add 2 tablespoons oil, then add pork; stir fry for 2–3 minutes or until pork is browned. Add green pepper; stir-fry for 3–4 minutes longer.
3. Add Chicken Broth to marinade, stir, and add to wok. Stir-fry for 2–3 minutes longer or until sauce boils and thickens. Serve immediately with hot cooked rice.

Spicy Stir-Fry

You can make your own stir-fries as mild or spicy as you like. If you really like hot food, try using a serrano or habanero pepper instead of the jalapeño pepper. The general rule is, the smaller the pepper, the hotter the fire. Mild green bell peppers, which are large, are always going to be less spicy than smaller jalapeño peppers.

Ham and Potato Casserole

 Serves 4

- ~ **TOTAL COST:** $6.47
- ~ **CALORIES:** 435.31
- ~ **FAT:** 21.53 g
- ~ **PROTEIN:** 19.90 g
- ~ **CHOLESTEROL:** 63.18 mg
- ~ **SODIUM:** 860.42 mg

1 tablespoon olive oil
2 tablespoons butter
1 onion, chopped
1 green bell pepper, chopped
2 tablespoons flour
½ teaspoon salt
⅛ teaspoon pepper
1 cup milk
1 cup shredded Swiss cheese
1 cup cubed cooked ham
4 potatoes, thinly sliced
3 tablespoons grated Parmesan cheese

This old fashioned recipe is pure comfort food. Make it when you have leftover ham after Easter or Christmas dinner.

1. Preheat oven to 350°F. In large saucepan, melt olive oil and butter over medium heat. Add onion; cook and stir for 3 minutes. Then add green bell pepper; cook and stir for 2 minutes longer. Remove vegetables from pan with slotted spoon and set aside.
2. Add flour to fat remaining in pan; cook and stir for 3 minutes. Add salt, pepper, and milk; bring to a simmer, stirring constantly with a wire whisk. Cook for 4–5 minutes or until sauce thickens. Remove from heat and stir in reserved vegetables, Swiss cheese, and ham.
3. Place ¼ cup sauce in the bottom of a 13" × 9" glass baking dish. Layer with ⅓ of the potatoes and top with ⅓ of the remaining sauce. Repeat layers, ending with sauce. Sprinkle with Parmesan cheese. Cover with foil and bake for 1 hour, then remove foil and bake 30–35 minutes longer or until potatoes are tender, casserole is bubbling, and top is beginning to brown. Cool for 10 minutes, then serve.

White Sauce

White sauces are the base for many recipes, including scalloped potatoes and gumbo. There are a few secrets to making the best white sauce. Be sure to cook the flour for at least 2 minutes so the starch granules swell and the "raw" taste goes away. And when adding the liquid, stir constantly with a wire whisk to prevent lumps.

Lemon Pork Scallops

Serves 4

~ **TOTAL COST:** $6.89
~ **CALORIES:** 264.98
~ **FAT:** 12.11 g
~ **PROTEIN:** 24.71 g
~ **CHOLESTEROL:** 88.89 mg
~ **SODIUM:** 391.23 mg

1 pound pork tenderloin
3 tablespoons flour
½ teaspoon salt
⅛ teaspoon pepper
½ teaspoon dried thyme leaves
2 tablespoon butter
1 tablespoon olive oil
4 cloves garlic, minced
3 tablespoons lemon juice
½ cup Chicken Broth (Chapter 6)
½ teaspoon grated lemon zest, if desired

This recipe would be delicious served with a rice pilaf and some roasted asparagus for a springtime meal.

1. Cut pork tenderloin into ¼-inch slices crosswise. Place on work surface and cover with waxed paper or parchment paper. Pound pork pieces until ⅛-inch thick. On shallow plate, combine flour, salt, pepper, and thyme. Coat pork in flour mixture.

2. In large saucepan, combine 1 tablespoon butter and olive oil over medium heat. When mixture is hot, add scallops. Cook for 2–3 minutes on each side, turning once, until pork is almost cooked. Remove to plate. Add shallot to saucepan; cook and stir for 2 minutes. Then add lemon juice, Chicken Broth, and lemon zest; bring to a boil. Boil for 3 minutes until sauce is reduced. Return pork to saucepan and cook over medium heat for 1–2 minutes until pork is thoroughly cooked

Sweet-and-Sour Pork

Serves 2–4*

~ **COST:** $2.67
~ **CALORIES:** 710
~ **FAT:** 33 g
~ **CARBOHYDRATES:** 32 g
~ **PROTEIN:** 70 g
~ **CHOLESTEROL:** 185 mg
~ **SODIUM:** 320 mg

1 pound lean boneless pork
½ large green or red bell pepper
¼ cup baby carrots
1 green onion, optional
⅓ cup white vinegar
2 tablespoons ketchup
3 tablespoons granulated sugar
⅓ cup, plus 2 tablespoons water
2 tablespoons vegetable oil
1 tablespoon cornstarch

1. Cut pork into cubes. Wash and drain all the vegetables. Cut bell pepper into cubes, and cut baby carrots in half. Dice the green onion, if using.

2. In a small bowl, combine the vinegar, ketchup, sugar, and ⅓ cup water, and set aside.

3. Heat the oil in a frying pan on medium to medium-high heat. When the oil is hot, add the pork cubes and brown. Drain off the fat from the pan and add the sauce. Reduce heat to medium-low, cover, and simmer for 45 minutes or until tender.

4. Combine the cornstarch and 2 tablespoons water in a small bowl. Increase heat to high and add the cornstarch mixture, stirring to thicken. Reduce heat to medium and add the green pepper and carrots. Cover and simmer for 10 minutes or until the vegetables are tender. Stir in the green onion if using. Serve hot over rice.

*Nutrition information and price per serving based on the recipe serving 2.

Pepperoni-Stuffed French Toast

Serves 4

- ~ **TOTAL COST:** $4.63
- ~ **CALORIES:** 582.82
- ~ **FAT:** 32.32 g
- ~ **PROTEIN:** 20.77 g
- ~ **CHOLESTEROL:** 190.83 mg
- ~ **SODIUM:** 1017.23 mg

½ loaf Whole Wheat French Bread (Chapter 3)
1 (3-ounce) package cream cheese, softened
¼ cup ricotta cheese
1 tablespoon heavy cream
1 (3-ounce) package pepperoni slices, chopped
¼ cup finely sliced green onion
⅓ cup milk
2 eggs
¼ teaspoon salt
⅛ teaspoon pepper
¼ cup grated Parmesan cheese
2 tablespoons butter
1 tablespoon olive oil
1 cup salsa

French Toast doesn't have to be sweet! This savory dish is a good choice for a cold winter's night. And remember, breakfast dishes for dinner are inexpensive and filling.

1. Slice bread into 1-inch slices. Cut a pocket in the side of each slice. In small bowl, combine cream cheese, ricotta cheese, and cream and beat until smooth. Stir in pepperoni and green onion. Stuff bread with this mixture.
2. In shallow bowl, combine milk, eggs, salt, cayenne pepper, and Parmesan cheese until combined. In large skillet, melt butter and olive oil over medium heat.
3. Dip stuffed bread pieces into egg mixture, turning once to coat. Then cook bread in skillet, turning once, until dark golden brown. Serve immediately with salsa.

Savory Stuffed French Toast
You can stuff a slice of French bread with just about anything. Instead of the cream cheese and pepperoni mixture, use a combination of cottage cheese and cooked onion, with some chopped cooked chicken and green onion. Use your imagination and you never have to serve the same dish twice—unless you want to!

Pork and Tomato Farfalle

Serves 4

~ **TOTAL COST:** $6.89
~ **CALORIES:** 395.79
~ **FAT:** 11.39 g
~ **PROTEIN:** 27.31 g
~ **CHOLESTEROL:** 67.25 mg
~ **SODIUM:** 753.63 mg

12 ounces pork tenderloin
½ teaspoon salt
⅛ teaspoon pepper
3 cloves garlic, minced
1 tablespoon vegetable oil
1 tablespoon butter
1 onion, chopped
1 (6-ounce) can tomato paste
¾ cup Chicken Broth (Chapter 6)
1 tablespoon sugar
½ teaspoon dried basil leaves
½ teaspoon dried thyme leaves
¼ cup evaporated milk
2 cups farfalle pasta
3 tablespoons grated Parmesan cheese

Any medium sized pasta can be used in this excellent skillet meal. Try medium shells, mostaccioli, or penne pasta.

1. Slice pork tenderloin crosswise into ¼-inch slices. In small bowl, combine salt, pepper, and garlic. Using back of spoon, crush garlic into spices until a paste forms. Rub this paste on the pork tenderloin slices.
2. In heavy skillet, heat oil and butter over medium heat and cook pork until browned, turning once, about 5 minutes; remove to clean plate. Then add onion to skillet and cook until crisp-tender. Bring a large pot of water to a boil.
3. Add tomato paste, Chicken Broth, sugar, basil, and thyme to skillet. Bring to a boil, reduce heat, cover pan, and simmer for 5 minutes to blend flavors. Return pork to skillet and bring back to a simmer. Simmer, covered, for 10–15 minutes or until pork is tender, then add evaporated milk and simmer 3 minutes longer.
4. Cook pasta according to package directions and drain, reserving ¼ cup cooking water. Add pasta to pork along with reserved pasta cooking water. Toss over medium heat for 1 minute, then serve with cheese.

Pork Fajitas

- **TOTAL COST:** $6.43
- **CALORIES:** 508.24
- **FAT:** 22.39 g
- **PROTEIN:** 24.36 g
- **CHOLESTEROL:** 58.78 mg
- **SODIUM:** 1047.23 mg

2 (4-ounce) boneless pork chops
1 tablespoon taco seasoning mix
½ teaspoon salt
⅛ teaspoon cayenne pepper
2 tablespoons vegetable oil
1 onion, sliced
1 zucchini, sliced
1 cup shredded Cheddar cheese
4 (10-inch) flour tortillas
¼ cup chopped cilantro

Instead of being slowly cooked, the pork in this simple recipe is stir-fried, so the fajitas are ready to eat in about 30 minutes.

1. Cut pork chops into thin strips and place in medium bowl. Sprinkle with taco seasoning mix, salt, and cayenne pepper; let stand for 15 minutes.
2. In heavy skillet, heat vegetable oil over medium heat. Stir-fry pork strips for 4–6 minutes until pork is cooked; remove from pan. Add onion and zucchini; stir-fry until crisp-tender, about 4 minutes. Return pork to pan and remove from heat.
3. Warm tortillas and fill with the pork mixture, Cheddar cheese, and cilantro; wrap and serve.

How to Warm Tortillas
Serve any dish that has a lot of sauce with a bunch of warmed flour or corn tortillas. To warm tortillas, wrap them in foil and place them in a 350°F oven for about 10 minutes. Or wrap in microwave-safe paper towels and microwave on high for 20–30 seconds for four tortillas. Place them in a tortilla warmer and serve.

CHAPTER 9

BEEF

Meatballs over Cornbread

Serves 4

- **TOTAL COST:** $4.93
- **CALORIES:** 501.35
- **FAT:** 20.34 g
- **PROTEIN:** 24.47 g
- **CHOLESTEROL:** 147.40 mg
- **SODIUM:** 469.74 mg

½ cup fresh soft bread crumbs
2 tablespoons grated Parmesan cheese
1 egg
¼ teaspoon onion salt
¾ pound 80% lean ground beef
½ cup chopped onion
2 tablespoons flour
⅛ teaspoon cayenne pepper
½ cup beef broth
1 cup water
4 (3" × 3") squares Double Cornbread (Chapter 3)

Tiny and tender meatballs in savory gravy served over hot split cornbread makes one of the most satisfying meals ever.

1. In medium bowl, combine bread crumbs, cheese, egg, and onion salt; beat until mixed. Add beef; work gently with hands until combined. Form into 30 meatballs.
2. In large skillet, brown meatballs, shaking pan frequently, and turning meatballs until they almost cooked. Remove with slotted spoon to plate. Add onion to drippings in skillet; cook and stir for 5 minutes.
3. Sprinkle flour and pepper into skillet; cook and stir for 1 minute. Add beef broth and water and bring to a simmer.
4. Return meatballs to skillet; simmer until beef registers 165°F on a meat thermometer.
5. If Cornbread was made earlier, reheat in the microwave 10 seconds on high per square. Split Cornbread, place bottom on serving plates, divide meatballs and sauce over all, and top with top of Cornbread. Serve immediately.

Old-Fashioned Beef Casserole

Serves 4

- ~ **TOTAL COST:** $4.83
- ~ **CALORIES:** 422.66
- ~ **FAT:** 17.16 g
- ~ **PROTEIN:** 24.42 g
- ~ **CHOLESTEROL:** 62.65 mg
- ~ **SODIUM:** 553.44 mg

¾ pound 80% lean ground beef
1 onion, chopped
1 (10-ounce) can cream of mushroom soup
1 cup milk
2 cups water
1 cup long grain rice
3 carrots, thinly sliced

Old-fashioned recipes are simple and very satisfying. You could add some dried herbs to this casserole to bring the flavor a bit more up to date; ½ teaspoon of thyme or oregano is perfect.

1. Grease a 2½ quart casserole dish and set aside. In large skillet, brown ground beef with onion; drain and set aside. Add soup, milk, water, and rice and bring to a simmer. Pour half of this mixture into prepared casserole.
2. Top with half of the onions and carrots. Sprinkle each layer with a bit of salt and pepper. Top with remaining beef mixture, then remaining onions and carrots.
3. Cover and bake at 350°F for 1 hour. Uncover and bake for 5–10 minutes longer until bubbly and vegetables are tender.

Ground Beef Tricks

A recommended serving size of beef is 3 ounces, not ¼ pound. So if you substitute ¾ pound of beef for a full pound in any recipe that serves four, save the ¼ pound in the freezer. Do this three times, and you'll have another portion of beef to use with little pain in your wallet.

Spaghetti with Meat Sauce

Serves 6

- ~ **TOTAL COST:** $6.57
- ~ **CALORIES:** 429.15
- ~ **FAT:** 12.16 g
- ~ **PROTEIN:** 24.45 g
- ~ **CHOLESTEROL:** 51.92 mg
- ~ **SODIUM:** 701.34 mg

¾ pound ground beef
1 onion, chopped
3 cloves garlic, minced
1 carrot, grated
1 teaspoon dried basil leaves
¼ teaspoon salt
1 (8-ounce) can tomato sauce
1 (10-ounce) can condensed tomato soup
½ cup water
1 teaspoon dried Italian seasoning
1 (12-ounce) package spaghetti pasta
⅓ cup grated Parmesan cheese

1. Brown ground beef with onion and garlic in heavy skillet over medium heat. Drain well, and then add carrot, basil, salt, and pasta sauce. Simmer for 10–15 minutes, stirring occasionally, until carrot is tender.
2. Bring a large pot of salted water to a boil. Cook pasta according to package directions until al dente while sauce is simmering. Drain pasta, return to pot, add 1 cup of sauce, and toss. Place on serving platter and pour remaining sauce over pasta. Sprinkle with cheese and serve immediately.

Reduced Sodium Products
Reduced sodium products are usually more expensive than their full-salt counterparts. For instance, low-sodium condensed soups are usually 10 to 20 cents more expensive than regular. You have to decide if the reduced sodium is worth it. To control what your family eats, you may be willing to pay a bit more.

Frito Pie

Serves 4

- **TOTAL COST:** $4.89
- **CALORIES:** 455.28
- **FAT:** 22.32 g
- **PROTEIN:** 16.81 g
- **CHOLESTEROL:** 41.42 mg
- **SODIUM:** 1033.66 mg

½ (15-ounce) bag Fritos corn chips
2 cups Homemade Chili, heated
½ cup chopped onion
1 cup shredded Cheddar cheese
8 pickled jalapeño slices, if desired

This unusual recipe may seem strange to you, but it's a Texas favorite. Attend any high school football game in Texas, and you'll see Frito Pie being enjoyed in the stands during halftime.

1. Divide corn chips among four bowls. Pour heated chili and onion over the chips and sprinkle with cheese and jalapeño slices. Serve immediately.
2. You can serve this by using individual 1.75-ounce bags of the corn chips. Split the bags along the side and add remaining ingredients. Eat right out of the bag with a plastic spoon.

Spicy Cube Steaks

Serves 4

- **TOTAL COST:** $6.74
- **CALORIES:** 314.48
- **FAT:** 11.52 g
- **PROTEIN:** 35.05 g
- **CHOLESTEROL:** 110.34 mg
- **SODIUM:** 657.76 mg

4 (4 ounce) cube steaks
3 tablespoons flour
1 tablespoon chili powder
½ teaspoon salt
⅛ teaspoon pepper
1 tablespoon olive oil
1 (14-ounce) can diced tomatoes with chiles

Cube steaks are a tougher cut of meat, like top round, that has been run through a machine that cuts through the fibers, making a tender dish. Serve over mashed potatoes for a true comfort-food meal.

1. Place cube steaks on waxed paper. In small bowl, combine flour, chili powder, salt, and pepper and mix well. Sprinkle half of flour mixture over steaks and pound into steak using a rolling pin or flat side of a meat mallet. Turn steaks, sprinkle with remaining flour mixture, and pound again.
2. Heat olive oil in large saucepan over medium-high heat. Add steaks; cook for 4 minutes on first side, until steaks release easily, then turn and cook for 2 minutes. Remove steaks from saucepan.
3. Pour tomatoes into pan; cook and stir to remove drippings from pan, until simmering. Add steaks back to pan and bring to a simmer again. Cover, and simmer for 15–20 minutes longer or until steaks are tender and sauce is thickened. Serve immediately.

Pesto Rice Meatballs

 Serves 5; 6 meatballs per serving

- ~ **TOTAL COST:** $5.98
- ~ **CALORIES:** 398.77
- ~ **FAT:** 25.31 g
- ~ **PROTEIN:** 26.49 g
- ~ **CHOLESTEROL:** 121.51 mg
- ~ **SODIUM:** 552.64 mg

¼ cup long grain rice
½ cup water
1 egg
⅓ cup Spinach Pesto (Chapter 2)
¼ cup grated Parmesan cheese
1 pound 80% lean ground beef
2 tablespoons olive oil
1 (10-ounce) can condensed tomato soup
1 cup water

Partially cooking the rice adds moisture to the meatballs and ensures that the rice becomes nice and tender, even on the inside of each meatball.

1. In small saucepan, combine rice and water. Bring to a boil, then reduce heat, cover, and simmer for 10 minutes to cook rice partially. Drain rice if necessary. Spread rice on a cookie sheet and freeze for 10 minutes.
2. In large bowl, combine rice, egg, Pesto, milk, and cheese and mix well. Add beef; mix gently but thoroughly until combined. Form into 1-inch meatballs.
3. Heat olive oil in large skillet over medium heat. Cook meatballs, turning frequently, until lightly browned, about 5 minutes. Drain pan, then add soup, water, and bring to a simmer. Stir gently, then cover and simmer for 20–30 minutes or until meatballs are thoroughly cooked. Serve immediately.

Leftover Meatballs

If you have leftover meatballs, they make fabulous sandwiches. Heat the meatballs with the sauce, or if you need more sauce, add some pasta or tomato sauce. Then split a couple of hoagie buns, toast them, top with the meatballs, sauce, and some cheese. Broil until the cheese melts and bubbles, then serve.

Taco Salad

Serves 4

~ **TOTAL COST:** $4.43
~ **CALORIES:** 334.81
~ **FAT:** 18.65 g
~ **PROTEIN:** 18.10 g
~ **CHOLESTEROL:** 56.40 mg
~ **SODIUM:** 614.33 mg

2 cups Homemade Chili (Chapter 6)
½ (15-ounce) can refried beans
5 cups shredded lettuce
1½ cups tortilla chips
1½ cups shredded Cheddar cheese

This recipe alone is a good reason to double the Homemade Chili recipe. Leftovers of that chili freeze beautifully, so you can make this dish in minutes.

1. In large saucepan, combine Chili and refried beans and stir over medium heat until hot, about 6–7 minutes.
2. Meanwhile, place lettuce on four plates and top with the tortilla chips. Spoon hot beef mixture over chips and top with the cheese. Serve immediately.

Tortilla Chips
You can make your own tortilla chips. Choose flavored or plain corn or flour tortillas and cut them into wedges using a pizza cutter. Heat 2 cups of vegetable oil in a large saucepan over medium-high heat and fry tortilla wedges until crisp, stirring frequently with a sieve or slotted spoon. Drain on paper towels and sprinkle with salt and seasonings.

Steak Quesadillas

Serves 4

~ **TOTAL COST:** $6.86
~ **CALORIES:** 310.34
~ **FAT:** 9.37 g
~ **PROTEIN:** 20.73 g
~ **CHOLESTEROL:** 53.46 mg
~ **SODIUM:** 771.57 mg

8 ounces sirloin tip steak
1 zucchini
½ cup salsa
½ (10.75-ounce) can condensed nacho cheese soup
4 (10-inch) flour tortillas

This price assumes $3.60 for ½ pound of steak. If you can find it cheaper than that, your cost will go down.

1. Grill or cook steak for 4–5 minutes on each side until medium, 145°F on a meat thermometer. Cover and let stand.
2. Slice zucchini into rounds and add to grill or pan that cooked the steak. Cook, turning once, until tender, about 4–5 minutes. Add salsa and soup to pan and bring to a simmer.
3. Slice steak thinly across the grain and add to pan. Remove from heat and make quesadillas with the tortillas. Serve immediately.

Spinach Beef Stir-Fry

Serves 4

- **TOTAL COST:** $6.91
- **CALORIES:** 358.74
- **FAT:** 22.19 g
- **PROTEIN:** 26.76 g
- **CHOLESTEROL:** 220.13 mg
- **SODIUM:** 744.80 mg

¾ pound 80% lean ground beef
1 cup sliced mushrooms
2 onions, chopped
4 cloves garlic, minced
½ teaspoon ground ginger
2 tablespoons soy sauce
1 (10-ounce) package frozen spinach, thawed
3 eggs
¼ cup milk
⅓ cup grated Parmesan cheese

This easy stir-fry recipe uses ingredients you probably already have around the house. You could add sliced summer squash, zucchini, or more mushrooms.

1. In large skillet, crumble ground beef. Cook and stir over medium heat for 3 minutes. Add mushrooms, onion, and garlic; cook and stir until beef is browned and vegetables are crisp-tender. Drain well.
2. Drain spinach thoroughly and add to skillet along with ginger and soy sauce; cook and stir for 2 minutes until hot.
3. In small bowl, combine egg, milk, and cheese and beat well. Add to skillet; stir-fry until eggs are cooked and set. Serve immediately.

Stir-Fry Tips
You don't need a wok to stir-fry; a large heavy-duty frying pan will do, preferably one without a non-stick surface. Have all the ingredients ready to cook and the sauces mixed. Heat the pan over high heat and add the ingredients in the order the recipe specifies. Keep the food moving with a sturdy spatula or wooden spoon. And be sure to serve immediately!

Pizza Burgers

Serves 4

- ~ **TOTAL COST:** $6.44
- ~ **CALORIES:** 587.82
- ~ **FAT:** 30.36 g
- ~ **PROTEIN:** 31.67 g
- ~ **CHOLESTEROL:** 104.90 mg
- ~ **SODIUM:** 1044.32 mg

¾ pound 80% lean ground beef
1 onion, chopped
1 tablespoon all-purpose flour
1 cup canned black beans, drained and chopped
1 (8-ounce) can tomato sauce
½ cup grated carrots
½ teaspoon dried Italian seasoning
½ teaspoon garlic salt
¼ cup grated Parmesan cheese
1 cup shredded Cheddar cheese, divided
3 English muffins, split
2 tablespoons butter, softened

Black beans and carrots stretch the meat and add rich flavor and nutrition to these simple open-faced sandwiches. You could serve the filling on toasted hamburger buns if you'd like too.

1. In a large saucepan, cook ground beef and onion together over medium heat, stirring occasionally, until meat is browned and cooked. Drain off excess fat and water.
2. Sprinkle flour over meat; cook and stir for 1 minute. Then add beans, tomato purée, carrots, Italian seasoning, and salt. Bring to a boil, reduce heat, and simmer for about 5–8 minutes until thickened. Stir in Parmesan cheese and ½ cup Cheddar cheese; remove from heat.
3. Preheat broiler. Spread split sides of English muffins with butter and toast under broiler. Remove from oven and divide beef mixture among muffins. Top with remaining Cheddar cheese. Broil 6 inches from heat for 4–5 minutes or until sandwiches are hot and cheese is melted and bubbly. Serve immediately.

Beef Risotto

- **TOTAL COST:** $6.95
- **CALORIES:** 342.04
- **FAT:** 11.67 g
- **PROTEIN:** 22.48 g
- **CHOLESTEROL:** 54.20 mg
- **SODIUM:** 438.81 mg

2 cups water
2 cups beef broth
1 tablespoon olive oil
½ pound sirloin steak, chopped
1 onion, minced
2 cloves garlic, minced
1½ cups long-grain white rice
2 tablespoons steak sauce
¼ teaspoon pepper
¼ cup grated Parmesan cheese
1 tablespoon butter

This elegant recipe is perfect for a spring dinner. It is a last-minute recipe, so don't start it until after your guests have arrived.

1. In medium saucepan, combine water and broth; heat over low heat until warm; keep on heat.
2. In large saucepan, heat olive oil over medium heat. Add beef; cook and stir until browned. Remove from pan with slotted spoon and set aside. Add onion and garlic to pan; cook and stir until crisp-tender, about 4 minutes.
3. Add rice; cook and stir for 2 minutes. Add the broth mixture, a cup at a time, stirring until the liquid is absorbed, about 15 minutes. When there is 1 cup broth remaining, return the beef to the pot and add the steak sauce, pepper, and asparagus.
4. Cook and stir until rice is tender, beef is cooked, and green beans are tender, about 5 minutes. Stir in Parmesan and butter and serve immediately.

Risotto

Risotto is easy to make and an expensive way to stretch any meat. It has a reputation for being difficult, but it is not. For the best risotto, have the liquid warming in a small saucepan while you cook the rice, keep stirring so the starch escapes from the grains of rice and thickens the sauce, and finish with a tiny bit of butter for extra creaminess.

Goulash

Serves 4

~ **TOTAL COST:** $6.97
~ **CALORIES:** 469.91
~ **FAT:** 18.12 g
~ **PROTEIN:** 23.36 g
~ **CHOLESTEROL:** 59.64 mg
~ **SODIUM:** 846.79 mg

¾ pound ground beef
1 onion, chopped
2 cloves garlic
⅛ teaspoon pepper
½ teaspoon dried oregano
1 (10-ounce) can condensed tomato soup
1 green bell pepper, chopped
1 (14-ounce) can diced tomatoes, undrained
2½ cups penne pasta

Goulash is just old fashioned comfort food. You can use any shape of pasta that's in your pantry. Serve this with a green salad and some breadsticks.

1. In large skillet, cook ground beef with onion and garlic until beef is browned and onion is tender. Drain well. Add pepper, oregano, soup, green pepper, and undrained tomatoes. Stir well and simmer, uncovered, for 10 minutes to blend flavors.
2. Cook pasta until almost al dente. Drain and stir pasta into mixture in skillet.
3. Bring mixture to a simmer; simmer, stirring frequently, for 8–10 minutes or until pasta is tender and mixture is blended. Serve immediately.

Beans and Meatballs

Serves 4

~ **TOTAL COST:** $5.60
~ **CALORIES:** 508.51
~ **FAT:** 19.44 g
~ **PROTEIN:** 24.59 g
~ **CHOLESTEROL:** 75.29 mg
~ **SODIUM:** 1093.34 mg

1 tablespoon olive oil
1 onion, chopped
2 cloves garlic, minced
½ cup ketchup
2 tablespoons brown sugar
3 tablespoons mustard
1 (15–ounce) can kidney beans
1 (15–ounce) can pork and beans
8 Sicilian Meatballs (this chapter), cooked

You can use any kind of canned beans you'd like in this easy recipe. Chili beans, chick peas, cannelloni beans, and black beans all work well. You do need one can of pork and beans, though.

1. Preheat oven to 350°F. In large saucepan, warm olive oil over medium heat. Add onion and garlic; cook and stir until tender, about 5 minutes. Add ketchup, brown sugar, and mustard and bring to a simmer.
2. Drain kidney beans and add with pork and beans to saucepan; mix well and remove from heat.
3. Cut Meatballs in half and add to bean mixture. Pour into 2–quart casserole. Bake for 50–60 minutes or until casserole is bubbling.

Spaghetti and Meatballs

Serves 4

- ~ **TOTAL COST:** $6.70
- ~ **CALORIES:** 696.78
- ~ **FAT:** 19.34 g
- ~ **PROTEIN:** 30.74 g
- ~ **CHOLESTEROL:** 65.34 mg
- ~ **SODIUM:** 1044.23 mg

12 Pesto Rice Meatballs (this chapter)
1 (26-ounce) jar pasta sauce
1 onion, chopped
1 large carrot, grated
1 (12-ounce) package spaghetti
5 tablespoons grated Parmesan cheese, divided

This simple recipe is full of vitamins C and A. Serve it with toasted Whole Wheat French Bread (Chapter 3) and some red wine.

1. Bring a large pot of water to a boil. Prepare the Pesto Rice Meatballs and bake. In large saucepan, combine pasta sauce, onion, and carrot and bring to a simmer. Simmer over low heat, stirring frequently, for 10–15 minutes until vegetables are tender.
2. Cook spaghetti in water according to package directions or until almost al dente. Drain spaghetti. Add Meatballs to simmering sauce along with spaghetti and 3 tablespoons of the cheese.
3. Simmer, stirring gently, for 5–6 minutes or until pasta is al dente. Sprinkle with the remaining 2 tablespoons Parmesan cheese and serve immediately.

Carrot in Spaghetti Sauce

Carrot may be a surprising ingredient in spaghetti sauce, but it helps thicken the sauce and adds nutrition and fiber. Make sure the carrot is finely shredded. Don't use the preshredded kind in the supermarket. Not only is it more expensive, but it won't melt into the sauce the way a hand-shredded carrot will.

Sicilian Meatballs

 Yields 16 meatballs; 4 per serving

- ~ **TOTAL COST:** $4.78
- ~ **CALORIES:** 416.49
- ~ **FAT:** 27.75 g
- ~ **PROTEIN:** 24.54 g
- ~ **CHOLESTEROL:** 135.70 mg
- ~ **SODIUM:** 305.32 mg

1 tablespoon olive oil
½ cup finely chopped onion
2 tablespoons tomato paste
2 tablespoons water
½ cup dried bread crumbs
3 tablespoons grated Parmesan cheese
1 teaspoon dried Italian seasoning
⅛ teaspoon nutmeg
1 egg
1 pound 80% lean ground beef

These meatballs are baked because it's less work and generates less waste. When meatballs are fried, you'll always lose a little bit that sticks to the pan.

1. Preheat oven to 350°F. In small saucepan, heat olive oil over medium heat. Add onion; cook and stir until onion is tender, about 4 minutes. Stir in tomato paste, lower heat to low, and cook, stirring occasionally, until the tomato paste begins to brown in spots (this adds a rich flavor to the meatballs).
2. When the tomato paste has begun to brown, add water to the saucepan; stir to loosen brown bits from the pan. Then remove the mixture to a large bowl. Add the bread crumbs, cheese, Italian seasoning, nutmeg, and egg and mix well. Then add the ground beef, working gently with hands to combine.
3. Form into 16 meatballs and place them on a broiler pan. Bake for 20–30 minutes or until meatballs are thoroughly cooked (165°F). Use immediately in a recipe or cool and chill for 1 day before using. Freeze for up to 3 months.

Meatballs

Meatballs can be used in so many ways. Combine a batch with some grape jelly and chili sauce in a slow cooker for a delicious appetizer. Add them to a sub sandwich for a meatball sub. You can also use them in Spaghetti and Meatballs (this chapter) or Beans and Meatballs (this chapter).

Top Sirloin with Black Beans and Mexican Salsa

 Serves 4

- ~ **PREP TIME:** 5 minutes
- ~ **COOK TIME:** 15 minutes
- ~ **TOTAL COST:** $6.96
- ~ **CALORIES:** 240
- ~ **FAT:** 6 g
- ~ **PROTEIN:** 29 g
- ~ **CHOLESTEROL:** 77 mg
- ~ **SODIUM:** 149 mg

1 tablespoon olive oil
¼ pound top round sirloin, cut into 2-inch cubes
1 clove fresh garlic, minced
½ teaspoon all-purpose seasoning
¼ cup frozen corn
1 tablespoon cilantro, chopped
½ cup beef broth
¼ cup celery, sliced
1 yellow onion, thinly sliced
1 cup salsa
1 (14-ounce) can black beans, canned
¼ teaspoon black pepper

Sliced in strips, this recipe could also be served as fajitas!

1. Coat a skillet with oil. Add sirloin, garlic, and all-purpose seasoning to skillet. Sauté on medium high for 8 minutes, stirring often.
2. Mix remaining ingredients and add to skillet. Simmer for 8 to 10 minutes. Add additional beef broth if mixture gets too dry.

Quick and Easy Tip
Using dried black beans from scratch takes a long time. Use the canned variety instead—they're still nutritious and much faster when every second counts.

Sautéed Beef with Sugar Snap Peas and Soy Sauce

 Serves 4

- ~ **PREP TIME:** 8 minutes
- ~ **COOK TIME:** 20 minutes
- ~ **TOTAL COST:** $6.95
- ~ **CALORIES:** 329
- ~ **FAT:** 14 g
- ~ **PROTEIN:** 31 g
- ~ **CHOLESTEROL:** 44 mg
- ~ **SODIUM:** 842 mg

1 tablespoon olive oil
¾ pound round sirloin steak, cut into 2-inch cubes
1 clove fresh garlic, minced
½ teaspoon all-purpose seasoning
3 tablespoons low-sodium soy sauce
1 cup chicken broth
½ cup hoisin sauce
1½ cups white or yellow onions, quartered
1 tablespoon cornstarch
1 tablespoon sesame oil
1½ tablespoons ground ginger
1½ cups sugar snap peas, fresh or frozen
2 carrots, carrots, sliced

Don't add salt to this recipe as there is plenty in the soy sauce, chicken broth, hoisin sauce, and oils.

1. Coat a skillet with olive oil. Add beef, garlic, and all-purpose seasoning to skillet. Sauté on medium high for 8 minutes, stirring often.
2. Mix remaining ingredients and add to skillet. Simmer for 8 to 10 minutes.

Quick and Easy Tip
Cornstarch is a natural thickener and should be mixed with equal parts water before cooking. It is used here to keep the sauce from getting too runny.

Spicy Beef with Onions

Serves 4

- **PREP TIME:** 10 minutes
- **COOK TIME:** 15 minutes
- **TOTAL COST:** $6.99
- **CALORIES:** 146
- **FAT:** 8 g
- **PROTEIN:** 35 g
- **CHOLESTEROL:** 63 mg
- **SODIUM:** 302 mg

1 tablespoon olive oil
¾ pound round sirloin, cut into 2-inch cubes
1 clove fresh garlic, minced
½ teaspoon all-purpose seasoning
½ teaspoon black pepper
1 teaspoon ground ginger
1 teaspoon jalapeño peppers, finely chopped
1 yellow onion, sliced
2 tomatoes, diced
1 tablespoon curry powder
1 teaspoon coriander
1 cup beef broth
1 cup sour cream

When cooking beef, the leaner cuts are top sirloin, eye of round, and bottom round, which have less than 3 grams of saturated fats per serving.

1. Coat a skillet with olive oil. Add beef, garlic, and all-purpose seasoning to skillet. Sauté on medium high for 8 minutes, stirring often.
2. Mix remaining ingredients except sour cream and add to skillet. Simmer for 8 to 10 minutes. Add sour cream and mix well. Simmer for another 5 minutes.

Easy Pot Roast with Potatoes and Carrots

Serves 4

- **PREP TIME:** 12 minutes
- **COOK TIME:** 35 minutes
- **TOTAL COST:** $6.99
- **CALORIES:** 239
- **FAT:** 5 g
- **PROTEIN:** 29 g
- **CHOLESTEROL:** 87 mg
- **SODIUM:** 237 mg

¾ pound top sirloin, cut into 2-inch cubes
1 teaspoon finely chopped fresh garlic
½ teaspoon all-purpose seasoning
1 cup yucca, chopped into 2-inch cubes
1 cup sliced carrots
1 baking potato, cut into 2-inch cubes
1½ cups beef broth
1 yellow onion, quartered
1 teaspoon fresh thyme, leaves chopped
½ teaspoon fresh sage, leaves chopped
1 bay leaf
½ teaspoon black pepper

Yucca is a plant native to hot and dry climates and can be found in the southwestern United States. It is the main ingredient in tapioca pudding and can be used in place of potatoes.

1. Add all ingredients to a large saucepan and cook on medium high for 8 to 10 minutes.
2. Reduce heat and simmer for 20 to 25 minutes. Add beef broth if gravy dries out.

> **Quick and Easy Tip**
> The best way to prepare yucca is by baking, boiling, or frying, much as you would a potato.

Grilled Fillet with Feta

 Serves 4

- ~ **PREP TIME:** 10 minutes
- ~ **COOK TIME:** 30 minutes
- ~ **TOTAL COST:** $7.00
- ~ **CALORIES:** 440
- ~ **FAT:** 12 g
- ~ **PROTEIN:** 41 g
- ~ **CHOLESTEROL:** 86 mg
- ~ **SODIUM:** 325 mg

2 tablespoons balsamic vinegar
3 tablespoons extra virgin olive oil
2 sprigs fresh thyme, leaves chopped
4 (4-ounce) beef tenderloin steaks
½ red onion, chopped
2 cloves garlic, chopped
4 tablespoons feta cheese, crumbled

Enjoy with Brussels Sprouts with Roasted Peanuts (Chapter 13) for a truly unique and delicious meal.

1. Preheat grill. In a mixing bowl, whisk together vinegar, ½ cup oil, and thyme. Then place steaks in a baking pan and pour vinegar mixture over steaks. Let stand at room temperature for 10 minutes. Meanwhile, in heavy saucepan, heat 1 tablespoon olive oil over medium heat and add onion and garlic. Sauté until tender, about 6 minutes. Remove from heat and set aside.
2. Place steaks on grill; cook on medium heat for approximately 7 minutes. Turn and cook for an additional 7 minutes or until desired doneness.
3. When serving, place steaks on platter or plate and top with feta cheese, then top with onion mixture and serve.

> **Quick and Easy Tip**
> For testing the doneness of meats, put your hand palm up and touch your thumb and index finger together. Feel the pad at the base of your thumb; that's what rare steaks feel like. Touch your thumb and middle finger together; the pad will feel like a medium-rare steak. Ring finger and thumb is medium, and thumb and pinky feels like a well-done steak.

Spicy Peppered Beef

Serves 4

~ **PREP TIME:** 10 minutes
~ **COOK TIME:** 20 minutes
~ **TOTAL COST:** $16.94
~ **CALORIES:** 362
~ **FAT:** 16 g
~ **PROTEIN:** 29 g
~ **CHOLESTEROL:** 71 mg
~ **SODIUM:** 302mg

¾ pound top sirloin
1 clove fresh garlic, minced
½ teaspoon all-purpose seasoning
1 can kernel corn, drained
1 red bell pepper, diced
½ yellow onion, diced
1 tablespoon fresh cilantro, chopped
1 tablespoon lemon juice
2 teaspoons brown sugar
½ teaspoon onion powder
1 teaspoon oregano
½ teaspoon paprika
½ teaspoon red pepper
½ teaspoon cumin
¼ teaspoon black pepper
1 cup beef broth

Quick and flavorful, this recipe is great with a side of pasta or rice.

1. Coat a skillet with nonstick spray. Add beef, garlic, and all-purpose seasoning to skillet. Sauté on medium-high heat for 8 minutes, stirring often.
2. Mix remaining ingredients and add to skillet. Simmer for 8 to 10 minutes.

Cubed Steaks with Tomatoes and Green Chilies

Serves 4

~ **PREP TIME:** 10 minutes
~ **COOK TIME:** 30 minutes
~ **TOTAL COST:** $6.52
~ **CALORIES:** 283
~ **FAT:** 10 g
~ **PROTEIN:** 26 g
~ **CHOLESTEROL:** 88 mg
~ **SODIUM:** 166 mg

3 tablespoons plain flour
1 tablespoon chili powder
Sea salt and black pepper to taste
¾ pound beef cube steaks
2 tablespoons olive oil
1 (14-ounce) can diced tomatoes with green chiles
½ cup sliced mushrooms

Cube steaks are typically round steaks that have been run through a machine that pierces the steak all over to break up connective tissue so the meat is more tender. You can pound your own round steaks using the pointed side of a meat mallet.

In a mixing bowl, combine flour, chili powder, salt, and pinch of pepper. Mix well. Place steaks on parchment paper and sprinkle half of flour mixture over steaks. Pound into steaks using a meat pounder or rolling pin. Turn steaks, sprinkle with remaining flour mixture, and pound again. In a large saucepan, heat olive oil over medium-high heat. Add steaks; sauté for 4 minutes, turn and sauté for 2 minutes. Remove steaks from saucepan. Pour tomatoes into pan; cook and stir until simmering, scraping browned bits. Add steaks along with mushrooms; simmer for 15 to 20 minutes, until tender.

Grilled Steak Skewers

Serves 4

- ~ **PREP TIME:** 10 minutes
- ~ **COOK TIME:** 20 minutes
- ~ **TOTAL COST:** $6.86
- ~ **CALORIES:** 204
- ~ **FAT:** 8 g
- ~ **PROTEIN:** 26 g
- ~ **CHOLESTEROL:** 56 mg
- ~ **SODIUM:** 360 mg

¾ pound sirloin steak
¾ cup barbeque sauce
2 tablespoons Coca-Cola
2 cloves garlic, chopped
½ teaspoon black pepper
6 cremini mushrooms, sliced
1 red bell pepper, seeded and cut into strips

The sugar acids in both the barbeque sauce and Coke blend well to add spice, flavor, and actually help cook the steak. Use as both a marinade and a basting sauce.

1. Cut steak into 1-inch cubes and combine with barbeque sauce, Coke, garlic, and black pepper. Mix well. Massage the sauce, or marinade, into the meat. Let stand for 10 minutes.
2. Meanwhile, prepare vegetables and preheat grill. Thread steak cubes, mushrooms, and bell peppers onto wooden or metal skewers. Place on grill over medium heat. Grill skewers and brush frequently with basting marinade for 7 to 10 minutes, until steak is desired doneness. Discard any remaining marinade when done.

Quick and Easy Tip
If you have time, prepare skewers the day before, pour marinade over all, and marinate overnight.

Grilled Fillet with Basil Pesto

Serves 2

- ~ **PREP TIME:** 8 minutes
- ~ **COOK TIME:** 20 minutes
- ~ **TOTAL COST:** $6.89
- ~ **CALORIES:** 416
- ~ **FAT:** 16 g
- ~ **PROTEIN:** 51 g
- ~ **CHOLESTEROL:** 72 mg
- ~ **SODIUM:** 391 mg

2 (4-ounce) fillet steaks, or tenderloin
1 pinch sea salt
1 pinch white pepper
½ cup basil pesto
¼ cup blue cheese
¼ cup fresh basil leaves, chopped

For a lighter version, leave off the blue cheese as pesto traditionally has Parmesan cheese already mixed in.

1. Prepare and heat grill. Place steaks on a platter and sprinkle both sides with salt and pepper.
2. Place steaks on grill and cook, over medium heat, for 5 minutes. Turn steaks, cover, and cook for 4 minutes. Top each steak with pesto and sprinkle blue cheese over the top of the pesto. Cover and grill for 4 minutes.
3. Meanwhile, roll basil leaves into a round shaped and cut into thin strips. Place steaks on a serving platter and sprinkle with basil chiffonade. Let rest for 5 minutes and serve.

Enchiladas with Beef and Beans

 Serves 4

- ~ **PREP TIME:** 10 minutes
- ~ **COOK TIME:** 25 minutes
- ~ **TOTAL COST:** $6.96
- ~ **CALORIES:** 711
- ~ **FAT:** 25 g
- ~ **PROTEIN:** 31 g
- ~ **CHOLESTEROL:** 85 mg
- ~ **SODIUM:** 1408 mg

1 pound flat iron steak
1 pinch sea salt
1 pinch cayenne pepper
1 tablespoon chili powder
1 teaspoon ground cumin
3 tablespoons olive oil
1 (16-ounce) cans pinto beans, drained
1 (16-ounce) can enchilada sauce
6 (10-inch) flour tortillas
1 cups pepper jack cheese, shredded or grated

Enchiladas are one of the most popular dishes requested for Mexican buffets.

1. Preheat oven to 400°F. Cut the steak, against the grain, into thin strips. Sprinkle steak with salt, pepper, chili powder, and cumin. Heat large saucepan or skillet over medium-high heat and add oil; heat oil until hot and add steak, cook for 3 minutes, or until steak is done.
2. Add drained beans and 1 cup enchilada sauce to steak and heat through. Divide mixture among flour tortillas and top with 1 cup cheese. Roll up tortillas to enclose tortillas and filling. Place in buttered casserole dish. Drizzle with remaining enchilada sauce and sprinkle with remaining cheese. Bake for 15 to 18 minutes, or until heated through.

> **Quick and Easy Tip**
> This is a great recipe to make even several days ahead as it freezes well.

Meatballs with Sesame-Ginger Vegetables

 Serves 6

- ~ **PREP TIME:** 4 minutes
- ~ **COOK TIME:** 35 minutes
- ~ **TOTAL COST:** $6.99
- ~ **CALORIES:** 345
- ~ **FAT:** 33 g
- ~ **PROTEIN:** 10 g
- ~ **CHOLESTEROL:** 74 mg
- ~ **SODIUM:** 275 mg

1 pound package frozen meatballs
3 tablespoons olive oil
1 yellow onion, chopped
2 cloves garlic, chopped
1 (16-ounce) package frozen Asian vegetables in sesame-ginger sauce
½ cup beef broth

Asian vegetables are usually sliced differently than other frozen mixed vegetables and come with their own sauce, saving both time and money.

Thaw meatballs overnight in the refrigerator. In a large saucepan, heat oil over medium-high heat. Add onion and garlic, and cook for 5 minutes. Add meatballs, vegetables, and beef broth, cover, reduce heat, and simmer for 7 minutes. Uncover and cook an additional 3 to 5 minutes, until mixture is slightly thickened. Serve immediately.

Quick and Easy Tip
These meatballs are great on their own or served with rice.

Chili with Jalapeños

Serves 6

- ~ **PREP TIME:** 8 minutes
- ~ **COOK TIME:** 20 minutes
- ~ **TOTAL COST:** $6.99
- ~ **CALORIES:** 333
- ~ **FAT:** 11 g
- ~ **PROTEIN:** 23 g
- ~ **CHOLESTEROL:** 47 mg
- ~ **SODIUM:** 978 mg

¾ pound ground beef
1 yellow onion, chopped
2 tablespoons plain flour
2 (14-ounce) cans diced tomatoes, undrained
1 (4-ounce) can chopped jalapeños, undrained
2 (8-ounce) cans tomato sauce with seasonings
1 cup water

If this chili is too spicy, leave out the jalapeños.

1. In a large saucepan, cook ground beef and onion over medium heat, stirring frequently to break up the meat, about 4 to 5 minutes. When beef is browned, drain off half the liquid and grease. Sprinkle flour over beef and cook for 2 minutes, stirring once.
2. Add remaining ingredients, bring to a simmer, and simmer for 10 to 15 minutes, until flavors are blended and liquid is thickened. Serve immediately.

Quick and Easy Tip
The flour helps thicken the chili, but be careful to not add too much or you'll create another recipe entirely!

Shepherd's Pie

 Serves 4

- ~ **PREP TIME:** 10 minutes
- ~ **COOK TIME:** 40 minutes
- ~ **TOTAL COST:** $7.00
- ~ **CALORIES:** 381
- ~ **FAT:** 21 g
- ~ **PROTEIN:** 18 g
- ~ **CHOLESTEROL:** 77 mg
- ~ **SODIUM:** 127 mg

2 baking potatoes, peeled, cut into 2-inch cubes
1 tablespoon canola oil
½ yellow onion, chopped
¾ pound ground beef
½ package taco seasoning
1 (16-ounce) package frozen broccoli, cauliflower, and carrots
¼ cup water or beef broth
¼ cup sour cream
¼ cup Parmesan cheese, grated

Shepherd's pie is traditionally a meat pie with a crust of mashed potatoes. It originated as a means of using leftover beef roast with mashed
potatoes.

1. Fill large-quart boiler ½ full with water and place over high heat.
   Add potatoes and boil until tender, about 15 to 20 minutes. Drain
   and mash with fork or potato masher. Set aside.
2. Preheat oven to 400°F. In a large saucepan over medium heat,
   heat 1 tablespoon canola oil. Add onion and sauté for 5 minutes.
   Add ground beef and taco seasoning and cook for approximately 7
   minutes or until beef is browned. Add frozen vegetables and ¼ cup
   water or broth and cook an additional 3 minutes. Add potatoes and
   sour cream and let cook for 5 more minutes.
3. Grease casserole dish with butter. Transfer beef mixture to casserole
   dish. Top with Parmesan cheese and bake for 15 minutes or until
   casserole is heated through.

Artichokes Stuffed with Herbs and Beef

Serves 4

~ **PREP TIME:** 10 minutes

~ **COOK TIME:** 45 minutes

~ **TOTAL COST:** $6.96

~ **CALORIES:** 378

~ **FAT:** 8 g

~ **PROTEIN:** 36 g

~ **CHOLESTEROL:** 84 mg

~ **SODIUM:** 649 mg

4 artichokes

4 slices Italian bread loaf

1 pound ground beef

½ yellow onion, chopped

2 cloves garlic, chopped

4 sprigs fresh oregano, leaves chopped

½ tablespoon fresh basil, leaves chopped

Sea salt and black pepper to taste

1 egg

2 tablespoons Parmesan cheese, grated

Artichokes can be prickly, so wear thick kitchen gloves if you have sensitive hands.

1. Preheat oven to 375°F. Cut the artichokes in half lengthwise, leaving stems on, and peel them with a vegetable peeler. Remove and discard the chokes (the prickly white and purple center). Bring a large boiler, ¾ filled with water, to a boil and add 1 tablespoon of salt. Add artichokes and boil them for 1 minute. Remove artichokes and transfer to a large bowl filled with ice water. Drain and set aside.
2. Separately, in a small bowl, soak bread in water for 1 minute, then squeeze out water. In a large mixing bowl, combine beef, onion, garlic, oregano, basil, pepper, salt, bread, egg, and cheese. Stuff the artichoke leaves with the beef mixture and place cut side down in a deep roasting pan.
3. Bake covered for 45 minutes. Uncover and bake for an additional 10 to 15 minutes.

Quick and Easy Tip
Artichokes are very healthy and are delicious when baked, steamed, grilled, or sautéed. Try marinated artichoke hearts when making pasta salad or serve them as is with fresh tomato slices.

Herbed Meatloaf of Beef and Pork

 Serves 6

~ **PREP TIME:** 10 minutes
~ **COOK TIME:** 60 minutes
~ **TOTAL COST:** $6.99
~ **CALORIES:** 335
~ **FAT:** 10 g
~ **PROTEIN:** 18 g
~ **CHOLESTEROL:** 97 mg
~ **SODIUM:** 328 mg

3 slices toasted Italian bread
¼ cup milk
2 Roma tomatoes, seeded and diced
1 yellow onion, chopped
3 cloves garlic, chopped
1 tablespoon fresh Italian parsley, chopped
1 teaspoon fresh thyme leaves, chopped
4 green olives, chopped
4 black olives, chopped
2 slices Swiss cheese, chopped
¾ pound ground beef
¾ pound ground pork
1 egg
1 tablespoon honey
Sea salt and black pepper to taste

Meatloaf is not something you may think of every day, but it is a great way to serve a hearty, filling, nutritious meal the family will enjoy.

Preheat oven to 375°F. In a mixing bowl, soak toast in milk, then squeeze out liquid. In a large mixing bowl, combine all ingredients. Mix together well and form into desired loaf shape. Place in greased loaf pan and bake for 45 to 60 minutes or until internal temperature reaches 170°F. Slice and serve.

Quick and Easy Tip
Make a ketchup glaze by combining ketchup, brown sugar, and a bit of Worcestershire sauce. Coat the meatloaf during the last 15 minutes of baking and allow to bake uncovered.

Curried Beef with Pine Nuts

Serves 4

- ~ **PREP TIME:** 10 minutes
- ~ **COOK TIME:** 15 minutes
- ~ **TOTAL COST:** $6.68
- ~ **CALORIES:** 585
- ~ **FAT:** 29 g
- ~ **PROTEIN:** 26 g
- ~ **CHOLESTEROL:** 77 mg
- ~ **SODIUM:** 398 mg

1 tablespoon olive oil
1 yellow onion, chopped
2 cloves garlic, chopped
1 pound ground beef
1 (4-ounce) package pine nuts
2 teaspoons curry powder
Sea salt and black pepper to taste
1 (8-ounce) can tomato sauce
1 cup water
¼ cup Italian parsley, chopped
4 cups cooked rice

Pine nuts are used in traditional pesto sauce. As an alternative, use crushed walnuts.

In a large saucepan over medium heat, add olive oil, onion, and garlic and cook until onions are tender. Add ground beef and cook until browned. Add pine nuts, curry, salt, pepper, tomato sauce, and water. Bring to a boil, then reduce heat and simmer until sauce is thickened. When ready to serve, stir in parsley. Serve over rice.

Quick and Easy Tip
Toasting nuts brings out their natural oils and flavors. Toast in a saucepan on stove top over low heat until nuts are slightly browned.

Tortellini Alfredo with Beef

Serves 4

- ~ **PREP TIME:** 5 minutes
- ~ **COOK TIME:** 18 minutes
- ~ **TOTAL COST:** $6.85
- ~ **CALORIES:** 534
- ~ **FAT:** 34 g
- ~ **PROTEIN:** 25 g
- ~ **CHOLESTEROL:** 98 mg
- ~ **SODIUM:** 987 mg

1 (16-ounce) package frozen beef-filled tortellini
¾ pound ground beef
1 yellow onion, chopped
½ (10-ounce) jar or package four-cheese Alfredo sauce
½ (9-ounce) container pesto sauce

Alfredo sauce is named for an Italian restaurateur, Alfredo, from Rome. A largely American dish now, Alfredo refers to a sauce made with melted cheese and butter.

1. Bring large-quart boiler filled ¾ with water to boil over high heat. Add pasta and cook as directed, about 5 to 8 minutes for fresh or fresh frozen pasta.
2. While waiting to boil, in a large saucepan over medium-high heat cook beef and onion, stirring to break up beef, about 5 minutes until beef is browned. Drain off grease. Combine beef with pasta and add Alfredo sauce to saucepan. Cook over medium heat for 5 minutes, stirring occasionally until mixture is combined and sauce bubbles. Stir in pesto, cover, remove from heat, let stand for 5 minutes, and serve.

Quick and Easy Tip
For a lighter version of this recipe, leave out the beef or substitute chicken or turkey.

Classic Beef Stroganoff

Serves 4

- **PREP TIME:** 5 minutes
- **COOK TIME:** 20 minutes
- **TOTAL COST:** $6.84
- **CALORIES:** 352
- **FAT:** 15 g
- **CARBOHYDRATES:** 5 g
- **PROTEIN:** 17 g
- **CHOLESTEROL:** 65 mg
- **SODIUM:** 283 mg

2 tablespoons olive oil
1 yellow onion, chopped
2 cloves garlic, chopped
1 pound ground beef
2 stalks celery, chopped
1 pound uncooked egg noodles
2 cups nonfat sour cream

Egg noodles are the traditional noodle for stroganoff. They are lighter, thinner, and cook faster than regular pasta noodles.

1. In large quart boiler filled ¾ with water, bring water to a boil over high heat. Meanwhile, heat olive oil in large saucepan over medium heat. Add onion and garlic, and cook for 4 minutes, until tender. Add beef and celery. Bring to a simmer and cook for 7 minutes, until beef is cooked and celery is tender.
2. When water is boiling, add egg noodles and cook until tender but not mushy, about 5 minutes. Drain and set aside.
3. Stir sour cream into beef mixture, cover, and remove from heat. Place noodles on serving platter and spoon beef mixture over.

Curried Apricot Beef over Rice

Serves 4

- **PREP TIME:** 10 minutes
- **COOK TIME:** 15 minutes
- **TOTAL COST:** $6.68
- **CALORIES:** 330
- **FAT:** 14 g
- **CARBOHYDRATES:** 16 g
- **PROTEIN:** 36 g
- **CHOLESTEROL:** 121 mg
- **SODIUM:** 398 mg

1 tablespoon olive oil
1 yellow onion, chopped
2 cloves garlic, chopped
1 pound ground beef
½ cup dried apricots, chopped
2 teaspoons curry powder
Sea salt and black pepper to taste
½ cup orange juice
¼ cup Italian flat-leaf parsley, chopped
4 cups cooked rice

This is another great recipe to use as a stuffing for bell peppers. Make the mixture first then prepare peppers by chopping off the stems and removing the seeds. Spoon in the beef/rice mixture and bake in a 400°F oven for about 12 minutes. This recipe should make 6 to 8 stuffed peppers. Enjoy!

In large saucepan over medium heat, add olive oil, onion, and garlic and cook until tender, about 5 minutes. Add ground beef and cook until browned, about 4 minutes. Add apricots, curry, salt, pepper, orange juice, and parsley. Bring to a boil, reduce heat, and simmer until sauce is reduced, about 5 minutes. Serve over rice.

Classic Swedish Meatballs

Serves 4

- ~ **PREP TIME:** 10 minutes
- ~ **COOK TIME:** 2¾ hours
- ~ **TOTAL COST:** $5.80
- ~ **CALORIES:** 416
- ~ **FAT:** 12 g
- ~ **CARBOHYDRATES:** 12 g
- ~ **PROTEIN:** 25 g
- ~ **CHOLESTEROL:** 135 mg
- ~ **SODIUM:** 305 mg

1½ cups plain bread crumbs
1 cup milk
½ pound ground beef
½ pound ground pork
2 eggs
1 yellow onion, chopped
Pinch sea salt
½ teaspoon steak seasoning
¼ teaspoon cardamom
1 (10 ½-ounce) can beef broth
Black pepper to taste
2 tablespoons butter, melted
2 tablespoons plain flour

Swedish meatballs are most commonly known as meatballs made with both beef and pork.

1. Soak bread crumbs in milk for 5 minutes in large mixing bowl. Preheat oven to 400°F. Add beef, pork, eggs, onion, pinch of salt, steak seasoning, and cardamom to bread crumbs. Mix well. Shape into 1-inch balls. Place on parchment-lined baking sheet and bake for 15 minutes.
2. In large-quart boiler, place cooked meatballs, ½ can beef broth, and pepper. Simmer over low heat for about 2 hours, adding broth or water as needed.
3. In small bowl, mix together melted butter and flour. Mix until a smooth paste forms. Add paste to ½ can beef broth and add to meatball mixture. Cook until thickened, about 25 minutes.

Beefy Fried Rice

 Serves 4

- ~ **TOTAL COST:** $4.19
- ~ **CALORIES:** 391.95
- ~ **FAT:** 22.44 g
- ~ **PROTEIN:** 19.08 g
- ~ **CHOLESTEROL:** 253.80 mg
- ~ **SODIUM:** 538.40 mg

½ pound 80 percent lean ground beef
1 onion, chopped
4 cloves garlic, minced
2 tablespoons vegetable oil
2 cups Vegetable Rice (Chapter 13)
2 tablespoons soy sauce
4 eggs, beaten

Any leftover rice or rice pilaf will work well in this super easy recipe. Or you could cook ¾ cup of instant rice and use it immediately.

1. In large saucepan or wok, combine ground beef with onion and garlic. Cook and stir over medium heat, stirring frequently, until beef is almost cooked. Remove from heat and drain thoroughly; wipe out saucepan or wok.
2. Return wok to heat and add oil; heat over medium high heat until oil ripples. Then add Rice; stir-fry for 1 minute. Sprinkle with soy sauce; stir-fry for 2–3 minutes longer.
3. Return ground beef mixture to saucepan. Then push food to the sides of the saucepan and pour eggs into the center. Cook eggs, stirring frequently, until set. Mix with rest of food in saucepan; stir-fry for 1–3 minutes until hot, then serve immediately.

> **Fried Rice**
> Fried rice is best when it has been cooked and thoroughly chilled; the grains will cook separately and heat thoroughly. You can use any leftover cooked meat or vegetable in a fried rice recipe; just make sure to add the cooked ingredients at the end of the stir-fry process because they only need to be heated through.

Chili French Bread Pizza

Serves 6

- ~ **TOTAL COST:** $6.25
- ~ **CALORIES:** 379.04
- ~ **FAT:** 17.58 g
- ~ **PROTEIN:** 19.66 g
- ~ **CHOLESTEROL:** 44.93 mg
- ~ **SODIUM:** 734.92 mg

1 tablespoon olive oil
1 onion, chopped
2 cups leftover Homemade Chili (Chapter 6)
1 (4–ounce) can mushroom pieces, drained
½ Whole Wheat French Bread (Chapter 3)
1 cup shredded Cheddar cheese
1 cup shredded part-skim mozzarella cheese
¼ cup grated Parmesan cheese

Any thick chili can be used in this easy and hearty recipe. You could even use a 16–ounce can of chili if you find it on sale.

1. Preheat broiler. In large skillet, heat olive oil over medium heat. Add onion; cook and stir until crisp-tender, about 4 minutes. Add Chili and drained mushrooms and bring to a simmer. Simmer for 10 minutes, stirring frequently.
2. Meanwhile, cut Bread in half lengthwise and place, cut side-up, on cookie sheet with sides. Broil 6 inches from the heat for 4–6 minutes or until toasted. Remove from oven; turn oven to 400°F. Spoon Chili mixture over crust and sprinkle with cheeses.
3. Bake for 20–25 minutes or until pizzas are hot and cheese is melted and beginning to brown. Let stand for 5 minutes, then cut and serve immediately.

Corned Beef Hash

Serves 6

- ~ **TOTAL COST:** $6.18
- ~ **CALORIES:** 352.41
- ~ **FAT:** 15.76 g
- ~ **PROTEIN:** 20.93 g
- ~ **CHOLESTEROL:** 61.87 mg
- ~ **SODIUM:** 703.76 mg

6 russet potatoes
1 tablespoon olive oil
2 tablespoons butter
1 onion, chopped
3 cloves garlic, minced
1 (12–ounce) can corned beef, diced
½ cup beef stock
1 tomato, chopped
¼ cup grated Parmesan cheese

You can top each serving of this hearty dish with a fried egg if you'd like for the classic finish, and an additional $1.09.

1. Scrub potatoes but do not peel. Cut potatoes into ½-inch pieces. In large skillet, combine olive oil and butter over medium heat. Add onion, garlic, and potatoes; cook and stir for 8–10 minutes or until potatoes are beginning to brown.
2. Add corned beef and beef stock; bring to a simmer. Cover and simmer for 10–15 minutes or until potatoes are tender. Uncover and add tomato; simmer for 3–4 minutes longer. Stir, sprinkle with cheese, and serve.

Mom's Meatloaf

Serves 6

- **TOTAL COST:** $5.76
- **CALORIES:** 359.20
- **FAT:** 22.57 g
- **PROTEIN:** 17.62 g
- **CHOLESTEROL:** 74.59 mg
- **SODIUM:** 719.40 mg

1 tablespoon olive oil
1 tablespoon butter
1 onion, chopped
½ cup mushrooms, chopped
⅓ cup sour cream
1 slice oatmeal bread, crumbled
1 teaspoon salt
⅛ teaspoon pepper
¾ pound ground beef
½ pound ground pork
⅓ cup ketchup
3 tablespoons mustard
2 tablespoons brown sugar

This meatloaf is pure comfort food. Leftovers are great crumbled into spaghetti sauce, or used for the classic meatloaf sandwich.

1. In small saucepan, heat olive oil and butter over medium heat. Add onion and mushrooms; cook and stir until vegetables are tender and mushrooms have given up their liquid. Continue cooking until the liquid evaporates. Remove to large bowl and let stand for 10 minutes.
2. Preheat oven to 350°F. Add sour cream, bread crumbs, salt, and pepper to mushroom mixture and mix well. Then add ground meats, mixing with your hands until combined. Form into two loaves and place on a broiler pan.
3. In small bowl, combine ketchup, mustard, and brown sugar and spoon over loaves. Bake for 60–70 minutes or until meat thermometer registers 165°F. Tent meatloaves with foil and let stand for 10 minutes before serving.

Meatloaf Tips

For the best meatloaf, be sure to combine all of the ingredients before you add the meat. Work the mixture as little as possible and don't compact it. Let it stand for 10 minutes, covered, after it's cooked. Be sure to refrigerate leftovers promptly. Leftover meatloaf can be used in place of meatballs in many recipes, and it makes a great sandwich.

Easy Meatloaf

Serves 6

- **PREP TIME:** 10 minutes
- **COOK TIME:** 30 minutes
- **TOTAL COST:** $6.96
- **CALORIES:** 359
- **FAT:** 23 g
- **PROTEIN:** 18 g
- **CHOLESTEROL:** 75 mg
- **SODIUM:** 719 mg

1 egg
½ teaspoon Italian seasoning
1 yellow onion, chopped
¼ teaspoon garlic pepper
¾ cup soft bread crumbs
¾ cup ketchup
1 pound ground beef
¾ cup shredded jack cheese, divided
Sea salt and black pepper as desired

Meatloaves made in muffin tins are cute, fun to make, and fun to eat. Serve with some ketchup and frozen French fries to give your kids a treat.

1. Preheat oven to 350°F. In a large bowl, combine egg, Italian seasoning, onion, garlic pepper, bread crumbs, and ½ cup ketchup and mix well. Add ground beef, cheese, salt and pepper, and mix gently but thoroughly to combine.
2. Press meat mixture, ⅓ cup at a time, into 12 muffin cups. Top each with bit of ketchup and remaining cheese. Bake at 350°F for 15 to 18 minutes, until meat is thoroughly cooked. Remove from muffin tins, drain if necessary, place on serving platter, cover with foil, and let stand 5 minutes before serving.

Quick and Easy Tip

Meatloaf mix can be substituted for the ground beef and is found in the meat aisle of the supermarket. It usually consists of one-third beef, one-third pork, and one-third veal, but read the label to find out what the blend is in your area. The veal lightens the mixture, and the pork adds a slightly different flavor and texture.

Meatloaf with Olives and Herbs

Serves 6

- ~ **PREP TIME:** 10 minutes
- ~ **COOK TIME:** 60 minutes
- ~ **TOTAL COST:** $6.97
- ~ **CALORIES:** 293
- ~ **FAT:** 9 g
- ~ **CARBOHYDRATES:** 34 g
- ~ **PROTEIN:** 18 g
- ~ **CHOLESTEROL:** 80 mg
- ~ **SODIUM:** 328 mg

3 slices bread, soaked in milk and squeezed
2 Roma tomatoes, seeded and diced
1 yellow onion, chopped
4 cloves garlic, chopped
2 tablespoons fresh Italian parsley, chopped
1 teaspoon fresh thyme leaves, chopped
6 green olives, chopped
6 black olives, chopped
2 slices Swiss cheese, chopped
1½ pounds ground beef
1 egg
1 tablespoon honey
Sea salt and black pepper to taste

Meatloaf often gets a bad rap, but it tastes great and is easy to make.

Preheat oven to 375°F. In mixing bowl, soak bread in water for up to 1 minute, then squeeze out liquid. In large mixing bowl, combine remaining ingredients with the bread. Mix together well and form into desired loaf shape. Place in greased loaf pan and bake for 45 to 60 minutes or until internal temperature reaches 170°F. Slice and serve.

> **Meatloaf Glaze**
> Make a glaze for your meatloaf by combining ketchup, brown sugar, and a bit of Worcestershire sauce. Coat the meatloaf during the last 15 minutes of baking and allow to bake uncovered.

Meatloaf with Cheese and Brown Sugar Glaze

 Serves 6

~ **PREP TIME:** 10 minutes
~ **COOK TIME:** 30 minutes
~ **TOTAL COST:** $6.76
~ **CALORIES:** 359
~ **FAT:** 23 g
~ **CARBOHYDRATES:** 19 g
~ **PROTEIN:** 18 g
~ **CHOLESTEROL:** 75 mg
~ **SODIUM:** 719 mg

1 egg
2 teaspoons Italian seasoning
1 yellow onion, chopped
¼ teaspoon garlic pepper
¾ cup soft bread crumbs
¾ cup ketchup
1 pound ground beef
½ cup shredded jack cheese
¼ cup brown sugar

If you have a large cupcake pan, make individual meatloaves by cooking them in cupcakes. Be sure to grease the cupcake tins if you don't have a nonstick pan.

1. Preheat oven to 350°F. In large bowl, combine egg, Italian seasoning, onion, garlic pepper, bread crumbs, ½ cup ketchup, beef, and cheese. Mix gently but thoroughly to combine.
2. Press meat mixture into nonstick meatloaf pan. In small bowl, combine ¼ cup ketchup with brown sugar. Mix together well. Spread on top of meatloaf. Cover loaf with aluminum foil and bake for 25 minutes. Uncover and bake an additional 15 to 20 minutes or until loaf is cooked through.

Barbecue Sirloin Skewers

 Serves 4

~ **PREP TIME:** 10 minutes
~ **COOK TIME:** 20 minutes
~ **TOTAL COST:** $6.87
~ **CALORIES:** 204
~ **FAT:** 8 g
~ **CARBOHYDRATES:** 5 g
~ **PROTEIN:** 26 g
~ **CHOLESTEROL:** 56 mg
~ **SODIUM:** 360 mg

¾ pound sirloin steak
¾ cup barbeque sauce
2 tablespoons Coca-Cola
2 cloves garlic, chopped
1 to 2 pinches of black pepper
8 cremini mushrooms, halved
1 red bell pepper, seeded and cut into 1-inch squares

The sugar acids in both the barbeque sauce and Coke blend well to add spice, flavor, and actually help cook the steak. Use as both a marinade and a basting sauce.

1. Cut steak into 1-inch cubes and combine with barbeque sauce, Coke, garlic, and black pepper. Mix well. Massage the sauce, or marinade, into the meat. Let stand for 10 minutes.
2. Meanwhile, prepare vegetables and preheat grill. Thread steak cubes, mushrooms, and bell peppers onto wooden or metal skewers. Place on grill over medium heat. Grill skewers and brush frequently with basting marinade for 7 to 10 minutes, until steak is desired doneness. Discard any remaining marinade when done.

Texas Ground Beef Bake

 Serves 4

- ~ **PREP TIME:** 10 minutes
- ~ **COOK TIME:** 35 minutes
- ~ **TOTAL COST:** $6.64
- ~ **CALORIES:** 336
- ~ **FAT:** 10 g
- ~ **CARBOHYDRATES:** 15 g
- ~ **PROTEIN:** 28 g
- ~ **CHOLESTEROL:** 134 mg
- ~ **SODIUM:** 472 mg

2 baking potatoes, chopped into 1-inch cubes
1 tablespoon olive oil
1 yellow onion, chopped
1 pound ground beef
1 package taco seasoning
¼ cup beef broth
1 (16-ounce) package frozen broccoli, cauliflower, and carrots
½ cup nonfat sour cream
½ cup Parmesan cheese, grated

The potatoes make this recipe super filling. It's pretty inexpensive to make, so this recipe is great for a crowd.

1. Fill large-quart boiler halfway with water and place over high heat. Add potatoes and boil until tender, about 10 to 15 minutes. Drain and mash with fork or potato masher. Set aside.
2. Preheat oven to 400°F. In large saucepan over medium heat, heat oil. Add onion and sauté for 5 minutes. Add ground beef and taco seasoning and cook for approximately 7 minutes or until beef is browned. Add frozen vegetables and cook an additional 3 minutes. Add in potatoes, ½ cup sour cream, and beef broth. Let cook for 5 more minutes.
3. Grease casserole dish with butter. Transfer beef mixture to casserole dish. Top with Parmesan cheese and bake for 15 minutes or until casserole is heated through.

Grandma's Cabbage Rolls

Serves 6

~ **TOTAL COST:** $6.41
~ **CALORIES:** 305.98
~ **FAT:** 12.40 g
~ **PROTEIN:** 19.64 g
~ **CHOLESTEROL:** 85.68 mg
~ **SODIUM:** 568.94 mg

½ head green cabbage
¾ pound ground beef
1 onion, chopped
3 cloves garlic, minced
1 cup cooked long-grain brown rice
2 tablespoons mustard
3 tablespoons ketchup
1 egg, beaten
¼ teaspoon pepper
1 (8-ounce) can tomato sauce
1 (10-ounce) can condensed tomato soup

Cabbage rolls are a thrifty old-fashioned recipe that is very good for you too. Any leftover shredded cabbage can be made into coleslaw.

1. Core cabbage and carefully remove 8 whole cabbage leaves from head. Soak leaves in hot water while preparing filling. Shred remaining cabbage; set aside 2 cups to use in filling.
2. Cook ground beef, onion, and garlic in heavy skillet until beef is browned and onion and garlic are tender; drain well. Remove from heat and add rice, mustard, and ketchup and mix well. Stir in egg, pepper, and shredded cabbage. Fill each cabbage leaf with filling and roll up.
3. Pour tomato sauce into 13" × 9" baking pan. Arrange cabbage rolls, seam-side down, in pan. Place any remaining filling around filled rolls. Pour condensed tomato soup over filled rolls.
4. Bake at 375°F for 30–40 minutes, until sauce bubbles, cabbage is tender, and rolls are thoroughly heated.

Steak with Mushrooms

 Serves 4

- **TOTAL COST:** $6.62
- **CALORIES:** 262.45
- **FAT:** 13.09 g
- **PROTEIN:** 25.33 g
- **CHOLESTEROL:** 71.6 mg
- **SODIUM:** 252.32 mg

1 pound shoulder round steak
3 tablespoons apple cider vinegar
1 tablespoon vegetable oil
1 tablespoon butter
1 onion, minced
1½ cups sliced mushrooms
2 tablespoons flour
1 cup beef broth
½ cup water
¼ teaspoon ground coriander
1 tablespoon Worcestershire sauce
⅛ teaspoon pepper

A rich mushroom sauce adds great flavor to tender marinated steak. This is a recipe for company!

1. In glass dish, combine steak, vinegar, and olive oil. Cover and marinate for at least 8–24 hours.
2. When ready to eat, Prepare and preheat grill. Drain steak, reserving marinade.
3. In large skillet, melt butter over medium heat. Add onion and mushrooms; cook and stir until liquid evaporates, about 8–9 minutes. Stir in flour; cook and stir for 2 minutes. Add beef broth, water, and marinade from beef and bring to a boil. Stir in Worcestershire and pepper; reduce heat to low and simmer while cooking steak.
4. Cook steak 6 inches from medium coals for 7–10 minutes, turning once, until steak reaches desired doneness. Remove from heat, cover, and let stand for 10 minutes. Slice thinly against the grain and serve with mushroom sauce.

Grilled Sirloin with Blue Cheese and Basil

 Serves 4

~ **PREP TIME:** 8 minutes
~ **COOK TIME:** 15 minutes
~ **TOTAL COST:** $6.99
~ **CALORIES:** 371
~ **FAT:** 12 g
~ **CARBOHYDRATES:** 14 g
~ **PROTEIN:** 41 g
~ **CHOLESTEROL:** 72 mg
~ **SODIUM:** 322 mg

2 bone-in sirloin steaks
3 tablespoons olive oil
Sea salt and lemon pepper to taste
¼ cup blue cheese
¼ cup fresh basil leaves, chopped

Sirloin is a quality cut of beef that is usually less expensive than filet mignon. Sirloin is great marinated and grilled or served largely chopped over mixed greens with a mustard vinaigrette.

Coat steaks with 2 tablespoons olive oil, and season with salt and lemon pepper as desired. In large saucepan over medium heat, heat 1 tablespoon oil. When hot, place steaks in pan. Cook about 5 minutes, turn once, and cook an additional 5 minutes. Top each steak with cheese and cook until steaks are cooked through and cheese is beginning to melt. Serve with fresh basil.

Grilling Steaks
Place meats on hot grill or grill pan and do not move! Let the meat naturally release from the heated surface. This is called searing the meat. Turn once and cook the other side, again, without moving it until done.

Herb-Crusted Roast of Beef with Potatoes

 Serves 6

~ **PREP TIME:** 12 minutes
~ **COOK TIME:** 35 minutes
~ **TOTAL COST:** $6.96
~ **CALORIES:** 339
~ **FAT:** 5 g
~ **CARBOHYDRATES:** 35 g
~ **PROTEIN:** 29 g
~ **CHOLESTEROL:** 94 mg
~ **SODIUM:** 537 mg

1½ pounds bottom round roast
Sea salt and lemon pepper to taste
1 teaspoon fresh thyme, leaves chopped
½ teaspoon fresh sage, leaves chopped
3 garlic cloves, chopped
2 carrots, peeled and chopped
2 medium baking potatoes, cut into 2-inch cubes
2 cups beef broth
1 yellow onion, quartered
1 bay leaf

Roasting meats may take a little while in the oven, but it is too simple to pass up. Use the roasting time to make a side dish or perhaps just relax!

Preheat oven to 350°F. Coat roast with salt, lemon pepper, thyme, and sage. Place in a roasting pan or aluminum pan. Add remaining ingredients, then cover and roast for 1 to 1½ hours, or until internal temperature reaches 145°F.

Marinated Flank Steak

 Serves 4

- **PREP TIME:** 9 minutes
- **COOK TIME:** 25 minutes
- **TOTAL COST:** $6.96
- **CALORIES:** 154
- **FAT:** 7 g
- **PROTEIN:** 8 g
- **CHOLESTEROL:** 2 mg
- **SODIUM:** 487 mg

2 garlic cloves, minced
¼ teaspoon sea salt
1 tablespoon grill seasoning such as Tony's or other
¼ teaspoon dry mustard
¼ teaspoon cayenne pepper
2 tablespoons balsamic vinegar
1 pound flank steak

Grill seasoning contains lots of spices, usually including cumin, oregano, pepper, garlic, and sugar. Use it for hamburgers as well as grilled steaks.

1. Preheat grill. In a small bowl, mash garlic and salt together and create a paste. Add remaining ingredients, except flank steak. Prick both sides of steak with fork and rub garlic mixture into the steak. Let stand for 10 minutes.
2. Place steak on grill over medium coals and cover. Grill for 5 minutes, turn steak, cover, and grill 5 minutes longer, until medium rare or medium. Let steak stand for 5 minutes, then slice against grain to serve.

Quick and Easy Tip

Flank steak refers to the steak from the belly portion of the cow. It is best when marinated or braised and is most widely used in the Mexican dish, fajitas. To ensure tenderness, mix together seasonings and wine and marinate overnight or up to 5 hours in the refrigerator. Remove when ready to grill.

Herb-Crusted New York Strip

 Serves 4

~ **PREP TIME:** 10 minutes

~ **COOK TIME:** 15 minutes

~ **TOTAL COST:** $7.00

~ **CALORIES:** 262

~ **FAT:** 9 g

~ **PROTEIN:** 45 g

~ **CHOLESTEROL:** 98 mg

~ **SODIUM:** 655 mg

4 (4- to 5-ounce) New York strip steaks

½ teaspoon sea salt and white pepper

2 tablespoons olive oil

2 tablespoons Worcestershire sauce

2 tablespoons fresh thyme leaves, chopped

½ teaspoon dried oregano leaves

¼ cup balsamic vinegar

2 tablespoons dry mustard

Worcestershire sauce is used a lot in steak recipes. It is a blend of different spices and ingredients, including anchovies.

1. Preheat grill. Place steaks on baking sheet and pierce all over with a fork. Sprinkle both sides with salt and pepper. In a small bowl, combine remaining ingredients and mix well. Pour over steaks, turning to coat, rubbing marinade into steaks with hands. Let stand for 10 minutes.
2. Place steaks on grill over medium heat and drizzle with any remaining marinade. Cover grill and cook for 5 minutes. Turn steaks and cook for 5 minutes longer or until desired doneness. Let stand 5 minutes, then serve.

> **Quick and Easy Tip**
> An instant-read meat thermometer is always a good utensil to have on hand. When grilling steaks, 140°F is rare, 145°F is medium rare, 160°F is medium, and 170°F is well done. Be sure to let the steak stand for a few minutes before carving and serving to let the juices redistribute.

New York Strip with Mustard Marinade

Serves 4

- ~ **PREP TIME:** 10 minutes
- ~ **COOK TIME:** 15 minutes
- ~ **TOTAL COST:** $7.00
- ~ **CALORIES:** 262
- ~ **FAT:** 13 g
- ~ **CARBOHYDRATES:** 0 g
- ~ **PROTEIN:** 34 g
- ~ **CHOLESTEROL:** 97 mg
- ~ **SODIUM:** 455 mg

4 (4- to 5-ounce) New York strip steaks
Sea salt and lemon pepper to taste
2 tablespoons olive oil
2 tablespoons Worcestershire sauce
2 tablespoons fresh thyme leaves, chopped
½ teaspoon dried oregano leaves
¼ cup balsamic vinegar
2 tablespoons dry mustard

Worcestershire sauce is used a lot in steak recipes. It is a blend of different spices and ingredients, including anchovies.

1. Season steaks with salt and pepper. In small bowl, combine remaining ingredients and mix well. Pour over steaks, turning to coat, rubbing marinade into steaks with hands. Let marinate for 30 minutes or up to 2 hours in refrigerator.
2. Heat grill pan. When hot, place steaks on pan and grill for 5 minutes; drizzle with marinade, if desired. Turn steaks and cook for 5 minutes longer, drizzling again with any remaining marinade. Cook until desired doneness. Remove from heat and let rest for 5 minutes, then serve.

Cooking Temperature Guide
An instant-read meat thermometer is a good utensil to have on hand. When grilling steaks, 140°F is rare, 145°F is medium rare, 160°F is medium, and 170°F is well done. Be sure to let the steak stand for a few minutes before carving and serving to let the juices redistribute.

Grilled London Broil with Merlot Marinade

 Serves 4

- ~ **PREP TIME:** 5 minutes
- ~ **COOK TIME:** 15 minutes
- ~ **TOTAL COST:** $7.00
- ~ **CALORIES:** 259
- ~ **FAT:** 13 g
- ~ **PROTEIN:** 37 g
- ~ **CHOLESTEROL:** 84 mg
- ~ **SODIUM:** 142 mg

1 cup dry red wine such as Merlot
1 tablespoon olive oil
1 teaspoon ground cinnamon
1 whole clove
Sea salt and black pepper to taste
¾ pound flank steak

It's not known how London Broil got its name because the dish originated in North America, not London. Flank steak is used and should be marinated or pounded to break down the otherwise tough proteins of this cut of beef. Always cut against the grain when serving.

Preheat grill. Mix together wine, oil, and seasonings. Coat the meat in the wine mixture and grill until desired doneness, 7 minutes per 1 inch of thickness.

Roast of Beef with Peppers and Onions

Serves 4

- ~ **PREP TIME:** 10 minutes
- ~ **COOK TIME:** 1 hour 10 minutes
- ~ **TOTAL COST:** $6.89
- ~ **CALORIES:** 376
- ~ **FAT:** 16 g
- ~ **PROTEIN:** 25 g
- ~ **CHOLESTEROL:** 56 mg
- ~ **SODIUM:** 278 mg

¾ pound bottom round steak
Sea salt and black pepper
1 teaspoon ground red pepper
1 teaspoon ground white pepper
2 tablespoons plain flour
¼ cup canola oil
1 yellow onion, chopped
1 red bell pepper, seeded and chopped
1 green bell pepper, seeded and chopped
1 celery rib, chopped
1 cup beef broth
2 cups cooked rice

If you have some at home, add some sliced cremini mushrooms.

Season roast with salt and peppers. Dust with flour on all sides. In a large heavy quart boiler, heat oil over medium heat. Add the round steak and brown on all sides. Remove the meat and pour off all but 1 teaspoon of the oil. Add half the onions, bell peppers, and celery. Mix well. Add the broth. Stir well and reduce heat to low. Return roast to the pot and add remaining vegetables. Cover and cook until the meat is very tender, about 1 hour and 15 minutes. Slice the meat, serve with rice and gravy from the pot.

Simple Beef Stroganoff

 Serves 4

- ~ **PREP TIME:** 5 minutes
- ~ **COOK TIME:** 14 minutes
- ~ **TOTAL COST:** $6.84
- ~ **CALORIES:** 352
- ~ **FAT:** 15 g
- ~ **PROTEIN:** 17 g
- ~ **CHOLESTEROL:** 65 mg
- ~ **SODIUM:** 283 mg

2 tablespoons olive oil
1 yellow onion, chopped
1 pound ground beef
1 (8-ounce) package frozen cut green beans, thawed and drained
1 pound uncooked egg noodles
2 cups sour cream

Egg noodles are the traditional noodle for stroganoff. They are lighter, thinner, and cook faster than regular pasta noodles.

1. In a large-quart boiler filled ¾ with water, bring water to a boil over high heat. Meanwhile, heat olive oil in a large saucepan over medium heat. Add onion and cook for 4 minutes, until tender. Add beef and brown, about 5 minutes. Add beans and simmer for 5 minutes.
2. When water is boiling, add egg noodles and cook until tender but not mushy, about 5 minutes. Drain and set aside.
3. Stir sour cream into beef mixture, cover, and remove from heat. Place noodles on serving platter and spoon beef mixture over.

> **Quick and Easy Tip**
> Packaged frozen beef tips with gravy are a quick way to make stroganoff or any recipe. If you have beef in your freezer, use that and add easy gravy mix to your recipe.

CHAPTER 10

SEAFOOD

Uptown Salmon Casserole

Serves 6

- ~ **TOTAL COST:** $6.77
- ~ **CALORIES:** 378.30
- ~ **FAT:** 14.50 g
- ~ **PROTEIN:** 19.72 g
- ~ **CHOLESTEROL:** 37.84 mg
- ~ **SODIUM:** 572.73 mg

3 tablespoons margarine, divided
1 onion, finely chopped
2 tablespoons all-purpose flour
½ teaspoon salt
1 teaspoon curry powder
1 cup milk
3 stalks celery, chopped
1 cup shredded Swiss cheese
2 cups small shells pasta
½ (15-ounce) can pink salmon, drained
1 cup red grapes, cut in half
1 slice oatmeal bread, toasted
2 tablespoons grated Parmesan cheese

With a homemade white sauce instead of canned condensed soup, this casserole has a more sophisticated flavor than most seafood casseroles.

1. Preheat oven to 375°F. Spray a 2-quart casserole with nonstick cooking spray and set aside. Bring a large pot of salted water to a boil.
2. Meanwhile, in large saucepan, melt 2 tablespoons margarine over medium heat. Add onion; cook and stir until tender, about 4 minutes. Add flour, salt, and curry powder; cook and stir until bubbly, about 3 minutes.
3. Stir in milk, whisking until smooth. Then add celery. Cook, stirring frequently, until sauce thickens. Stir in Swiss cheese and remove from heat.
4. Cook pasta according to package directions until al dente. Drain and add along with salmon and grapes to milk mixture. Pour into prepared casserole.
5. Melt remaining 1 tablespoon margarine. Crumble the toasted bread and combine with the butter and Romano cheese. Sprinkle on top of casserole. Bake for 20–30 minutes or until casserole is bubbly and topping is browned and crisp.

Gemelli Tuna Salad

Serves 6

- ~ **TOTAL COST:** $4.93
- ~ **CALORIES:** 326.09
- ~ **FAT:** 6.17 g
- ~ **PROTEIN:** 19.38 g
- ~ **CHOLESTEROL:** 13.55 mg
- ~ **SODIUM:** 265.25 mg

1 (16–ounce) package gemelli pasta
⅔ cup mayonnaise
½ cup plain yogurt
2 teaspoons Old Bay Seasoning
2 tablespoons mustard
2 tablespoons lemon juice
¼ cup milk
2 cups frozen peas
¼ cup chopped green onions
1 cup sliced radishes
1 (6–ounce) can light tuna, drained

Remember, "light" tuna is not only less expensive, but contains less mercury than albacore.

1. Bring a large pot of salted water to a boil. Meanwhile, in large bowl combine mayonnaise, yogurt, Old Bay Seasoning, mustard, lemon juice, and milk, and mix with wire whisk until blended.
2. Place frozen peas in a colander. Cook pasta in boiling water according to package directions until al dente. Pour over peas in colander to drain and to thaw peas. Add to mayonnaise mixture along with green onions and radishes and stir to coat.
3. Flake tuna and add to salad; toss gently. Cover and chill for 2–3 hours before serving on lettuce cups.

Old Bay Seasoning
If you can't find Old Bay Seasoning or don't want to buy a large container, make this substitute for this recipe. Combine ½ teaspoon celery salt with ¼ teaspoon dry mustard, a pinch of cloves, nutmeg, ginger, allspice, red pepper flakes, mace, and ½ teaspoon paprika. Increase these amounts to make your own Old Bay to store for other recipes.

Tuna Salad on Ciabatta Bread

 Serves 2

~ **PREP TIME:** 12 minutes
~ **CHILL TIME:** 1 hour
~ **TOTAL COST:** $6.98
~ **CALORIES:** 406
~ **FAT:** 14 g
~ **PROTEIN:** 27 g
~ **CHOLESTEROL:** 25 mg
~ **SODIUM:** 783 mg

½ medium crisp apple, cored and chopped
Juice of ½ lemon
1 hard-boiled egg, diced
½ red onion, chopped
1 cans tuna in water, drained
1 tablespoon chopped walnuts
1 tablespoon extra virgin olive oil
½ tablespoon balsamic vinegar
Sea salt and black pepper to taste
½ loaf Italian bread such as ciabatta
2 to 4 green or red lettuce leaves

Ciabatta bread is a traditional Italian bread that tastes great drizzled with a little extra virgin olive oil.

1. In a mixing bowl, combine apple, lemon juice, and water. Toss well and then drain. Add the egg and onion to the apples. Toss well. Add tuna, nuts, oil, vinegar, and pinch of salt and pepper. Slice the bread in half lengthwise, then layer lettuce and mound the tuna mixture on top.
2. Wrap loaf tightly with plastic wrap and refrigerate for 1 hour. Slice into 6 equal portions and serve.

Quick and Easy Tip
For extra crunch, toast the bread.

Fish Chowder

 Serves 4

~ **PREP TIME:** 10 minutes
~ **COOK TIME:** 15 minutes
~ **TOTAL COST:** $6.99
~ **CALORIES:** 136
~ **FAT:** 4 g
~ **PROTEIN:** 13 g
~ **CHOLESTEROL:** 137 mg
~ **SODIUM:** 518 mg

1 tablespoon olive oil
1 large baking potatoes, peeled and cut into 1- to 2-inch cubes
1 ears corn, kernels cut off cob
1 large tomatoes, chopped
½ leek, trimmed and sliced
¾ pound whitefish such as tilapia
1 teaspoon curry powder
Black pepper to taste
¼ cup white wine such as Sauvignon Blanc
16 ounces chicken broth plus 16 ounces water
½ head fresh kale, washed and chopped
½ teaspoon capers

Fish chowder can be made so many ways—try adding corn and leeks.

In a large-quart boiler, heat oil on medium. Add the potatoes, stir in corn, tomatoes, leeks, and fish; sauté until leeks begin to wilt, about 6 minutes. Add curry and pepper, then add wine and reduce the wine by half, about 20 minutes. Pour in the broth and water and simmer for 45 minutes. Add kale and simmer for 5 minutes, then remove from heat. Ladle into serving bowls and sprinkle with capers.

Quick and Easy Tip
Use frozen corn off the cob and save time on chopping without sacrificing flavor.

Baked Tortillas with Crab and Basil

 Serves 6

~ **PREP TIME:** 5 minutes
~ **COOK TIME:** 20 minutes
~ **TOTAL COST:** $6.60
~ **CALORIES:** 225
~ **FAT:** 15 g
~ **PROTEIN:** 9 g
~ **CHOLESTEROL:** 42 g
~ **SODIUM:** 309 mg

6 ounces canned crab meat, drained
8 basil leaves, chopped
Pinch black pepper
1½ cups sour cream
2 large flour tortillas
Nonstick cooking spray

Serving anything with crab at parties is always a hit! There are many different types of crab meat available in stores, so shop for which is most cost effective for you. My favorite is pasteurized Maryland blue crab.

Preheat oven to 375°F. Flake the crabmeat. In a mixing bowl, combine crab, basil, pepper, and sour cream. Spray pie dish or pie pan with cooking spray. Place 1 tortilla on the bottom. Spoon in crab mixture, top with second tortilla, then spray with more cooking spray. Bake for 20 minutes. Let stand 5 minutes, slice then serve.

Quick and Easy Tip
Make sure to use fresh basil with this recipe. Dried basil doesn't have the crispness of fresh and will make the dish taste a little bitter.

Tuna Mac

 Serves 4

~ **TOTAL COST:** $3.84
~ **CALORIES:** 367.03
~ **FAT:** 14.12 g
~ **PROTEIN:** 20.67 g
~ **CHOLESTEROL:** 49.78 mg
~ **SODIUM:** 631.89 mg

3 tablespoons butter
½ cup chopped onion
½ cup chopped celery
½ cup chopped green bell pepper
1 (7.25-ounce) package macaroni and cheese mix
¼ cup milk
¼ cup sour cream
½ teaspoon paprika
1 (6-ounce) can light tuna, drained

A box of macaroni and cheese turns into dinner with a few additions. You could use any vegetables you have on hand, but the "holy trinity" of bell pepper, onion, and celery add nice flavor.

1. Bring a large pot of water to a boil. Meanwhile, in large saucepan, melt butter over medium heat. Add onion, celery, and bell pepper; cook and stir until crisp-tender, about 4 minutes.
2. Cook macaroni from mix until al dente; drain and add to pan with vegetables along with cheese packet, milk, sour cream, and paprika. Stir until combined, then gently stir in tuna. Cook for 2–3 minutes until hot, then serve immediately.

Risotto with Shrimp

Serves 6

~ **PREP TIME:** 10 minutes
~ **COOK TIME:** 20 minutes
~ **TOTAL COST:** $6.99
~ **CALORIES:** 212
~ **FAT:** 6 g
~ **PROTEIN:** 14 g
~ **CHOLESTEROL:** 88 mg
~ **SODIUM:** 486 mg

2 teaspoons olive oil
½ yellow onion, chopped
2 cloves garlic, minced
1 cups arborio rice
2 tablespoons dry white wine
2½ cups vegetable or chicken broth
¾ pound cooked shrimp
¼ cup Parmesan cheese
¼ bunch fresh Italian parsley, chopped

Risotto is delicious cooked most any way. The secret is to stir continuously and wait until most liquid is absorbed before adding more. Arborio rice is a short, thick-grain rice that seems to absorb as much liquid as you give it, so keep adding until you reach the consistency you desire.

In a large saucepan, heat oil over medium heat and add onion. Cook for 3 minutes. Add the garlic and cook an additional 1 more minute. Add the rice and stir into the mixture, combining well. Pour in the wine and let reduce by half. Add the broth, ½ cup at a time, stirring each until liquid is fully incorporated before adding more. Continue the process until all liquid is used. Remove from heat. Stir in shrimp and cheese. Sprinkle with parsley and serve.

Shrimp in Wontons with Fresh Gingerroot

Serves 6

~ **PREP TIME:** 15 minutes
~ **COOK TIME:** 5 minutes
~ **TOTAL COST:** $5.99
~ **CALORIES:** 125
~ **FAT:** 2 g
~ **PROTEIN:** 10 g
~ **CHOLESTEROL:** 62 mg
~ **SODIUM:** 353 mg

½ pound cooked shrimp, peeled and chopped
1 bunch scallions, chopped
6 cloves garlic, chopped
1 tablespoon fresh ginger, peeled and chopped
½ cup white wine such as Sauvignon Blanc
Juice of 1 lemon
1 cup fish broth
2 tablespoons soy sauce
1 package square wonton wrappers

Wontons are great to have on hand. Try brushing them with olive oil, sprinkling with Parmesan cheese, and baking until golden for easy Parmesan crisps that are perfect by themselves or for dips.

1. In a mixing bowl, combine shrimp, half the scallions, half the garlic, and ginger. Spoon mixture into wonton wrappers, seal edges by wetting slightly with water, fold wonton in half, and press to seal.
2. In a large saucepan, combine remaining garlic and ginger. Heat over medium heat and add wine, lemon juice, broth, and soy sauce. Bring to a simmer. Add the filled wontons and simmer about 2 minutes. Serve with remaining broth, garnish with remaining scallions.

Polenta with Serrano Peppers and Whitefish

 Serves 4

- ~ **PREP TIME:** 10 minutes
- ~ **COOK TIME:** 35 minutes
- ~ **TOTAL COST:** $6.99
- ~ **CALORIES:** 265
- ~ **FAT:** 7 g
- ~ **PROTEIN:** 22 g
- ~ **CHOLESTEROL:** 66 mg
- ~ **SODIUM:** 812 mg

2 tablespoons olive oil
½ serrano chili pepper, seeded and diced
3 cups fish broth or vegetable broth
1 cup cornmeal or masa meal
¾ pound whitefish such as cod or tilapia
Sea salt and black pepper to taste
2 tablespoons Parmigiano-Reggiano or Parmesan cheese
1 tablespoon apple cider vinegar

Many people do not realize that cornmeal is the same as polenta and is very affordable. Substitute it virtually anywhere you would use rice.

1. Preheat grill to medium heat. Heat 1½ tablespoons olive oil in a stockpot on medium. Lightly sauté the chili, then add the broth and bring to a boil.
3. Whisk in the cornmeal slowly and cook for about 20 to 30 minutes, stirring frequently, adding more broth if necessary.
4. While polenta cooks, lightly dip the fish in the remaining olive oil and place on rack to drain. Season with salt and pepper.
5. When the polenta is finished cooking, remove it from the heat and add the cheese; keep warm.
6. Grill fish for 3 to 5 minutes on each side, depending on the thickness of the fish.
7. To serve, spoon out generous dollop of polenta on each serving plate and arrange the fish on top. Drizzle with the vinegar.

Quick and Easy Tip
You can substitute salmon in this recipe if you prefer.

Almond-Crusted Salmon on Tortilla Crisps

Serves 3

- ~ **PREP TIME:** 10 minutes
- ~ **COOK TIME:** 12 minutes
- ~ **TOTAL COST:** $6.45
- ~ **CALORIES:** 452
- ~ **FAT:** 16 g
- ~ **PROTEIN:** 29 g
- ~ **CHOLESTEROL:** 50 mg
- ~ **SODIUM:** 825 mg

3 flour or corn tortillas
½ serrano pepper, minced
2 tablespoons almonds, chopped
1 teaspoon chili powder
¼ cup milk
½ pound salmon fillet, rinsed and cut into 3 portions
1 tablespoon extra virgin olive oil, plus extra for drizzling
Honey

Nuts add protein, flavor, and crunch! If serving for a party, however, it's a good idea to ask if any of your guests are allergic.

1. Toast tortillas under the broiler. Mix together the serrano pepper, almonds, and chili powder. In a mixing bowl, pour in milk. Dip salmon into milk and then dredge the salmon into the almond mixture.
2. In a large saucepan over medium heat, add olive oil and heat until hot but not smoking. Add salmon and cook each side for approximately 5 minutes, until cooked. Serve on tortillas drizzle with extra virgin olive oil and honey.

Quick and Easy Tip
Buying chopped almonds is about the same price as whole. Save yourself a step and buy them prechopped.

Grilled Fish Sandwich

Serves 4

- ~ **PREP TIME:** 12 minutes
- ~ **COOK TIME:** 10 minutes
- ~ **TOTAL COST:** $5.60
- ~ **CALORIES:** 314
- ~ **FAT:** 9 g
- ~ **PROTEIN:** 18 g
- ~ **CHOLESTEROL:** 44 mg
- ~ **SODIUM:** 565 mg

4 slices bacon
1 red onion, chopped
½ pound whitefish
8 slices whole-wheat bread
1 tablespoon extra virgin olive oil
8 lettuce leaves
1 large tomato, sliced

Sandwiches are great for lunch or dinner, or try mini-sandwiches for afternoon parties in the summer.

1. In a large saucepan, cook bacon until crisp. Drain bacon on paper towels, crumble, and set aside. Drain off all but 2 tablespoons bacon drippings. Cook onion in drippings over medium heat for 3 to 4 minutes. Add fish and cook for about 3 minutes per side, depending upon thickness. Turn once.
2. Toast bread slices and brush with olive oil. Layer one bread slice with lettuce, onion, bacon, tomatoes, and fish. Top with additional bread slice.

Quick and Easy Tip
Leave onions raw, if you like, for a crisp, fresh alternative.

Broiled Oysters with Lemon

 Serves 4

~ **PREP TIME:** 5 minutes
~ **COOK TIME:** 5 minutes
~ **TOTAL COST:** $6.99
~ **CALORIES:** 92
~ **FAT:** 3 g
~ **PROTEIN:** 11 g
~ **CHOLESTEROL:** 56 mg
~ **SODIUM:** 120 mg

1 pound fresh shelled oysters
1 tablespoon olive oil
Black pepper to taste
1 teaspoon grated lemon zest
¼ bunch fresh parsley, minced
Sea salt to taste

Do not eat oysters raw unless you know they come from a quality source and have been stored properly.

Preheat oven broiler. Place cleaned and opened oysters on broiler pan and drizzle each with olive oil, sprinkle with pepper and lemon zest. Place under broiler for 2 minutes or until oysters are fully cooked. The oyster meat should feel firm but not hard. Top with parsley and salt, and serve.

> **Quick and Easy Tip**
> To save time, purchase oysters from a seafood market out of the shell. Add Parmesan cheese to these before broiling for extra flavor.

Mussels in Red Wine Sauce

 Serves 4

~ **PREP TIME:** 10 minutes
~ **COOK TIME:** 10 minutes
~ **TOTAL COST:** $7.00
~ **CALORIES:** 122
~ **FAT:** 5 g
~ **PROTEIN:** 15 g
~ **CHOLESTEROL:** 38 mg
~ **SODIUM:** 563 mg

1 dozen mussels, cleaned and rinsed
1 tablespoon olive oil
1 shallots, chopped
2 cloves garlic, chopped
2 large tomatoes, chopped
½ cup dry red wine
½ cup fish broth, canned
¼ teaspoon dried red pepper flakes
1 teaspoon dried oregano

This is a quick and satisfying seafood dish.

Clean the mussels. In a large-quart boiler, heat oil over medium heat. Add shallots, garlic, and tomatoes. Cook for 5 minutes. Add mussels, wine, broth, pepper flakes, and oregano; simmer until mussels open. Serve.

> **Quick and Easy Tip**
> Purchase mussels in the shell at your local seafood market or in the seafood section. Be sure to debeard them (pull the fibers off) and rinse them. Discard any open shells before cooking.

Oven-Roasted Freshwater Bass with Black Olive Chutney

 Serves 6

- ~ **PREP TIME:** 10 minutes
- ~ **COOK TIME:** 20 minutes
- ~ **TOTAL COST:** $6.12
- ~ **CALORIES:** 116
- ~ **FAT:** 4 g
- ~ **PROTEIN:** 13 g
- ~ **CHOLESTEROL:** 72 mg
- ~ **SODIUM:** 615 mg

1 shallot, peeled and chopped
1 stalk celery, chopped
Sea salt and black pepper to taste
1 pound bass fillet
½ cup dry white wine
1 cup fish broth or vegetable broth
¼ cup kalamata olives, chopped
2 cloves garlic, chopped
¼ teaspoon fresh-grated lemon zest

Try to find black bass or freshwater bass. You can also use Chilean sea bass, but it is significantly more expensive.

1. Preheat oven to 400°F. In ovenproof baking dish, add shallots and celery to bottom of dish. Sprinkle with salt and pepper. Place fish on top and add the wine and broth. Cover and bake for 15 to 20 minutes.
2. While the fish cooks, prepare chutney by combining olives, garlic, and lemon zest. Remove the fish from the cooking liquid and serve with a spoonful of chutney.

Quick and Easy Tip
Chutneys are thick, usually sweet, low-fat sauces that are made of fruits with spices. They are great for cooking as they add lots of flavor and texture to your recipes.

Pan-Fried Flounder with Balsamic Reduction

 Serves 2

~ **PREP TIME:** 5 minutes
~ **COOK TIME:** 15 minutes
~ **TOTAL COST:** $6.25
~ **CALORIES:** 75
~ **FAT:** 2.5 g
~ **PROTEIN:** 27 g
~ **CHOLESTEROL:** 54 mg
~ **SODIUM:** 94 mg

2 cups balsamic vinegar
¼ cup plain flour
¼ cup cornmeal
½ pound flounder fillet
1 tablespoon olive oil
Black pepper to taste

A flat, whitefish, flounder is not overly fishy tasting and is good baked, broiled, grilled, or fried.

1. In a small-quart boiler, add balsamic vinegar and simmer over medium heat until liquid is reduced by two-thirds, about 15 minutes.
2. While vinegar is reducing, in a mixing bowl, combine flour and cornmeal and coat the flounder. In a large saucepan over medium heat, heat oil. Add flounder and cook about 7 minutes on each side. Serve fish by drizzling with balsamic reduction and sprinkle with pepper.

Quick and Easy Tip
If your market does not have flounder, use halibut or tilapia fillets.

Pan-Fried Trout

 Serves 4

~ **PREP TIME:** 10 minutes
~ **COOK TIME:** 15 minutes
~ **TOTAL COST:** $7.00
~ **CALORIES:** 165
~ **FAT:** 5 g
~ **PROTEIN:** 23 g
~ **CHOLESTEROL:** 66 mg
~ **SODIUM:** 79 mg

½ cup plain flour
¼ cup cornmeal
½ teaspoon garlic powder
Sea salt and black pepper to taste
2 egg whites
1 tablespoon cold water
4 small prepared trout
2 tablespoons olive oil
¼ bunch fresh Italian parsley

Trout is usually cooked whole. Be careful when eating to discard any bones.

1. In a small bowl, combine flour, cornmeal, garlic powder, and pepper. In a separate bowl, mix together egg whites and water. Coat trout with cornmeal mixture, then dip in egg mixture, then dip again in cornmeal mixture. Shake off excess.
2. Heat oil to medium temperature in a large skillet. Cook trout about 5 minutes on each side until golden brown and cooked through. Remove trout from pan and drain on rack covered with paper towels. Sprinkle with parsley and salt before serving.

Quick and Easy Tip
Trout is a wonderful fish when smoked. If you have a stovetop smoker, smoke trout for 20 to 25 minutes using cherry wood chips.

Shrimp-Stuffed Halibut with Lime and Cilantro

Serves 2

- ~ **PREP TIME:** 12 minutes
- ~ **COOK TIME:** 8 minutes
- ~ **TOTAL COST:** $7.00
- ~ **CALORIES:** 184
- ~ **FAT:** 4 g
- ~ **PROTEIN:** 35 g
- ~ **CHOLESTEROL:** 122 mg
- ~ **SODIUM:** 145 mg

½ pound halibut fillet
¼ pound shrimp, peeled and deveined, chopped
1 lime, zested and juiced
1 tablespoon fresh cilantro, stems removed, leaves chopped
2 cloves garlic, chopped
1 tablespoon extra virgin olive oil
Black pepper to taste

Halibut is a perfect fish for grilling. Because halibut has a flaky texture when cooked, try to turn it only once when cooking, especially on the grill.

1. Soak 12 wooden skewers in water for about 1 hour. Preheat grill.
2. Butterfly the halibut fillet lengthwise to make a ½- to ¾-inch thick fillet. Lay the fillet out, then layer the shrimp, half the lime zest, half the cilantro, and garlic. Gently roll up the stuffed filet, then cut into 6 pinwheels. Insert 2 skewers into each pinwheel, forming an X to hold the pinwheels together. Brush with half of the oil, and grill for 4 minutes on each side.
3. To serve, sprinkle each with pepper and the remaining zest and cilantro. Drizzle with remaining olive oil.

> **Quick and Easy Tip**
> Use a grill basket to grill the halibut as it makes the fish easy to turn.

Peppercorn-Crusted Tuna

Serves 2

- **PREP TIME:** 4 minutes
- **COOK TIME:** 5 minutes
- **TOTAL COST:** $6.99
- **CALORIES:** 150
- **FAT:** 2 g
- **PROTEIN:** 26 g
- **CHOLESTEROL:** 51 mg
- **SODIUM:** 110 mg

½ cup balsamic vinegar
2 tablespoons freshly cracked peppercorns
½ pound tuna steaks, sliced into 2 equal portions
Pinch sea salt
2 tablespoons unsalted butter, chilled
Lemon wedges

Tuna is a delicious fish and can be cooked so many ways. When buying, make sure to purchase top-grade tuna, sushi grade if possible.

1. Heat the vinegar in a small saucepan and bring to a boil. Lower heat and cook until vinegar is reduced to about 3 tablespoons. Set aside. Press the cracked peppercorns firmly into one side of each tuna steak. Sprinkle the tuna lightly with salt. Heat 1 tablespoon of the butter in a large nonstick skillet over medium-high heat and cook the fish, peppered side down, until seared, about 3 minutes. Turn fish and cook for 1 to 2 minutes, until the fish is seared on the outside yet still very pink in the center. Transfer the fish to a plate and cover loosely with foil to keep warm.
2. Add the remaining butter and reduced vinegar to the saucepan. Whisk constantly and cook over high heat until thick, about 1 to 2 minutes. To serve, place tuna steak, peppered side up, on serving plate and drizzle with balsamic sauce. Garnish with lemon wedges.

Quick and Easy Tip
Place peppercorns in a Ziploc bag and crush using a rolling pin.

Broiled Whitefish with Lemon Dijon

 Serves 4

- **PREP TIME:** 7 minutes
- **COOK TIME:** 7 minutes
- **TOTAL COST:** $6.74
- **CALORIES:** 143
- **FAT:** 8 g
- **PROTEIN:** 18 g
- **CHOLESTEROL:** 51 mg
- **SODIUM:** 247 mg

1 stick (½ cup) unsalted butter
2 tablespoons shallots, chopped
Juice of ½ lemon
1 teaspoon paprika
2 tablespoons Dijon mustard
Pinch sea salt and black pepper
¾ pound cod fillets
1 tablespoon fresh Italian parsley, chopped

Cod is a light, flaky whitefish that tends to take on the flavors of the ingredients around it. Salmon and halibut are also great fish to pair with this sauce.

1. Preheat broiler. Heat butter in a small saucepan over medium-low heat. Add shallots and cook until soft, about 2 minutes. Add lemon juice, paprika, mustard, salt, and pepper. Remove from heat and whisk until creamy and well blended. Transfer the butter sauce to a small bowl.
2. Dip the fillets in butter sauce, coating both sides. Place the fillets in a single layer in shallow broiler pan. Spoon any remaining butter sauce over tops of fillets.
3. Broil the fish until browned and cooked through, about 4 to 5 minutes. Baste with pan juices several times during the cooking process. To serve, transfer fillets to a platter and pour pan juices over the fish. Top with parsley.

Quick and Easy Tip
If the fresh fish selection does not look as fresh as it should, substitute frozen.

Salmon Patties

Serves 5

- ~ **TOTAL COST:** $5.28
- ~ **CALORIES:** 296.77
- ~ **FAT:** 15.80 g
- ~ **PROTEIN:** 20.39 g
- ~ **CHOLESTEROL:** 103.32 mg
- ~ **SODIUM:** 776.76 mg

⅓ cup brown rice
⅔ cup water
1 tablespoon olive oil
½ cup finely chopped onion
½ cup shredded carrot
2 tablespoons ground almonds
2 tablespoons flour
2 tablespoons sour cream
½ teaspoon salt
⅛ teaspoon pepper
1 egg
1 (14-ounce) can salmon, drained
3 tablespoons grated Parmesan cheese
2 tablespoons butter

Serve these old-fashioned patties with Creamy Mashed Potatoes (Chapter 13) and a green salad for a retro meal. Pink salmon is much less expensive than red sockeye, and in a recipe like this, it's hard to tell the difference.

1. In small saucepan, combine rice and water. Bring to a boil, reduce heat, cover, and simmer for 30–40 minutes or until rice is tender and liquid is absorbed.
2. In large saucepan, heat olive oil over medium heat. Add onion and carrot; cook and stir for 4 minutes. Remove from heat and combine with almonds, flour, sour cream, salt, pepper, and egg in a medium bowl. Stir in cooked rice, then add salmon and stir gently. Add cheese and mix.
3. Form mixture into four patties. Wipe out large saucepan and melt butter over medium heat. Add patties and cook for 3–5 minutes on each side, turning once, until patties are crisp and brown. Serve immediately.

Freezing Fish

Leftover canned fish, like salmon and tuna, freezes very well. If you don't use a whole can, remove the rest from the can and place it in a freezer bag or container, seal, label, and freeze for up to 3 months. To thaw, place in refrigerator overnight. Never store fish in the can, even in the refrigerator or freezer.

Salmon Smothered with Onions, Mushrooms, and Zucchini

Serves 2

- ~ **PREP TIME:** 10 minutes
- ~ **COOK TIME:** 10 minutes
- ~ **TOTAL COST:** $6.14
- ~ **CALORIES:** 239
- ~ **FAT:** 15 g
- ~ **PROTEIN:** 29 g
- ~ **CHOLESTEROL:** 80 mg
- ~ **SODIUM:** 259 mg

1 cup chicken broth
1 tomato, chopped
½ green bell pepper, seeded and chopped
½ yellow onion, chopped
1 cup sliced cremini mushrooms
1 zucchini, sliced
1 clove garlic, chopped
2 teaspoons Italian seasoning
Sea salt and black pepper to taste
½ pound skinless salmon fillets
2 tablespoons grated Parmesan cheese

Salmon is packed full of omega-3 fatty acids, which help give your skin a healthy glow, and it tastes delicious and is very filling.

1. Combine the broth, tomatoes, peppers, onions, mushrooms, zucchini, garlic, seasoning, salt, and pepper in a large saucepan, and heat over medium-high heat. Cover and bring to a boil.
2. Using wooden spoon, move vegetables aside and add the salmon fillets. Reduce heat to medium, cover, and gently simmer until the fish is opaque and firm throughout, about 8 to 10 minutes. Transfer salmon to serving plates, spoon vegetables over salmon and sprinkle with Parmesan cheese.

> **Quick and Easy Tip**
> Buy whole salmon fillets and cut into individual serving sizes and freeze.

Pan-Grilled Salmon with Wasabi

 Serves 2

- ~ **PREP TIME:** 9 minutes
- ~ **COOK TIME:** 12 minutes
- ~ **TOTAL COST:** $7.00
- ~ **CALORIES:** 270
- ~ **FAT:** 17 g
- ~ **PROTEIN:** 34 g
- ~ **CHOLESTEROL:** 117 mg
- ~ **SODIUM:** 34 mg

½ pound salmon fillets
Pinch sea salt
2 tablespoons butter
¼ cup heavy cream, room temperature
Juice of 1 lemon
1 tablespoon wasabi paste
Black pepper to taste
1 tablespoon fresh chives, chopped

Wasabi paste is available in the Asian or ethnic section of your grocery store.

1. Season salmon with salt. In a large saucepan over medium heat, heat butter until melted. Add salmon, skin side down. Cook about 4 minutes or until skin begins to brown. Flip salmon and cook an additional 4 minutes. Transfer salmon to plate and cover loosely with foil.
2. Add the cream and lemon juice to the pan and stir to blend. Bring to a simmer and cook for 2 minutes. Remove from heat and let cool for 2 minutes. Add the wasabi paste and stir to blend well. Adjust seasoning as desired. Transfer salmon to serving platter and top with wasabi mixture, pinch of pepper, and chives.

Quick and Easy Tip

Bring cream to room temperature; however, don't let it sit out too long. If you get distracted and find you are cooking later, put the cream back in the refrigerator.

Tuna Lasagna Rolls

 Serves 6

~ **TOTAL COST:** $6.80

~ **CALORIES:** 487.23

~ **FAT:** 25.42 g

~ **PROTEIN:** 23.51 g

~ **CHOLESTEROL:** 84.49 mg

~ **SODIUM:** 759.32 mg

6 lasagna noodles

1 potato, peeled

2 tablespoons butter

1 onion, diced

2 cloves garlic, minced

1 cup frozen peas

1 cup shredded carrots

1 (6-ounce) can light tuna, drained

1 (8 ounce) package cream cheese

½ cup milk

1 cup shredded Cheddar cheese

1 (8 ounce) can tomato sauce

½ teaspoon dried Italian seasoning

¼ cup grated Parmesan cheese

These lovely little rolls are filled with a cheesy tuna and vegetable blend. You could substitute any other seafood or vegetable in this recipe if you'd like.

1. Preheat oven to 350°F. Bring a large pot of salted water to a boil. Dice potato and add to large skillet along with butter. Cook over medium heat until potato starts to soften, about 5 minutes. Add onion and garlic; cook and stir until onion is tender, about 5 minutes longer.
2. Cook lasagna noodles according to package directions until tender. Drain and rinse with cold water; drain again. Add peas, carrots, and tuna to potato mixture; cook and stir for 3 minutes.
3. In microwave safe bowl, combine cream cheese, milk, and vegetable broth and microwave on high for 2 minutes until cheese is melted; stir with wire whisk. Add Colby cheese and stir. Add ⅓ cup of this mixture to the vegetables in skillet.
4. Arrange noodles on work surface. Spread each with some of the vegetable mixture. Spoon half of cream cheese sauce into 12" × 8" glass baking dish and arrange filled noodles on sauce. Pour remaining sauce over, then top with tomato sauce; sprinkle with seasoning and Parmesan cheese. Bake for 35–40 minutes or until casserole is bubbling. Serve immediately.

Spicy Fish Tacos

Serves 4

~ **TOTAL COST:** $5.55
~ **CALORIES:** 597.85
~ **FAT:** 25.50 g
~ **PROTEIN:** 23.72 g
~ **CHOLESTEROL:** 77.84 mg
~ **SODIUM:** 872.73 mg

½ cup sour cream
1 tablespoon lemon juice
2 ounces canned chopped green chiles, drained
¾ cup frozen corn, thawed and drained
½ cup salsa
16 frozen fish fingers
2 teaspoons chili powder
⅛ teaspoon cayenne pepper
½ teaspoon paprika
4 large taco shells
1½ cups shredded lettuce
1 cup shredded Cheddar cheese
½ cup Big Batch Guacamole (Chapter 2)

These crisp and creamy tacos are full of flavor and color. For a splurge, add some halved cherry tomatoes and fresh chopped avocado.

1. Preheat oven to 400°F. In medium bowl, combine sour cream, lemon juice, green onion, and corn; mix well. Add salsa; stir and set aside.
2. Place fish fingers on cookie sheet. In small bowl combine chili powder, cayenne pepper, and paprika; mix well. Sprinkle this mixture over the fish fingers and toss to coat. Bake fish according to package directions.
3. Heat taco shells in oven according to package directions as soon as fish is done; for about 4–5 minutes or until hot.
4. Assemble tacos by starting with the sour cream mixture, adding some fish fingers, then topping with lettuce, cheese, and Guacamole. You can let diners assemble their own tacos. Serve immediately.

Fish Fingers

Fish fingers are usually sold in very large packages, about 3–5 pounds. Store the package in the coldest part of your freezer, and be sure to reseal the package carefully after you remove some food. And be sure to abide carefully by the use by dates on the package. Shop around for the best deal; these products often go on sale.

Broiled Halibut with Basil Pesto and Tomatoes

 Serves 4

- ~ PREP TIME: 4 minutes
- ~ COOK TIME: 14 minutes
- ~ TOTAL COST: $6.99
- ~ CALORIES: 405
- ~ FAT: 6 g
- ~ PROTEIN: 50 g
- ~ CHOLESTEROL: 1 mg
- ~ SODIUM: 1041 mg

¾ pound halibut fillets
1 tablespoon olive oil
Sea salt and black pepper to taste
2 cups chopped, seeded tomatoes
¾ cup pesto sauce
¼ cup Parmesan cheese, grated

Halibut is among the largest fish in the sea and is dominant in the Pacific Northwest. It is a whitefish and is delicious, not overly fishy tasting, and flakes nicely when cooked properly.

1. Preheat broiler. Place fillets on broiler pan lined with aluminum foil and brush with half the olive oil; sprinkle with salt and pepper. In a small bowl, combine tomatoes, remaining olive oil, pesto, and Parmesan cheese; season with salt and pepper.
2. Broil halibut fillets for 10 to 12 minutes or until fish is firm when touched. Top with tomato mixture and broil an additional 1 to 2 minutes being careful not to burn.

Quick and Easy Tip
Allow about 10 minutes cooking time per 1 inch of thickness for any type of fish.

Cornmeal Fried Fish

 Serves 4

- ~ TOTAL COST: $6.44
- ~ CALORIES: 264.10
- ~ FAT: 11.58 g
- ~ PROTEIN: 24.70 g
- ~ CHOLESTEROL: 115.48 mg
- ~ SODIUM: 425.62 mg

¼ cup all-purpose flour
3 tablespoons cornmeal
½ teaspoon salt
⅛ teaspoon pepper
1 tablespoon butter
1 egg
3 tablespoons milk
4 (4-ounce) fish fillets, thawed if frozen
⅓ cup vegetable oil

If you have a fisherman in your family, the cost will drop to about 47 cents!

1. In small bowl, combine flour, cornmeal, salt, and pepper and mix well. Cut butter into small pieces and add to flour mixture; cut in with two knives until mixture is finely blended. In shallow bowl, combine egg and milk and beat well.
2. Pat fish dry. Dip into egg mixture, then into cornmeal mixture, coating both sides. Let stand on a wire rack for 10 minutes.
3. Heat oil in large skillet until it reaches 375°F. Fry fish over medium heat, turning once, until golden brown, about 8–12 minutes. Drain on paper towels and serve immediately.

Tex-Mex Mackerel Pasta Salad

 Serves 6

- ~ **TOTAL COST:** $6.89
- ~ **CALORIES:** 428.03
- ~ **FAT:** 10.60 g
- ~ **PROTEIN:** 32.78 g
- ~ **CHOLESTEROL:** 73.99 mg
- ~ **SODIUM:** 727.43 mg

⅓ cup mayonnaise
⅓ cup plain yogurt
¼ cup milk
½ cup chunky hot salsa
2 teaspoons chili powder
1 green bell pepper, chopped
1 jalapeño pepper, minced
1 (15-ounce) can mackerel, drained
½ cup crumbled feta cheese
2 cups frozen corn
1 (12-ounce) package small shell pasta

Pasta salads are a great choice during the summer months. Mackerel is a strong-tasting fish, so it works well in this spicy salad.

1. In large bowl, combine mayonnaise, yogurt, milk, salsa, and chili powder and mix well. Stir in bell pepper, jalapeño pepper, mackerel, and cheese and mix well. Place corn and peas on top of salad mixture.
2. Cook pasta according to package directions, drain, and pour over salad mixture while hot. Stir gently to coat all ingredients with dressing, cover, and refrigerate for 1–2 hours to blend flavors.

Mackerel
Mackerel is a fatty fish, one of those health foods that you should include in your diet. It's high in omega-3 fatty acids, which help protect against heart disease by lowering blood pressure and keeping your arteries clear. Look for Jack and Atlantic mackerel, and avoid King mackerel, which can be high in mercury.

Salmon Soufflé

 Serves 4

- **TOTAL COST:** $3.63
- **CALORIES:** 261.36
- **FAT:** 14.28 g
- **PROTEIN:** 20.77 g
- **CHOLESTEROL:** 290.34 mg
- **SODIUM:** 285.03 mg

1 (7-ounce) can pink salmon, drained
1 tablespoon olive oil
½ cup finely chopped onion
2 tablespoons flour
¼ teaspoon salt
⅛ teaspoon pepper
½ cup milk
¼ cup sour cream
5 egg yolks
2 tablespoons lemon juice
½ teaspoon dried dill weed
5 egg whites
¼ teaspoon cream of tartar

Did you know that eating foods high in cholesterol, like eggs, won't increase your cholesterol count? Eating a healthy diet over all, including varied foods, is more important.

1. Preheat oven to 400°F. Remove skin and bones from salmon; flake salmon and set aside.
2. In small pan, heat olive oil over medium heat. Add onion; cook and stir until tender, about 5 minutes. Add flour, salt, and pepper; cook and stir for 1 minute. Add milk and sour cream; cook and stir until thick, about 3 minutes. Stir in egg yolks and remove from heat. Add salmon, lemon juice, and dill weed; do not stir, but set aside.
3. In large bowl, combine egg whites with cream of tartar; beat until stiff peaks form. Stir salmon mixture to combine.
4. Fold egg whites into salmon mixture. Spray the bottom of a 2-quart casserole with nonstick cooking spray. Pour salmon mixture into dish. Bake for 20 minutes, then lower heat to 350°F and bake for 20–30 minutes longer or until soufflé is puffed and deep golden brown. Serve immediately.

Baked Fish in Mustard Sauce

 Serves 4

- ~ **TOTAL COST:** $6.50
- ~ **CALORIES:** 229.84
- ~ **FAT:** 8.38 g
- ~ **PROTEIN:** 23.88 g
- ~ **CHOLESTEROL:** 96.29 mg
- ~ **SODIUM:** 414.35 mg

4 (4-ounce) pollock fillets, thawed if frozen
¼ teaspoon salt
⅛ teaspoon pepper
1 tablespoon lemon juice
½ teaspoon dried tarragon leaves
2 tablespoons butter or margarine, melted
¼ cup milk
2 tablespoons mustard
1 slice whole wheat bread, crumbled

Combining breadcrumbs with milk to form a sauce is a trick from Scandinavian cooks.

1. Preheat oven to 400°F. Spray a 1-quart baking dish with nonstick cooking spray. Place fish into dish and sprinkle with salt, pepper, and lemon juice.
2. In small bowl, combine tarragon, melted butter, milk, and mustard, and whisk until blended. Stir in the breadcrumbs. Pour this sauce over the fish.
3. Bake for 20–25 minutes, or until fish flakes when tested with fork and sauce is bubbling. Serve immediately.

Cheapest Fish

Certain cuts of fish are cheaper than others. Pollock, a mild white fish, is one of the least expensive. The more exotic fish, like orange roughy and red snapper, can cost up to $14.00 a pound. If you have a fisherman in the family, encourage the sport! But make sure that you heed warnings posted by states about water quality and fish safety.

Wine-Poached Salmon with Tomatoes and Zucchini

 Serves 4

- ~ **PREP TIME:** 10 minutes
- ~ **COOK TIME:** 15 minutes
- ~ **TOTAL COST:** $6.97
- ~ **CALORIES:** 239
- ~ **FAT:** 15 g
- ~ **CARBOHYDRATES:** 8 g
- ~ **PROTEIN:** 17 g
- ~ **CHOLESTEROL:** 40 mg
- ~ **SODIUM:** 359 mg

¾ cup chicken stock
¼ cup white wine such as Sauvignon Blanc
2 large tomatoes, chopped
1 yellow onion, chopped
1 zucchini, sliced
1 clove garlic, chopped
2 teaspoons Italian seasoning
Sea salt and black pepper to taste
4 (4-ounce) skinless salmon fillets
2 tablespoons grated Parmesan cheese (optional)

You can enjoy salmon smoked, grilled, baked, poached, or marinated with vegetables or rice or on salads.

1. Combine the broth, wine, tomatoes, onions, zucchini, garlic, Italian seasoning, salt, and pepper in a large saucepan, and heat over medium-high heat. Cover and bring to a boil.
2. Using wooden spoon, move vegetables aside and add the salmon fillets. Reduce heat to medium, cover, and gently simmer until the fish is opaque and firm throughout, about 8 to 10 minutes. Transfer salmon to serving plates, spoon vegetables over salmon, and sprinkle with Parmesan cheese, if desired.

Health Benefits of Salmon

When cooked properly, salmon doesn't taste fishy and it's great for your skin as it is high in omega-3 fatty acids.

Lime-Poached Halibut with Cilantro

 Serves 4

- ~ **PREP TIME:** 12 minutes
- ~ **COOK TIME:** 8 minutes
- ~ **TOTAL COST:** $7.00
- ~ **CALORIES:** 241
- ~ **FAT:** 11 g
- ~ **CARBOHYDRATES:** 11 g
- ~ **PROTEIN:** 33 g
- ~ **CHOLESTEROL:** 2 mg
- ~ **SODIUM:** 210 mg

¾ pound halibut fillet
Sea salt and black pepper to taste
2 tablespoons extra-virgin olive oil
2 cloves garlic, chopped
2 limes, zested and juiced
1 tablespoon fresh cilantro, stems removed, leaves chopped
¼ cup white wine such as Sauvignon Blanc
¼ cup chicken or vegetable broth

This dish is especially light and healthy, as halibut is naturally low in fat, high in protein, and contains no carbs. The lime, cilantro, and other ingredients greatly enhance the flavor of the fish without adding fat or calories.

Season halibut with salt and pepper. In large saucepan, heat oil over medium heat and add garlic. Sauté until fragrant, about 1 minute. Add remaining ingredients, including halibut, then cover and cook until halibut is flaky, about 8 minutes.

> **Halibut**
> Halibut is a type of flatfish known to the northern waters of the Pacific and the Atlantic. It is a meaty fish that becomes flaky when cooked properly. Pay attention not to overcook as the fish becomes dry and tough.

Scallops Sautéed in White Wine and Butter

Serves 4

~ **PREP TIME:** 5 minutes
~ **COOK TIME:** 10 minutes
~ **TOTAL COST:** $7.00
~ **CALORIES:** 343
~ **FAT:** 9 g
~ **CARBOHYDRATES:** 12 g
~ **PROTEIN:** 40 g
~ **CHOLESTEROL:** 75 mg
~ **SODIUM:** 212 mg

2 tablespoons olive oil
4 cloves garlic, chopped
2 scallions, chopped
1 cup dry white wine such as Sauvignon Blanc
¾ pound sea scallops
Pinch sea salt and lemon pepper
Zest and juice of ½ lemon (zest first, then juice)
2 tablespoons butter

As an appetizer, substitute small bay scallops, add some finely chopped apple, and serve on spoons arranged on a platter.

1. In large saucepan, heat olive oil over medium heat. Add garlic and scallions. Cook for 2 to 3 minutes, stirring occasionally. Add wine, reduce heat to low, and simmer for 2 minutes. Add scallops, pinch of salt and pepper, and lemon zest and juice. Cover and simmer for 3 minutes or until scallops turn opaque in color and are slightly firm. Be careful not to overcook as the scallops will become tough.
2. When scallops are cooked, stir in butter until melted and serve.

Scallops

Scallops are bivalved mollusks, some of which have beautiful shells. They can be found in waters all over the world. The three major kinds of scallops are sea scallops, which are the largest, bay scallops, which are smaller and more sweet in flavor, and calico scallops, which are the smallest of the scallop family and are not widely used in cooking as they are darker in color and tougher in texture.

Pan-Grilled Salmon with Baby Bok Choy

 Serves 4

~ **PREP TIME:** 10 minutes
~ **COOK TIME:** 12 minutes
~ **TOTAL COST:** $6.98
~ **CALORIES:** 263
~ **FAT:** 6 g
~ **CARBOHYDRATES:** 2 g
~ **PROTEIN:** 34 g
~ **CHOLESTEROL:** 89 mg
~ **SODIUM:** 125 mg

¾ pound salmon fillet, cut into 4 equal portions
4 tablespoons olive oil
Sea salt and lemon pepper
1 green onion, chopped
2 baby bok choy, finely sliced lengthwise
¼ cup white wine
Juice of ½ lemon

Bok choy is also known as Chinese cabbage or snow cabbage and is part of the turnip family. It should not be confused with Napa Chinese cabbage, which is lighter in texture and color than bok choy.

Coat salmon fillets with 3 tablespoons olive oil, then season with salt and lemon pepper. Heat remaining 1 tablespoon oil in large saucepan over medium heat. Add green onion and sauté for 1 minute. Add salmon, bok choy, wine, and lemon juice. Cover, reduce heat to medium low, and cook salmon for 10 minutes, or until cooked through.

Breaded Tilapia Fillet with Balsamic Syrup

 Serves 4

~ **PREP TIME:** 5 minutes
~ **COOK TIME:** 25 minutes
~ **TOTAL COST:** $6.79
~ **CALORIES:** 285
~ **FAT:** 11 g
~ **CARBOHYDRATES:** 3 g
~ **PROTEIN:** 27 g
~ **CHOLESTEROL:** 91 mg
~ **SODIUM:** 251 mg

3 cups balsamic vinegar
½ cup plain flour
¼ cup cornmeal
¾ pound tilapia fillet
1 tablespoon olive oil
Black pepper to taste

Balsamic syrup is an easy and inexpensive way to add unique flavor to fish. It is not limited to fish, however, as it tastes great with other proteins such as chicken and even with fresh berries. See the dessert recipe Strawberries with Toasted Pecans and Balsamic Syrup, Chapter 15.

1. In small-quart boiler, add balsamic vinegar and simmer over medium heat until liquid is reduced by two-thirds, about 15 minutes.
2. While vinegar is reducing, in mixing bowl combine flour and cornmeal and coat the tilapia. In large saucepan over medium heat, heat oil. Add tilapia and cook about 5 minutes on each side. Serve fish by drizzling with balsamic reduction and sprinkle with pepper.

Spiced Tuna with Mustard and Crushed Peppercorns

Serves 2

- ~ **PREP TIME:** 8 minutes
- ~ **COOK TIME:** 6 minutes
- ~ **TOTAL COST:** $6.84
- ~ **CALORIES:** 150
- ~ **FAT:** 2 g
- ~ **CARBOHYDRATES:** 12 g
- ~ **PROTEIN:** 15 g
- ~ **CHOLESTEROL:** 17 mg
- ~ **SODIUM:** 610 mg

½-pound tuna steak, sliced into 2 equal portions
3 tablespoons prepared mustard
Pinch sea salt
4 tablespoons freshly cracked peppercorns, crushed
1 tablespoon olive oil
4 lemon wedges

Fresh tuna is naturally low in fat and high in protein. The meatiness of the flesh makes it more filling than other lighter fish, such as tilapia. Fresh fish can get a little expensive, so look for specials and freeze it for later use.

Coat tuna with mustard on both sides. Season lightly with salt. Press the cracked peppercorns firmly into each side of tuna steak. Heat 1 tablespoon oil in a large nonstick skillet over medium-high heat and cook the fish, peppered side down, until seared, about 2 minutes. Turn fish and cook for 2 minutes, until the fish is seared on the outside yet still very pink in the center. Transfer the fish to a plate and cover loosely with foil to keep warm. Serve with lemon wedges.

> **Crushed Peppercorns**
> An easy way to crush peppercorns without making a huge mess is to place peppercorns in a Ziploc bag and crush using a rolling pin.

Baked Salmon with Shallots and Horseradish Dijon

 Serves 2

- ~ **PREP TIME:** 7 minutes
- ~ **COOK TIME:** 12 minutes
- ~ **TOTAL COST:** $6.96
- ~ **CALORIES:** 245
- ~ **FAT:** 15 g
- ~ **PROTEIN:** 35 g
- ~ **CHOLESTEROL:** 80 mg
- ~ **SODIUM:** 228 mg

½ pound salmon fillets, skin on
2 tablespoons olive oil
Pinch sea salt and black pepper
4 tablespoons butter, room temperature
2 tablespoons prepared horseradish
1 tablespoon Dijon grainy mustard
½ large shallot, peeled and minced
1 tablespoon fresh chives, chopped

Some chefs consider the skin side of fish to be "presentation side," but you can plate it skinless or skin side down if you prefer.

1. Preheat oven to 375°F. Line a baking sheet with parchment paper and place salmon skin side down. Drizzle with olive oil and season with salt and pepper. bake salmon for about 12 minutes.
2. Separately, combine butter, horseradish, mustard, and shallot in a small bowl and blend well. Season with salt and pepper. Serve baked salmon with a dollop of butter mixture. Top with chopped chives.

Quick and Easy Tip
There are lots of ways to spice up butter, and this recipe is great for meats, poultry, and fish. If you find you really like this one, make a double batch of the butter mixture and use with other foods.

Sautéed Shrimp with Curry

Serves 4

~ **PREP TIME:** 8 minutes
~ **COOK TIME:** 5 minutes
~ **TOTAL COST:** $6.99
~ **CALORIES:** 130
~ **FAT:** 4 g
~ **PROTEIN:** 23 g
~ **CHOLESTEROL:** 172 mg
~ **SODIUM:** 182 mg

1 pound shrimp, peeled and deveined
1½ tablespoons curry powder
Pinch chili powder
1 tablespoon olive oil
¼ cup scallions, chopped
½ cup chili sauce
Sea salt and black pepper to taste

Shrimp are perfect to use for a quick meal because they cook in 2 minutes or less! Keep some in your freezer for last-minute meals.

In a mixing bowl, combine shrimp, curry, and chili powder, and toss to coat. Heat oil in a large skillet over medium heat. Add shrimp and cook, stirring often, until shrimp turns pink, about 2 minutes. Add scallions and chili sauce and stir. Cook until heated through, about 3 minutes. Season to taste with salt and pepper.

Quick and Easy Tip
Serve this over pasta or rice as a tasty alternative.

Lime-Jalapeño Grouper

Serves 4

~ **PREP TIME:** 8 minutes
~ **COOK TIME:** 10 to 12 minutes
~ **TOTAL COST:** $7.00
~ **CALORIES:** 225
~ **FAT:** 84 g
~ **PROTEIN:** 36 g
~ **CHOLESTEROL:** 34 mg
~ **SODIUM:** 75 mg

½ stick (¼ cup) unsalted butter, room temperature
2 tablespoons jalapeños, seeded and chopped
Juice of 1 lime
Sea salt and black pepper to taste
¾ pound grouper fillets
¼ cup plain flour
3 tablespoons olive oil

Grouper is a whitefish known to the Gulf and Atlantic coasts. It is very mild in flavor and is great for grilling, broiling, or poaching.

1. In a small bowl, combine butter, jalapeños, lime juice, and salt (for a smoother butter, combine in food processor). Set aside. Season fillets with salt and pepper. Place flour in a small bowl and coat the fish in the flour.
2. In a large saucepan over medium-high heat, add the oil and fish and cook until browned, about 3 to 5 minutes. Carefully turn the fish and cook for an additional 3 to 4 minutes or until fish is golden on both sides and texture is flaky. When serving, dollop fish with jalapeño butter.

Quick and Easy Tip
When seeding jalapeños, be sure to wear gloves. If you accidentally seed them without gloves, soak your hands in milk to calm the burn.

Prosciutto-Wrapped Shrimp with Honey and Lemon

Serves 4

- ~ **PREP TIME:** 10 minutes
- ~ **COOK TIME:** 5 minutes
- ~ **TOTAL COST:** $6.94
- ~ **CALORIES:** 173
- ~ **FAT:** 6 g
- ~ **PROTEIN:** 22 g
- ~ **CHOLESTEROL:** 142 mg
- ~ **SODIUM:** 445 mg

2 ounces prosciutto, thinly sliced, cut into ½-inch-wide x 3-inch-long strips
¾ pound shrimp, peeled and deveined
2 tablespoons olive oil
Black pepper to taste
¼ cup chicken broth
1 tablespoon lemon juice
1 tablespoon honey

Prosciutto-wrapped shrimp is popular at parties. Before wrapping, spread a little Dijon mustard on the prosciutto for another layer of flavor.

1. Wrap prosciutto around shrimp and press lightly to seal. In a large saucepan, heat oil over medium-high heat. Add shrimp and cook, turning once, until shrimp turn pink, about 3 minutes. Season with pepper. Transfer shrimp to plate and cover loosely.
2. Add the broth, lemon juice, and honey to the pan and bring to a simmer. Add the shrimp and any accumulated juices to the pan and stir to coat the shrimp evenly, being careful not to damage the prosciutto wrapping. Heat through, about 1 to 2 minutes. Season to taste.

Quick and Easy Tip
Honey is a natural sweetener. Use in place of sugar for sauces and even some desserts.

Whitefish with Caper Cream Sauce

 Serves 4

- **PREP TIME:** 10 minutes
- **COOK TIME:** 12 minutes
- **TOTAL COST:** $7.00
- **CALORIES:** 335
- **FAT:** 25 g
- **PROTEIN:** 29 g
- **CHOLESTEROL:** 51 mg
- **SODIUM:** 80 mg

¾ pound whitefish fillets
Sea salt and black pepper to taste
3 tablespoons plain flour
4 tablespoons unsalted butter
1 tablespoon shallots, chopped
½ cup dry white wine
2 tablespoons capers, rinsed and drained
2 teaspoons grain mustard
½ cup heavy cream, room temperature

If you'd rather not use heavy cream (it tastes good but is typically expensive and high in fat and calories), use ½ cup low-fat sour cream and ½ cup milk.

Season each fillet with salt and pepper. Sprinkle both sides with flour. In a large saucepan, heat 3 tablespoons of butter over medium heat. Add the fish, and cook until cooked through, about 2 minutes per side. Remove fillets and set aside. Add shallots to the pan and additional butter. Cook for about 1 minute, until soft but not browned. Add wine, capers, and mustard and simmer for about 3 minutes, until sauce starts to thicken. Slowly add cream, stirring constantly until incorporated. Cook about 6 minutes until the sauce begins to thicken. Adjust seasoning as desired. Serve by placing fish on platter and pouring sauce over.

> **Quick and Easy Tip**
> When cooking with any kind of cream sauce, stir frequently to avoid burning.

Shrimp and Sausage Jambalaya

 Serves 4

~ **PREP TIME:** 6 minutes
~ **COOK TIME:** 30 minutes
~ **TOTAL COST:** $6.48
~ **CALORIES:** 366
~ **FAT:** 19 g
~ **PROTEIN:** 26 g
~ **CHOLESTEROL:** 40 mg
~ **SODIUM:** 952 mg

1 8-ounce package yellow rice mix
2 tablespoons olive oil
1 yellow onion, chopped
1 (14-ounce) can diced tomatoes with green chilies, undrained
½ pound frozen cooked shrimp, thawed
1 Italian or Polish sausage, cooked and sliced into ½-inch slices

Jambalaya is traditional to New Orleans and is a combination of Spanish and French culture. Jambalaya is the New World answer to Old World paella.

Prepare rice mix as directed on package. Meanwhile, in a large saucepan heat olive oil over medium heat. Add onion; cook and stir for 4 to 5 minutes, until tender. Add tomatoes, shrimp, and sliced sausage; bring to a simmer, and cook for 3 to 4 minutes. When rice is cooked, add to saucepan; cook and stir for 8 minutes, until blended. Serve immediately.

Quick and Easy Tip
Add any combination of vegetables to this dish to create your own version. In the South, we add okra and green beans.

Sautéed Shrimp with Artichokes

 Serves 4

~ **PREP TIME:** 8 minutes
~ **COOK TIME:** 6 minutes
~ **TOTAL COST:** $7.00
~ **CALORIES:** 251
~ **FAT:** 5 g
~ **CARBOHYDRATES:** 42 g
~ **PROTEIN:** 17 g
~ **CHOLESTEROL:** 120 mg
~ **SODIUM:** 220 mg

1 tablespoon olive oil
¼ cup scallions, chopped
¾ pound shrimp
Pinch chili powder
½ cup chili sauce
½ can artichoke hearts, drained and chopped
sea salt and black pepper to taste

Use these same ingredients to make shrimp dip. Just substitute cooked bay shrimp for the uncooked, large shrimp here and add a cup of mayonnaise. Mix all the ingredients together and don't cook, as the shrimp are already cooked! Just be sure the shrimp are drained before combining.

In large skillet over medium heat, add oil and heat until fragrant. Add scallions and sauté for 1 minute. Add shrimp and cook for 2 minutes. Add chili powder, chili sauce, and artichoke hearts. Cook an additional 3 minutes or until sauce is heated through. Season with salt and pepper as desired. Serve with rice.

Cooking Shrimp
If budget allows, buy peeled and deveined shrimp. If not, peel shrimp and remove tails before cooking.

Scallops in White Wine and Peppers

 Serves 4

- ~ **PREP TIME:** 5 minutes
- ~ **COOK TIME:** 10 minutes
- ~ **TOTAL COST:** $7.00
- ~ **CALORIES:** 398
- ~ **FAT:** 9 g
- ~ **PROTEIN:** 40 g
- ~ **CHOLESTEROL:** 75 mg
- ~ **SODIUM:** 212 mg

2 tablespoons olive oil
4 cloves garlic, chopped
1 serrano pepper, seeded and minced
1 cup dry white wine such as Sauvignon Blanc
¾ pound sea scallops
Pinch sea salt
Pinch cayenne pepper
2 tablespoons butter

There are three major kinds of scallops. Sea scallops are the largest, with a yield of anywhere between 20 to 30 per pound. Allow 1 to 3 per person, depending upon size. Bay scallops are smaller, sweet in flavor, yield about 50 per pound, and are great for appetizers. Calico scallops are the smallest of the scallop family and are not widely used in cooking, as they are darker in color and more tough in texture.

1. In a large saucepan, heat olive oil over medium heat. Add garlic and serrano pepper; cook for 2 to 3 minutes, stirring occasionally. Add wine, reduce heat to low, and simmer for 2 minutes. Add scallops, salt, and cayenne pepper, cover, and simmer for 3 minutes or until scallops turn opaque in color and are slightly firm. Be careful not to overcook as the scallops will become tough.
2. When scallops are cooked, stir in butter until melted and serve.

Quick and Easy Tip

For cooking, the general rule is cook with a wine you would drink. However, I can guarantee you that I am not going to cook with my 1988 Tuscan Sangiovese from Chianti! Be realistic. Select a wine that is bottled—no cooking with wine in a box—and that suits the dish you are preparing. The heavier in flavor the dish, the more robust the wine. The lighter the dish, the lighter the wine.

Penne Pasta with Basil Cream Sauce and Crab

 Serves 4

- ~ **PREP TIME:** 5 minutes
- ~ **COOK TIME:** 20 minutes
- ~ **TOTAL COST:** $7.00
- ~ **CALORIES:** 239
- ~ **FAT:** 8 g
- ~ **CARBOHYDRATES:** 8.43 g
- ~ **PROTEIN:** 17 g
- ~ **CHOLESTEROL:** 122 mg
- ~ **SODIUM:** 559 mg

½ tablespoon salt
1 pound penne pasta, uncooked
Drizzle olive oil
2 cups nonfat sour cream
1 tablespoon fresh basil, chopped
1 teaspoon Crazy Jane salt or other salt seasoning
½ pound canned crab meat, drained

Believe it or not, there really is a salt seasoning called Crazy Jane. It is usually found in the herbs and seasoning section of the grocery store. Use it for dips, stews, or anywhere you would use seasoned salt.

1. Fill large-quart boiler ¾ with water and add ½ tablespoon salt. Bring to a boil and add pasta. Add a drizzle of olive oil. Cook until al dente, then drain.
2. In large saucepan over medium heat, add sour cream, basil, and seasoned salt. Heat until just bubbling. Reduce heat and add drained crab meat. Cook until heated. Toss with pasta and serve.

Cheese Ravioli with Shrimp

 Serves 4

- ~ **PREP TIME:** 8 minutes
- ~ **COOK TIME:** 15 minutes
- ~ **TOTAL COST:** $7.00
- ~ **CALORIES:** 498
- ~ **FAT:** 6 g
- ~ **CARBOHYDRATES:** 85 g
- ~ **PROTEIN:** 45 g
- ~ **CHOLESTEROL:** 43 mg
- ~ **SODIUM:** 410 mg

1 tablespoon olive oil
½ pound frozen shrimp, peeled and deveined
1 (9-ounce) package refrigerated or frozen cheese ravioli
¾ cup pesto sauce
½ cup grated Parmesan cheese

Make your own ravioli by using wonton wrappers. Place cheese or other filling in the center of one wrapper and top with a second wrapper. Seal the edges by coating them lightly with water and pressing together. Buying premade ravioli saves time.

1. In large saucepan over medium heat, heat olive oil. Add shrimp and cook for about 4 minutes, until shrimp turn pinkish. Remove all from skillet and set aside.
2. Add ravioli with 2 cups water to skillet. Bring to a boil over high heat. Reduce heat to medium, cover, and simmer for 5 minutes, until ravioli are hot, stirring occasionally. Drain pasta. Return pasta and shrimp to skillet. Stir in pesto sauce, mixing gently so as not to break ravioli. Cook until heated, about 1 to 2 minutes, then top with Parmesan cheese.

Salmon Rice Loaf

Serves 4

- ~ **TOTAL COST:** $4.67
- ~ **CALORIES:** 307.12
- ~ **FAT:** 14.30 g
- ~ **PROTEIN:** 27.63 g
- ~ **CHOLESTEROL:** 180.34 mg
- ~ **SODIUM:** 929.83 mg

1 tablespoon butter
½ cup finely chopped onion
¼ cup shredded carrot
¼ cup brown rice
½ cup water
2 eggs, beaten
1 (14-ounce) can pink salmon, drained
½ cup shredded Swiss cheese
1 teaspoon dried dill weed
1 tablespoon lemon juice
½ teaspoon salt
⅛ teaspoon white pepper

This soothing, homey dish is true classic comfort food. Serve with mashed potatoes and peas sautéed in butter.

1. Preheat oven to 350°F. Grease a 9" × 5" loaf pan with butter and set aside. In medium skillet, melt butter over medium heat. Add onion; cook and stir for 3 minutes. Add carrot; cook and stir for 2 minutes longer. Add brown rice; cook and stir for 2 minutes. Add Vegetable Broth and bring to a boil. Reduce heat, cover, and simmer for 25–30 minutes or until rice is almost tender.
2. When rice is done, add eggs, drained and flaked salmon, cheese, and seasonings to pan; stir well. Spoon into prepared pan and smooth top. Bake for 40–50 minutes or until loaf is set and top is browned. Let cool for 5 minutes, then slice and serve.

Canned Salmon
The skin and bones you'll find in a can of salmon are edible. You can eat them and get lots of calcium, or discard them; it's your choice! Canned salmon comes in two varieties: pink, which is less expensive, and red sockeye, which is more expensive but very flavorful. You can also now find salmon in a pouch, which has less liquid.

Sweet and Sour Fish

Serves 4

- ~ **TOTAL COST:** $6.31
- ~ **CALORIES:** 393.88
- ~ **FAT:** 11.46 g
- ~ **PROTEIN:** 10.16 g
- ~ **CHOLESTEROL:** 18.24 mg
- ~ **SODIUM:** 779.48 mg

4 frozen crunchy fish fillets
1 cup long grain rice
2 cups water
1 tablespoon olive oil
1 onion, chopped
2 cloves garlic, minced
1 green bell pepper, chopped
1 cup sliced carrot
1 (8-ounce) can pineapple tidbits
⅓ cup ketchup
2 tablespoons sugar
2 tablespoons apple cider vinegar
2 tablespoons cornstarch
2 tablespoons soy sauce
½ teaspoon ground ginger
⅛ teaspoon cayenne pepper

The trick to stir-frying is to have all the ingredients prepared and ready to go before you start heating anything. Then this complete dinner is ready in about 20 minutes!

1. In large saucepan, combine rice and water and bring to a boil. Reduce heat, cover, and simmer for 20–25 minutes or until rice is tender and liquid is absorbed. Preheat oven to 350°F. Prepare fish as directed on package.
2. Meanwhile, in large saucepan heat olive oil over medium heat. Add onion and garlic; stir-fry for 3 minutes. Add bell pepper and carrot; stir-fry for 3–5 minutes longer.
3. Drain pineapple, reserving juice. Add pineapple to saucepan and stir. In small bowl, combine reserved pineapple juice, ketchup, sugar, vinegar, cornstarch, soy sauce, ginger, and pepper and mix well. Add to saucepan, bring to a simmer, and cook until thickened, about 3–5 minutes.
4. When rice is done, place on serving plate and top with vegetable mixture. Cut fish fillets in half and place on top of vegetables; serve immediately.

Crisp Polenta with Salmon Cream

 Serves 4

- ~ **TOTAL COST:** $6.89
- ~ **CALORIES:** 412.65
- ~ **FAT:** 25.09 g
- ~ **PROTEIN:** 18.62 g
- ~ **CHOLESTEROL:** 77.99 mg
- ~ **SODIUM:** 875.23 mg

⅔ cup sour cream
3 green onions, chopped
¼ cup grated Parmesan cheese
2 (3-ounce) salmon fillets
¼ teaspoon salt
⅛ teaspoon pepper
2 tablespoons butter
1 tablespoon olive oil
4 (3" × 3") squares polenta
1 cup salsa

The combination of flavors and textures in this simple recipe is sublime. For a splurge, use more salmon.

1. In medium bowl, combine sour cream, onions, and cheese; mix well and set aside. Sprinkle salmon fillets with salt and pepper.
2. Combine olive oil and butter in large skillet over medium heat. Add salmon fillets; cook for 4 minutes, then carefully turn salmon and cook for 2–4 minutes longer or until just cooked. Remove to plate and cover with foil to keep warm.
3. Add Polenta squares to pan; cook until brown and crisp, about 4 minutes, then turn and cook on second side until brown and crisp, about 3 minutes.
4. Flake salmon and add to sour cream mixture. Spoon over hot Polenta and top with salsa. Serve immediately.

Canned, Fresh, or Frozen?
When it comes to seafood, canned is going to be the least expensive. You can substitute canned for fresh or frozen when the recipe calls for flaking the fish after it is cooked. Unless you live on the coast, fresh seafood in your grocer's case has been frozen; usually it's frozen on the boat or the same day it's caught.

Salmon Pizza

Serves 6

- ~ **TOTAL COST:** $6.98
- ~ **CALORIES:** 561.86
- ~ **FAT:** 28.76 g
- ~ **PROTEIN:** 22.48 g
- ~ **CHOLESTEROL:** 89.51 mg
- ~ **SODIUM:** 850.32 mg

1 Yeast Pizza Crust (Chapter 3), prebaked
½ cup milk
1 (8 ounce) package cream cheese
1 tablespoon cornstarch
½ teaspoon salt
⅛ teaspoon pepper
1 teaspoon dried dill weed
1 tablespoon butter
4 cloves garlic, minced
3 green onions, chopped
½ (15-ounce) can pink salmon, drained
1 cup shredded Swiss cheese
3 tablespoons grated Parmesan cheese

Gourmet pizza at home! This rich pizza is loaded with salmon. You can substitute cooked fish filets or shrimp for some of the salmon if you'd like.

1. Preheat oven to 400°F. Place Pizza Crust on cookie sheet and set aside. Cut cream cheese into cubes and, in medium microwave-safe bowl, combine with milk. Microwave on 50 percent power for 1 minute; remove and stir. Return to microwave and cook on 50 percent power for 1–2 minutes longer, or until cheese is melted. Stir with wire whisk until smooth, then add cornstarch, salt, pepper, and dill weed. Set aside.
2. In large saucepan, melt butter over medium heat. Add garlic and green onion; cook and stir until crisp tender, about 3 minutes. Add salmon and remove from heat.
3. Spread cream cheese mixture over Pizza Crust. Remove salmon and vegetables from saucepan with slotted spoon and arrange over crust. Sprinkle with cheeses.
4. Bake for 20–25 minutes or until cheese melts and begins to brown. Let stand for 5 minutes, then cut into slices to serve.

Salmon Stuffed Potatoes

 Serves 6

- ~ **TOTAL COST:** $6.60
- ~ **CALORIES:** 371.58
- ~ **FAT:** 17.04 g
- ~ **PROTEIN:** 18.15 g
- ~ **CHOLESTEROL:** 67.09 mg
- ~ **SODIUM:** 830.34 mg

3 baking potatoes
½ (15-ounce) can salmon, drained
3 tablespoons butter
½ cup finely chopped onion
2 cloves garlic, minced
⅓ cup light cream
½ teaspoon salt
⅛ teaspoon pepper
1½ cups shredded Swiss cheese
½ teaspoon paprika

You can serve these elegant potatoes as a main dish, or serve them alongside a grilled steak for a surf and turf dinner. Save the salmon to make Uptown Salmon Casserole (this chapter).

1. Preheat oven to 400°F. Rinse potatoes, dry, and prick with fork. Place on baking rack and bake for 40–45 minutes, until soft when pressed with fingers. Remove potatoes from oven and let cool for 30 minutes.
2. Meanwhile, in medium saucepan, melt butter. Add onion and garlic; cook and stir until crisp tender, about 4 minutes. Add fish; cook until opaque, about 2 minutes. Remove from heat and add shrimp.
3. When potatoes are cool enough to handle, cut in half lengthwise. Scoop out the flesh, leaving a ¼-inch thick shell. Place flesh in large mixing bowl. Drain butter from shrimp and vegetables and add to potatoes; mash until smooth. Add cream, salt, and cayenne pepper and beat well.
4. Fold in shrimp mixture and cheese. Pile mixture back into potato shells. Sprinkle with paprika. Bake potatoes for 15–20 minutes longer or until hot and potatoes begin to brown. Serve immediately.

Baking Potatoes

The best potatoes for baking are russet potatoes, those oblong, golden brown globes. Before they are put into the oven, wash them well, dry, and prick with a fork to prevent explosions in the oven. You can rub them with a bit of olive oil or butter for a crisper skin, but it's not necessary.

Fish 'n Chips Dinner

Serves 4

- ~ **TOTAL COST:** $5.94
- ~ **CALORIES:** 445.75
- ~ **FAT:** 17.98 g
- ~ **PROTEIN:** 14.94 g
- ~ **CHOLESTEROL:** 41.98 mg
- ~ **SODIUM:** 862.32 mg

3 cups shredded cabbage
1 carrot, shredded
⅓ cup mayonnaise
⅓ cup buttermilk
½ teaspoon dried dill weed
3 cups frozen French-fried potatoes
1 tablespoon chili powder
28 frozen breaded fish sticks

This is a complete meal, for under $1.50 per serving. The fresh coleslaw is a great contrast to the hot and crisp potatoes and fish.

1. In large bowl, combine cabbage and carrots. In small bowl combine mayonnaise, buttermilk, and dill weed and blend well. Pour over cabbage mixture and stir to coat; cover and refrigerate.
2. Preheat oven to 425°F. Place French fries on a cookie sheet and sprinkle with the chili powder. Toss to coat. Spread in an even layer, and arrange the fish sticks on the same pan.
3. Bake for 25–35 minutes or until the fish and potatoes are golden brown and crisp. Serve with the coleslaw.

Pesto Fish en Papillote

Serves 4

- ~ **TOTAL COST:** $6.99
- ~ **CALORIES:** 256.97
- ~ **FAT:** 12.08 g
- ~ **PROTEIN:** 23.12 g
- ~ **CHOLESTEROL:** 70.77 mg
- ~ **SODIUM:** 594.83 mg

4 (4 ounce) pollock filets
½ teaspoon salt
⅛ teaspoon white pepper
½ cup Spinach Pesto (Chapter 2)
2 tablespoons butter, melted

This dish is a good choice for a birthday party because it's another present to unwrap! You could add thinly sliced zucchini or small peas to the packets.

1. Preheat oven to 400°F. Cut four large rectangles of heavy-duty foil; fold in half and cut half a heart shape. Unfold. Place one fish filet close to the fold on one side of the heart.
2. Sprinkle fish with salt and pepper and spread pesto evenly on each filet, then drizzle with melted butter.
3. Fold heart shapes in half and crimp to close by folding the foil over tightly at the edge. Place on large cookie sheets and bake for 12–15 minutes, rotating cookie sheets halfway through baking time. Let your guests unwrap the bundles themselves, warning them to be careful of the steam.

Crabby Corn Pie

 Serves 6

- ~ **TOTAL COST:** $5.95
- ~ **CALORIES:** 439.94
- ~ **FAT:** 22.08 g
- ~ **PROTEIN:** 19.44 g
- ~ **CHOLESTEROL:** 118.31 mg
- ~ **SODIUM:** 708.02 mg

2 tablespoons butter

1 onion, chopped

2 tablespoons all-purpose flour

½ teaspoon salt

½ teaspoon dried basil leaves

1 cup milk

2 cups frozen corn, thawed and drained

2 eggs, beaten

1 (8-ounce) package frozen surimi flakes, thawed

1 cup shredded Swiss cheese

1 Angel Pie Crust (Chapter 15), prebaked

This elegant pie would be delicious for brunch on the porch, accompanied by a molded gelatin salad and a spinach salad.

1. Preheat oven to 350°F. In medium bowl, combine cracker crumbs with melted butter. Mix well, then press into bottom and up sides of a 9-inch pie pan. Set aside.
2. In large skillet, heat olive oil over medium heat. Add onion; cook and stir until tender, about 4 minutes. Add flour, salt, and basil; cook and stir for 3 minutes. Add milk; cook and stir until thickened. Add corn and eggs; stir well. Cook for 1 minute.
3. Drain surimi, then arrange with cheese in pie crust. Carefully pour in corn mixture. Bake for 30–40 minutes or until the pie is set, puffed, and golden brown. Let stand for 5 minutes, then serve.

Surimi

Imitation crab legs, or *surimi*, are made from mild white fish, colored and flavored so it tastes like crab. And it does, especially when combined with other ingredients. You can find it shaped to look like crab legs, or already flaked, which is cheaper. Sometimes you can find surimi flavored and shaped to look like shrimp.

Polenta Shrimp Casserole

 Serves 4

- **TOTAL COST:** $6.90
- **CALORIES:** 363.10
- **FAT:** 20.95 g
- **PROTEIN:** 19.46 g
- **CHOLESTEROL:** 118.50 mg
- **SODIUM:** 729.10 mg

3 tablespoons butter, divided
1 yellow summer squash, sliced
1 onion, chopped
1 tablespoon flour
3 tablespoons yellow cornmeal
½ teaspoon salt
⅛ teaspoon white pepper
½ teaspoon dried thyme leaves
1½ cups chicken broth
½ cup sour cream
½ cup shredded Swiss cheese
5 ounces frozen 60-count shrimp, thawed
2 slices Hearty White Bread (Chapter 3)
3 tablespoons grated Romano cheese

This elegant casserole layers polenta with sautéed squash, zucchini, and shrimp. You can make it ahead of time—add 10–15 minutes to the baking time.

1. Preheat oven to 350°F. In large saucepan, melt 2 tablespoons butter over medium heat. Add onion; cook and stir until crisp tender, about 4 minutes. Add yellow squash; cook and stir until squash begins to soften. Remove squash and onions with slotted spoon and set aside.
2. Add flour, cornmeal, salt, pepper, and thyme leaves to drippings remaining in saucepan. Cook and stir until mixture bubbles. Gradually stir in broth; cook and stir until thickened. Then add sour cream and Swiss cheese; remove from heat.
3. Grease a 2-quart casserole with unsalted butter. Place half of the vegetable mixture into the bottom of the casserole. Add ¾ of the shrimp, then half of the cornmeal mixture. Top with remaining vegetable mixture, remaining shrimp, then remaining cornmeal mixture. Melt remaining 1 tablespoon butter. Make crumbs out of bread and mix with melted butter and Romano cheese; sprinkle over casserole.
4. Bake for 35–45 minutes or until casserole bubbles and bread crumb topping is golden brown. Let stand for 5 minutes before serving.

Tangy Fish Fillets

Serves 4

~ **TOTAL COST:** $6.30
~ **CALORIES:** 400.95
~ **FAT:** 20.59 g
~ **PROTEIN:** 18.69 g
~ **CHOLESTEROL:** 57.31 mg
~ **SODIUM:** 853.40 mg

1 (20-ounce) package breaded fish fillets
¼ cup mayonnaise
2 tablespoons mustard
2 tablespoons lemon juice
⅓ cup grated Parmesan cheese

Dressing up breaded fish fillets is a delicious way to add flavor and fun to your meals. And it's so inexpensive!

1. Preheat oven to 400°F, or as package directs. Place fish fillets in a 15" × 10" jelly roll pan. Bake for 10 minutes, or half the cooking time.
2. Meanwhile, in small bowl, combine remaining ingredients except cheese and mix well.
3. Remove fish from oven and spread each with some of the mayonnaise mixture. Sprinkle with Parmesan cheese. Return to oven and bake for 8–10 minutes longer or until fish is thoroughly cooked and topping is bubbling.

Seafood Fillets

Most seafood is very expensive. Breaded fish portions are the exception, because they are made from pieces of fish that are combined to form a fillet shape. You're still getting a nice serving of seafood along with all its omega-3 fatty acids and nutrition, but the cost is much lower. You can dress up this food with sauces, herbs, spices, and cheeses.

CHAPTER 11

VEGETARIAN

Classic Cheese Soufflé

Serves 4

~ **TOTAL COST:** $2.76
~ **CALORIES:** 334.21
~ **FAT:** 24.82 g
~ **PROTEIN:** 17.83 g
~ **CHOLESTEROL:** 269.81 mg
~ **SODIUM:** 729.07 mg

3 tablespoons butter
¼ cup finely chopped onion
3 tablespoons all-purpose flour
½ teaspoon salt
⅛ teaspoon pepper
1 tablespoon mustard
1 cup milk
4 eggs, separated
1 cup shredded Cheddar cheese
3 tablespoons grated Parmesan cheese

Believe it or not, soufflés are one of the cheapest entrées you can make. They're made of eggs, butter, cheese, flour, and milk; that's it!

1. Preheat oven to 350°F. Grease the bottom of a 1-quart soufflé or casserole dish. Tear off a strip of aluminum foil 3 inches longer than the circumference of the dish. Fold in thirds so you have a long thin strip and butter one side. Wrap the foil around the top of the dish, buttered-side in, so 2 inches extend above the top of the dish.
2. In small saucepan, combine butter and onion. Cook and stir over medium heat until onion is very tender, about 5 minutes. Add flour, salt, and pepper; cook and stir for 3 minutes. Then add mustard and milk; cook and stir until thick and bubbly. Remove from heat and stir in egg yolks, one at a time. Then stir in cheeses. Set aside.
3. In medium bowl, beat egg whites until stiff peaks form. Stir a dollop of the whites into the cheese mixture. Then carefully fold in remaining egg whites. Pour into prepared pan. Bake for 50–55 minutes or until soufflé is puffed and deep golden brown. Serve immediately.

Soufflé Tips

For the best soufflés, here are a few rules. Be sure that the flour is thoroughly cooked in the butter before you add the milk. Stir sauce with a wire whisk to avoid lumps. Beat the egg whites last; don't make them first and let them sit. You can vigorously stir the first dollop of egg whites in the cheese sauce, but carefully fold the rest in.

Spanish Rice

~ **TOTAL COST:** $5.36
~ **CALORIES:** 318.71
~ **FAT:** 12.99 g
~ **PROTEIN:** 6.67 g
~ **CHOLESTEROL:** 61.54 mg
~ **SODIUM:** 885.51 mg

1 tablespoon olive oil
1 tablespoon butter
1 onion, chopped
3 cloves garlic, minced
1 green bell pepper, chopped
1½ cups rice
1 cup vegetable broth
2 cups water
⅓ cup sliced green olives
1 (8-ounce) can tomato sauce
1 (4-ounce) can chopped green chiles, drained
1 egg, beaten
½ teaspoon salt
⅛ teaspoon cayenne pepper

You can make this with leftover rice too; just sauté the onion, garlic, and green pepper, add the rice, then add remaining ingredients and bake the dish.

1. In large saucepan, heat olive oil and butter over medium heat. Add onion and garlic; cook and stir until crisp-tender, about 4 minutes. Add bell pepper and rice; cook, stirring, for 3–4 minutes to brown the rice.
2. Add vegetable broth and water and bring to a boil. Cover, reduce heat, to medium low, and simmer for 15 minutes or until rice is almost tender.
3. Meanwhile, spray a 2-quart casserole with nonstick cooking spray and preheat oven to 375°F. Remove saucepan from heat and stir in olives, tomato sauce, chiles, egg, salt, and pepper and mix gently. Pour into prepared casserole and bake for 20–25 minutes or until bubbly.

Spinach-Ricotta Omelet

 Serves 4

- ~ **TOTAL COST:** $4.29
- ~ **CALORIES:** 335.61
- ~ **FAT:** 22.32 g
- ~ **PROTEIN:** 23.87 g
- ~ **CHOLESTEROL:** 353.81 mg
- ~ **SODIUM:** 695.03 mg

½ (10-ounce) package frozen spinach, thawed and drained
½ cup part-skim ricotta cheese
3 tablespoons grated Parmesan cheese
⅛ teaspoon nutmeg
6 eggs
¼ cup milk
½ teaspoon salt
⅛ teaspoon pepper
1 tablespoon olive oil
1 tablespoon butter
½ cup finely chopped onion
1 cup shredded part-skim mozzarella cheese

Yes, you can have an omelet! Even though egg yolks are high in cholesterol, just one in this omelet adds some body and flavor while still keeping cholesterol low.

1. Press spinach between layers of paper towel to remove all excess moisture. Set aside. In small bowl, combine ricotta with Parmesan cheese and nutmeg; set aside.
2. In medium bowl, beat eggs with milk, salt, and pepper until smooth. Heat a nonstick skillet over medium heat. Add olive oil, then add spinach and onion; cook and stir until onion is crisp-tender, about 4 minutes.
3. Add egg mixture to skillet; cook, running spatula around edges to let uncooked mixture flow underneath, until eggs are set but still moist.
4. Spoon ricotta mixture and mozzarella cheese on top of eggs; cover pan, and let cook for 2 minutes. Then fold omelet and serve immediately.

Omelet Variety

You can add just about any cooked vegetable or meat to omelets, and you can vary the cheese as well. Just make sure that the vegetables and meats are well drained so they don't water down the omelet. Omelets should be served immediately, so make sure your family is waiting for the omelet rather than the other way around.

Rich Baked Beans

 Serves 8

- ~ **TOTAL COST:** $2.89
- ~ **CALORIES:** 382.92
- ~ **FAT:** 1.12 g
- ~ **PROTEIN:** 13.24 g
- ~ **CHOLESTEROL:** 0.0 mg
- ~ **SODIUM:** 543.65 mg

1 pound navy beans
1 onion, finely chopped
1 teaspoon salt
3 tablespoons mustard
½ cup brown sugar
½ cup ketchup
½ cup molasses
¼ teaspoon pepper

On the coldest day of winter, simmer these beans in the oven to fill your home with warmth and fabulous aroma. Serve with warm Brown Bread (Chapter 3) for a meal under $4.00 for eight people.

1. Sort the beans and rinse well; drain. Cover with cold water and soak overnight. The next day, drain the beans well and rinse again. Place beans in a large soup pot and cover with more cold water; bring to a boil over medium heat.
2. Simmer, uncovered, for 1½ hours. Then drain beans, reserving liquid.
3. Pour beans into a 3-quart casserole dish and add salt, mustard, brown sugar, ketchup, tomato paste, molasses, and pepper and mix thoroughly until well combined.
4. Add reserved bean liquid to just cover the beans. Cover the dish tightly with aluminum foil and place in oven. Bake at 325°F for 4 hours, checking once during cooking time and adding reserved bean liquid as necessary, until mixture is thick and beans are tender. Serve immediately.

Sicilian Bread Salad

 Serves 4

~ **TOTAL COST:** $4.86

~ **CALORIES:** 435.01

~ **FAT:** 15.50 g

~ **PROTEIN:** 12.50 g

~ **CHOLESTEROL:** 2.38 mg

~ **SODIUM:** 1017.13 mg

4 cups cubed Cornmeal Focaccia (Chapter 3)

2 tablespoons olive oil

½ cup canned mushroom pieces, drained

¼ cup Spinach Pesto (Chapter 2)

1 (15-ounce) can red beans, drained

½ (14.5-ounce) can diced tomatoes, drained

4 tablespoons zesty Italian salad dressing

3 cups torn lettuce leaves

You need a good hearty bread for this recipe; don't try to make it with wimpy white bread.

1. Preheat oven to 350°F. Make sure to include some crust with each cube of the Focaccia. Place on cookie sheet and drizzle with the olive oil; toss to coat. Bake for 12–15 minutes, turning once, until golden brown and crisp. Cool completely on wire rack.
2. In large bowl, combine mushrooms, Pesto, and beans; toss until coated. Let stand for 10 minutes.
3. Add bread and tomatoes and toss to coat. Drizzle with salad dressing and add lettuce; toss gently and serve immediately.

> **Versatile Salads**
> One of the things that make salads such a good use for leftovers is that they are so versatile. Combine just about any cooked leftover with some spicy salad dressing and a "filler" ingredient like greens or pasta or rice and you have an easy, satisfying meal. For complete protein in a vegetarian salad, combine beans with grains or rice.

Potato Tacos

Serves 4

~ **TOTAL COST:** $5.90
~ **CALORIES:** 468.99
~ **FAT:** 91.28 g
~ **PROTEIN:** 20.89 g
~ **CHOLESTEROL:** 35.10 mg
~ **SODIUM:** 955.49 mg

2 russet potatoes
1 onion, chopped
3 cloves garlic, minced
1 tablespoon olive oil
½ teaspoon salt
⅛ teaspoon pepper
1 (12-ounce) can evaporated milk
½ (4-ounce) can chopped green chiles, undrained
2 tablespoons flour
4 large taco shells
½ cup Big Batch Guacamole (Chapter 2)
1 cup shredded Cheddar cheese

Tacos are delicious, inexpensive, and easy on the cook. Let diners assemble their own tacos.

1. Preheat oven to 400°F. Scrub potatoes and cut into 1-inch pieces, including some of the skin on each piece. Combine in roasting pan with onion and garlic. Drizzle with olive oil and sprinkle with salt and pepper and toss to coat. Roast for 30 minutes, then turn vegetables with a spatula and roast for 15–20 minutes longer until potatoes are tender and browned.
2. When potatoes are done, combine evaporated milk, undrained chiles, and flour in a large saucepan. Bring to a boil over high heat, then reduce heat to low and simmer for 5 minutes or until mixture begins to thicken.
3. Stir in potato mixture until coated. Heat taco shells in the oven until crisp, about 3–4 minutes. Make tacos with potato mixture, Guacamole, and cheese.

Toasted Cornbread Salad

 Serves 6

- ~ **TOTAL COST:** $6.59
- ~ **CALORIES:** 425.84
- ~ **FAT:** 22.61 g
- ~ **PROTEIN:** 12.92 g
- ~ **CHOLESTEROL:** 54.41 mg
- ~ **SODIUM:** 458.14 mg

½ (9-inch square) Double Cornbread (Chapter 3)
1 (15-ounce) can pinto beans, rinsed
1 green bell pepper, chopped
2 cups frozen corn, thawed and drained
1 tomato, chopped
½ cup Spanish peanuts
⅓ cup ranch salad dressing
⅓ cup salsa
⅓ cup plain yogurt
½ cup cubed pepper jack cheese

Add anything you'd like to this versatile and delicious main-dish salad. Leftover cooked rice, more cheese, or vegetables can be used.

1. Preheat oven to 375°F. Cut corn bread into 1-inch cubes and place on baking sheet. Bake for 10–15 minutes or until cubes are light golden brown and toasted. Set aside.
2. Drain the beans and prepare vegetables. In medium bowl, combine salad dressing, salsa, and yogurt, and blend well. Combine with all ingredients in large serving bowl and toss gently. Serve immediately.

Give Your Salad Some Crunch
Most corn bread salads are made by layering crumbled corn bread with vegetables, cheese, meat, and dressing, chilling for a few hours, then tossing at the last minute. By toasting leftover cornbread cut into cubes and serving immediately, the salad retains crunch and texture. You could use some toasted or pine nuts instead of the peanuts.

Pumpkin Soufflé

Serves 4

~ **TOTAL COST:** $3.06
~ **CALORIES:** 242.34
~ **FAT:** 13.74 g
~ **PROTEIN:** 12.19 g
~ **CHOLESTEROL:** 219.20 mg
~ **SODIUM:** 603.14 mg

2 tablespoons vegetable oil
1 onion, chopped
4 cloves garlic, minced
2 tablespoons flour
¼ teaspoon salt
⅛ teaspoon pepper
½ cup milk
1 (13-ounce) can solid-pack pumpkin
4 egg yolks
½ teaspoon dried thyme leaves
4 egg whites
¼ teaspoon cream of tartar
7 tablespoons grated Parmesan cheese

This beautiful little entrée is wonderful for entertaining. Serve it with a crisp green salad and some breadsticks for a light lunch.

1. Preheat oven to 425°F. Grease the bottom of a 1½-quart soufflé dish with a bit of oil and set aside. In small saucepan, heat vegetable oil over medium heat. Add onion and garlic; cook and stir until tender, about 5 minutes.
2. Add flour, salt, and pepper; cook and stir for 1 minute. Blend in milk; cook and stir until thick, about 2–3 minutes. Place in large bowl and let cool for 10 minutes. Blend in pumpkin, egg yolk, and thyme until smooth.
3. In medium bowl, combine egg whites, salt, and cream of tartar and beat until stiff peaks form. Stir a spoonful of the beaten egg whites into pumpkin mixture, then fold in remaining egg whites along with the Parmesan cheese. Pour into prepared soufflé dish.
4. Bake for 15 minutes, then reduce heat to 350°F and bake for another 20–25 minutes or until soufflé is puffed and golden brown. Serve immediately.

Tex-Mex Potato Salad

Serves 5

- ~ **TOTAL COST:** $6.75
- ~ **CALORIES:** 341.40
- ~ **FAT:** 10.28 g
- ~ **PROTEIN:** 9.62 g
- ~ **CHOLESTEROL:** 19.10 mg
- ~ **SODIUM:** 425.24 mg

8 russet potatoes
1 onion, chopped
4 cloves garlic, chopped
2 tablespoons olive oil
1 tablespoon chili powder
½ cup plain yogurt
½ cup mayonnaise
½ cup salsa
½ teaspoon salt
2 cups frozen corn, thawed and drained
1 green bell pepper, chopped
1 jalapeño pepper, minced
½ cup feta cheese, crumbled

This updated potato salad has a lot of colorful vegetables. Serve it with lettuce in a tostada shell for a nice presentation.

1. Preheat oven to 400°F. Scrub potatoes and cut into cubes. Place in large baking pan along with red onion and garlic. Drizzle with olive oil; toss using hands, coating vegetables with oil. Bake at 400°F for 50–65 minutes, turning once with spatula, until potatoes are tender inside and crisp outside.
2. Meanwhile, in large bowl combine chili powder, yogurt, mayonnaise, salsa, and salt, and mix well. Add corn, bell pepper, and jalapeño and mix well. When potatoes are done, stir into mayonnaise mixture along with cheese, turning gently to coat.
3. Cover salad and refrigerate for at least 3 hours until chilled. Or you can serve the salad immediately.

Ethnic Potato Salad

You can flavor potato salads any way you'd like. Instead of the Tex-Mex flavors, use chopped bell peppers, crumbled goat cheese, and olives for a Greek variation. Use five spice powder, cilantro, bok choy, and green onions for an Asian Potato Salad. With your imagination and a few ingredients, you don't have to serve the same salad twice.

Spanish Omelet

Serves 4

~ **TOTAL COST:** $5.91
~ **CALORIES:** 344.03
~ **FAT:** 24.03 g
~ **PROTEIN:** 18.57 g
~ **CHOLESTEROL:** 352.28 mg
~ **SODIUM:** 453.12 mg

2 tablespoons vegetable oil, divided
1 onion, minced
3 cloves garlic, minced
1 stalk celery, chopped
½ chopped green bell pepper
1 jalapeño pepper, minced
½ teaspoon dried oregano
2 tomatoes, chopped
¼ teaspoon salt
⅛ teaspoon pepper
6 eggs
¼ cup milk
3 tablespoons sour cream
1 cup grated Cheddar cheese

If you remove the seeds from the jalapeño, the sauce will be milder. Like it hot? Leave the seeds on.

1. For the sauce, in a small saucepan heat 1 tablespoon olive oil over medium heat. Add onion, garlic, celery, bell pepper, and jalapeño pepper; cook and stir for 4 minutes until crisp-tender. Add oregano, tomatoes, salt, and pepper, and bring to a simmer. Reduce heat to low and simmer for 5 minutes.
2. In large bowl, combine eggs, milk, and sour cream and beat until combined. Heat 1 tablespoon oil in nonstick skillet and add egg mixture. Cook, moving spatula around pan and lifting to let uncooked mixture flow underneath, until eggs are set but still moist.
3. Sprinkle with Cheddar and top with half of the tomato sauce. Cover and cook for 2–4 minutes longer, until bottom of omelet is golden brown. Fold over, slide onto serving plate, top with remaining tomato sauce, and serve.

Spicy Mexican Bean Salad

Serves 4

- ~ **TOTAL COST:** $6.54
- ~ **CALORIES:** 372.72
- ~ **FAT:** 14.09 g
- ~ **PROTEIN:** 13.68 g
- ~ **CHOLESTEROL:** 0.0 mg
- ~ **SODIUM:** 1008.45 mg

½ pound green beans
1 (15-ounce) can black beans, rinsed
1 (15-ounce) can pinto beans, rinsed
½ cup minced onion
4 green onions, chopped
¼ cup olive oil
¼ cup lemon juice
2 tablespoons mustard
2 tablespoons sugar
1 jalapeño pepper, minced
½ teaspoon salt
⅛ teaspoon cayenne pepper
2 teaspoons chili powder
6 lettuce leaves

Three-bean salad typically has a sweet-and-sour dressing coating green beans and wax beans. This recipe adds pinto beans, black beans, and the spice of minced jalapeño peppers.

1. Trim green beans and steam over boiling water for 8–12 minutes until crisp-tender. Remove and place in serving bowl. Rinse and drain black beans and pinto beans and add to bowl along with onion and green onions.
2. In small bowl, combine olive oil, lemon juice, mustard, sugar, jalapeño pepper, salt, cayenne pepper, and chili powder and mix with wire whisk until blended. Pour over bean mixture, stir gently, cover, and refrigerate for at least 2 hours to blend flavors. Serve on lettuce leaves with hot Cornbread.

> **Complete Protein**
> This salad doesn't provide complete protein because it only has legumes, with no grain, nuts, or seeds. It's the combination of beans with these other ingredients that has the correct amino acids for best nutrition. Serve it with Double Cornbread (Chapter 3) for complete protein, or add some chopped peanuts or pine nuts.

Onion Quiche

 Serves 6

- ~ **TOTAL COST:** $4.64
- ~ **CALORIES:** 384.79
- ~ **FAT:** 22.03 g
- ~ **PROTEIN:** 12.85 g
- ~ **CHOLESTEROL:** 147.60 mg
- ~ **SODIUM:** 619.99 mg

1 tablespoon butter
1 onion, chopped
1 onion, sliced
½ cup sour cream
⅓ cup milk
3 eggs, beaten
½ teaspoon salt
⅛ teaspoon pepper
2 tablespoons grated Parmesan cheese
1 cup shredded Muenster cheese
1 Angel Pie Crust (Chapter 15)

For onion lovers! This vegetarian quiche is a good choice for brunch; serve it with some homemade pastries and lots of fruit salad.

1. Preheat oven to 375°F. In large skillet, heat olive oil over medium heat. Add chopped and sliced onion; cook and stir for 8–9 minutes or until onions are translucent. Remove from heat and set aside.
2. In medium bowl, combine sour cream, milk, eggs, salt, and pepper and beat well. Sprinkle Romano cheese in bottom of Pie Crust. Add onions and arrange in an even layer. Sprinkle with Muenster cheese, then top with egg mixture. Bake for 35–45 minutes or until filling is set and golden brown in spots. Let stand for 5 minutes, then serve.

Quiche

Quiche is a good choice for breakfast or brunch. It freezes well. Simply cut the completely cooled quiche into slices, wrap well in freezer wrap, label, and freeze up to 6 months. To defrost, reheat each individual slice on 50 percent power for 2–4 minutes, then on 100% power for 1 minute, until hot. Let stand for 3 minutes, then serve.

Veggie Omelet

Serves 4

- ~ **TOTAL COST:** $4.19
- ~ **CALORIES:** 367.12
- ~ **FAT:** 21.50 g
- ~ **PROTEIN:** 20.99 g
- ~ **CHOLESTEROL:** 411.25 mg
- ~ **SODIUM:** 648.82 mg

2 tablespoons butter
1 onion, finely chopped
3 cloves garlic, minced
1 cup roasted vegetables
7 eggs
⅓ cup milk
½ teaspoon salt
⅛ teaspoon pepper
1 cup shredded Swiss cheese

This recipe is a great way to use up any leftover vegetables. Or you could just sauté any combination along with the onions.

1. In large nonstick skillet, melt butter over medium heat. Add onion and garlic; cook and stir until crisp tender, about 4 minutes. Add Roasted Vegetables; cook and stir just until hot. Remove vegetables from skillet with slotted spoon and set aside.
2. In medium bowl, combine eggs, cream, salt, and pepper and beat well until foamy. Place same skillet over medium heat and pour in egg mixture. Cook for 3 minutes without stirring, then run a spatula around the edges of the egg mixture, lifting to let uncooked egg flow underneath.
3. Continue cooking egg until bottom is lightly browned and egg is just set, about 3–6 minutes longer. Add reserved vegetables to omelet and sprinkle cheese over all. Carefully fold omelet in half, cover, and let cook for 2 minutes to melt cheese. Serve immediately.

Veggie Risotto

Serves 6

- ~ **TOTAL COST:** $5.42
- ~ **CALORIES:** 407.35
- ~ **FAT:** 13.83 g
- ~ **PROTEIN:** 12.64 g
- ~ **CHOLESTEROL:** 30.84 mg
- ~ **SODIUM:** 428.53 mg

1 tablespoon olive oil
3 tablespoons butter, divided
3 cups vegetable broth
2 cup water
1 onion, finely chopped
3 cloves garlic, minced
½ cup chopped mushrooms
1 cup frozen chopped spinach, thawed
½ teaspoon salt
2 cups long grain rice
¼ cup grated Parmesan cheese
½ cup grated Muenster cheese

Here's a shocker: you can make risotto with regular long grain rice. You don't need to buy that expensive Arborio rice. Just keep stirring!

1. In large saucepan, combine olive oil and 1 tablespoon butter. In a medium saucepan, bring the broth and water to a very slow simmer.
2. When the butter melts, add the onion, garlic, and mushrooms. Cook, stirring frequently, until tender, about 5 minutes. Then add the drained spinach and salt; cook and stir for 3–4 minutes longer. Add the rice; cook and stir for 3 minutes.
3. Add broth mixture, ½ cup at a time, stirring frequently and cooking until the rice absorbs the broth. Continue adding broth mixture, stirring, until the rice is tender. Add the cheese and remaining 2 tablespoons butter; cover and remove from heat. Let stand for 4 minutes, then stir and serve.

Cooking Risotto

When rice is cooked slowly and manipulated by stirring, the starch cells break open and thicken the liquid. Arborio rice is usually used because it's very high in starch. But regular rice works just as well. You do have to keep an eye on the rice, and stir very frequently, both to help release the starch and to prevent the risotto from burning.

Vegetable Lasagna Rolls

Serves 6

~ **TOTAL COST:** $5.95
~ **CALORIES:** 460.03
~ **FAT:** 22.23 g
~ **PROTEIN:** 16.81 g
~ **CHOLESTEROL:** 75.99 mg
~ **SODIUM:** 560.43 mg

6 lasagna noodles
2 potatoes, peeled
2 tablespoons butter
1 onion, diced
2 cloves garlic, minced
1 cup frozen peas
1 carrot, shredded
1 (8-ounce) package cream cheese
¾ cup milk
1 cup shredded Cheddar cheese
1 (8-ounce) can tomato sauce
½ teaspoon dried Italian seasoning
¼ cup grated Parmesan cheese

These lovely little rolls are filled with a cheesy vegetable blend. You could substitute any other vegetable in this recipe if you'd like.

1. Preheat oven to 350°F. Bring a large pot of salted water to a boil. Dice potatoes and add to large skillet along with butter. Cook over medium heat until potatoes start to soften, about 5 minutes. Add onion and garlic; cook and stir until onion is tender, about 5 minutes longer.
2. Cook lasagna noodles according to package directions until tender. Drain and rinse with cold water; drain again. Add peas and carrots to potato mixture; cook and stir for 3 minutes.
3. In microwave safe bowl, combine cream cheese, milk, and vegetable broth and microwave on high for 2 minutes until cheese is melted; stir with wire whisk. Add Colby cheese and stir. Add ⅓ cup of this mixture to the vegetables in skillet.
4. Arrange noodles on work surface. Spread each with some of the vegetable mixture. Spoon half of cream cheese sauce into 12" × 8" glass baking dish and arrange filled noodles on sauce. Pour remaining sauce over, then top with tomato sauce; sprinkle with seasoning and Parmesan cheese. Bake for 35–40 minutes or until casserole is bubbling. Serve immediately.

Sicilian Stuffed Cabbage

Serves 6

- ~ **TOTAL COST:** $6.95
- ~ **CALORIES:** 318.88
- ~ **FAT:** 12.05 g
- ~ **PROTEIN:** 13.00 g
- ~ **CHOLESTEROL:** 97.24 mg
- ~ **SODIUM:** 787.32 mg

1 head cabbage
¾ cup brown rice
2 cups water
1 teaspoon salt
¼ cup mustard
2 eggs
1 cup shredded Swiss cheese
2 tablespoons butter
1 onion, chopped
3 cloves garlic, minced
1 (14-ounce) can diced tomatoes, undrained
1 (10.75-ounce) can tomato soup

Stuffed cabbage is probably the ultimate comfort food. Make it on a cold winter night and serve it with chocolate bread pudding.

1. Remove the outer layers of the cabbage and discard. Cut out the core and gently remove the outside eight leaves. Place in a large bowl and cover with hot water; set aside. Chop remaining cabbage.
2. In large saucepan, combine brown rice and water. Bring to a boil, then cover, reduce heat, and simmer for 30–40 minutes or until rice is almost tender. Drain and add salt, mustard, eggs, and cheese and mix well. Add chopped cabbage.
3. In large skillet, heat butter over medium heat. Add onion and garlic; cook and stir until crisp-tender, about 4 minutes. Add tomatoes and tomato soup and bring to a simmer.
4. Drain cabbage leaves and place on work surface. Divide rice filling among leaves, using about ½ cup for each, and roll up. Place, seam side down, in 13" × 9" glass baking dish. Pour tomato mixture over everything. If there is leftover rice mixture, arrange around stuffed leaves.
5. Place in oven and turn heat to 350°F. Bake for 60–70 minutes or until casserole is bubbly. Serve immediately.

Vegetable Pancakes

Serves 6

- ~ **TOTAL COST:** $5.83
- ~ **CALORIES:** 523.84
- ~ **FAT:** 28.44 g
- ~ **PROTEIN:** 17.57 g
- ~ **CHOLESTEROL:** 147.13 mg
- ~ **SODIUM:** 673.33 mg

10 Easy Crepes (Chapter 15)
1 tablespoon vegetable oil
1 onion, chopped
1½ cups frozen hash brown potatoes, thawed
1 cup frozen peas
½ teaspoon dried tarragon leaves
½ teaspoon salt
⅛ teaspoon pepper
1 cup sour cream, divided
1 cup shredded Cheddar cheese
½ cup shredded Swiss cheese

Crepes filled with vegetables and topped with sour cream and cheese are a taste treat that doesn't seem like a budget meal.

1. Prepare crepes or defrost if frozen. In medium saucepan, heat oil over medium heat. Add onions; cook and stir for 3 minutes. Then add potatoes and peas; cook and stir until vegetables are hot and potatoes begin to brown, about 4–5 minutes longer. Remove from heat and sprinkle with tarragon, salt, and pepper.
2. Add half of the sour cream and mix well. Fill crepes with this mixture; roll to enclose filling. Place in a microwave-safe 9" × 13" baking dish. Spread crepes with remaining sour cream and sprinkle with cheese.
3. Microwave, covered, for 3–6 minutes on 70% power, rotating once during cooking time, until cheese is melted and crepes are hot. Serve immediately.

Versatile Crepes

Once you have some Crepes on hand, you can make dinner from almost anything; leftover chili, chopped beef mixed with a bottled cheese sauce, or chicken and pesto. Fill the crepes with the mixture, roll up, then place in a baking dish. You can bake them, covered, at 350°F for 20–30 minutes until warmed through.

Bean Burritos

Serves 5

- ~ **TOTAL COST:** $6.95
- ~ **CALORIES:** 373.59
- ~ **FAT:** 16.67 g
- ~ **PROTEIN:** 13.29 g
- ~ **CHOLESTEROL:** 23.73 mg
- ~ **SODIUM:** 939.52 mg

2 tablespoons vegetable oil
1 onion, chopped
3 cloves garlic, minced
1 jalapeño, minced
1 (15-ounce) can pinto beans, rinsed
1 tablespoon chili powder
1 (15-ounce) can enchilada sauce
10 corn tortillas
1 cup shredded Cheddar cheese

Refried beans have a wonderful rich texture and a hearty, meaty taste; they add so much to this simple recipe. Serve with a fruit salad and some orange fizz.

1. Preheat oven to 350°F. In heavy skillet, heat oil and cook onion and garlic over medium heat, stirring frequently, for 3–4 minutes. Add chile, kidney and pinto beans, cumin, and ½ cup enchilada sauce; mash some of the beans and cook and stir mixture for 3–4 minutes.
2. Place a thin layer of enchilada sauce in 13" × 9" glass baking dish. Dip each tortilla into more enchilada sauce, top with ⅓ cup bean filling, roll up, and place in dish. Top with cheese; bake at 350°F for 20–30 minutes or until hot and bubbly.

Tomato Noodle Bake

Serves 4

- ~ **TOTAL COST:** $5.82
- ~ **CALORIES:** 368.29
- ~ **FAT:** 15.24 g
- ~ **PROTEIN:** 14.52 g
- ~ **CHOLESTEROL:** 45.96 mg
- ~ **SODIUM:** 984.50 mg

1 onion, chopped
3 cloves garlic, chopped
2 tablespoons olive oil
2 carrots, grated
1 (14-ounce) can diced tomatoes, undrained
1 (6-ounce) can tomato paste
1½ cups water
1 (4-ounce) jar mushroom pieces, undrained
⅛ teaspoon red pepper flakes
2 teaspoons sugar
2 cups elbow macaroni noodles
1 cup shredded Colby cheese

This rich and hearty casserole doesn't need cheese, but you can top it with some grated Parmesan or Cheddar before baking for a nice crust.

1. Brown ground beef, onions, and garlic in large skillet. Drain well, then add remaining ingredients. Bring to a boil, then partially cover pan and simmer over low heat for 25–30 minutes to blend flavors, stirring frequently.
2. Meanwhile, bring a large pot of water to a boil and cook noodles until almost al dente. Drain well and stir into mixture in skillet.
3. Pour into greased 3-quart casserole and sprinkle with cheese Bake for 30–40 minutes or until casserole is bubbling and hot. Serve immediately.

Corn-and-Chili Pancakes

Serves 4

- ~ **TOTAL COST:** $3.06
- ~ **CALORIES:** 399.21
- ~ **FAT:** 14.20 g
- ~ **PROTEIN:** 14.16 g
- ~ **CHOLESTEROL:** 130.66 mg
- ~ **SODIUM:** 484.32 mg

½ cup buttermilk
1 tablespoon butter, melted
2 eggs
½ cup grated Cheddar cheese
1 jalapeño pepper, minced
1 cup frozen corn, thawed
½ cup cornmeal
1 cup all-purpose flour
1½ teaspoons baking powder
½ teaspoon baking soda
1 tablespoon sugar
1 tablespoon chili powder
1 tablespoon vegetable oil

Top these spicy pancakes with some nonfat sour cream and salsa, or some warmed maple syrup.

1. In large bowl, combine buttermilk, olive oil, eggs, Cheddar cheese, and jalapeño pepper and beat well. Add corn add to buttermilk mixture along with cornmeal, flour, baking powder, baking soda, sugar, and chili powder; mix until combined. Let stand for 10 minutes.
2. Heat griddle or frying pan over medium heat. Brush with the butter, then add the batter, ¼ cup at a time. Cook until bubbles form and start to break and the sides look dry, about 3–4 minutes. Carefully flip pancakes and cook until light golden brown on second side, about 2–3 minutes. Serve immediately.

Fresh Fennel Bulb with Lemon and Asiago Cheese

 Serves 4

- ~ **PREP TIME:** 7 minutes
- ~ **COOK TIME:** none
- ~ **TOTAL COST:** $6.68
- ~ **CALORIES:** 65
- ~ **FAT:** 3 g
- ~ **PROTEIN:** 3 g
- ~ **CHOLESTEROL:** 1 mg
- ~ **SODIUM:** 345 mg

2 bulbs fresh fennel, cleaned
½ fresh lemon
1 (4-ounce) wedge Parmigiano-Reggiano or asiago cheese
1 tablespoon high-quality extra virgin olive oil
Pinch sea salt

Simple and Italian, just the way they like it!

Trim fennel stems and wispy fronds from fennel tops. Break the bulbs apart, layer by layer, using your hands to make long, bite-size pieces. Discard the core. Arrange the pieces onto a serving platter. Squeeze lemon over fennel. Using a vegetable peeler, shave curls of cheese over fennel, allowing them to fall where they may. Make about 10 curls. Drizzle olive oil over all and sprinkle with salt.

Quick and Easy Tip
Precut fennel and keep in the refrigerator. Fennel is a vegetable that has a licorice taste. The citric acid in the lemon and tart flavor help balance the bitterness of fresh fennel.

Roasted Red Pepper Omelet with Fresh Mint Leaves

 Serves 2

- **PREP TIME:** 10 minutes
- **COOK TIME:** 5 minutes
- **TOTAL COST:** $2.83
- **CALORIES:** 325
- **FAT:** 28 g
- **CARBOHYDRATES:** 4 g
- **PROTEIN:** 15 g
- **CHOLESTEROL:** 471 mg
- **SODIUM:** 480 mg

2 tablespoons unsalted butter
½ yellow onion, chopped
½ red bell pepper, seeded and chopped
½ tablespoon fresh mint leaves, chopped
4 eggs, well beaten
2 ounces Gorgonzola cheese, crumbled
Sea salt and black pepper to taste

Gorgonzola is an Italian blue cheese originally from the town of Gorgonzola near Milan, Italy, which is northern Italy. Made from cow's milk, it is typically firm yet crumbly and has a strong, salty flavor.

1. Heat a 10-inch nonstick pan over medium-high heat; add 1 table-spoon butter and heat until just melted. Add onion and sauté about 1 minute. Add bell pepper and sauté an additional 1 minute. In small bowl, whisk in mint leaves with eggs. Remove onion mixture from pan and set aside.
2. Place pan over medium heat and add remaining tablespoon of but-ter. Pour egg mixture into pan and tilt pan to distribute evenly. Place onion mixture on one side of omelet. Top the mixture with cheese. Season with salt and pepper. Cook until the consistency is like cus-tard. Run spatula along sides of omelet, tilting pan to let liquid eggs in center drain off to bottom of omelet. Then carefully but quickly flip plain side of omelet over side with cheese and peppers. Cut in half and serve.

Asian Crepes with Snow Peas and Water Chestnuts

Serves 4

- **PREP TIME:** 7 minutes
- **COOK TIME:** 15 minutes
- **TOTAL COST:** $4.83
- **CALORIES:** 223
- **FAT:** 8 g
- **PROTEIN:** 12 g
- **CHOLESTEROL:** 125 mg
- **SODIUM:** 263 mg

4 eggs
2¼ cups milk
2 cups plain flour
Pinch sea salt
¼ cup (half a stick) melted butter, plus 2 to 3 tablespoons for cooking
¼ cup peanut oil
1 pound snow pea pods, ends trimmed slightly
½ fresh lemon, zested and juiced
1 8-ounce can sliced water chestnuts, drained
½ cup roasted, unsalted peanuts
2 tablespoons soy sauce
1 tablespoon fresh gingerroot, minced
Tabasco or other red pepper sauce as desired

Did you know that water chestnuts are not related to the nut family at all? Water chestnuts are actually an aquatic vegetable that grows in marshes and are native to China. That's why you always see them in Chinese food!

1. In a medium mixing bowl, whisk together eggs, milk, flour, butter, and salt. Mix to combine well, but don't overly mix. In nonstick skillet, add ½ to 1 tablespoon of the butter and heat over medium heat. Swirl pan to coat. Pour in ¼ cup of batter and swirl to cover pan. Cook for 1 to 1½ minutes, lifting edges with spatula. Crepe should easily slide out of pan. As crepes are cooked, transfer to plate to hold, stacking them is okay.
2. In a large saucepan or nonstick skillet, heat oil over medium-high heat. Add snow pea pods, lemon zest and juice, and stir to coat. Add water chestnuts and peanuts, and stir occasionally, cooking for 5 minutes. Add remaining ingredients, mix well and serve with crepes.
3. To wrap crepes, place crepe flat on plate, add ⅓ cup filling, fold crepe in half, then fold again.

Quick and Easy Tip
If you are nervous about making crepes, buy flour tortillas instead. They are inexpensive and will save you time.

Asparagus Frittata with Cheese

Serves 8

- ~ **PREP TIME:** 7 minutes
- ~ **COOK TIME:** 15 minutes
- ~ **TOTAL COST:** $6.75
- ~ **CALORIES:** 225
- ~ **FAT:** 21 g
- ~ **PROTEIN:** 21 g
- ~ **CHOLESTEROL:** 312 mg
- ~ **SODIUM:** 340 mg

1 (10-ounce) box frozen chopped asparagus
6 eggs
½ cup Cheddar cheese, grated
¼ cup Monterey Jack cheese, shredded
Fine zest of one lemon
Sea salt and black pepper to taste
2 tablespoons butter, unsalted

Asparagus contains no fat or cholesterol and is low in calories and sodium. It's also a good source of folic acid, potassium, and fiber.

1. In a large ovenproof saucepan over medium heat, add asparagus and cook for 2 to 3 minutes or until heated through. Drain, chop, and set aside in a separate bowl.
2. Preheat broiler. In another bowl, beat eggs and then mix in cheeses, lemon zest, salt, and pepper. Mix well. In the large saucepan, heat butter over medium heat. Add egg mixture, then distribute asparagus throughout egg mixture and reduce heat, cooking slowly for about 10 minutes. To finish cooking, place saucepan under broiler for about 30 seconds to finish cooking and brown very slightly on top.

Quick and Easy Tip

If you do not have an ovenproof saucepan or skillet, don't worry. When cooking the frittata, use a spatula to run around the sides of the frittata to lift. Tilt the pan and let some of the runny egg mixture in the center of the frittata run to the sides. This is similar to cooking an omelet; however, a frittata is easier in that you don't have to flip it.

Parmesan-Stuffed Mushrooms

 Serves 6

- ~ **PREP TIME:** 7 minutes
- ~ **COOK TIME:** 12 minutes
- ~ **TOTAL COST:** $5.05
- ~ **CALORIES:** 125
- ~ **FAT:** 11 g
- ~ **PROTEIN:** 6 g
- ~ **CHOLESTEROL:** 5 mg
- ~ **SODIUM:** 145 mg

1 pound cremini mushrooms, stems removed and
  reserved
3 tablespoons butter, unsalted
1 yellow onion, chopped
¾ cup bread crumbs
Sea salt and black pepper to taste
1 teaspoon dried thyme leaves
¼ cup Parmesan cheese, grated
2 tablespoons fresh Italian parsley, chopped

Get a jump-start on this recipe by making the filling
mixture the day before. Wait, however, to broil the
mushrooms until just before serving.

1. Preheat broiler. Chop mushroom stems. In a large
   saucepan over medium heat, melt butter. Add onion
   and cook for 2 minutes. Add mushroom stems and
   cook 2 to 3 minutes more. Stir in bread crumbs,
   salt, pepper, and thyme. Cook an additional 1 minute. Remove from heat and stir in cheese.
2. Using a small spoon, fill each mushroom cap with
   mushroom mixture. Place filled mushrooms on a
   baking sheet and put under preheated broiler for 6
   minutes, or until tops are browned and caps have
   softened slightly and become juicy. Sprinkle tops
   with parsley.

Roasted Fresh Beets with Feta

 Serves 4

- ~ **PREP TIME:** 10 minutes
- ~ **COOK TIME:** 45 to 55 minutes
- ~ **TOTAL COST:** $5.62
- ~ **CALORIES:** 181
- ~ **FAT:** 4 g
- ~ **PROTEIN:** 3 g
- ~ **CHOLESTEROL:** 12 mg
- ~ **SODIUM:** 125 mg

2 pounds fresh beets, washed and cut into 2-inch cubes
1 tablespoon olive oil
Sea salt and black pepper to taste
1 cup feta cheese
1 bunch fresh Italian flat-leaf parsley, chopped

Most people hear "roasted beets" and think, yuk!
Boy are they wrong! This is one of my most popular
dishes in my cooking classes.

1. Heat oven to 375°F. Toss beets with olive oil, salt,
   and pepper. Spread onto parchment-lined baking
   sheet in single layer. Roast in middle rack of oven
   for 45 minutes or until tender. Check about halfway through cooking and toss if needed.
2. Remove from oven, toss with feta and parsley,
   and serve.

> **Quick and Easy Tip**
> Add a little lemon zest to perk up the flavor, if you
> like.

Sautéed Parsnips and Pears with Mango Chutney

 Serves 4

~ **PREP TIME:** 12 minutes

~ **COOK TIME:** 21 minutes

~ **TOTAL COST:** $6.35

~ **CALORIES:** 245

~ **FAT:** 2 g

~ **PROTEIN:** 5 g

~ **CHOLESTEROL:** 2 mg

~ **SODIUM:** 205 mg

1½ pounds parsnips, cut into 1-inch pieces

2 tablespoons olive oil

1 red onion, thinly sliced

2 Bosc pears, cored and thinly sliced

1 teaspoon curry powder

½ teaspoon ground coriander

Sea salt and black pepper to taste

¼ cup plain yogurt

¼ cup mango chutney

2 tablespoons fresh cilantro, chopped

Coriander is the seed that fresh cilantro is grown from. Native to Southwest Asia and North Africa, coriander is used in many cooking cultures including Middle Eastern, Mediterranean, and Indian.

Partially boil the parsnips, about 5 minutes. In a large saucepan over medium heat, add oil. Add onion, pears, curry, and coriander and cook for about 10 minutes, stirring regularly. Add the parsnips and season with sea salt and pepper, and cook an additional 5 minutes, until parsnips brown lightly. Remove from heat and then stir in yogurt, chutney, and cilantro. Serve.

> **Quick and Easy Tip**
> Parsnips are root vegetables related to carrots. They typically grow in cold climates, not warm, as frost enhances their flavor.

Sweet Potatoes with Candied Gingerroot

 Serves 4

- ~ **PREP TIME:** 10 minutes
- ~ **COOK TIME:** 25 minutes
- ~ **TOTAL COST:** $5.36
- ~ **CALORIES:** 249
- ~ **FAT:** 3 g
- ~ **PROTEIN:** 5 g
- ~ **CHOLESTEROL:** 1 mg
- ~ **SODIUM:** 422 mg

4 large sweet potatoes, peeled and cut into 2- to 3-inch cubes
¼ cup milk
2 tablespoons butter
1 tablespoon mashed candied ginger, or 1 tablespoon brown sugar plus ½ teaspoon ground ginger

Sweet potatoes, found in North and South America, are commonly confused with yams, which are native to Africa and Asia. A tasty alternative to baking potatoes, sweet potatoes are loaded with beta carotene and vitamin C.

Place potatoes in a large-quart boiler filled ¾ with water. Bring to a boil and cook potatoes until tender, about 20 minutes. Drain and return to pan. In a small saucepan, heat the milk with the butter. Add milk mixture to potatoes, along with candied ginger. Mash by hand using potato masher or with an electric mixer.

Quick and Easy Tip
Fresh ginger is the underground stem of the ginger plant. This root can be candied and eaten as a snack or combined with other foods as a spice. Fresh gingerroot can be kept in the refrigerator for up to three weeks or in the freezer for up to five months.

Grilled Portobello Mushrooms

 Serves 4

- ~ **PREP TIME:** 15 minutes
- ~ **COOK TIME:** 6 minutes
- ~ **TOTAL COST:** $6.20
- ~ **CALORIES:** 120
- ~ **FAT:** 1 g
- ~ **PROTEIN:** 7 g
- ~ **CHOLESTEROL:** 2 mg
- ~ **SODIUM:** 199 mg

4 large portabello mushrooms, stems removed
½ cup extra virgin olive oil
1 cup red wine vinegar
2 tablespoons soy sauce
1 tablespoon sugar
½ cup variety fresh herbs, chopped, such as parsley, thyme, rosemary, chives

Portabello mushrooms are like a vegetarian burger! Try using them as "bread" for a portabello mushroom sandwich layering cheese, mixed greens, and tomato slices.

1. Brush any dirt from the mushrooms, but do not wash them. Whisk together olive oil, vinegar, soy sauce, sugar, and herbs. In shallow dish, pour the marinade over the mushrooms; marinate 10 minutes, turning after 5 minutes.
2. Preheat grill. Grill 2 to 3 minutes on each side. Serve whole or sliced with leftover marinade.

Quick and Easy Tip
Add a tablespoon or slice of Gruyère or Swiss cheese and cook until melted for an extra culinary treat.

Olive-Stuffed Artichokes

Serves 4

~ **PREP TIME:** 12 minutes
~ **COOK TIME:** 35 minutes
~ **TOTAL COST:** $6.32
~ **CALORIES:** 153
~ **FAT:** 9 g
~ **PROTEIN:** 3 g
~ **CHOLESTEROL:** 1 mg
~ **SODIUM:** 201 mg

4 large artichokes, trimmed and split lengthwise
4 quarts water
½ fresh lemon, zested and juiced
1 cup cooked white rice
7 green olives, chopped
7 kalamata olives, chopped
Sea salt and black pepper to taste
2 tablespoons fresh Italian flat-leaf parsley, chopped
3 tablespoons butter, melted
1 egg
1 clove garlic, minced

I always use Italian flat-leaf parsley, as it has a better flavor and texture than curly parsley. Besides, among chefs, curly parsley is a bit out of fashion.

1. Boil the artichokes in 4 quarts of water with lemon juice and lemon zest for 20 minutes. Drain and place on a parchment-lined baking sheet, cut side up.
2. Preheat oven to 350°F. Mix the rest of the ingredients together in a large bowl. Spoon filling over the artichokes, pressing between the leaves. Bake for 15 minutes or until hot.

Quick and Easy Tip
Artichokes can be a little tricky. Wear gloves to tear off the outer leaves and trim the stem. Either steam them, boil them, or bake them to make them tender.

Baked Potatoes Stuffed with Spinach and Cheese

Serves 4

~ **PREP TIME:** 10 minutes
~ **COOK TIME:** 1 hour 5 minutes
~ **TOTAL COST:** $5.50
~ **CALORIES:** 249
~ **FAT:** 3 g
~ **PROTEIN:** 5 g
~ **CHOLESTEROL:** 1 mg
~ **SODIUM:** 422 mg

4 baking potatoes
1 (10-ounce) package frozen chopped spinach, thawed, with excess water squeezed out
1 cup sour cream
Pinch nutmeg
1 cup white American cheese, grated
Sea salt and black pepper to taste
½ cup sharp Cheddar cheese, shredded

Stuffed potatoes are easy, filling, and taste great! Add crispy bacon crumbles and chopped chives for a truly delicious potato.

Preheat the oven to 350°F. Bake the potatoes for 40 minutes. Cool the potatoes and split them in half lengthwise. Spoon out the insides of the potatoes, leaving skin intact. Place potato filling in a mixing bowl and add the spinach. Stir in sour cream and nutmeg. Add the American cheese and season with salt and pepper. Restuff the potato skins and arrange Cheddar cheese on top. Bake for another 20 minutes, and serve hot.

Quick and Easy Tip
When scooping out the potato, scoop out as much as possible but leave a slight potato edge along the skin. This helps keep the potato skin from breaking.

Veggie Burger-Stuffed Red Bell Peppers

Serves 4

- ~ **PREP TIME:** 5 minutes
- ~ **COOK TIME:** 33 minutes
- ~ **TOTAL COST:** $6.96
- ~ **CALORIES:** 277
- ~ **FAT:** 5 g
- ~ **PROTEIN:** 5 g
- ~ **CHOLESTEROL:** 12 mg
- ~ **SODIUM:** 324 mg

4 large garlic cloves, minced
1 large onion, minced
¼ cup olive oil
2 veggie burgers, frozen
Sea salt and black pepper to taste
4 large red bell peppers

When shopping for bell peppers, stick with buying red or green as the yellow and orange bell peppers are slightly more rare and are usually more expensive. You do not sacrifice flavor by buying red or green ones.

1. Sauté the garlic and onion for 3 minutes in a large saucepan with 1 tablespoon olive oil over medium heat. Add veggie burgers, breaking up with a wooden spoon, and cook until heated through and broken down, about 4 minutes. Add salt and pepper as desired. Preheat oven to 350°F.
2. Cut the peppers in half lengthwise and scoop out seeds and cores. Fill with the burger mixture, drizzle with remaining olive oil, and place on parchment-lined baking sheets and bake for 25 minutes.

Quick and Easy Tip

If you don't have veggie burgers, substitute firm tofu or extra vegetables with rice or other grain. If you don't have sesame oil or just don't like it, leave it out of this recipe and add grated Parmesan cheese. Add any combination of your favorite ingredients to customize your recipe.

Burritos with Black Beans, Broccoli, and Cauliflower

 Serves 4

- ~ **PREP TIME:** 5 minutes
- ~ **COOK TIME:** 14 minutes
- ~ **TOTAL COST:** $4.60
- ~ **CALORIES:** 175
- ~ **FAT:** 8 g
- ~ **PROTEIN:** 14 g
- ~ **CHOLESTEROL:** 1 mg
- ~ **SODIUM:** 421 mg

2 tablespoons olive oil
1 yellow onion, chopped
½ teaspoon crushed red pepper flakes or hot sauce
2 cups frozen broccoli and cauliflower combo, thawed
1 (15-ounce) can black beans, drained
4 (10-inch) flour tortillas
1½ cups shredded Pepper Jack cheese

This is a healthy way to enjoy Mexican food. If you have some sour cream in your refrigerator, add a dollop.

1. In a large saucepan over medium heat, heat olive oil and add onion. Cook about 4 minutes, until tender. Sprinkle with red pepper flakes and stir together. Drain vegetables and add to onion mixture. Cook for about 4 minutes. Stir in black beans, cover, and let simmer for 4 minutes.
2. Meanwhile, warm tortillas by layering in microwave-safe paper towels and microwaving on high for 1 to 2 minutes. Spread tortillas on cutting board or other work surface and divide vegetable mixture amongst tortillas. Sprinkle with cheese, fold in sides, and roll up.

> **Quick and Easy Tip**
> Other great ingredients for this recipe are chopped green beans, corn, and red bell peppers. Add extra spice by adding chili powder or cayenne pepper.

Vegetarian Chili

Serves 6

- ~ **PREP TIME:** 3 minutes
- ~ **COOK TIME:** 20 minutes
- ~ **TOTAL COST:** $5.88
- ~ **CALORIES:** 324
- ~ **FAT:** 11 g
- ~ **PROTEIN:** 24 g
- ~ **CHOLESTEROL:** 0 mg
- ~ **SODIUM:** 437 mg

2 (15-ounce) cans spicy chili beans, undrained
1 (14-ounce) can diced tomatoes with green chilies, undrained
1 (12-ounce) jar tomato salsa
1 tablespoon chili powder
1 green bell pepper, chopped
1 cup water

As a chef you grow to love tasty, easy recipes like this one. Perfect for a Super Bowl party!

In heavy saucepan, combine all ingredients. Bring to a boil, then reduce heat and simmer for 15 to 20 minutes, stirring occasionally, until peppers are crisp-tender and mixture is heated and blended. Serve immediately, topped with sour cream, grated cheese, and chopped green onions, if desired.

Quick and Easy Tip
Use this chili on taco salad or baked potatoes!

Linguine with Brie and Tomatoes

Serves 4

- ~ **PREP TIME:** 5 minutes
- ~ **COOK TIME:** 15 minutes
- ~ **TOTAL COST:** $6.20
- ~ **CALORIES:** 241
- ~ **FAT:** 10 g
- ~ **PROTEIN:** 5 g
- ~ **CHOLESTEROL:** 36 mg
- ~ **SODIUM:** 180 mg

5 large tomatoes
¼ cup olive oil
1 (12-ounce) box linguine pasta
Pinch sea salt
¼ fresh basil, chopped
1 (6-ounce) wedge Brie cheese

Soft cheeses include Brie, Camembert, and Reblochon. When you need to slice these cheeses, place them in the freezer for about 15 minutes. The cheese will harden and it will be easier to handle.

Cut tomatoes in half and squeeze out seeds. Coarsely chop tomatoes and combine in a large bowl with olive oil. Bring large pot of water to a boil and cook linguine pasta as directed on package. Meanwhile, add salt and basil to tomatoes and toss gently. Cut Brie into small cubes and add to tomatoes. Drain pasta and immediately add tomato mixture. Toss, using tongs, until mixed.

Quick and Easy Tip
Hothouse tomatoes are good for this recipe as are tomatoes from the vine, which tend to be the most flavorful.

Teriyaki Vegetables

 Serves 4

- ~ **PREP TIME:** 5 minutes
- ~ **COOK TIME:** 18 minutes
- ~ **TOTAL COST:** $5.32
- ~ **CALORIES:** 228
- ~ **FAT:** 1 g
- ~ **PROTEIN:** 9 g
- ~ **CHOLESTEROL:** 0 mg
- ~ **SODIUM:** 379 mg

1 cup broccoli florets
1 cup sugar snap peas
½ cup sliced water chestnuts, drained
½ cup baby corn, drained
1 cup cauliflower, in chunks
1 cup shiitake mushrooms, sliced
⅓ cup low-sodium teriyaki sauce

If you prefer to use frozen vegetables instead of fresh, you may have to increase your cooking time about 5 minutes to allow for thawing.

1. Coat a skillet with nonstick spray. Add all ingredients, except teriyaki sauce, to skillet.
2. Cook vegetables for 15 minutes on medium high or until broccoli is tender. Pour teriyaki on veggies and simmer for 3 minutes.

Quick and Easy Tip
Did you know that shiitake mushrooms traditionally sprout off of logs? They're the most common type of mushroom used in Asian dishes, and they add a deep flavor and chewy texture. If you prefer an even more intense flavor from your mushrooms, buy your shiitake mushrooms dried instead of fresh.

Baked Sweet Potato Fries

Serves 6

- ~ **PREP TIME:** 5 minutes
- ~ **COOK TIME:** 30 minutes
- ~ **TOTAL COST:** $4.50
- ~ **CALORIES:** 136
- ~ **FAT:** 3 g
- ~ **PROTEIN:** 2 g
- ~ **CHOLESTEROL:** 0 mg
- ~ **SODIUM:** 14 mg

2 pounds peeled sweet potatoes
2 teaspoons ground cinnamon
1 tablespoon olive oil

This recipe offers a nutritional step up from regular baked fries because the sweet potatoes are packed full of beta carotene. And they are a tasty alternative.

1. Preheat oven to 450°F. Cut potatoes into matchsticks, about ½-inch thick. Toss potatoes, cinnamon, and olive oil in a bowl.
2. Coat a large cookie sheet with nonstick spray. Bake for 25 to 30 minutes or until potatoes are fairly crispy.

Quick and Easy Tip
These make a great snack food for kids!

Sautéed Squash with Mushrooms and Goat Cheese

 Serves 4

- ~ **PREP TIME:** 5 minutes
- ~ **COOK TIME:** 12 minutes
- ~ **TOTAL COST:** $6.95
- ~ **CALORIES:** 122
- ~ **FAT:** 3 g
- ~ **CARBOHYDRATES:** 14 g
- ~ **PROTEIN:** 11 g
- ~ **CHOLESTEROL:** 5 mg
- ~ **SODIUM:** 201 mg

2 tablespoons olive oil
1 yellow onion, chopped
3 yellow squash, sliced
1 zucchini squash, sliced
2 cups cremini or button mushrooms, cleaned and sliced
1 red bell pepper, seeded and chopped
Salt and lemon pepper to taste
4 ounces goat cheese

Use a medley of mushrooms such as baby portobellos, shitake, and morel, if your budget allows.

In large sauté pan over medium heat, add olive oil. Heat oil until fragrant, then add onion and sauté for 3 minutes. Add both squash, mushrooms, and peppers. Season with salt and pepper. Cover and reduce heat to medium low. Simmer for about 5 to 6 minutes. Uncover, stir, and stir in goat cheese. Cook until heated through. If too much liquid, cook uncovered about 1 to 2 minutes longer, or leave liquid and serve over brown or white rice.

> **Goat Cheese**
> Goat cheese is a delicious cheese made from goat's milk. The tart flavor comes from its unique chain of fatty acids.

Baked Stuffed Artichokes

 Serves 4

- ~ **PREP TIME:** 12 minutes
- ~ **COOK TIME:** 35 minutes
- ~ **TOTAL COST:** $6.32
- ~ **CALORIES:** 153
- ~ **FAT:** 9 g
- ~ **CARBOHYDRATES:** 12 g
- ~ **PROTEIN:** 3 g
- ~ **CHOLESTEROL:** 1 mg
- ~ **SODIUM:** 156 mg

4 large artichokes, trimmed and split lengthwise
½ fresh lemon
4 quarts water
¾ cup Parmesan cheese, grated
10 pitted black olives, chopped
1 red bell pepper, seeded and chopped
1 clove garlic, finely chopped
1 teaspoon fresh thyme, leaves chopped
1 yellow squash, finely chopped
Sea salt and lemon pepper to taste
1 tablespoon olive oil

If artichokes aren't your thing or you are pressed for time, use this mixture to stuff red bell peppers or large tomatoes. If you do, it is not necessary to boil the peppers or tomatoes.

1. Boil the artichokes in 4 quarts of water, squeezing in lemon juice, then placing in lemon half. Boil for 20 to 25 minutes. Drain and place on a parchment-lined baking sheet, cut side up.
2. Preheat oven to 350°F. Scoop out choke, using any heart pieces in vegetable mixture. In a large mixing bowl, combine remaining ingredients, tossing with the olive oil. Divide filling into artichokes, pressing between the leaves where needed. Bake for 15 minutes or until hot.

Artichoke Tip
Artichokes can be a little tricky to work with because they have prickly little tips like roses. Wear gloves to tear off the outer leaves and trim the stem. Either steam, boil, or bake them to make them tender. Enjoy them alone with some melted butter or dipping sauce.

Two-Cheese Twice-Baked Potatoes with Spinach

 Serves 4

~ **PREP TIME:** 12 minutes

~ **COOK TIME:** 1 hour 5 minutes

~ **TOTAL COST:** $5.45

~ **CALORIES:** 249

~ **FAT:** 3 g

~ **CARBOHYDRATES:** 53 g

~ **PROTEIN:** 5 g

~ **CHOLESTEROL:** 2 mg

~ **SODIUM:** 422 mg

4 baking potatoes, wrapped in foil

1 tablespoon olive oil

½ yellow onion, chopped

1 (10-ounce) package frozen chopped spinach, thawed, excess water
   squeezed out

Pinch nutmeg

1 cup nonfat sour cream

1 cup white American cheese, grated

Sea salt and black pepper to taste

½ cup Parmesan cheese, grated

Cheddar, provolone, and Gruyère cheeses also work well for this
recipe. If you are looking to add a few calories and fat, top with crispy,
crumbled bacon.

1. Preheat the oven to 350°F. Bake the potatoes for 40 minutes. While
   baking, heat oil in large saucepan over medium heat. Add onion
   and sauté until just tender, about 2 minutes. Then add spinach and
   nutmeg, and sauté until heated and moisture has cooked out, about
   4 minutes. Add sour cream and American cheese. Cook until cheese
   is just melting, about 1 minute. Turn off heat.
2. Cool the potatoes and split them in half lengthwise. Spoon out
   the insides of the potatoes, leaving skin intact. Place potato filling
   in saucepan with spinach mixture, season with salt and pepper,
   and combine well. Restuff the potato skins and arrange Parmesan
   cheese on top. Bake for another 20 minutes, and serve hot.

Potato Filling
Twice-baked potatoes require a sturdy potato skin to support the filling.
Be sure to leave about a ¼" to ½" edge of potato when scooping out the
center and make every effort not to break the sides.

Squash Casserole with Saltine Crust

 Serves 6

- ~ **PREP TIME:** 5 minutes
- ~ **COOK TIME:** 45 minutes
- ~ **TOTAL COST:** $6.42
- ~ **CALORIES:** 122
- ~ **FAT:** 3 g
- ~ **PROTEIN:** 11 g
- ~ **CHOLESTEROL:** 72 mg
- ~ **SODIUM:** 156 mg

10 medium yellow squash, sliced
1 yellow onion, chopped
Salt and black pepper to taste
6 ounces shredded Cheddar cheese
2 eggs
10 saltine crackers, crushed

If you love this recipe but are looking for a change, try substituting zucchini for the yellow squash. These vegetables are traditionally interchangeable because of similar flavors and textures.

1. Coat a 9" x 13" baking dish with nonstick spray. Place squash and onion in dish. Sprinkle with salt and pepper and bake at 350°F for 15 minutes.
2. Drain water from veggies and stir in cheese. Beat eggs and mix into veggies. Stir in crackers until thick. Return dish to oven and bake at 325°F for 30 minutes.

Oven-Roasted Sweet Potatoes with Carrots

 Serves 6

- ~ **PREP TIME:** 5 minutes
- ~ **COOK TIME:** 30 minutes
- ~ **TOTAL COST:** $6.51
- ~ **CALORIES:** 189
- ~ **FAT:** 3 g
- ~ **CARBOHYDRATES:** 27 g
- ~ **PROTEIN:** 2 g
- ~ **CHOLESTEROL:** 0 mg
- ~ **SODIUM:** 14 mg

2 pounds peeled sweet potatoes
1 pound carrots, peeled
Sea salt and lemon pepper to taste
2 tablespoons olive oil

Kids love sweet potatoes and carrots, so this recipe is a natural for family dinners. If you have leftovers, save them for your kids' after-school snacks.

1. Preheat oven to 450°F. Cut potatoes and carrots into matchsticks, about ½-inch thick. Toss potatoes, carrots, salt, pepper, and olive oil in a bowl.
2. Line baking sheet with parchment paper. Bake for 25 to 30 minutes or until potatoes and carrots are tender and fairly crispy, turning once if necessary.

Roasting Vegetables
Roasting vegetables is a low-cal, low-fat way to add flavor to vegetables while at the same time maintaining their nutrients. Plus it's simple and easy on cleanup! Keep some in your refrigerator for a quick, healthy and tasty snack.

Sautéed Asian Vegetables with Peanuts

 Serves 4

- ~ **PREP TIME:** 8 minutes
- ~ **COOK TIME:** 18 minutes
- ~ **TOTAL COST:** $5.42
- ~ **CALORIES:** 228
- ~ **FAT:** 4 g
- ~ **CARBOHYDRATES:** 55 g
- ~ **PROTEIN:** 9 g
- ~ **CHOLESTEROL:** 9 mg
- ~ **SODIUM:** 379 mg

1 tablespoon sesame oil
1 green onion, chopped
1 cup broccoli florets, largely chopped
1 cup sugar snap peas
½ cup sliced water chestnuts, drained
½ cup baby corn, drained
1 cup cauliflower, chopped
1 cup cremini or button mushrooms, sliced
½ cup roasted, salted peanuts, finely chopped
2 tablespoons soy sauce

Peanuts are often used in preparing Asian cuisine. However, feel free to substitute walnuts, hazelnuts, pecans, or almonds, depending upon your flavor preference.

Heat oil in large saucepan over medium heat. Add onion and sauté about 1 minute. Add remaining ingredients, then cover and reduce heat. Simmer vegetables until tender, about 15 minutes.

Fresh Fennel with Pecorino Romano Cheese

 Serves 4

- ~ **PREP TIME:** 7 minutes
- ~ **COOK TIME:** none
- ~ **TOTAL COST:** $6.78
- ~ **CALORIES:** 65
- ~ **FAT:** 3 g
- ~ **CARBOHYDRATES:** 6 g
- ~ **PROTEIN:** 3 g
- ~ **CHOLESTEROL:** 1 mg
- ~ **SODIUM:** 345 mg

2 bulbs fresh fennel, cleaned
½ fresh lemon
½ cup Pecorino Romano cheese, shaved
2 tablespoons extra-virgin olive oil

Fennel is actually an herb. Harvested for many culinary uses, the fresh fennel bulb may be eaten raw, as in this recipe, or stewed, sautéed, grilled, or braised. Fennel seeds are used in rye bread and fennel is the primary ingredient used in absinthe.

Trim fennel stems and wispy fronds from fennel tops. Break the bulbs apart, layer by layer, using your hands to make long, bite-size pieces. Discard the core. Arrange the pieces onto a serving platter. Squeeze lemon over fennel. Sprinkle with cheese and drizzle olive oil.

Pecorino Romano Cheese
Pecorino Romano is a hard, salty sheep's milk cheese from the region of Sardinia, Italy, one of the most beautiful places on earth! Because of the cheese's salty nature, it is not necessary to add salt to this fennel recipe.

Potato Latkes with Basil

 Serves 4

- ~ **PREP TIME:** 12 minutes
- ~ **COOK TIME:** 12 minutes
- ~ **TOTAL COST:** $4.56
- ~ **CALORIES:** 274
- ~ **FAT:** 8 g
- ~ **CARBOHYDRATES:** 24 g
- ~ **PROTEIN:** 4 g
- ~ **CHOLESTEROL:** 20 mg
- ~ **SODIUM:** 310 mg

2 large eggs
3 large baking potatoes, peeled and grated
1 yellow onion, grated
Sea salt and lemon pepper to taste
½ tablespoon fresh basil, chopped
2 tablespoons plain flour, plus a little extra if needed
Canola oil for frying

Overworking the potato mixture will result in overly wet "dough" and will require more flour. Try to avoid this, as adding more flour will cause your latkes to taste more like flour than potatoes.

1. Beat eggs in large bowl. After grating potatoes, squeeze out as much excess water from potatoes as possible. Combine potato, onion, salt, pepper, and basil. Mix well. Add in flour and toss together, being careful not to overwork the mixture.
2. In a large saucepan over medium-high heat, pour in oil about ¼-inch deep. Heat oil to hot but not burning. From potato batter, make 8 pancakes. Gently squeeze out any excess water and place pancakes in batches into hot oil. Cook slowly, without moving them for the first 5 minutes. Loosen with spatula and turn after about 8 minutes. When the top appears to be about ⅓ cooked, flip pancake and finish cooking, about 4 more minutes. Drain on paper towels and serve.

> **Potato Latkes**
> Potato latkes, or pancakes, are usually served for Jewish holidays and are traditionally served with sour cream and applesauce. Another way to serve them is with sour cream and caviar.

Oven-Broiled Portobello Mushrooms with Fresh Herbs and Provolone

 Serves 4

- ~ **PREP TIME:** 15 minutes
- ~ **COOK TIME:** 8 minutes
- ~ **TOTAL COST:** $6.20
- ~ **CALORIES:** 120
- ~ **FAT:** 1 g
- ~ **CARBOHYDRATES:** 4 g
- ~ **PROTEIN:** 7 g
- ~ **CHOLESTEROL:** 26 mg
- ~ **SODIUM:** 123 mg

4 large portabello mushrooms, stems removed
½ cup extra-virgin olive oil, plus more if needed
Sea salt and black pepper to taste
½ cup variety fresh herbs, chopped, such as parsley, thyme, rosemary, chives
½ cup provolone cheese, sliced

If you are unable to locate portobello mushrooms, buy a variety of mushrooms and broil them together. Because they will most likely be smaller in size than the portobellos, your cooking time may be shortened.

1. Preheat broiler. Brush any dirt from the mushrooms, but do not wash them. Place mushrooms on parchment-lined baking sheet, stem side down to start. Drizzle with olive oil and season lightly with salt and pepper. Place under broiler for 4 minutes.
2. Remove mushrooms from broiler and place pan on stovetop. Turn mushrooms over, drizzle with additional olive oil, and top with herbs, season lightly with salt and pepper. Top with cheese slices. Return to broiler and broil until cheese melts.

Portobello Mushrooms

Portobello mushrooms are really just super large cremini mushrooms! They are so large and meaty they are like eating a vegetarian burger. Being the Bikini Chef with a focus on figure-flattering flavors, I use them as "bread" for a portobello mushroom sandwich (see Grilled Portobello Mushroom Panini, Chapter 14), layering cheese, mixed greens, and often red bell pepper for a truly low-cal, low-fat meal.

Parsnips and Leeks with Fresh Herbs

 Serves 4

- ~ **PREP TIME:** 12 minutes
- ~ **COOK TIME:** 21 minutes
- ~ **TOTAL COST:** $5.35
- ~ **CALORIES:** 215
- ~ **FAT:** 1 g
- ~ **CARBOHYDRATES:** 46 g
- ~ **PROTEIN:** 5 g
- ~ **CHOLESTEROL:** 0 mg
- ~ **SODIUM:** 50 mg

1½ pounds parsnips, cut into 1-inch pieces
2 tablespoons olive oil
1 red onion, thinly sliced
1 leek, cleaned, trimmed, and chopped
2 Bosc pears, unpeeled, cored, and thinly sliced
1 teaspoon fresh thyme, leaves chopped
Sea salt and lemon pepper to taste

Italian parsley, fresh rosemary, or flavored fresh thyme such as lemon thyme are also great herbs for this recipe.

1. Partially boil the parsnips, about 5 minutes. Drain and set aside.
2. Heat oil in large saucepan over medium heat. Add onion and leeks. Sauté for 4 minutes. Add pears, thyme, and parsnips. Season with salt and pepper. Cover and cook about 10 minutes, stirring regularly. Uncover and cook an additional 2 minutes or until parsnips are tender.

Parsnips

Parsnips are root vegetables related to carrots. They typically grow in cold climates, not warm, as frost enhances their flavor.

Tomatoes, Basil, and Camembert with Linguine

 Serves 4

- ~ **PREP TIME:** 5 minutes
- ~ **COOK TIME:** 15 minutes
- ~ **TOTAL COST:** $6.49
- ~ **CALORIES:** 241
- ~ **FAT:** 8 g
- ~ **CARBOHYDRATES:** 28 g
- ~ **PROTEIN:** 5 g
- ~ **CHOLESTEROL:** 12 mg
- ~ **SODIUM:** 180 mg

1 (12-ounce) box linguine pasta
¼ cup olive oil
5 large tomatoes, seeded and diced
Sea salt and black pepper to taste
¼ fresh basil, chopped
1 cup Camembert cheese, chopped, room temperature

Camembert is a softer cheese that is made from cow's milk and is traditionally from the Normandy region of France. It has a mild but distinctive flavor and creamy texture. It is one of my favorite cheeses to cook with as it pairs nicely with many types of foods.

1. Bring large-quart boiler filled ¾ with water to a boil, add in pinch of salt and a drizzle of olive oil. Cook linguine pasta until al dente. Drain and set aside.
2. In large saucepan over medium heat, heat oil. Add tomatoes and simmer 1 minute; season with salt and pepper. Return pasta to large-quart boiler. Add tomato mixture, basil, and cheese. Toss well and serve.

Barley Casserole with Root Vegetables

 Serves 6

~ **PREP TIME:** 10 minutes
~ **COOK TIME:** 1 hour
~ **TOTAL COST:** $6.76
~ **CALORIES:** 218
~ **FAT:** 3 g
~ **CARBOHYDRATES:** 46 g
~ **PROTEIN:** 14 g
~ **CHOLESTEROL:** 10 mg
~ **SODIUM:** 401 mg

1 large yellow onion, chopped
1 leek, cleaned, rinsed and chopped
1 carrot, peeled and chopped
1 beet, peeled and chopped
1 parsnip, peeled and chopped
2 tablespoons fresh cilantro, chopped
1 tablespoon olive oil
1 cup barley
½ teaspoon ground cumin
4 cups vegetable stock
Sea salt and black pepper to taste

Root vegetables, such as beets and parsnips, are typically a winter food but enjoy them anytime. In this recipe, they are baked but root vegetables are terrific in soups and stews.

Preheat oven to 350°F. Combine all the ingredients in a large casserole dish greased with oil. Cover tightly and bake for 60 minutes.

Healthy Stuffed Potato

 Serves 2

~ **COST:** $0.41
~ **CALORIES:** 130
~ **FAT:** 0.5 g
~ **CARBOHYDRATES:** 29 g
~ **PROTEIN:** 6 g
~ **CHOLESTEROL:** 0 mg
~ **SODIUM:** 70 mg

2 potatoes
4 tablespoons plain yogurt, divided
¼ teaspoon cayenne pepper
1 teaspoon tomato sauce
1 canned artichoke heart, finely chopped
Salt and pepper, to taste
1 tablespoon soy cheese, optional

1. Preheat oven to 400°F.
2. Wash the potatoes and scrub to remove any dirt. Poke a few holes in each potato. Place directly on the middle oven rack.
3. Bake the potatoes for 45 minutes, or until done. To test for doneness, pierce the potatoes with a fork. It should go through easily. Remove from the oven. Cut each potato in half lengthwise while still hot.
4. Remove the pulp from the potatoes and set aside the skins. Place the pulp in a bowl and add 2 tablespoons of the yogurt, cayenne pepper, tomato sauce, artichoke, and salt and pepper. Use a fork to whip the potatoes until fluffy. Add as much of the remaining 2 tablespoons yogurt as needed while whipping to reach desired consistency.
5. Scoop the potato mixture into the reserved potato skins. Sprinkle with the soy cheese, if desired. Bake for about 15 minutes or until the cheese melts. Serve hot.

CHAPTER 12

PASTA AND PIZZA

Pepperoni Pizza

 Serves 6

- ~ **TOTAL COST:** $5.76
- ~ **CALORIES:** 476.12
- ~ **FAT:** 20.90 g
- ~ **PROTEIN:** 17.99 g
- ~ **CHOLESTEROL:** 36.48 mg
- ~ **SODIUM:** 949.24 mg

1 onion, chopped
2 cloves garlic, minced
1 tablespoon olive oil
1 (6-ounce) can tomato paste
¾ cup Chicken Broth (Chapter 6)
1 teaspoon Italian seasoning
2 tablespoons mustard
1 (12-inch) pizza crust, prebaked
1 (3-ounce) package pepperoni slices
1 cup shredded part-skim mozzarella cheese
½ cup shredded Cheddar cheese

A take-out pepperoni pizza, which will not feed six people this well, costs at least $8.00. And who knows what's in it? Control your budget and your family's health.

1. In heavy skillet sauté onion and garlic in olive oil until crisp-tender. Add tomato sauce, tomato paste, chicken broth, and Italian seasoning. Simmer for 8–10 minutes to blend flavors. Stir in mustard.
2. Spread cooled sauce over pizza crust and top with pepperoni slices. Sprinkle cheeses over pepperoni.
3. Preheat oven to 400°F. Bake pizza for 15–20 minutes, until crust is crisp, pizza is hot, and cheese is melted and beginning to brown.

Designer Pizzas
You can use just about any meat to top your own pizza. Just make the sauce for the Pepperoni Pizza or the Sausage Pizza, then use leftover cooked hamburgers, crumbled, Polish sausage that you grilled the night before, or cooked ground sausage. And add vegetables too; sliced mushrooms and bell peppers cooked in some butter add great flavor and nutrition.

Sausage Pizza

Serves 6

- ~ **TOTAL COST:** $6.91
- ~ **CALORIES:** 475.25
- ~ **FAT:** 24.91 g
- ~ **PROTEIN:** 17.86 g
- ~ **CHOLESTEROL:** 39.63 mg
- ~ **SODIUM:** 849.87 mg

8 ounces pork sausage

1 onion, chopped

1 cup sliced mushrooms

1 green bell pepper, chopped

1 (8-ounce) can tomato sauce

3 tablespoons tomato paste

¼ cup water

1 teaspoon dried Italian seasoning

1 Quick Pizza Crust (page XX), prebaked

1½ cups shredded part-skim mozzarella cheese

3 tablespoons grated Parmesan cheese

This rich pizza is very nutritious and filling. Serve it with a green salad and some fresh corn on the cob.

1. Preheat oven to 400°F. Crumble pork sausage into saucepan and place over medium heat. Cook until sausage is browned, stirring frequently. Remove pork from saucepan and drain excess fat, but do not wipe saucepan.
2. Add onion, mushrooms, and bell pepper to saucepan; cook, stirring to loosen drippings, for 3–4 minutes or until crisp-tender. Add tomato sauce, tomato paste, water, dried Italian seasoning, and pork sausage; cook and stir for 2 minutes.
3. Place pizza crust on cookie sheet and top with pork mixture. Sprinkle with cheeses. Bake for 20–25 minutes or until pizza is hot and cheese is melted and beginning to brown. Let stand for 5 minutes, then serve.

Meatball Pizza

Serves 2

- ~ **PREP TIME:** 5 minutes
- ~ **COOK TIME:** 15 minutes
- ~ **TOTAL COST:** $6.89
- ~ **CALORIES:** 678
- ~ **FAT:** 33 g
- ~ **PROTEIN:** 21 g
- ~ **CHOLESTEROL:** 41 mg
- ~ **SODIUM:** 1670 mg

2 (6-inch) prepared pizza crust, such as Boboli

1 cup pizza sauce

½ teaspoon dried oregano leaves

½ teaspoon dry mustard

4 ounces frozen meatballs, thawed and cut in half

½ cup frozen vegetables of onion and bell pepper stir-fry combo

1 cup shredded mozzarella

Boboli pizza crusts are delicious, convenient, and inexpensive. They're also great for kids' pizza parties!

Preheat oven to 400°F. Place pizza dough on work surface. In a small bowl, combine pizza sauce with oregano and dry mustard. Mix well. Spread over pizza dough. Cut meatballs in half and arrange, cut side down, on pizza sauce. Sprinkle onion and bell pepper on pizza and top with cheese. Place pizza directly on rack in center of oven. Bake for 15 minutes or until crust is golden brown and cheese has melted and begins to brown.

Quick and Easy Tip

Buying precooked frozen meatballs is the way to go for any meatball recipe unless you have lots of helping hands to roll them out. You can always add your own special touch to the sauce!

Three-Cheese Pizza

Serves 2

- ~ **PREP TIME:** 7 minutes
- ~ **COOK TIME:** 15 minutes
- ~ **TOTAL COST:** $6.98
- ~ **CALORIES:** 410
- ~ **FAT:** 18 g
- ~ **PROTEIN:** 6 g
- ~ **CHOLESTEROL:** 94 mg
- ~ **SODIUM:** 824 mg

1 cup pizza marinara sauce
2 (6-inch) prepared pizza crust such as Boboli
1 cup shredded provolone cheese
1 cup shredded mozzarella cheese
1 cup pepper jack cheese
6 cloves fresh garlic, minced
1 tablespoon olive oil

The Italians in Napoli (Naples) claim to be the originators of pizza. I don't know if they were the first ones to create pizza, but theirs sure taste delicious.

Preheat oven to 425°F. Ladle the sauce over the dough, spreading it out evenly over the surface. Top with the cheeses, and sprinkle with garlic. Drizzle with olive oil. Place directly in oven on center rack. Bake for 15 minutes, until cheese is melted and dough is cooked through.

Quick and Easy Tip

If you prefer to use fresh pizza dough, lots of stores now have premade, fresh, unbaked pizza dough, and it is not very expensive.

Pepperoni Pizza on English Muffin

Serve 6 to 8

- ~ **PREP TIME:** 5 minutes
- ~ **COOK TIME:** 5 minutes
- ~ **TOTAL COST:** $6.36
- ~ **CALORIES:** 278
- ~ **FAT:** 11 g
- ~ **CARBOHYDRATES:** 33 g
- ~ **PROTEIN:** 13 g
- ~ **CHOLESTEROL:** 21 mg
- ~ **SODIUM:** 475 mg

8 English muffins, split and toasted
1½ cups pizza sauce
1 (6-ounce) jar sliced mushrooms, drained
1 cup pepperoni, sliced
2 cups shredded mozzarella cheese

The perfect snack size, English muffins are a healthy, quick, easy way to enjoy the "feel" of a pizza without having to make or buy a whole pizza. Plus you will tend to eat less of it when there are only two "slices"!

Preheat oven to broil. Place English muffin halves on baking sheet and top each one with pizza sauce. Layer mushrooms and pepperoni over pizza sauce. Sprinkle cheese over pizzas. Broil pizzas, 4 to 6 inches from heat source, for 2 to 4 minutes or until pizzas are hot and cheese is melted, bubbly, and beginning to brown. Serve immediately.

Pizza with Herbs and Black Olives

 Serves 2

- **PREP TIME:** 5 minutes
- **COOK TIME:** 15 minutes
- **TOTAL COST:** $6.89
- **CALORIES:** 320
- **FAT:** 10 g
- **PROTEIN:** 13 g
- **CHOLESTEROL:** 25 mg
- **SODIUM:** 670 mg

2 (6- to 8-inch) prepared pizza crusts such as Boboli
½ cups tomato sauce
1 cup shredded mozzarella cheese
¼ cup grated romano cheese
4 sprigs fresh basil, chopped
4 sprigs fresh oregano, leaves chopped
¼ cup chopped black olives
Black pepper to taste
1 tablespoon olive oil

Boboli pizza crusts come in small and large sizes. Use the small ones for pizza parties so everyone can make their own individual pizzas! It's easy, fun, and easy on cleanup, which is the best part of all.

Preheat oven to 425°F. Place dough on work surface. Ladle sauce over the dough, spreading out evenly over entire surface. Top with cheese, herbs, olives, and pepper. Drizzle with oil and place in center of oven directly on rack. Bake about 15 minutes or until dough is cooked through.

Quick and Easy Tip
If you are planning a pizza party, purchase your ingredients a day or two ahead of time and prep the day before.

Barbecue Chicken Pizza
Serves 2

- **PREP TIME:** 5 minutes
- **COOK TIME:** 15 minutes
- **TOTAL COST:** $6.99
- **CALORIES:** 458
- **FAT:** 11 g
- **PROTEIN:** 24 g
- **CHOLESTEROL:** 85 mg
- **SODIUM:** 600 mg

2 (6- to 8-inch) Boboli pizza crusts
1 tablespoon olive oil
1 cup cooked boneless, skinless chicken breasts, chopped into 1-inch chunks
1 cup barbeque sauce
1 cup mozzarella cheese

Preheat oven to 425°F. Place pizza dough on work surface. Brush dough with olive oil. In a mixing bowl, toss chicken with barbecue sauce to coat. Spread chicken on pizza dough and top with cheese. Bake directly on rack in center of oven for 15 minutes or until crust is crispy and golden.

Hawaiian-Style Pizza with Pineapple

 Serves 2

~ **PREP TIME:** 5 minutes
~ **COOK TIME:** 15 minutes
~ **TOTAL COST:** $6.97
~ **CALORIES:** 375
~ **FAT:** 19 g
~ **PROTEIN:** 32 g
~ **CHOLESTEROL:** 126 mg
~ **SODIUM:** 563 mg

2 (6- to 8-inch) Boboli pizza crusts
1 tablespoon olive oil
1½ cups thick deli ham, chopped
1½ cups canned, chopped pineapple, drained
1½ cups mozzarella cheese

This is a great recipe to add basil or thyme. Be sure to use fresh herbs for this recipe, however, as the dried herbs would taste a little bitter.

Preheat oven to 425°F. Place pizza crust on work surface. Brush with olive oil. Top with ham, pineapple, and cheese. Bake directly on rack in oven for about 15 minutes or until crust is golden and crispy.

Pizza with Roasted Red Peppers

Serves 2

~ **PREP TIME:** 5 minutes
~ **COOK TIME:** 15 minutes
~ **TOTAL COST:** $1
~ **CALORIES:** 310
~ **FAT:** 10 g
~ **PROTEIN:** 8 g
~ **CHOLESTEROL:** 59 mg
~ **SODIUM:** 641 mg

2 (6- to 8-inch) Boboli pizza crusts
2 tablespoons olive oil
1 jar roasted red bell peppers, drained and chopped
1 bunch fresh basil, chopped
Sea salt and black pepper to taste
1½ cups shredded mozzarella

Add chopped or sliced fresh or canned mushrooms to this pizza for extra flavor and color. If you use canned mushrooms, make sure they are well drained.

Preheat oven to 425°F. Place pizza crust on work surface. Brush with 1 tablespoon olive oil. In a mixing bowl, toss peppers with basil and season with salt and pepper as desired. Spread onto pizza. Top with cheese and drizzle with remaining olive oil. Place in oven directly on center rack. Bake for 15 minutes or until pizza is crisp and golden.

Spinach Mushroom Pizza

Serves 2

- ~ **PREP TIME:** 5 minutes
- ~ **COOK TIME:** 15 minutes
- ~ **TOTAL COST:** $6.98
- ~ **CALORIES:** 321
- ~ **FAT:** 9 g
- ~ **PROTEIN:** 6 g
- ~ **CHOLESTEROL:** 72 mg
- ~ **SODIUM:** 689 mg

2 (6- to 8-inch) Boboli pizza crusts
2 tablespoons olive oil
1 cup frozen spinach, thawed and well drained
1 cup canned sliced mushrooms, well drained
1 cup shredded mozzarella

Add black olives, tomatoes, feta cheese, or even goat cheese for extra delicious flavor without a lot of work!

Preheat oven to 425°F. Place pizza crust on work surface. Brush with 1 tablespoon olive oil. Top pizza with spinach, mushrooms, and cheese. Drizzle with remaining olive oil. Place directly on rack in center of oven. Bake for 15 minutes or until done.

Pizza Margherita

Serves 2

- ~ **PREP TIME:** 5 minutes
- ~ **COOK TIME:** 15 minutes
- ~ **TOTAL COST:** $6.69
- ~ **CALORIES:** 306
- ~ **FAT:** 18 g
- ~ **PROTEIN:** 6 g
- ~ **CHOLESTEROL:** 64 mg
- ~ **SODIUM:** 499 mg

2 (6- to 8-inch) Boboli pizza crusts
1 tablespoon olive oil
½ cup shredded mozzarella
1 bunch basil, chopped
3 Roma tomatoes, sliced
Sea salt and black pepper to taste

Feel free to add cooked sausage for tons of flavor and protein!

Preheat oven to 425°F. Place pizza crust on work surface. Brush with olive oil. Top with cheese, basil, and tomatoes. Season with salt and pepper as desired. Bake in center rack of oven directly on rack for 15 minutes or until dough is cooked through.

Pita Pizza with Eggplant and Gorgonzola

 Serves 2

- ~ **PREP TIME:** 5 minutes
- ~ **COOK TIME:** 6 to 8 minutes
- ~ **TOTAL COST:** $5.78
- ~ **CALORIES:** 138
- ~ **FAT:** 4 g
- ~ **PROTEIN:** 8 g
- ~ **CHOLESTEROL:** 28 mg
- ~ **SODIUM:** 429mg

1 large whole wheat pita
2 tablespoons marinara sauce
¼ cup eggplant, peeled and diced
1 tablespoon sun-dried tomatoes, chopped
2 tablespoons shredded mozzarella cheese
1 tablespoon Gorgonzola cheese

The combination of eggplant and tomatoes is a lycopene dream. Lycopene is great for both your heart and your vision.

Preheat oven to 350°F. Top pita with marinara, eggplant, tomatoes, mozzarella, and Gorgonzola. Place on parchment-lined baking sheet and bake for 6 to 8 minutes or until cheese has melted.

Quick and Easy Tip
Pita bread is also good sliced into triangles and baked until crispy. Mix all these ingredients together, except for pita, and serve as an eggplant salsa with pita crisps.

Pita Pizza with Spinach and Feta

Serves 2

- ~ **PREP TIME:** 5 minutes
- ~ **COOK TIME:** 6 to 8 minutes
- ~ **TOTAL COST:** $4.24
- ~ **CALORIES:** 118
- ~ **FAT:** 2 g
- ~ **PROTEIN:** 8 g
- ~ **CHOLESTEROL:** 26 mg
- ~ **SODIUM:** 313 mg

1 large whole wheat or plain pita
3 tablespoons shredded mozzarella cheese
1 tablespoon feta cheese
½ cup fresh spinach, chopped
2 tablespoons Roma tomatoes, chopped
½ teaspoon fresh garlic, minced

Just like it did for Popeye, spinach will make you strong. It's full of iron, vitamin A, and fiber, which is helpful in blood cell production and brain cell development.

Preheat oven to 350°F. Top pita with mozzarella, feta, spinach, tomatoes, and garlic. Place on parchment-lined baking sheet and cook for 6 to 8 minutes or until cheese has melted.

Quick and Easy
The often-used feta and spinach combination is popular in Greek cuisine. Add mushrooms, peppers, and your favorite cheese as an alternative to this tasty, healthy dish.

Ricotta Cheese Pita Pizza

Serves 2

~ **PREP TIME:** 5 minutes
~ **COOK TIME:** 6 to 8 minutes
~ **TOTAL COST:** $4.16
~ **CALORIES:** 110
~ **FAT:** 1 g
~ **PROTEIN:** 8 g
~ **CHOLESTEROL:** 35 mg
~ **SODIUM:** 257 mg

1 large whole wheat or plain pita
2 tablespoons shredded mozzarella cheese
2 tablespoons ricotta cheese
2 tablespoons Roma tomatoes, sliced
½ teaspoon fresh garlic, minced

Ricotta cheese is an Italian sheep milk or cow milk cheese and is generally lower in fat than other cheeses. Ricotta means "recooked" as it is produced from the whey (the liquid that separates from the cheese) of cheese when in production.

Preheat oven to 350°F. Top pita with mozzarella, ricotta, tomatoes, and garlic. Place pita on parchment-lined baking sheet. Place in oven and bake for 6 to 8 minutes or until cheese has melted.

> **Quick and Easy**
> Add fresh basil to this for a truly Italian meal.

Pita Pizza with Thanksgiving Turkey and Sweet Potatoes

Serves 2

~ **PREP TIME:** 5 minutes
~ **COOK TIME:** 5 to 6 minutes
~ **TOTAL COST:** $2.10
~ **CALORIES:** 205
~ **FAT:** 3 g
~ **PROTEIN:** 12 g
~ **CHOLESTEROL:** 24 mg
~ **SODIUM:** 223 mg

1 whole wheat or plain pita
¼ cup leftover sweet potatoes or leftover sweet potato casserole
2 ounces leftover oven-roasted turkey breast, cut in small chunks
1 tablespoon leftover turkey gravy
Sea salt and black pepper as needed

Tired of turkey sandwiches? This is a delicious alternative to holiday leftovers.

Preheat oven to 350°F. Top pita with sweet potatoes, turkey, and top with gravy. Season with salt and pepper, if desired. Transfer to a parchment-lined baking sheet and bake until heated through, about 5 minutes.

> **Quick and Easy Tip**
> This proves that pizzas can be made with just about everything. Create your own at home using whatever leftovers are in your refrigerator!

Pita Pizza with Buffalo Chicken Wings

 Serves 2

~ **PREP TIME:** 5 minutes
~ **COOK TIME:** 6 to 8 minutes
~ **TOTAL COST:** $3.02
~ **CALORIES:** 170
~ **FAT:** 2 g
~ **PROTEIN:** 17 g
~ **CHOLESTEROL:** 59 mg
~ **SODIUM:** 471 mg

1 large whole wheat pita
2 tablespoons Crystal Wing Sauce
1 cup cooked, boneless chicken wings (available in the freezer section)
1 ounce shredded mozzarella cheese

The combination of crispy chicken, wing sauce, and cheese makes for a wildly flavorful and textured pizza. Make it for football parties!

Preheat oven to 350°F. Top pita with sauce, chicken, and mozzarella in that order. Place on parchment-lined baking sheet and place in oven. Bake for 6 to 8 minutes or until cheese has melted.

> **Quick and Easy Tip**
> Substitute your favorite wing sauce, if you like. And in true Buffalo wing fashion, serve with celery and blue cheese dressing.

Barbecue Chicken Pizza on Pita

 Serves 2

~ **PREP TIME:** 3 minutes
~ **COOK TIME:** 6 to 8 minutes
~ **TOTAL COST:** $4.00
~ **CALORIES:** 187
~ **FAT:** 11 g
~ **PROTEIN:** 14 g
~ **CHOLESTEROL:** 75 mg
~ **SODIUM:** 301 mg

1 cup cooked chicken breast, boneless, skinless, chopped
2 tablespoons sweet barbecue sauce
1 large whole-wheat pita
¼ cup shredded mozzarella cheese
Sea salt and pepper to taste

Making pizzas using pita bread is a great way to cut down on costs, calories, and fat without sacrificing flavor.

Preheat oven to 350°F. In a bowl, mix together chicken and barbecue sauce. Top pita with chicken mixture, mozzarella, salt, and pepper. Place on parchment-lined baking sheet and cook in oven for 6 to 8 minutes or until cheese has melted.

> **Quick and Easy Tip**
> Use whole-wheat or regular pita, depending upon your taste.

Pita Pizza with Ricotta Cheese and Chopped Tomatoes

 Serves 2

- ~ **PREP TIME:** 5 minutes
- ~ **COOK TIME:** 6 to 8 minutes
- ~ **TOTAL COST:** $3.58
- ~ **CALORIES:** 110
- ~ **FAT:** 1 g
- ~ **CARBOHYDRATES:** 19 g
- ~ **PROTEIN:** 8 g
- ~ **CHOLESTEROL:** 35 mg
- ~ **SODIUM:** 257 mg

1 large whole wheat or plain pita
2 tablespoons shredded mozzarella cheese
2 tablespoons ricotta cheese
1 Roma tomato, chopped
½ teaspoon fresh garlic, minced

Customize your pita pizza with red onion, fresh basil leaves, or maybe fresh asparagus tips.

Preheat oven to 350°F. Top pita with mozzarella, ricotta, tomatoes, and garlic. Place pita on parchment-lined baking sheet. Place in oven and bake for 6 to 8 minutes or until cheese has melted.

Boboli Pizza with Smoked Salmon

Serves 2

- ~ **PREP TIME:** 10 minutes
- ~ **COOK TIME:** 20 minutes
- ~ **TOTAL COST:** $7.00
- ~ **CALORIES:** 256
- ~ **FAT:** 8 g
- ~ **CARBOHYDRATES:** 33 g
- ~ **PROTEIN:** 13 g
- ~ **CHOLESTEROL:** 12 mg
- ~ **SODIUM:** 783 mg

1 (8-inch) Boboli pizza crust
4 ounces garlic and herb soft cream cheese
4 ounces smoked salmon
½ red bell pepper, sliced
½ cup provolone cheese, shredded or chopped

Not traditionally thought of for pizza, this smoked salmon flavor makes this pizza one not to miss! Add some capers and freshly chopped red onion for an added treat.

1. Heat oven to 400°F. Place pizza crust on parchment-lined baking sheet. Spread with cream cheese and arrange smoked salmon and bell pepper slices on top. Sprinkle evenly with provolone cheese.
2. Bake for 18 to 22 minutes or until crust is hot and crisp and cheese is melted. Serve immediately.

Mexican Pizza with Chicken

Serves 8

- ~ **PREP TIME:** 7 minutes
- ~ **COOK TIME:** 20 minutes
- ~ **TOTAL COST:** $6.81
- ~ **CALORIES:** 480
- ~ **FAT:** 13 g
- ~ **CARBOHYDRATES:** 50 g
- ~ **PROTEIN:** 43 g
- ~ **CHOLESTEROL:** 27 mg
- ~ **SODIUM:** 581 mg

8 flour tortillas
1 (16-ounce) can refried beans
½ cup taco sauce
½ teaspoon dried oregano
1 tablespoon chili powder
2 cups cooked chicken breast, diced
2 cups shredded Pepper Jack cheese

Fresh avocado slices are a naturally delicious addition to this already tasty meal. And remember, avocados are filled with the good fat our bodies need and have no cholesterol!

1. Preheat oven to 400°F. Place tortillas on two parchment-lined baking sheets. Bake for 5 to 8 minutes until tortillas are crisp, switching the baking sheets halfway through cooking and turning tortillas once.
2. In small bowl combine beans, taco sauce, oregano, and chili powder and mix well. Spread evenly over baked tortillas. Top with chicken and cheese. Bake for 12 to 18 minutes or until pizzas are hot and cheese is melted and beginning to brown.

Turkey Pizza

Serves 6

- ~ **TOTAL COST:** $6.20
- ~ **CALORIES:** 398.70
- ~ **FAT:** 18.08 g
- ~ **PROTEIN:** 14.50 g
- ~ **CHOLESTEROL:** 27.19 mg
- ~ **SODIUM:** 735.62 mg

1 (6- to 8-inch) Boboli pizza crust
1 (8-ounce) can tomato sauce
½ teaspoon dried basil leaves
½ teaspoon dried thyme leaves
1 (8-ounce) can pineapple tidbits, drained
1 cup cubed cooked turkey
1 cup shredded Swiss cheese
3 tablespoons grated Parmesan cheese

This easy pizza is a variation of the classic ham and pineapple pizza. Make it when you have leftover Thanksgiving turkey.

1. Preheat oven to 400°F. Place pizza crust on cookie sheet or pizza stone. In small bowl, combine tomato sauce, basil, and thyme leaves; spread over crust. Top with pineapple, turkey, Swiss, and Parmesan cheeses.
2. Bake pizza for 15–20 minutes or until the crust is browned and cheese is melted and beginning to brown. Let stand for 5 minutes, then cut into wedges to serve.

Homemade Pizza Sauce
You can easily make your own classic pizza sauce with just a can of tomato sauce and seasonings. This costs about 70 cents a cup, while premade pizza sauce costs $1.02 a cup. Adding a spoonful of mustard will perk up the homemade mixture even more, for another 5 cents.

Chicken Calzones

 Serves 8

~ **TOTAL COST:** $6.31
~ **CALORIES:** 433.34
~ **FAT:** 22.04 g
~ **PROTEIN:** 17.28 g
~ **CHOLESTEROL:** 50.37 mg
~ **SODIUM:** 560.36 mg

2 Angel Pie Crusts (Chapter 15), unbaked
2 Slow Cooker Simmered Chicken Breasts (Chapter 7), cubed
1 cup shredded Swiss cheese
1 cup frozen peas, thawed
¼ cup sliced green onion
½ cup sour cream
1 tablespoon milk
2 tablespoons grated Parmesan cheese

Calzones are like stuffed pizzas. You can fill them with anything you'd like. This is a great way to use up leftovers.

1. Preheat oven to 400°F. Divide the pie dough into eight pieces and roll out between waxed paper to 6-inch rounds. Meanwhile, in medium bowl combine remaining ingredients except Parmesan cheese; mix well.
2. Place the dough circles on cookie sheets and place filling on half of each round, leaving a ½-inch border. Fold unfilled half over filled half and press edges with a fork to seal. Cut slits or decorative shapes in the top of each calzone.
3. Brush calzones with milk and sprinkle with Parmesan cheese. Bake for 17–23 minutes or until crust is golden brown and filling is hot. Let cool on wire racks for 5 minutes, then serve.

Spaghetti with Creamy Tomato Sauce

Serves 6–8

~ **TOTAL COST:** $4.95
~ **CALORIES:** 462.12
~ **FAT:** 10.19 g
~ **PROTEIN:** 15.46 g
~ **CHOLESTEROL:** 19.07 mg
~ **SODIUM:** 892.32 mg

1 recipe Spaghetti Sauce (Chapter 12)
½ cup light cream
1 (16-ounce) package spaghetti pasta
½ cup grated Parmesan cheese

You can serve this simple and flavorful recipe to family or friends. Serve it with some Whole Wheat French Bread (Chapter 3), sliced, buttered, and toasted.

1. Bring a large pot of water to a boil. Prepare or reheat Spaghetti Sauce as directed. During last 5 minutes of cooking time, stir in the light cream and stir to blend.
2. Cook the pasta in the boiling water until al dente according to package directions. Drain and add to Spaghetti Sauce; cook and stir for 1 minute to let the pasta absorb some of the sauce. Sprinkle with Parmesan and serve immediately.

Tomatoes

Tomatoes are an excellent heart-healthy food, high in vitamins C and A, and with little or no fat or cholesterol. You can find them in canned tomato sauce, tomato paste, diced tomatoes, stewed tomatoes, and pureed tomatoes. Any will work in a pasta sauce; just look for those on sale. Be sure to write the purchase date right on the cans; use within one year.

Pita Pizza with Grilled Vegetables

 Serves 6

- **PREP TIME:** 8 minutes
- **COOK TIME:** 6 to 8 minutes
- **TOTAL COST:** $6.78
- **CALORIES:** 117
- **FAT:** 1 g
- **PROTEIN:** 8 g
- **CHOLESTEROL:** 15 mg
- **SODIUM:** 347 mg

1 tablespoon olive oil
1 yellow onion, diced
1 red bell pepper, seeded and diced
½ cup broccoli florets, chopped
2 tomatoes, seeded and diced
Sea salt and black pepper as needed
6 large whole wheat pita
6 tablespoons marinara sauce
½ cup shredded mozzarella cheese
1 tablespoon fresh basil, chopped

Grilled vegetables are great on anything. If you don't have any leftover grilled vegetables on hand, buy fresh or use some frozen vegetables from your freezer.

1. In a large sauté pan over medium heat, add olive oil and heat until warmed, about 15 seconds. Add onion, bell pepper, broccoli, and tomatoes, and season with salt and pepper as desired. Cook until tender, about 5 minutes.
2. Place pita on parchment-lined baking sheet. Top pita with marinara, mozzarella, basil, and vegetables. Place in oven and bake for 6 to 8 minutes or until cheese has melted.

> **Quick and Easy Tip**
> This is the perfect recipe for any leftover grilled vegetables from a summer cookout or another recipe you made earlier in the week.

Hash Brown Pizza

 Serves 6

- ~ **TOTAL COST:** $6.62
- ~ **CALORIES:** 354.09
- ~ **FAT:** 15.55 g
- ~ **PROTEIN:** 15.71 g
- ~ **CHOLESTEROL:** 37.97 mg
- ~ **SODIUM:** 1032.57 mg

1 tablespoon olive oil
1 tablespoon butter, melted
3 potatoes, shredded
1 onion, finely chopped and divided
½ teaspoon salt
⅛ teaspoon pepper
1 (8-ounce) can tomato sauce
2 tablespoons tomato paste
1 tablespoon mustard
1 teaspoon dried Italian seasoning
1 cup shredded Cheddar cheese
1 cup shredded part-skim mozzarella cheese
¼ cup grated Parmesan cheese

Shred potatoes directly into a bowl of ice water to keep them from turning brown, then drain well before tossing with the onion. For a splurge, add pepperoni!

1. Preheat broiler. Brush a 12-inch ovenproof skillet with olive oil and melted butter. In large bowl, toss potatoes with half of onion, salt, and pepper. Heat skillet over medium-high heat until very hot. Carefully add potatoes; arrange in an even layer and press down with a spatula.
2. Cook for 5 minutes, occasionally shaking the pan so the potatoes don't stick, until potatoes are golden brown on the bottom. Transfer to the broiler; broil for 3–6 minutes or until top is golden brown. Set aside. Turn oven to bake at 425°F.
3. In small bowl, combine tomato sauce, tomato paste, mustard, and Italian seasoning; mix well. Spread over potatoes and sprinkle with cheeses. Bake pizza for 15–20 minutes or until hot and cheese is melted and bubbling.

Spicy Thai Peanut Noodles

 Serves 8

~ **TOTAL COST:** $5.99
~ **CALORIES:** 548.42 g
~ **FAT:** 24.02 g
~ **PROTEIN:** 20.38 g
~ **CHOLESTEROL:** 0.0 mg
~ **SODIUM:** 492.59 mg

1 tablespoon olive oil
1 onion, chopped
5 cloves garlic, minced
1 (16-ounce) package spaghetti pasta
⅔ cup Chicken Stock (Chapter 6) or water
⅔ cup peanut butter
½ teaspoon ground ginger
2 tablespoons brown sugar
3 tablespoons soy sauce
⅛ teaspoon cayenne pepper
1 cup chopped peanuts

To make this even spicier, you could add a minced jalapeño pepper, or some crushed red pepper flakes if you have some on hand.

1. Bring a large pot of salted water to a boil. In large saucepan, heat olive oil over medium heat. Add onion and garlic; cook and stir until tender, about 5 minutes.
2. When water comes to a boil, add the spaghetti and cook according to package directions until al dente. Meanwhile, add Stock, peanut butter, ginger, brown sugar, soy sauce, and cayenne pepper to onions. Bring to a simmer and cook, stirring, for 3 minutes.
3. When pasta is done, drain, reserving ½ cup pasta cooking water. Add pasta to saucepan; cook and stir until pasta is coated, about 1–2 minutes. Add reserving cooking water as needed to make a smooth sauce. Sprinkle with peanuts and serve immediately.

Salmon Linguine

Serves 6

- **TOTAL COST:** $6.00
- **CALORIES:** 526.42
- **FAT:** 19.79 g
- **PROTEIN:** 22.55 g
- **CHOLESTEROL:** 49.57 mg
- **SODIUM:** 367.40 mg

3 slices bacon
3 cloves garlic, minced
½ cup light cream
1 (3-ounce) package cream cheese, softened
1 (16-ounce) package linguine
½ cup Spinach Pesto (Chapter 2)
1 (7-ounce) can pink salmon, drained
1½ cups frozen peas, thawed
⅓ cup coarsely chopped walnuts

Bacon and salmon has to be one of the most perfect combination of flavors and textures in the world. Keep these ingredients on hand for a fabulous dinner.

1. Bring a large pot of salted water to a boil. Meanwhile, in large saucepan cook bacon until crisp. Remove bacon, crumble, and set aside. Drain bacon drippings from pan but do not wipe pan. Add garlic; cook and stir until fragrant, about 2 minutes. Add cream and cream cheese; remove from heat.
2. Cook pasta according to package directions until al dente. Drain, reserving ⅓ cup pasta cooking water, and add pasta to saucepan with cream mixture.
3. Return saucepan to medium heat and add Pesto, salmon, and peas. Toss gently with tongs until sauce is blended, adding some reserved pasta water as necessary to make a smooth sauce. Sprinkle with walnuts and serve.

About Seafood

You can substitute most seafood for other types in most recipes. Crab is a good substitute for shrimp, which is a good substitute for clams or mussels. Seafood should always smell sweet or slightly briny, never "fishy." If you buy it fresh, use it within 1–2 days or freeze it immediately in freezer proof bags or wraps.

Seafood Stuffed Shells

 Serves 4

- ~ **TOTAL COST:** $6.45
- ~ **CALORIES:** 404.62
- ~ **FAT:** 22.35 g
- ~ **PROTEIN:** 25.73 g
- ~ **CHOLESTEROL:** 101.05 mg
- ~ **SODIUM:** 665.05 mg

1 tablespoon butter
1 onion, finely chopped
1 green bell pepper, chopped
12 tablespoons cream cheese
½ cup milk
½ teaspoon salt
⅛ teaspoon pepper
½ teaspoon dried thyme leaves
1 (6-ounce) can light tuna, drained
2 ounces frozen small shrimp, thawed and chopped
2 tablespoons grated Parmesan cheese
12 jumbo macaroni shells
½ cup shredded Swiss cheese

Now this is one elegant dish! You will be proud to serve it to guests, even the director of the board. For a splurge, add more shrimp

1. Preheat oven to 400°F. Bring a large pot of salted water to a boil. In medium saucepan, melt butter over medium heat. Add onion and bell pepper; cook and stir until crisp-tender, about 4 minutes.
2. Cut cream cheese into cubes and add to saucepan along with milk, salt, pepper, and thyme. Bring to a simmer and cook, stirring, until sauce blends. Reserve ½ cup sauce. Drain tuna and add to mixture in saucepan along with shrimp and Parmesan cheese.
4. Cook shells in water until almost al dente according to package directions. Drain, rinse shells in cold water and drain again. Stuff shells with seafood mixture.
5. Pour half of the sauce in 2-quart baking dish. Top with the stuffed shells, then pour over remaining sauce and sprinkle shells with Swiss cheese. Bake for 20–25 minutes or until dish is hot and cheese melts and begins to brown.

Spaghetti Sauce

 Yields 5 cups; serving size ½ cup

- ~ **TOTAL COST:** $2.69
- ~ **CALORIES:** 97.45
- ~ **FAT:** 2.56 g
- ~ **PROTEIN:** 2.66 g
- ~ **CHOLESTEROL:** 0.0 mg
- ~ **SODIUM:** 443.32 mg

1 tablespoon olive oil
1 onion, chopped
2 cloves garlic, minced
1 (6-ounce) can tomato paste
1 (14-ounce) can diced tomatoes, undrained
1 tablespoon dried Italian seasoning
½ cup grated carrots
⅛ teaspoon salt
⅛ teaspoon pepper
1 cup water

Grated carrots add nutrition and fiber to this rich sauce, and help reduce the problem of sauce separation.

1. In large saucepan, heat olive oil over medium heat. Add onion and garlic; cook and stir until crisp-tender, about 4 minutes.
2. Add tomato paste; let paste brown a bit without stirring (this adds flavor to the sauce). Then add remaining ingredients and stir gently but thoroughly.
3. Bring sauce to a simmer, then reduce heat to low and partially cover. Simmer for 30–40 minutes, stirring occasionally, until sauce is blended and thickened. Serve over hot cooked pasta or couscous, or use in recipes.

Whole Wheat Pasta with Basil and Tomato Pesto

Serves 2

- ~ **COST:** $2.50
- ~ **CALORIES:** 960
- ~ **FAT:** 79 g
- ~ **CARBOHYDRATES:** 48 g
- ~ **PROTEIN:** 19 g
- ~ **CHOLESTEROL:** 20 mg
- ~ **SODIUM:** 310 mg

1½ cups rigatoni pasta
1 ounce fresh basil leaves
3 garlic cloves
1 large tomato
⅓ cup pine nuts
½ cup grated Parmesan cheese
½ cup olive oil

1. Cook the pasta in boiling salted water until tender but still firm (al dente). Drain.
2. Chop the basil leaves to make 1 cup. Smash, peel, and chop the garlic. Wash and chop the tomato, reserving the juice.
3. Process the garlic and pine nuts in a food processor. One at a time, add and process the tomato and basil leaves. Slowly add the olive oil and keep processing until the pesto is creamy. Add the grated Parmesan cheese. Pour half the pesto sauce over the cooked pasta. Store the remaining pesto sauce in a sealed container in the refrigerator for up to 7 days.

Amatriciana

Serves 4

- **TOTAL COST:** $6.48
- **CALORIES:** 590.82
- **FAT:** 17.12 g
- **PROTEIN:** 30.88 g
- **CHOLESTEROL:** 33.45 mg
- **SODIUM:** 1078.23 mg

3 slices bacon
4 links pork sausage
1 tablespoon vegetable oil
2 onions, chopped
1 jalapeño pepper
4 cloves garlic, minced
1 (14-ounce) can diced tomatoes
1 (6-ounce) can tomato paste
¼ teaspoon red pepper flakes
1 (12-ounce) package linguine
⅓ cup grated Romano cheese

This classic Italian dish is usually prepared with pancetta instead of bacon and without onions. For a splurge, you can make it that way too.

1. Bring a large pot of salted water to a boil. Meanwhile, cook bacon in a large skillet until crisp. Remove bacon from pan, crumble, and set aside. Cook sausage in drippings remaining in skillet, turning frequently, until browned. Remove to paper towel and cut into ½-inch pieces.
2. Drain fat from skillet but do not clean. Add olive oil and heat over medium heat. Add onions, jalapeño, and garlic and cook for 5 minutes. Add undrained tomatoes, tomato paste, and red pepper flakes and cook, stirring frequently, until blended; add reserved bacon and sausage.
3. When water comes to a boil, cook pasta until al dente according to package directions. Drain pasta, reserving ½ cup cooking water. Add cooking water to saucepan to help thin the sauce. Add pasta and toss over medium heat for 2–3 minutes. Sprinkle with cheese and serve immediately.

Greek Pasta

 Serves 4

- ~ **TOTAL COST:** $5.54
- ~ **CALORIES:** 527.31
- ~ **FAT:** 15.20 g
- ~ **PROTEIN:** 18.82 g
- ~ **CHOLESTEROL:** 31.95 mg
- ~ **SODIUM:** 990.34 mg

1 tablespoon olive oil
2 tablespoons butter
2 onions, chopped
3 cloves garlic, minced
1 (10-ounce) package frozen chopped spinach, thawed
1 (14-ounce) can diced tomatoes, undrained
½ teaspoon salt
⅛ teaspoon pepper
1 (12-ounce) package linguine
⅓ cup crumbled feta cheese

You can turn pasta into any ethnic cuisine just with the ingredients you choose. This Greek pasta is flavorful and delicious.

1. Bring a large pot of salted water to a boil. Meanwhile, in large saucepan combine olive oil and butter over medium heat. When butter melts, add onion and garlic; cook and stir until crisp-tender, about 4 minutes.
2. Add spinach to pan; cook and stir until water evaporates. Add undrained tomatoes, salt, and pepper and bring to a simmer. Reduce heat and cover.
3. Cook pasta until al dente according to package directions. Drain pasta, reserving ¼ cup cooking water. Add pasta to saucepan and toss gently, adding some of the reserved cooking water if necessary. Sprinkle with feta and serve immediately.

Al Dente

Al dente is the Italian term that translates literally as "to the tooth." This means that the pasta is tender to the bite, but still has a slightly give in the center. It's important to not overcook pasta or it will become gummy. Start testing the pasta a couple of minutes before the package says it is done to be sure it's perfect.

Linguine with Clam Sauce

 Serves 4

- ~ **TOTAL COST:** $6.49
- ~ **CALORIES:** 486.14
- ~ **FAT:** 16.48 g
- ~ **PROTEIN:** 12.88 g
- ~ **CHOLESTEROL:** 30.60 mg
- ~ **SODIUM:** 296.45 mg

3 tablespoons butter
1 tablespoon olive oil
1 onion, chopped
5 cloves garlic, minced
1 (12-ounce) package linguine
1 (6.5-ounce) cans minced clams, undrained
1 (4-ounce) can mushroom pieces, undrained
½ teaspoon dried basil leaves
3 tablespoons lemon juice
¼ cup sour cream
1 tablespoon cornstarch
¼ cup minced parsley

If you love garlic, add more! This creamy clam sauce is delicious served blended with perfectly cooked pasta. Just add some garlic bread and eat.

1. Bring a large pot of salted water to a boil. Meanwhile, in large saucepan, combine butter and olive oil over medium heat. When butter melts, add onion and garlic; cook and stir until tender, about 5 minutes.
2. Add pasta to boiling water and cook until almost al dente according to package directions. Meanwhile, add undrained clams, mushrooms, basil, and lemon juice to saucepan and bring to a simmer.
3. When pasta is done, drain and add to saucepan with sauce. In small bowl, combine lemon juice, sour cream, and cornstarch and blend with wire whisk. Add to saucepan; cook and stir until mixture bubbles, about 4–6 minutes. Sprinkle with parsley and serve.

Creamy Fettuccine

Serves 6

- ~ **TOTAL COST:** $4.92
- ~ **CALORIES:** 461.93
- ~ **FAT:** 13.50 g
- ~ **PROTEIN:** 19.25 g
- ~ **CHOLESTEROL:** 172.51 mg
- ~ **SODIUM:** 394.87 mg

½ cup heavy cream
¼ cup milk
4 eggs
¼ cup grated Parmesan cheese
½ teaspoon salt
⅛ teaspoon pepper
2 cups frozen peas
1 (16-ounce) package fettuccine
⅓ cup shredded Parmesan cheese

This super simple recipe is perfect for the days when all you have is pasta, cheese, eggs, and milk on hand.

1. Bring a large pot of salted water to a boil. Meanwhile, in medium bowl combine cream, milk, eggs, cheese, salt, and pepper and mix with wire whisk; set aside.
2. Place peas in colander and place in sink. Cook fettuccine until al dente according to package directions. Drain over peas in colander and return to pot.
3. Stir egg mixture again and add to pot. Toss together with pasta and peas over medium heat for 2–3 minutes or until sauce forms and mixture is hot. Sprinkle with shredded Parmesan cheese and serve immediately.

Parmesan Cheese

The cheapest Parmesan cheese is the pregrated kind in the green can. This can be used in complex recipes, like lasagna, or in sandwich spreads and salads, where the flavor isn't as important. In simple recipes like this one, buy a chunk of good Parmesan cheese and grate some. It will keep for a long time, and you can use the rind in soup.

Spaghetti Pizza

Serves 8

~ **TOTAL COST:** $6.69
~ **CALORIES:** 378.61
~ **FAT:** 12.19 g
~ **PROTEIN:** 18.31 g
~ **CHOLESTEROL:** 102.38 mg
~ **SODIUM:** 554.02 mg

1 tablespoon olive oil
1 onion, chopped
3 cloves garlic, minced
1 (4-ounce) can mushroom pieces
1 (8-ounce) can tomato sauce
1 teaspoon dried Italian seasoning
½ teaspoon salt
⅛ teaspoon cayenne pepper
1 (16-ounce) package spaghetti pasta
3 eggs
½ cup milk
1 cup shredded part-skim mozzarella cheese
1 cup shredded Cheddar cheese

This hearty meatless casserole serves a crowd for very little money. For a splurge, add cooked sausage or pepperoni to the tomato sauce.

1. Preheat oven to 350°F. Spray a 13" × 9" glass baking dish with non-stick cooking spray and set aside. Bring a large pot of salted water to a boil.
2. In medium saucepan, heat olive oil over medium heat. Add onion, garlic, and drained mushrooms; cook and stir until crisp tender, about 5 minutes. Add tomato sauce, Italian seasoning, salt, and pepper; cook for 15 minutes, stirring occasionally.
3. When water boils, cook pasta until al dente according to package directions. In large bowl, combine eggs and milk and beat well. When pasta is done, drain and immediately add to bowl with egg mixture; toss with tongs to coat.
4. Pour spaghetti mixture into prepared dish and spread evenly. Spoon tomato sauce over all, then sprinkle with cheeses. Bake 30–40 minutes or until casserole is hot and cheeses are melted and beginning to brown. Let stand for 5 minutes, then cut into squares to serve.

Garlic Broccoli Sauce over Pasta

 Serves 4

- **TOTAL COST:** $4.79
- **CALORIES:** 484.00
- **FAT:** 10.33 g
- **PROTEIN:** 21.78 g
- **CHOLESTEROL:** 17.96 mg
- **SODIUM:** 549.91 mg

1 (16-ounce) package frozen broccoli cuts, thawed
1 tablespoon olive oil
4 cloves garlic, minced
1 cup Chicken Stock (Chapter 6) or water
½ cup plain yogurt
1 tablespoon lemon juice
½ teaspoon salt
⅛ teaspoon pepper
½ teaspoon dried basil leaves
12 ounces linguine pasta
6 tablespoons grated Parmesan cheese

This smooth sauce has lots of flavor and a beautiful green color. This can be served as the main dish in a vegetarian meal, or as a side dish with any grilled meat.

1. Bring a large pot of salted water to a boil. Meanwhile, in large skillet, heat olive oil over medium heat. Add broccoli and garlic; stir-fry until broccoli is bright green, about 4–5 minutes. Add Stock or water, bring to a simmer, cover pan, and cook for 3 minutes.
2. Add pasta to boiling water. In food processor, combine all of the broccoli mixture with yogurt, lemon juice, salt, pepper, and basil, and blend until smooth.
3. When pasta is done, drain, reserving ¼ cup pasta water. Return pasta to pot. Add broccoli mixture and enough reserved pasta water to make a sauce; toss together over medium heat for 2 minutes. Serve with Parmesan cheese.

Pasta Sauces

Pasta sauces can be as complicated as a tomato sauce simmered for hours, or some garlic sautéed in oil with salt and pepper. Use your imagination and you can turn leftovers into pasta sauce. This recipe is an excellent use for leftover broccoli or asparagus. Or toss leftover vegetables into tomato sauce for another main dish.

Pasta and Wilted Spinach

Serves 6

- **TOTAL COST:** $5.72
- **CALORIES:** 449.99
- **FAT:** 10.88 g
- **PROTEIN:** 21.08 g
- **CHOLESTEROL:** 127.39 mg
- **SODIUM:** 356.28 mg

6 slices bacon
4 cloves garlic, minced
1 pound spaghetti pasta
2 tablespoons sugar
2 tablespoons white vinegar
1 tablespoon apple cider vinegar
4 cups chopped spinach
3 eggs, beaten
¼ cup heavy cream
½ cup grated Parmesan cheese, divided

Wilted spinach salad takes on a new twist when served as a hot pasta dish. This super quick recipe is delicious.

1. Bring a large pot of salted water to a boil. Meanwhile, in large skillet cook bacon until crisp. Remove bacon from skillet and drain on paper towels; crumble and set aside. Remove all but 3 tablespoons bacon drippings from skillet. Add garlic to hot skillet and remove from heat.
2. Add pasta to water and cook according to package directions. Meanwhile, beat eggs, cream, and ¼ cup Parmesan cheese in small bowl. When pasta is done, drain and return to pot. Add egg mixture; toss for 2 minutes.
3. Working quickly, place skillet with bacon drippings over medium high heat. Add sugar, vinegars, salt, and pepper and bring to a boil. Add spinach; toss until spinach starts to wilt.
4. Add all of spinach mixture to the pasta mixture. Toss over low heat for 2 minutes or until mixture is hot and spinach is wilted. Serve immediately with more Parmesan cheese.

Dark Greens

You can substitute other dark greens for spinach if you'd like. Bok choy, collard greens, kale, and mustard greens would all work well. If the recipe calls for cooking the dark greens, these other vegetables need to be cooked about 40–50% longer than spinach because they are sturdier. Be sure to prepare the greens the same way.

Pasta Carbonara with Bread Crumbs

 Serves 6

- ~ **TOTAL COST:** $3.19
- ~ **CALORIES:** 468.67
- ~ **FAT:** 10.64 g
- ~ **PROTEIN:** 17.86 g
- ~ **CHOLESTEROL:** 150.29 mg
- ~ **SODIUM:** 210.39 mg

1 tablespoon olive oil
1 tablespoon butter
4 cloves garlic, minced
3 slices Hearty White Bread (Chapter 3)
1 pound spaghetti pasta
4 eggs
¼ cup milk
⅓ cup grated Parmesan cheese
¼ teaspoon pepper
2 tablespoons chopped fresh parsley

The garlicky bread crumbs substitute for the bacon in this super easy and delicious pasta dish.

1. Bring a large pot of salted water to a boil. Meanwhile, in large saucepan, heat olive oil and butter over medium heat. Add garlic; cook and stir until garlic is fragrant, about 3 minutes. Add bread crumbs. Cook and stir over medium heat for 6–9 minutes until bread crumbs are toasted. Remove bread crumbs from pan and place on plate.
2. Add pasta to boiling water and cook until al dente according to package directions. Meanwhile, in medium bowl, combine eggs, cream, cheese, and pepper and mix well.
3. Drain pasta and place in pan used to saute bread crumbs; place over medium heat. Add egg mixture all at once; toss pasta with tongs for 2 minutes (heat will cook eggs). Add half of the bread crumbs and toss. Place on serving plate and sprinkle with remaining bread crumbs and parsley; serve immediately.

Tex-Mex Fettuccine

Serves 6

- ~ **TOTAL COST:** $6.62
- ~ **CALORIES:** 432.85
- ~ **FAT:** 16.19 g
- ~ **PROTEIN:** 17.16 g
- ~ **CHOLESTEROL:** 44.08 mg
- ~ **SODIUM:** 589.83 mg

½ pound pork sausage
1 onion, chopped
3 cloves garlic, minced
1 jalapeño pepper, minced
1 green bell pepper, chopped
1 (14-ounce) can diced tomatoes, undrained
2 tablespoons flour
½ cup light cream
12 ounces fettuccine pasta
⅓ cup grated Cotija cheese

This simple fettuccine dish is spicy, creamy, and flavorful. Serve it with a crisp green salad and a fruit salad for a cooling contrast.

1. Bring a large pot of salted water to a boil. Meanwhile, cook pork sausage along with onion and garlic over medium heat, stirring until sausage is brown and vegetables are tender. Drain well. Add jalapeño pepper, bell pepper, and tomatoes; bring to a simmer.
2. Cook pasta according to package directions until al dente. When pasta is almost done, combine flour and cream in a small bowl and beat well. Add to tomato mixture; bring to a boil and simmer for 3 minutes.
3. Drain pasta and add to saucepan with sauce. Toss for 2 minutes, then sprinkle with cheese and serve.

> **Cotija Cheese**
> Cotija cheese is an aged hard grating cheese similar to Parmesan and Romano cheeses, but with a stronger flavor It's usually less expensive too. You can find it in Mexican markets and sometimes at the regular grocery store. When the cheese is less aged, it resembles feta cheese. It freezes well, like all hard cheeses; grate some and store it in the freezer to use anytime.

Pasta with Spinach Pesto

 Serves 6

- ~ **TOTAL COST:** $3.63
- ~ **CALORIES:** 435.57
- ~ **FAT:** 15.09 g
- ~ **PROTEIN:** 15.86 g
- ~ **CHOLESTEROL:** 24.64 mg
- ~ **SODIUM:** 377.29 mg

1 cup Spinach Pesto (Chapter 2)
1 (3-ounce) package cream cheese, softened
Pinch grated nutmeg
1 tablespoon lemon juice
2 tablespoons heavy cream
1 pound fettuccine pasta
½ cup grated Romano cheese

Romano cheese is made from goat's milk and has a slightly richer, sharper taste than Parmesan cheese.

1. In food processor or blender, combine Pesto, cream cheese, nutmeg, lemon juice, and heavy cream; process or blend until smooth.
2. Bring a large pot of salted water to a boil. Add fettuccine; cook until al dente according to package directions. Drain pasta, reserving about ¼ cup of the pasta cooking water.
3. Return pasta to pot and stir in the pesto mixture along with reserved cooking water. Cook and stir over low heat until sauce is creamy and coats pasta. Sprinkle with Romano cheese and serve.

Vermicelli with Tuna

Serves 4

- ~ **TOTAL COST:** $3.91
- ~ **CALORIES:** 474.08
- ~ **FAT:** 7.05 g
- ~ **PROTEIN:** 26.42 g
- ~ **CHOLESTEROL:** 18.25 mg
- ~ **SODIUM:** 654.51 mg

1 tablespoon olive oil
1 onion, chopped
3 cloves garlic, minced
½ (29-ounce) can tomato puree
1 teaspoon dried oregano leaves
1 (12-ounce) package vermicelli pasta
1 (6-ounce) can white chunk tuna, drained
⅓ cup grated Parmesan cheese
2 tablespoons chopped flat-leaf parsley

Vermicelli is thinner than spaghetti and is a good choice for light sauces that won't weigh it down.

1. Bring a large pot of water to a boil. In large skillet, heat oil over medium heat. Add onion and garlic; cook and stir until tender, about 6 minutes. Add tomato puree carefully along with oregano and stir; simmer for 5–8 minutes.
2. Cook pasta in boiling water until al dente according to package directions. Drain, reserving ⅓ cup pasta cooking water.
3. Add pasta to tomato mixture along with tuna; cook and stir over medium heat for 2–3 minutes, adding reserved cooking water as necessary, until sauce bubbles. Sprinkle with cheese and parsley and serve immediately.

Chicken Puttanesca

Serves 4

- **TOTAL COST:** $5.89
- **CALORIES:** 481.48
- **FAT:** 10.22 g
- **PROTEIN:** 18.38 g
- **CHOLESTEROL:** 17.87 mg
- **SODIUM:** 910.92 mg

s vegetable oil
2 boneless, skinless chicken thighs
2 tablespoons all-purpose flour
½ teaspoon salt
⅛ teaspoon cayenne pepper
4 cloves garlic, minced
1 anchovy fillet in oil, mashed
1 (14-ounce) can diced tomatoes, undrained
¼ cup tomato paste
½ teaspoon dried Italian seasoning
½ cup chopped green olives
1 (12-ounce) package spaghetti

Chicken thighs and olives add a rich flavor to this easy and delicious pasta recipe.

1. Bring a large pot of salted water to a boil over high heat. Meanwhile, in large skillet heat oil over medium heat. Sprinkle chicken with flour, salt, and pepper. Add chicken to skillet and cook for 5 minutes without moving. Turn chicken and cook for 3 minutes on the second side; remove to a platter.
2. To drippings remaining in skillet, add garlic and anchovy; cook and stir to melt anchovy for 2–3 minutes. Add tomatoes and tomato paste and bring to a simmer. Shred chicken and return to sauce. Simmer sauce for 10 minutes.
3. Cook pasta as directed on package until al dente. Stir olives into sauce and continue simmering. Drain pasta and add to skillet with sauce. Toss over low heat for 2 minutes, then serve.

Puttanesca

Puttanesca literally means "pasta of the ladies of the evening." Where did the name originate? History is blurry on this subject. It may be because the dish is hot and spicy, or because it's an inexpensive dish that can be made quickly. The dish always includes anchovies, garlic, and some hot spice, either cayenne pepper, Tabasco sauce, or red pepper flakes.

Pesto Pasta with Peas

Serves 4

~ **TOTAL COST:** $4.69
~ **CALORIES:** 595.89
~ **FAT:** 22.35 g
~ **PROTEIN:** 23.30 g
~ **CHOLESTEROL:** 19.73 mg
~ **SODIUM:** 448.91 mg

1 tablespoon olive oil
1 tablespoon butter
2 cloves garlic, minced
½ cup chopped onion
1½ cups frozen peas
¼ cup water
12 ounces rotini pasta
½ cup Spinach Pesto (Chapter 2)
⅓ cup chopped walnuts
⅓ cup grated Romano cheese

This simple dish can be made in minutes and it's a great supper when the cupboard is almost bare. Keep these ingredients on hand to feed your family fast.

1. Bring a large pot of salted water to a boil. In large saucepan, heat olive oil over medium heat. Add garlic and onion; cook and stir until vegetables begin to brown, about 6 minutes. Add frozen peas and water; bring to a simmer. Cover pan, reduce heat, and simmer for 3–4 minutes.
2. Cook pasta according to package directions until al dente. Drain, reserving ¼ cup cooking water, and add to saucepan with peas. Add Pesto and walnuts and reserved pasta water, if necessary, and toss over medium heat for 2–3 minutes, until pasta is coated. Serve with Romano cheese.

Tortellini Pasta with Tomatoes and Kalamata Olives

Serves 8

~ **PREP TIME:** 10 minutes
~ **COOK TIME:** 10 minutes
~ **TOTAL COST:** $6.57
~ **CALORIES:** 389
~ **FAT:** 8 g
~ **CARBOHYDRATES:** 29 g
~ **PROTEIN:** 5 g
~ **CHOLESTEROL:** 62 mg
~ **SODIUM:** 410 mg

1 (8-ounce) package frozen or fresh cheese tortellini
¼ cup extra-virgin olive oil
¼ cup Parmesan cheese, grated
2 large tomatoes, seeded and diced
1 cup kalamata olives, chopped
Sea salt and pepper to taste

Tortellini pasta is typical to the north-central region of Italy and is customarily filled with a meat such as prosciutto. Tortelloni pasta is of the same shape but larger in size.

Cook tortellini as directed on package. Drain well. Separately, in medium bowl, whisk together oil and cheese. Add in tomatoes and olives, season as desired with salt and pepper. Add pasta and toss well to coat. Cover and refrigerate for 20 minutes.

Dressed-Up Macaroni and Cheese

 Serves 6

~ **TOTAL COST:** $4.78
~ **CALORIES:** 386.69
~ **FAT:** 10.95 g
~ **PROTEIN:** 15.19 g
~ **CHOLESTEROL:** 31.30 mg
~ **SODIUM:** 768.48 mg

¼ cup butter or margarine
1 cup chopped onion
2 (7.25-ounce) boxes macaroni and cheese mix
⅔ cup milk
3–4 tablespoons mustard
2 cups frozen peas, thawed

This recipe assumes that each box of Mac and Cheese costs $1.09. When you find it on sale for 50¢ a box, your cost will drop to $3.60.

1. In medium saucepan, melt butter over medium heat. Add onion; cook and stir until tender, about 5 minutes.
2. Meanwhile, bring a large pot of water to boil. Add macaroni from package and cook according to package directions until al dente. Drain macaroni and return to pot.
3. Stir in powdered mix from package, cooked onions with butter, milk, mustard, and peas and stir until sauce is creamy and mixture is hot. Serve immediately.

Gnocchi of Barley and Spinach

 Serves 6

~ **PREP TIME:** 18 minutes
~ **COOK TIME:** 8 minutes
~ **TOTAL COST:** $3.86
~ **CALORIES:** 326
~ **FAT:** 6 g
~ **CARBOHYDRATES:** 42 g
~ **PROTEIN:** 8 g
~ **CHOLESTEROL:** 13 mg
~ **SODIUM:** 265 mg

¼ cup cooked spinach
¼ cup cooked barley
1 whole egg
1 egg white
½ teaspoon extra-virgin olive oil
1 teaspoon dry white wine
½ cup semolina
½ cup unbleached all-purpose flour
Sea salt and pepper to taste

Gnocchi is an Italian dumpling usually made from semolina flour or potato. The barley used here is a healthy, lighter version of this Italian favorite.

1. In a blender or food processor, purée the spinach and barley, then add the eggs, oil, and wine; continue to blend until thoroughly smooth.
2. Sift together the semolina, flour, salt, and pepper. Incorporate the spinach mixture with the flour mixture.
3. Bring 1 gallon water to a boil. Drop the gnocchi into the boiling water and cook for approximately 8 minutes, until al dente.

Frittata of Fettuccini, Tomatoes, and Basil

 Serves 8

~ **PREP TIME:** 8 minutes
~ **COOK TIME:** 15 minutes
~ **TOTAL COST:** $6.80
~ **CALORIES:** 187
~ **FAT:** 5 g
~ **PROTEIN:** 5 g
~ **CHOLESTEROL:** 73 mg
~ **SODIUM:** 650 mg

1 tomato, diced
½ pound package egg fettuccini noodles
3 tablespoons prepared pesto
3 eggs, lightly beaten
¼ cup milk
1 tablespoon fresh basil, leaves chopped
½ cup Parmesan cheese, grated

This unique twist on a traditional frittata is delicious and filling. Substitute your favorite ingredients or, even better, whatever you have leftover in your refrigerator.

1. Bring large pot of water to boiling, add the dried tomatoes and noodles. Cook until al dente, about 8 to 10 minutes. Drain well. Return to the pot. Add the pesto and toss until pasta is well coated.
2. In a small bowl, beat together the eggs and milk until blended. Pour over the noodle mixture. Cook over medium heat, gently turning with a spatula until the eggs are thickened and cooked. Serve with fresh basil and cheese.

Penne Pasta with Garlic and Tomatoes

 Serves 8

~ **PREP TIME:** 8 minutes
~ **COOK TIME:** 18 minutes
~ **TOTAL COST:** $6.32
~ **CALORIES:** 382
~ **FAT:** 25 g
~ **PROTEIN:** 12 g
~ **CHOLESTEROL:** 20 mg
~ **SODIUM:** 266 mg

2 tablespoons olive oil, plus a drizzle for cooking pasta
6 cloves garlic, chopped
3 cups chicken broth
6 Roma tomatoes, chopped
¼ fresh Italian parsley, chopped
8 scallions, white part and half the green tops, chopped
Sea salt and black pepper to taste, plus 1 tablespoon salt for pasta water
¼ cup unsalted butter, softened
1 pound penne pasta

As a delicious alternative, add cooked, chopped chicken breasts.

1. In a large saucepan over medium heat, heat olive oil and add garlic, sauté until golden. Add chicken broth, tomatoes, parsley, and scallions. Add salt and pepper as desired. Bring to a boil and reduce over medium-high heat, about 5 to 8 minutes. Whisk in butter, a little at a time, to thicken sauce. Remove from heat and keep warm.
2. Meanwhile, in a large pot filled ¾ with water, bring water to a boil. Add 1 tablespoon of salt and a drizzle of oil. Add pasta and stir to prevent sticking. Cook until al dente, about 8 to 10 minutes. Drain. Transfer pasta to serving bowl and toss with sauce.

Tortellini Pasta with Salmon

 Serves 8

~ **PREP TIME:** 10 minutes
~ **CHILL:** 2 to 4 hours
~ **TOTAL COST:** $6.97
~ **CALORIES:** 283
~ **FAT:** 6 g
~ **PROTEIN:** 20 g
~ **CHOLESTEROL:** 53 mg
~ **SODIUM:** 410 mg

1 (8-ounce) package frozen or fresh cheese tortellini
1 zucchini, sliced
1 red bell pepper, cut into narrow strips (julienned)
1 (6.5-ounce) cans salmon, drained and flaked
½ cup plain yogurt
¼ cup Parmesan cheese, grated
¼ cup fresh Italian parsley, chopped
1 teaspoon dried oregano, crumbled

When it comes to fresh or frozen, pasta is one of those food products that freezes well. Use whichever is the most cost effective for your budget.

1. Cook tortellini as directed on package. Drain well. In a medium bowl, toss together pasta, zucchini, and bell pepper. Add salmon and mix to combine.
2. In a small bowl, stir together yogurt, cheese, parsley, and oregano. Mix well. Add to pasta mixture and toss gently to coat. Cover and refrigerate for several hours before serving so dairy ingredients thicken.

> **Quick and Easy Tip**
> Using canned salmon is a cost-effective and time-saving way to enjoy this healthy fish.

Rotini Pasta with Red Bell Peppers, Peas, and Green Onions

Serves 8

~ **PREP TIME:** 15 minutes
~ **CHILL:** 2 hours
~ **TOTAL COST:** $6.35
~ **CALORIES:** 199
~ **FAT:** 6 g
~ **PROTEIN:** 6 g
~ **CHOLESTEROL:** 22 mg
~ **SODIUM:** 349 mg

1 cup plain nonfat yogurt
½ cup low-fat mayonnaise
½ cup grated Parmesan cheese
1 tablespoon fresh basil, leaves chopped
2 cloves garlic, chopped
Sea salt and black pepper to taste
2 red bell peppers, seeded and chopped
1 cup blanched peas
½ cup chopped green onions
1 pound rotini pasta, cooked and drained

Pasta salad is great for parties. It is inexpensive, filling, and goes a long way when it comes to serving.

In a large bowl, blend yogurt, mayonnaise, Parmesan cheese, basil or dill, garlic, salt, and pepper. Add the bell peppers, peas, and green onions, and mix well. Add pasta and toss to coat. Cover and refrigerate for 2 hours.

> **Quick and Easy Tip**
> Keep cooked pasta on hand in the refrigerator for quick and easy meals. Cook pasta, drain, and drizzle with 1 teaspoon of olive oil to coat, then refrigerate. The oil helps keep pasta from sticking together.

Pasta with Mushrooms and Crispy Bacon

 Serves 8

- ~ **PREP TIME:** 8 minutes
- ~ **COOK TIME:** 23 minutes
- ~ **TOTAL COST:** $5.23
- ~ **CALORIES:** 125
- ~ **FAT:** 8 g
- ~ **PROTEIN:** 6 g
- ~ **CHOLESTEROL:** 8 mg
- ~ **SODIUM:** 366 mg

2 tablespoons olive oil, plus a drizzle for pasta
2 slices bacon, chopped
½ yellow onion, chopped
2 cups fresh cremini or button mushrooms, sliced
1½ cups frozen peas
1 teaspoon unsalted butter
2 cups chicken broth
Sea salt and black pepper to taste, plus 1 tablespoon salt for pasta water
1 pound pasta shells or penne pasta
½ cup Parmesan cheese, grated

The bacon adds a wonderful flavor to this recipe. If your budget allows, substitute the bacon for more traditional Italian prosciutto. Dice the prosciutto as you would the bacon; however, the cooking time for the prosciutto will be less because prosciutto is traditionally sliced thinner than bacon.

1. In a large skillet or saucepan, heat oil over medium heat. Add bacon and onion and cook until bacon is crisp and onion is tender. Add mushrooms and cook until the moisture has almost all evaporated, about 5 minutes. Add peas, butter, and broth. Simmer until liquid is reduced by half, about 10 minutes. Season with salt and pepper to taste.
2. Meanwhile, in a large pot, bring at least 4 quarts of water to a rolling boil. Add 1 tablespoon salt and a drizzle of olive oil. Add the pasta, stir to separate, and cook until not quite al dente, about 8 minutes or so. Drain. Transfer pasta to skillet and combine with the hot sauce. Cook briefly to heat through. Transfer all to large bowl and toss with the Parmesan.

> **Quick and Easy Tip**
> Adding olive oil to the pasta before cooking helps keep the pasta from sticking together. Just be sure not to use too much. A small drizzle is fine.

CHAPTER 13

VEGETABLES AND SIDE DISHES

Polenta—Two Ways

Serves 12

- ~ **TOTAL COST:** $1.82
- ~ **CALORIES:** 135.41
- ~ **FAT:** 5.50 g
- ~ **PROTEIN:** 3.25 g
- ~ **CHOLESTEROL:** 8.02 mg
- ~ **SODIUM:** 259.12 mg

7 cups water
2 cups yellow cornmeal
1 teaspoon salt
½ cup grated Parmesan cheese
2 tablespoons butter
2 tablespoons olive oil

You can serve this polenta immediately, or chill it, slice it, and fry it to crisp perfection to be used in recipes like Crisp Polenta with Salmon Cream (Chapter 10).

1. In large saucepan, combine water and salt and bring to a rolling boil. Add cornmeal slowly, stirring constantly with a wire whisk. Cook, stirring constantly, over medium heat until the cornmeal thickens, about 12–17 minutes. Remove from heat and add cheese and butter, stirring until mixture is smooth.
2. You can now serve the polenta immediately, or chill it to fry the next day.
3. To chill, butter a 9" × 13" pan and spread polenta in an even layer. Cover and chill until very firm, at least 8 hours.
4. The next day, cut polenta into 3-inch squares. Heat olive oil in a large skillet over medium heat. Fry polenta squares until crisp and golden brown, turning once, about 2–3 minutes per side. Serve immediately. You can freeze the chilled polenta up to 3 months; fry while frozen until hot and golden.

Polenta

Polenta, also known as cornmeal mush, has been nourishing populations for centuries. Its mild flavor means you can flavor it a thousand different ways. And, if you serve it with beans, wheat, or legumes, you're serving foods that can be used by your body as complete proteins, making it the ideal vegetarian main dish idea.

Creamy Mashed Potatoes

Serves 4

- ~ **TOTAL COST:** $1.57
- ~ **CALORIES:** 208.27
- ~ **FAT:** 11.54 g
- ~ **PROTEIN:** 5.40 g
- ~ **CHOLESTEROL:** 28.93 mg
- ~ **SODIUM:** 310.42 mg

2 cups water
⅓ cup milk
¼ teaspoon salt
3 tablespoons butter
2 cups potato flakes
⅓ cup sour cream
¼ cup grated Parmesan cheese

Dried potato flakes are made from 100% potatoes, and they are delicious and nutritious. These additions make them taste even better.

1. In large saucepan, combine water, milk, salt, and butter over high heat. Bring to a rolling boil, then add potatoes flakes and remove from heat.
2. Let stand for 1 minute, then whip with a fork. Stir in sour cream and Parmesan cheese, cover, and let stand for 2 minutes, then serve.

Vegetable Rice

Serves 6

- ~ **TOTAL COST:** $2.54
- ~ **CALORIES:** 196.92
- ~ **FAT:** 4.60 g
- ~ **PROTEIN:** 4.67 g
- ~ **CHOLESTEROL:** 5.02 mg
- ~ **SODIUM:** 259.77 mg

1 tablespoon butter
1 tablespoon olive oil
1 onion, chopped
2 cloves garlic, minced
1 large carrot, shredded
2 cups long grain rice
4 cups water
½ teaspoon salt
⅛ teaspoon pepper
1½ cups frozen peas, thawed

Adding vegetables to rice makes them a heartier accompaniment. Serve this dish with any main dish, or use leftovers in Beefy Fried Rice (Chapter 9).

1. In large saucepan, heat butter and olive oil over medium heat. Add onion; cook and stir until crisp-tender, about 4 minutes. Add carrot and rice; cook and stir for 2–3 minutes longer.
2. Add water, salt, and pepper. Bring to a boil, then cover, reduce heat to low, and simmer for 15 minutes, then stir in peas. Bring back to a simmer, cover, and cook for 5–8 minutes or until rice is tender. Remove from heat and let stand for 5 minutes, then fluff rice with fork and serve.

Confetti Slaw

- **TOTAL COST:** $6.01
- **CALORIES:** 138.99
- **FAT:** 4.28 g
- **PROTEIN:** 7.42 g
- **CHOLESTEROL:** 20.80 mg
- **SODIUM:** 279.21 mg

½ cup mayonnaise
½ cup buttermilk
½ cup plain yogurt
¼ cup crumbled feta cheese
1 teaspoon dried dill weed
⅛ teaspoon pepper
2 tablespoons prepared horseradish
½ head red cabbage, shredded
½ head green cabbage, shredded
3 stalks celery, sliced
1 green bell pepper, chopped
2 cups frozen peas, thawed

Cabbage is one of the cheapest foods available, and it is delicious; crisp, crunchy, and slightly sweet. This salad feeds a bunch!

1. In large bowl, combine mayonnaise, buttermilk, yogurt, feta, dill, pepper, and horseradish and mix until blended.
2. Prepare cabbage and vegetables, adding them to the mayonnaise mixture as you work. When everything is added, toss gently to coat. Cover and refrigerate for at least 2 hours before serving. Store in refrigerator up to 4 days.

Asian Slaw

- **PREP TIME:** 15 minutes
- **CHILL:** 1 hour
- **TOTAL COST:** $5.70
- **CALORIES:** 103
- **FAT:** 7 g
- **PROTEIN:** 1 g
- **CHOLESTEROL:** 22 mg
- **SODIUM:** 170 mg

1 head Chinese cabbage, shredded
½ (8.25-ounce) can crushed pineapple, drained
1 (8-ounce) can sliced water chestnuts
1 large bunch fresh Italian parsley, chopped
¼ green onions, chopped
¼ cup mayonnaise
1 tablespoon prepared mustard
1 teaspoon fresh gingerroot, minced

Chinese cabbage is also called snow cabbage. It is lighter in texture than American cabbage and has a sweeter flavor.

Combine cabbage, pineapple, water chestnuts, parsley, and onion. Cover and chill. For the dressing, combine mayonnaise, mustard, and gingerroot. Cover and chill separately. When ready to serve, pour dressing over cabbage and toss to coat.

Quick and Easy Tip
Chinese cabbage is great for salads and for stir-frying with other vegetables. Treat as you would American cabbage or other leafy vegetable.

Three Bean Salad

 Serves 6

~ **TOTAL COST:** $4.32
~ **CALORIES:** 281.31
~ **FAT:** 12.59 g
~ **PROTEIN:** 7.98 g
~ **CHOLESTEROL:** 0.0 mg
~ **SODIUM:** 521.53 mg

2 cups frozen green beans
1 (15-ounce) can chickpeas, rinsed
1 (15-ounce) can kidney beans, rinsed
⅓ cup olive oil
3 tablespoons lemon juice
3 tablespoons sugar
½ teaspoon celery seed
¼ teaspoon salt
⅛ teaspoon white pepper

This salad can be served as a vegetarian main course by serving it over mixed salad greens or chilled marinated couscous. You could add some chopped toasted walnuts too, for flavor and crunch.

1. Prepare green beans as directed on package. Drain well and place in serving bowl along with drained chickpeas and kidney beans.
2. In small bowl, combine olive oil, lemon juice, sugar, celery seed, salt, and pepper and mix well with wire whisk. Drizzle over vegetables and stir to coat. Cover and refrigerate at least 4 hours, stirring occasionally, before serving.

Substituting Beans
Most beans and legumes are good substitutes for each other. Green beans, yellow wax beans, and snap peas are equivalent.

Potato Salad

Serves 8

~ **PREP TIME:** 8 minutes
~ **COOK TIME:** none
~ **TOTAL COST:** $5.54
~ **CALORIES:** 272
~ **FAT:** 6 g
~ **CARBOHYDRATES:** 22 g
~ **PROTEIN:** 3 g
~ **CHOLESTEROL:** 22 mg
~ **SODIUM:** 400 mg

¾ cup mayonnaise
1 teaspoon sugar
2 teaspoons Dijon-style mustard
2 pounds potatoes (any variety), peeled, cut into 2-inch cubes, and boiled
1 small carrot, peeled and grated
Salt and white pepper to taste
1 tablespoon roughly chopped Italian parsley

When making potato salad, don't overboil the potatoes, as they become mushy and will cause your potato salad to have a consistency similar to mashed potatoes.

Whisk together mayonnaise, sugar, and mustard in a small bowl. Add potatoes and carrots; toss them gently to coat. Season to taste with salt and white pepper. Garnish with chopped parsley.

Asian Cucumber Salad

Serves 4

- **PREP TIME:** 10 minutes
- **COOK TIME:** none
- **TOTAL COST:** $2.79
- **CALORIES:** 103
- **FAT:** 7 g
- **CARBOHYDRATES:** 10 g
- **PROTEIN:** 1 g
- **CHOLESTEROL:** 1 mg
- **SODIUM:** 170 mg

¼ cup rice wine vinegar
1 teaspoon sugar
1 teaspoon chopped jalapeño pepper
1 European-style long cucumber or 1 large regular
   cucumber
Sesame oil

Chopped tomatoes are also a good addition to this healthy, flavorful salad.

Whisk together rice vinegar, sugar, and chopped jalapeño. If using a European cucumber, it is not necessary to peel, but if using an American cucumber, peel it. Halve the cucumber lengthwise; remove seeds. Slice seeded cucumber very thinly into half-moons. Combine with vinegar mixture, drizzle in a few drops of sesame oil, and toss to coat. Marinate for at least 10 minutes before serving.

Slaw of Summer Vegetables

Serves 8

- **PREP TIME:** 15 minutes
- **COOK TIME:** none
- **TOTAL COST:** $6.98
- **CALORIES:** 158
- **FAT:** 3 g
- **CARBOHYDRATES:** 9 g
- **PROTEIN:** 2 g
- **CHOLESTEROL:** 0 mg
- **SODIUM:** 158 mg

1 small head napa cabbage, grated or chopped
1 carrot, peeled and chopped
¼ pound snow peas, sliced
1 red bell pepper, seeded and chopped
12 green beans, ends trimmed, chopped
1 small red onion, chopped
1 ear fresh sweet corn, shucked, kernels cut off cob
½ teaspoon sugar
¼ cup apple cider vinegar
1 tablespoon olive oil
Pinch celery seeds
Salt and black pepper to taste

This vegetable combination is great served fresh, as with this recipe, or heat the tablespoon of olive oil in a large skillet and sauté the ingredients for about 5 minutes.

Combine all vegetables in a large mixing bowl; toss with sugar, vinegar, oil, celery seeds, salt, and pepper. Allow to sit at least 10 minutes before serving.

Napa Cabbage
Napa cabbage is Chinese cabbage and is lighter in texture and flavor than American cabbage.

Pasta Salad with Lemon Balsamic Vinaigrette and Red Bell Peppers

 Serves 8

- ~ **PREP TIME:** 15 minutes
- ~ **CHILL TIME:** 2 hours
- ~ **TOTAL COST:** $6.35
- ~ **CALORIES:** 199
- ~ **FAT:** 6 g
- ~ **CARBOHYDRATES:** 28 g
- ~ **PROTEIN:** 6 g
- ~ **CHOLESTEROL:** 22 mg
- ~ **SODIUM:** 349 mg

¼ cup extra-virgin olive oil
¼ cup balsamic vinegar
Sea salt and black pepper to taste
2 cloves garlic, chopped
Fine zest of 1 lemon
1 pound rotini pasta, cooked and drained
1 red onion, chopped
2 red bell peppers, seeded and chopped
½ cup grated Parmesan cheese
1 tablespoon fresh basil, leaves chopped

This recipe for pasta salad is a great base for any pasta salad. Add chopped prosciutto, fresh kernel corn, chopped asparagus tips or green beans, chopped black olives . . . creating your own recipes in the kitchen is part of the fun of cooking!

In large bowl, whisk together oil, vinegar, salt, pepper, garlic, and lemon zest. Mix well. Add pasta, onion, peppers, Parmesan, and basil and toss well to coat.

Tabbouleh

 Serves 6

- ~ **PREP TIME:** 8 minutes
- RESTING TIME: 2 HOURS, 15 MINUTES
- ~ **TOTAL COST:** $6.39
- ~ **CALORIES:** 124
- ~ **FAT:** 11 g
- ~ **CARBOHYDRATES:** 12 g
- ~ **PROTEIN:** 3 g
- ~ **CHOLESTEROL:** 1 mg
- ~ **SODIUM:** 75 mg

1 cup cracked (bulgur) wheat
1 quart water
1 small cucumber, chopped
3 scallions, finely chopped
2 ripe tomatoes, seeded and chopped
2 tablespoons chopped chives
1 cup chopped Italian parsley
½ cup extra-virgin olive oil
Juice of 2 lemons
Sea salt and black pepper to taste

Other great ingredients for this recipe are red or yellow bell pepper, yellow squash, and fresh peas.

1. Soak the wheat in 1 quart water for 15 minutes (or overnight). Drain and squeeze out excess moisture by tying up in a cheesecloth or clean kitchen towel.
2. Combine wheat with cucumber, scallions, tomatoes, chives, and parsley in a mixing bowl. Toss with olive oil, lemon juice, salt, and pepper. Set aside to marinate for 2 to 3 hours before serving.

Tabbouleh
Middle Eastern bulgur wheat absorbs water quickly, giving it a pliable and chewy texture unlike anything else in the world. This is an everyday dish in Egypt, and it goes perfect with stuffed grape leaves.

Barley Corn Salad

Serves 8

- ~ **PREP TIME:** 5 minutes
- ~ **COOK TIME:** 35 minutes
- ~ **TOTAL COST:** $5.84
- ~ **CALORIES:** 127
- ~ **FAT:** 6 g
- ~ **CARBOHYDRATES:** 36 g
- ~ **PROTEIN:** 4 g
- ~ **CHOLESTEROL:** 2 mg
- ~ **SODIUM:** 129 mg

1 cup barley
2 quarts lightly salted water
1 (16-ounce) package frozen sweet corn kernels
1 carrot, chopped finely
2 ribs celery, chopped finely
1 medium red onion, chopped finely
1 tablespoon red wine vinegar or cider vinegar
2 tablespoons extra-virgin olive oil
½ cup chopped fresh herbs, such as parsley, chives, basil, oregano, mint, and cilantro
Salt and freshly ground black pepper to taste

Barley can be substituted for brown rice, white rice, or another of your favorite grains.

1. Boil the barley in 2 quarts lightly salted water until it is very tender, about 30 minutes. Drain and spread on a platter to cool. Heat a dry cast-iron pan or skillet over a high flame for 1 minute. Add the corn and cook without stirring until some kernels attain a slight char and the corn has a smoky aroma, about 5 minutes.
2. Combine the barley, corn, carrot, celery, and onion in a mixing bowl. Add remaining ingredients and toss well to coat.

Old-Fashioned Apples and Onions

Serves 4

- ~ **TOTAL COST:** $3.41
- ~ **CALORIES:** 162.36
- ~ **FAT:** 9.29 g
- ~ **PROTEIN:** 0.70 g
- ~ **CHOLESTEROL:** 15.26 mg
- ~ **SODIUM:** 336.66 mg

2 tablespoons butter
1 tablespoon olive oil
2 onions, chopped
2 cloves garlic, minced
2 Granny Smith apples, sliced
2 tablespoons brown sugar
1 tablespoon apple cider vinegar
½ teaspoon salt
⅛ teaspoon pepper

This sweet and tart side dish is perfect served with a grilled steak or some sautéed chicken breasts.

1. In large saucepan, combine butter and olive oil over medium heat. When butter melts, add onions and garlic. Cook and stir for 5–6 minutes until soft. Add apples; cook and stir for 1 minute.
2. Sprinkle with brown sugar, vinegar, salt, and pepper. Cover saucepan and cook for 5–7 minutes, shaking pan occasionally, until apples are just tender. Stir gently and serve.

Cheesy Home Fries

Serves 6

- ~ **TOTAL COST:** $3.73
- ~ **CALORIES:** 324.11
- ~ **FAT:** 13.02 g
- ~ **PROTEIN:** 7.24 g
- ~ **CHOLESTEROL:** 34.20 mg
- ~ **SODIUM:** 825.77 mg

4 russet potatoes
⅓ cup grated Parmesan cheese
¼ cup flour
½ teaspoon salt
¼ teaspoon pepper
½ teaspoon dried Italian seasoning
6 tablespoons butter, melted

These fabulous potatoes are tender, crisp, and beautifully seasoned. Don't serve them with ketchup!

1. Preheat oven to 350°F. Prepare a large bowl full of ice water. Peel potatoes and cut into French fry–size strips, dropping into the bowl of ice water as you work. When all the potatoes are prepared, remove from ice water and dry, first with kitchen towels, then with paper towels.
2. In large bowl, combine cheese, flour, salt, pepper, and Italian seasoning and mix well. Add potatoes, half at a time, and toss well to coat. Place butter in 15" × 10" jelly roll pan and place in oven to melt. Place coated potatoes on butter in pan and sprinkle with remaining cheese mixture. Bake potatoes for 50–60 minutes, turning three times with a spatula, until brown and crisp. Serve immediately.

Honey Carrots

Serves 6

- ~ **TOTAL COST:** $2.06
- ~ **CALORIES:** 123.68
- ~ **FAT:** 4.99 g
- ~ **PROTEIN:** 1.05 g
- ~ **CHOLESTEROL:** 15.26 mg
- ~ **SODIUM:** 301.52 mg

8 carrots, peeled and sliced
2 cups water
3 tablespoons butter
2 cloves garlic, minced
3 tablespoons honey
½ teaspoon salt
⅛ teaspoon pepper

Remember, whole carrots are the best value, but if you're pressed for time, you could substitute prepared sliced carrots or frozen sliced carrots.

1. In large saucepan, combine carrots and water and bring to a boil. Reduce heat, cover, and simmer for 4–5 minutes or until carrots are just barely tender. Drain and place carrots in serving bowl.
2. Return pan to heat and add butter and garlic. Cook and stir over medium heat until garlic is fragrant. Return carrots to pot and add honey, salt, and pepper. Cook and stir for 2–3 minutes until carrots are glazed. Serve immediately.

Spinach and Rice

 Serves 6

- **TOTAL COST:** $4.46
- **CALORIES:** 353.69
- **FAT:** 14.69 g
- **PROTEIN:** 13.42 g
- **CHOLESTEROL:** 43.39 mg
- **SODIUM:** 681.73 mg

2 tablespoons butter
1 onion, chopped
1½ cups long-grain white rice
1 teaspoon salt
2½ cups water
½ teaspoon dried thyme leaves
pinch ground nutmeg
1 (10-ounce) package frozen spinach
½ cup light cream
1 cup grated Parmesan cheese
½ cup grated Swiss cheese

The combination of spinach with rice and cheese is so delicious. The touch of nutmeg really brings the flavors together.

1. In large saucepan, melt butter over medium heat. Add onion; cook and stir until crisp tender, about 5 minutes. Add rice; cook and stir for 2 minutes longer. Sprinkle salt over all and add water and thyme leaves. Bring to a boil, reduce heat to low, cover, and simmer for 20–25 minutes or until rice is tender.
2. Meanwhile, thaw spinach and drain well in colander; then squeeze with your hands to drain thoroughly. Stir into rice mixture along with nutmeg, cream, and cheeses. Cook and stir until spinach is hot and cheeses are melted, about 5–8 minutes.

> **Thawing Spinach**
> Frozen chopped spinach and frozen cut leaf spinach both contain a lot of water. If the recipe calls for draining the spinach, take time to do it properly or the recipe will be ruined. Thaw the spinach, then place it in a colander and squeeze with your hands. Then wrap the spinach in a kitchen towel and twist to remove the last bits of moisture.

Roasted Potatoes

Serves 8

- ~ **TOTAL COST:** $4.61
- ~ **CALORIES:** 319.04
- ~ **FAT:** 5.37 g
- ~ **PROTEIN:** 5.84 g
- ~ **CHOLESTEROL:** 0.0 mg
- ~ **SODIUM:** 953.23 mg

5 pounds russet potatoes
3 tablespoons olive oil
2 onions, chopped
4 cloves garlic, minced
1 teaspoon salt
⅛ teaspoon pepper

If you don't peel the potatoes you won't have any waste, and the dish will have more vitamins and fiber.

1. Preheat oven to 400°F. Scrub potatoes and cut into 1-inch pieces. Place in large roasting pan and drizzle with olive oil. Sprinkle with onion, garlic, salt, and pepper and toss with hands until vegetables are coated with oil.
2. Bake, uncovered, for 30 minutes. Using a large spatula, turn the vegetables; arrange in even layer. Bake for 30–40 minutes longer or until potatoes are tender and beginning to brown and crisp. Serve immediately.

Red Potatoes with Herbs

Serves 6

- ~ **PREP TIME:** 6 minutes
- ~ **COOK TIME:** 15 minutes
- ~ **TOTAL COST:** $4.76
- ~ **CALORIES:** 197
- ~ **FAT:** 3 g
- ~ **PROTEIN:** 4 g
- ~ **CHOLESTEROL:** 2 mg
- ~ **SODIUM:** 351 mg

1 pound baby red potatoes
¼ cup butter
3 cloves garlic, minced
2 tablespoons fresh thyme leaves, chopped
2 tablespoons fresh Italian parsley, chopped
Sea salt and pepper to taste

Baby potatoes cook fast because they are so small. Removing a strip of skin from the middle of the potato helps prevent them from splitting as they cook.

1. Peel a strip of skin from the middle of each potato. Place potatoes in a large pot, cover with water, and bring to a boil over high heat. Cook until tender when pierced with a fork, about 15 minutes.
2. Meanwhile, combine butter and garlic in a small saucepan. Cook over medium heat for 2 to 3 minutes, until garlic is fragrant. Remove from heat.
3. When potatoes are done, drain thoroughly, then return potatoes to pot. Place pot over medium heat and pour butter mixture over potatoes. Sprinkle with remaining ingredients, toss gently, then serve.

Quick and Easy Tip
To prepare fresh herbs that have tiny leaves, such as oregano, rosemary, marjoram, and thyme, simply pull the leaves backward off the stem. Chop the leaves to open up the natural oils and flavors of the herb.

Pan-Fried Rosemary New Potatoes

 Serves 4

- ~ **PREP TIME:** 5 minutes
- ~ **COOK TIME:** 22 minutes
- ~ **TOTAL COST:** $4.55
- ~ **CALORIES:** 189
- ~ **FAT:** 3 g
- ~ **CARBOHYDRATES:** 18 g
- ~ **PROTEIN:** 2 g
- ~ **CHOLESTEROL:** 0 mg
- ~ **SODIUM:** 201 mg

1 pound golf-ball–size red-skinned new potatoes
2 tablespoons extra-virgin olive oil
3 sprigs fresh rosemary
Sea salt and freshly ground black pepper

These potatoes tastes great baked, as well. To bake, cut into quarters and then toss with ingredients. Bake until tender, about 25 minutes.

1. Heat oven to 375°F. Slice the potatoes into ½-inch-thick rounds, and boil them in lightly salted water until crisp-tender, about 7 minutes. Drain well, and dry very well with a towel.
2. Heat the olive oil in a large, heavy, ovensafe skillet until it shimmers but does not smoke. Add the rosemary sprigs (they should sizzle), and then slip in the potatoes. Cook without disturbing for 5 minutes. Once potatoes have browned lightly on the first side, turn them over and put the pan in the oven. Cook 10 minutes. Transfer potatoes to a serving platter, season with salt and pepper, and garnish with additional rosemary sprigs.

Garlic Mashed Potatoes

 Serves 6

- ~ **PREP TIME:** 8 minutes
- ~ **COOK TIME:** 30 minutes
- ~ **TOTAL COST:** $6.13
- ~ **CALORIES:** 205
- ~ **FAT:** 2 g
- ~ **CARBOHYDRATES:** 24 g
- ~ **PROTEIN:** 3 g
- ~ **CHOLESTEROL:** 10 mg
- ~ **SODIUM:** 122 mg

3 heads garlic, top chopped, peel left on
2 pounds potatoes, peeled and chopped into 2-inch pieces
8 tablespoons butter
½ cup low-fat milk
1½ teaspoons salt
White pepper (optional)

Everyone loves garlic mashed potatoes. The secret, however, is to roast the garlic first. Raw garlic flavor is very pungent and may overpower your potatoes otherwise.

1. Heat oven to 400°F. Wrap all three garlic heads into a pouch fashioned from aluminum foil, and place in the center of the oven. Roast until garlic is very soft and yields to gentle finger pressure, about 45 minutes. Turn off heat.
2. In large-quart boiler, boil potatoes in lightly salted water until tender, about 20 minutes. Using your hands, squeeze out the roasted garlic. Heat the butter and milk together in a small pan until the butter melts. Drain the potatoes well, then return them to the pot. Mash them with a potato masher or stiff wire whisk. Add the roasted garlic, season with salt and pepper, and add the milk mixture. Mix just enough to incorporate.

Polenta with Fresh Basil and Garlic

 Serves 6

- ~ **PREP TIME:** 10 minutes
- ~ **COOK TIME:** 15 minutes
- ~ **TOTAL COST:** $6.72
- ~ **CALORIES:** 156
- ~ **FAT:** 2 g
- ~ **CARBOHYDRATES:** 32 g
- ~ **PROTEIN:** 4 g
- ~ **CHOLESTEROL:** 5 mg
- ~ **SODIUM:** 222 mg

¼ cup olive oil
2 cloves fresh garlic, chopped
Sea salt and black pepper to taste
2 cups finely ground cornmeal
4 tablespoons unsalted butter, room temperature
1 tablespoon fresh basil, leaves chopped
½ cup Parmesan cheese, grated

Making polenta is easy and it tastes great. Cooked polenta can be shaped into balls, sticks, or patties, and fried in oil. Although this method tastes great, I don't recommend it regularly if you desire to consume fewer calories and fat. You can enjoy it fried on occasion, though. Everything in moderation!

Bring 8½ cups water to a boil in large heavy boiler. Add olive oil, garlic, salt, and pepper. Slowly add cornmeal (polenta) and stir continuously. After all cornmeal has been added, cook and stir over low heat until polenta pulls away from sides of boiler. This should only take a few minutes, as the water is absorbed quickly. Polenta should be thick, smooth, and creamy. Stir in basil, butter, and cheese.

> **Polenta**
> Polenta is a dish made from cornmeal and is popular in many European cuisines, especially northern Italian foods. When I worked at Beccofino Ristorante and Wine Bar in Florence, Italy, we served a similar baked version with sun-dried tomatoes.

Long-Grain Rice with Fresh Thyme

Serves 6

- ~ **PREP TIME:** 5 minutes
- ~ **COOK TIME:** 25 minutes
- ~ **TOTAL COST:** $6.84
- ~ **CALORIES:** 192
- ~ **FAT:** 2 g
- ~ **PROTEIN:** 4 g
- ~ **CHOLESTEROL:** 1 mg
- ~ **SODIUM:** 13 mg

1 tablespoon olive oil

1 yellow onion, chopped

2 ribs celery, chopped

1 clove garlic, minced

1 tablespoon fresh thyme, stems removed, leaves chopped

1 bay leaf

2½ cups water

1 cup uncooked long-grain rice

My nickname for thyme is tedious thyme because it takes a lot of time to remove the leaves from thyme! This recipe requires only a small amount of fresh thyme, thankfully. For those that require more thyme, have your family help you remove the leaves.

In a large saucepan over medium heat, heat oil until warm. Add onion, celery, garlic, and thyme. Sauté for 5 minutes until tender. Add bay leaf and water. Bring to a boil and add the rice. Cover and simmer for 20 minutes or until all the water is absorbed and the rice is tender. Remove the bay leaf and serve.

Quick and Easy Tip

Thyme is one of my favorite herbs and I use it in almost everything I make. I combine it with fresh rosemary on most occasions. Both thyme and rosemary will last up to 3 weeks in your refrigerator. Just keep them wrapped loosely with a damp paper towel.

Couscous with Herbs

 Serves 6

- ~ **PREP TIME:** 3 minutes
- ~ **COOK TIME:** 15 minutes
- ~ **TOTAL COST:** $5.75
- ~ **CALORIES:** 244
- ~ **FAT:** 6 g
- ~ **PROTEIN:** 8 g
- ~ **CHOLESTEROL:** 1 mg
- ~ **SODIUM:** 376 mg

2 tablespoons olive oil
1 yellow onion, finely chopped
2 cups chicken broth
½ teaspoon dried oregano leaves
½ teaspoon dried marjoram leaves
1 cup couscous

If you end up with soggy couscous, don't worry; you can salvage it. Spread it out on parchment-lined baking sheets and dry it out in a 375°F oven for 10 minutes. Couscous is all about the balance of grain versus moisture. If you have too much moisture, just dry it out.

In a large saucepan, heat oil over medium heat. Add onion and cook until tender, about 5 minutes. Add chicken broth and herbs and bring to a boil. Stir in couscous, cover pan, and remove from heat. Let stand for 5 to 10 minutes, until liquid is absorbed. Fluff couscous with fork and serve.

> **Quick and Easy Tip**
> Couscous is actually not a grain. It is ground semolina pasta that is usually precooked. Because the ground pasta is precooked, it absorbs hot liquid extra fast making for super-fast cooking when combined with other ingredients.

Citrus Green Beans

 Serves 4

- ~ **TOTAL COST:** $2.52
- ~ **CALORIES:** 100.17
- ~ **FAT:** 5.07 g
- ~ **PROTEIN:** 2.40 g
- ~ **CHOLESTEROL:** 15.26 mg
- ~ **SODIUM:** 191.76 mg

1 (16-ounce) package frozen cut green beans, thawed
⅔ tablespoons butter
3 cloves garlic, minced
¼ cup orange juice
2 tablespoons lemon juice
¼ teaspoon salt
⅛ teaspoon white pepper

Tender and crisp green beans are perked up with lemon and orange juice in this simple side dish recipe.

1. Drain beans well and dry with paper towel; set aside.
2. In large skillet, melt butter and add garlic. Cook over medium heat until garlic is fragrant, about 2 minutes. Then add green beans; cook and stir for 2–3 minutes or until beans are crisp-tender. Stir in lemon juice, orange juice, orange zest, salt, and pepper, and heat through. Serve immediately.

Sautéed Green Beans and Red Bell Peppers with Fresh Thyme

Serves 6

~ **PREP TIME:** 6 minutes
~ **COOK TIME:** 9 to 10 minutes
~ **TOTAL COST:** $4.18
~ **CALORIES:** 59
~ **FAT:** 4 g
~ **PROTEIN:** 4 g
~ **CHOLESTEROL:** 1 mg
~ **SODIUM:** 18 mg

2 tablespoons olive oil
1 onion, finely chopped
3 cups frozen green beans
1 red bell pepper, seeded and cut into strips
Juice of ½ lemon
Sea salt and black pepper to taste
1 teaspoon fresh thyme leaves, stems removed, leaves chopped

Nutritionists teach that a colorful plate is a healthy plate, and this recipe helps prove that theory. Enjoy good nutrition and color with this easy-to-follow recipe.

In heavy saucepan, heat oil over medium heat. Add onion and cook until onion is tender, about 5 minutes, stirring occasionally. Add green beans and sauté for about 1 minute. Add bell pepper, lemon juice, salt, pepper, and thyme leaves. Stir occasionally while cooking about 3 minutes, or until peppers are tender and beans are heated through.

Quick and Easy Tip
Use fresh or frozen vegetables to make this simple yet flavorful dish.

Sautéed Green Beans with Garlic

Serves 6

~ **PREP TIME:** 5 minutes
~ **COOK TIME:** 13 minutes
~ **TOTAL COST:** $4.68
~ **CALORIES:** 92
~ **FAT:** 8 g
~ **PROTEIN:** 4 g
~ **CHOLESTEROL:** 8 mg
~ **SODIUM:** 21 mg

4 cups water
1 pound green beans, ends trimmed, beans washed and dried
1 tablespoon olive oil
1 tablespoon butter
6 cloves garlic, chopped
1 shallot, chopped
Sea salt and pepper to taste

Garlic is good for your immune system but not for your breath. If you find yourself consuming lots of fresh garlic, make sure you have equal amounts of fresh parsley around to freshen your breath.

1. In a large saucepan over medium-high heat, add water and bring to a boil. Add green beans and lower heat to simmer. Simmer for 7 minutes, until beans are tender but still crisp.
2. Meanwhile, in a separate saucepan, combine oil, butter, garlic, and shallots. Heat over medium-high heat and cook until fragrant, about 2 minutes. Drain beans well and add to garlic mixture. Season with salt and pepper. Cook an additional 4 minutes. Serve.

Green Beans with Blue Cheese and Walnuts

 Serves 4

~ **PREP TIME:** 4 minutes
~ **COOK TIME:** 6 minutes
~ **TOTAL COST:** $7.00
~ **CALORIES:** 103
~ **FAT:** 2 g
~ **PROTEIN:** 4 g
~ **CHOLESTEROL:** 6 mg
~ **SODIUM:** 129 mg

1 pound green beans, ends trimmed, cut into 2-inch pieces
4 slices bacon
4 ounces blue cheese, crumbled
¼ cup walnut pieces, toasted

Try adding a squeeze of lemon to enhance the already delicious flavors.

1. Bring medium-sized saucepan of salted water to a boil. Add the beans and cook until crisp and tender, about 4 minutes. drain and set aside.
2. Cook until bacon is crisp, drain on paper towels. To assemble, place beans on serving platter and sprinkle with a few bacon pieces and cheese, then add walnuts on top.

Quick and Easy Tip
For extra flavor, after draining the beans, chop the bacon and then sauté the beans with the bacon. Yum!

Sautéed Sugar Snap Peas

 Serves 6

~ **PREP TIME:** 5 minutes
~ **COOK TIME:** 8 minutes
~ **TOTAL COST:** $4.24
~ **CALORIES:** 56
~ **FAT:** 4 g
~ **PROTEIN:** 2 g
~ **CHOLESTEROL:** 0 mg
~ **SODIUM:** 8 mg

3 cups sugar snap peas
2 tablespoons olive oil
½ teaspoon dried marjoram leaves
½ teaspoon garlic salt
½ teaspoon black pepper

Sugar snap peas are very sweet peas that are completely edible, pod included. Look for bright green peas with no dark or light spots, and select the pods that are plump and crisp. Pay attention not to cook them too long; 2 minutes in boiling water is plenty of time!

Preheat oven to 425°F. Place peas (in pods) on parchment-lined baking sheet. Sprinkle with remaining ingredients. Mix together with your hands until peas are well coated. Place in oven and roast for 6 minutes, until peas begin to brown a little and are tender but crisp.

Quick and Easy Tip
Use these delicious, naturally sweet peas in any stir-fry recipe, Asian or non-Asian.

Broccoli with Sesame Seeds

 Serves 5

- ~ **PREP TIME:** 2 minutes
- ~ **COOK TIME:** 15 minutes
- ~ **TOTAL COST:** $3.98
- ~ **CALORIES:** 30
- ~ **FAT:** 5 g
- ~ **PROTEIN:** 2 g
- ~ **CHOLESTEROL:** 3 mg
- ~ **SODIUM:** 8 mg

4 cups water
1 head broccoli, stems chopped, florets only
2 tablespoons olive oil
1 tablespoon butter
1 yellow onion, chopped
3 cloves garlic, chopped
2 tablespoons toasted sesame seeds

Bring out the color by boiling the broccoli in water for about 1 minute. Not only does this bring out the color, it makes the broccoli tender but not mushy. Easy!

1. In a large saucepan over medium-high heat, add water and bring to a boil. Once boiling, reduce heat to simmer, add broccoli, and simmer for 6 minutes.
2. Meanwhile, place olive oil and butter in a separate saucepan over medium heat. Add onion and garlic. Cook and stir for 5 minutes. Drain broccoli and add to onion and garlic mixture. Sprinkle with sesame seeds, toss to coat, and serve.

Quick and Easy Tip
In place of sesame seeds, use pine nuts, cashews, or almonds for an added crunch and extra protein.

Oven-Roasted Beets

 Serves 5

- ~ **PREP TIME:** 5 minutes
- ~ **COOK TIME:** 25 minutes
- ~ **TOTAL COST:** $5.20
- ~ **CALORIES:** 137
- ~ **FAT:** 8 g
- ~ **PROTEIN:** 3 g
- ~ **CHOLESTEROL:** 8 mg
- ~ **SODIUM:** 108 mg

1 pound baby beets
2 tablespoons olive oil
Sea salt and pepper to taste
3 tablespoons butter
1 tablespoon fresh oregano leaves

Beets are a root vegetable not commonly thought of for everyday meals. When most people think of beets, they think of canned beets in vinegar. However, beets can be truly flavorful if grilled, baked, and tossed with fresh herbs, olive oil, or cheese.

Preheat oven to 400°F. Cut off beet tops and root, if attached. Scrub beets and then cut in half. Place beets in a large roasting pan, drizzle with olive oil, and sprinkle with salt and pepper. Toss to coat. Place in oven and roast for 25 minutes or until beets are tender when pierced with a fork. Place in serving bowl and toss with butter and oregano.

Quick and Easy Tip
You can find baby beets in most grocery stores and at farmer's markets. Look for red and white striped candy-cane beets, golden, or white beets.

Sautéed Vegetables with Quinoa

 Serves 6

- ~ **PREP TIME:** 10 minutes
- ~ **COOK TIME:** 32 minutes
- ~ **TOTAL COST:** $5.36
- ~ **CALORIES:** 318
- ~ **FAT:** 9 g
- ~ **CARBOHYDRATES:** 31 g
- ~ **PROTEIN:** 6 g
- ~ **CHOLESTEROL:** 1 mg
- ~ **SODIUM:** 258 mg

1 tablespoon olive oil
1 yellow squash, chopped
1 zucchini squash, chopped
1 eggplant, chopped
4 cloves garlic, chopped
¾ cup quinoa
2 ½ cups vegetable broth
½ tablespoon tarragon, leaves chopped
Black pepper to taste
1 teaspoon capers, smashed

Healthy grains don't have to be boring and this recipe proves just that! Tarragon has a slightly licorice flavor, so use basil if you prefer a lighter flavor.

Heat the oil to medium temperature in a medium-size saucepan, then add the vegetables and garlic; sauté for 3 minutes. Add the quinoa, and stir for 1 minute. Add the stock and simmer for approximately 30 minutes with lid slightly ajar, until the quinoa is thoroughly cooked. Remove from heat and add the tarragon, black pepper, and capers.

Sweet Peas with Fresh Mint Leaves

 Serves 4

- ~ **PREP TIME:** 5 minutes
- ~ **COOK TIME:** 5 minutes
- ~ **TOTAL COST:** $3.65
- ~ **CALORIES:** 102
- ~ **FAT:** 1 g
- ~ **CARBOHYDRATES:** 29 g
- ~ **PROTEIN:** 2 g
- ~ **CHOLESTEROL:** 24 mg
- ~ **SODIUM:** 35 mg

2 cups shelled fresh peas (about 2 pounds unshelled)
½ teaspoon sugar
2 tablespoons butter
Salt and pepper to taste
3 tablespoons fresh mint leaves, chopped

Shelling peas may sound like a time-consuming task but it really is easier than you think. If you are cooking for lots of people, have a friend help you or teach your kids how to do it. They will learn about fresh vegetables and help you in the process!

Simmer the peas and sugar until bright green and tender, about 5 minutes; drain. Toss peas with butter, salt, pepper, and mint.

Acorn Squash with Tarragon

 Serves 4

- ~ **PREP TIME:** 5 minutes
- ~ **COOK TIME:** 20 minutes
- ~ **TOTAL COST:** $4.08
- ~ **CALORIES:** 102
- ~ **FAT:** 1 g
- ~ **PROTEIN:** 2 g
- ~ **CHOLESTEROL:** 24 mg
- ~ **SODIUM:** 35 mg

1 acorn squash
2 tablespoons water
2 tablespoons butter, unsalted
2 tablespoons brown sugar
1 tablespoon honey
½ teaspoon dried tarragon leaves
Sea salt and white pepper to taste

Acorn squash is the perfect squash to serve as a side dish or an entrée. It is very filling, flavorful, and packed full of nutrients. A very hard squash, acorn squash requires quite a bit of baking time to soften. Bake ahead and reheat for serving the next day.

1. Cut squash in half lengthwise, then cut in half again crosswise. Remove seeds and fibers from center. Place the squash halves, cut side down, on work surface and cut crosswise into 1-inch pieces. Place skin side down, in microwave safe dish. Sprinkle with 2 table-spoons water. Cover with plastic wrap, vent one corner, and micro-wave on high for 12 to 15 minutes, until flesh is tender when tested with fork. Uncover and drain. Set aside. to reheat.
2. Separately, in a small boiler, combine remaining ingredients and heat over medium heat, stirring until smooth. Keep warm over low heat. To serve, place acorn squash half on plate and pour sauce over.

> **Quick and Easy Tip**
> Acorn squash is a winter squash that has a hard rind that is only edible after cooking.

Braised Swiss Chard

Serves 4

- ~ **PREP TIME:** 8 minutes
- ~ **COOK TIME:** 15 minutes
- ~ **TOTAL COST:** $5.53
- ~ **CALORIES:** 62
- ~ **FAT:** 1 g
- ~ **CARBOHYDRATES:** 2 g
- ~ **PROTEIN:** 2 g
- ~ **CHOLESTEROL:** 2 mg
- ~ **SODIUM:** 25 mg

1 cup vegetable broth
1 large bunch red or green Swiss chard, stems chopped, leaves cut into bite-size pieces
Sea salt and black pepper to taste
1 tablespoon olive oil
2 medium shallots, finely chopped
1 tablespoon unsalted butter
Lemon wedges

Another culinary curveball for most people, swiss chard can be enjoyed braised, as here, sautéed, or even grilled. Don't be afraid to experiment with it to discover how you like it best.

1. In large skillet, bring the broth to a boil; add the chard stem pieces. Season with salt and pepper; cook until tender, about 6 minutes. Transfer them to a bowl or plate, reserving their cooking liquid. Wipe out the skillet.
2. Return the skillet to medium heat. Add olive oil and shallots. Cook 1 minute until they sizzle and soften slightly. Add the chard leaves, and cook only until they wilt, about 5 minutes. Add back the stems, plus 2 tablespoons of their cooking liquid. Bring to a simmer, and swirl in the butter. Taste for seasoning. Serve with lemon wedges.

Swiss Chard

Swiss chard is a leafy vegetable from the same species as beets. It is one of the healthiest foods you can eat as it is packed full of vitamins and minerals. It is naturally low in calories, fat, and carbs.

Buttered Brussels Sprouts with Nutmeg

 Serves 4

- ~ **PREP TIME:** 2 minutes
- ~ **COOK TIME:** 15 minutes
- ~ **TOTAL COST:** $3.12
- ~ **CALORIES:** 30
- ~ **FAT:** 1 g
- ~ **CARBOHYDRATES:** 9 g
- ~ **PROTEIN:** 3 g
- ~ **CHOLESTEROL:** 20 mg
- ~ **SODIUM:** 88 mg

1 pint Brussels sprouts
½ stick unsalted butter
Salt and white pepper
Pinch nutmeg
Lemon wedges (optional)

If cooked properly, Brussels sprouts taste remarkably good and they are so good for you!

1. Remove outer leaves from sprouts, and trim the stems so that they're flush with the sprout bottoms. Halve the sprouts by cutting through the stem end. Don't worry about loose leaves— include them.
2. Boil in small batches, in 4 quarts of well-salted, rapidly boiling water for 10 minutes. Drain well.
3. In a medium saucepan over medium heat, melt the butter and add the cooked sprouts, tossing with the salt, pepper, and nutmeg to coat. Sauté for about 5 minutes. Serve with lemon wedges.

Grilled Radicchio

 Serves 4

- ~ **PREP TIME:** 5 minutes
- ~ **COOK TIME:** 4 minutes
- ~ **TOTAL COST:** $4.89
- ~ **CALORIES:** 9
- ~ **FAT:** 0 g
- ~ **CARBOHYDRATES:** 2 g
- ~ **PROTEIN:** 1 g
- ~ **CHOLESTEROL:** 0 mg
- ~ **SODIUM:** 9 mg

4 heads radicchio
1 tablespoon extra-virgin olive oil
1 lemon, halved
Sea salt and black pepper to taste

Radicchio has brightly colored red leaves that have a natural white vein to them. Add to other grilled vegetables or enjoy fresh in salads. Grilled radicchio would also be a nice topping to burgers, which are in the next chapter.

1. Quarter the radicchio heads through the root end. In a mixing bowl, drizzle the olive oil over the pieces, squeeze on the lemon juice, and season with salt and pepper; toss to coat.
2. Heat a grill or stovetop grill pan to medium heat. Lay the radicchio, cut side down, across the grill. Cook until wilting is visible from the sides, only about 2 minutes. Turn and cook for 1 or 2 minutes more, pulling it from the grill before it goes completely limp. Serve with extra lemon wedges on the side.

Radicchio
Radicchio is a leafy vegetable also known as Italian chicory. It has a spicy bitter taste that mellows when grilled. As with so many other foods, balsamic vinegar pairs nicely with radicchio.

Rapini with Garlic

Serves 4

- ~ **PREP TIME:** 5 minutes
- ~ **COOK TIME:** 9 minutes
- ~ **TOTAL COST:** $5.23
- ~ **CALORIES:** 59
- ~ **FAT:** 1 g
- ~ **CARBOHYDRATES:** 3 g
- ~ **PROTEIN:** 2 g
- ~ **CHOLESTEROL:** 0 mg
- ~ **SODIUM:** 12 mg

1 pound rapini, bottoms trimmed
2 tablespoons olive oil
3 cloves garlic, finely chopped
Pinch crushed red pepper flakes
Sea salt and black pepper to taste
Lemon wedges

Sauté yellow onion slices and mushrooms and add to the rapini for another tasty side dish.

1. Fill large-quart boiler ¾ with water; add 1 table-spoon salt and bring to a boil. Add rapini and boil for 3 minutes. Drain and transfer to ice bath to stop the cooking process. Drain well and set aside.
2. In large saucepan over medium heat, heat olive oil. Add the garlic and red pepper flakes and sauté for 2 minutes. Add all of the rapini at once; toss to coat. Season well with salt and pepper. When the rapini is hot, serve with lemon wedges on the side.

Rapini
A relative of the turnip family, rapini is also known as broccoli raab (or rabe). It is commonly used in Chinese, Italian, and Portuguese cooking and is high in vitamins A and C and iron.

Cumin-Roasted Butternut Squash

Serves 8

- ~ **PREP TIME:** 6 minutes
- ~ **COOK TIME:** 40 minutes
- ~ **TOTAL COST:** $5.69
- ~ **CALORIES:** 103
- ~ **FAT:** 1 g
- ~ **CARBOHYDRATES:** 9 g
- ~ **PROTEIN:** 2 g
- ~ **CHOLESTEROL:** 0 mg
- ~ **SODIUM:** 10 mg

1 medium butternut squash (2–3 pounds)
2 tablespoons ground cumin
2 tablespoons olive oil
Sea salt and black pepper to taste
1 tablespoon fresh Italian flat-leaf parsley, chopped

Butternut squash is also delicious when baked with honey, cinnamon, and butter.

1. Preheat oven to 375°F. Cut the butternut squash in two, crosswise, just above the bulbous bottom. Place the cut side of the cylindrical barrel down on a cutting board and peel it with a knife or potato peeler, removing all rind. Repeat with the bottom part, then cut bottom in half and remove seeds.
2. Dice squash into 1-inch chunks. In a large mixing bowl, toss squash with cumin, oil, salt, and pepper.
3. Spread into a single layer on a parchment-lined baking sheet. Bake (or roast) in oven for 40 minutes, turning after 25 minutes, until browned and tender. Serve sprinkled with chopped parsley.

Chinese String Beans

Serves 4

- ~ **PREP TIME:** 10 minutes
- ~ **COOK TIME:** 15 to 20 minutes
- ~ **TOTAL COST:** $5.83
- ~ **CALORIES:** 110
- ~ **FAT:** 5 g
- ~ **CARBOHYDRATES:** 8 g
- ~ **PROTEIN:** 3 g
- ~ **CHOLESTEROL:** 3 mg
- ~ **SODIUM:** 191 mg

Oil for deep-frying
1 pound fresh green beans, stem ends trimmed
2 tablespoons peanut oil
½ cup scallions, chopped
1 (1-inch) piece fresh ginger, peeled and finely chopped
3 cloves garlic, chopped
1 teaspoon sugar
1 teaspoon white vinegar
Sea salt to taste
Asian sesame oil

Frying green beans is easy. Just be sure they are completely dried before placing them in the hot oil or the oil will spatter on you while frying and you might get burned. Ouch!

1. In large skillet, heat 2 inches of oil until hot but not smoking. Carefully fry the green beans in 4 small batches. They will shrivel as they cook—they take about 5 minutes per batch.
2. In a separate skillet, heat the peanut oil. Add the scallions, ginger, garlic, sugar, and vinegar. Cook 1 minute, until the garlic turns white. Add the green beans; toss to coat. Season with salt and sesame oil.

Cauliflower with Red and Orange Bell Peppers

 Serves 6

- ~ **PREP TIME:** 7 minutes
- ~ **COOK TIME:** 17 minutes
- ~ **TOTAL COST:** $6.86
- ~ **CALORIES:** 91
- ~ **FAT:** 2 g
- ~ **PROTEIN:** 2 g
- ~ **CHOLESTEROL:** 5 mg
- ~ **SODIUM:** 88 mg

3 tablespoons olive oil
1 red onion, chopped
½ teaspoon turmeric
3 cups cauliflower florets
2 green chili peppers, seeded and chopped
1 each red and orange bell pepper, seeded and sliced into ¼-inch strips
Sea salt and black pepper to taste

Turmeric provides intense color and subtle flavor to this dish and is traditional to Indian cuisine.

Heat oil on nonstick skillet over medium-high heat. Add red onion and cook until soft, about 3 minutes. Add turmeric, stir and cook for 1 minute. Add the cauliflower and reduce heat to medium, cook, stirring occasionally, for about 8 minutes. Add the chili and bell peppers, cook about 5 minutes, until peppers are tender. Season with salt and pepper to taste. Serve hot.

Quick and Easy Tip
Chili peppers add great flavor to recipes and are very affordable. Just be sure to seed them while wearing gloves so the seeds don't burn your hands.

Creamed Spinach with Nutmeg

 Serves 4

- ~ **PREP TIME:** 5 minutes
- ~ **COOK TIME:** 9 minutes
- ~ **TOTAL COST:** $4.20
- ~ **CALORIES:** 166
- ~ **FAT:** 10 g
- ~ **PROTEIN:** 16 g
- ~ **CHOLESTEROL:** 35 mg
- ~ **SODIUM:** 80 mg

2 tablespoons butter, unsalted
1 pound baby spinach leaves
1 tablespoon water
Sea salt and black pepper to taste
2 tablespoons plain flour
½ cup evaporated milk
Pinch ground nutmeg

Creamed spinach is great when paired with a juicy steak.

1. Melt butter in a medium nonstick skillet over medium-high heat. Tip skillet to coat bottom with butter. Reduce heat to medium and add spinach leaves. Add water and stir. Cook until leaves start to wilt, about 3 minutes. Season with salt and pepper.
2. Sprinkle flour over spinach and stir to evenly distribute. Add evaporated milk and nutmeg, and stir. Cook, uncovered, until sauce starts to thicken, about 5 minutes. Serve hot.

Quick and Easy Tip
As an alternative to evaporated milk, substitute sour cream. It adds flavor and creaminess, and you can use it in other recipes more easily than evaporated milk.

Brussels Sprouts with Roasted Peanuts

 Serves 4

- ~ **PREP TIME:** 5 minutes
- ~ **COOK TIME:** 15 minutes
- ~ **TOTAL COST:** $5.42
- ~ **CALORIES:** 75
- ~ **FAT:** 1 g
- ~ **PROTEIN:** 5 g
- ~ **CHOLESTEROL:** 4 mg
- ~ **SODIUM:** 89 mg

2 cups quartered Brussels sprouts, ends trimmed
¼ cup coarsely chopped unsalted dry roasted peanuts
1 tablespoon olive oil
Sea salt and black pepper to taste

Lots of people cringe when they hear you are serving Brussels sprouts; however, there are many ways to make people fall in love with them. Use this recipe as a base and then try alternative ingredients such as balsamic vinegar and honey.

1. Add 1 inch of salted water to a medium-sized saucepan fitted with a vegetable steamer. Bring to a boil and add the Brussels sprouts. Cover and cook over medium heat until crisp and tender, about 7 minutes. Set aside.
2. Add peanuts to a large nonstick skillet. Toast the nuts over medium heat, tossing frequently, about 3 minutes. Add the sprouts, oil, salt, and pepper. Sauté until heated through, about 5 minutes. Taste and adjust the seasoning as desired and serve.

Quick and Easy Tip
Brussels sprouts are best when tender but not mushy. No matter how you cook them—baked, sautéed, steamed, or boiled,—don't overcook them.

Roasted Scalloped Corn

Serves 6

~ **TOTAL COST:** $4.25

~ **CALORIES:** 295.06

~ **FAT:** 15.24 g

~ **PROTEIN:** 10.55 g

~ **CHOLESTEROL:** 98.44 mg

~ **SODIUM:** 444.13 mg

1 (16-ounce) package frozen corn, thawed

2 tablespoons olive oil, divided

1 tablespoon butter

1 onion, finely chopped

2 cloves garlic, minced

2 slices Hearty White Bread (Chapter 3), toasted

1 (15-ounce) can creamed corn

2 eggs, beaten

½ teaspoon salt

⅛ teaspoon pepper

¾ cup shredded Cheddar cheese

¼ cup grated Parmesan cheese

Scalloped corn is an old-fashioned recipe that is excellent served with ham or pork. Add a green salad for a nice dinner.

1. Preheat oven to 425°F. Spray a 9-inch casserole dish with nonstick cooking spray and set aside. Drain thawed corn and place on cookie sheet. Drizzle with 1 tablespoon olive oil and toss to coat. Roast for 10–20 minutes or until corn just starts to turn color. Remove from oven and set aside. Reduce oven temperature to 350°F.
2. In large saucepan, heat remaining 1 tablespoon olive oil with butter over medium heat. Add onion and garlic; cook and stir until tender, about 5 minutes. Remove from heat and set aside.
3. Crumble the toasted bread to make fine crumbs; reserve ¼ cup. Stir crumbs into onion mixture along with roasted corn and creamed corn; mix well. Add eggs, salt, and pepper, beating well to combine. Stir in Cheddar cheese.
4. Pour into prepared casserole dish. In small bowl, combine reserved crumbs with the Parmesan cheese and sprinkle over the top of the corn mixture. Bake for 20–30 minutes or until casserole is set and beginning to brown.

Scalloped Vegetables

Scalloped means to cook in a cream sauce or a white sauce. You can achieve the same effect without making a white sauce; just beat together eggs and milk and stir that into cooked vegetables, then pour into a casserole and bake. This is a great way to turn leftover vegetables into another dish.

Hawaiian Carrots

Serves 6

~ **TOTAL COST:** $3.40
~ **CALORIES:** 166.26
~ **FAT:** 9.94 g
~ **PROTEIN:** 1.30 g
~ **CHOLESTEROL:** 20.35 mg
~ **SODIUM:** 303.31 mg

1 (16-ounce) package large carrots
2 tablespoons butter
1 onion, finely chopped
1 (8-ounce) can pineapple tidbits
2 tablespoons cornstarch
1 tablespoon lemon juice
2 tablespoons butter
½ teaspoon salt
½ cup toasted coconut

The natural sweetness of carrots is complemented by sweet and tart pineapple and lemon juice in this fresh side dish recipe.

1. Peel and slice carrots and place in microwave-safe 2 quart dish along with 1 cup water. Cover and microwave for 4–6 minutes on high power, stirring once during cooking, until tender. Set aside.
2. In medium saucepan, combine butter and onion; cook and stir over medium heat until crisp tender, about 4 minutes. Drain pineapple, reserving juice. Add pineapple and carrots to saucepan and cook over medium heat for 3 minutes. Stir in reserved pineapple juice, cornstarch, lemon juice, butter, and salt; bring to a simmer. Simmer for 5 minutes, stirring frequently, until thickened. Sprinkle with coconut and serve.

Roasted Cauliflower Crunch

Serves 6

~ **TOTAL COST:** $4.73
~ **CALORIES:** 200.05
~ **FAT:** 14.91 g
~ **PROTEIN:** 6.29 g
~ **CHOLESTEROL:** 27.53 mg
~ **SODIUM:** 252.95 mg

1 head cauliflower
¼ cup dried bread crumbs
¼ cup ground walnuts
3 tablespoons grated Parmesan cheese
½ teaspoon dried oregano leaves
½ teaspoon seasoned salt
⅛ teaspoon pepper
⅓ cup butter, melted

Roasting cauliflower makes it tender and creamy. The crisp coating is a nice contrast.

1. Preheat oven to 400°F. Remove leaves from cauliflower and cut into individual florets. On shallow plate, combine bread crumbs, walnuts, cheese, oregano, salt, and pepper and mix well. Dip cauliflower florets into melted butter, then roll in bread crumb mixture to coat.
2. Arrange in single layer on 15" × 10" jelly roll pan. Roast for 15–20 minutes or until cauliflower is tender and coating is browned.

About Dried Bread Crumbs

Purchased bread crumbs are available in plain and Italian flavored versions. To make your own; simply dry bread in a 300°F oven for 15–25 minutes, then cool and grind in a food processor. Store covered in an air-tight for up to 1 week, or freeze up to 3 months.

Black Beans and Corn

> Serves 6

~ **TOTAL COST:** $3.60
~ **CALORIES:** 211.05
~ **FAT:** 4.71 g
~ **PROTEIN:** 7.38 g
~ **CHOLESTEROL:** 10.18 mg
~ **SODIUM:** 791.48 mg

2 tablespoons butter or bacon grease
1 onion, chopped
1 (15-ounce) can black beans, rinsed
1 (15-ounce) can corn, drained
1 (15-ounce) can creamed corn
¼ teaspoon salt
Dash cayenne pepper
2 tablespoons chopped parsley

This simple side dish is excellent served with grilled hamburgers. It can also be part of a vegetarian lunch, as a light main dish.

1. In heavy skillet, melt butter and cook onion over medium heat until crisp-tender, about 4 minutes.
2. Rinse and drain black beans and add to skillet along with drained corn, undrained creamed corn, salt, and pepper.
3. Cover and bring to a simmer; simmer for 4–5 minutes until thoroughly heated. Stir in cilantro, and parsley and serve.

Green Rice Bake

> Serves 6

~ **TOTAL COST:** $4.40
~ **CALORIES:** 251.43
~ **FAT:** 13.05 g
~ **PROTEIN:** 12.89 g
~ **CHOLESTEROL:** 104.02 mg
~ **SODIUM:** 278.87 mg

2 tablespoons butter
1 onion, chopped
2 cloves garlic, minced
1 cup white long-grain rice
2 cups vegetable broth
½ cup chopped parsley
5 tablespoons grated Parmesan cheese
1 cup grated Swiss cheese
½ teaspoon dried basil leaves
½ teaspoon dried thyme leaves
½ cup milk
2 eggs, beaten

This creamy casserole turns rice into an elegant side dish. Serve it with Crispy Chicken Patties (Chapter 7) and some fresh fruit

1. Preheat oven to 375°F. In large oven proof saucepan, melt butter over medium heat. Add onion and garlic; cook and stir until crisp tender, about 4 minutes. Stir in rice; cook and stir for 2 minutes. Add vegetable broth; bring to a simmer, cover, and simmer for 15 minutes.
2. Stir in parsley, bell pepper, cheeses, and seasonings and mix well. Stir in milk and eggs. Bake, uncovered, for 40–50 minutes or until casserole is set and top begins to brown.

Rice with Salsa and Black Beans

 Serves 6

- ~ **PREP TIME:** 12 minutes
- ~ **COOK TIME:** 15 minutes
- ~ **TOTAL COST:** $5.60
- ~ **CALORIES:** 204
- ~ **FAT:** 5 g
- ~ **PROTEIN:** 12 g
- ~ **CHOLESTEROL:** 3 mg
- ~ **SODIUM:** 466 mg

1 tablespoon olive oil
½ yellow onion, diced
2 cloves garlic, minced
1 strip bacon, chopped
2 (16-ounce) cans black beans, undrained
½ cup picante salsa
Sea salt and black pepper to taste
4 cups cooked long-grain white rice

Rice is a good base as a side dish as you can enjoy it as is with olive oil or butter, or add fresh herbs, asparagus, green beans, red bell peppers, mushrooms, or your favorite ingredients.

In a large saucepan over medium heat, heat oil and add onions. Sauté (cook) until tender, about 5 minutes. Add garlic and bacon and cook until bacon is cooked but not crisp, about 3 minutes. Stir in the beans and salsa. Mix well and simmer about 10 minutes. Cover, stirring occasionally. Add salt and pepper to taste. Serve over rice in a bowl.

> **Quick and Easy Tip**
> Add some fresh cilantro for extra flavor and color.

Italian Risi e Bisi with Parmesan

 Serves 6

- ~ **PREP TIME:** 5 minutes
- ~ **COOK TIME:** 25 minutes
- ~ **TOTAL COST:** $5.75
- ~ **CALORIES:** 192
- ~ **FAT:** 2 g
- ~ **PROTEIN:** 4 g
- ~ **CHOLESTEROL:** 2 mg
- ~ **SODIUM:** 341 mg

2 tablespoons olive oil
1 onion, finely chopped
1½ cups long-grain white rice
2 (10-ounce) cans chicken broth
½ cup water
1 cup frozen peas
½ cup Parmesan cheese, grated

Risi e bisi, or rice and peas, is a popular Italian dish. Stick to the simplicity of this dish rather than adding ingredients and trying to change it.

1. In heavy saucepan, heat olive oil over medium heat. Add onion; cook and stir until onion is tender, about 5 minutes. Add rice; stir to combine and cook about 2 minutes. Add chicken broth and water and bring to a boil. Cover pan, reduce heat, and simmer for an additional 15 minutes, until rice is almost tender.
2. Add peas, cover, and cook over medium-low heat until peas are hot and rice is tender, about 3 to 4 minutes. Stir in cheese and serve.

Lemon Pesto Pilaf

Serves 4

~ **TOTAL COST:** $2.03
~ **CALORIES:** 186.94
~ **FAT:** 7.05 g
~ **PROTEIN:** 5.80 g
~ **CHOLESTEROL:** 11.78 mg
~ **SODIUM:** 281.72 mg

1 tablespoon butter
1 cup long-grain white rice
2 cups Chicken Stock (Chapter 6) or water
2 tablespoons lemon juice
½ teaspoon lemon zest, if desired
¼ cup Spinach Pesto (Chapter 2)

This simple pilaf has so much flavor and the most beautiful color. You could use prepared pesto from the supermarket if you'd like, for 50 cents more.

1. In heavy saucepan, melt butter over medium heat. Add onion; cook and stir until tender, about 5 minutes. Add rice; cook and stir for 3–4 minutes or until rice is opaque.
2. Add Stock or water, stir well, cover, bring to a simmer, and reduce heat to low. Simmer for 15–20 minutes, until rice is tender. Stir in juice, zest, and pesto; remove from heat and cover; let stand for 3–4 minutes. Fluff with fork and serve.

Sautéed Corn

Serves 6

~ **TOTAL COST:** $2.53
~ **CALORIES:** 140.12
~ **FAT:** 8.27 g
~ **PROTEIN:** 2.49 g
~ **CHOLESTEROL:** 20.35 mg
~ **SODIUM:** 250.99 mg

1 (16-ounce) package frozen corn, thawed
¼ cup butter
1 onion, chopped
½ teaspoon salt
⅛ teaspoon white pepper
½ teaspoon dried basil leaves

Corn is a staple for busy moms; almost every child will eat it. Preparing it this way adds extra flavor and should coax even picky eaters to try some.

Drain corn well. In medium saucepan, melt butter over medium heat. Add onion; cook and stir until tender, about 5 minutes. Add corn; cook and stir for 4–6 minutes or until corn is hot and tender. Sprinkle with salt, pepper, and basil and serve.

Thawing Frozen Vegetables
When thawing frozen vegetables it's best to do it gently. One of the fastest ways that preserves the color and texture is to open the package and place the vegetables in a colander. Run cool water over the vegetables until they thaw. Be sure to drain the vegetables well before adding them to the recipe.

Spanish Rice

Serves 6

- ~ **TOTAL COST:** $3.11
- ~ **CALORIES:** 167.92
- ~ **FAT:** 5.14 g
- ~ **PROTEIN:** 3.35 g
- ~ **CHOLESTEROL:** 0.0 mg
- ~ **SODIUM:** 473.40 mg

2 tablespoons vegetable oil
1 onion, chopped
3 cloves garlic, minced
1 jalapeño pepper, minced
1½ cups long-grain white rice
2½ cups water
1 (14-ounce) can diced tomatoes, undrained
1 tablespoon chili powder
½ teaspoon cumin
½ teaspoon salt
Dash pepper

Rice cooked with onions, garlic, peppers, and tomatoes is a fabulous side dish—you can serve it with everything from grilled steaks to chicken soup.

1. In large saucepan, heat vegetable oil over medium heat and cook onion, garlic, and pepper until crisp-tender. Add rice; cook and stir for 5–8 minutes until rice becomes opaque.
2. Stir in remaining ingredients and bring to a boil. Cover, reduce heat, and simmer for 20–30 minutes or until rice is tender. Let stand off heat for 5 minutes. Fluff with fork and serve.

Steamed Asparagus and Carrots with Lemon

Serves 6

- ~ **PREP TIME:** 2 minutes
- ~ **COOK TIME:** 20 minutes
- ~ **TOTAL COST:** $6.78
- ~ **CALORIES:** 74
- ~ **FAT:** 0 g
- ~ **PROTEIN:** 4 g
- ~ **CHOLESTEROL:** 0 mg
- ~ **SODIUM:** 194 mg

½ pound baby carrots, rinsed
1 (8-ounce) package frozen asparagus spears
2 tablespoons lemon juice
1 teaspoon lemon pepper
Pinch sea salt (optional)

Steaming is a great way to cook vegetables as it brings out their color and maintains their nutrients. Plus, it's easy on clean up, which is perhaps the best thing of all!

1. Place carrots in a steamer basket above boiling water. Cover and steam about 15 minutes or till crisp tender. Rinse the carrots in cold water; drain.
2. Meanwhile, cook the frozen asparagus spears according to package directions. Rinse the asparagus in cold water; drain. Place both carrots and asparagus in serving bowl and drizzle with lemon juice and pepper; add salt if desired. Cover and chill until ready to serve.

> **Quick and Easy Tip**
> The perfect make-ahead recipe for any dinner occasion. Add a teaspoon of fresh thyme if you have some on hand.

Yellow Squash Croquettes

~ **PREP TIME:** 10 minutes
~ **COOK TIME:** 4 minutes
~ **TOTAL COST:** $3.81
~ **CALORIES:** 156
~ **FAT:** 5 g
~ **CARBOHYDRATES:** 10 g
~ **PROTEIN:** 2 g
~ **CHOLESTEROL:** 35 mg
~ **SODIUM:** 200 mg

2 cups yellow squash, skin on, finely chopped
1 large yellow onion, chopped
1 egg, beaten
Sea salt and black pepper to taste
Pinch of cayenne pepper
½ cup plus 1 tablespoon plain flour
Canola oil for frying

Another way to test the heat of oil is to place the tip of a wooden spoon into the hot oil. If the oil bubbles around the spoon, the oil is hot and ready for frying.

Combine first 5 ingredients and mix well. Stir in flour, being careful not to overmix. In iron skillet or other deep saucepan, heat canola oil (about ½ to 1 inch deep) until hot. Test by placing a small pinch of squash mixture into hot oil. If bubbling rapidly, oil is hot. Drop mixture by teaspoonfuls into the hot oil. Cook until browned, turning once. Remove from oil with slotted spoon and transfer to paper towels. Once drained, serve hot.

Wild Mushroom Ragout in Puff Pastry Shells

Serves 8

~ **PREP TIME:** 5 minutes
~ **COOK TIME:** 25 minutes
~ **TOTAL COST:** $7.00
~ **CALORIES:** 192
~ **FAT:** 2 g
~ **CARBOHYDRATES:** 38 g
~ **PROTEIN:** 4 g
~ **CHOLESTEROL:** 44 mg
~ **SODIUM:** 301 mg

24 pieces frozen puff pastry hors d'oeuvre shells
1 tablespoon unsalted butter
2 cups cremini mushrooms, chopped
½ teaspoon salt
2 sprigs fresh rosemary, leaves picked and chopped
¼ cup vegetable stock or water
1 teaspoon cornstarch dissolved in 1 tablespoon cold water
Freshly ground black pepper to taste
Squeeze of lemon
Sea salt to taste

If you love cheese, add a little grated parmesan cheese to the top or in the ragout.

Bake puff pastry shells according to package directions. In a medium skillet over medium heat, melt the butter. Add the mushrooms and cook, without stirring, for 5 minutes, until a nice brown coating has developed. Add salt and rosemary; cook 3 minutes more. Add the stock and cornstarch; stir until thickened and bubbling. Remove from heat; adjust seasoning with black pepper, a few drops of lemon, and salt to taste. Spoon ½ teaspoon of mushroom ragout into each shell and serve.

CHAPTER 14

SANDWICHES

Chili Quesadillas

Serves 4–6

- ~ **TOTAL COST:** $6.36
- ~ **CALORIES:** 408.21
- ~ **FAT:** 20.26 g
- ~ **PROTEIN:** 14.92 g
- ~ **CHOLESTEROL:** 50.58 mg
- ~ **SODIUM:** 876.44 mg

8 (8-inch) flour tortillas
½ cup sour cream
1 (4-ounce) can green chiles, drained
1 cup shredded Cheddar cheese
½ cup shredded Swiss cheese
2 tablespoons butter
1 cup Homemade Chili (Chapter 6)

This hearty dish could serve 8–10 as an appetizer (cut into eighths). If you'd like, top it with sour cream and more cheese.

1. In small bowl, combine sour cream with green chiles and mix well. Place tortillas on work surface. Spread mixture onto all tortillas. Top with cheeses, then put tortillas together to make four quesadillas.
2. Melt butter on large skillet over medium heat until sizzling. Add quesadillas and cook, turning once, until tortillas are toasted and cheese is melted. While quesadillas are cooking, heat chili in microwave until hot.
3. Cut quesadillas into quarters and place on serving dish; spoon hot Chili over all. Serve immediately.

Two Bean Sandwiches

Yields 6 Sandwiches

- ~ **TOTAL COST:** $3.90
- ~ **CALORIES:** 206.57
- ~ **FAT:** 3.65 g
- ~ **PROTEIN:** 9.74 g
- ~ **CHOLESTEROL:** 0.0 mg
- ~ **SODIUM:** 712.25 mg

1 tablespoon olive oil
4 cloves garlic, minced
1 (15-ounce) can kidney beans, drained
2 tablespoons lemon juice
½ teaspoon salt
⅛ teaspoon cayenne pepper
1 (15-ounce) can black beans, drained
1 cup chopped celery
1 cup shredded carrots
6 (8-inch) corn tortillas

This spread is really good (and provides complete protein!) when you serve it on corn tortillas. You could add some sour cream or cheese to the sandwiches.

1. In small saucepan, heat olive oil over medium heat. Add garlic; cook and stir until fragrant, about 2–3 minutes. Place in medium bowl and add garbanzo beans, lemon juice, salt, and pepper. Mash until mixture is mostly smooth.
2. Stir in black beans, kidney beans, celery, and carrot. Make sandwiches with the spread and toasted sandwich bread and serve immediately.

Raspberry Chicken Sandwiches

 Serves 4

- ~ **TOTAL COST:** $4.70
- ~ **CALORIES:** 453.83
- ~ **FAT:** 21.21 g
- ~ **PROTEIN:** 23.09 g
- ~ **CHOLESTEROL:** 55.26 mg
- ~ **SODIUM:** 1040.34 mg

2 slices bacon
2 Slow Cooker Simmered Chicken Breasts (Chapter 7)
⅓ cup mayonnaise
8 slices wheat bread
3 tablespoons margarine
4 lettuce leaves
¼ cup raspberry jam

Using raspberry jam is an inexpensive way to get the taste of raspberries in this delicious sandwich.

1. In small skillet, cook bacon until crisp; crumble and set aside. Cut chicken into ½-inch cubes. In medium bowl, combine chicken, bacon, and mayonnaise and stir gently to coat chicken.
2. Spread bread with margarine on both sides and toast in a toaster oven or under the broiler. Make sandwiches with the toasted bread, the chicken mixture, lettuce, and raspberry jam. Slice diagonally and serve immediately.

Substituting Meats

With sandwiches, it's easy to substitute one meat for another. If you don't have chicken on hand, use turkey or ham, or even roast beef. Canadian bacon or sausage can be substituted for plain bacon. "Taste" the recipe in your mind. If you think a substitution will work well, go ahead.

Fried Egg Sandwiches

Serves 4

- ~ **TOTAL COST:** $1.79
- ~ **CALORIES:** 250.10
- ~ **FAT:** 9.49 g
- ~ **PROTEIN:** 12.11 g
- ~ **CHOLESTEROL:** 220.75 mg
- ~ **SODIUM:** 530.02 mg

1 tablespoon butter
4 eggs
2 tablespoons ketchup
1 tablespoon mayonnaise
1 tablespoon mustard
8 slices toasted whole wheat bread

Fried egg sandwiches are so quick and easy, and perfect for breakfast or lunch. For more nutrition, add thinly sliced tomatoes, and make sure you use whole wheat bread.

1. In large skillet, melt butter over medium heat. Add eggs and cook until whites are opaque. Carefully cut through the eggs, dividing them into four quarters, and flip. Cook on second side until the yolks are just set.
2. In small bowl, combine ketchup, mayonnaise, and mustard and mix well. Spread on each slice of bread; top with fried egg. Top with second slice of toasted bread and press together gently. Serve immediately.

Grilled Tuna Apple Melts

Serves 4

- ~ **TOTAL COST:** $3.26
- ~ **CALORIES:** 357.95
- ~ **FAT:** 20.61 g
- ~ **PROTEIN:** 22.35 g
- ~ **CHOLESTEROL:** 43.57 mg
- ~ **SODIUM:** 879.45 mg

1 (6-ounce) can tuna, drained
2 green onions, sliced
½ cup chopped apple
¼ cup chopped celery
2 teaspoons mustard
¼ cup mayonnaise
6 slices American cheese, divided
4 slices whole wheat bread
2 tablespoons butter or margarine

These melted sandwiches are open-faced, saving you both money and carbs because you only eat one slice of bread.

1. In medium bowl, combine tuna, onions, apple, celery, mustard, and mayonnaise and mix gently but thoroughly. Dice two slices of American cheese.
2. Preheat broiler. On broiler pan, place Bread slices and spread with butter. Broil for 2–4 minutes or until bread is toasted. Turn Bread slices over. Top each with a slice of cheese, then divide the tuna mixture and place on top. Sprinkle with the diced cheese.
3. Broil sandwiches 6 inches from heat source for 3–6 minutes, watching carefully, until the cheese melts and tuna mixture is hot. Serve immediately.

What Kind of Tuna?

Canned tuna varies in cost depending on the type and form. Solid pack tuna is the most expensive. Albacore, or white tuna, is the most expensive packed tuna because the fish is larger and costs more to catch. "Light" tuna is the other type most commonly sold in the United States. It is darker and less expensive, and actually contains less mercury than the larger albacore.

Triple Cheese Quesadillas

 Serves 4

- ~ **TOTAL COST:** $3.14
- ~ **CALORIES:** 331.97
- ~ **FAT:** 23.24 g
- ~ **PROTEIN:** 17.88 g
- ~ **CHOLESTEROL:** 75.63 mg
- ~ **SODIUM:** 443.24 mg

1 cup grated Cheddar cheese
1 cup grated Swiss cheese
⅓ cup grated Parmesan cheese
½ teaspoon dried Italian seasoning
8 (8-inch) flour tortillas
2 tablespoons butter, softened

Quesadillas are so easy to make and you can vary the recipe in countless ways. For example, you can use colored or corn tortillas or vary the cheese. To splurge, add ingredients like cooked ground beef, chicken, or bacon.

1. In small bowl, combine cheeses and Italian seasoning; toss well. Place four tortillas on work surface; divide cheese mixture among them. Top with remaining tortillas.
2. Heat a large skillet over medium heat. Spread butter on both sides of each quesadilla and place in skillet. Cook, pressing down gently with a spatula, until first side is golden brown, about 3–5 minutes. Carefully turn each quesadilla and cook, pressing down with a spatula, until cheese is melted and second side is golden brown, about 2–5 minutes. Remove to serving plate, cut into quarters, and serve, with salsa for dipping, if you like.

Tortillas

Tortillas freeze beautifully and they thaw in minutes. Make sure that you put them into a freezer bag; don't freeze them in the original wrapper. You might want to separate each one with some waxed paper so you can remove them individually. To thaw, microwave on 30% power for about 30 seconds.

Tuna Avocado Pitas

 Serves 4

- ~ **TOTAL COST:** $5.95
- ~ **CALORIES:** 425.19
- ~ **FAT:** 20.82 g
- ~ **PROTEIN:** 29.69 g
- ~ **CHOLESTEROL:** 69.80 mg
- ~ **SODIUM:** 486.78 mg

4 whole wheat pita breads, unsplit
4 slices Swiss cheese
1 avocado
1 (6-ounce) can chicken, drained
½ cup grated carrot
¼ cup mayonnaise
1 cup shredded Swiss cheese, divided
½ teaspoon dried thyme leaves

Carrot and avocado add nutrition to a chicken sandwich served on a toasted pita bread.

1. Preheat oven to 400°F. Toast pita breads in oven until crisp, about 5 minutes. Remove from oven and top each with a slice of Swiss cheese.
2. Peel avocado and mash slightly, leaving some chunks. Spread this on top of the Swiss cheese. In small bowl, combine chicken, carrot, mayonnaise, and ¼ cup cheese. Spread on top of avocado.
3. Sprinkle sandwiches with remaining cheese and the thyme. Bake for 7–11 minutes, until cheese melts and starts to bubble and brown. Serve immediately.

"Neat" Sloppy Joes

Serves 4

- ~ **TOTAL COST:** $4.81
- ~ **CALORIES:** 321.16
- ~ **FAT:** 13.42 g
- ~ **PROTEIN:** 16.41 g
- ~ **CHOLESTEROL:** 39.94 mg
- ~ **SODIUM:** 888.59 mg

1½ cups Homemade Chili (Chapter 6), chilled
1 cup shredded carrot
1 cup shredded Cheddar cheese
¼ cup grated Parmesan cheese
1 (8-ounce) can refrigerated crescent roll dough

This is a great way to remake any thick chili or casserole. Just add more cheese and encase it in some flaky rolls. Yum!

1. Preheat oven to 375°F. In small bowl, combine Chili with Cheddar and Parmesan cheeses; mix well.
2. Unroll dough on work surface and separate into four rectangles. Press the perforations to seal. Divide Chili mixture among the rectangles, keeping it on one half of the dough. Fold other half of dough over Chili mixture, pressing edges to seal. Prick top with fork.
3. Bake for 15–25 minutes or until sandwiches are deep golden brown. Let cool for 5 minutes, then serve.

Crescent Roll Dough

In recent years, generic forms of crescent roll dough have appeared on the market. These products are just as good as the brand names, and they offer a significant cost savings. Unfortunately, you can't freeze unbaked crescent roll dough, so be sure to buy just what you can use by the expiration dates.

Chicken Barbecue Cornbread Melts

 Serves 4

- ~ **TOTAL COST:** $4.82
- ~ **CALORIES:** 347.78
- ~ **FAT:** 15.46 g
- ~ **PROTEIN:** 24.00 g
- ~ **CHOLESTEROL:** 98.97 mg
- ~ **SODIUM:** 842.17 mg

2 squares Double Cornbread (Chapter 3)
2 chopped Slow Cooker Simmered Chicken Breasts
   (Chapter 7)
½ cup barbecue sauce
¼ cup mayonnaise
1 cup chopped celery
1 cup shredded sharp Cheddar cheese

These rich little open-faced sandwiches use split corn bread as the bread. They're inexpensive and fabulous!

1. Preheat broiler. Carefully cut Cornbread in half horizontally. Place cut side up on cooking sheet or broiler pan.
2. In small bowl, combine chopped Chicken, barbecue sauce, mayonnaise, and celery. Spoon onto split Cornbread. Sprinkle with cheese. Broil sandwiches 6 inches from heat for 2–4 minutes or until sandwiches are hot and cheese is melted and bubbling. Serve immediately.

Tex-Mex Burgers

 Serves 4

- ~ **TOTAL COST:** $6.80
- ~ **CALORIES:** 617.13
- ~ **FAT:** 33.45 g
- ~ **PROTEIN:** 38.83 g
- ~ **CHOLESTEROL:** 127.48 mg
- ~ **SODIUM:** 758.49 mg

2 tablespoons diced canned green chiles, undrained
½ cup tortilla chip crumbs
¼ cup minced onion
¼ teaspoon cayenne pepper
1 pound 80 percent lean ground beef
4 (1-ounce) slices Pepper Jack cheese
4 flour tortillas
⅓ cup salsa
⅓ cup sour cream

These burgers could also be served in toasted hamburger buns with salsa, sour cream, and guacamole, if you shape them into rounds instead of ovals.

1. Prepare and preheat grill. In large bowl, combine chiles, tortilla chip crumbs, onion, and cayenne pepper and stir. Add ground beef; mix gently but thoroughly. Form into 4 oval shapes about 3" × 5".
2. Grill hamburgers for 10–14 minutes, turning once, until meat is thoroughly cooked and instant-read thermometer registers 165°F. Top with Pepper Jack cheese and a few pepper slices, cover grill, and heat for 2–3 minutes to melt cheese. Wrap in tortillas with salsa and sour cream and serve immediately.

Turkey Cheeseburger on Whole Wheat Bun

Serves 4

- ~ **PREP TIME:** 10 minutes
- ~ **COOK TIME:** 11 minutes
- ~ **TOTAL COST:** $6.99
- ~ **CALORIES:** 424
- ~ **FAT:** 15 g
- ~ **CARBOHYDRATES:** 42 g
- ~ **PROTEIN:** 29 g
- ~ **CHOLESTEROL:** 121 mg
- ~ **SODIUM:** 403 mg

½ cup breadcrumbs
1 egg, beaten
½ teaspoon salt
¼ teaspoon cayenne pepper
¼ teaspoon cumin
1 teaspoon chili powder
1 pound ground turkey
4 slices Pepper Jack cheese
4 whole-wheat hamburger buns

Lots of spices make these burgers very flavorful. You could make a Tex-Mex sandwich spread to put on the hamburger buns by combining mayonnaise with some chopped chipotle peppers and adobo sauce.

1. Preheat grill or broiler. In large bowl, combine breadcrumbs, egg, salt, cayenne, and chili powder and mix well. Add turkey and mix gently but thoroughly until combined. Form into 4 patties.
2. Cook patties, covered, 4 to 6 inches from medium heat for about 10 minutes, turning once, until thoroughly cooked. Top each with a slice of cheese, cover grill, and cook for 1 minute longer, until cheese melts. Meanwhile, toast the cut sides of hamburger buns on the grill; make sandwiches with turkey patties and buns.

Make Recipes Your Own

Once you get the hang of making a recipe quickly, think about varying the ingredients to make it your own. For instance, spicy turkey cheeseburgers could be made with chutney, curry powder, and Havarti or provolone cheese. Or make them Greek burgers with feta cheese, chopped olives, and some dried oregano leaves.

Lemon Pepper Dijon Burger

 Serves 4

- ~ **PREP TIME:** 15 minutes
- ~ **COOK TIME:** 12 minutes
- ~ **TOTAL COST:** $5.81
- ~ **CALORIES:** 307
- ~ **FAT:** 20 g
- ~ **CARBOHYDRATES:** 0 g
- ~ **PROTEIN:** 29 g
- ~ **CHOLESTEROL:** 99 mg
- ~ **SODIUM:** 128 mg

1¼ pounds ground beef
¾ teaspoon seasoned salt
⅛ teaspoon lemon pepper
1 tablespoon fresh Italian flat-leaf parsley, chopped
3 tablespoons butter
1 tablespoon Dijon mustard
Juice of ½ a lemon
2 teaspoons quality steak sauce

Dijon mustard enhances the flavor of the beef and blends nicely with the steak sauce. Use grainy Country Dijon if you prefer.

1. Lightly mix the ground beef with the seasoned salt, lemon pepper, and chopped parsley, and form into 4 evenly sized patties. Melt the butter in a medium-sized nonstick skillet over medium-high heat. Add the mustard and quickly blend to combine. Add the burgers to the skillet and cook for about 4 minutes per side, turning once. Transfer the burgers to a plate and tent with foil to keep warm. (Burgers will be returned to the pan for additional cooking.)
2. Add the lemon juice and steak sauce to the pan and blend to combine. Return the burgers and any accumulated juices to the pan and let simmer for 2 to 3 minutes while basting. Remove the pan from heat and allow the burgers to rest for 2 to 3 minutes. Serve with sauce ladled over the top; serve hot, plain, or with your favorite bun.

Onion Garlic Burgers

Serves 5

- ~ **TOTAL COST:** $4.61
- ~ **CALORIES:** 322.79
- ~ **FAT:** 20.00 g
- ~ **PROTEIN:** 25.50 g
- ~ **CHOLESTEROL:** 114.22 mg
- ~ **SODIUM:** 562.44 mg

1 tablespoon olive oil
½ cup chopped onion
3 cloves garlic, minced
¼ cup dried bread crumbs
1 egg
1 tablespoon water
1 tablespoon soy sauce
½ teaspoon salt
⅛ teaspoon pepper
1 pound 80% lean hamburger

Ground beef is cheapest when you buy it in larger quantities of three or four pounds. And when it's on sale, it's an even better buy.

1. In small saucepan, heat olive oil over medium heat. Add onion and garlic; cook and stir until very tender, about 6 minutes. Remove from heat and let cool for 15 minutes. Place onion mixture in blender or food processor and add bread crumbs, egg, water, soy sauce, and salt and pepper. Blend or process until smooth and remove to large bowl.
2. Add hamburger to puréed mixture, gently mixing with hands just until combined. Cover and refrigerate for at least 4 hours.
3. Preheat grill or broiler. Form hamburger mixture into 5 patties and grill or broil until meat thermometer registers 165°F, turning carefully once. Serve on toasted buns with relish, mustard, and ketchup.

Burger with Sauerkraut and Cheese

Serves 4

- ~ **PREP TIME:** 12 minutes
- ~ **COOK TIME:** 12 to 14 minutes
- ~ **TOTAL COST:** $6.78
- ~ **CALORIES:** 354
- ~ **FAT:** 23 g
- ~ **CARBOHYDRATES:** 1 g
- ~ **PROTEIN:** 33 g

1¼ pounds ground beef
½ teaspoon seasoned salt
⅛ teaspoon black pepper
¼ cup sauerkraut, rinsed and drained
8 slices low-fat Muenster cheese

If sauerkraut doesn't strike your fancy, use freshly grated cabbage or toss fresh cabbage with a little Italian dressing.

1. Lightly mix the ground beef with the seasoned salt and pepper; form into 4 evenly sized patties. Clean and oil grill rack and preheat grill to medium high. Cook the burgers for about 5 minutes on each side for medium.
2. During the last 2 minutes of cooking, top each burger with 1 tablespoon kraut and 2 slices of cheese per burger. Transfer the burgers to a plate and tent with foil to keep warm. Let rest for 1 to 2 minutes to allow the juices to reabsorb. Serve hot, plain, or with favorite bun.

Southwestern Burger

Serves 4

- ~ **PREP TIME:** 15 minutes
- ~ **COOK TIME:** 15 minutes
- ~ **TOTAL COST:** $6.97
- ~ **CALORIES:** 342
- ~ **FAT:** 22 g
- ~ **CARBOHYDRATES:** 2 g
- ~ **PROTEIN:** 31 g
- ~ **CHOLESTEROL:** 102 mg
- ~ **SODIUM:** 189 mg

1¼ pounds ground beef
½ teaspoon garlic salt
¼ teaspoon red pepper flakes
¼ cup shredded Pepper Jack cheese
½ cup mild, medium, or hot salsa
¼ cup canned jalapeño slices
¼ cup fresh cilantro, leaves chopped

Jack cheese is common in Southwestern cuisine as are spicy peppers. For a milder version, leave out the red pepper flakes and add in onion powder.

1. Lightly mix the ground beef with the garlic salt and pepper flakes; form into 4 evenly sized patties. Clean and oil grill rack and preheat grill to medium high.
2. Cook the burgers for about 5 minutes on each side for medium. During the last 2 minutes of cooking, top each burger with cheese. Transfer the burgers to a plate and tent with foil to keep warm. Let rest for 1 to 2 minutes to allow the juices to reabsorb. Serve hot, topped with the salsa, jalapeños, and cilantro leaves, as is or with your favorite bun.

Grilled Steak Sandwich

Serves 2

- ~ **PREP TIME:** 8 minutes
- ~ **COOK TIME:** 6 minutes
- ~ **TOTAL COST:** $6.13
- ~ **CALORIES:** 390
- ~ **FAT:** 17 g
- ~ **CARBOHYDRATES:** 36 g
- ~ **PROTEIN:** 30 g
- ~ **CHOLESTEROL:** 164 mg
- ~ **SODIUM:** 840 mg

8 ounces grilled flank steak
½ cup roasted red peppers, drained
4 slices French bread
1 cup shredded Muenster cheese
2 tablespoons butter

Steak sandwiches are the perfect solution to leftover steak. Toss in some chopped onion with the roasted red bell peppers for extra flavor.

1. Cut steak into ¼-inch-thick pieces against the grain. Slice the red peppers into strips. Place 4 bread slices on work surface and top each with ¼ cup cheese. Arrange one-fourth of the steak strips and red peppers on top of each. Top each with another ¼ cup cheese, then top with remaining bread slices. Spread butter on the outsides of the sandwiches.
2. Grill in iron skillet or other heavy skillet for 5 to 6 minutes, turning once, until sandwiches are hot and cheese is melted.

Slicing Bread for Sandwiches
When you're slicing French or Italian bread for sandwiches, be sure to cut the bread on the diagonal. Use a serrated bread knife and grasp the bread firmly with your nondominant hand.

Grilled Portobello Mushroom Panini

 Serves 2

~ **PREP TIME:** 5 minutes
~ **COOK TIME:** 5 to 6 minutes
~ **TOTAL COST:** $5.35
~ **CALORIES:** 95
~ **FAT:** 3 g
~ **CARBOHYDRATES:** 15 g
~ **PROTEIN:** 5 g
~ **CHOLESTEROL:** 2 mg
~ **SODIUM:** 65 mg

4 portobello mushrooms
3 cloves garlic, chopped
1 tablespoon olive oil
Sea salt and black pepper to taste
½ cup mixed greens
2 slices provolone cheese

Portobello mushrooms are so meaty they can be used as a healthy substitute for bread. Because of their size and density, portobello mushrooms are very filling as well.

1. Preheat broiler. Clean off the mushrooms with damp paper towels or a mushroom brush, and scrape out the black membrane on the underside of the cap. Mince the garlic.
2. Mix together the oil and garlic; coat each mushroom with oil mixture. Season with salt and pepper. Top two mushrooms each with ¼ cup greens and slice of cheese. Place all on aluminum foil and broil until cheese is melted. To serve, top each stuffed mushroom with the plain mushroom.

Panini
A panini is a grilled sandwich made from loaf bread.

Barbecue Beef Sandwich

 Serves 6

~ **PREP TIME:** 5 minutes
~ **COOK TIME:** 12 minutes
~ **TOTAL COST:** $6.79
~ **CALORIES:** 318
~ **FAT:** 19 g
~ **PROTEIN:** 16 g
~ **CHOLESTEROL:** 53 mg
~ **SODIUM:** 361 mg

1 tablespoon olive oil
½ yellow onion, chopped
6 tablespoons steak sauce
1 (8-ounce) can tomato sauce
1 pound thinly sliced cooked deli roast beef, largely chopped
6 sandwich buns, toasted

Perfect for using up leftover roast beef, this recipe can also be used with chicken.

In heavy skillet, heat oil over medium heat. Add onion and cook, stirring frequently for 5 minutes. Add steak sauce and tomato sauce and bring to a simmer. Stir in roast beef and simmer an additional 5 minutes, stirring frequently until sauce thicken slightly and roast beef is heated through.

Corned Beef on Rye with Swiss Cheese

Serves 4

~ **PREP TIME:** 3 minutes
~ **COOK TIME:** none
~ **TOTAL COST:** $6.80
~ **CALORIES:** 381
~ **FAT:** 22 g
~ **PROTEIN:** 17 g
~ **CHOLESTEROL:** 53 mg
~ **SODIUM:** 428 mg

¼ cup mustard
¼ cup mayonnaise
8 slices deli pumpernickel rye swirl bread
¾ pound corned beef
2 cups deli coleslaw
4 slices deli Swiss Cheese

These are perfect sandwiches for St. Patrick's Day parties. Serve with a pickle and side of potato salad.

In a small mixing bowl, combine mustard and mayo. Spread mustard mixture onto bread slices and make sandwiches with the corned beef, coleslaw, and Swiss cheese. Cut in half and serve.

Quick and Easy Tip
When you're using any kind of prepared salads in sandwich recipes, you may need to drain the salad by placing it in a colander and letting it stand for a few minutes, or use a slotted spoon to scoop the salad out of the container. If you're making sandwiches ahead of time, leave the salad out and add it just before serving.

Seafood Slaw Sandwiches

Serves 4

~ **TOTAL COST:** $5.17
~ **CALORIES:** 365.94
~ **FAT:** 16.94 g
~ **PROTEIN:** 20.08 g
~ **CHOLESTEROL:** 56.46 mg
~ **SODIUM:** 845.08 mg

1 (8-ounce) package imitation flake crab meat
2 cups Confetti Slaw (Chapter 13)
1 cup shredded Swiss cheese
4 hot dog buns, sliced
2 tablespoons butter, softened

Imitation crab meat is real fish. It's made from a species called *surimi*, and flavored and shaped to look like crab. It's a good inexpensive substitute for real crab in this tasty sandwich.

1. In medium bowl, combine crab, Confetti Slaw, and cheese and mix gently until combined.
2. Spread cut sides of buns with butter and toast under a broiler or in a toaster oven. Make sandwiches with the toasted buns and the crab filling; serve immediately.

Crispy Grilled Sandwich of Ham, Turkey, and Cheese

 Serves 4

- ~ **PREP TIME:** 5 minutes
- ~ **COOK TIME:** 8 minutes
- ~ **TOTAL COST:** $4.32
- ~ **CALORIES:** 535
- ~ **FAT:** 24 g
- ~ **PROTEIN:** 18 g
- ~ **CHOLESTEROL:** 34 mg
- ~ **SODIUM:** 460 mg

¼ pound thinly sliced deli ham
¼ pound thinly sliced deli turkey
¼ pound thinly sliced deli Colby cheese
8 slices whole grain bread
1 cup fish batter mix
¼ cup oil as needed

Grilled sandwiches taste great with a dipping sauce. For a spicy dip, combine ½ cup mayonnaise with 2 tablespoons honey Dijon mustard and a teaspoon of chili sauce. Blend well and enjoy.

1. Make sandwiches using ham, turkey, and cheese on bread. In shallow bowl, prepare batter mix as directed on package.
2. Pour oil into heavy saucepan and heat over medium heat until drop of water sizzles and evaporates. Dip sandwiches in batter mixture and place immediately in oil. Cook over medium heat, turning once, until bread is golden brown and cheese has melted, about 4 minutes per side. Cut sandwiches in half and serve.

Quick and Easy Tip

You can find fish batter mix near the seafood section in the grocery store.

Crescent Ham Salsa Sandwiches

 Serves 4

- ~ **TOTAL COST:** $6.89
- ~ **CALORIES:** 349.75
- ~ **FAT:** 16.86 g
- ~ **PROTEIN:** 15.79 g
- ~ **CHOLESTEROL:** 43.40 mg
- ~ **SODIUM:** 1097.25 mg

3 (2-ounce) packages shaved ham
½ cup Suave Fruit Salsa (Chapter 2), divided
½ cup shredded Muenster cheese
¼ cup sour cream
1 (8-ounce) can refrigerated crescent rolls

Once you have this basic recipe down, you can vary it to make a hundred different versions. It's quick, easy, and delicious.

1. Preheat oven to 375°F. Place ham on cutting board and chop into fine pieces. Drain ¼ cup of the Fruit Salsa and chop finely. Combine with ham, Muenster cheese, and sour cream in small bowl.
2. Separate crescent dough into 4 rectangles, firmly pressing perforations to seal. Divide ham mixture among rectangles. Fold dough in half to make a triangular shape, sealing edges with a fork. Place on ungreased cookie sheet.
3. Bake 15–20 minutes until sandwiches are golden brown. Serve with remaining Fruit Salsa.

Crescent Dough

In recent years, generic forms of crescent roll dough have appeared on the market. These products are just as good as the brand names, and they offer a significant cost savings.

Salmon and Avocado on Pita

 Serves 4 to 8

- **PREP TIME:** 8 minutes
- **COOK TIME:** none
- **TOTAL COST:** $6.93
- **CALORIES:** 408 per two pockets
- **FAT:** 4 g
- **CARBOHYDRATES:** 44 g
- **PROTEIN:** 39 g
- **CHOLESTEROL:** 65 mg
- **SODIUM:** 630 mg

1 (7-ounce) pouch pink salmon, drained
1 avocado, peeled and diced
½ cup mayonnaise
½ teaspoon dried basil leaves
½ cup chopped tomato
4 pita pockets, halved

Using low-fat or nonfat mayonnaise helps to cut down on the calories and fat in this recipe. Or, use soynnaise, which is a soy-based mayonnaise product that is more healthy for you and tastes great.

In small bowl, combine all ingredients except pita and mix gently but thoroughly. Divide mixture evenly between pita pockets.

Shrimp Salad on Sourdough Loaf

 Serves 8

- **PREP TIME:** 10 minutes
- **COOK TIME:** none
- **TOTAL COST:** $6.76
- **CALORIES:** 312
- **FAT:** 11 g
- **CARBOHYDRATES:** 42 g
- **PROTEIN:** 8 g
- **CHOLESTEROL:** 50 mg
- **SODIUM:** 342 mg

2 (3-ounce) packages low-fat cream cheese, softened
¼ cup nonfat sour cream
½ teaspoon dried dill
3 (6-ounce) cans small shrimp, drained
1½ cups chopped celery hearts
4 small sourdough loaves bread

Season the shrimp mixture lightly with Crazy-Jane or other seasoned salt, if desired. Or, to cut down on sodium, squeeze in a little lemon juice.

1. In medium bowl, beat cream cheese with sour cream and dill until smooth and fluffy. Stir in shrimp and chopped celery hearts.
2. Using serrated knife, cut sourdough loaves in half horizontally. Spread bottom layer with cream cheese mixture and top with top layer. Cut in half and serve.

> **Canned Seafood**
> Canned seafood can have a salty taste. Rinse before use, but be sure to drain it very well, and don't soak it. Canned salmon, crab meat, and tuna, as well as surimi, or frozen fake crab, can all be substituted for canned shrimp in just about any recipe.

Tuna Salad with Red Seedless Grapes on Whole Grain Toast

 Serves 4

~ **PREP TIME:** 12 minutes
~ **CHILL TIME:** 1 hour
~ **TOTAL COST:** $6.78
~ **CALORIES:** 288
~ **FAT:** 3 g
~ **CARBOHYDRATES:** 35 g
~ **PROTEIN:** 27 g
~ **CHOLESTEROL:** 20 mg
~ **SODIUM:** 483 mg

1 hard-boiled egg, diced
½ red onion, chopped
1 cup red seedless grapes, halved
Zest of 1 lemon
1½ cups canned tuna
¼ cup chopped walnuts
¾ cup low-fat mayonnaise
1 tablespoon balsamic vinegar
Sea salt and black pepper to taste
1 head green or red leaf lettuce
8 slices whole grain bread, toasted

Chopped celery and apples are also natural additions to tuna salad, which can be served chilled or warmed.

In mixing bowl, combine all ingredients except lettuce and bread. Toss well. Cover with plastic wrap and refrigerate about an hour. When ready to serve, layer lettuce on 1 slice of bread, mound the tuna mixture on top, and top with other slice of bread. Or skip the bread and serve tuna salad on lettuce leaf.

Grilled Whitefish BLTs on Sourdough

 Serves 4

~ **PREP TIME:** 12 minutes
~ **COOK TIME:** 10 minutes
~ **TOTAL COST:** $6.97
~ **CALORIES:** 251
~ **FAT:** 11 g
~ **CARBOHYDRATES:** 21 g
~ **PROTEIN:** 6 g
~ **CHOLESTEROL:** 11 g
~ **SODIUM:** 361 mg

2 slices bacon, cooked crisp then crumbled, drippings reserved
¾ pound grilled whitefish
8 mini sourdough rolls, sliced in half
3 tablespoons extra-virgin olive oil
4 green or red leaf lettuce leaves, torn into large pieces
½ red onion, chopped
1 tomato, sliced

The term whitefish can refer to a variety of white flesh fish but is most commonly associated with Atlantic whitefish and other whitefish varieties.

1. In large saucepan, heat bacon drippings. Add fish and cook for about 3 minutes per side, depending upon thickness. Turn once.
2. Lightly toast bread slices, then brush with olive oil. Layer one bread slice with lettuce, onion, bacon, tomatoes, and fish. Top with additional bread slice.

Open-Face Meatball Hoagies

Serves 4

~ **PREP TIME:** 10 minutes
~ **COOK TIME:** 11 minutes
~ **TOTAL COST:** $6.63
~ **CALORIES:** 280
~ **FAT:** 12 g
~ **CARBOHYDRATES:** 31 g
~ **PROTEIN:** 13 g
~ **CHOLESTEROL:** 23 mg
~ **SODIUM:** 795 mg

½ (16-ounce) package frozen meatballs, thawed overnight in refrigerator
½ (15-ounce) jar pasta sauce
½ cup frozen onion and pepper stir-fry combo, thawed and drained
2 hoagie rolls, sliced and toasted
½ (6-ounce) package sliced provolone cheese

Meatball sandwiches are delicious and fun. Packaged frozen meatballs are usually on the smaller side, so you may want to squeeze on a few more if you love meatballs like I do!

1. Cut thawed meatballs in half and place in heavy saucepan with pasta sauce. Cook over medium heat, stirring occasionally, until sauce bubbles and meatballs are hot.
2. Stir in onion and pepper stir-fry combo; cook and stir for 3 to 5 minutes, until vegetables are hot and tender. Preheat broiler.
3. Top each hoagie roll half with meatball mixture and place on broiler rack. Top each with a slice of cheese. Broil 6 inches from heat source for 3 to 6 minutes, until cheese is melted and bubbly. Serve immediately.

Provolone Cheese
Provolone cheese is a mild cheese with a slightly smoky taste that's made from cow's milk. It is usually aged for a few months so the texture is slightly firm. You can buy provolone aged for up to a year. This aged cheese has a more intense flavor and firm texture, similar to Parmesan cheese.

The Simply Delicious Burger

 Serves 4

- ~ **PREP TIME:** 12 minutes
- ~ **COOK TIME:** 12 minutes
- ~ **TOTAL COST:** $5.03
- ~ **CALORIES:** 305
- ~ **FAT:** 20 g
- ~ **CARBOHYDRATES:** 0 g
- ~ **PROTEIN:** 29 g
- ~ **CHOLESTEROL:** 99 mg
- ~ **SODIUM:** 108 mg

1¼ pounds ground beef
½ teaspoon seasoned salt
Black pepper, to taste
2 tablespoons oil

Use this burger as a base for any other style burger you would like to make. With this as a base, top with sauces such as roasted red pepper or a simple Thousand Island dressing.

Lightly mix the ground beef with salt and pepper and form into 4 evenly sized patties. On stovetop, heat 2 tablespoons oil in a nonstick skillet over medium-high heat. Cook for about 5 minutes per side for medium, turning once. Transfer burgers to a plate and tent with foil to keep warm. Let rest for 1 to 2 minutes to allow the juices to reabsorb. Serve hot plain or with your favorite bun.

Two More Easy Ways to Cook Burgers
To grill: Clean grill rack and lightly oil to prevent sticking. Preheat grill to medium high. Cook for about 5 minutes per side for medium, turning once. Transfer burgers to a plate and tent with foil to keep warm. Let rest for 1 to 2 minutes to allow the juices to reabsorb.
To broil: Clean broiler rack and lightly oil to prevent sticking. Set broiler rack 4 inches from heat source. Preheat broiler to medium high. Cook for about 5 minutes per side for medium, turning once. Transfer burgers to a plate and tent with foil to keep warm. Let rest for 1 to 2 minutes to allow the juices to reabsorb.

Refried Bean Burgers

Serves 4

- ~ **TOTAL COST:** $6.58
- ~ **CALORIES:** 507.34
- ~ **FAT:** 25.93 g
- ~ **PROTEIN:** 26.90 g
- ~ **CHOLESTEROL:** 77.32 mg
- ~ **SODIUM:** 873.12 mg

½ cup minced onion
⅓ cup tortilla chips crumbs
1 tablespoon chili powder
½ cup refried beans
¾ pound 80% lean ground beef
4 whole wheat hamburger buns
4 slices American cheese

Refried beans add their rich smooth taste and texture to hamburgers cooked on the grill. This recipe takes a little bit of organization; read it through a few times before you begin.

1. In large bowl, combine onion, tortilla chip crumbs, chili powder, and half of the refried beans; mix well. Add ground beef; mix gently with your hands until blended. Form into 8 hamburger patties and refrigerate.
2. Prepare and preheat grill, using mesquite or apple wood chips if you'd like. Cut hamburger buns in half and toast, cut side down, on grill until crisp. Remove from grill. Add hamburgers to grill, cover, and cook for 5 minutes on first side.
3. Meanwhile, combine remaining refried beans and taco sauce in an ovenproof saucepan; place on grill and heat. Turn hamburgers and cover again. Place 1 slice of cheese on each hamburger bun half; place cheese side up on grill to melt. Remove hamburgers when internal temperature reaches 165°F, about 5 minutes longer.
4. Assemble hamburgers by spreading heated refried bean mixture onto each cheese-topped hamburger bun half; top with cooked hamburgers and second half of bun. Serve immediately.

Burger Tips

All ground meat recipes must be cooked until well done—that is, 165°F on an instant-read thermometer. For moist and tender burgers, handle the meat as little as possible and don't press down on the burgers while they are cooking. Toast the buns on the grill during the last few minutes of cooking time for more crunch and flavor.

Meatball Marinara Sandwiches

 Serves 4

- ~ **TOTAL COST:** $6.19
- ~ **CALORIES:** 501.92
- ~ **FAT:** 25.92 g
- ~ **PROTEIN:** 28.45 g
- ~ **CHOLESTEROL:** 120.44 mg
- ~ **SODIUM:** 1015.93 mg

¾ pound 80% lean ground beef
¼ cup dry bread crumbs
3 tablespoons milk
1 egg
1 teaspoon dried Italian seasoning
½ teaspoon salt
⅛ teaspoon pepper
½ (26-ounce) jar tomato pasta sauce
4 hoagie buns
1 cup shredded Monterey Jack or Cheddar cheese

Meatball sandwiches are hearty and filling, and are easy to make. You can make the meatballs ahead of time, then reheat in the sauce before assembling the sandwiches.

1. In large bowl combine beef, bread crumbs, milk, egg, salt, and pepper and mix gently but thoroughly. Form into 24 meatballs and place on baking sheet. Bake at 350°F for 20–30 minutes, until meatballs are thoroughly cooked. combine
2. In large saucepan, heat the pasta sauce over low heat. Add meatballs and simmer for 4–5 minutes.
3. Toast sliced hoagie buns under broiler. Place meatballs and sauce on one half of each toasted bun and top with cheese. Place filled halves of hoagie buns on broiler pan and broil 4–6 inches from heat for 4–5 minutes, until cheese melts. Assemble sandwiches and serve.

> **Sharp or Mild Cheese?**
> Whether you buy sharp or mild cheese is really all about your tastes. If you want a lot of impact with less cheese, either for financial or health reasons, choose a sharper flavor cheese. About a cup of sharp Cheddar cheese will flavor an entire casserole or pizza.

Tex-Mex Pitas

Serves 4

- ~ **TOTAL COST:** $6.84
- ~ **CALORIES:** 207.01
- ~ **FAT:** 13.06 g
- ~ **PROTEIN:** 20.23 g
- ~ **CHOLESTEROL:** 54.31 mg
- ~ **SODIUM:** 415.39 mg

1 cup chopped deli roast beef
1 green bell pepper, chopped
2 jalapeño peppers, diced
3 green onions, chopped
⅓ cup salsa
1 cup shredded Cheddar cheese
2 cups lettuce leaves
½ cup refried beans
2 large pita breads, cut in half

You can substitute leftover chopped roast beef or steak for the deli meat in this delicious sandwich recipe, or use corn tortillas or onion buns instead of the pitas.

1. In medium bowl, combine beef, peppers, green onions, salsa, and cheese and blend well.
2. Spread refried beans evenly inside each pita and top with lettuce. Tuck beef mixture into each bread and serve.

Hummus Sandwiches

Serves 6

- ~ **TOTAL COST:** $6.41
- ~ **CALORIES:** 357.05
- ~ **FAT:** 17.11 g
- ~ **PROTEIN:** 10.55 g
- ~ **CHOLESTEROL:** 10.18 mg
- ~ **SODIUM:** 539.92 mg

1 (15-ounce) can garbanzo beans, drained
2 tablespoons lemon juice
3 tablespoons olive oil
⅛ teaspoon pepper
½ teaspoon paprika
¼ cup toasted sesame seeds
¼ cup chopped green onions
12 slices whole wheat bread
2 tablespoons butter, softened
6 lettuce leaves
6 slices tomato

This recipe for hummus also makes a delicious appetizer dip for fresh vegetables or as a sandwich spread for chicken or roast beef sandwiches. Store it, well covered, in the refrigerator for up to 1 week.

1. In food processor or blender, combine drained garbanzo beans, lemon juice, olive oil, pepper, and paprika and process until almost smooth. Remove from processor to medium bowl and stir in toasted sesame seeds and green onions.
2. Spread one side of each slice of bread with butter and divide hummus among bread slices. Top with lettuce leaves and tomato and make sandwiches. Cut in half diagonally and serve immediately.

Curried Chicken Salad Wraps

Serves 4

~ **TOTAL COST:** $5.39
~ **CALORIES:** 356.28
~ **FAT:** 11.34 g
~ **PROTEIN:** 23.43 g
~ **CHOLESTEROL:** 59.27 mg
~ **SODIUM:** 799.22 mg

1 (12-ounce) can dark and light meat chicken, drained
¼ cup mayonnaise
¼ cup Apple Chutney (Chapter 2)
1 teaspoon curry powder
⅓ cup golden raisins
¼ cup chopped green onions
⅓ cup crushed pineapple, well drained
4 (8-inch) flour tortillas

Mango chutney is the expensive ingredient in this recipe, so making it yourself saves a lot of money. Freeze the chutney in small amounts and use as needed.

1. In medium bowl combine all ingredients except flour tortillas and mix well to blend. Place flour tortillas on work surface and divide chicken mixture among them.
2. Roll up each tortilla, enclosing filling; then cut in half crosswise. Serve immediately.

Chutney

Chutney is a cooked mixture of fruits and spices used in Indian and Middle Eastern cuisine. It adds a lot of flavor, but is expensive. You can make it yourself, using any fruit you'd like. Chutney can be made with blueberries, peaches, nectarines, grapes, mangoes, even tomatoes.

Simple Chicken Wraps

Serves 4

~ **PREP TIME:** 8 minutes
~ **TOTAL COST:** $5.52
~ **CALORIES:** 272
~ **FAT:** 19 g
~ **PROTEIN:** 11 g
~ **CHOLESTEROL:** 2 mg
~ **SODIUM:** 181 mg

3 ounces cream cheese, room temperature
1 tablespoon mayonnaise
1 tablespoon fresh lemon juice
Pinch sea salt and black pepper
2 (8-inch) flour tortillas, room temperature
2 cups cooked chicken, cubed
½ red onion, diced
1 cup baby spinach leaves

Wraps are perfect for afternoon appetizer parties. Wrap the finished wrap tightly in plastic and refrigerate for about 1 hour. Remove from plastic and slice into 1-inch slices.

1. Mix together cream cheese, mayonnaise, lemon juice, salt, and pepper in a small bowl. Mix well until smooth.
2. Place tortillas on clean work surface. Spread half the cream cheese mixture on the upper third of each tortilla, about ½ inch from edge. Place half of the chicken on the lower third of each tortilla. Top each with onions and spinach. Roll up each wrap starting from the bottom and fold the tortilla over the filling and roll upward. Compress lightly to form a firm roll. Press at the top to seal the wrap closed with cream cheese mixture. Cut sandwich in half and wrap in plastic film. Refrigerate until ready to serve.

Roast Beef Wrap with Red Bell Peppers and Blue Cheese

 Serves 4

- ~ **PREP TIME:** 10 minutes
- ~ **TOTAL COST:** $4.36
- ~ **CALORIES:** 176
- ~ **FAT:** 10 g
- ~ **PROTEIN:** 4 g
- ~ **CHOLESTEROL:** 10 mg
- ~ **SODIUM:** 361 mg

3 ounces cream cheese, room temperature
1 tablespoon mayonnaise
2 ounces blue cheese crumbles
Sea salt and black pepper to taste
2 (8-inch) flour tortillas, room temperature
⅓ pound deli roast beef, cut into ½-inch strips
¼ cup diced roasted red bell peppers
1cup romaine lettuce, chopped

Flour or whole wheat tortillas are the best for making wraps. Use them at room temperature for ease in folding.

1. In a small mixing bowl, combine cream cheese, mayonnaise, blue cheese, salt, and pepper. Blend until smooth. Place tortilla on clean work surface. Spread half of cream cheese mixture on upper third of each tortilla, about ½ inch from edge. Place half the roast beef on the lower third of each tortilla. Top each with peppers and lettuce.
2. Roll up each wrap starting from the bottom and fold tortilla over the filling, compressing slightly to form a firm roll. Press at the top to seal the wrap closed with the cream cheese mixture. Cut the sandwich in half and wrap in plastic film. Refrigerate until ready to serve.

Honey-Roasted Turkey Wraps with Mixed Greens

 Serves 4

- ~ **PREP TIME:** 7 minutes
- ~ **COOK TIME:** none
- ~ **TOTAL COST:** $4.38
- ~ **CALORIES:** 389
- ~ **FAT:** 9 g
- ~ **PROTEIN:** 8 g
- ~ **CHOLESTEROL:** 24 mg
- ~ **SODIUM:** 324 mg

3 ounces cream cheese, room temperature
1 tablespoon mayonnaise
2 tablespoons cranberry sauce
Sea salt and black pepper to taste
2 (8-inch) flour tortillas
⅓ pound deli sliced honey-roasted turkey breast
¼ pound Cheddar cheese, shredded (about ½ cup)
1 cup mixed greens

Consider using smoked meats in place of regular meats. Smoked meats add an extra layer of flavor without adding fat or calories.

1. Mix together cream cheese, mayonnaise, cranberry sauce, salt, and pepper in a small bowl. Place tortillas on clean work surface. Spread half the cream cheese mixture on upper third of each tortilla, about ½ inch from the edge. Place half the turkey on the lower third of each tortilla. Top each with Cheddar cheese and greens.
2. Roll up each wrap starting from the bottom and fold the tortilla over the filling, compressing slightly to form a firm roll. Press at the top to seal wrap closed with the cream cheese mixture. Cut the sandwich in half and wrap in plastic film. Refrigerate until ready to serve.

Grilled Vegetable Sandwiches

 Serves 6

- ~ **PREP TIME:** 5 minutes
- ~ **COOK TIME:** 5 minutes
- ~ **TOTAL COST:** $6.99
- ~ **CALORIES:** 263
- ~ **FAT:** 9 g
- ~ **PROTEIN:** 4 g
- ~ **CHOLESTEROL:** 10 mg
- ~ **SODIUM:** 361 mg

¼ cup olive oil
½ eggplant, cubed
1 red bell pepper, seeded and diced
1 sweet red onion, diced
Sea salt and black pepper to taste
6 club sandwich rolls
2 ounces goat cheese, room temperature

Goat cheese is a very flavorful cheese that tastes even better when warmed!

1. Heat 1 tablespoon olive oil on grill pan over medium heat. Add all vegetables to grill; season with salt and pepper. Grill until cooked but al dente, about 5 minutes.
2. Brush rolls with remaining oil. Spread goat cheese onto rolls. Layer grilled vegetables onto roll. Serve a whole sandwich to 6 persons or cut in half and serve 12 persons.

Quick and Easy Tip
This is great recipe for using leftover grilled vegetables. Use any combination of vegetables you have. Reheat the vegetables by grilling as instructed above but for only 3 minutes.

Sandwich of Pita with Cucumbers and Feta Cheese

 Serves 6

- ~ **PREP TIME:** 6 minutes
- ~ **COOK TIME:** none
- ~ **TOTAL COST:** $5.88
- ~ **CALORIES:** 181
- ~ **FAT:** 8 g
- ~ **PROTEIN:** 5 g
- ~ **CHOLESTEROL:** 11 mg
- ~ **SODIUM:** 321 mg

6 pita bread
2 cucumbers, peeled and diced
1 large red onion, chopped
¼ bunch fresh oregano, leaves chopped
3 ounces feta cheese, crumbled
1 tablespoon olive oil
Fresh ground black pepper

Feta is a very salty cheese so you most likely do not need to add any salt to this recipe to enjoy.

Slice each pita in half and then open to create a pita pocket. Stuff pocket with cucumber, onion, oregano, and feta. Drizzle with oil and sprinkle with black pepper.

Quick and Easy Tip
A great recipe for a weekend lunch. Mix all ingredients ahead of time, let marinate, and then stuff pita pockets just before serving. Add sliced black olives for a truly Greek dish.

Egg Salad Supreme Sandwiches

Serves 4

- ~ **TOTAL COST:** $4.29
- ~ **CALORIES:** 300.21
- ~ **FAT:** 12.74 g
- ~ **PROTEIN:** 15.06 g
- ~ **CHOLESTEROL:** 333.99 mg
- ~ **SODIUM:** 572.52 mg

6 eggs
¼ cup minced red bell pepper
¼ cup minced green onion
2 tablespoons drained pickle relish
⅛ teaspoon salt
Pinch pepper
⅓ cup plain yogurt
¼ cup mayonnaise
2 tablespoons butter, softened
4 (8-inch) crusty hoagie buns, sliced
4 romaine lettuce leaves

If you don't like pickle relish, omit it and add 1 table-spoon lemon juice to the egg salad filling.

1. Place eggs in medium saucepan and cover with cold water. Bring to a boil over high heat; then cover pan, remove from heat, and let stand 15 min-utes. Place pan in sink and run cold water into pan until eggs have cooled. Crack eggs slightly against the side of pan and let sit another 5 minutes in the cold water. Peel eggs and coarsely chop.
2. Combine chopped eggs with remaining ingredi-ents except lettuce, butter, and hoagie buns and mix gently. Spread a thin layer of butter on cut sides of hoagie buns and toast in toaster over or under broiler. Make sandwiches with the egg salad and lettuce.

Turkey Pesto Sandwiches

Serves 4

- ~ **TOTAL COST:** $5.29
- ~ **CALORIES:** 352.59
- ~ **FAT:** 19.44 g
- ~ **PROTEIN:** 15.43 g
- ~ **CHOLESTEROL:** 59.93 mg
- ~ **SODIUM:** 553.23 mg

1 (3-ounce) package cream cheese
¼ cup mayonnaise
⅓ cup Spinach Pesto (Chapter 2)
¼ cup grated Parmesan cheese
1 cup chopped smoked turkey
8 slices cracked wheat bread
2 tablespoons butter, softened
4 slices tomato

You can substitute plain cooked turkey or chicken for the smoked turkey in these easy and flavorful sandwiches.

1. In medium bowl, combine cream cheese and Miracle Whip and beat until well blended. Add pesto and Parmesan cheese and mix well. Stir in turkey and stir to blend.
2. Spread one side of each slice of bread with soft-ened butter. Divide turkey mixture among bread slices, top with tomato slices, and put together to make sandwiches. Serve immediately.

Packaged Meats

Be sure to compare unit pricing for precooked, sliced meats that you buy in your grocer's meat department. Sometimes the least expensive pack-age has the most expensive meat. Also consider how the meat is sliced. Shaved meat can deliver a bigger taste than plain slices, since there is more surface area available for your taste buds to sense.

Tex-Mex Grilled Cheese

 Serves 4

~ **TOTAL COST:** $4.99
~ **CALORIES:** 516.38
~ **FAT:** 34.04 g
~ **PROTEIN:** 19.11 g
~ **CHOLESTEROL:** 73.59 mg
~ **SODIUM:** 679.23 mg

8 slices whole wheat bread
¼ cup butter
4 slices American cheese
¼ cup salsa
1 avocado, diced
2 pickled jalapeños, sliced
4 slices Pepper Jack cheese

These quick and easy sandwiches are nice for lunch on a busy day. Serve them with apple and pear slices and a root beer float.

1. Place bread on work surface. Spread one side of each piece with butter. Turn bread slices over. Place American cheese on half of the slices. Top with salsa, avocado, and pickled jalapeño slices. Cover salsa with Pepper Jack cheese. Top with other half of bread slices, buttered side up.
2. Cook sandwiches for 4–5 minutes on each side on heated griddle, turning once, or in dual contact grill for 4–5 minutes total until bread is brown and crisp and cheeses are melted.

Ham and Muenster on Pita

 Serves 4

~ **PREP TIME:** 10 minutes
~ **COOK TIME:** 2 minutes
~ **TOTAL COST:** $6.85
~ **CALORIES:** 210
~ **FAT:** 3 g
~ **CARBOHYDRATES:** 26 g
~ **PROTEIN:** 12 g
~ **CHOLESTEROL:** 20 mg
~ **SODIUM:** 945 mg

4 pita pocket breads
3 tablespoons olive oil, divided
2 tablespoons mustard
6 ounces sliced cooked ham
6 ounces sliced Muenster cheese
½ cup sliced roasted red peppers, drained

Roasted red peppers are sold in jars in the condiment aisle of the supermarket.

1. Preheat broiler. Using a sharp knife, split the pocket breads into 2 round pieces. In small bowl, combine 1 tablespoon olive oil and the mustard and mix well. Spread this mixture on inside halves of the pita breads.
2. Layer ham, Muenster cheese, roasted red peppers, and more Muenster cheese on one side of each pita bread. Top with remaining pita bread sides. Spread outside of sandwiches with remaining 2 tablespoons olive oil.
3. Place each sandwich on aluminum foil and place under broiler. Broil 2 minutes, or until cheese is melted and bread is golden brown and toasted. Cut sandwiches in half and serve.

Avocado and Muenster Sandwich on Hoagie Bun

 Serves 2 to 4

- ~ **PREP TIME:** 10 minutes
- ~ **COOK TIME:** 5 minutes
- ~ **TOTAL COST:** $6.29
- ~ **CALORIES:** 280
- ~ **FAT:** 13 g
- ~ **CARBOHYDRATES:** 30 g
- ~ **PROTEIN:** 6 g
- ~ **CHOLESTEROL:** 26 mg
- ~ **SODIUM:** 275 mg

2 avocados
¼ cup creamy Italian salad dressing
2 hoagie buns, sliced and toasted
2 plum tomatoes, sliced
4 slices Muenster cheese

Hoagie buns can be a bit large for some appetites, so that's why they are perfect for slicing into smaller portions and sharing with a friend or serving as appetizers.

1. Preheat broiler. Peel and seed avocados; place in small bowl along with salad dressing. Mash, using a fork, until almost blended but with still some pieces of avocado visible.
2. Place bottom halves of buns on broiler pan and spread with half of avocado mixture. Top with tomato slices and cover with cheese slices. Broil 6 inches from heat source for 2 to 5 minutes or until cheese is melted and begins to bubble. Spread top halves of buns with remaining avocado mixture and place on top of cheese. Serve immediately.

Spinach and Cheese Bagel Pizza

Serves 6 to 8

- ~ **PREP TIME:** 12 minutes
- ~ **COOK TIME:** 11 minutes
- ~ **TOTAL COST:** $6.23
- ~ **CALORIES:** 360
- ~ **FAT:** 8 g
- ~ **CARBOHYDRATES:** 61 g
- ~ **PROTEIN:** 16 g
- ~ **CHOLESTEROL:** 5 mg
- ~ **SODIUM:** 620 mg

6 bagels, split and toasted
2 tablespoons olive oil
½ yellow onion, chopped
1 (8-ounce) can pizza sauce
Pinch ground nutmeg
1 cup frozen chopped spinach, thawed
1 cup shredded mozzarella cheese

A healthy alternative to sometimes heavy pizza dough, bagels provide a crunchy and substantial crust and are the perfect size for an individual pizza.

1. Preheat broiler. Place bagels on a parchment-lined baking sheet. In heavy saucepan, heat olive oil over medium heat and add onion; cook and stir for 4 to 6 minutes, until onion is tender. Add pizza sauce and nutmeg; bring to a simmer.
2. Meanwhile, drain the thawed spinach in a colander or strainer, then drain again by pressing between paper towels. Spread bagel halves with pizza sauce mixture and top evenly with the spinach. Sprinkle with cheese. Broil 6 inches from heat for 4 to 7 minutes, until cheese melts and sandwiches are hot.

Hearty Grilled Cheese Sandwich

 Serves 1

- ~ **COST:** $0.90
- ~ **CALORIES:** 380
- ~ **FAT:** 24 g
- ~ **CARBOHYDRATES:** 26 g
- ~ **PROTEIN:** 16 g
- ~ **CHOLESTEROL:** 45 mg
- ~ **SODIUM:** 940 mg

2 slices bacon
About 2 teaspoons butter or margarine
2 slices bread
Pinch paprika
¼ cup grated Cheddar cheese
2 teaspoons (or to taste) mustard

1. Cook the bacon in a frying pan until crisp. Drain on paper towels. Do not clean out the pan.
2. Spread the butter or margarine over one side of a slice of bread. Sprinkle with the paprika and add the grated cheese on top. Lay the bacon slices over the top. Spread the mustard over one side of the other slice of bread. Close the sandwich.
3. Return the frying pan to the stovetop and heat on medium. Add the sandwich to the frying pan. Cook until the bottom is golden brown, about 1 to 2 minutes. Press down gently on the sandwich with a spatula while it is cooking.
4. Turn the sandwich over and cook on the other side until browned and the cheese is nearly melted, about 1 to 2 minutes. Remove the sandwich from the pan and cut in half.

Ultimate Submarine Sandwich

Serves 1

- ~ **COST:** $4.75
- ~ **CALORIES:** 790
- ~ **FAT:** 38 g
- ~ **CARBOHYDRATES:** 57 g
- ~ **PROTEIN:** 58 g
- ~ **CHOLESTEROL:** 140 mg
- ~ **SODIUM:** 2070 mg

1 (8-inch) whole wheat sub bun
1 tablespoon mustard
1 tablespoon mayonnaise
1½ tablespoons finely chopped red onion
1 romaine lettuce leaf
2 slices cooked ham
1 ounce Cheddar cheese, thinly sliced
2 slices turkey
1 ounce mozzarella cheese, thinly sliced
½ tomato, sliced
2 pickles

1. Slice the sub bun in half lengthwise.
2. Spread the mustard on the inside of one half. Spread the mayonnaise on the inside of the other half.
3. Fill with the red onion, lettuce leaf, sliced ham, Cheddar cheese, sliced turkey, mozzarella cheese, sliced tomato, and pickles.

CHAPTER 15

DESSERT

Oatmeal Raisin Cookies

 Yields 48 cookies

- ~ **TOTAL COST:** $3.95
- ~ **CALORIES:** 102.76
- ~ **FAT:** 4.38 g
- ~ **PROTEIN:** 1.52 g
- ~ **CHOLESTEROL:** 8.81 mg
- ~ **SODIUM:** 56.37 mg

1 cup regular oatmeal
¼ cup margarine
½ cup oil
1 cup brown sugar
½ cup sugar
2 tablespoons honey
2 eggs
1 cup leftover Nutty Oatmeal (Chapter 4)
1½ cups all-purpose flour
½ cup whole wheat flour
1½ teaspoons baking soda
½ cup chopped walnuts
1 cup chopped raisins

Two kinds of oatmeal make these cookies nice and chewy. Grinding some of the uncooked oatmeal adds a great texture to these lunch box cookies.

1. Preheat oven to 350°F. Place the quick cooking oatmeal and rolled oatmeal on a cookie sheet and bake 5–10 minutes, stirring frequently, until oatmeal is fragrant and light golden brown around the edges. Remove from cookie sheet and cool. Grind ⅓ cup of the oatmeal in food processor.
2. In large bowl, combine margarine, oil, brown sugar, and sugar and beat until smooth. Stir in honey, eggs, and leftover oatmeal and mix well. Add flour and baking soda and mix. Then stir in toasted regular and ground oatmeal and walnuts.
3. Drop by teaspoons onto greased cookie sheets. Bake 10–13 minutes or until cookies are set and golden brown around the edges. Cool on pans for 3 minutes, then remove to wire racks to cool. Store covered at room temperature.

Oatmeal: Quick or Regular?
Regular oatmeal is made from groats, or whole oat kernels, which have been hulled. Quick oatmeal is a more finely cut version. It does make a difference which type you use. The regular oatmeal will be more separate and discrete in cookies, while the quick oatmeal will blend more with the batter.

Grandma's Banana Fruit Pudding

Serves 8

- ~ **TOTAL COST:** $5.79
- ~ **CALORIES:** 398.76
- ~ **FAT:** 11.51 g
- ~ **PROTEIN:** 6.29 g
- ~ **CHOLESTEROL:** 85.32 mg
- ~ **SODIUM:** 220.74 mg

1 (15-ounce) can fruit cocktail
1 cup sugar, divided
¼ cup all-purpose flour
¼ teaspoon salt
3 eggs, separated
1 cup milk
1 tablespoon butter or margarine
2 teaspoons vanilla
2 cups vanilla wafer cookies
2 large bananas
⅓ cup toffee bits

Fruit cocktail adds flavor to the homemade pudding and the banana mixture in this classic old-fashioned recipe.

1. Preheat oven to 350°F. Spray a 2-quart baking dish with nonstick cooking spray and set aside.
2. Drain fruit cocktail, reserving juice. Place fruit in a small mixing bowl and set aside. In medium saucepan, combine 1 cup reserved fruit juice, ¾ cup sugar, flour, salt, and egg yolks and beat well. Gradually add milk, stirring until combined. Cook pudding over medium heat until mixture thickens and boils, stirring constantly, about 8 minutes.
3. Remove pudding from heat and stir in butter and vanilla. Put a layer of vanilla wafer cookies in the bottom of prepared baking dish. Slice bananas and combine with reserved fruit and toffee bits in small bowl. Spoon half of banana mixture over cookies in dish.
4. Top with half of pudding mixture; repeat layers, ending with pudding. Refrigerate while preparing meringue.
5. In medium bowl, beat egg whites until foamy. Gradually beat in remaining ¼ cup sugar until stiff peaks form. Top pudding with meringue mixture, spreading to cover and sealing meringue to sides of dish. Bake for 15–20 minutes or until meringue is browned. Remove from oven and chill for at least 4 hours before serving.

Caramel Mandarin Orange Cake

 Serves 16

~ **TOTAL COST:** $4.17
~ **CALORIES:** 351.97
~ **FAT:** 15.68 g
~ **PROTEIN:** 3.34 g
~ **CHOLESTEROL:** 63.31 mg
~ **SODIUM:** 262.48 mg

2 (9-ounce) boxes yellow cake mix
4 eggs
⅔ cup vegetable oil
1 (11-ounce) can mandarin oranges, undrained
½ cup coconut
1¼ cups brown sugar
2 tablespoons honey
5 tablespoons butter
6 tablespoons milk
2 teaspoons vanilla

Adding fruit to cake mix not only adds flavor, but moistness too. The caramel topping is the perfect finishing touch.

1. Preheat oven to 350°F. Spray a 9" × 13" cake pan with cooking spray containing flour and set aside.
2. In large bowl, combine cake mix, eggs, oil, and undrained oranges. Beat on low speed until combined, then beat at medium speed for 3 minutes. Fold in coconut. Pour into pan. Bake for 25–35 minutes or until cake pulls away from sides of pan and top springs back when lightly touched. Place on wire rack.
3. While cake is cooling, make caramel topping. In medium saucepan, combine brown sugar, dark corn syrup, butter, and milk. Bring to a boil, stirring constantly with wire whisk. Boil for 3 minutes.
4. Using a chopstick, poke about 20 holes evenly in the warm cake. Add vanilla to caramel topping and slowly pour over cake, spreading evenly if necessary. Cool completely before serving.

> **Compare Prices**
> Compare prices between the different brands of cake mix. There are some differences, and when the mixes are on sale, stock up. You may get a better deal by using two smaller cake mixes instead of just one big two-layer box. The ingredients and quality are the same.

Date Nut Chews

Serves 24

~ **TOTAL COST:** $5.33
~ **CALORIES:** 139.95
~ **FAT:** 5.01 g
~ **PROTEIN:** 3.10 g
~ **CHOLESTEROL:** 26.93 mg
~ **SODIUM:** 83.50 mg

3 eggs
½ cup sugar
½ cup brown sugar
2 tablespoons corn syrup
1 teaspoon vanilla
¾ cup flour
½ teaspoon salt
1 tablespoon cornstarch
1 teaspoon baking powder
½ cup oatmeal, ground
½ cup white chocolate chips, ground
1 cup chopped dates
1 cup chopped walnuts
powdered sugar

Finely ground oatmeal and white chocolate chips add chewy texture to these fabulous bar cookies.

1. Preheat oven to 350°F. Grease a 9" x 13" pan with unsalted butter and set aside. In large bowl, beat eggs until frothy. Gradually add sugar and brown sugar, beating until mixture becomes very thick. Beat in corn syrup and vanilla. Then stir in flour, salt, cornstarch, and baking powder and mix well.
2. Stir in ground oatmeal, ground white chocolate chips, dates, and walnuts. Spoon batter into prepared pan. Bake for 25–35 minutes or until bars are set and light golden brown. Cool for 30 minutes, or until cool enough to handle, then cut into bars. Roll bars in powdered sugar to coat; place on wire rack to cool completely.

Honey Double Gingerbread

Serves 16

- **TOTAL COST:** $6.84
- **CALORIES:** 264.73
- **FAT:** 9.83 g
- **PROTEIN:** 3.39 g
- **CHOLESTEROL:** 63.79 mg
- **SODIUM:** 262.07 mg

⅔ cup butter or margarine, softened
¾ cup brown sugar
½ cup sugar
¾ cup honey
3 eggs
2 cups all-purpose flour
2 teaspoons ground ginger
½ teaspoon salt
1 teaspoon cinnamon
½ teaspoon nutmeg
1 teaspoon baking soda
1 teaspoon baking powder
1 tablespoon minced candied ginger
¾ cup milk
¼ cup heavy cream

Gingerbread should be served warm from the oven. Top it with softly whipped heavy cream or coffee ice cream.

1. Preheat oven to 350°F. Spray a 9" x 13" pan with nonstick cooking spray, then dust with flour and set aside.
2. In large bowl, combine butter, brown sugar, sugar, and honey and beat well. Add eggs, one at a time, beating well after each addition. Stir in flour, ginger, salt, cinnamon, nutmeg, baking soda, and baking powder. Then add the candied ginger and milk, stirring until batter is smooth.
3. Pour batter into prepared pan and bake for 45–55 minutes or until gingerbread springs back when lightly touched in center and begins to pull away from sides of pan. Cool for 30 minutes, then serve.

Candied Ginger

You can make your own candied ginger; it's much less expensive than store-bought. Gingerroot is found in the produce aisle of the supermarket. To candy it, combine ½ cup sugar with ½ cup water and 1 tablespoon lemon juice. Bring to a simmer, then add ⅓ cup chopped fresh gingerroot. Simmer for 20 minutes, then cool, drain, and roll the ginger pieces in sugar. Store in the refrigerator up to 3 weeks.

Peanut Butter Crunch Cake

Serves 16

- ~ **TOTAL COST:** $6.74
- ~ **CALORIES:** 449.30
- ~ **FAT:** 22.64 g
- ~ **PROTEIN:** 9.06 g
- ~ **CHOLESTEROL:** 54.92 mg
- ~ **SODIUM:** 223.06 mg

½ cup butter, softened
1 cup peanut butter
1½ cups brown sugar
½ cup sugar
2 cups flour
½ cup applesauce
3 eggs
1 teaspoon baking powder
½ teaspoon baking soda
1½ teaspoons vanilla
2 cups semisweet chocolate chips
½ cup chopped peanuts

Applesauce replaces some of the butter in this delicious cake with the built-in streusel topping.

1. Preheat oven to 350°F. Spray a 9" x 13" baking pan with nonstick cooking spray containing flour and set aside. In large bowl, combine butter, peanut butter, brown sugar, sugar, and flour and mix until crumbly. Reserve 1 cup of this crumbly mixture and place in medium bowl.
2. To crumbs remaining in large bowl, add applesauce, eggs, baking powder, baking soda, and vanilla. Stir until combined, then beat for 3 minutes at medium speed. Pour batter into prepared pan. Add chocolate chips and peanuts to crumbs reserved in medium bowl and mix well. Sprinkle over batter.
3. Bake for 35–45 minutes or until cake begins to pull away from edges of pan and springs back when touched lightly in center. Cool completely; store covered at room temperature.

Easy Crepes

 Yields 8 crepes

~ **TOTAL COST:** $1.36
~ **CALORIES:** 110.54
~ **FAT:** 4.51 g
~ **PROTEIN:** 4.02 g
~ **CHOLESTEROL:** 61.33 mg
~ **SODIUM:** 98.60 mg

1½ cups all-purpose flour
3 eggs
1 cup milk
¼ cup water
¼ teaspoon salt
3 tablespoons butter, melted

With some frozen crepes in the freezer, you can whip up dessert in seconds. Thaw and fill them with ice cream, pudding, or fresh fruit, then roll up and top with chocolate sauce.

1. In medium bowl, combine all ingredients. Beat at low speed until batter is smooth, about 1 minute. Cover and let stand for 30 minutes.
2. Heat a 6-inch nonstick skillet over medium heat for 1 minute. Lightly brush with oil, then pour in 3 tablespoons of batter, using a ¼ cup measure so you add the batter all at once. Swirl and tilt the pan so the batter evenly covers the bottom.
3. Cook crepe for 2–3 minutes or until bottom turns light golden brown. Using a fork, loosen the crepe from the pan and flip over; cook for 30 seconds on second side. Let cool on kitchen towels.
4. When crepes are completely cool, stack them with waxed paper or parchment paper between each crepe. Place in heavy duty freezer bags, label, and freeze up to 3 months. To use, unwrap crepes and separate. Let stand at room temperature for 20–30 minutes.

Citrus Angel Pie

Serves 8

~ **TOTAL COST:** $3.95
~ **CALORIES:** 396.87
~ **FAT:** 18.02 g
~ **PROTEIN:** 7.10 g
~ **CHOLESTEROL:** 126.96 mg
~ **SODIUM:** 249.68 mg

1 Angel Pie Crust (this chapter)
⅓ cup all purpose flour
1 cup sugar
1½ cups milk
1 (8-ounce) package cream cheese
3 egg yolks
3 tablespoons butter
½ teaspoon lemon zest
½ teaspoon orange zest
¼ cup lemon juice
½ cup orange juice

The creamy citrus filling is piled into a meringue crust for a pie perfect for summer. Follow directions to the letter so the filling sets properly. You can omit the lemon and orange zest if you'd rather use bottled juice.

1. In large saucepan, combine flour, sugar, and salt and blend well with wire whisk. Gradually add milk, stirring constantly. Place over medium heat and cook and stir until mixture thickens and comes to a full boil. Lower heat to low and cook for 2 minutes longer, stirring constantly. Cut cream cheese into cubes and add to milk mixture along with egg yolks. Cook and stir for 2 more minutes.
2. Remove from heat and stir in remaining ingredients, beating well until combined. Cool for 30 minutes, then chill for 1 hour until mixture mounds when dropped from a spoon. Stir again if necessary and spoon into pie shell. Cover and chill for at least 4 hours before serving.

Chocolate Cream–Filled Cupcakes

Yields 24 cupcakes

- **TOTAL COST:** $5.05
- **CALORIES:** 258.66
- **FAT:** 10.14 g
- **PROTEIN:** 2.62 g
- **CHOLESTEROL:** 40.44 mg
- **SODIUM:** 141.99 mg

¾ cup butter, softened
1 cup sugar
¼ cup brown sugar
2 teaspoons vanilla, divided
2 eggs
2¼ cups flour, divided
1 teaspoon baking powder

½ teaspoon salt, divided
1½ cups milk, divided
2 (1-ounce) squares unsweetened chocolate, chopped
⅓ cup butter, softened
4 cups powdered sugar

The cream filling for these cupcakes is made from a flour base. This adds body and creamy texture to the filling while reducing the overall fat content. A package of six of those highly processed cream-filled chocolate cupcakes costs $3.99!

1. Preheat oven to 375°F. Line 24 muffin cups with paper liners. In large bowl, combine ¾ cup butter, 1 cup sugar, brown sugar, and 1 teaspoon vanilla and beat until fluffy. Add eggs, one at a time, beating well after each addition. Add 2 cups flour, baking powder, ¼ teaspoon salt, and 1 cup milk; beat until blended, then beat at medium speed for 2 minutes.

2. Fill prepared muffin cups ⅔ full with cake batter. Bake for 20–25 minutes or until cupcakes are light golden brown and top springs back when lightly touched with finger. Remove from muffin tins and cool completely.

3. In medium saucepan, combine ¼ cup flour and ½ cup milk; cook over medium low heat, stirring constantly, until the mixture thickens. When milk mixture begins to boil, add chopped chocolate and remove from heat. Stir until chocolate melts and mixture is smooth. Cool completely.

4. For chocolate cream, in large bowl, combine ⅓ cup butter with 1 teaspoon vanilla, ¼ teaspoon salt, and milk mixture and beat until fluffy. Gradually add enough powdered sugar for desired spreading consistency. Place half of mixture into pastry bag with large round tip. Insert tip into the top of each cupcake; gently squeeze bag until cupcake expands slightly. Repeat with remaining cupcakes. Frost cupcake tops with remaining cream mixture.

Devil's Food Cupcakes

Yields 24 cupcakes

- ~ **TOTAL COST:** $2.43
- ~ **CALORIES:** 160.27
- ~ **FAT:** 7.00 g
- ~ **PROTEIN:** 2.24 g
- ~ **CHOLESTEROL:** 9.63 mg
- ~ **SODIUM:** 187.74 mg

1 cup sugar
½ cup brown sugar
½ cup cocoa powder
1 egg
⅔ cup corn oil
1 cup buttermilk
½ cup coffee or water
2 teaspoons vanilla
2¼ cups flour
½ teaspoon salt
2 teaspoons baking soda
1 teaspoon baking powder

Using cocoa powder and vegetable oil not only reduces the saturated fat content to almost nothing, but makes cupcakes that are velvety and smooth.

1. Preheat oven to 350°F. Line 24 muffin cups with paper liners and set aside. In large mixing bowl, combine sugar, brown sugar, cocoa powder, egg, vegetable oil, buttermilk, coffee, and vanilla and mix well until smooth.
2. Sift together flour, salt, baking soda, and baking powder and add all at once to sugar mixture. Stir with a wire whisk until batter is smooth. Using a ¼ cup measure, pour batter into prepared muffin cups. Bake for 15–20 minutes or until cakes spring back when lightly touched in center. Cool in pans for 5 minutes, then remove to wire racks to cool completely. Frost with Buttercream Frosting (this chapter) or sprinkle with powdered sugar.

Lemon Meringues

Yields 30 cookies

- ~ **TOTAL COST:** $0.68
- ~ **CALORIES:** 35.91
- ~ **FAT:** 0.38 g
- ~ **PROTEIN:** 0.39 g
- ~ **CHOLESTEROL:** 0.0 mg
- ~ **SODIUM:** 7.62 mg

3 egg whites
Pinch of salt
1 teaspoon lemon juice
1 cup sugar
1 teaspoon lemon zest
5 round lemon candies, finely crushed

Save some cookies (or make another batch!) to make Lemon Meringue Parfaits (this chapter). Use the egg yolks to make Pots de Crème (this chapter).

1. Preheat oven to 250°F. In large bowl, beat egg whites with salt and lemon juice until foamy. Gradually beat in sugar until stiff peaks form and sugar is dissolved. Fold in lemon zest and the finely crushed candies.
2. Drop by teaspoonfuls onto a baking sheet lined with parchment paper. Bake for 50–60 minutes or until meringues are set and crisp and very light golden brown. Cool on the cookie sheets for 3 minutes, then carefully peel off the parchment paper and place on wire racks to cool.

Lemon Meringue Parfaits

 Serves 6

- ~ **TOTAL COST:** $4.90
- ~ **CALORIES:** 549.06
- ~ **FAT:** 32.40 g
- ~ **PROTEIN:** 9.68 g
- ~ **CHOLESTEROL:** 184.66 mg
- ~ **SODIUM:** 123.12 mg

3 eggs
⅓ cup lemon juice
¾ cup sugar
¼ cup butter, divided
¾ cup heavy whipping cream
⅓ cup brown sugar
1 cup coarsely chopped walnuts
12 Lemon Meringues (this chapter)

This spectacular dessert is perfect for a special occasion. You have to make it ahead of time, so all you have to do is take it out of the fridge.

1. In heavy saucepan, combine eggs with lemon juice and sugar. Beat with wire whisk until smooth. Cook over low heat, stirring constantly, until mixture thickens and bubbles, about 10–15 minutes. Remove from heat and strain into a small bowl. Stir in 2 tablespoons butter, then place a sheet of plastic wrap directly on the surface and chill until cold.

2. In medium microwave-safe bowl, combine 2 tablespoons butter and brown sugar. Microwave on high until melted and stir until blended. Stir in chopped walnuts and microwave on high for 2–3 minutes, stirring once during cooking time, until walnuts are glazed. Spread on waxed paper and cool completely.

3. In small bowl, beat cream until stiff peaks form. Beat the chilled lemon mixture with same beaters and fold in cream. Break Lemon Meringues into pieces. In six parfait glasses, layer the lemon cream, pecans, and Meringues. Cover and chill for at least 3 hours before serving.

Glazed Cinnamon Apple Cake

Serves 10

- ~ **TOTAL COST:** $6.86
- ~ **CALORIES:** 319.85
- ~ **FAT:** 12.38 g
- ~ **PROTEIN:** 2.95 g
- ~ **CHOLESTEROL:** 52.29 mg
- ~ **SODIUM:** 289.00 mg

10 tablespoons butter, softened, divided
½ cup brown sugar
1 egg
1 teaspoon vanilla
1¼ cups flour
1½ teaspoons baking powder
½ teaspoon salt
2 ½ teaspoons cinnamon, divided
½ cup milk
4 apples, peeled and chopped
2 tablespoons lemon juice
1 cup sugar, divided
1 tablespoon cornstarch
¾ cup water

Lots of apples add great flavor and moistness to this delicious dessert that's a cross between apple pie and cake.

1. Preheat oven to 350°F. Grease a 10-inch springform pan with solid shortening and set aside. In large bowl, combine 6 tablespoons butter and brown sugar; beat until fluffy. Add egg and vanilla and beat until combined. Place flour, baking powder, salt, and ½ teaspoon cinnamon in a sifter. Sift ⅓ of flour mixture over butter mixture and beat. Then add ⅓ of the milk. Repeat, beating after each addition.
2. Spread batter into prepared pan. Prepare apples and sprinkle with lemon juice, ¼ cup sugar and 1 teaspoon cinnamon over; toss. Spread over batter in pan.
3. In small heavy saucepan, combine ¾ cup sugar, cornstarch, and water and mix well. Add ¼ cup butter and 1 teaspoon cinnamon; cook over medium heat, stirring constantly, until thick. Spoon over apples. Bake for 40–50 minutes or until cake pulls away from sides of pan and apples and glazed. Cool for 30 minutes; serve warm.

Working with Butter

When butter is used in baked goods, it needs to be softened. If any of the butter melts during the softening process, the texture of the final product will change. To soften butter properly, let it stand at room temperature for about an hour before using. Do not use the microwave; the hot and cold spots means part of the butter always melts.

Date Torte

 Serves 6

- ~ **TOTAL COST:** $2.97
- ~ **CALORIES:** 236.02
- ~ **FAT:** 8.75 g
- ~ **PROTEIN:** 6.54 g
- ~ **CHOLESTEROL:** 105.75 mg
- ~ **SODIUM:** 116.95 mg

3 eggs
½ cup sugar
1 teaspoon vanilla
3 tablespoons flour
pinch salt
1 teaspoon baking powder
½ cup finely chopped dates
½ cup chopped walnuts

This recipe isn't a layered torte. It's a simple dessert with a light and chewy texture made by beating eggs until very light and fluffy. Serve it with whipped cream or ice cream.

1. Preheat oven to 350°F. Grease a 9-inch pie pan with unsalted butter and set aside. In large bowl, beat eggs until light in color. Gradually add sugar, beating until mixture is light and fluffy. Stir in vanilla, then fold in flour, salt, and baking powder. Add dates and walnuts.
2. Spread mixture into prepared pan. Bake for 25–35 minutes or until torte begins to pull away from sides of pan. Cool for 1 hour, then cut into wedges and serve warm.

Chocolate Truffles

Yields 36 truffles

- ~ **TOTAL COST:** $5.48
- ~ **CALORIES:** 140.80
- ~ **FAT:** 9.55 g
- ~ **PROTEIN:** 1.33 g
- ~ **CHOLESTEROL:** 13.14 mg
- ~ **SODIUM:** 20.99 mg

1 cup heavy whipping cream
1 (1-ounce) square unsweetened chocolate
1 cup semisweet chocolate chips
1½ cups milk chocolate chips
2 tablespoons butter
1 teaspoon vanilla
¾ pound white chocolate candy coating

Chocolate truffles are a decadent treat, but they aren't expensive to make. Gourmet chocolates like these cost $20.00 a pound in some stores; this recipe makes two pounds of candy for under $6.00.

1. In heavy saucepan, heat cream until it just begins to simmer around the edges. Meanwhile, chop the chocolate square into chip-size bits. When the cream begins to simmer, remove from the heat and add all of the chocolates and the butter. Stir until chocolate melts and mixture is smooth. Add vanilla, cover and chill until firm.
2. When mixture is firm, scoop out balls with a small cookie scoop or melon baller; place on parchment paper. Chill again until firm. Cut candy coating into small pieces and melt as package directs. Dip the truffles into the candy coating and place on parchment; chill until hardened. Store at room temperature.

Buttercream Frosting

 Yields 3 cups; serving size ¼ cup

~ **TOTAL COST:** $3.10
~ **CALORIES:** 340.00
~ **FAT:** 16.37 g
~ **PROTEIN:** 0.30 g
~ **CHOLESTEROL:** 44.01 mg
~ **SODIUM:** 141.34 mg

1 cup butter, softened
5 cups powdered sugar
pinch salt
1 teaspoon vanilla
3 to 5 tablespoons light cream

Tubs of prepared buttercream frosting cost just about as much as this recipe, but you only get two cups per tub. And homemade tastes so much better!

In large bowl, beat butter until fluffy. Gradually add 1 cup powdered sugar, beating until fluffy. Stir in vanilla. Then add remaining powdered sugar alternately with the whole milk, until desired spreading consistency is reached. Fills and frosts two 9-inch cake layers, or frosts one 9" × 13" cake.

Buttercream Frosting Flavorings
To this basic frosting recipe, you can add 2 squares of melted unsweetened chocolate for Chocolate Frosting, or add 6 tablespoons of cocoa powder. For a Peanut Butter Frosting, reduce the butter amount to ⅓ cup and add ⅓ cup peanut butter (you may need to add more milk). For Peppermint Frosting, crush some peppermint candies and fold into the frosting. You get the idea!

Pots de Crème

Serves 6

~ **TOTAL COST:** $3.49
~ **CALORIES:** 286.30
~ **FAT:** 18.35 g
~ **PROTEIN:** 3.96 g
~ **CHOLESTEROL:** 133.81 mg
~ **SODIUM:** 48.34 mg

1 cup heavy cream
¾ cup milk
⅓ cup sugar
pinch salt
1 cup semisweet chocolate chips
3 egg yolks
1 teaspoon vanilla

These super-rich little cups of chocolate cream are decadent and so delicious. It's hard to believe they're a budget recipe!

1. Preheat oven to 325°F. Grease 6 custard cups with butter and place on sturdy cookie sheet; set aside.
2. In large saucepan, combine the cream, milk, sugar, and salt. Cook over medium heat, whisking frequently, until the mixture comes to a boil. Add the chocolate chips and remove from heat; whisk until smooth.
3. In small bowl, beat the egg yolks until smooth. Add ¼ cup of the hot chocolate mixture to the egg yolks, beating well until smooth. Then add the egg yolk mixture to the chocolate mixture in the saucepan, whisking constantly.
4. Strain the mixture into the custard cups. Bake for 25–30 minutes or until the mixture is just set. Cool on wire racks for 45 minutes, then remove to refrigerator to cool. Chill for 3–4 hours before serving.

Crumb Cake

Serves 16

- **TOTAL COST:** $4.90
- **CALORIES:** 283.74
- **FAT:** 11.95 g
- **PROTEIN:** 3.41 g
- **CHOLESTEROL:** 50.56 mg
- **SODIUM:** 245.69 mg

2 cups brown sugar

2 cups flour

¾ cup butter

1 cup buttermilk

1 teaspoon baking soda

2 eggs

½ teaspoon salt

1 teaspoon cinnamon

¼ teaspoon nutmeg

2 teaspoons vanilla

½ cup chopped pecans

¼ cup powdered sugar

This classic cake was inspired by a now-defunct frozen crumb cake by a famous company. It's light yet rich, velvety smooth, and crunchy all at the same time!

1. Preheat oven to 350°F. Grease a 9" × 13" pan with unsalted butter and set aside. In large bowl, combine brown sugar and flour and mix well. Cut butter into small pieces and add to flour mixture; mixing with pastry blender or two knives until crumbs form. Remove ¾ cup crumb mixture and set aside.
2. To remaining crumb mixture, add buttermilk, baking soda, eggs, salt, cinnamon, and nutmeg and stir until combined. Then beat at medium speed for 2 minutes. Spoon into prepared pan. To reserved crumbs, add pecans and mix well. Sprinkle over cake.
3. Bake for 25–35 minutes or until cake begins to pull away from sides of pan and top springs back when lightly touched. Cool cake completely, then place powdered sugar in small strainer and sprinkle heavily over cake.

Buttermilk

You can purchase buttermilk in small packages, including ½ pint, to use in baking. If you don't have buttermilk, it's easy to make a substitute. Put 2 tablespoons of apple cider vinegar or lemon juice in a cup measure. Then add enough regular milk to fill the cup. Let the mixture stand for 5 minutes, then use in the recipe.

Apple-Date Turnovers

~ **TOTAL COST:** $5.66

~ **CALORIES:** 197.61

~ **FAT:** 9.65 g

~ **PROTEIN:** 2.52 g

~ **CHOLESTEROL:** 15.26 mg

~ **SODIUM:** 103.68 mg

2 Granny Smith apples, peeled and chopped

½ cup finely chopped dates

1 teaspoon lemon juice

1 tablespoon flour

3 tablespoons brown sugar

1½ teaspoons cinnamon, divided

12 (15" × 19") sheets frozen filo dough, thawed

½ cup finely chopped walnuts

5 tablespoons sugar, divided

6 tablespoons butter or margarine, melted

Traditionally, turnovers are made of puff pastry, which is loaded with saturated fat. Using filo dough reduces the fat and increases the crispness.

1. In medium bowl, combine apples, dates, lemon juice, flour, brown sugar, and 1 teaspoon cinnamon, and mix well; set aside. Place thawed filo dough on work surface and cover with waxed paper, then a damp kitchen towel to prevent drying. Work with one sheet at a time. In small bowl, combine walnuts and 3 tablespoons sugar.
2. Lay one sheet filo on work surface; brush with butter. Sprinkle with 2 tablespoons of the walnut mixture. Place another sheet of filo on top, brush with butter, and sprinkle with 1 tablespoon of the walnut mixture. Cut into two 4½" × 18" strips.
3. Place 2 tablespoons of the apple filling at one end of dough strips. Fold a corner of the dough over the filling so edges match, then continue folding dough as you would fold a flag. Place on ungreased cookie sheets and brush with more butter. Repeat process with remaining strips, walnut mixture, apple filling, and melted butter.
4. Preheat oven to 375°F. In small bowl, combine remaining 2 tablespoons sugar and ½ teaspoon cinnamon and mix well. Sprinkle over turnovers. Bake for 20–30 minutes or until pastries are golden-brown and crisp. Remove to wire racks to cool.

Apple Pear–Nut Crisp

 Serves 8

~ **TOTAL COST:** $6.36
~ **CALORIES:** 337.06
~ **FAT:** 12.70 g
~ **PROTEIN:** 4.03 g
~ **CHOLESTEROL:** 30.53 mg
~ **SODIUM:** 141.06 mg

2 apples, sliced
3 pears, sliced
2 tablespoons lemon juice
¼ cup sugar
1 teaspoon cinnamon
½ teaspoon nutmeg
1½ cups quick-cooking oatmeal
¾ cup flour
⅔ cup brown sugar
⅛ teaspoon salt
½ cup butter or margarine, melted

Leave the skins on the apples and pears for more fiber and nutrition. You can peel them, if you'd like.

1. Preheat oven to 350°F. Spray a 9-inch round cake pan with nonstick cooking spray and set aside.
2. Prepare apples and pears, sprinkling with lemon juice as you work. Combine in medium bowl with sugar, cinnamon, and nutmeg. Spoon into prepared cake pan.
3. In same bowl, combine oatmeal, flour, whole-wheat flour, and brown sugar and mix well. Add melted butter and mix until crumbly. Sprinkle over fruit in dish.
4. Bake for 35–45 minutes or until fruit bubbles and topping is browned and crisp. Let cool for 15 minutes before serving.

Chocolate Tassies

Yields 48 cookies

~ **TOTAL COST:** $6.88
~ **CALORIES:** 129.02
~ **FAT:** 6.80 g
~ **PROTEIN:** 1.69 g
~ **CHOLESTEROL:** 7.92 mg
~ **SODIUM:** 57.88 mg

1 (12-ounce) package semisweet chocolate chips, divided
2½ cups finely crushed graham crackers
½ cup finely chopped walnuts
½ cup butter
1 (13-ounce) can evaporated milk
1 cup brown sugar

Tassies are little cakes and cookies that are baked in muffin tins. It's essential that you use mini muffin tins in this recipe; in regular tins, the mixture will not bake through.

1. Preheat oven to 375°F. Spray mini muffin cups with nonstick baking spray containing flour and set aside. In medium microwave-safe bowl, melt 1 cup of the semisweet chocolate chips at 50 percent power; stir until smooth; set aside. In large bowl, combine remaining semisweet chocolate chips, graham crackers, and walnuts.
2. In medium bowl, combine butter, margarine, and brown sugar and beat until fluffy. Gradually add melted chocolate, then evaporated milk, beating thoroughly. Pour over graham cracker mixture; stir until combined. Fill each muffin tin about ⅔ full. Bake 8–12 minutes or until set. Let cool in muffin tins for 3 minutes, then carefully remove and cool completely on wire rack.

Raisin Bars

Yields 36 bars

- **TOTAL COST:** $4.55
- **CALORIES:** 135.11
- **FAT:** 4.28 g
- **PROTEIN:** 1.52 g
- **CHOLESTEROL:** 22.06 mg
- **SODIUM:** 85.53 mg

1½ cups dark raisins
1½ cups water
¾ cup butter or margarine
¾ cup sugar
¼ cup brown sugar
1 tablespoon lemon juice
½ cup milk, divided
2 eggs
2 teaspoons vanilla, divided
2⅓ cups all-purpose flour
1 teaspoon cinnamon
¼ teaspoon nutmeg
½ teaspoon salt
½ teaspoon baking soda
2 cups powdered sugar

These old-fashioned bars have the best flavor; the combination of soft raisins and spices with the tender cookie is really wonderful.

1. Preheat oven to 350°F. Spray a 10" × 15" jelly roll pan with baking spray containing flour and set aside. In large saucepan, combine raisins with water and bring to a boil. Remove from heat and stir in margarine, sugar, brown sugar, lemon juice, and ¼ cup milk; stir until margarine is melted. Add egg and 1 teaspoon vanilla and beat well.
2. Stir in flour, spices, salt, and baking soda and mix well. Pour into prepared pan. Bake 20–35 minutes or until bars are light golden brown and spring back when lightly touched with finger. Let cool until warm.
3. While bars are still warm, combine powdered sugar, ¼ cup milk, and 1 teaspoon vanilla in small bowl and beat until smooth. Spoon and spread over warm bars. Let cool completely, then cut into squares. Store covered at room temperature.

Frosted Ginger Cookies

Yields 48 cookies

- ~ **TOTAL COST:** $4.42
- ~ **CALORIES:** 109.10
- ~ **FAT:** 3.52 g
- ~ **PROTEIN:** 0.93 g
- ~ **CHOLESTEROL:** 8.95 mg
- ~ **SODIUM:** 92.90 mg

½ cup butter, softened
1 cup brown sugar
½ cup sour cream
½ cup buttermilk
½ cup light molasses
2½ cups all-purpose flour
¼ teaspoon salt
1½ teaspoons ground ginger
1 teaspoon cinnamon
¼ teaspoon nutmeg
2 teaspoons baking soda
¼ cup butter
⅓ cup brown sugar
¼ cup milk
1 teaspoon vanilla
2–3 cups powdered sugar

Soft ginger cookies should always be frosted! This browned butter frosting adds a richness and depth of flavor to these spicy cookies.

1. In large bowl, combine butter with brown sugar and beat well. Then add sour cream, buttermilk, and molasses and beat again. Stir in flour, salt, ginger, cinnamon, nutmeg, and baking soda until a dough forms. Cover dough and chill for at least 1 hour in the fridge.

2. Preheat oven to 375°F. Roll dough into 1-inch balls and place on ungreased cookie sheets. Flatten slightly with palm of hand. Bake 8–13 minutes or until cookies are puffed and set. Let cool on baking sheet 2–3 minutes, then remove to wire racks to cool.

3. For frosting, in heavy saucepan melt butter over medium heat. Continue cooking butter, stirring frequently, until butter just begins to brown, about 7–9 minutes. Remove from heat and add brown sugar and milk; stir with wire whisk. Then add vanilla. Stir in enough powdered sugar until spreading consistency. Frost cooled cookies.

Angel Pie Crust

1 Crust; serves 8

- ~ **TOTAL COST:** $0.57
- ~ **CALORIES:** 92.91
- ~ **FAT:** 1.42 g
- ~ **PROTEIN:** 1.40 g
- ~ **CHOLESTEROL:** 3.82 mg
- ~ **SODIUM:** 103.44 mg

3 egg whites
½ teaspoon lemon juice
¾ cup sugar
¼ teaspoon salt
1 teaspoon vanilla
1 tablespoons butter
1 teaspoon flour

This practically fat-free pie crust is perfect piled high with ice cream balls and different types of ice cream topping.

1. Preheat oven to 275°F. Separate eggs while cold; let egg whites stand at room temperature for 45 minutes before beating (for better volume). Beat egg whites with lemon juice until foamy. Gradually add ¼ cup sugar, beating until soft peaks form. Add salt and vanilla and beat well. Then gradually add remaining ½ cup sugar, beating until stiff peaks form.
2. Heavily butter a 9-inch pie plate and dust with flour. Place meringue in prepared plate and form a shell, building up the sides to about ½-inch over top rim of pie plate. Bake for 1 hour, until crust is very light golden. Turn off oven and let meringue cool for 1 hour, then cool completely on wire rack.
3. You can also shape this pie on a Silpat-lined cookie sheet. Spread meringue into a 10-inch circle at least 1-inch thick, then spoon more meringue on the edges and build up a 2-inch rim that is 2 inches wide. Bake at 275°F for 45 minutes, then cool for 30 minutes in oven; remove and cool completely on wire rack.

Leftover Egg Yolks
Leftover egg yolks can be frozen. Just beat slightly and divide into ice cube trays. Freeze until solid, then package into freezer bags. To thaw, let stand in the refrigerator overnight. You can use egg yolks to make Pots de Crème (this chapter) or Citrus Angel Pie (this chapter), but don't freeze them first. Frozen, thawed egg yolks are great fried, then chopped and added to egg or spinach salad.

Chocolate Oatmeal Pie

Serves 12

~ **TOTAL COST:** $5.91
~ **CALORIES:** 447.41
~ **FAT:** 27.58 g
~ **PROTEIN:** 7.78 g
~ **CHOLESTEROL:** 77.28 mg
~ **SODIUM:** 241.48 mg

1 Angel Pie Crust (this chapter)
½ cup butter
1½ cups semisweet chocolate chips, divided
¾ cup brown sugar
¼ cup corn syrup
3 eggs
2 tablespoons flour
¼ teaspoon salt
1 cup chopped walnuts, toasted
1 cup quick cooking oatmeal

Oatmeal takes the place of nuts in this simple yet very rich pie. Serve it with a scoop of ice cream or a dollop of whipped cream.

1. Preheat oven to 350°F. Do not prebake pie crust. In large saucepan, combine butter with ¾ cup of the chocolate chips, brown sugar, and corn syrup. Cook and stir over low heat until butter and chocolate chips melt. Remove from heat. Add eggs, one at a time, beating well after each addition.
2. Stir in flour, salt, walnuts, oatmeal, and remaining ¾ cup of chocolate chips. Pour into prepared crust. Bake for 40–50 minutes or until pie is set and pie crust is golden brown. Cool for 45 minutes, then serve warm or cool.

Strawberry Angel Food Cake

Serves 8

~ **PREP TIME:** 5 minutes
~ **FREEZE TIME:** 15 minutes
~ **TOTAL COST:** $7.00
~ **CALORIES:** 364
~ **FAT:** 6 g
~ **PROTEIN:** 6 g
~ **CHOLESTEROL:** 8 mg
~ **SODIUM:** 432 mg

1 whole angel food cake
2 cups strawberry frozen yogurt, thawed slightly
1 pint strawberries, stemmed and sliced

Angel food cake is great for making all kinds of desserts. Used here with strawberry, this cake is also great with chocolate syrup and whipped cream.

Cut the cake in half horizontally. Spread the strawberry yogurt on bottom half of cake. Place half of strawberry slices on top of yogurt. Replace top half of the cake. Place more strawberry slices on top of cake. Freeze 15 minutes before serving.

> **Quick and Easy Tip**
> If you prefer, substitute your favorite frozen fruit yogurt and combine the corresponding fresh fruit, say raspberry, for example.

Chocolate Peanut Butter Truffle Tart

 Serves 16

- **TOTAL COST:** $6.40
- **CALORIES:** 332.03
- **FAT:** 20.19 g
- **PROTEIN:** 6.30 g
- **CHOLESTEROL:** 28.27 mg
- **SODIUM:** 92.15 mg

¼ cup butter, softened
¾ cup peanut butter, divided
½ cup sugar
1 teaspoon vanilla
1 egg
1⅓ cups flour
1 (12-ounce) package semisweet chocolate chips
1 cup milk chocolate chips
½ cup heavy cream

Wow—this super rich tart should be saved for a special occasion. You have to cut it into tiny pieces because it's so rich.

1. Preheat oven to 350°F. In medium bowl, combine butter, ¼ cup peanut butter and sugar and beat until combined. Add vanilla and egg and mix well. Stir in flour until a dough forms. Press dough into bottom and up sides of 10-inch tart pan with removable bottom. Bake for 15–20 minutes or until set and light golden brown. Cool completely.
2. In large microwave safe bowl, combine ½ cup peanut butter, semi-sweet chocolate chips, milk chocolate chips, and cream. Microwave on high for 2 minutes; remove and stir. Continue microwaving for 30-second intervals, stirring after each interval, until chocolate is melted and mixture is smooth.
3. Pour into cooled pie crust. Cover and chill for at least 4 hours. Let stand at room temperature for 15–20 minutes before serving to make cutting easier.

Measuring Brown Sugar
Brown sugar is measured differently than other sugars. Because it has a high moisture content, it must be packed firmly into the measuring cup, not spooned in like granulated or powered sugar. When the sugar is turned out of the cup, it should retain the shape of the cup. Measure tablespoons and teaspoons the same way.

Chocolate Candy Bar Cookies

 Serves 12

- ~ **PREP TIME:** 10 minutes
- ~ **COOK TIME:** 15 minutes
- ~ **TOTAL COST:** $4.36
- ~ **CALORIES:** 399
- ~ **FAT:** 22 g
- ~ **PROTEIN:** 7 g
- ~ **CHOLESTEROL:** 37 mg
- ~ **SODIUM:** 210 mg

1¼ cups plain flour

¾ teaspoon baking powder

¼ teaspoon sea salt

½ cup unsalted butter, softened

½ cup sugar

1 egg

1 teaspoon vanilla extract

1 cup chopped chocolate-covered candy bars (about 6 ounces, ½-inch thick pieces)

Heath bars work great for this recipe, and Baby Ruth bars also work well. Just be sure you don't eat all the candy bars before you need them for the recipe.

Preheat oven to 325°F. In a bowl, sift together flour, baking powder, and salt. In a large bowl, using an electric mixer set on medium, beat together butter and sugar until fluffy and smooth, about 30 seconds. Mix in egg and vanilla and beat for 1 minute, stopping mixer halfway through to scrape down the sides with rubber spatula. Reduce speed to low and add flour mixture, mixing just until incorporated. Gently mix in the candy bar pieces. Drop the batter by large tablespoons onto ungreased baking sheets. Bake for 15 minutes, or until lightly browned. Remove while warm to prevent sticking. Cool on wire racks.

Simplest Ever Chocolate Mousse

Serves 6

- ~ **PREP TIME:** 10 minutes
- ~ **CHILL:** 2 hours
- ~ **TOTAL COST:** $4.02
- ~ **CALORIES:** 307
- ~ **FAT:** 12 g
- ~ **PROTEIN:** 3 g
- ~ **CHOLESTEROL:** 54 mg
- ~ **SODIUM:** 135 mg

1 (6-ounce) package chocolate pudding mix

¾ cup milk

1 teaspoon instant coffee powder

1 (8-ounce) package cream cheese, cubed

Lots of people are intimidated just by the thought of making chocolate mousse. But this recipe is so simple you can make it with your kids!

In a medium saucepan, combine pudding mix, milk, and instant coffee and stir well. Place over medium heat and cook, stirring constantly, until the mixture comes to a boil. Add the cream cheese and beat until blended. Pour into a 1-quart mold. Chill before serving.

Quick and Easy Tip
Nothing goes better with chocolate than fresh berries. Add some fresh raspberries when serving for a beautiful dish that tastes delicious!

Cream Cheese Pound Cake

Serves 10

- ~ **PREP TIME:** 15 minutes
- ~ **COOK TIME:** 1½ hours
- ~ **TOTAL COST:** $7.00
- ~ **CALORIES:** 502
- ~ **FAT:** 38 g
- ~ **PROTEIN:** 8 g
- ~ **CHOLESTEROL:** 173 mg
- ~ **SODIUM:** 368 mg

1½ cups butter
3 cups sugar
1 (8-ounce) package cream cheese
6 eggs
1 teaspoon vanilla
3 cups cake flour
1 tablespoon powdered sugar, for serving

Pound cakes taste delicious, slice easily, and hold up well for parties.

1. Preheat oven to 300°F. Grease a bundt pan with softened butter, dusted with flour. Tap out the excess flour from the pan.
2. With mixer, cream together butter, sugar, and cream cheese until light and fluffy. Add eggs one at a time, beating well after each one. Then add the vanilla. Mix well. Add flour slowly until combined. Pour into bundt pan and bake for 1½ hours. When serving, dust with powdered sugar.

Quick and Easy Tip
Pound cake can be used in strawberry shortcakes as a substitute for angel food cake.

Oven-Baked Peaches with Brown Sugar Crust

Serves 4

- ~ **PREP TIME:** 10 minutes
- ~ **COOK TIME:** 45 minutes
- ~ **TOTAL COST:** $4.56
- ~ **CALORIES:** 202
- ~ **FAT:** 7 g
- ~ **PROTEIN:** 12 g
- ~ **CHOLESTEROL:** 124 mg
- ~ **SODIUM:** 263 mg

1 (20-ounce) can sliced peaches, drained
Zest of ½ lemon
¼ cup dry pie crust mix
¾ cup packed brown sugar
2 tablespoons butter, cut into pieces
Whipped cream

Lemon zest is the rind of the lemon that has been grated off. When grating, use the small side of a large grater or invest in a zester, and be sure to stop when you see the white pith of the lemon. The pith has a bitter taste that will transfer to your food.

Preheat oven to 325°F. Place peaches in a medium-sized baking dish. Add lemon zest. Crumble pie crust mix into a bowl. Add the brown sugar and mix well. Dust peaches with pie-crust mixture and dot liberally with the butter. Bake for 45 minutes or until top is crusty. Serve warm with whipped cream or ice cream.

Quick and Easy Tip
Using canned peaches certainly saves time, but if you have some helpers, use fresh peaches that you have peeled and the removed the pits.

Oatmeal-Crusted Baked Apples

 Serves 6

- ~ **PREP TIME:** 5 minutes
- ~ **COOK TIME:** 20 minutes
- ~ **TOTAL COST:** $4.14
- ~ **CALORIES:** 298
- ~ **FAT:** 6 g
- ~ **PROTEIN:** 3 g
- ~ **CHOLESTEROL:** 31 mg
- ~ **SODIUM:** 91 mg

1 (21-ounce) can apple pie filling
¾ cup brown sugar
1 teaspoon cinnamon
¼ teaspoon nutmeg
½ cup plain flour
½ cup oatmeal
¼ cup butter, melted

The secret that makes this recipe good is the crumbly sugary crust on top.

1. Preheat oven to 400°F. Place pie filling into 1½-quart casserole dish. In a medium bowl, combine sugar, cinnamon, nutmeg, flour, and oatmeal and mix well. Add melted butter and mix until crumbs form. Sprinkle crumbs over pie filling.
2. Bake for 15 to 20 minutes or until pie filling bubbles and crumb mixture is browned.

Quick and Easy Tip
Apple pie filling, or any canned pie filling, can also be added to cake mixes for a more dense, flavorful cake. Add the same crumbly crust to the top of the cake before baking. Yum!

Easy No-Bake Chocolate Custard

Serves 6

- ~ **PREP TIME:** 5 minutes
- ~ **FREEZE TIME:** 4 hours
- ~ **TOTAL COST:** $4.52
- ~ **CALORIES:** 127
- ~ **FAT:** 7 g
- ~ **PROTEIN:** 1 g
- ~ **CHOLESTEROL:** 6 mg
- ~ **SODIUM:** 2 mg

1 cup chocolate syrup
1 (15-ounce) can sweetened condensed milk
1 (16-ounce) container frozen whipped topping, thawed
½ teaspoon vanilla
¼ cup sliced almonds, toasted

Whenever a recipe calls for vanilla, use real vanilla extract as opposed to imitation vanilla, even if you are shopping on a budget. Imitation vanilla has very little flavor, and you end up using five times as much to try to get the same amount of flavor.

In a large bowl, combine syrup and sweetened condensed milk and beat until smooth. Fold in whipped topping and vanilla. Sprinkle with almonds and serve immediately as a custard or place in casserole dish, top with almonds, and freeze until hardened.

Quick and Easy Tip
Pour this mixture into a prepared pie crust (ready-made crust, available in the freezer section) and freeze until solid. Top with chocolate shavings.

Peanut Butter Cup Pie with Chocolate Ice Cream

 Serves 8

- ~ **PREP TIME:** 10 minutes
- ~ **FREEZE TIME:** 4 hours
- ~ **TOTAL COST:** $7.00
- ~ **CALORIES:** 495
- ~ **FAT:** 29 g
- ~ **PROTEIN:** 13 g
- ~ **CHOLESTEROL:** 144 mg
- ~ **SODIUM:** 383 mg

30 fudge-covered graham crackers
¼ cup butter, melted
2½ pints chocolate ice cream
¾ cup peanut butter
4 ounces peanut butter cups, chopped

This is a great dessert for parties as it usually appeals to a lot of people.

1. Crush graham crackers and combine with butter. Press crumbs into a 9-inch pie pan and set aside.
2. In a blender or food processor, combine ice cream and peanut butter. Blend or process until combined. Fold in chopped peanut butter cups until mixed well. Pour into pie crust and freeze until firm.

Quick and Easy Tip

For best results when serving, remove from freezer and let stand for about 10 minutes. Slice and then serve.

Chocolate Parfait with Oatmeal Cookies and Crumbled Toffee

Serves 4

- ~ **PREP TIME:** 10 minutes
- ~ **COOK TIME:** none
- ~ **TOTAL COST:** $4.89
- ~ **CALORIES:** 269
- ~ **FAT:** 8 g
- ~ **PROTEIN:** 3 g
- ~ **CHOLESTEROL:** 26 mg
- ~ **SODIUM:** 88 mg

1 (3-ounce) package instant chocolate pudding mix
1 cup chocolate milk
1 cup whipping cream
5 oatmeal cookies, broken into pieces
¼ cup toffee candy bits

Substitute any type of cookie you wish for this dessert or change the flavor of pudding mix.

1. In a medium bowl, combine pudding mix and chocolate milk. Mix well. With wire whisk, whisk until smooth and thickened. In a small bowl, beat cream until stiff peaks form. Fold into pudding mixture.
2. Layer pudding mixture, cookies, and candy bits into parfait, martini, or wine glasses. Serve immediately or refrigerate.

Grilled Bananas with Honey

 Serves 6

- ~ **PREP TIME:** 5 minutes
- ~ **COOK TIME:** 6 minutes
- ~ **TOTAL COST:** $4.25
- ~ **CALORIES:** 132
- ~ **FAT:** 1 g
- ~ **PROTEIN:** 1 g
- ~ **CHOLESTEROL:** 0 mg
- ~ **SODIUM:** 3 mg

6 bananas, peeled
Cooking spray
2 tablespoons honey
¼ cup almonds, whole or chopped
¼ cup light brown sugar
2 teaspoons fresh cilantro, leaves chopped

There are hundreds of types of bananas. The most familiar banana is the Cavendish banana; however, some markets may carry red bananas, which are sweeter, or the Manzano banana, which has an apple flavor.

1. Preheat grill. Spray bananas with cooking spray and place on grill. Turn them while grilling to get crossed grill marks on the bananas. Grill them for 3 minutes on each side.
2. When serving, slice bananas on bias, fan on plate, drizzle with honey, and sprinkle with almonds, brown sugar, and cilantro.

> **Quick and Easy Tip**
> Grilled bananas whole, with peel on, if you prefer, until black. Peel back and serve as outlined above.

Cider-Poached Apples with Raisins

 Serves 6

- ~ **PREP TIME:** 5 minutes
- ~ **COOK TIME:** 45 minutes
- ~ **TOTAL COST:** $5.72
- ~ **CALORIES:** 164
- ~ **FAT:** 4 g
- ~ **PROTEIN:** 0 g
- ~ **CHOLESTEROL:** 1 mg
- ~ **SODIUM:** 91 mg

6 Granny Smith apples, peeled
1 cup apple cider
¼ cup sweet white wine such as Reisling
Zest and juice of 1 lemon (zest first, then juice)
3 whole cloves or ¼ teaspoon ground cloves
2 cinnamon sticks or ½ teaspoon ground cinnamon
¼ cup golden raisins

When a recipe requires both lemon zest and lemon juice, be sure to zest the lemon first, then roll the lemon on a hard surface to break up the juices inside, and then juice the lemon. Trying to get the zest off a juiced lemon is near to impossible and will most likely result in an injury to your hand.

1. Place apples in a large saucepan with the cider, wine, lemon juice, zest, cloves, and cinnamon. Simmer, covered, on medium heat for 30 to 45 minutes, until apples are fork tender. Remove apples and set aside.
2. Reduce cooking liquid in half. Serve apples sprinkled with raisins and drizzled with remaining liquid.

Easy Lime Tart

 Serves 8

- ~ **PREP TIME:** 8 minutes
- ~ **COOK TIME:** 25 minutes
- ~ **TOTAL COST:** $5.20
- ~ **CALORIES:** 103
- ~ **FAT:** 4 g
- ~ **PROTEIN:** 1 g
- ~ **CHOLESTEROL:** 26 mg
- ~ **SODIUM:** 100 mg

3 limes, zested and juiced
3 eggs, beaten
2 tablespoons cornstarch
½ cup granulated sugar
1 cup water
1 ready-made frozen pie crust

For this recipe, prebaking the pie crust is essential to a crispy tart. Placing the filling into an unbaked pie crust will result in an undone or uncooked pie crust bottom.

1. Mix together all ingredients well, except pie crust, and place in a medium-quart boiler over medium heat. Bring to slow simmer and stir mixture constantly so the eggs don't curdle until it becomes thick.
2. Pour lime mixture into pie crust and bake for 15 minutes.

Quick and Easy Tip
Substitute lemons if you prefer.

Zabaglione with Marsala Wine and Peaches

Serves 6

- ~ **PREP TIME:** 10 minutes
- ~ **COOK TIME:** 10 minutes
- ~ **TOTAL COST:** $6.97
- ~ **CALORIES:** 198
- ~ **FAT:** 8 g
- ~ **PROTEIN:** 8 g
- ~ **CHOLESTEROL:** 159 mg
- ~ **SODIUM:** 308 mg

3 pounds fresh ripe peaches, peeled, halved, pits removed
¼ cup granulated sugar
3 large egg yolks, room temperature
2 tablespoons water
¼ cup Marsala wine

Zabaliogne, or sabayon, is a thin custard-like sauce for berries or other fruits. It is delicious when poured into a martini glass and topped with fresh berries. Make the day before and keep in the refrigerator overnight.

1. Slice peaches into 1/8-inch slices and fan out on plate to serve.
2. Combine sugar and yolks in top of double boiler over medium heat. Using an electric mixer, beat mixture until frothy. Add water and wine. Continue to cook over simmering water, beating constantly with mixer at medium speed until mixture thickens, about 8 minutes. When serving, pour sauce over peaches and serve hot.

Piña Colada Grilled Pineapple

Serves 6

- ~ **PREP TIME:** 10 minutes
- ~ **COOK TIME:** 10 minutes
- ~ **TOTAL COST:** $6.12
- ~ **CALORIES:** 259
- ~ **FAT:** 1 g
- ~ **PROTEIN:** 1 g
- ~ **CHOLESTEROL:** 2 mg
- ~ **SODIUM:** 9 mg

3 tablespoons dark rum
½ ripe medium pineapple, peeled and cut crosswise into 6 slices, ¾-inch thick
1 tablespoon brown sugar
1 cup frozen whipped topping
¼ cup shredded coconut

Try serving this in the shape of a butterfly for an impressive presentation!

Preheat grill to medium. Drizzle rum over pineapple slices and sprinkle with brown sugar. Grill pineapple, with grill cover down, for 5 minutes per side, turning only once. Serve with whipped topping and shredded coconut.

Quick and Easy Tip
If you are making this for a party, slice the pineapple the day before and then have your friends help with the grilling for fun!

Lemon Drop Cookies

 Serves 16

- ~ **PREP TIME:** 12 minutes
- ~ **COOK TIME:** 10 minutes
- ~ **TOTAL COST:** $4.75
- ~ **CALORIES:** 120
- ~ **FAT:** 8 g
- ~ **PROTEIN:** 2 g
- ~ **CHOLESTEROL:** 1 g
- ~ **SODIUM:** 33 mg

1 cup granulated sugar
2 sticks unsalted butter, softened
3 teaspoons lemon juice
1 large egg
¾ teaspoon baking soda
¼ teaspoon sea salt
2 cups plain flour
⅓ cup powdered sugar

These lemon cookies are a perfect complement to the end of a delicious meal.

1. Preheat oven to 350°F. Line a baking sheet with parchment paper. In a large bowl, combine sugar and butter and cream together until smooth. Add lemon juice and combine. Beat in egg.
2. In a separate bowl, add baking soda, salt, and flour. Stir to blend. Using an electric mixer at low speed, gradually add flour mixture to butter mixture until just blended into a soft dough. Drop by heaping teaspoonfuls onto baking sheet. Place cookies about 1½ inches apart.
3. Bake on middle rack in oven 9 to 10 minutes until a toothpick inserted into center comes out clean. Do not overcook. Dust cookies with powdered sugar while warm. Let cool for 2 minutes and remove from baking sheet.

Oatmeal Cranberry Chews

Serves 12

~ **PREP TIME:** 10 minutes
~ **COOK TIME:** 12 minutes
~ **TOTAL COST:** $4.75
~ **CALORIES:** 345
~ **FAT:** 11 g
~ **PROTEIN:** 3 g
~ **CHOLESTEROL:** 23 mg
~ **SODIUM:** 103 mg

1 cup butter
½ cup granulated sugar
½ cup brown sugar
1 egg, plus 1 extra if needed
½ teaspoon baking soda
½ teaspoon baking powder
¾ teaspoon ground cinnamon
½ teaspoon ground nutmeg
1 cup plain flour
1½ cups quick-cooking oatmeal
½ cup dried cranberries

These little cookies are great as a snack as they are fairly healthy and taste great.

1. Preheat oven to 350°F. Line a baking sheet with parchment paper. In a large bowl, cream together butter and sugars. Beat in 1 egg. In a separate bowl, sift together the baking soda, baking powder, cinnamon, and nutmeg with the flour. Blend well. Add flour mixture to butter mixture and blend thoroughly. Stir in oatmeal and dried cranberries. If dough is too dry, beat in remaining egg.
2. Drop by heaping teaspoonfuls onto baking sheet, placing cookies about 2 inches apart. Bake for 10 to 12 minutes or until done.

Parfait of Raspberries and Pecans

Serves 6

~ **PREP TIME:** 8 minutes
~ **COOK TIME:** none
~ **TOTAL COST:** $6.99
~ **CALORIES:** 311
~ **FAT:** 18 g
~ **PROTEIN:** 4 g
~ **CHOLESTEROL:** 69 mg
~ **SODIUM:** 152 mg

1½ cups whipping cream
½ cup powdered sugar
½ teaspoon vanilla
2 pints raspberries
½ cup chopped pecans, toasted
½ cup grated semisweet chocolate

You can use Cool Whip for some recipes, but making your own whipped cream is so much more fun and you can add your own flavors to it. As a guide, 1 cup unwhipped cream equates to about 2 cups whipped!

1. Place cream in a large mixing bowl. Begin whipping over high speed with electric mixer. While whipping, add sugar and vanilla. Beat until stiff peaks form. In a separate small bowl, add raspberries and crush them slightly so some are puréed and some are still whole.
2. Layer raspberries with whipped cream mixture, pecans, and grated chocolate in 6 parfait, martini, or wine glasses. Serve immediately or cover and refrigerate.

Amaretto Bread Pudding

 Serves 10

~ **PREP TIME:** 15 minutes
~ **COOK TIME:** 45 minutes
~ **TOTAL COST:** $7.00
~ **CALORIES:** 594
~ **FAT:** 26 g
~ **PROTEIN:** 12 g
~ **CHOLESTEROL:** 190 mg
~ **SODIUM:** 361 mg

¼ cup unsalted butter
1 large loaf day-old or toasted Italian bread
6 eggs
1½ cups whole milk
1½ cups heavy cream
¼ cup amaretto liqueur
¼ cup honey
¼ cup granulated sugar

Bread pudding is a simple dessert that can be made with raisins, berries, nuts, or any combination of the above. Just add bread pieces, milk, sugar, and eggs and you have the makings of bread pudding.

1. Preheat oven to 375°f. Lightly grease a rectangular 13" x 9" baking dish with 1 teaspoon of butter. Melt remaining butter. Tear bread into large 2-inch pieces. Combine with melted butter in a bowl. Beat eggs in a separate bowl. Whisk in milk, cream, liqueur, honey, and sugar. Place bread mixture in prepared pan. Pour egg mixture over top and stir to combine.
2. Bake for 30 minutes, uncovered. Stir, and return to oven. Bake for about 15 to 20 minutes longer until set. Serve warm with whipped cream or ice cream.

Oven-Baked Pears with Whipped Cream

Serves 6

~ **PREP TIME:** 10 minutes
~ **COOK TIME:** 30 minutes
~ **TOTAL COST:** $6.90
~ **CALORIES:** 268
~ **FAT:** 8 g
~ **PROTEIN:** 4 g
~ **CHOLESTEROL:** 95 mg
~ **SODIUM:** 123 mg

Juice of 1 lemon
6 pears, peeled and cored
2 to 4 tablespoons sugar
Ready whipped cream as desired

Pears also taste terrific when grilled. If grilling, grill on each side about 2 minutes. Grilling the pears saves time, adds flavor and color to the pears, and doesn't heat your house as much as the oven does.

Preheat oven to 375°F. In a 2-quart baking dish, combine lemon juice with enough water to cover the bottom. Add the pears, cover, and bake for 15 to 20 minutes, or until tender. Remove from oven. Uncover and sprinkle each pear with 1 to 2 teaspoons sugar. Bake, uncovered, for 10 minutes. Serve warm or chilled with whipped cream.

> **Quick and Easy Tip**
> For a truly Italian dish, substitute the whipped cream with mascarpone, an Italian cream cheese, if your budget allows. Mascarpone is a little more expensive than whipped cream and provides a less sweet flavor to the pears.

Fresh Fruit with Orange Honey Compote

Serves 4

- **PREP TIME:** 10 minutes
- **COOK TIME:** 10 minutes
- **TOTAL COST:** $5.86
- **CALORIES:** 78
- **FAT:** 1 g
- **CARBOHYDRATES:** 11 g
- **PROTEIN:** 2 g
- **CHOLESTEROL:** 0 mg
- **SODIUM:** 6 mg

1 orange, segmented
¼ cup fresh-squeezed orange juice
1½ tablespoons honey
Pinch ground cinnamon
1 cup wild berries such as blackberries and raspberries
2 cups cantaloupe, diced
1 tablespoon fresh mint, leaves chopped

A compote is a dessert of fruit in sugared syrup. When heating, be careful not to boil the fruit in the syrup rapidly or the fruit will break down and disintegrate.

1. In small boiler over medium heat, combine the orange, orange juice, honey, and cinnamon and bring to a gentle boil. Boil for 2 minutes, remove from heat, and set aside.
2. Place fresh fruit in mixing bowl, pour orange mixture over and lightly toss to coat evenly. Serve with fresh mint.

> **Segmenting Fruit**
> Segmenting an orange or any similar fruit means to cut the fruit away from the pith. The pith tastes bitter and also, segmenting makes the fruit look prettier in your dish!

Blueberries with Melon and Whipped Lemon Cream

Serves 4

- **PREP TIME:** 15 minutes
- **COOK TIME:** none
- **TOTAL COST:** $4.09
- **CALORIES:** 100
- **FAT:** 17.5 g
- **CARBOHYDRATES:** 15 g
- **PROTEIN:** 1 g
- **CHOLESTEROL:** 63 mg
- **SODIUM:** 16 mg

½ cup heavy cream
⅛ teaspoon light, sugar-free or regular lemonade drink mix
2 cups cantaloupe, peeled and cut into 1-inch cubes
2 cups fresh blueberries
Fine zest of 1 lemon

Sugar-free lemonade mix is a great way to add flavor to this dessert and keep it light on calories. As an alternative, substitute other flavored drink mixes such as cherry or strawberry.

1. Combine the cream and lemonade mix in a medium-sized bowl; whip using standing mixer or hand mixer until soft peaks form.
2. Place cantaloupe and berries in a wine glass or martini glass. Top with lemon cream. Garnish with lemon zest.

Brownies with Chopped Pecans

Serves 16

- ~ **PREP TIME:** 10 minutes
- ~ **COOK TIME:** 35 minutes
- ~ **TOTAL COST:** $6.08
- ~ **CALORIES:** 138
- ~ **FAT:** 7 g
- ~ **PROTEIN:** 2 g
- ~ **CHOLESTEROL:** 39 mg
- ~ **SODIUM:** 11 mg

¼ teaspoon sea salt
½ teaspoon baking powder
½ teaspoon ground cinnamon
½ cup plain flour
1 stick unsalted butter
4 ounces semisweet chocolate pieces
2 large eggs
1 teaspoon vanilla extract
¾ cup granulated sugar
1 cup chopped pecans

Even though I am known as the Bikini Chef, sometimes chocolate and ice cream really do the trick! Leave out the pecans if you are allergic to nuts or are bringing these to a party.

1. Preheat oven to 325°F. Grease a 9" x 9" baking pan. In a bowl, combine the salt, baking powder, and cinnamon with the flour until well blended.
2. Fill heavy quart boiler 1½ inches deep with water. Place butter in a metal bowl that fits securely on top of the boiler. Place boiler with bowl on stove over medium heat. Heat until butter is beginning to melt. Add chocolate to butter and melt together, stir only occasionally. Once both butter and chocolate are melted, remove from heat and beat in eggs. Add vanilla extract. Stir in sugar, then blend in flour mixture. Stir in pecans.
3. Spread batter evenly into prepared pan. Bake on the middle rack of oven for 30 minutes or until toothpick inserted comes out nearly clean. Let cool and cut into 16 bars.

> **Quick and Easy Tip**
> This recipe is better slightly undercooked than overcooked. Overcooking causes the brownies to dry out.

Caramelized Pears with Brown Sugar and Almonds

Serves 4

- **PREP TIME:** 10 minutes
- **COOK TIME:** 6 minutes
- **TOTAL COST:** $2.73
- **CALORIES:** 114
- **FAT:** 12 g
- **CARBOHYDRATES:** 25 g
- **PROTEIN:** 2 g
- **CHOLESTEROL:** 1 mg
- **SODIUM:** 48 mg

3 pears, ripe but still firm, sliced

1½ tablespoons brown sugar, plus 1 tablespoon for garnish

2 tablespoons almonds, whole or chopped

½ cup vanilla yogurt

Carmelizing sugar means to lightly brown the sugar. Pay attention when broiling, as the sugar can burn quickly.

1. Preheat broiler. Fan the pear slices in shallow ovenproof dish. Sprinkle 1½ tablespoons brown sugar over the pears. Broil until the sugar is caramelized but not burned, about 4 to 5 minutes. Sprinkle the almonds on top and broil for 1 more minute, until golden.
2. To serve, divide the pears among 4 serving plates. Top each with equal parts of the yogurt and garnish with remaining sugar.

Wild Berry Parfait

Serves 4

- **PREP TIME:** 12 minutes
- **COOK TIME:** none
- **TOTAL COST:** $3.41
- **CALORIES:** 227
- **FAT:** 11 g
- **CARBOHYDRATES:** 30 g
- **PROTEIN:** 2 g
- **CHOLESTEROL:** 42 mg
- **SODIUM:** 48 mg

1½ cups wild berries such as raspberries, blackberries, and blueberries

½ cup whipping cream

2 tablespoons powdered sugar

½ cup raspberry or blackberry jam

4 fresh mint leaves, for garnish

If you don't have enough room in your refrigerator for martini glasses, layer mixture in a decorative, deep serving bowl. Present dessert in center of table before serving so everyone can enjoy your beautiful creation.

1. Divide 1 cup of the berries equally between 4 chilled martini glasses or ramekins.
2. In standing mixer, pour in cream and whip until just combined. Add sugar and continue whipping until soft peaks form. In medium bowl, gently mix together whipped cream and jam. Dollop the mixture on top of the fruit. Top cream mixture with remaining berries and finish with fresh mint leaf.

Substitute Granulated Sugar

If you don't have powdered sugar, you can use granulated sugar. The only difference is the powdered sugar dissolves into the cream making it perfectly smooth.

Petit Wild Berry Fruit Tarts

Makes 24 tarts, serves 6

- ~ **PREP TIME:** 10 minutes
- ~ **COOK TIME:** 15 minutes
- ~ **TOTAL COST:** $6.99
- ~ **CALORIES:** 342
- ~ **FAT:** 9 g
- ~ **CARBOHYDRATES:** 45 g
- ~ **PROTEIN:** 3 g
- ~ **CHOLESTEROL:** 0 mg
- ~ **SODIUM:** 290 mg

24 frozen mini phyllo tart shells
½ cup apple jelly
½ teaspoon chopped fresh thyme leaves
½ cup fresh blueberries
½ cup fresh raspberries

Your grocer's freezer section is a gold mine of pre-pared pie and tart shells. If it is within your budget, stock up on a few different types to make pies and tarts in minutes.

1. Preheat oven to 375°F. Place tart shells on a parchment-lined baking sheet and bake according to package directions. Remove to wire racks to cool.
2. Meanwhile, heat apple jelly and thyme in a medium saucepan over low heat until jelly melts. Remove from heat and stir in berries. Put a couple of teaspoons of berry mixture into each tart shell and serve.

Fresh Herbs
Fresh herbs go with everything, including desserts. Thyme is used here because of its slightly minty, lemony fragrance. Rosemary is also a natural complement to fruit desserts such as pears, lemon, and even in shortbreads.

Easy Cheesecake with Fresh Raspberries

Serves 6

- ~ **PREP TIME:** 15 minutes
- ~ **CHILL TIME:** 2 hours up to 8 hours before serving
- ~ **TOTAL COST:** $6.98
- ~ **CALORIES:** 505
- ~ **FAT:** 24 g
- ~ **CARBOHYDRATES:** 62 g
- ~ **PROTEIN:** 10 g
- ~ **CHOLESTEROL:** 61 mg
- ~ **SODIUM:** 333 mg

1 (14-ounce) can sweetened condensed milk
1 (8-ounce) package cream cheese, softened
¼ cup lemon juice
1 (9-inch) graham cracker pie crust
1 cup fresh berries, such as raspberries

Another way to enjoy this recipe is to place cream cheese mixture in wine or parfait glasses and chill. To serve, top with crumbled graham cracker crust and fresh berries.

1. In standing mixer or large bowl, combine condensed milk, cream cheese, and lemon juice; beat on low speed until smooth and combined. Pour into graham cracker crust. Place in freezer for 10 minutes.
2. Place berries on cream cheese filling and serve, or cover and chill the pie in the refrigerator for up to 8 hours. Store leftovers in the refrigerator.

Traditional Cheesecakes
Making traditional cheesecakes from scratch takes a lot of time and can be expensive. The main ingredient to cheesecake is naturally the cream cheese. Here you can enjoy the flavor of a homemade cheesecake with a lot less effort and expense!

Strawberries with Toasted Pecans and Balsamic Syrup

 Serves 6

- ~ **PREP TIME:** 15 minutes
- ~ **COOK TIME:** 30 minutes
- ~ **TOTAL COST:** $6.22
- ~ **CALORIES:** 161
- ~ **FAT:** 13 g
- ~ **CARBOHYDRATES:** 7 g
- ~ **PROTEIN:** 3 g
- ~ **CHOLESTEROL:** 13 mg
- ~ **SODIUM:** 2 mg

1 cup balsamic vinegar or 1 teaspoon high-quality aged balsamic vinegar
3 cups strawberries, stemmed and sliced
1 cup sour cream
½ cup brown sugar
¼ cup toasted pecans

This recipe tastes so good you could actually skip the sour cream to lower the calories and fat.

1. For balsamic syrup, in small boiler over medium-low to low heat, pour in 1 cup vinegar and let simmer for 30 minutes or until vinegar is reduced to about ¼ cup (or skip this step if using high-quality aged balsamic). Set aside.
2. In glass serving bowl, place one-third of the strawberries. Top with one-third of the sour cream, and sprinkle with one-third of the brown sugar. Repeat layers, ending with brown sugar. Top with toasted pecans, drizzle with balsamic syrup, and serve. Or cover and refrigerate up to 8 hours, reserving balsamic syrup until serving time.

Italian Bread Pudding with Frangelico

 Serves 10

- ~ **PREP TIME:** 15 minutes
- ~ **COOK TIME:** 45 minutes
- ~ **TOTAL COST:** $6.99
- ~ **CALORIES:** 594
- ~ **FAT:** 26 g
- ~ **CARBOHYDRATES:** 82 g
- ~ **PROTEIN:** 12 g
- ~ **CHOLESTEROL:** 190 mg
- ~ **SODIUM:** 361 mg

¼ cup unsalted butter
1 large loaf day-old or toasted Italian bread
6 eggs
2 cups whole or low-fat milk
2 cups heavy cream
¼ cup Frangelico liqueur
¼ cup honey
¼ cup granulated sugar

Bread pudding is a simple dessert that can be made with raisins, berries, nuts, or any combination of the above. Just add bread pieces, milk, sugar, and eggs and you have the makings of bread pudding.

1. Preheat oven to 375°F. Lightly grease a rectangular 13" x 9" baking dish with 1 teaspoon butter. Melt remaining butter. Tear bread into large 2-inch pieces. Combine with melted butter in a bowl. Beat eggs in separate bowl. Whisk in milk, cream, liqueur, honey, and sugar. Place bread mixture in prepared pan. Pour egg mixture over top and stir to combine.
2. Bake for 30 minutes, uncovered. Stir and return to oven. Bake for about 15 to 20 minutes longer until set. Serve warm with whipped cream or ice cream.

Easy Italian Panna Cotta

Serves 5–6*

- ~ **COST:** $0.50
- ~ **CALORIES:** 260
- ~ **FAT:** 22 g
- ~ **CARBOHYDRATES:** 12 g
- ~ **PROTEIN:** 3 g
- ~ **CHOLESTEROL:** 80 mg
- ~ **SODIUM:** 40 mg

¼ cup warm water
1 envelope unflavored gelatin, such as Knox
1½ cups whipping cream or heavy cream
¼ cup granulated sugar
2 teaspoons vanilla extract
¾ cup milk

1. Pour the warm water into a small bowl. Pour the gelatin over the water and let it stand 5 minutes to soften.
2. In a medium-sized saucepan, bring the cream, sugar, and vanilla extract to a boil over medium heat. Reduce heat to low and simmer for 2 to 3 minutes, stirring occasionally to make sure all the sugar is dissolved. Add the milk and simmer for another 2 to 3 minutes.
3. Remove the saucepan from the heat and stir in the softened gelatin (check to make sure the cream and milk mixture is not boiling when you add the gelatin). Stir until the gelatin is completely dissolved.
4. Pour the mixture into a bowl. Set the bowl inside another bowl filled with ice water. Cool for 15 minutes, stirring regularly. Pour the liquid into 4-ounce ramekins or custard cups and refrigerate overnight.
5. To serve, dip the bottom of each ramekin briefly in a bowl of hot water, and use a knife to cut around the bottom of the panna cotta, loosening the edges. Dry the bottom of the ramekin and invert the panna cotta onto a plate. Enjoy as is, or top with seasonal fresh fruit.

*Nutrition information and price per serving based on the recipe serving 6.

INDEX

the hungry Editor

Foodies Unite!

Bring your appetite and follow The Hungry Editor who really loves to eat. She'll be discussing (and drooling over) all things low-fat and full-fat, local and fresh, canned and frozen, highbrow and lowbrow. . .

When it comes to good eats, The Hungry Editor (and her tastebuds) do not discriminate!

It's a Feeding Frenzy—dig in!

Sign up for our newsletter at

www.adamsmedia.com/blog/cooking

and download our free **Top Ten Gourmet Meals for $7** recipes!